VideoCentral ⊙

bedfordstmartins.com
/newsreporting

Watch **"Going Visual: Video,
Radio and the Web."**

- Why are some radio stations
  shooting and sharing videos
  online? What do they hope
  to accomplish with this?

- Do you visit radio station
  websites and watch videos?
  If not, will you do so in the
  future? Explain.

and expense of a second inauguration? President Obama had already been sworn in as president. Author Sally Quinn explains, "We want to see the flags wave and the bands play, the parades march along and the leader of the free world standing before our Capitol dome."

Television and online media help us do that.

WHAT RADIO AND TELEVISION DO BEST

During major news events, radio and television newscasters repeat their reports and update their audiences as the news develops. If you tune in to CNN, not only do you see what's happening and listen to commentary, you also see additional headlines streaming below the picture on a ticker. You can pay attention to the news you are most interested in, and you feel as if you are witnessing history.

Of course, much of the time, journalists must write and report news after it has occurred. Many, if not most, radio and television stations provide at least some news that is written by journalists working for the wire services, such as the Associated Press or Reuters.

In addition, radio and television journalists might publish updates all day leading up to news broadcasts, using new media sources like Twitter, Facebook and YouTube. They also often produce news for podcasts, blogs or wikis. And some have found ways to take content that used to be available only online and merge it with traditional newscasts. Information and reactions posted on social media are often shared during newscasts.

⊙ INTEGRATED MEDIA WITH VIDEOCENTRAL

News Reporting and Writing doesn't just cover the integration of print and digital media — it practices it, too, with the new VideoCentral feature. Throughout the book, call-outs in the margins link to a series of thought-provoking online videos that expand on the material covered in the print chapters with an insider's look at journalism. Topics include legal rights of bloggers, real news versus satiric fake news, citizen journalism, shield laws and more, all accompanied by discussion questions. Turn to the inside back cover for more information on how to access VideoCentral.

EXPANDED DIGITAL MEDIA COVERAGE

Digital media coverage has been expanded throughout the book, reflecting the prominence of digital media in the new journalism landscape. Chapter 12, Writing News for the Web, for example, includes new coverage reflecting the convergence of print and online media, with material on writing for social media, search engine optimization and blogs, in addition to more traditional news sites.

News Reporting and Writing

Eleventh Edition

The Missouri Group

Brian S. Brooks

George Kennedy

Daryl R. Moen

Don Ranly

School of Journalism
University of Missouri

Bedford/St. Martin's
Boston • New York

For Bedford/St.Martin's
Publisher for Communication: Erika Gutierrez
Developmental Editors: Jesse Hassenger, Linda Stern
Publishing Services Manager: Andrea Cava
Production Supervisor: Samuel Jones
Marketing Manager: Stacey Propps
Project Management: Books By Design, Inc.
Photo Researcher: Creative Compliance, LLC
Text Design: Glenna Collett
Cover Design: Marine Miller
Cover Art: © Getty Images
Composition: Books By Design, Inc.
Printing and Binding: RR Donnelley and Sons

President, Bedford/St. Martin's: Denise B. Wydra
Director of Development: Erica T. Appel
Director of Marketing: Karen R. Soeltz
Production Director: Susan W. Brown
Director of Rights and Permissions: Hilary Newman

Manufactured in the United States of America.
8 7 6 5 4 3
f e d c b a

For information, write: Bedford/St.Martin's, 75 Arlington Street, Boston, MA 02116 (617-399-4000)

ISBN 978-1-4576-5354-4

Preface

WHAT DOES IT MEAN to be a journalist today? Has the image of the print newspaper reporter wielding a trusty pen and notebook been replaced by a journalist updating Twitter from a mobile device? How do students get their news? From a print newspaper, a network or cable news broadcast or a news blog—or from one another's Facebook links? These are important questions in the dramatically changing world of journalism. Consider the many forms today's journalism encompasses: 24-hour channels and news sites, traditional and online newspapers, podcasts and blogs, and even satiric programs like *The Colbert Report* and *The Daily Show with Jon Stewart*. What do these changes mean for today's journalism students? How can they best prepare for a successful career in this evolving industry?

The staff of today's converged newsrooms can agree on one answer: Editors want journalists who can report fully and write clearly, whether for an online news outlet, a professional blog, a cable news show or a print newspaper. The keys to being a good journalist are still as fundamental as that. We have revised the 11th edition of *News Reporting and Writing* to reflect the ways these essential skills are applied across this changing field. To this end, we have added more—and better integrated—coverage of reporting news across various media.

When it comes to integrated media, we practice what we preach: The new edition of *News Reporting and Writing* combines print and digital media into a single accessible package. Callouts in the book's margins link to online videos that offer insider perspectives on issues of modern journalism, including the legal rights of bloggers, journalistic ethics, the common ground between real news and satiric fake news, and the power of images. Our integrated media program takes *News Reporting and Writing* beyond the limits of the printed page.

Even as we expand further into the digital realm, we continue to stress the essential reporting and writing skills that are the foundations of our profession—past, present and future, no matter the medium. We've also updated our current examples and issues, while still modeling in these examples—and in our own writing—the clear and descriptive writing journalism students must learn. Our emphasis on these topics in the textbook, combined with robust online support and practice opportunities, ensures that students will have more opportunities than ever before to practice and refine their skills.

New to This Edition

Revisions to the 11th edition of *News Reporting and Writing* address changes to the journalism landscape and provide additional opportunities for students to refine their reporting and writing skills in today's world. Specifically, this new edition offers the following features:

» **An increased and strengthened focus on Web writing and digital media.** Chapter 12, "Writing News for the Web," has been expanded to include more coverage of social media writing, search-engine optimization and blogs, in addition to traditional news sites. The coverage of digital media is integrated throughout the book, addressing digital media alongside print and recognizing its prominence in the new journalism landscape.

» **An even greater array of writing models.** In keeping with the growing focus on digital media, our annotated models now include samples that track a story across multiple media formats—including Twitter, blogs, print and the Web—showing students how to adapt their core skills for different audiences. All models have useful annotations in the margins of the stories explaining best practices for reporting, writing and editing.

» ⓞ **Bedford Integrated Media.** *News Reporting and Writing* now includes integrated videos that expand on the material covered in the book's print chapters. These online videos get students thinking critically about news media by giving them an insider's look at journalism from a variety of provocative angles. Topics include shield laws and nontraditional journalists, media ownership, the culture of specialization in magazines, citizen journalism and more—and they're all accompanied by thought-provoking discussion questions. These videos come automatically with every new copy of *News Reporting and Writing*; turn to the inside back cover for more information on how to access them.

» **Nine new "On the Job" boxes that prepare students for contemporary careers.** In every chapter, a working journalist illustrates how the skills students learn in class will prepare them for careers across the media and in public relations—even in today's challenging and evolving job market. The journalists profiled have wide-ranging careers, from working the White House beat to writing long-form stories for ESPN. Many of the newest boxes focus on new job opportunities and challenges created by a field in transition; they discuss how a journalist's role can change and expand unexpectedly because of technology, and they suggest ways journalists can embrace that change and stay engaged with their work. For example, one writer explains how he graduated with a degree in magazine journalism but wound up working for a startup rather than a larger corporation, and a producer for a local NBC affiliate discusses taking on additional investigative responsibilities.

» **New digital formats.** The Bedford e-Book to Go for *News Reporting and Writing* includes the same content as the print book, offering an affordable, tech-savvy PDF e-book option for students. Instructors can customize the e-book by adding their own content and deleting or rearranging chapters. Learn more about custom Bedford e-Books to Go at **www.bedfordstmartins.com/ebooks**, where you can also learn more about other e-book formats for *News Reporting and Writing*.

Enduring Features of the Text

Users of *News Reporting and Writing* have come to expect that every new edition of our textbook will be readable and current as well as deeply focused on journalistic essentials. We are proud to continue to offer the following features:

» **Comprehensive coverage of all aspects of reporting and writing the news.** *News Reporting and Writing* teaches students the elements of good reporting and writing and provides the basic tools they need to become journalists across various media platforms, including advice on how to conduct interviews and research, employ media-enriched reporting techniques and create rich and well-crafted stories for the basic beats.

» **A focus on storytelling.** From life stories to world-news reports, local meetings to national press conferences, good journalism means good writing. We use real-life examples, up-to-the-minute news story samples and a consistent focus on writing essentials to show students how to craft rich and interesting stories. In addition, Chapter 10, "Writing to Be Read," helps students master coherence, effective language and other techniques central to captivating an audience.

» **Thorough coverage of media convergence and online journalism.** *News Reporting and Writing* ensures that students learn how to prepare stories effectively for multiple forms of media. Reflecting changes to the journalism landscape, this book covers the rising role of technology, convergence and the emergence of integrated newsrooms, the challenges to legacy media and the future of online journalism.

» **Unparalleled discussion of legal and ethical issues.** Throughout the book, we offer students a framework for critically assessing the ethical questions they will face as journalists. In addition, we dedicate Chapters 21 and 22 to legal and ethical matters.

» **A chapter on math for journalists.** *News Reporting and Writing* includes a chapter on "Reporting with Numbers," which stresses the importance of using and understanding data—a vital skill for political and business news writers in particular.

» **Coverage of common grammar issues, Associated Press style, and proofreading and copy editing symbols—in print and with the best online tools.** The appendices provide helpful information students need to turn in polished, professionally edited copy, and an easy-to-find reference for proofreading and copy editing symbols is located at the end of the book. In addition, thousands of accompanying online exercises offer students additional opportunities to improve their grammar and AP style knowledge (**www.bedfordstmartins.com/newsreporting**).

Resources for Students and Instructors

As before, *News Reporting and Writing* is supported by a range of effective resources for students and instructors. For more information, please visit the online catalog at www.bedfordstmartins.com/newsreporting/catalog. The following ancillaries are available with this edition:

» *News Reporting and Writing* website (**www.bedfordstmartins.com/newsreporting**). Here students can find links to research tools, online exercises, and all of the online videos from the book's integrated media program. Students can also access *Exercise Central for AP Style*, a free database offering more than

2,500 questions on wire-service style and on the 20 grammar and usage errors most commonly made by journalism students.

» **Workbook for *News Reporting and Writing*, 11th Edition.** Supplementing the exercises at the end of each text chapter, the revised workbook gives students extra practice mastering the principles of journalism.

» **Instructor's Manual for *News Reporting and Writing*, 11th Edition.** This revised and updated manual contains a sample syllabus; additional teaching resources; and chapter-specific overviews, teaching tips, lecture outlines, classroom activities and discussion questions, as well as answers to the end-of-chapter exercises from the main text and answers to the workbook exercises. The Instructor's Manual is available for immediate download at **www.bedfordstmartins.com /newsreporting/catalog**.

Acknowledgments

Our colleagues and students at the University of Missouri have given us invaluable feedback on the book, for which we are grateful.

We especially appreciate the contributions of Dr. Charles Davis, a faculty colleague, who revised the law chapter; Marty Steffens, who holds the Society of American Business Editors and Writers Chair in Business and Financial Journalism, for revising our business chapter; and Jennifer Reeves of our radio-television faculty for reviewing the chapter on writing for radio and television. We are grateful to Karl Grubaugh of American River College and Granite Bay High School for his superb work on the workbook and Instructor's Manual for this edition.

We thank all of the instructors who thoughtfully reviewed the text: Mary Elizabeth Carey, University of Massachusetts; Justin Catanoso, Wake Forest University; Rory Faust, Northern Arizona University; Peter Friederici, Northern Arizona University; Joe Grimm, Michigan State University; Alec Klein, Northwestern University; Anup Kumar, Cleveland State University; Kimberley Mangun, The University of Utah; Suzanne McBride, Columbia College Chicago; Jean Reid Norman, University of Nevada, Las Vegas; Leland "Buck" Ryan, University of Kentucky; Scott A. Strain, Laney College; and Margaret Tebo, Columbia College Chicago.

We also thank those who reviewed previous editions: Betsy B. Alderman, University of Tennessee at Chattanooga; Anne Becker, Oakland University; Mark Berkey-Gerard, Rowan University; JoAnne C. Broadwater, Towson University; Betty S. Clapp, Cleveland State University; Jan Barry Crumb, Rutgers University; Helene DeGross, Lake Forest College; Dee Drummond, University of Toledo; Sandra Fish, University of Colorado; Jennifer Follis, University of Illinois; Gwen R. Fowler, Coastal Carolina University; Eddye Gallagher, Tarrant County College; Patrick Harwood, College of Charleston; Ron Hollander, Montclair State University; Amani Ismail, California State University, Northridge; Elena Jarvis, Daytona State College; Kevin R. Kemper, University of Arizona; Laura Krantz, Tyler Junior College; Linda Loomis, State University of New York, Oswego; Therese Lueck, University of Akron; Carole McNall, St. Bonaventure University; Kristi Nies, Peru State College; Carolyn Olson, Maryville

University; Debra Patterson, Motlow State Community College; Richard Puffer, Coker College; Cathy Stablein, College of DuPage; Cynthia Thomas, Grand Valley State University; Tracy Warner, Indiana-Purdue, Fort Wayne; Thomas E. Winski, Emporia State University; and Vallorie Wood, Kennesaw State University.

We have worked with editors at Bedford/St. Martin's for more than 30 years now. With each edition, they have challenged us to improve, and we appreciate their efforts. We would like to acknowledge the expert work of our developmental editor, Linda Stern, who kept us in line and on time. Thanks are also due to Erika Gutierrez, Jesse Hassenger, Karen Schultz Moore, Erica Appel, and Caitlin Crandell. We are equally grateful to the production team, which includes Andrea Cava and Nancy Benjamin of Books By Design, as well as our photo researcher, Tyler Thompson. We'd like to extend further thanks to our marketing team, led by Stacey Propps and including Allyson Russell.

As always, we value your comments. You can reach us via email at Brooksbs @missouri.edu; Kennedyg@missouri.edu; Moend@missouri.edu; or Ranlyd@missouri .edu.

Brian S. Brooks
George Kennedy
Daryl R. Moen
Don Ranly

Brief Contents

Preface   v

PART ONE   JOURNALISM AND JOURNALISTS

1 The Nature of News   3

2 The Changing Media Landscape   21

3 The Emerging Media   41

PART TWO   REPORTING TOOLS

4 Interviewing   59

5 Handling Quotations and Attributions   81

6 Gathering and Verifying Information   111

7 Finding the News in News Releases   131

8 Reporting with Numbers   149

PART THREE   STORYTELLING

9 The Inverted Pyramid   167

10 Writing to Be Read   193

11 Alternatives to the Inverted Pyramid   219

PART FOUR   WRITING FOR SPECIFIC MEDIA

12 Writing News for the Web   241

13 Writing News for Radio and Television   265

PART FIVE   BASIC STORIES

14 Covering a Beat   287

15 Speeches, News Conferences and Meetings   313

16 Other Types of Local Stories   329

17 Business and Consumer News   365

PART SIX   SPECIALIZED TECHNIQUES

18 Social Science Reporting   387

19 Investigative Reporting   401

20 Working in Public Relations   419

PART SEVEN   RIGHTS AND RESPONSIBILITIES

21 Media Law   443

22 Ethics   465

Appendix 1   20 Common Errors of Grammar and Punctuation   489

Appendix 2   Wire-Service Style Summary   499

Appendix 3   Society of Professional Journalists' Code of Ethics   506

Glossary   509

Index   521

Annotated Models   543

Copy Editing and Proofreading Symbols   544

VideoCentral Clips (by chapter)   546

Contents

Preface   v

PART ONE   **JOURNALISM AND JOURNALISTS**

1   **The Nature of News**   3

Convergence in Journalism   4
    ⊙ VideoCentral: Convergence and Essential Skills   5
What News Is   5
    Elements of a Good News Story   5
    How Different Media Present the News   7
    The Rise of Citizen Journalism   7
    ⊙ VideoCentral: Newspapers Now: Balancing Citizen Journalism and
       Investigative Reporting   8
The Role of Journalism   8
    Challenges to American Journalism   8
    ON THE JOB   A Career Crosses Media Lines   9
    Principles of Good Journalism   10
    Journalists' Responsibilities in a Democracy   10
Accuracy, Fairness and Bias   12
    Accuracy and Fairness   13
    Dealing with Bias   14
The Issue of Objectivity   15
What Is *Not* News   17

Suggested Readings   17
Suggested Websites   18
Exercises   18

2   **The Changing Media Landscape**   21

News Consumption in the Age of Mobile Devices   21
    Mobile's Role in Consumers' Move to the Web   21
    Increasing News Audiences   22
Greater Media Fragmentation   23

Financial Challenges to Legacy Media   24

Smaller Audiences as a Result of Media Proliferation   24

Lower Advertising Revenues and Higher Debt   25

◉ VideoCentral: Internet Media Entrepreneurs: Newsy.com   27

Newspapers: The Source of Most News   27

Journalism's Role in a Democracy   28

How People Consume News Today   28

ON THE JOB Editing Online News   29

Types of News Audiences   29

Can Web-Based News Replace Newspaper Reporting?   30

Distrust of the Media   31

Convergence as a Response to Media Fragmentation   32

Enhanced Web Coverage   33

Synchronized Media Coverage   34

Embracing Citizen Journalism   35

Problems with Citizen Journalism   36

Forms of Citizen Journalism   37

The Future of Journalism   38

Suggested Readings   38

Suggested Websites   39

Exercises   39

3   The Emerging Media   41

Changes in the Business of Journalism   42

Not-for-Profit Business Models   44

Financially Successful Not-for-Profit Sites   45

Financially Problematic Nonprofit Sites   46

◉ VideoCentral: User Generated Content   46

ON THE JOB The Lure of the Web   47

For-Profit Media Models   47

Experimentation on the Web   48

◉ VideoCentral: Newspapers and the Internet: Convergence   48

Niche Journalism Sites   49

Sports Sites   49

Business Sites   50

General News Sites   50

San Diego: Pioneering New Media Prototypes   51

Building Audiences as the Key to Success   52

Jobs in Journalism   53

Suggested Readings   56
Suggested Websites   56
Exercises   56

PART TWO   **REPORTING TOOLS**

4   Interviewing   59

Preparing for the Interview   60
   The News Story   61
   The Profile   62
   ON THE JOB   Getting the Tough Interview   63
   The Investigative Piece   63
      Gathering Information   64
      Requesting an Interview   64

Doing an Audio or Video Interview   64
   ◉ VideoCentral: **Radio: Yesterday, Today and Tomorrow**   65

Using the Telephone, Email, Instant Messaging or Skype for Interviews   66

Setting Up the Interview   68

Preparing Questions   68
   Researching Questions   68
   Phrasing Questions   69
      Open-Ended Questions   70
      Closed-Ended Questions   71

Establishing Rapport   72
   Interview Approaches   73
   ON THE JOB   Relating to Your Subject   74
   Other Practical Considerations   74

Ensuring Accuracy and Fairness   75
   Using a Recorder   75
   Taking Notes   76
   Verifying Information   76
   Observing   77
   Asking Follow-Up Questions   77
   Using Other Techniques   78

Ending the Interview   78

Suggested Readings   79
Suggested Websites   79
Exercises   79

5   Handling Quotations and Attributions   81

What to Quote Directly   82
Unique Material   83
Use Good Judgment in Selecting Quotes   83
Don't Use Direct Quotes for Straight Facts   83
Use Quotes That Move the Story Forward   83
Consider Using Dialogue to Tell Part of the Story   84
The Unique Expression   84
Important Quotes by Important People   85

Accuracy and Fairness in Direct Quotations   85
ANNOTATED MODEL   Using Quotes Effectively   86
Verification   87
VideoCentral: Computer Assisted Reporting   87
Quoting from Email, Social Media, the Internet and Chat Rooms   87
Using Someone Else's Direct Quotations   88
Practicing Prepublication Review   89

Altering Quotations   91
Paraphrasing Quotes   91
Using Partial Quotes   91
Capturing Dialect or Accent   92
Mixing and Matching Questions and Answers   94
Correcting Grammar in Quotes   95
The Case for Correcting Grammar   95
The Case Against Correcting Grammar   95
Removing Redundancies   96
Deleting Obscenity, Profanity and Vulgarity   97
Avoiding Made-Up Quotes   98

Attributing Direct and Indirect Quotes   98
When to Attribute   98
How to Attribute   99
ANNOTATED MODEL   Using Anonymous Sources   100
Attributing Written Sources   103

Handling On- and Off-the-Record Information   104
Problems with Anonymous Sources   104
ON THE JOB   Off the Record   105
Disagreement About Terminology   105
Background Interviews   106

Suggested Readings   107
Suggested Websites   107
Exercises   107

6 **Gathering and Verifying Information   111**

Accurate Information: The Basis of a Good Story   112
  ◉ VideoCentral: The Objectivity Myth   112
  The Discipline of Multiple Sources   112
  ANNOTATED MODEL   Integrating Multiple Sources into a Story   113
  The Discipline of Verification   114

Online Sources of Information   115
  News Archives: The Place to Start   117
  Search Engines   118
  News Sites, Social Media and Content Aggregators   119
  ◉ VideoCentral: Media Effects Research   119
  Commercial Database Services   119
  Government Databases   120
  Special-Interest Databases   122
  Custom Databases   122
  ON THE JOB   The Challenges of Editing for the Web   123

Traditional Sources of Information   124
  The Traditional Newsroom Library   125
  Other Traditional Sources   126

Suggested Readings   128
Suggested Websites   128
Exercises   128

7 **Finding the News in News Releases   131**

The Importance of News Releases   131

Types of News Releases   132
  ◉ VideoCentral: Filling the News Hole: Video News Releases   133
  Announcement Releases   133
  ON THE JOB   Reading News Releases: Sweat the Small Print   134
  Cause-Promoting Releases   135
  Image-Building Releases   135

Handling News Releases   136
  Rewriting an Announcement Release   137
  Rewriting a Cause-Promoting Release   139
  Rewriting an Image-Building Release   139

Rewriting a News Release — An Example   141
  Read the News Release Carefully   142
  Check for Accuracy and Fairness   142
  Do Additional Research and Interviews   142
  Get Back to the News Release Contact with Questions   143

Write the Story   144
ANNOTATED MODEL   Integrating News Release Information   145

Suggested Readings   146
Suggested Websites   146
Exercises   146

8 Reporting with Numbers   149

Proportion   151
Percentages and Percentage Change   151
Populations, Samples and Margins of Error   151
Percentage Change and Percentage Points   152
Averages and Medians   153
Rates   154

Interest and Compounding   155

Inflation   156

Taxes   157
Sales Taxes   157
Income Taxes   157
ON THE JOB   Working with Numbers   158
Property Taxes   159

Budgets   159
Budget Basics   160
Finding Stories in Budget Changes, Trends and Comparisons   160

Financial Reports   162

Mixing Numbers and Words   164
VideoCentral: Freedom of Information   164

Suggested Readings   164
Suggested Websites   165
Exercises   165

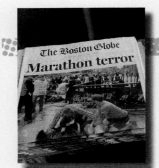

PART THREE   STORYTELLING

9 The Inverted Pyramid   167

Importance of the Inverted Pyramid Story   168
VideoCentral: Magazine Specialization Today   170

Finding the Lead   170
Writing the Inverted Pyramid Lead   171
Emphasizing Different News Values   174

ANNOTATED MODEL   A Sample Inverted Pyramid Story   175
What, So What and What's Next   175

Variations on the Inverted Pyramid Lead   176
The "You" Lead   176
The Immediate-Identification Lead   176
The Delayed-Identification Lead   177
The Summary Lead   178
The Multiple-Element Lead   179
ON THE JOB   Inverted Pyramid—A Basic Tool   180
Danger Signals   182
Leads with Flair   182

Story Organization   183
The One-Subject Story   183
The Memo-Structure Story   183
ANNOTATED MODEL   A Single-Subject Inverted Pyramid Story   184
ANNOTATED MODEL   A Memo-Structure Story   185
The Multiple-Element Story   185

Writing a Story Across Media Platforms   187
Tweeting Breaking News   187
Initial Online Story   187
ANNOTATED MODEL   The Classic Inverted Pyramid Story   188
Full Story with Ongoing Updates   188

Checking Accuracy and Attributions   189

Suggested Readings   190
Suggested Websites   190
Exercises   190

10   Writing to Be Read   193
VideoCentral: Community Voices: Weekly Newspapers   195

Good Writing Begins with Good Reporting   195
ON THE JOB   Setting the Hook in the Opening   196

Accurate, Specific Details   196
Use Concrete Examples   196
Show, Don't Just Tell   197
Use Words Precisely   198

Coherence   199
Decide on the Order of Elements   199
Select the Proper Sentence Structure   200
Use the Precise Conjunction   200

Use Transitions   201
ANNOTATED MODEL   Using Transitions   202

Conciseness and Simplicity   203
Be Concise   204
ANNOTATED MODEL   Editing for Conciseness   205
Keep It Simple   205

Correct and Effective Language   206
Figures of Speech   206
Careful Word Choice   207
Bias-Free Language   207
Correct Grammar and Punctuation   209

The Tools of Narration   210
Scenes   210
Dialogue   212
Anecdotes   213
Foreshadowing   214

Suggested Readings   216
Suggested Websites   216
Exercises   216

11   Alternatives to the Inverted Pyramid   219

Chronology   220
Where to Start   221
A Sample Outline   221
The Nut Paragraph, Foreshadowing and the "To Be Sure"   224
The Ending   225

News Narrative   226
News Narrative with News Emphasis   226
ANNOTATED MODEL   News Narrative with News Emphasis   227
News Narrative with Narrative Emphasis   228

Focus Structure   228
ANNOTATED MODEL   News Narrative with Narrative Emphasis   229
Writing the Lead   230
Writing the Setup   230
The Transition and the Nut Paragraph   230
Foreshadowing   231
The "So What"   232
The "To Be Sure"   233
ON THE JOB   Tips for Writing   234
Writing the Body   234
Writing the Ending   235

bedfordstmartins.com/newsreporting

Service Journalism 235

 VideoCentral: Narrowcasting in Magazines 238

Suggested Readings 238
Suggested Websites 238
Exercises 239

PART FOUR   WRITING FOR SPECIFIC MEDIA

12   Writing News for the Web   241

The Web as a Unique Media Form 242

Readers' Expectations of the Digital Media 243
   Readers Want the News Right Away 244
   Readers Want to Have Their Say 244
    VideoCentral: Going Viral: Political Campaigns and Video 244
   Readers Want Multimedia Variety 245
   Readers Want the News Upfront 246
   Readers Want to Customize Content 247
   The Audience Is International 248
   Structure Is All-Important 248
   ANNOTATED MODEL   Layering Content on a Web Page 250

Guidelines for Writing for the Web 251
   Think Immediacy 251
   Save Readers Time 251
   ON THE JOB   An Online Career 252
   Provide Information That's Quick and Easy to Get 252
   Think Both Verbally and Visually 253
   Cut Your Copy 253
   Use Lots of Lists and Bullets 253
   Write in Chunks 254
   Use Hyperlinks 255
      Internal Connections 256
      External Connections 256
   Give Readers a Chance to Talk Back 257
   Don't Forget the Human Touch 257

Writing with Search Engines in Mind 258

Writing for Blogs 259
   Wide-Ranging Subject Matter 259
    VideoCentral: Net Neutrality 260
   Professional Standards 261

Promoting News on Facebook and Twitter 261

 bedfordstmartins.com/newsreporting

Tomorrow's Readers   262

Suggested Readings   262
Suggested Websites   263
Exercises   263

13   **Writing News for Radio and Television**   265

What Radio and Television Do Best   266
    ◉ VideoCentral: Going Visual: Video, Radio and the Web   266
Criteria for Selecting Radio and Television News   266
Timeliness   267
Information Rather Than Explanation   267
Audio or Visual Impact   267
Emphasis on People   268
Writing Radio and Television News   268
Characteristics of Radio and Television News Writing   268
    Immediacy   268
    ANNOTATED MODEL   Use of Verb Tenses in a TV Story   270
    Conversational Style   270
    Tight Phrasing   271
    Clarity   272
Story Structure   273
    Writing the Radio and Television Lead   273
    Writing Lead-Ins and Wrap-Ups   274
    Writing to the Video   275
    ◉ VideoCentral: Television Networks Evolve: Cable, Satellite, Broadband   276
Using Social Media in Radio and Television   276
Blending Online with On-Air   276
ON THE JOB   Writing News for Radio, Television and More   277
Guidelines for Using Social Media   277
ON THE JOB   Be Ready to Meet the Challenge   278
Preparing Radio and Television News Copy   278
Format   278
Names and Titles   279
Pronunciation   281
Abbreviations   281
Symbols and Numbers   282
Quotations and Attributions   282
Punctuation   283

Suggested Readings   283
Suggested Websites   284
Exercises   284

PART FIVE   BASIC STORIES

14   Covering a Beat   287
  ⊙ VideoCentral: Agenda Setting & Gatekeeping   288
Principles for Reporters on a Beat   288
  Be Prepared   289
    Reading for Background   289
    Talking to Sources   290
  ON THE JOB His Beat: The White House   291
  Be Alert   291
  Be Persistent   293
    Insisting on a Responsive Answer   293
    Following Up on Slow Developments   294
  Be There   294
  Be Wary   296
Beat Reporting Across Media Platforms   296
    ANNOTATED MODEL   A Crime Story Across Media Platforms   297
Covering the Most Important Local Beats   299
  City and County Government   300
  The Schools   301
  Higher Education   304
  Police   305
  Sports   306
    Sports Reporting *Is* Beat Reporting   307
    Developing Contacts   308
    Digging for the Real Story   309

Suggested Readings   310
Suggested Websites   311
Exercises   311

15   Speeches, News Conferences and Meetings   313
  ⊙ VideoCentral: What Makes Public Television "Public"?   314
Distinguishing Among Speeches, News Conferences and Meetings   314
Getting Ready to Cover the Story   314
  Preparing for the Speech Story   314

Preparing for the News Conference Story   315
Preparing for the Meeting Story   316

Covering Speeches, News Conferences and Meetings   316
The Medium Matters   317
Getting the Content Correct   318
Describing the Participants   318
Being Observant   319
Arriving, Positioning Yourself and Staying On   319

Structuring and Writing Your Story   321
Writing the Speech Story   321
ANNOTATED MODEL   Speech Story   322
Writing the News Conference Story   323
Writing the Meeting Story   324
ON THE JOB   Speeches, News Conferences and Meetings   325

Suggested Readings   326
Suggested Websites   326
Exercises   327

16   Other Types of Local Stories   329

Your Preparation   330
Preparing for the Crime Story   330
Preparing for Accident and Fire Stories   332
Preparing for the Court Story   333

Writing the Story   333
The Crime Story   333
ANNOTATED MODEL   Comparison of a Breaking News Story and a
    Follow-Up Story   335
Accident and Fire Stories   337
The Court Story   340
Avoiding Libelous Statements   340
ON THE JOB   "Every Story Is Important"   341
Types of Courts and Cases   342
A Breaking-News Tweet   342
A Typical First Story   343
Follow-Up Story: First Court Appearance   343
Follow-Up Story: Preliminary Hearing   344
Follow-Up Story: Arraignment   345
Follow-Up Story: First Day of the Trial   346
Follow-Up Story: Trial Testimony   347
Follow-Up Story: Verdict   348
Sentencing and Appeals   348

bedfordstmartins.com/newsreporting

Other Issues in Crime and Court Reporting   349

   The Free Press/Fair Trial Controversy   349

   Gag Orders and Closed Trials   349

   Covering Sex Crimes   350

      Sex Crime Victims   350

      Sex Crime Offenders   350

   Press-Bar Guidelines   351

   Cameras in the Courtroom   352

   Coverage of Minority Groups   352

   Coverage of Terrorism   353

   ⊚ VideoCentral: Fake News/Real News: A Fine Line   353

   Issues of Taste and Ethics   353

      Reporting Details of a Crime   353

      Reporting Confessions and Prior Convictions   353

      Identifying Juveniles   354

Obituaries and Life Stories   354

   Crafting a Lead   356

   Building the Story   356

   Writing Life Stories   357

   Sources of Information   357

      The Mortuary Form   357

   ANNOTATED MODEL   A Life Story   358

      The Newsroom Library   360

      Interviews with Family and Friends   361

   Cause of Death   361

   Private or Embarrassing Information   361

Suggested Readings   362

Suggested Websites   363

Exercises   363

17   Business and Consumer News   365

The Growing Importance of Business Journalism   366

   Specialized Business News   367

   ⊚ VideoCentral: The Money Behind the Media   367

   Global Reach   367

   Wide Range of Topics   368

How to Report Business Stories   369

   Avoiding Jargon and Finding the "So What"   369

   Putting Sources at Ease   370

   Watching Out for Biases and Conflicts of Interest   370

   ON THE JOB   Translating Business into English   371

Where to Find Business Stories   371
   Records and Reports   372
      Corporate Data   372
      Investment Data   372
      Financial Ratios   372
      Company Filings   372
      Trade Press   373
      Newsletters   374
      Court Records   374
      Local Regulators   374
      Other Sources   374
   Human Sources   375
      Company Executives   375
      Public Relations Sources   376
      Academic Experts   377
      Trade Associations   377
      Chamber of Commerce Officials   377
      Former Employees   377
      Labor Leaders   377
      Other Sources   377
   Announcements and Meetings   378
   Reporter Enterprise   378

Looking at the Numbers   378

Covering Consumer News   381
   Where to Find Consumer News   381
      Government Agencies   381
      Consumer Groups   382
      Private Businesses   382
   How to Report Consumer Stories   383

Suggested Readings   384
Suggested Websites   384
Exercises   385

PART SIX   **SPECIALIZED TECHNIQUES**

18   Social Science Reporting   387

Computer-Assisted Reporting   388
   ◉ VideoCentral: Computer-Assisted Reporting   388

Participant Observation   389
   The Problem of Invasion of Privacy   389

◉ bedfordstmartins.com/newsreporting

The Problem of Involvement   390
The Problem of Generalization   390

Systematic Study of Records   390

Field Experiments   391

State the Hypothesis and Identify the Variables   391

ON THE JOB   Computer-Assisted Reporting Has Many Uses   392

Control the Experiment and Choose Subjects Randomly   392

Public Opinion Polls   393

The Margin of Error   393
Poll Information to Share   394
Caution in Interpreting Polls   396

Suggested Readings   398
Suggested Websites   398
Exercises   399

19   Investigative Reporting   401

Investigative Reporting: An American Tradition   401

VideoCentral: Investigative Reporting Resources   402

The Process   403

Beginning the Investigation   404
Carrying Out the Investigation   404
Getting It Right   405
Writing the Story   405

Selecting an Effective Story Structure and Lead   407
Including Proof of the Story's Credibility   408
Striving for Clear, Simple Explanations   408

ON THE JOB   A TV Reporter Sets the Investigative Pace   409

The Sources   410

Human Sources   410
Written Sources   412

Public Records   413
Nonpublic Records   414

VideoCentral: Shield Laws and Non-Traditional Journalists   415

Problems with Written Sources   415

New Tools, Traditional Goals   415

Suggested Readings   416
Suggested Websites   416
Exercises   417

20 Working in Public Relations 419

Public Relations: A Different Approach to News 420

Defining Public Relations 420

A Range of Interests 422

Objectivity and Public Relations Writing 422

◉ VideoCentral: Give and Take: Public Relations and Journalism 423

The Main Focus of Public Relations Writing 423

The Message 423

The Audience 424

ANNOTATED MODEL News Release Responding to a Crisis 425

ON THE JOB Public Relations Writing 428

The Media 428

Television, Radio and Newsstand Publications 429

The Internet: An All-in-One Medium 429

Social Networking Media 429

Internal Publications, Brochures and Billboards 430

Persuasive Writing 430

Your Attitude 430

Credibility and Trust 431

News Releases That Get Attention 432

Know What News Is and How to Write It 432

Know the Structure and Operations of Newsrooms 433

Know the People in the News Media and the Jobs They Hold 433

Know the Style of Writing That Fits the Medium 434

Know How to Distribute Information Online 435

Digital News Releases 435

ANNOTATED MODEL Social Media News Release 437

Some Final Advice 439

Suggested Readings 439

Suggested Websites 440

Exercises 440

PART SEVEN   RIGHTS AND RESPONSIBILITIES

21 Media Law 443

The First Amendment: Journalists' Rights and Responsibilities 443

Libel 445

Identifying Libel 445

Libel Suit Defenses 446

Truth 446

Privilege 448

 bedfordstmartins.com/newsreporting

Fair Comment and Criticism   449
The Actual Malice Test and Public Officials   449
The Actual Malice Test and Public Figures   450
ON THE JOB The Keys to Avoiding Libel   451
The Negligence Test and Private Citizens   453
Libel Remains a Danger   453
Libel and the Internet   453

Invasion of Privacy   454
Trespassing   455
Portraying in a "False Light"   455
Causing Unwanted Publicity Offensive to a Person of Ordinary Sensibilities   455

Protection of Sources and Notes   456
◉ VideoCentral: **Bloggers & Legal Rights**   456

Access to Courts   459

Copyright and Fair Use   460

Suggested Readings   462
Suggested Websites   462
Exercises   462

22 **Ethics   465**
The Public Perception of Journalism Ethics   466
Bloggers as Watchdogs   466
Journalism Codes of Ethics   466
◉ VideoCentral: **Journalism Ethics: What News Is Fit to Print?**   466

Three Ethical Philosophies   467
The Ethics of Duty   467
The Ethics of Final Ends or Consequences   468
ON THE JOB Develop Your Ability to Identify Ethical Situations   469
Situation Ethics: The Ethics of Specific Acts   469
No Moral Absolutes   469
Love of Neighbor   470
The Greatest Good for the Greatest Number   470
Ayn Rand's Rational Self-Interest   470

Resolving Ethical Issues   470

Ethical Problems for Journalists   473
Deceit   473
Conflicts of Interest   474
Friendship   474
Payola   474
Freebies   475
Checkbook Journalism   475

ON THE JOB Nurturing a Healthy Ethical Process in an Ever-Changing
Environment   476
  Participation in the News   477
Advertising Pressure   477
Magazines and "New Financial Pillars"   478
Invasion of Privacy   478
  Crime Victims   479
  Juvenile Offenders   480
  Victims of Child Abuse and Their Families   480
  Sexual Orientation   481
  Public Figures   481
  Photos and Video   481
Withholding Information   482
Incorrect and Incomplete Information   483

Plagiarism   484

Twitter Ethics   486

Suggested Readings   487
Suggested Websites   487
Exercises   487

Appendix 1   20 Common Errors of Grammar and Punctuation   489
Appendix 2   Wire-Service Style Summary   499
Appendix 3   Society of Professional Journalists' Code of Ethics   506

Glossary   509
Index   521

Annotated Models   543
Copy Editing and Proofreading Symbols   544
VideoCentral Clips (by chapter)   546

News Reporting and Writing

The Nature of News

CHANCES ARE GOOD that you got some news today from a **Facebook** posting or a **Twitter** feed. The chances also are good that the news report you read originated with a newspaper, which put it up on a website, where it was grabbed by an aggregator. A friend of yours may have spotted it on Google and forwarded it to you and dozens of others. After reading, you may have added a comment and replied. This is the way the public conversation that is journalism works today.

The benefits of this new world of news include instant communication and the ability to share with friends, reflecting a change from the days when journalism was a one-way lecture. Mixed with those blessings, however, are serious problems. The traditional news organizations that still produce most original content are losing audience and income. The truthfulness, or even the actual source, of those Facebook posts and Twitter feeds can be difficult to discover. The uncertainty surrounding the craft and the business of journalism has never been greater.

According to the Project for Excellence in Journalism, "News organizations—old and new—still produce most of the content audiences consume. But each technological advance has added a new layer of complexity—and a new set of players—in connecting that content to consumers and advertisers."

Those new players include aggregators, such as Google and HuffingtonPost.com, that collect, reorganize and often link to work originally done by others—sometimes without full credit and usually without payment. The new players also include Facebook, which in 2012 reached 1 billion users worldwide. The social network allows participants to exchange news, commentary, gossip and personal information without the involvement of professional journalists.

The professionals have added to their traditional tasks new roles—curator and fact checker—as they scramble to assess the accuracy and identify the sources of news that is as likely to be announced by Twitter as by the Associated Press.

Here's just one example of how the news flows through journalism's new conversation. After the first televised debate of the 2012 presidential campaign, the consensus among professional commentators in print and on the air was that Gov. Mitt Romney had soundly defeated President Barack Obama. But on social media, the verdict was just the opposite. A national study of 5.9 million tweets showed Obama was favored 35-22, with another 17 percent being jokes. Of the 262,000 Facebook posts examined, Obama led 40-36.

In this chapter you will learn:

1. How convergence and the forces of technology are reshaping journalism.

2. What the news is, including the elements of a good story, the presentation of news in different media and the rise of citizen journalism.

3. What roles journalism plays in a democracy, including contemporary challenges, principles of good journalism and journalists' responsibilities.

4. How to apply principles of accuracy and fairness and how to avoid bias.

5. How to think about the issue of objectivity.

6. How to distinguish news from commentary and opinion.

Because users of Twitter and Facebook tend to be younger than television viewers or newspaper readers, these results suggest what could be a significant disparity based on age and medium.

It's hard to imagine a more interesting or more confusing time to be practicing or studying journalism.

CONVERGENCE IN JOURNALISM

Convergence is the term that describes efforts to use the different strengths of different media to reach broader audiences and tell the world's stories in new ways. Convergence demands of journalists new skills and new flexibility. Print reporters find themselves summarizing their stories into a television camera and tweeting while an event unfolds before them. Videographers find themselves selecting images to be published in the partner newspaper. Both print and broadcast journalists look for Web links to connect their stories to the worldwide audience and nearly infinite capacity of the Internet. Smartphones provide new outlets and require new storytelling techniques.

The technological revolution also has exploded traditional definitions of just who is a journalist. Millions of people across the world have launched blogs—online journals or columns. Although one estimate is that only 5 percent of those sites include original reporting, and although most have tiny audiences, many have become influential voices in the public conversation. In an effort to add personality and encourage interactivity with audience members, traditional news organizations are encouraging staff members to write blogs.

Increasingly, members of the public are being invited to respond to stories that are published or broadcast. Citizens are even being enlisted as amateur reporters. **Crowdsourcing**, as it is called, has become a reporting tool at news organizations from North Dakota to Florida. Readers and viewers are invited to submit their own stories, photographs and video. They are sometimes asked to lend their expertise to help solve community problems.

The Public Insight Network takes crowdsourcing to the next logical step. Pioneered by public radio, the Public Insight Network is, as the name suggests, a network of citizens who agree to share their knowledge and their insights with professional reporters. National Public Radio and *The New York Times* have teamed up in a new Public Insight Network. So have the investigative nonprofit ProPublica and local news organizations, such as the online *St. Louis Beacon*. Network members may be experts in any field of public interest. Some have professional credentials; others have valuable life experience. They join the network as volunteers. Their pay is the satisfaction they derive from enriching the content and improving the accuracy of journalism.

Even the fundamentals of journalism are evolving as technology speeds up the communication process, provides new sources for both reporters and audiences, and

> " Traditional newsrooms, meanwhile, are different places than they were before the recession. They are smaller, their aspirations have narrowed and their journalists are stretched thinner. But their leaders also say they are more adaptive, younger and more engaged in multimedia presentation, aggregation, blogging and user content. In some ways, new media and old, slowly and sometimes grudgingly, are coming to resemble each other. "
>
> —Project for Excellence in Journalism, "The State of the News Media, 2011"

reshapes journalism from a one-way flow of information to a give-and-take with audiences and competitors. One element that hasn't changed, however, is the importance of accuracy and fairness. And the essential role of journalism in a democratic society remains the one assigned to it by James Madison in 1822: "A popular government without popular information or the means of acquiring it is but a prologue to a farce or a tragedy, or perhaps both."

The basic skills required of every journalist haven't changed either, despite the revolution in technology. Whatever the medium, the skills of news gathering and storytelling are essential to good journalism.

WHAT NEWS IS

The criteria that professional reporters and editors use to decide what news is can be summarized in three words:

- » Relevance
- » Usefulness
- » Interest

Relevance, usefulness and interest for a specific audience are the broad guidelines for judging the news value of any event, issue or personality. These criteria apply generally, but each journalist and each news organization uses them in a specific context that gives them particular meaning. That context is supplied by the audience — the reader, listener or viewer. Journalists always determine newsworthiness with a particular audience in mind.

Elements of a Good News Story

Within the broad news standards of relevance, usefulness and interest, journalists look for more specific elements in each potential story. The most important elements are these:

- » **Impact.** The potential impact of a story is another way of measuring its relevance and usefulness. How many people are affected by an event or idea? How seriously does it affect them? The wider and heavier the impact, the better the story. Sometimes, of course, impact isn't immediately obvious. Sometimes it isn't very exciting. The challenge for good journalism is making such dull but important stories lively and interesting. That may require relying on the next three elements.
- » **Conflict.** Conflict is a recurring theme in all storytelling, whether the stories told are journalism, literature or drama. Struggles between people, among nations or with natural forces make fascinating reading and viewing. Conflict is such a basic element of life that journalists must resist the temptation to overdramatize or oversimplify it.

» **Novelty.** Novelty is another element common to journalism and other kinds of stories. People or events may be interesting and therefore newsworthy just because they are unusual or bizarre.

» **Prominence.** Names make news. The bigger the name, the bigger the news. Ordinary people have always been intrigued by the doings of the rich and famous. Both prominence and novelty can be, and often are, exaggerated to produce "news" that lacks real relevance and usefulness.

» **Proximity.** Generally, people are more interested in and concerned about what happens close to home. When they read or listen to national or international news, they often want to know how it relates to their own community. Some news organizations are turning to hyperlocal coverage as they seek to reconnect with readers; they report at the neighborhood level, sometimes by soliciting contributions from residents or citizen journalists. Independent websites devoted to this kind of extremely local coverage are springing up across the country. Increasingly, however, journalists and scholars are recognizing that communities organized around a particular interest—a sport, a hobby or an issue—are at least as important as geographic communities.

» **Timeliness.** News is supposed to be new. With the Internet and cable and satellite television, "new" means instantaneous. Events are reported as they happen, and this poses a challenge for journalists. Speed conflicts with thoughtfulness and thoroughness. Opportunities for error multiply. Perspective and context are needed today more than ever, but both are more difficult to supply with little time for thinking. Despite the drawbacks of 24/7 news coverage, it's clear that for news to be relevant and useful, it must be timely. For example, it is much more useful to write about an issue facing the city council before the issue is decided than afterward. Timely reporting can give people a chance to be participants in public affairs rather than remain mere spectators.

The digital age, with its often-confusing multitude of sources, splintering of audiences and growing complaints about negative news, has inspired most journalists to add two new criteria for assessing the value of stories:

» **Engagement.** When news was only broadcast or printed on paper, the flow of information was one-way—from journalists to audiences. No more. Today, a news report is often just the beginning of the conversation. Audience members online respond to, correct and criticize the journalism. Many reporters and commentators maintain blogs and invite responses on social networking media such as Twitter and Facebook to encourage such involvement. Increasingly, a goal of both individual journalists and news organizations is to engage the public with the news and with the news provider.

» **Solutions.** Scholars and audiences alike complain that journalists too often report problems and controversies without offering solutions. Political scientist Thomas Patterson has even argued that the negative tone of much coverage of politics and government has the effect of increasing cynicism and decreasing participation in the most basic activities of citizenship, such as voting. More and more journalists are seeking out expert sources and inviting audience members not only to explain complex problems but also to suggest solutions.

How Different Media Present the News

The preceding list suggests two important things about news. First, not all news is serious, life-and-death stuff. The journalistic conversation that holds a society together includes talk of crime, politics and world affairs, of course, but it also includes talk of everyday life. It includes humor and gossip. All of that can be news. Second, news is more than a collection of facts. Telling the news usually means telling stories. The narrative, the humanity and the drama of storytelling make up the art of journalism. To gather the facts for their stories, journalists use many of the same techniques used by sociologists, political scientists and historians. But to tell their stories so that those facts can be understood, journalists often use the techniques of other storytellers, such as novelists and screenwriters.

> *"* If you have any message at all, in any form, that you want to convey to the world, you now have a platform to do so. . . . Your fans and supporters are never more than a click or two away, and they're ready to help you make history — or change it. *"*
>
> —David Mathison, *Be the Media*

The different news media give different weights to the criteria for assessing the value of news stories and require different approaches to telling those stories. For example, newspapers and magazines are better than television or radio for explaining the impact of an issue or the causes of a conflict. Scholars have learned that, although most people say they get most of their news from television, few can remember very much of what they've seen or heard on a newscast. But print can't compete with television in speed or emotional power. The differing strengths and limitations of each medium make it more likely that you'll find a lengthy explanatory story in a newspaper or magazine, while you're more likely to learn of an event from television, radio or the Internet. A newspaper lets you read the details of a budget or a box score, but television shows you the worker whose job was cut or the player scoring the winning basket. The unique power of online journalism is that it brings together the immediacy of television and the comprehensive authority of print, with endless opportunities for users to pursue their interests through the Web. Social media create new communities of interest and allow nonjournalists to join the public conversation.

The Rise of Citizen Journalism

We've already seen how **citizen journalists**, not employed by traditional news organizations and often not professionally trained, use the new technology and social media to report and comment on the news. Some of these citizen journalists have gone further and have created their own news sites online. The focus may be on local communities, as is the case with *The Sacramento Press*, which has three full-time staffers and 1,500 unpaid "community contributors." Or it may be broader, as with the activist indymedia.us, which describes itself as a "network of collectively run media outlets for the creation of radical, accurate and passionate tellings of the truth."

Few of these citizen journalism outlets are profitable, and many are deliberately nonprofit. Their goal, whether local or international, is to cover communities and issues that even local newspapers and broadcast stations don't reach. Their staffs are a mix of trained journalists and interested amateurs. Their audiences are people who don't feel adequately served by the traditional media. Some observers have likened citizen journalists to the pamphleteers who pioneered American journalism two centuries ago.

Some critics of mainstream, traditional journalism hope that these citizen journalists can fill the gaps left by reduced professional staffs or even replace the traditional sources altogether. However, research by two University of Missouri scholars shows that few of the new sites are even close to filling either role. The researchers studied citizen journalism sites and sites sponsored by traditional, or legacy, media—newspapers, magazines, broadcast television, radio and the like—in 46 randomly selected cities. Their conclusion was that the citizen sites "are much more narrow in their content and focus than the **legacy media** sites in those cities." Two-thirds of the citizen sites they studied were blogs rather than news sites.

THE ROLE OF JOURNALISM

VideoCentral ▶

Scott Gold

bedfordstmartins.com /newsreporting

Watch **"Newspapers Now: Balancing Citizen Journalism and Investigative Reporting."**

- What are some strengths and weaknesses of citizen journalism? When are citizen journalists useful?

- Will citizen journalism ever replace traditional journalism? Explain.

The First Amendment to the U.S. Constitution protects the five freedoms that the nation's founders considered essential to a democracy: freedom of speech, religion, the press, petition and assembly. In the 1830s, French aristocrat Alexis de Tocqueville came to study the U.S. and wrote his classic *Democracy in America*. He was struck by the central role played by the only journalism available then: newspapers. "We should underrate their importance if we thought they just guaranteed liberty; they maintain civilization," he wrote.

Challenges to American Journalism

More than 200 years after they were guaranteed, the First Amendment freedoms are still essential and still under threat. After the terrorist attacks of Sept. 11, 2001, a new emphasis on national and personal security tempted government officials and citizens alike to question just how much freedom is compatible with safety. The role of journalism in guaranteeing liberty and maintaining civilization is challenged by those who make news and those who need it.

American journalism is also under threat from growing public skepticism about how well today's journalists are fulfilling their historic roles. National surveys by the Pew Research Center for the People and the Press show, for example, that more than half the public sees bias in the news. About half say that journalists' reports are often inaccurate. Fewer than half say journalism protects democracy, and about one-third

ON THE JOB

A Career Crosses Media Lines

Teri Finneman, a multimedia correspondent for four daily newspapers and two TV stations in North Dakota, graduated from college in 2003. Five years later, she felt compelled to return to school. New technology had provided new challenges and new opportunities. She needed new skills.

"Multimedia wasn't even in my vocabulary at that time," she says. "You focused on print, broadcast or public relations. It never occurred to me once to take a broadcast class or learn how to work a video camera. After all, I was planning to work in newspapers." Times and technology change.

When she returned to the field, Finneman spent as much time shooting video, managing a blog and juggling multiple tools and multiple media as writing for print. And her perspective changed as well.

"Multimedia reporting has helped level the playing field among media outlets," she says. "No longer does TV have the advantage of being able to provide visual images of the 5-year-old singing sensation or the aftermath of dangerous weather. Now, newspapers send out their own videographers and offer the same footage on their websites.

"Likewise, TV stations that used to only be able to tell 30 to 90 seconds of a story can now write full-length pieces and put them online to give viewers the same amount of information that the newspaper can provide.

"Knowing a range of media also gives you flexibility in deciding the best one to use to tell a story. If you're covering overcrowding at an animal shelter, for example, a video story is likely going to give your audience a better understanding and experience of the event than a print story can. If you're going to a political speech outlining a new complicated program, being able to write a full-length print piece is beneficial."

She adds, "Using various media also allows for audience engagement like never before and helps the community feel part of their local media."

Finneman has this message for today's journalism students: "My advice would be to become as well-rounded as possible. There are an increasing number of jobs that combine print and online responsibilities, and you will be at an advantage if you can do both."

Now she is following her own advice and studying for her Ph.D.

say journalism is hurting democracy. In assessing coverage of the 2012 election, voters gave journalists only a grade of C–. Views of the press increasingly vary with political affiliation. Republicans are much more critical than Democrats. And those who get their news online rate the major Internet sources—such as Google, Yahoo, AOL and Slate.com—even lower than the traditional media.

On the other hand, the same surveys show that credibility has improved, at least a little, from historic lows. Comfortable majorities say they believe all or most of what they read in newspapers and see on television news. Most people give higher ratings to the particular newspaper or TV station they use than to the news media in general. And two-thirds rate journalists as highly professional. (For regular samplings of public opinion about journalism, visit www.people-press.org, the website of the Pew Research Center.)

Principles of Good Journalism

What these citizens seem to be saying is that the work journalists do is important, but journalists aren't doing it well enough. The past decade has seen the emergence of several major efforts to improve the performance of American journalism.

One of those efforts has been driven by an informal association called the Committee of Concerned Journalists and the related Project for Excellence in Journalism. The project conducts regular research on journalism, and it issues reports that can be accessed on its website, Journalism.org. Among the reports are annual "State of the News Media" assessments, as well as regular reports on the public's news consumption and on journalists' performance. Another product of these reformers is a book that every journalism student and practitioner should read: *The Elements of Journalism* by Bill Kovach and Tom Rosenstiel, two leaders of the committee and the project.

The book argues that "the purpose of journalism is to provide people with the information they need to be free and self-governing." It proposes 10 principles to achieve this purpose:

1. Journalism's first obligation is to the truth.
2. Its first loyalty is to citizens.
3. Its essence is a discipline of verification.
4. Its practitioners must maintain independence from those they cover.
5. Journalism must serve as an independent monitor of power.
6. It must provide a forum for public criticism and compromise.
7. It must strive to make the significant interesting and relevant.
8. It must keep the news comprehensive and proportional.
9. Its practitioners must be allowed to exercise their personal conscience.
10. Citizens, too, have rights and responsibilities when it comes to the news.

In these principles, you can hear echoes of the Journalist's Creed, written nearly a century before by Walter Williams, founding dean of the world's first journalism school, at the University of Missouri. Williams wrote that "the public journal is a public trust . . . (and) acceptance of a lesser interest than the public interest is a violation of that trust."

Journalists' Responsibilities in a Democracy

The efforts to reform or restore journalism recognize these vital functions of journalists in a free society:

» **Journalists report the news.** News reporting, the first and most obvious function of journalists, is the foundation of the rest. Reporters cover Congress and council meetings, describe accidents and disasters, and show the horrors of war and the highlights of football games. This reporting takes many forms: tweets, live television, online bulletins, next-day newspaper analyses and long-form magazine narratives. In 2009, the *Houston Chronicle* was a finalist for journalism's highest honor, the Pulitzer Prize, for its staff coverage of a hurricane threatening the city. Nearly all the reporting, plus blogs by staff and citizens, appeared online rather than on paper. No wonder journalism has been called the first rough draft of history.

» **Journalists monitor power.** The power that Americans most often are concerned about is the power of government. Lately, private power has become more of a worry and more of a source of news. Alexandra Berzon and her colleagues at the *Las Vegas Sun* won the Pulitzer Prize for public service for their investigation of lax inspections that led to high rates of death and injury among construction workers on the Las Vegas Strip. Monitoring is required even if power is used legitimately—when governments raise taxes or take us to war, for example, or when businesses close plants or cut health care benefits for employees. When the power is used illegally or immorally, another important function comes into play.

» **Journalists uncover injustice.** A television reporter pursues a tip and eventually uncovers a pattern of sexual abuse and nonenforcement that changes the culture at the nation's military academies. A newspaper discovers that prisoners on death row were convicted unfairly. In those cases and thousands more, journalists bring to light dangerous or illegal abuses that might otherwise go unchecked.

» **Journalists tell compelling stories that delight us and some that dismay us.** For example, the husband-and-wife team of Nicholas D. Kristof and Sheryl WuDunn told the horrifying and hopeful stories of women struggling to overcome discrimination and abuse in the developing world for *The New York Times* and in a book, *Half the Sky: Turning Oppression into Opportunity for Women Worldwide*. Television's *60 Minutes* and *Frontline* tell the stories of true-life dramas. Bloggers bring firsthand experiences and often great passion to their posts.

» **Journalists sustain communities.** These communities may be small towns, cities or even virtual communities of people connected only by the Internet. Through their reporting, monitoring, revealing and storytelling, journalists serve as the nervous system of the community. They convey information as well as argument.

» **Journalists curate information.** With so much material from so many unknown sources flooding the Internet, an increasingly important role for journalists is that of curator—collecting, sorting and verifying information. Now that professional journalists are not the sole, and sometimes not even the primary, providers of news, their duty has expanded to include checking the facts asserted by others.

» **Journalists set the record straight.** When the candidates for president met in televised debates in 2012, every television network and major newspaper deployed fact checkers whose assignment was to assess the accuracy of the candidates' claims and of the charges they exchanged. At least two national organizations, FactCheck.org and PolitiFact.com, have full-time staff members who do nothing but separate fact from fiction in political argument.

Scholars have used other terms for this combination of vital functions. One is "agenda setting," the placing of issues on the public agenda for discussion and decision. Another is "gatekeeping," the process by which some events and ideas become news and others do not. Today the gatekeeping function has largely evolved into curating or navigating, guiding readers and viewers through oceans of fact, rumor and fantasy in search of solid meaning. Bloggers such as Matt Drudge and Josh Marshall sometimes serve as agenda setters for mainstream journalists. Entertainers such as Jon Stewart serve as sources not only of laughs but of information. Even in the Internet age, however, the news you read on Google or some other website probably was first reported in one of the traditional newsrooms.

ACCURACY, FAIRNESS AND BIAS

The goal toward which most journalists strive has seldom been expressed better than in a phrase used years ago by Bob Woodward, then an editor at *The Washington Post*. Woodward was defending in court an investigative story published by *The Post*. The story, he said, was "the best obtainable version of the truth."

A grander-sounding goal would be "the truth," unmodified. But Woodward's phrase, while paying homage to the ideal, recognizes the realities of life and the limitations of journalism. Despite centuries of argument, philosophers and theologians are still unable to agree on what truth is. Even if there were agreement on that basic question, how likely is it that the Roman Catholic Church and the Planned Parenthood organization would agree on the "truth" about abortion, or that a president and an opposition presidential candidate would agree on the "truth" about the state of the American economy?

> " The new media tools and techniques are wonderful ways to generate information much, much faster. They don't so much take away from the actual reporting as they allow the reporter to know so much more. "
>
> —Karen Dillon, reporter, *The Kansas City Star*

In American daily journalism, that kind of dispute is left to be argued among the partisans on all sides, on the editorial pages and in commentaries. The reporter's usual role is simply to find and write the facts. The trouble is, that task rarely turns out to be simple.

Sometimes it's hard to get the facts. The committee searching for a new university president announces that the field of candidates has been narrowed to five, but the names of the five are not released. Committee members are sworn to secrecy. What can you do to get the names? Should you try?

Sometimes it's hard to tell what the facts mean. The state supreme court refuses to hear a case in which legislators are questioning the constitutionality of a state spending limit. The court says only that there is no "justiciable controversy." What does that mean? Who won? Is the ruling good news or bad news, and for whom?

Sometimes it's even hard to tell what is fact. After a yearlong study, a presidential commission says there is no widespread hunger in America. Is that conclusion a fact? Or is the fact only what the commission said? And how can you determine whether the commission is correct?

Daily journalism presents still more complications. As a reporter, you usually have only a few hours—or at most a few days—to try to learn as many facts about an event as possible. Then, even in such a limited time, you may accumulate information enough for a story of 2,000 words, only to be told that there is space or time enough for only 1,000 words or fewer. The new media offer more space but no more time for reporting. When you take into account all these realities and limitations, you can see that reaching the best obtainable version of the truth is challenge enough for any journalist.

How can you tell when that goal has been reached? Seldom, if ever, is there a definitive answer. But there are two questions every responsible journalist should ask about every story before being satisfied: Is it accurate? Is it fair?

Accuracy and Fairness

Accuracy is the most important characteristic of any story, great or small, long or short. Every name must be spelled correctly; every quote must be just what was said; every set of numbers must add up. And that still isn't good enough. You can get the details right and still mislead unless you are accurate with context, too. The same statement may have widely different meanings depending on the circumstances in which it was uttered and the tone in which it was spoken. Circumstances and intent affect the meaning of actions as well. You will never have the best obtainable version of the truth unless your version is built on accurate reporting of detail and context.

Nor can you approach the truth without being fair. Accuracy and fairness are related, but they are not the same. Being fair requires asking yourself if you have done enough to uncover all the relevant facts and have delivered those facts in an impartial manner, without favoring one side or another in a story. The relationship between accuracy and fairness—and the differences between them—is shown clearly in this analogy from the world of sports.

The referee in a basketball game is similar, in some ways, to a reporter. Each is supposed to be an impartial observer, calling developments as he or she sees them. (Of course, the referee's job is to make judgments on those developments, while the reporter's job is just to describe them. Rendering judgment is the role of columnists, bloggers and other opinion writers.) Television has brought to sports the instant replay, in which a key play—for example, one in which a player may have been fouled while taking a shot—can be examined again and again, often from an angle different from the referee's line of sight. Sometimes the replay shows an apparent outcome different from the one the official called. Perhaps the players actually didn't make contact. Perhaps what looked like an attempted shot was really a pass. The difference may be due to human error on the official's part, or it may be due to the differences in angle and in viewpoint. Referees recognize this problem. They try to deal with it by obtaining the best possible view of every play and by conferring with their colleagues on some close calls. Still, every official knows that an occasional mistake will be made. That is unavoidable. What can, and must, be avoided is unfairness. Referees must be fair, and both players and fans must believe they are fair. Otherwise, their judgments will not be accepted; they will not be trusted.

With news, too, there are different viewpoints from which every event or issue can be observed. Each viewpoint may yield a different interpretation of what is occurring and of what it means. There is also, in journalism as in sports, the possibility of human error, even by the most careful reporters.

Fairness requires that you as a reporter try to find every viewpoint on a story. Rarely will there be only one; often there are more than two. Fairness requires that you allow ample opportunity for response to anyone who is being attacked or whose integrity is being questioned in a story. Fairness requires, above all, that you make every effort to avoid following your own biases in your reporting and your writing (see Figure 1.1). However, neither fairness nor objectivity requires that every viewpoint receive the same amount of time or space.

Dealing with Bias

The research summarized earlier in this chapter suggests that citizens don't think journalists do enough to keep bias—conscious or unconscious—out of the news. More than eight out of 10 respondents in a national survey said they see bias at least

		News Stories	Commentaries
Accuracy		• Make sure facts (events, names, dates, statistics, places, quotes) are correct. • Verify facts with multiple sources. • Use reliable sources for statistics. • Use facts as the substance of the story. • Discover and include all necessary facts.	• Make sure facts (events, names, dates, statistics, places, quotes) are correct. • Include all the facts needed to prove a point of view. • Possibly leave out facts that don't support the argument but ideally provide context or ideas that explain the facts.
Fairness		• Provide context for facts. • Give all relevant sides of a story. • Strive for balance.	• Provide context for facts. • Use facts and reason to persuade the audience of a point of view. • Appeal to emotion, but not by distorting the facts.
Bias		• Leave personal bias out of the story. • Use neutral language.	• Support personal bias with facts and reasoning. • Acknowledge and rebut other points of view. • Use civil language, not highly charged language or personal attacks.

FIGURE 1.1

Accuracy, fairness and lack of bias are essential in news stories. Writers of commentaries (editorials, blogs, written and spoken essays, reviews and letters to the editor) must also be accurate and fair in order to be credible.

sometimes. Of those, about twice as many said the bias seemed to be culturally and politically liberal as thought it conservative. A chorus of critics claims that journalists lean to the left. A smaller chorus complains of a rightward tilt. Books and cable television talk shows add heat, if not light, to the criticism. How valid is it?

One answer is that American journalism has many biases built into it. For example, journalists are biased toward conflict. War is a better story than peace. Journalists are biased toward novelty. Airplanes that don't crash are seldom reported. Journalists are biased toward celebrity. The lives and deaths of celebrities are chronicled in detail on the network news as well as in fan magazines.

There's a less obvious but even more important bias that probably accounts for much of the criticism. It is hidden in the job description of journalism. What do journalists say they do? What are they proudest of? What do they honor?

Journalists describe themselves as the outside agitators, the afflicters of the comfortable and the comforters of the afflicted. They see their job as being the watchdog against the powerful, the voice of the voiceless, the surrogate for the ordinary citizen, the protector of the abused and downtrodden. Journalists expect themselves to be forever skeptical, consistently open-minded, respectful of differences, sensitive to what sociologists call "the other." Neither patriotism nor religion should be exempt from their critical examination.

Does that job description seem more "liberal" or more "conservative"?

Consider that conservatives generally are respectful of authority and supportive of the status quo. Is it any surprise, then, that the overwhelming majority of conservatives and many liberals see a liberal bias in journalism? Notice that this bias has little or nothing to do with partisan politics.

Now suppose we had a journalism that wasn't questioning, disrespectful of authority, open to new ideas, dogging the powerful and speaking for the weak. Who would benefit, and who would suffer? Would society and democracy be better or worse off?

At a deeper level, however, American journalism is profoundly conservative. Journalists seldom examine critically the foundation stones on which the American way of life is based. Among these are capitalism, the two-party system, the concepts of the ethnic melting pot and of social mobility. When was the last time you saw any of those ideas questioned seriously in the mainstream press?

One conclusion suggested by this analysis is that in societies that aren't free—such as America before independence—a free press is a revolutionary instrument. In a society such as 21st-century America, which considers itself free and is overall self-satisfied, the free press becomes, at a fundamental level, conservative.

THE ISSUE OF OBJECTIVITY

The rules that mainstream journalists follow in attempting to arrive at the best obtainable version of the truth—to report accurately, fairly and without bias—are commonly summarized in the concept of objectivity. Objectivity has been and still is accepted as a working credo by most American journalists, as well as by students and teachers of journalism. It has been exalted by leaders of the profession as an essential, if unattainable, ideal. Its critics, by contrast, have attacked objectivity as, in the phrase of sociologist Gaye Tuchman, a "strategic ritual" that conceals a multitude of professional sins while producing superficial and often misleading coverage.

In his classic *Discovering the News*, Michael Schudson traces the rise of objectivity to the post–World War I period, when scholars and journalists alike turned to the methods and the language of science in an attempt to make sense of a world that was being turned upside down by the influence of Sigmund Freud in psychology and Karl Marx in politics, the emergence of new economic forces and the erosion of traditional values. Objectivity was a reliance on observable facts, but it was also a methodology for freeing factual reporting from the biases and values of source, writer or reader. It was itself a value, an ideal.

Schudson writes, "Journalists came to believe in objectivity, to the extent that they did, because they wanted to, needed to, were forced by ordinary human aspiration to seek escape from their own deep convictions of doubt and drift."

Objectivity, then, was a way of applying to the art of journalism the methods of science. Those methods emphasized reliance on observable fact. They also included the use of a variety of transparent techniques for pursuing truth and verifying facts. In science, transparency means that the researchers explain their objectives, their methods, their findings and their limitations. In journalism, only part of that methodology is usually followed. Journalists seldom describe their methods or discuss the limits of their findings. If they did, at least some members of the public might be less suspicious and less critical.

In *The Elements of Journalism*, Kovach and Rosenstiel worry that a kind of phony objectivity has replaced the original concept. The objectivity of science does not require neutrality or the artificial balance of two sides in a dispute. Scientists are free, and expected, to state their conclusions, as long as they report how they reached those conclusions. However, as usually practiced today, journalistic objectivity employs both neutrality and balance, sometimes instead of the kind of openness that is essential in science. This misunderstanding or misapplication of the real principles of objectivity has opened the way for critics to call for its abandonment. Journalists would be more honest, these critics argue, if they were open about their biases. In much of Europe, for example, journalists practice openly biased reporting, which their audiences expect.

The problem with that approach is easy to see in European journalism or, closer to home, in the opinionated journalism of partisan publications, cable television or many blogs. One-sided reports appeal to audiences that share the writer's bias, but they repel those that don't. Fairness and accuracy too often are casualties in this journalism of assertion rather than of verification.

Properly understood, objectivity provides the journalistic method most likely to yield the best obtainable version of the truth. True objectivity, Kovach and Rosenstiel argue, would add scientific rigor to journalistic art. Without that, journalists and audiences alike can be misled.

WHAT IS *NOT* NEWS

Though there's debate about just how objective a reporter can possibly be, journalists and scholars all agree about one thing: Reporting the news is not the same as expressing an opinion. The primary goal of a news story is to inform. Whether in print, on television or radio, or online, a reporter's job is to communicate pertinent facts, together with enough background information to help the audience understand those facts. Accuracy and fairness are paramount. By contrast, the primary goal of opinion writers and speakers is to persuade. Accuracy and fairness are still important—though they sometimes get lost in argument. A commentator is expressing a point of view rather than reporting the views of others.

To see for yourself the differences in style and substance, watch Brian Williams deliver the *NBC Nightly News*. Then, later in the evening, switch to MSNBC, a sister network, and listen to Rachel Maddow discuss the same events. Now move to Fox and Bill O'Reilly. The events of the day, as Williams reported them, haven't changed, but their context and meaning sound very different from the viewpoints of the political left (Maddow) and right (O'Reilly). For another clear example of the differences between reporting and commentary, compare a front-page story in *The New York Times* with an editorial on the same subject on the newspaper's opinion page. The former is seeking to inform you, the latter to persuade you.

Because the aims are different, news stories and commentary approach accuracy, fairness and bias differently.

In 1947, the Hutchins Commission on freedom of the press concluded that what a free society needs from journalists is "a truthful, comprehensive and intelligent account of the day's events in a context which gives them meaning." The goal of this chapter is to show you how the journalists of today and tomorrow understand that need, how they are trying to meet it, and how complex the task is. The rest of the book helps you develop the skills you'll need to take up the challenge. There are few challenges as important or as rewarding.

SUGGESTED READINGS

Journalism reviews: Every issue of *Columbia Journalism Review*, *American Journalism Review*, *Quill* and *The American Editor*, the bulletin of the American Society of News Editors, offers reports and analyses of the most important issues of contemporary journalism.

Kovach, Bill, and Tom Rosenstiel. *The Elements of Journalism: What Newspeople Should Know and the Public Should Expect*. New York: Three Rivers Press, 2007. This little book is packed with practical advice and inspiration, a kind of applied ethics for journalists in any medium.

Schudson, Michael. *Discovering the News: A Social History of American Newspapers*. New York: Basic Books, 1978. This well-written study traces the development of objectivity in American journalism.

Wurman, Richard Saul. *Information Anxiety*. New York: Doubleday, 1990. This guide for consumers of information can also serve as a guide for journalists as they seek to provide understanding.

SUGGESTED WEBSITES

www.asne.org

The American Society of News Editors is the most important of the industry's professional organizations. This website gives you access to the society's landmark credibility project, including the results of a major study of Americans' attitudes toward, and uses of, journalism. You'll find that study in the "Archives" section.

www.bedfordstmartins.com/newscentral

When you visit News Central, you will find up-to-the-moment RSS feeds, research links and exercises to help you improve your grammar and AP style usage. In addition, the site's Video-Central: Journalism section hosts the videos highlighted in this chapter as well as additional clips of leading professionals discussing important media trends.

www.cjr.org

Columbia Journalism Review is the oldest of the magazines devoted to the critical analysis of journalists' performance. You'll find critiques of major stories, essays on ethics, book reviews and trade news. *American Journalism Review* (www.ajr .org) offers similar content.

www.journalism.org

The site of the Pew Research Center's Project for Excellence in Journalism contains relevant research and articles on the current state of journalism. See especially the "State of the News Media" reports for the most comprehensive look at the current performance of all the major news media.

www.people-press.org

The site of the Pew Research Center for the People and the Press is a reliable source for frequent reports on public attitudes toward journalism, as well as on topics in the news.

www.politifact.com

This site is one of the best fact-checking sites. It is operated by the *Tampa Bay Times* in Florida and staffed by professional journalists. Its analyses usually provide not only fact but context.

www.poynter.org

This site is an excellent starting point for journalism students. The Poynter Institute is the leading center of continuing professional education for journalists. On this site you'll find not only a guide to the services and resources of the institute itself but also links to the sites of every major professional organization and a variety of other useful resources.

EXERCISES

1. **Team project.** As a group, compare your sources of news. Does anyone read an actual newspaper or watch the nightly news on television? How do you assess the accuracy of news items you receive from Twitter or Facebook? Where do those items originate?

2. Now change your news habits for a week. Stay off Facebook and Twitter, at least as news sources. Instead, read a newspaper every day, and watch the nightly news on television. Which approach leaves you better informed? Which is more enjoyable?

3. Spend some time with the citizen journalists at www .voiceofsandiego.org and www.indymedia.us. Compare what you find with the stories in the mainstream media from those geographic areas. Where do you see overlapping coverage, and what stories are different in each medium? Which sources seem to serve the citizens best?

4. Most Americans say they get most of their news from television. Watch an evening newscast on one of the major networks. Read the print edition of *The New York Times* or *USA Today* for the same day. Compare the number of stories, the topics covered and the depth of coverage. How well informed are television-dependent Americans?

5. Get copies or visit the websites of your local newspaper, a paper from a city at least 50 miles away and a paper of national circulation, such as *USA Today* or *The Wall Street Journal*. Analyze the front page or home page according to the criteria discussed in this chapter, and answer the following questions:

   a. What does the selection of stories on the front page or home page tell you about the editors' understanding of each paper's audience?

   b. If you find stories on the same topic on the front page or home page of two or more newspapers, determine whether the stories were written differently for different audiences.

   c. On the basis of what you've learned in this chapter, do you agree or disagree with the editors' news judgments? Why?

6. As a class project, visit or invite to your class the editor of your local paper and the news director of a local television station. Study their products ahead of time, and then interview them about how they decide the value of news stories, how they assess the reliability of sources and how they try to ensure accuracy.

7. **Journalism blog.** Create your own blog for the class (www .blogger.com is a good place to start). For your first post, write about your goals for the blog. Email the blog's name and link to your classmates and instructor. Use your blog throughout the term to discuss the issues raised in this and other chapters, especially the tricky ones such as objectivity and fairness.

2

The Changing Media Landscape

WHEN A GUNMAN fatally shot 20 children and six adult staff members at Sandy Hook Elementary School in Newtown, Conn., in late 2012, many first got the news through the traditional media. But a record number also got the news on the fastest-growing news platforms in the U.S.: smartphones and tablet computers, often lumped together as **mobile media** or, simply, mobile.

A Pew Research Center study concluded that 27 percent of Americans were regularly turning to mobile devices to get their news by 2012. According to Pew, the age of mobile arrived in 2011—a new era in which "people are connected to the Web wherever they are." Almost nine in 10 Americans now own mobile phones, and 44 percent of those devices are **smartphones**, which enable users to access the Web and its audio and video capabilities. Twenty-two percent of Americans owned **tablet computers** in 2012, up from just 4 percent two years earlier.

NEWS CONSUMPTION IN THE AGE OF MOBILE DEVICES

According to the Pew study, this new era is encouraging for the news industry. The study found that "mobile devices are adding to people's news consumption, strengthening the lure of traditional news brands and providing a boost to long-form journalism. Eight in 10 who get news on smartphones or tablets . . . get news on personal computers as well. People are taking advantage, in other words, of having easier access to news throughout the day—in their pocket, on their desks and in their laps." At the same time, the news from the survey was mixed: Consumption of traditional media—newspapers, radio and television, in particular—continued to decline.

Mobile's Role in Consumers' Move to the Web

The arrival of mobile as a major force in news adds momentum to the sweeping changes taking place in the media industry. Asked in 2012 to choose whether radio, television, newspapers or the Web was most essential to their lives, a whopping 46 percent of Americans ranked the Web first; newspapers were a distant fourth. Among Americans aged 12 to 34, the response was even more pronounced: 68 percent ranked

In this chapter you will learn:

1. How major changes in news consumption are affecting the U.S. media.

2. How fragmentation hurts the bottom line of legacy media companies.

3. How financial problems affect the gathering of news.

4. Why newspapers are the source of most news.

5. Where journalism fits in our democracy.

6. How people consume news today.

7. Why people distrust the media.

8. Why convergence is a response to media fragmentation.

9. How citizen journalism is changing American journalism.

10. How journalists view the future of their profession.

the Web as most essential. That 2012 study by TV ratings agency Arbitron Inc. and Edison Research seems to depict quite accurately what's happening to media in the U.S.: People increasingly look to the Web to satisfy their need for news, getting there however they can—through personal computers, smartphones and tablets.

Increasing News Audiences

Fueling this change in media consumption is the arrival of faster and easier access to the Web, not only through mobile devices but also within the home. When Arbitron and Edison conducted a similar study 10 years earlier, in 2002, 72 percent of Americans reported being able to access the Web from almost anywhere, but only 13 percent reported having broadband (high-speed) Web access at home. By 2012, the landscape had shifted significantly: 70 percent reported having broadband access, and 76 percent even had their own **Wi-Fi** (wireless Internet access) connection at home. This combination makes access easier and faster, and it allows multiple connections to the Web from within the home. Broadband access also enables the streaming of audio and video over the Web, which has the effect of reducing the market for traditional radio and television while increasing the overall radio and television audience.

Something similar is happening with newspaper companies. Fewer people are buying or subscribing to the traditional print product, but more and more readers access newspaper websites, which has the effect of increasing the overall newspaper audience.

Social media are important to the media mix, too. More than 56 percent of Americans now have a profile on a social networking site such as Facebook or LinkedIn.

Newspaper publishers hope that e-readers like the Kindle will spark new interest in newspaper reading.

And while young people dominate the use of social media, the fastest growth rate in social media usage in 2012 was among those 45 and older. Increasingly, people learn about breaking news when someone, often a media company employee, posts about it on Facebook, Twitter or other social media sites.

All that raises the question: What does this mean to those who provide news and news-related information? First, it's quite obvious that both the size of the audience and its appetite for news are growing. Second, it's also true that the way in which that audience wants to receive news is shifting from traditional media toward mobile and online media. It's extremely important, then, for those who produce news to understand this shift and to provide news the way the public wants it. Consumption patterns are shifting so significantly that it's plausible to declare that we are in the midst of nothing less than a media revolution.

GREATER MEDIA FRAGMENTATION

Many have misread what's happening. In almost any story about the current state of the media, the recurring theme is likely to be, "Everyone is tuning out." You've heard it: Young people don't consume news. Newspapers are on their deathbeds. Local television will be the next to die. There's just one thing wrong with that conventional wisdom: It isn't true.

What is true is that consuming news is just one of many things people choose to do on their smartphones and tablets. One study of smartphones by comScore Inc. showed that users reported these activities as most important on those devices:

1. Accessing email.
2. Checking the weather.
3. Accessing social networks and blogs.
4. Playing games.
5. Searching for information.
6. Accessing maps.
7. Accessing news.
8. Listening to music.
9. Using instant messaging services.
10. Doing work.

Indications are that consuming news is even more important to users of tablets. Almost one-third of those who buy tablets read more news from more sources than they read before, according to a study conducted by the Pew Research Center's Project for Excellence in Journalism. Consuming news is the second most popular activity for tablet users after email.

So, accessing news is far more important to users than many suggest. That may well account for the dozens of news-based computer applications, or **apps,** for iPhones and iPads found in Apple's online store. Similar apps exist for the Android and Windows markets.

The U.S. population also continues to increase, and the size of the audience for news is growing with it. While audiences decline for newspapers and local television, consumers are flocking to the Web for news—often using smartphones and tablets to access it. The problem for news companies is not that people are tuning out or using media less frequently. Instead, the problem is **media fragmentation**. This proliferation of media outlets has led to smaller audiences for individual media companies. There are many more places to get news today than there were 25 years ago.

Smaller audiences are resulting in less advertising, or reduced prices for it, which has put great financial stress on those media, particularly newspapers and local television. Indeed, in its 2012 report on the State of the News Media, Pew concluded, "The transformation of the nation's news landscape has already taken a heavy toll on print news sources, particularly print newspapers. But there are now signs that television news—which so far has held onto its audience through the rise of the Internet—also is increasingly vulnerable, as it may be losing its hold on the next generation of news consumers." So there's no lack of interest in news, and the audience is increasing. But the news industry has a broken business model.

FINANCIAL CHALLENGES TO LEGACY MEDIA

For the better part of two centuries, owning a newspaper was virtually a license to print money. Great fortunes were made by media barons like William Randolph Hearst, who owned large newspapers, and Donald W. Reynolds, who owned small ones. Their businesses were lucrative: For much of the 20th century, newspapers turned a profit of 20 to 25 cents—sometimes even more—on each dollar that came through the door.

When radio and television came along, those media built on this legacy. Both quickly became profitable, and owning television networks and stations eventually became even more lucrative than owning newspapers. Magazines also found a home in the American media landscape. As advertisers began to covet their ability to deliver targeted audiences, the number of magazines proliferated.

Trouble was brewing, however, and by the end of the 20th century, it became clear that audience fragmentation was becoming a significant problem.

Smaller Audiences as a Result of Media Proliferation

When radio and television came along, they fit into the media landscape with little harm to newspapers and magazines. But by the time the Web and cable television arrived, media outlets were proliferating and media consumption patterns were shifting. Younger people started turning away from newspapers in favor of the Web and its thousands of information sources. Cable television took viewers from local stations. In the end, the proliferation of media outlets began to slice audiences, even growing ones, into smaller and smaller fragments, taking ad revenue from the traditional legacy media.

Today, it's clear that legacy media—newspapers, magazines, radio and broadcast television—are being damaged severely by newer media forms such as cable television, the Web and mobile devices. Newspaper revenues have fallen precipitously, and local television stations are now feeling the pinch caused by a proliferation of cable channels. Magazines are still generally healthy, thanks to their ability to target audiences more efficiently than newspapers or local television. Still, even magazines are threatened by the changes. In late 2012, *Newsweek*, first published in 1933, announced it would quit putting out a print edition and move to all-electronic distribution; the digital edition was later put up for sale. Magazines, like newspapers, suffer from high production and distribution costs. As a result, their long-term prognosis is uncertain. To hedge their bets, magazine publishers, like their newspaper counterparts, are embracing the Web.

William Randolph Hearst (1863–1951) made a fortune as the owner of large newspapers.

Lower Advertising Revenues and Higher Debt

Newspapers are costly to produce, and revenue trends are headed in the wrong direction. Classified advertising, long a big moneymaker at newspapers, has been devastated by websites like craigslist.org. Help-wanted advertising, in particular, has plummeted. Newspapers are manufactured products that consume large amounts of expensive paper and ink. They are labor-intensive not only in news reporting but also in printing and distribution. They are, in effect, an increasingly inefficient—and costly—way to deliver news.

Nevertheless, despite what many would have you believe, most newspapers are *still* profitable. Those that have failed or are suffering mostly fall into two categories: Either they are the second newspaper in a two-newspaper city, or they have been purchased by corporations and have amassed huge debt. Many well-known newspapers have closed, including the *Rocky Mountain News* of Denver and the *Seattle Post-Intelligencer*. Some, like *The (New Orleans) Times-Picayune*, have opted for less-frequent publishing schedules, often three or four days a week. Still others—the *Chicago Tribune*, the *Los Angeles Times* and *The Boston Globe* among them—are in trouble because of heavy debt incurred when they were purchased.

More than 1,700 daily newspapers existed as late as 1980, but today the number hovers around 1,380. Daily newspaper circulation declined almost 29 percent from 1990 to 2011. More than 15,000 newspaper journalists lost their jobs between 2000 and 2010, and some cities, like Ann Arbor, Mich., home to about 115,000 people and a major university, don't have a daily newspaper anymore.

Many forecast a similar pending contraction of local television. No one is predicting that local television stations will disappear, but it's likely that fewer stations will offer local news in the years ahead.

Despite all this, the typical U.S. newspaper still turns a nice profit of about 5 cents on the dollar, and most local television stations are still profitable, too. When you consider that many industries operate quite comfortably on much lower profit margins, newspapers and local television are far from dying. The trend, though, is in the wrong direction for legacy media companies, which still derive about 90 percent of their income from their original platforms rather than from the Web because print advertising is more profitable than Web advertising.

NEWSPAPERS: THE SOURCE OF MOST NEWS

Although people prefer different news *platforms*, what they are *not* doing is rejecting traditional *sources* of news—news provided by legacy media, companies that specialize in traditional media forms such as newspapers, magazines, radio and broadcast television.

So while it's tempting to dismiss newspapers as a product of a bygone era and suggest that we simply move on to newer and better ways of getting news, the larger problem is that newspapers are the source of most of the news we consume. Indeed, most of the information found on Yahoo or Google News originated with legacy media operations, most often newspapers. The same is true with most other news websites.

In fact, several studies have concluded that the vast majority of all news consumed in the U.S., regardless of where it was consumed, originated with newspapers. The reason? Newspapers have the best news-gathering apparatus in almost every city in the country. They typically employ more journalists than all the radio and television stations in that city combined.

So for more than a century, the legacy media have funded the extensive news-gathering operation that exists in the U.S. and much of the rest of the world. Yet increasingly, because of the diminished audiences for print journalism, newspapers and television companies are trimming the size of their staffs in an effort to survive. Clearly, a new business model is needed.

As we go about this task of creating a new business model for the news media, what we must save is not specific newspapers and television programs, and not the companies that own them, but the high-quality reporting they produce.

Most of that news is **spot news**—breaking news that occurred today. Replacing spot news might not be too tough. After all, if a plane crashes, some blogger or citizen journalist, if no one else, is bound to report it. More problematic is the potential loss of what journalist Alex S. Jones calls "the creation of new awareness provided by either months of investigation or relentlessly regular coverage."

Jones is the Laurence M. Lombard Lecturer in the Press and Public Policy and the director of the Joan Shorenstein Center on the Press, Politics and Public Policy at Harvard University. In his book *Losing the News: The Future of the News That Feeds Democracy*, he praises the technological changes that are altering the journalism landscape, but he fears the loss of the "iron core of news that serves as a watchdog over government, holds the powerful accountable, and gives citizens what they need." He's hopeful and optimistic that the "iron core" can be saved.

In a review of Jones' book in *The New York Times*, Harold Evans, former editor of *The Sunday Times of London* and *The Times of London*, points out what happens when this kind of news doesn't get enough attention: "the insufficiently monitored housing bubble; the neglect in New Orleans, leading to the devastation after Katrina; or the formation of Al Qaeda in Afghanistan, leading to 9/11."

JOURNALISM'S ROLE IN A DEMOCRACY

While the overall size of the news audience is growing, not all consumers are embracing the new media. Indeed, some young people, in particular, don't consume news at all, and that merely adds to the problems of legacy media.

College student Kendra Logan, 19, is among an increasing number of young people who don't consume news. "I don't read newspapers, I don't watch television news, and I rarely look at news on the Internet," she says. She's among the disengaged, and she's not alone. According to a study by the Pew Research Center, Logan is among the 34 percent of those younger than 25 who get no news daily, up from 25 percent just 10 years earlier.

That's troubling to those who worry about the foundations of U.S. democracy. Ill-informed members of the public can't make good decisions in the voting booth, if indeed they vote at all. They can't possibly understand the big issues of the day—among them conflicts with extremists, health care availability, failing schools, illegal immigration and poverty. In short, they can't be good citizens. To actively participate in democracy requires knowledge of what's going on in the world, the nation, the state and the community.

Logan is one of millions of uninformed Americans who are tuning out the news as the U.S. experiences the biggest shift in media consumption patterns since colonial times. That's bad for the media, but it's also bad for the country, which depends on an informed citizenry to make good decisions in the voting booth. With that in mind, it's important for today's journalist to understand audiences—how and why people decide to consume news and why some choose not to do so.

HOW PEOPLE CONSUME NEWS TODAY

It's clear that legacy media are falling out of favor at an increasing pace. But if there are losers, there also must be winners. As noted earlier, those winners are the Web and mobile and, to a lesser extent, cable television. According to a 2012 Pew study, television continues to reign as America's favorite news source—55 percent of respondents reported consuming news on television the day before being surveyed. That percentage, however, had dropped from 68 percent in 1991. While cable television audiences remained stable, local television audiences continued to decline.

ON THE JOB
Editing Online News

Sarah Rupp graduated with a degree in newspaper journalism but immediately found herself working at online sites.

Right out of school, she landed an internship at msnbc.com in Redmond, Wash. She later worked at other online sites, including ABCNews.com, before landing at seattlepi.com, which operates 24/7.

"I usually work a day shift, which means that I have to keep the site fresh with new articles, story updates, breaking news and photos," Rupp says. "Throughout the day we add new wire stories, staff stories, photo galleries and other Web-only features. . . . Besides doing the daily stuff, I also get to work on special projects like producing video and putting together new content channels for the site."

She enjoys the work: "The great thing about working for a news website is you get the chance to do a little of everything — writing, editing, choosing stories, designing graphics, building Web pages, posting photos and editing audio clips.

"There are a lot of exciting things going on in online journalism. . . . No longer are reporters the only people who report the news. That means the very definition of what 'news' is has changed and will continue to change."

The second most popular source of news? That would be the combination of Web and mobile devices, up to 39 percent in 2012. That's an increase of about 16 percent since 2006. Thirty-three percent listened to radio news, and only 29 percent read a newspaper. So, in that six-year period from 2006 to 2012, Web-based news, whether accessed through computers or mobile devices, passed both radio and newspapers in popularity.

Types of News Audiences

A 2008 Pew study placed news consumers in one of four audience segments. Understanding those segments helps us understand the shifts in news consumption that affect the future of journalism. They are the following:

» **Traditionalists.** This group is older, less affluent and not as well-educated as the typical news consumer. Members of this group are heavy consumers of television news at all times of the day and understand news best by seeing pictures rather than reading or hearing. Traditionalists have a strong interest in the weather and relatively low interest in science and tech news. Most have computers, but few of them get news online on a typical day. This group makes up the largest part of the total audience (46 percent when the study was conducted).

» **Integrators.** These well-educated, affluent and mostly middle-aged people get news from legacy media, the Web and mobile devices. They are more engaged in public affairs than other news consumers are, and they are more sophisticated and sought after by advertisers. Television is a main news source for this group, but most also get news online each day. This group made up 23 percent of the public.

» **Net-Newsers.** This group is affluent, well-educated and relatively young. Members are more likely to read political blogs than watch network news, and their Web use soars during the day. They are frequent online news viewers and heavy technology users, and they have a strong interest in technology news. Fifty-eight percent of them are men, and the group as a whole made up 13 percent of the audience.

» **The Disengaged.** This group stands out for its low levels of news interest and news consumption. This group made up 14 percent of the public.

These segments account for 96 percent of the U.S. public. Of the remaining 4 percent, Pew reported that 2 percent did not name either a traditional source or the Web as their main source of news. An additional 2 percent named the Web as a main source but rarely go online for news.

Can Web-Based News Replace Newspaper Reporting?

Perhaps most telling about those numbers is that no single group of consumers leans toward newspapers as a primary source of news. Television—particularly cable television—and the Web dominate, with the growing Net-Newsers group relying heavily on the Web and its mobile-accessible content. Those who read newspapers or watch network news and local television are older. As that generation starts to die and as younger generations mature into news consumers (or non-news consumers), the Web and mobile stand to be the big winners. Cable television shows resiliency and continues to maintain its market share.

In the view of most journalists, both cable television and many sites on the Web have credibility problems. It's difficult to tell what's news and what's opinion on much of cable television, and determining the veracity of websites is far from easy. Despite that, readers and viewers have spoken. They want to consume news through the new outlets, and as we learned in Chapter 1, some citizen journalists (nonprofessionals who function as journalists) want to participate in the news-gathering process. Still others may not want to report the news but want to engage professional journalists and others in a discussion of that news. Journalists must determine where they fit in that process and adapt.

Most journalists are reluctantly embracing this changing environment, even while they're troubled by what it portends. Almost certainly, there will be fewer jobs in the legacy media. But almost as certainly, there will be new opportunities in the emerging media, which we will discuss in Chapter 3.

This doesn't necessarily mean that newspapers will disappear or that local television will consolidate into one or two stations per market. But the importance of both outlets is declining, and with that decline comes a major transformation of the American media landscape.

DISTRUST OF THE MEDIA

At least some of the shift in media consumption patterns can be traced to the public's increasing distrust of the legacy media. According to a Gallup study, in 1998, 55 percent of Americans expressed a great deal or a fair amount of trust and confidence in the media, but by 2012 that had fallen to 40 percent. Fifty-eight percent of Democrats expressed trust in the media, while only 31 percent of independents and 26 percent of Republicans did so.

Journalists are perplexed about the public's attitude, and there are no clear answers about why distrust of the media is growing. Some likely causes have been suggested:

» People fail to distinguish between reporters (who report, as Bob Woodward says, "the best obtainable version of the truth") and columnists (who offer opinion).

» The decline of profitability of newspapers and local television has led to reduced staffing, which in turn has damaged the media's ability to report well and ensure accuracy.

» As newspapers have moved away from fact-based writing in the inverted pyramid format (see Chapter 9), they have given reporters greater license to stylize stories with narrative writing. Descriptive writing is often mistaken for opinion-based journalism.

» On cable television, in particular, the lines blur between news programs and talk shows where opinion, not fact, dominates.

» Cable television and talk radio are dominated by right-wing and left-wing talk-show hosts, many of whom, like Rush Limbaugh and Rachel Maddow, make no pretense of objectivity. Many consumers would consider Limbaugh and Maddow journalists, a description that makes most journalists cringe.

» Some people even argue that news coverage itself is tilted leftward or rightward depending on the political slant of the media outlet. Most journalists deny this, but the public perception remains.

Indeed, Pew studies of press accuracy continue to show that Democrats have the most favorable view of CNN and MSNBC, while Republicans tilt heavily toward Fox News. That doesn't seem to bother any of the three outlets. Nor does it bother their respective viewers. Some have suggested this marks a return to the partisan press that existed in this country before and just after the American Revolution.

There's a major disconnect between how the public and those in the media view various news outlets. Most journalists would consider the reporting and accuracy of *The New York Times* and *The Wall Street Journal* to be far superior to that of CNN, Fox News, MSNBC and network television. The public disagrees. Among those media outlets, network television has the highest favorable ratings, followed by CNN, Fox and MSNBC. *The Times* and *The Journal* are last and next to last, respectively. Even widely respected National Public Radio ranks below CNN, Fox and MSNBC.

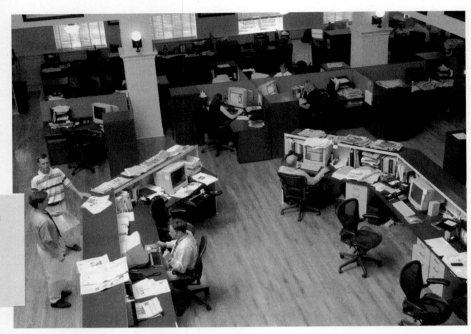

In 2001, the *Lawrence (Kan.) Journal-World* became one of the first media organizations to house its print, online and television news reporting groups in one converged newsroom.

In recent years, much of the criticism of the press has come from Republicans, particularly those on the far right, who consider most journalists to be left-wing activists who favor Democratic positions. Now, Democrats are increasingly skeptical, too.

But there is good news in all this. Most Americans have favorable views of local television news (73 percent), the daily newspaper they read most often (65 percent) and network television news (64 percent). So while there is great criticism of the press in general, most news consumers have no problem with the media they choose to consume. The prevailing attitude seems to be this: "The media in general are lousy and incompetent, but my newspaper or television station is not so bad."

CONVERGENCE AS A RESPONSE TO MEDIA FRAGMENTATION

As shifting media consumption patterns upset the business models of news companies, many are responding by expanding their product offerings and shifting their emphasis away from legacy media and into growth areas, particularly the Web. If the public wants to read news on the Web, or even on tablets or mobile phones, news companies intend to provide that option.

Journalists call this phenomenon—the coordination of print, broadcast and online reporting in a news operation—convergence. It's the transformation of traditional media into something entirely new, a 24/7 news operation where the Web, not the traditional product, comes first. The concept is that consumers should be able

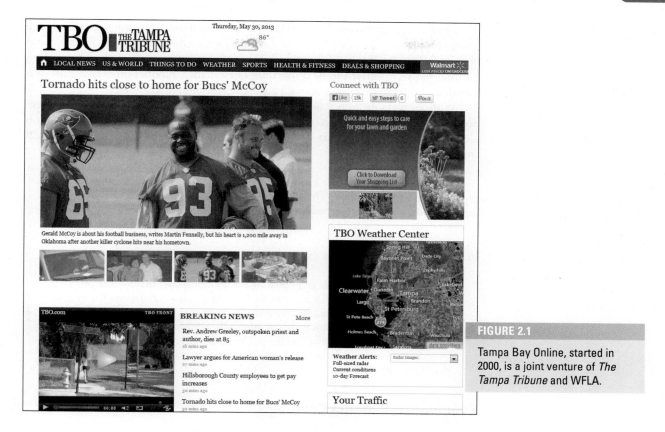

FIGURE 2.1

Tampa Bay Online, started in 2000, is a joint venture of *The Tampa Tribune* and WFLA.

to get news on their terms, however and whenever they want it. Radio and television stations put their recorded newscasts online, and some consumers watch them on the Web. Sometimes these Web-based newscasts even contain material that didn't make it into the traditional newscast, including, for example, a full-length video of the mayor's press conference. Sometimes such material is included even on a newspaper website. And the Web, of course, permits users to interact with databases of public information, such as property tax bills, driver's license records and records of the salaries of public officials and schoolteachers. Neither print nor broadcast outlets can provide this information as effectively. The *Tampa Tribune*-WFLA-Tampa Bay Online convergence effort in Florida is one of the oldest experiments in convergence, having started in 2000 (see Figure 2.1).

Enhanced Web Coverage

Increasingly, many news operations—even newspapers—think "Web first." An editor of *The Philadelphia Inquirer* wrote, "Let's break as much news as we can online, particularly if it's a story, column or review that readers might get from another source, or that benefits from the strengths of the Web."

Many newspapers have become Web-first, 24-hour-a-day operations that embrace citizen journalism. As news breaks, the reporter writes the story first for the Web and mobile devices and posts it for public consumption as soon as it's ready. Then, when it's time to put together the next morning's newspaper, production efforts shift. If a member of the public comes up with a story before a reporter, so be it.

Without a doubt, more and more media companies are headed in this direction. The Gannett Co. did so with the creation of what it calls Gannett Information Centers. Gannett CEO Craig Dubow described the concept in a letter to Gannett employees:

> The Information Center is a way to gather and disseminate news and information across all platforms, 24/7. The Information Center will let us gather the very local news and information that customers want, then distribute it when, where and how our customers seek it.

In Dubow's opinion, the concept is working:

> Breaking news on the Web and updating for the newspaper draws more people to both those media. Asking the community for help gets it—and delivers the newspaper into the heart of community conversations once again. Rich and deep databases with local, local information gathered efficiently are central to the whole process. The changes impact all media, and the public has approved. Results include stronger newspapers, more popular websites and more opportunities to attract the customers advertisers want.

Synchronized Media Coverage

"Convergence" is the hottest buzzword in the media industry these days, but defining it isn't easy. In the definition of some, convergence occurs when a newspaper or television station starts publishing material on the Web. According to others, convergence occurs when print reporters start carrying digital voice recorders and produce material for radio as well as the newspaper, or when reporters use a video camera to record a press conference for the newspaper's website.

While those may indeed be forms of convergence, in its most complete sense convergence involves the coming together of four communication forms:

» Text.
» Video and audio.
» The Web.
» Mobile phones and other wireless devices such as tablets.

Take a look at newspaper sites on the Web, and you will see this happening. Some of the best uses of video anywhere can be found on the website of *The New York Times,* something you might not expect. Interactive graphics that help readers visualize processes in new ways also dazzle readers on the *Times* site. If *The Times* is

Anyone with a video camera or smartphone can post observations to a site like CNN's iReport. To combat false reports, media outlets are beginning to moderate what gets posted.

often seen as gray and stodgy, its website certainly is not. Want news on your iPhone? *The Times* has an app for that. Want breaking news delivered to your phone through instant messaging? The Associated Press has an app for that.

Newspaper companies aren't the only ones doing convergence. The BBC, CNN, CBS, ESPN and others have created stellar websites that not only give users the news but also add to their understanding of it—often in far more detail than they can provide on their traditional newscasts and sportscasts.

EMBRACING CITIZEN JOURNALISM

The best of the legacy media companies are embracing the public's involvement in the news-gathering process and allowing the public to critique stories on the Web. The old "one provider to many consumers" model of newspapers and television is increasingly becoming a thing of the past.

When terrorists planted bombs on a London subway, the first images of the disaster came from survivors who used their mobile phones to take photos and transmit them to the outside world from below ground. When an airplane struck birds during takeoff and was forced to land, nearly miraculously, on New York's Hudson River, some of the first images came from nearby apartment dwellers who took photos and video from their windows. When the Arab Spring uprisings occurred in the Middle East, citizen reporting through social media sometimes was the only source of news as repressive governments banned reporters from the scenes. Social media allowed citizens to provide eyewitness accounts, which were picked up and distributed by mainstream media.

This form of citizen journalism—the gathering and reporting of the news by nonjournalists—is cropping up on websites around the world, much of it on sites of established media companies. For example, when the BBC asked users around the world to snap photos of scheduled anti-war protests and send them in, hundreds of photos were submitted. When an F-15 fighter crashed, a citizen in Virginia shot photos that she sent to a local television station. The photo taken immediately following the impact was used in the newscast along with video footage taken later.

Much of the video and still footage taken by people who happen to be on the scene finds its way to **moblogs**, a form of blogging in which the user publishes blog entries directly to the Web from a mobile phone or tablet. But when it finds its way onto the sites of mainstream media, as the examples above show, citizen journalists effectively serve as an extension of the media outlet's traditional reporting staff.

> " Responding to the question, 'Do you ever envision a time when your organization will not publish a print edition,' 62 percent of newspaper publishers replied 'no.' One-third said 'yes' and 5 percent said 'maybe.' "
>
> —Mike Jenner, Reynolds Journalism Institute

A notable example of a community-oriented site with citizen-generated blogs is BlufftonToday.com, produced by the *Bluffton Today* newspaper in South Carolina. BlufftonToday.com contains community blogs, expert blogs and staff blogs. As a result, everyone is part of the dialogue.

Problems with Citizen Journalism

Citizen journalism often works, but occasionally it goes awry, just like professional journalism. Some journalists have devoted a lot of effort to dismissing the idea of citizen journalism, citing the likelihood of inaccuracies. But it may be telling that some 10 years after the advent of citizen journalism, relatively few instances of major errors have been found in national media. One significant one was a false report posted in 2008 on CNN's iReport.cnn.com that Apple CEO Steve Jobs had suffered a heart attack. The erroneous story, which rattled investors, led to a $12 decline in Apple's stock price before the company debunked it three hours later. Jobs later died, but in 2008 he was very much alive.

The iReport site is almost completely open and permits users to post "news"—unedited and unvetted—after a minimal registration process. Observed Scott Karp of Publishing 2.0, a blog that reports on the evolution of media, "The problem is—and this is something that advocates of citizen journalism typically overlook—that if a platform is open, and anyone can participate, that means not only can well-intentioned citizens participate but so can bad actors, spammers, liars, cheats and thieves." Despite such warnings, the 2008 report about Jobs' death remains one of the few examples of false reporting on a national story by a citizen journalist.

Although most mainstream media outlets are allowing citizens to participate, they are moderating what goes onto their sites. As a result, back in the newsroom, journalists often find that their roles have changed. Not only do they perform their traditional roles, but they also edit stories, photos and videos shot by readers and viewers; moderate Web-based discussion forums; write blogs; and post breaking news on Facebook and Twitter. As a result, newsrooms have begun to look different from those of the past, and the websites of traditional media companies are getting more and more attention. That means more and more journalists—even in newspaper newsrooms—are being trained in digital audio and video editing. Some find themselves in front of television cameras to create mini-newscasts that will appear on the website.

Forms of Citizen Journalism

While some citizen journalism finds its way onto the sites of legacy media, today's Web publishing environment makes it easy for citizens to create their own sites and cut out the legacy media entirely. Anyone, it seems, can become a publisher. In an article in *Online Journalism Review*, J.D. Lasica sorted the media forms used in citizen journalism into six types:

» **Audience participation** (user comments attached to news stories, personal blogs, photos or video footage captured from mobile phone cameras, local news written by members of the community). Mainstream media outlets such as msnbc.com give readers the chance to post comments and other items on their sites.

» **Independent news or information websites** (such as the Drudge Report). These sites are published by those not normally associated with traditional media.

» **Participatory news sites** (*Northwest Voice*). Here, readers get to write, take photos and publish their work, perhaps even in newspaper format, with the assistance of professional editors.

» **Collaborative and contributory news sites** (Slashdot.org). These sites, often featuring a specific subject-matter area, are based on reader comments and contributions.

» **Thin media** (mailing lists, email newsletters). Through thin media, targeted news content is directed to those with narrowly defined interests.

» **Personal broadcasting sites** (JustinTV.com). On these sites, the operators provide news-based subject matter in a specific area of interest, such as technology. The result is downloadable audio or video.

There are more sources of information than ever before, and the public is embracing those alternatives. Many websites target specific groups of readers with great precision. Interested in the latest in football recruiting at your favorite university? There's probably a site for that. Interested in a nontraditional take on local politics? There may well be a blog for that. All of these new alternatives are eroding the strength of legacy media.

THE FUTURE OF JOURNALISM

As we've learned, despite the belief of many that journalism is a dying profession, the audience for journalists' work is actually growing. That reality leads many in the profession to believe that the future of journalism is bright, not dismal.

Even if newspapers—or at least most of them—are indeed destined to die, as some believe, many newspaper *companies* are almost certain to survive. A 2012 study of U.S. newspaper publishers found that 65 percent were "very optimistic" or "somewhat optimistic" about the future of their industry; 31 percent were neutral on the issue, and only 4 percent said they were "not optimistic." Not a single publisher in that study, conducted by the Reynolds Journalism Institute, reported being "not optimistic at all."

Perhaps that's because many in the newspaper business realize there is still a strong and growing market for the content they produce. In the future, that content may not be delivered on newsprint, but newspaper publishers have high hopes that e-book readers like the Kindle Fire and the growth of tablet computers like the iPad will spark new interest in news consumption. Publishers hope to find a successful business model to support the expensive process of news gathering. Indications are that their hopes have merit. The chore ahead of them, then, is to continue to improve the product and maximize its appeal for delivery on tablets and smartphones while refining the business model.

As mentioned earlier, in almost any city in the U.S., the one newspaper (and usually there is only one) employs more journalists than all the radio and television stations combined. So while the number of newspapers may be declining, newspaper companies are far from dead and are still eager to hire young people who can help them make the transition from print to the Web and mobile phones.

Not all legacy media will disappear—not by a long shot. Some will continue to succeed in their legacy forms, including many newspapers and local television stations, and others will make the transition to the Web and find ways to make it profitable. Still others will create niche sites to create new revenue streams, and others will find totally new models for delivering their content over devices like mobile phones, tablet computers and e-book readers. Meanwhile, information-based Web startups are likely to become increasingly profitable, and foundation-funded, not-for-profit news companies are being tested nationwide (see Chapter 3). With all this comes the need to hire journalists to create the original content consumers demand.

The way journalism is distributed is changing, but the market for good journalism continues to grow.

SUGGESTED READINGS

Croteau, David, and William Hoynes. *The Business of Media: Corporate Media and the Public Interest*. Thousand Oaks, Calif.: Pine Forge Press, 2006. This is a good treatise on the impact of changing economic models on the media industry.

Gillmor, Dan. *Mediactive*. Self-published, 2010. In this book, Gillmor discusses the changes occurring in traditional media and the democratization of new media forms.

Gillmor, Dan. *We the Media: Grassroots Journalism by the People, for the People*. Sebastopol, Calif.: O'Reilly Media, 2006. This book on the value of citizen journalism was written by a longtime newspaper reporter and editor.

Jones, Alex S. *Losing the News: The Future of the News That Feeds Democracy*. New York: Oxford Univ. Press, 2009. This is a superb review of why legacy media are so critical to democracy.

Meyer, Philip. *The Vanishing Newspaper: Saving Journalism in the Information Age.* 2nd ed. Columbia: Univ. of Missouri Press, 2009. In this excellent book, Meyer discusses the importance of newspapers in the news-gathering process.

Wollan, Robert, Nick Smith and Catherine Zhou. *The Social Media Management Handbook: Everything You Need to Know to Get Social Media Working in Your Business.* Hoboken, N.J.: John Wiley and Sons, 2011. This is a good primer on incorporating social media into a business model.

SUGGESTED WEBSITES

www.grady.uga.edu/annualsurveys
The University of Georgia issues an annual report on the employment patterns of journalism graduates nationwide.

www.journalists.org
The Online News Association was organized in 1999.

www.magazine.org
The Association of Magazine Media is the professional organization for magazine journalists.

www.naa.org
The Newspaper Association of America, a leading trade association for the industry, tracks trends in newspaper consumption.

www.nab.org
The National Association of Broadcasters is the primary trade organization of the broadcast industry.

www.people-press.org
The Pew Research Center for the People and the Press is an excellent source that tracks the changing attitudes of the American people toward the press. Pew's research can be found here.

www.rtdna.org
The Radio Television Digital News Association, a leading trade group for broadcast journalists, tracks trends in that field.

EXERCISES

1. **Team project.** Your instructor will divide the class into groups of three or four. As a team, choose a news aggregator site, such as Google News. On your own, read the top five stories; then read the top five stories on your local newspaper's site. What are the differences and similarities? What does each site do well? What does each do poorly? Discuss your findings in your group, and rate the sites on how well they fulfill the need for news to be relevant, useful and interesting.

2. Find two newspaper websites that carry staff-generated blogs. Compare and contrast them. Are the writers responsive to readers' comments? Is the discussion lively or slow? What role do readers' comments play on these blogs?

3. Analyze a citizen journalism site in your community or in your area. How does the information in the top three stories compare with the information in the top three stories on the local newspaper's website? If there are no citizen journalism sites in your community, find one in a large city nearby.

4. Provide a revised definition of news using the new realities of citizen journalism. Define it for different audiences, including you and your friends, and your parents.

5. Interview two college students to determine their top three sources of news. Then do the same with two people 40 or older. Write a one-page report on the differences you found in media consumption patterns.

6. The Web, in addition to being a place to publish, is a useful source of information for journalists. Using the Web, locate information on the most recent U.S. census, and report the following:

   a. The population of your state.
   b. The population of your city.
   c. The range of income levels and percentages of population that fall within those income levels in your city.
   d. The demographic breakdown of your city by race.

7. Research two legacy media companies, one that is primarily print-oriented and one that is broadcast-oriented. Using publicly available reports, describe any differences you find in the commitment of those companies to online news.

8. **Journalism blog.** Go to a news site or discussion board, and follow one thread of discussion. For the blog you set up in Chapter 1, write a post describing how the information you found on the news site might be useful to a reporter. Also describe how you would verify the information you found there.

3

The Emerging Media

WHEN MARGARET FRIEVOGEL took a buyout from the *St. Louis Post-Dispatch* in 2005 with about 40 other journalists, she realized that the world of journalism was changing—and not for the better, she felt: "What was happening at the *Post-Dispatch* was happening all over the country, and it amounted to less reporting."

Frievogel and several former *Post-Dispatch* colleagues decided that the citizens of St. Louis needed more reporting, not less, so in 2008 they founded the *St. Louis Beacon* (stlbeacon.com), a website modeled after successful news websites formed in other cities like Minneapolis-St. Paul (MinnPost.com) and New York (Gotham Gazette.com).

Frievogel was a good choice as founding editor because of her 34 years of experience as a reporter, editor and Washington correspondent for the *Post-Dispatch*. She and her colleagues believed they could produce a high-quality news product for St. Louis on the Web without being burdened by the high costs of publishing a newspaper. Support for the effort comes mostly from large and small donations, sponsorships and advertising. Several years after its launch, the *Beacon* seems to be doing well.

The *Beacon* doesn't attempt to cover everything the *Post-Dispatch* does. Instead, it focuses on politics, the economy, health, education and the arts. It does so through its website and its related forums, partnerships with other media, social media and email.

It also creates opportunities for citizens to meet in person with subject-matter experts and staff members. The *Beacon* regularly stages a popular event called Beacon & Eggs, a town-hall style meeting at which topics of community interest are discussed. Topics have ranged from attempts to understand political polling to disaster preparedness.

This new form of not-for-profit journalism, in which journalists attempt to connect closely to their audience, is one promising alternative to reductions in the number of journalists hired by the legacy media. There also are encouraging signs that for-profit news-based Web startups can thrive when not burdened by the costs of operating legacy media. In this chapter, we'll examine promising and not-so-promising alternatives to traditional media, including some that appear to be succeeding and some that have failed. We'll also look at attempts by legacy media to break the mold and form new ventures.

In this chapter you will learn:

1. How the business of journalism is changing.

2. How not-for-profit business models are evolving.

3. How for-profit media models are developing.

4. Where new business models are being pioneered.

5. Why building audiences is the key to success.

6. What new types of jobs are available in legacy and emerging media.

CHANGES IN THE BUSINESS OF JOURNALISM

Print and broadcast companies understand the shift away from legacy media for consumers of news. Most news companies now see themselves as Web-first operations, and they are embracing the idea of breaking news by transmitting it wirelessly to mobile phones and tablets. But as we've learned, it's also true that they still derive the lion's share of their revenue (usually around 90 percent) from their legacy products — primarily newspapers or television — not from their websites or mobile phone services. Income from traditional sources is declining, but so far Web and mobile revenue is not increasing rapidly enough to replace it.

It's clear that legacy media companies are embracing the idea of delivering the news whenever, wherever and however consumers want it. What's not clear is how they can prosper doing so. As noted in Chapter 2, newspapers still finance much of the massive news-gathering apparatus needed to cover the news both in this country and around the world. That raises a question: If newspapers continue their downward spiral, can that capacity for news gathering be financed only by revenue from newer media operations?

Many believe it is possible. Legacy media companies are making a major commitment to the Web in hopes that they can find a solution to their problems. Newspapers, radio and television stations, and even magazines now have substantial news sites online. Often, the news hits there first.

Still, not all segments of the legacy media are struggling. Many magazines still thrive because of their ability to target audiences that advertisers covet. Indeed, there's a magazine for almost any demographic: *Boating* for boaters, *PC World* for computer aficionados, *The Bridge World* for bridge players.

Like magazines, many small and medium-sized newspapers still do well, too, thanks to their intensely local coverage. They provide content that readers want and are relatively free of competition in smaller communities nationwide. And as we learned in Chapter 2, cable television is doing well, too.

Another bright spot is National Public Radio, whose audience has grown dramatically over the last decade. Local NPR stations also are thriving, and many affiliates are expanding their staffs to try to fill the vacuum left by other stations that have reduced or abandoned local news. Some are teaming up with Web startups or even local newspapers.

So even as some parts of the legacy media struggle to make the difficult transition to the digital economy, other parts thrive. There are still thousands of jobs to be had in legacy media companies. Young people right out of school who are armed with knowledge of the Web are prime candidates for those jobs.

Some entrepreneurial journalists are trying to fill the void as legacy media retrench or scale back on providing costly investigative reporting. They seek financing through various means and hope to turn a profit. Still others create sites altruistically

> " Paper won't disappear (in the future), but paperless media will soak up more of our time. We will eventually become paperless the way we once became horseless. Horses are still around, but they are ridden by hobbyists, not consumers. "
>
> — Paul Saffo, Institute for the Future

There is a magazine for every interest, from knitting to Web design.

with little or no hope of turning a profit. Several models for these new forms of Web-based journalism are emerging:

» **Financed by venture capital.** Some sites, like HuffingtonPost.com and Newsy.com, received startup financing from private investors and became nationally popular, attracting significant amounts of advertising. Some also charge for subscriptions to premium content.

» **Funded by foundations.** ProPublica.org, which seeks to do investigative reporting nationwide, and similar sites are financed by grants from foundations and operate as not-for-profit corporations.

» **Financed with hybrid models.** Some sites, like stlbeacon.org and MinnPost.com, are hybrids funded by advertisers, corporate sponsors and individual donors.

» **Financed as an old media/new media hybrid.** Politico.com and other sites sell ads to support their free Web content while publishing traditional products. *Politico* is both a website and a Washington-based political newspaper.

» **Financed by individual entrepreneurs.** Other sites, like WestSeattleBlog.com, were established with spare change and hope to attract enough advertising to survive.

» **Not financed at all.** Still other sites, like ColumbiaHeartBeat.com, don't seek advertising or attempt to make a profit. The publishers of such sites operate them without expectation of profit and often have separate jobs.

Arianna Huffington co-founded the news site HuffingtonPost.com, which follows the classic financial model of relying on private investment and advertising.

Some of the founders of these sites don't even think of themselves as journalists; they're merely filling a perceived void in news coverage in their communities. Others are displaced journalists with formal training and significant experience in news gathering.

NOT-FOR-PROFIT BUSINESS MODELS

For the most part, private citizens, families or publicly traded companies own the legacy media operations in the U.S. As a result, these companies continue to exist only if they earn a profit. Traditionally, most revenue has come from advertising, with some additional revenue from newsstand sales and subscriptions. Many of the new Web-based journalism sites aim to follow the same model by supporting themselves through advertising or subscriptions. Not-for-profit sites, however, seek only to support their operations—to pay staff and other costs—not to make a profit for owners or investors.

Financially Successful Not-for-Profit Sites

The not-for-profit models in which foundations are a key source of funding are relatively new, and in some circles they are controversial. Jack Shafer of Slate.com, an online magazine, says, "There's something disconcerting about wanting to divorce the newspaper (or a news website) from market pressures." Others disagree. ProPublica .org, a foundation-funded nonprofit site, produces journalism of unquestioned high quality (see Figure 3.1). Its editors explain how they operate:

> Profit-margin expectations and short-term stock market concerns, in particular, are making it increasingly difficult for the public companies that control nearly all of our nation's news organizations to afford—or at least think they can afford—the sort of intensive, extensive and uncertain efforts that produce great investigative journalism.

ProPublica relies on grants from foundations, including a major one from the Sandler Foundation, to "support the work of 34 working journalists, all of them dedicated to investigative reporting on stories with significant potential for major impact." The model is working. In 2011, ProPublica won a Pulitzer Prize for national reporting for a series on Wall Street bankers who enrich themselves at the expense of their clients and sometimes even their own companies. The year before,

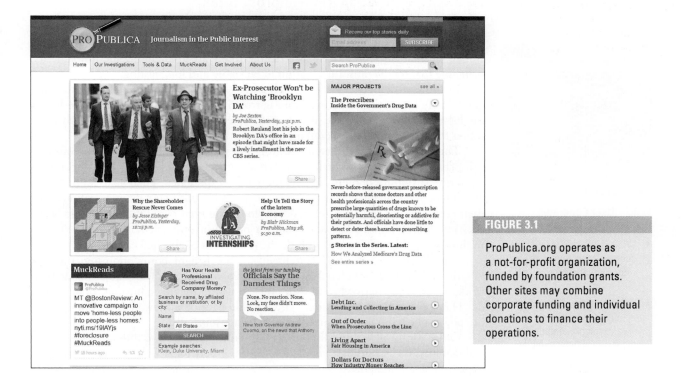

FIGURE 3.1

ProPublica.org operates as a not-for-profit organization, funded by foundation grants. Other sites may combine corporate funding and individual donations to finance their operations.

ProPublica won a Pulitzer in the investigative reporting category when it discovered that doctors at a New Orleans hospital had engaged in euthanasia following Hurricane Katrina.

ProPublica typically offers its stories to legacy media operations, free of charge, for publication or broadcast. After a period of exclusivity for the partner organization, the story appears on the ProPublica site. The New Orleans story, for example, appeared first in *The New York Times Magazine*. This totally new model works because the credentials of ProPublica's reporters are outstanding. Without that credibility, no legacy media organization would publish or broadcast its stories.

MinnPost.com, formed largely by laid-off journalists in the Minneapolis-St. Paul area, accepts donations from corporations and individuals but also sells advertising. It is professionally staffed and designed, and it operates as a not-for-profit corporation. The *St. Louis Beacon* (stlbeacon.com), *Gotham Gazette* in New York City (GothamGazette.com) and a growing group of other sites operate similarly.

The Investigative News Network was formed in 2009 in an effort to promote investigative reporting, often the hallmark of such sites. More than 20 nonpartisan, nonprofit news sites gathered in New York to form the organization, and it has already grown to more than 60 members throughout North America.

Financially Problematic Nonprofit Sites

For every high-quality news site like ProPublica.org, MinnPost.com or the *St. Louis Beacon*, there are dozens of other civic blogs or websites that are much less professional and that carry little or no advertising. Many are challenging the fundamental principle that media must turn a profit to be viable and long-lasting.

In the first definitive study of such sites, researchers Esther Thorson and Margaret Duffy found that most are more narrow in content and focus than the legacy media sites in the cities where they operate. The citizen sites are predominantly blogs rather than news sites. They contain little advertising.

The site owners they interviewed were not particularly interested in the business side of their operations. Few of them rated making money, or even covering their costs, as a priority. Two-thirds of them had had journalism experience. Their goals for their sites are well-defined: giving citizens a voice, providing fair and accurate information about their communities and enabling residents to decide their own futures. In many ways, such efforts are a logical extension of citizen journalism embraced by legacy media. But in this case, publication comes outside the purview of established companies.

The Thorson-Duffy study, produced for the Knight Foundation and the Pew Charitable Trusts, concluded that while such site owners are clearly dedicated to their work, they operate narrowly and with no clear way of making a business of what they do. Thorson and Duffy conclude, "These results cannot be viewed as encouraging for the power of citizen journalism to replace legacy journalism."

Other forms of startups also are well-intentioned but have little or no commercial viability. Neighborhood newsletters and intensely local websites may have great appeal to small audiences, but they have little hope of becoming profitable. Niche

bedfordstmartins.com /newsreporting

Watch **"User Generated Content."**

- What is "user generated content," and does it differ from content created by a media organization?

- Will user generated content eliminate the demand for "professional" content? Will there be a different role for traditional media producers?

ON THE JOB
The Lure of the Web

Adam Falk graduated with a degree in magazine journalism, but he knew he wouldn't be entering the magazine world right away. There was too much more he wanted to try.

In college, he'd focused on building a new-media skill set to tell stories in innovative ways. Just after graduation he took a Web design internship with the Media Policy Center, a nonprofit film company in Los Angeles. But he eventually found himself in the startup world. He currently works for Newsy, a video news company headquartered in Columbia, Mo.

"When I chose to go from Los Angeles to a college town, some scratched their heads," Falk says. "I wanted to work at a place and with people who moved as fast as I did."

He says he got even more than he bargained for. The 24/7 nature of startup work is a challenge. Still, he adds, "I've had the chance to change some things here. My co-worker and I just redesigned the website, mobile apps and graphics in the videos."

"The best thing about working for a startup is your presence makes an impact and your work gets seen. Chances are, I wouldn't have the same opportunities working an entry-level job at a larger media company," Falk says.

As for his average day: "My day-to-day activity looks different the longer I work here. I'm definitely not bored."

Now, Falk is back in Los Angeles helping to start a small Newsy studio in a big city.

publications that attempt to attract micro audiences also are unlikely to become profitable unless they are extended to large geographic areas and are able to attract the larger audiences for which advertisers are willing to pay.

Unquestionably, some good publications have emerged on the Web that could best be described as the products of people with a passion for informing their neighbors. Trained journalists produce some; others are less polished and perhaps less professional. Still, all of them employ journalistic techniques in reporting the news. To dismiss any of them would be a mistake.

But whether journalism can be sustained for long periods in the absence of good business models remains to be seen. In the end, as the Thorson-Duffy study shows, profit-based media—or those funded by foundations—are probably the only long-term answer to society's need for top-quality information. Determining how to pay the cost of providing good journalism is problematic.

FOR-PROFIT MEDIA MODELS

Because their costs are high, newspapers and television stations in major markets must have hundreds of thousands of readers or viewers to be profitable for their owners and investors. But with much lower costs on the Web, luring large numbers is not nearly as critical. And if a Web-based venture is successful, it too can attract a large audience without all those legacy-media costs.

Experimentation on the Web

Jim Spencer saw a new way to approach journalism on the Web. His concept was to create a video-centric website that gives users a look at the news from multiple viewpoints, both foreign and domestic. The result is Newsy.com, a multiperspective website that's growing rapidly.

Newsy takes news from various existing outlets and repackages it to show how different media are covering a story. A story on Afghanistan, for example, may include video snippets from Fox News, the BBC and Al Jazeera, the independent television news station headquartered in Qatar that serves the Middle East. The video clips may be packaged with links to today's story from *The New York Times* or another from Germany's *Frankfurter Allgemeine Zeitung*. Each one of the "borrowed" news snippets is short, usually less than 12 seconds of video or a mere sentence or two from the print sources. That enables Newsy.com to use the material under the fair-use provisions of copyright law.

"We're trying to ride the wave of popularity of Internet video," Spencer says in explaining his marketing concept. Newsy staffers do no original reporting, although they do original research by scouring the Web for background and context. They compile the most interesting and useful perspectives from other media, write a script and then use an anchor to deliver the story on the Web in the style of television news. Consumers are finding the concept helpful in understanding complex stories and ensuring that they don't get a one-dimensional perspective.

Innovative forms of new media like Newsy.com are popping up all over the Web. Most are being launched by entrepreneurs like Spencer rather than by legacy media companies. That's unfortunate in a way, because legacy media companies need those types of innovations to help protect their costly news-gathering capability.

Content aggregators like Newsy.com and more established Web aggregators like Google News and Yahoo News have been vilified by newspaper publishers as "newspaper killers." Former Google CEO Eric Schmidt denies that. The problem with newspapers, Schmidt says, is the Web in general, not just companies like Google and Yahoo. "We need these content partners to survive," Schmidt said. "We need their content. We are not in the content business."

In 2009, Schmidt started putting those words into action by launching an experimental news hub called Google Fast Flip that allowed users to view news articles from major publishers and flip through them quickly, something closely akin to flipping through print newspaper pages but delivered on the Web. Google placed ads around the news articles and shared the revenue with publishers. The experiment was a failure, and Google killed it in late 2011.

A few legacy media companies have made inroads toward profitability on the Web. Gannett, for example, which owns more newspapers than any other U.S. media company, also owns the successful USAToday.com and CareerBuilder.com websites. It also boasts some successful Web-based niche products that are localized by its newspapers around the country, including one targeted to mothers.

For the most part, however, innovation on the Web is coming not from legacy media companies but from entrepreneurs like Spencer and from veteran journalists who left legacy media companies to create startup Web ventures. Often, these successful for-profit sites do not provide news of almost every type as newspapers do. Instead, they focus on particular niches within the news.

Niche Journalism Sites

In his remarkable book *Be the Media: How to Create and Accelerate Your Message . . . Your Way*, entrepreneur David Mathison outlines dozens of examples of people making money by attracting intensely loyal followers in relatively small numbers. He argues that someone who can attract 1,000 "true fans" can make a profit in almost any business. True fans are those who like your content so much they are willing to pay for it, not only on the Web but in other forms such as books, music or other merchandise.

Sports Sites

Will the true-fan model work for news content? Perhaps so. It clearly is working for sports content. Three websites—Rivals.com, Scout.com and 247Sports.com—compete head-to-head for information on football and basketball recruiting at colleges nationwide. All do other things, but recruiting coverage, something that legacy media do poorly, is at the heart of their businesses. Discussion boards abound where fans discuss their teams and watch every step in the battle for the nation's best high school players. Users pay premium rates of around $100 a year for access, and they come by the tens of thousands. Advertising boosts profit even more. Most college and university subsidiary sites have independent operators, often trained as journalists, who in turn are connected in the national network. As the sites attract more users, the operators' incomes increase.

While some websites are financed on a shoestring, others have corporate backing. MLB.com was financed with the deep pockets of Major League Baseball. Its team sites employ journalists to give fans an insider's view of what's happening with the Yankees, Marlins, Angels and other teams. Fans outside the local television viewing area can even watch the games on Web-based video.

Then there are the general sports sites on the Web, including ESPN.com, CBSSports.com, Fox Sports on MSNBC (msn.foxsports.com) and dozens of others. Such sites give hope to aspiring sports journalists that there will be jobs for them when they graduate, even if those jobs are not at a newspaper or a television station.

Business Sites

Something similar is happening in business journalism. Sites such as Bloomberg .com, various Dow Jones sites and MarketWatch.com are attracting readers—often at premium rates—because of their ability to produce information that readers desire and are willing to pay for. Such sites create increasing numbers of Web-based jobs for journalism graduates. In some cases, related cable television channels create even more jobs for television majors.

General News Sites

Clearly, though, most general news sites are not making money. Some newspaper companies report covering the costs of producing their websites with advertising income, but for the most part the legacy media continue to pay the salaries of those who gather the news.

Some argue that newspapers made a big mistake by giving away their news on websites, and today many are trying to change that by erecting pay walls and charging for at least some content. It's a tough uphill battle at this point. The public is accustomed to getting news for free on the Web, and many believe companies will find it hard to succeed by suddenly charging for content users are accustomed to getting for free. Nonetheless, pay walls are becoming increasingly common. They will create some revenue, without doubt, but will this model generate enough to rescue legacy media companies? The jury is still out.

A key to Web profitability, then, would seem to come in niche areas like sports and business that attract highly interested readers. Those seeking to provide general news probably will continue to struggle until a feasible economic model is found. Finding that model is the holy grail of the media industry today, and lots of schemes are under consideration. Among them are these:

» Entrepreneurs and journalists have created entirely new national news websites like Politico.com. These conceivably could fill a significant void in national news coverage if legacy media organizations continue to fail or cut back.
» More and more papers, *The Wall Street Journal* and the *Arkansas Democrat-Gazette* of Little Rock among them, charge for most Web content. This seems to work for those publications, but some that have tried this model have failed.
» Some companies are considering micropayments. In other words, they attract readers with some free content and then charge for select news content, much as Apple does with songs on iTunes. Indeed, versions of this model are most popular among those creating pay walls.
» One small paper, the *Antelope Valley Press* in Palmdale, Calif., offers only headlines and brief news summaries on its website. The full articles are available only in print.
» Rupert Murdoch's News Corp., which owns *The Wall Street Journal*, the *New York Post* and other newspapers, is talking with other publishers about founding a consortium that would collect fees for Web-based news products.

SAN DIEGO: PIONEERING NEW MEDIA PROTOTYPES

Many not-for-profit as well as for-profit concepts are being tested in San Diego. When a series of budget cuts sliced the size of *The San Diego Union-Tribune* reporting staff in half, a local businessman, Buzz Woolley, financed the startup of an online-only news organization called Voice of San Diego (see Figure 3.2). There, a dozen or so reporters pursue key issues facing the community, including housing, government, the environment and education. Voice of San Diego, a nonprofit corporation, is financed by donors like Woolley, foundations, advertising, corporate sponsorships and citizen "members" who donate to keep the enterprise going, in much the same way that listeners give to National Public Radio.

Yet another group started the San Diego News Network, a for-profit local news site that ultimately failed in 2010. Aggregating news from its own staff, freelancers, radio and television stations, bloggers and others, the site covered much of the same ground as *The Union-Tribune* and did so with a website that resembled the newspaper's.

Investigative Newsource (inewsource.org) is perhaps the most unusual of San Diego's startups. It's an independent nonprofit investigative reporting project based on the campus of San Diego State University. Lorie Hearn, a former *Union-Tribune*

FIGURE 3.2

The not-for-profit Voice of San Diego exemplifies how news organizations are changing their financing and news-delivery methods.

editor, persuaded her former company's owner to contribute money to the startup. The effort is staffed largely by former *Union-Tribune* reporters, with the assistance of San Diego State journalism students. It was founded as The Watchdog Institute and changed its name when it became affiliated with KPBS, the public broadcasting station in San Diego.

Whether any of these schemes will prove successful in maintaining the watchdog function of the press in an era of declining profits remains to be seen. In the short term, it appears that the publication of niche products on the Web or foundation-supported media are the most likely ways to underwrite the significant costs of covering general news.

The primary alternatives to the for-profit model would seem to be either government-financed media, which for the most part is an unpopular and unwelcome idea in the U.S., or foundation-backed media. ProPublica remains the primary example of foundation financing, while National Public Radio and the Public Broadcasting System remain the only good examples of government-financed media. Of course, both NPR and PBS also have hundreds of thousands of listeners and viewers who contribute money to help pay the bills.

BUILDING AUDIENCES AS THE KEY TO SUCCESS

Those who start news-oriented websites and blogs need to know how to attract audiences. They cannot simply create a site and hope the world flocks to it. As a result, skills that once were never taught to aspiring journalists are being incorporated into courses at many schools of journalism.

Succeeding as an entrepreneurial journalist requires a knowledge of tagging, linking and promotion of sites through viral marketing; the ability to report and edit text, audio and video; an understanding of audiences; knowledge of how to gather reader comments and contributions; and the ability to write headlines, subsidiary decks and text to optimize the chances of being found by search engines.

Search-engine optimization is critical. In newspapers, it's not really important to use the word "baseball" in a headline about the Giants beating the Dodgers. But doing so might well be essential to ensuring that a search engine finds and properly categorizes your story. Understanding **metadata**, keywords that don't necessarily appear in the story but help search engines index it, is just as important. It's all part of building and maintaining an audience.

The good news is that Web advertising revenue and Web subscription revenue both are rising. Much of that revenue today goes to sites unrelated to media companies—often pornography, gambling and shopping sites. But also hugely popular are social media sites such as Facebook, MySpace and LinkedIn.

No one would suggest that journalists use pornography or gambling to promote their products, but using social media sites is an option worth considering. Some media companies are now putting video clips or links to news stories on Facebook, which in turn causes readers to click to their news sites. Increasing traffic is the key to profitability, so viral marketing of this type is increasingly common.

Similarly, texts to smartphones can have embedded links that drive readers to news websites. Most believe that mobile phones and tablets—collectively known simply as "mobile"—will be the next great platform on which people will consume news. With tablets like Apple's iPad and smartphones like Apple's iPhone and the Samsung Galaxy, the power of mobile-delivered news is becoming ever more evident.

JOBS IN JOURNALISM

While people like Jim Spencer are forming their own companies in the new media economy, others are finding more traditional types of jobs—sometimes at legacy media companies and sometimes elsewhere. (See Figure 3.3 for insight into the range of jobs and salaries available for journalism graduates.)

When Jenifer Langosch went to journalism school, she thought she'd end up working as a newspaper sports writer. Instead, she found a job covering the Pittsburgh Pirates and St. Louis Cardinals for MLB.com. Troy Wolverton did end up in a legacy media job, writing a personal technology column for the *San Jose Mercury News*. But he did so only after years in Web-based media, including CNET.com.

"I learned a long time ago that the Web was going to open opportunities . . . that never existed before," Jim Spencer says. "There's a whole new world out there. Aspiring journalists have all sorts of jobs to lure them that never even existed a decade ago."

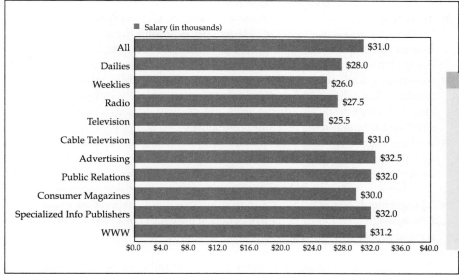

FIGURE 3.3

Median yearly salaries for 2011 bachelor's degree recipients with full-time jobs.

Source: Lee B. Becker, Tudor Vlad, and Konrad Kaplen, "2011 Annual Survey of Journalism and Communication Graduates," James M. Cox Jr. Center for International Mass Communication Training and Research, Grady College of Journalism and Mass Communication, University of Georgia, 2012. Available at www.grady.uga.edu/annualsurveys.

Training to become a journalist prepares you for many jobs. Some are obvious, some are not. Most jobs, regardless of the medium, fall into one of these categories:

» **Writing and reporting.** Newspaper reporters and magazine writers are examples. At newspapers, most writing jobs are full-time staff positions, but many magazines rely much more heavily on freelance writers who are paid by the story. The skills of reporting and writing go together. No one in journalism can be a good writer without first being a good reporter.

» **Editing.** Great jobs abound for those who can edit well. Newspapers, magazines, radio and television stations and some websites have copy editors, assignment editors and editorial assistants. At newspapers, the entry-level position of copy editor often pays more than the entry-level position of reporter. Copy editors are in greater demand than reporters.

» **Photography and video.** Print publications and websites use lots of photographs and therefore need photographers. At newspapers, most photographers are staff members, but at many magazines freelance photographers are more common. Video is becoming important for all media operations that run websites. No longer is video merely the province of television.

» **Art and design.** Designers are needed in all media. There are jobs for newspaper and magazine designers and Web designers. Even television stations need Web designers. There also is an increasing demand for information graphics specialists—people who produce maps, charts and graphs.

» **Production.** Television producers are in high demand. It's quite possible to become a news producer right out of journalism school. Web producers are also in demand, and additional production jobs exist in the print media, particularly for those who can edit audio and video.

» **Tech support.** Those who combine a knowledge of journalism with computer literacy can find jobs anywhere. Media outlets around the world have a strong interest in computer-literate journalists. To increase their marketability, journalism students should consider a minor or double major in information technology.

» **Advertising and public relations.** Advertising and public relations often are taught within schools and departments of journalism. Jobs in this field abound, and they range from advertising sales and creative design to account management and Internet marketing and promotion.

» **Audience development.** Many websites now have teams of people trained to expand the site's audience. Through the use of viral marketing, audience development specialists post messages on Facebook and Twitter with links to the site. This helps drive traffic and enhances prospects for advertising revenue.

» **Management.** Many who enter journalism eventually become assignment editors, managing editors or executive editors. Those jobs pay more and are part of a natural progression for reporters and copy editors.

As in any period of transition, there are opportunities as well as wrong turns. Those who position themselves to excel in this environment will find success in journalism—even at legacy media companies.

Jobs in Journalism

Jobs in Legacy Media

Jobs abound for those who seek to enter the legacy media. Here are a few of the possibilities for each medium. Asterisks (*) identify entry-level jobs that beginners are likely to land.

Newspapers (Daily and Weekly)	Magazines	Television	Radio	Online Media	Other Jobs
Reporter*	Writer*	Reporter*	Reporter*	Writer*	Advertising sales*
Copy editor*	Fact checker*	Producer*	Producer*	Producer*	Advertising copy writer*
Page designer*	Editorial assistant*	Desk assistant*	Anchor	Graphics specialist*	Advertising account manager*
Information graphics specialist*	Copy editor*	Videographer*	News director	Executive producer (titles vary)	Public relations practitioner*
Photographer*	Page designer*	Anchor			Account executive
Assignment editor	Senior writer	News director			Art director
News editor	Senior editor	Executive producer			Media critic
Managing editor	Contributing writer				Foreign correspondent
Executive editor	Managing editor				
Columnist	Editor				
	Columnist				

Jobs in Emerging Media

Jobs are rapidly increasing for those who seek work in emerging media. In addition to starting your own website, here are a few of the possibilities for paid jobs in Web-based media. Many jobs listed under "Jobs in Legacy Media" also exist in emerging media. All of the jobs listed below are entry-level jobs that beginners are likely to land.

Websites	Entrepreneurial Activities
Reporter	News software designer
Copy editor	Ad software designer
Designer	E-zine editor
Writer	Multimedia designer
Producer	Newsletter editor
Graphics specialist	
Advertising sales	
Advertising design	

SUGGESTED READINGS

Briggs, Mark. *Entrepreneurial Journalism: How to Build What's Next for News*. Thousand Oaks, Calif.: Sage, 2012. This is a good reference for starting your own news publication.

Chaney, Paul. *The Digital Handshake: Seven Proven Strategies to Grow Your Business Using Social Media*. Hoboken, N.J.: John Wiley, 2009. This excellent book discusses the importance of social media in spreading the word about new websites.

Mathison, David. *Be the Media: How to Create and Accelerate Your Message . . . Your Way*. New Hyde Park, N.Y.: Natural E Creative Group, 2009. Mathison offers an excellent discussion about how to become an entrepreneur and build a circle of "true fans."

Pavlik, John. *Media in the Digital Age*. New York: Columbia Univ. Press, 2008. This is a thorough treatise on how digital media are transforming society.

SUGGESTED WEBSITES

www.huffingtonpost.com
The Huffington Post is one of the premier news sites on the Web. It was founded with venture capital and designed to be free of the weight of legacy media.

www.minnpost.com
This hybrid site accepts both advertising and foundation support. It's a not-for-profit designed to provide high-quality journalism for the Minneapolis-St. Paul area.

www.politico.com
Politico.com is an excellent example of a new politically oriented media site supported by advertising. It has a companion newspaper that is traditional in nature.

www.propublica.org
This excellent foundation-supported site brings together some of the nation's top journalists to pursue investigative reporting.

www.stlbeacon.org
This site, formed by veteran journalists who left the *St. Louis Post-Dispatch*, has become increasingly popular with news consumers in the St. Louis area.

EXERCISES

1. **Team project.** Your instructor will divide the class into teams of three or four. With the other members of your group, brainstorm a list of ideas for a news website that you could create. Research a few of the ideas on the Web, and then decide together which is the most viable one. Plan your site: What would its purpose be? Who would its audience be? What would the site be like? Would it have video, animation or audio? What text features would you provide? Where would you get your content? How large a staff would you need? How would you support the site? As a team, write a detailed plan for your proposed site, answering these and any other questions you think are relevant.

2. Research two companies engaged in producing new forms of media, and provide a report on how they operate. Describe any efforts the companies are making to find new revenue streams.

3. **Journalism blog.** Find a blog or website that tries to cover local news with intensity. Interview the editor about the nature of the site. Does it make money? Does he or she care? Why? Post your findings on your own journalism blog and invite comments from your classmates.

4. Go to www.minnpost.com, and do an analysis of the news indexed on the front page. How does this differ from what you see on the front page of www.startribune.com, the website of the Minneapolis newspaper?

5. Go to www.politico.com. Choose a political story from that site, and contrast how the same story is covered on www.washingtonpost.com.

6. Contrast the kinds of stories you see on www.westseattle blog.com to those published in *The Seattle Times* or on its website, http://seattletimes.nwsource.com. Which seems to provide more government coverage?

7. Follow a local news provider on Twitter for a day. Then write a two-page, double-spaced account of how the provider uses Twitter to tease content on its main site or in its publication.

8. Describe in one page, double-spaced, how Twitter or Facebook might be used to drive traffic to your school newspaper's website.

Interviewing

**In this chapter
you will learn:**

1. How to prepare for
   an interview for a
   news story, profile or
   investigative piece.

2. How to conduct an audio
   or video interview.

3. How to evaluate the
   pros and cons of doing
   interviews by telephone,
   email, instant messaging
   or Skype.

4. How to set up an
   interview.

5. How to prepare your
   questions.

6. How to establish rapport
   with a source.

7. How to ensure accuracy.

8. How to end an interview.

JOURNALISTS GET most of their information by asking people questions. Sometimes, though, the hardest part is just getting a source to agree to talk to you. One of the masters of getting people to open up is Mike McGraw, the Pulitzer Prize–winning projects reporter of *The Kansas City Star*. McGraw is a persistent reporter who has been known to work for months to convince a source to talk with him. "I couldn't get a lawyer to talk to me for the longest time," McGraw says. "I finally learned he was active as an adult leader in the Boy Scouts, as I was. So I brought up our common connection in an email one day. We both valued the organization, he emailed me back, and we began a dialogue that finally ended in an interview."

Persistence is just one of many techniques McGraw uses to get people to talk.

"I once wanted to talk to workers at a turkey processing plant," McGraw says. "I put my business cards under windshield wipers in the parking lot and asked them to join me for a beer. About 12 showed up."

Often, reporters get sources to talk by first making them feel at ease. Many are not accustomed to speaking with a reporter and find the experience intimidating. "I look for pictures of grandkids on someone's desk and find other things we might have in common," McGraw says.

"Sometimes I actually start off saying (the conversation) is off the record, which puts them at ease and gets me closer to the truth. I am honest and forthright with them, and I often convince them to go on the record."

McGraw often makes it clear that he's not going to quit working on a story until he gets the interview. "I often tell them, 'Look, I'm going to be looking into this for a long time. I'm going to find the flaws and the positives. Take this journey with me—help educate me—and at the end I promise you a chance to respond to everything I write that affects you. I won't show you the story, but I'll tell you what's in it. No, you won't like all of it, but it won't be lopsided, either.'"

Interviewing—having conversations with sources—is the key to most stories you will write. Your ability to make people feel comfortable with you is often the difference between mediocre reporting and good reporting. A face-to-face interview is always preferable to a telephone interview, which in turn is preferable to having a source answer questions by email. Face-to-face interviews allow you to develop a rapport with a source that is difficult, if not impossible, to achieve over the telephone or by email or instant messaging. If you meet sources in their offices, like McGraw you might find photos or objects that give you a way to break the ice with a nonthreatening conversation.

Of course, when a deadline looms on a breaking news story, you may be forced to settle for a telephone interview. (See "Using the Telephone, Email, Instant Messaging or Skype for Interviews" in this chapter.) That also may be necessary if you and the source are not in the same city or area. Least desirable of all is the email interview, which does not allow any sort of rapport to be established. You'll often get dry and uninformative answers to questions posed by email, and you won't have an opportunity to ask the follow-up questions you may have asked during a face-to-face interview.

Information is the raw material of a journalist. While some of it is gathered from records and some from observation, most is gathered in one-on-one conversations. You try first to talk to **primary sources**, those who witnessed the event or have authority over documents. If you can't get to a primary source, you may be forced to go to a **secondary source**, someone who talked to a witness, such as a public safety official, a lawyer or a next-door neighbor.

Even when you are doing a profile, determine how your source knows your profile subject. Does your source work with the subject? If so, he's probably not much of an authority on the subject's after-hours activities. Does she play poker with the subject? If so, she probably doesn't know the subject in the workplace. Once you know how your source knows what he or she knows, then you can start the conversation. If you're interviewing for television, broadcast or **webcast** (an audio or video report published on the Web), your goals and techniques may be different from those of a print reporter, but the basics are the same.

PREPARING FOR THE INTERVIEW

How you prepare for an interview depends in part on what kind of story you intend to write. (Figure 4.1 shows a checklist you can use in doing interviews.) You may be doing a news story, a personality profile or an investigative piece. In each case, you check the newspaper library and search online databases, talk to other reporters and, if there's enough time, read magazine articles and books. Social media sites such as Facebook offer you information on some people you might not otherwise be able to contact. Don't print information off these sites without verification, though. Interviews are best used to solicit reactions and interpretations, not to gather facts. Good reporters gather their facts before an interview.

To prepare for a news story, you pay more attention to clips about the subject of the story than those about the personality of the interviewee. To prepare for a profile, you look for personality quirks and information about the subject's interests, family, friends, travels and habits. To prepare for an investigative piece, you want to know both your subject matter and the person you are interviewing. In all these stories, do not overlook other reporters and editors who know something about the person or subject. Let's look more closely at each of these types of common stories.

Interviewing Checklist

Before the Interview

1. Know the topic.
   - Seek specific information.
   - Research the topic.
   - List the questions.

2. Know the person.
   - Find salient biographical information.
   - Understand the person's expertise regarding the topic.

3. Set up the interview.
   - Set the time.
     - Schedule at the interviewee's convenience, but suggest a time.
     - Estimate the length of time needed.
     - Ask about possible return visits.
   - Set the place.
     - Choose the interviewee's turf or neutral turf.

4. Discuss arrangements.
   - Will you bring a digital recorder?*
   - Will you bring a photographer or a videographer?*
   - Will you let the interviewee check the accuracy of quotes?

During the Interview

1. When you arrive
   - If possible, control the seating arrangement.
   - Place your digital recorder at the optimum spot.
   - Warm up the person briefly with small talk.
   - Set the ground rules: Everything is on the record once the recorder is turned on.

2. The interview itself
   - Use good interviewing techniques.
     - Ask open-ended questions, which require the source to elaborate rather than give simple yes or no answers.
     - Allow the person to think and to speak; pause.
     - Don't be threatening in voice or manner.
     - Control the conversational flow, but be flexible.
   - Take good notes.
     - Be unobtrusive.
     - Be thorough.
   - Use the digital recorder.
     - Make sure it's on and working, but take notes, too.
     - Note the number on the digital counter at important parts in the interview so you can find quotes easily.

3. Before you leave
   - Ask if there's anything else the interviewee wants to say.
   - Check facts: spellings, dates, statistics and quotes.
   - Set a time for rechecking facts and quotes.
   - Discuss when and where the interview might appear.
   - For a print publication, ask if the interviewee wants extra copies.

After the Interview

1. Organize your notes immediately.

2. Craft a proper lead.

3. Write a coherent story.

4. Check facts for accuracy with the interviewee.

*Some sources may feel uncomfortable being recorded, videotaped or photographed.

FIGURE 4.1

Successful interviews require careful preparation.

The News Story

Usually, reporters don't have much time to prepare to cover a news story. You'll be lucky if you have a few minutes to dig into your newsroom's digital archive for background on the event or the issue. With a few more minutes, you can go online to see what other reporters have written on similar topics. Those hurried searches will provide a bit of background and perhaps some context. Then you're out the door. Still, there are three important mental steps you can take as you chase the news.

First, review in your head what you've turned up in your quick background research. If you're off to meet a political candidate, a public official or a celebrity, when was the person last in the news? For what? What will your audience (or your boss) most likely want to know now? If you're headed for a crime scene or a disaster, what do you know about the neighborhood? Has anything like this happened lately? With what results?

Second, plan your approach. Whom will you seek out at the scene? Who's likely to be in charge? What do you know about that person and her or his attitude toward reporters? Are you alone on this assignment and expected to capture audio or video? If so, double-check your equipment. Will you be reporting live on camera? If so, double-check your appearance.

Finally, plan out your first few questions. Sometimes, those are obvious. If the news is a crime or disaster, you'll want to know what happened. Was anybody hurt? What's the damage? If the story is focused on an issue or a person, you'll have some choices to make. Ideally, your backgrounding has gotten you past the most basic "Who are you?" and "Why are you here?" questions. So you may want to start with something like "What are you hoping to accomplish here?" or "Why do you think this issue is so important?"

Most news interviews aren't adversarial, but if you have tough questions, save them for the end of the conversation. That way, they won't keep you from getting most of what you need.

From there, follow your instincts and your training to find the story.

The Profile

Lane DeGregory, a staff writer for the *Tampa Bay (Fla.) Times*, was writing a profile story about a Largo, Fla., city manager who was fired when he announced he was going to have sex-reassignment surgery. DeGregory's first hurdle was getting the city manager to talk at length with her. The next hurdle was convincing the manager's wife to talk with her. Says DeGregory, "It came to this: 12 days, 10 phone calls, a two-page letter, a note, two stories, immeasurable groveling and a lot of luck."

Sometimes, journalism is hard work.

Describing to Poynter.org how she obtained the key interviews for the remarkable story, DeGregory said she typed a two-page letter to the wife to explain why she wanted to interview her and added a handwritten note and then delivered it to the house. She finally got the interview one evening when she called the former city manager, who handed the phone to the wife. DeGregory said the wife was at first reluctant. She progressed from yes and no answers to sentences. She started to relax. They talked for four hours.

Not every interview is that difficult, time-consuming or important. But every successful interview begins with establishing trust and ends with telling a story.

DeGregory says that writing previous stories on gender issues helped her establish rapport and gain the trust of the city manager. She knew the language, for one thing. She also knew the issues.

"I knew for most transgendered people, it isn't about who they want to have sex with but about who they feel they really are. So I didn't have to ask any dumb 'I-don't-get-it' questions, and I could speak with some authority on the subject."

ON THE JOB
Getting the Tough Interview

Derek Kravitz has worked as a reporter for *The Washington Post* and the Associated Press, but a story he did years ago while on his first job at the *Columbia (Mo.) Daily Tribune* is a constant reminder of how important it is to be persistent to get people to open up and talk. He explains:

Alan Farha was wanted by Columbia police for scamming area churches, so he was on the move. I found a phone number for his father in Georgetown, Texas, and left a voice mail. Later that night, I got a call from Farha on my cellphone. We spent the next hour discussing why I not only shouldn't interview him (he said he had nothing to say and his case was unimportant) but why we shouldn't focus resources on a larger story on his case (it could affect his fragile sobriety, he said, and he could fall into a deeper hole with his drug addictions).

I told him that many people, not just in Columbia, but across many states and in countless churches, thought he was a con man. He said he wasn't. I gave him the opportunity to tell his story, and after laying out the Police Department's case against him, he described his addictions and how he had resorted to asking people for money to get by. That didn't make him a con man, he said. That made him a beggar. And a Columbia police detective I spoke to agreed.

We ran the story. Farha left Columbia and has been charged with (but not arrested for) scamming churches . . . in Indiana, Texas and New Hampshire.

The *Tribune* story seems to follow him because every time he hits a new town, I get an email or a link from a local newspaper asking about him. He hasn't stopped, but his story is now well-known, mainly thanks to Google.

Oddly enough, I also got a "friend request" from Farha on LinkedIn recently. His profile says he's still struggling with his addictions.

If you don't have the background on your subject that DeGregory had on hers, you will need to research the subject and the person you will be profiling. For most profiles, you will be talking not only to your subject but also to his or her friends, family and co-workers. In many cases, you will get their names from your subject. Ask how your subject knows them: co-worker, social acquaintance, recent or lifelong friend? Then ask the co-worker or friend how he or she knows your profile subject. With this information, you won't ask inappropriate questions—you don't want to ask about your subject's love for hunting if the interviewee only knows the person from work, for example—and you can properly evaluate the information you are getting.

The Investigative Piece

The casual conversations you want to have for profile interviews are not always possible for the investigative reporter. An adversarial relationship determines both the preparation required for an investigative piece and the atmosphere of the interview itself. An investigative reporter is like an attorney in a courtroom. Wise attorneys know in advance what the answers to their questions will be. Investigative reporters often do, too, but they also are open-minded enough to switch gears if sources convince them they are on the wrong track. Regardless, preparation is essential.

Lowell Bergman, a veteran investigative reporter who worked in both print and television, advises, "Learn as much about the subject before you get there, regardless of whether you play dumb because you want them to explain it to you, or whether you just want them to know that you're not going to waste their time."

Gathering Information

In the early stages of the investigation, you conduct some fishing-expedition interviews: Because you don't know how much the source knows, you cast around. Start with people on the fringes. Gather as much as you can from them. Study the records. Only after you have most of the evidence should you confront your central character. You start with a large circle and gradually draw it smaller.

Requesting an Interview

DeGregory had difficulty getting her interview because she wanted to ask questions about a personal topic. Investigative reporters frequently have problems getting the interview because the information they seek is often damaging to the person. Sources who believe you are working on a story that will be critical of them or their friends often try to avoid you. Steve Weinberg, author of an unauthorized biography of industrialist Armand Hammer, had to overcome the suspicion of many former Hammer associates. Their former boss had told them not to talk to Weinberg. Instead of calling, Weinberg approached them by mail. "I sent letters, examples of my previous work, explained what I wanted to cover and why I was doing it without Hammer's blessing," Weinberg says.

He recommends that you use a letter or an email to share some of what you know about the story that might surprise or impress the source. For instance, a reference such as "And last week, when I was checking all the land records . . ." indicates the depth of your research.

In his letter to former Hammer assistants, Weinberg talked about how Hammer was one of the most important people in the history of business. The letters opened doors to all seven of Hammer's former executive assistants whom Weinberg contacted.

Weinberg, like DeGregory, has shown former stories as a way of trying to gain the subject's confidence. Weinberg also offers to show the sources relevant portions of his manuscript as an accuracy check. (An *accuracy check* just verifies the facts. It does not give the source the option of choosing what goes in and what stays out of a story.) He makes it clear in writing that he maintains control of the content.

Requesting an interview in writing can allow you to make your best case for getting it. And an offer to allow your sources to review the story assures them that you are serious about accuracy. Email makes both the request and the offer simpler and faster.

DOING AN AUDIO OR VIDEO INTERVIEW

When you're interviewing someone in front of a camera, the basic rules of preparation and interviewing don't change. For instance, Bob Schieffer, longtime host of

Face the Nation on CBS, says the most important thing before every interview is to know as much about the story as possible.

Some of your objectives and techniques, however, do change. Television journalists, at least those who appear on camera, are also performers. Sure, they have to report and write, but they also have to be able to tell their stories with both words and body language to people who are watching and listening—not reading. An important part of the television reporter's performance is the interview.

Reporters who conduct interviews that will appear on radio, in a podcast or online, also are performers. They must ask questions and respond to answers smoothly.

Both print and television reporters often interview to develop information that can be used in further reporting. Interviews conducted on camera usually have a different goal. That goal is the **sound bite**, the few seconds of words with accompanying video that convey not only information but also emotion. Print is a medium that mainly provides information. Television is a medium of emotion. The best interviews for television are those that reveal how a situation feels to the participants or witnesses.

Al Tompkins, the Poynter Institute's group leader for broadcast and online journalism, offers what he calls "a new set of interviewing tools" intended to produce better storytelling for television. You can find these and other tools at www.poynter .org. Here are some tips that show both the similarities and differences between print and television interviewing:

» **Ask both objective and subjective questions.** To gather facts, ask objective questions: "When?" "Where?" "How much?" But subjective questions usually produce the best sound bites: "Why?" "Tell me more about . . ." "Can you explain . . . ?"

» **Focus on one issue at a time.** Vague, complicated questions produce vague, complicated, hard-to-follow answers. Remember that readers can reread until they understand, but viewers generally can't rewind an interview. (These days, many broadcast organizations, including PBS, are posting interviews online.) Help viewers follow the story by taking your interviewee through it one step at a time.

» **Ask open-ended questions.** For print, you occasionally want a simple yes or no. That kind of answer stops a television interview. Open-ended questions encourage conversation, and conversation makes for a good interview. (For more on this, see "Open-Ended Questions" later in this chapter.)

» **Keep questions short.** Make the interviewee do the talking. Tompkins points out that short questions are more likely to produce focused responses. They also keep the viewer's attention on the person being interviewed and on what she or he has to say.

» **Build to the point.** The best interviews are like the best stories. They don't give away the punch line in the first few words. Ask soft, easy questions to encourage the interviewee to relax and trust you. Then move to the heart of the issue.

» **Be honest.** As true for television as for print and online, the importance of honesty is too often overlooked by rookie reporters. You do neither your source nor yourself a favor if you lead the source to expect an interview about softball when

VideoCentral

**bedfordstmartins.com
/newsreporting**

Watch **"Radio: Yesterday, Today and Tomorrow."**

• The video talks about ways in which radio has changed over the last 80 years. What other changes can you think of?

• Will the Internet (and online music sources) be the end of radio, or will radio stations still be around decades from now? What example from the video supports your view?

you have an indictment in mind. Tell the source ahead of time that you'll want to ask some tough questions. Say that you want to get the whole story, to be fair—and mean it. Then politely but firmly dig in. As Tompkins notes, honesty has the added benefit of helping you defend yourself against any later accusations of malice.

USING THE TELEPHONE, EMAIL, INSTANT MESSAGING OR SKYPE FOR INTERVIEWS

Interviews, as noted earlier, are always more successful if conducted in person. But when you have to interview by phone, there are at least three points to remember. These are more important for feature stories, profiles and investigative work than for standard news stories, though some news stories require more time and effort during interviews than others.

First, just as you do in person, if this is the first time you've spoken to the source, attempt to establish rapport. Don't immediately start firing questions. Express your appreciation for the person's time. Explain why you are calling and how important the interviewee is to the story. If you have talked to others who know this person, mention that to help your source relax.

Second, depending on how much time and how important this interview is, you may want to record it. You must seek the permission of the person you are interviewing: "Is it OK to record this conversation? I want to make sure I get it accurately, and this way, I can concentrate more fully on the content." Put the request on the recording. In most states, it is illegal to record a phone conversation without the other person's consent. Remember to take notes even if you are recording an interview. If the recorder malfunctions, you'll still have material for your story.

Third, just as in any other interview, try to have a conversation rather than a Q&A session. (A Q&A—question and answer—story is more or less a verbatim transcript of an interview. The interview material isn't digested and reworked into a story.) React to what is said with affirmations. Laugh when appropriate. Admit when you don't understand, and ask for more explanation.

The phone can be a friend, but it can never replace personal contact. Neither can email, but reporters are using email more frequently because they are facing more deadline pressure than ever as they feed websites, often in addition to another medium.

Email interviews have many weaknesses. They don't permit you to establish rapport. And you need to be certain the person with whom you are corresponding is the person you think he or she is. The classic *New Yorker* cartoon shown on page 67 explains the risk.

On the other hand, email is quick and convenient as a follow-up to personal or phone interviews. Email can also be effective for a Q&A story. The email captures the original questions and preserves the responses. Once you've made contact and established identity, an email interview can be useful and even surprisingly revealing.

"On the Internet, nobody knows you're a dog."

> You can't be sure who's on the other end of an email message, or that other people aren't helping the interviewee respond to your questions.

Some people will say things at a keyboard they wouldn't say face to face. Some get carried away by the power of their own prose. Some, of course, are cryptic and not forthcoming.

Instant messaging has the same strengths and weaknesses as email except that it is faster. You can best use IM for follow-up questions, clarifications and checking information to ensure accuracy.

Don't forget that email and IM are permanent. Don't ask or say anything you wouldn't want to see forwarded to others. Do make your questions clear and grammatically correct. The permanence works *for* you, too. The answers are equally permanent. They can't be taken back or denied later. And it's hard to misquote an email.

Skype **online videoconferencing** offers the advantages of email and eliminates one major drawback. With Skype, you're communicating in real time with someone you can actually see. And you're talking as opposed to typing. So you can be more comfortable that you have the right person on the other end of the link, and you can add the visual information that's missing from an email interview. Soldiers deployed overseas use Skype to stay in touch with families. Reporters can use the same technology to interview sources they might never see in the flesh.

This reporter dresses to fit in with the marchers he is interviewing; he gains their confidence by being friendly and attentive.

SETTING UP THE INTERVIEW

All this homework is important, but something as trifling as your appearance may determine whether you will have a successful interview. You would hardly wear cutoff shorts into a university president's suite, and you wouldn't wear a three-piece suit to talk to underground revolutionaries.

Most interviews are conducted in the source's office. If the story is a profile or a feature, however, it usually is better to get the source away from his or her work. If you are doing a story about a rabbi's hobby of collecting butterflies, seek a setting appropriate to the topic. Suggest meeting where the rabbi keeps the collection.

In some interviews, it is to your advantage to get the source on neutral territory. If you have questions for the provost or a public official, suggest meeting in a coffee shop at a quiet time. A person has more power in his or her official surroundings.

It is important, too, to let the source know how much time you need and whether you expect to return for further information. And if you don't already know how the source might react to a recording device, ask when you are making the appointment.

PREPARING QUESTIONS

You have now done the appropriate homework. You are properly attired. You have made an appointment and told the source how much time you need. Before you leave to meet your source, you may want to write down a list of questions to ask. They will guide you through the interview and prevent you from missing important topics altogether. The best way to encourage a spontaneous conversation is to have your questions prepared. You'll be more relaxed. Having questions prepared relieves you of the need to be mentally searching for the next question as the source is answering the last one. If you are trying to think of the next question, you cannot pay close attention to what is being said, and you might miss the most important part of the interview.

Researching Questions

Preparing the questions for an interview is hard work, even for veterans. If you are writing for your campus newspaper, seek suggestions from other staff members. You will find ideas in the newspaper's electronic database. If you anticipate a troublesome interview with the chancellor, you might want to seek advice from faculty members, too. What questions would they ask if they were you? Often, they have more background knowledge, or they might have heard some of the faculty talk around campus. Staff members are also valuable sources of information.

Although you may ask all of your prepared questions in some interviews, in most you probably will use only some of them. Still, you will have benefited from preparing the questions in two important ways. First, even when you don't use many, the work you did thinking of the questions helped prepare you for the interview. Second, sources who see that you have a prepared list often are impressed with your seriousness.

On the basis of the information you have gathered already, you know what you want to ask. Now you must be careful about how you phrase the questions.

Phrasing Questions

A young monk who asked his superior if he could smoke while he prayed was rebuked sharply. A friend advised him to rephrase the question. "Ask him if you can pray while you smoke," he said. The young monk was discovering that how questions are structured often determines the answer. Journalists face the same challenge. Reporters have missed many stories because they didn't know how to ask their questions. Quantitative researchers have shown how only a slight wording change affects the results of a survey. If you want to know whether citizens favor a city plan to beautify the downtown area, you can ask the question in several ways:

- Do you favor the City Council's plan to beautify the downtown area?
- The City Council plans to spend $3 million beautifying the downtown area. Are you in favor of this?
- Do you think the downtown area needs physical changes?
- Which of the following actions do you favor?
  - Prohibiting all automobile traffic in an area bounded by Providence Road, Ash Street, College Avenue and Elm Street.
  - Having all the downtown storefronts remodeled to carry out a single theme and putting in brick streets, shrubbery and benches.
  - None of the above.

How you structure that question may affect the survey results by several percentage points. Similarly, how you ask questions in an interview may affect the response.

With the phrasing of the question, many reporters signal the response they expect or the prejudices they have. For instance, a reporter who says, "Don't you think that the City Council should allocate more money to the Parks and Recreation Department?" is not only asking a question but also influencing the source or betraying a bias. Another common way of asking a leading question is this: "Are you going to vote against this amendment like the other City Council members I've talked to?" A neutral phrasing would be "Do you think the City Council should allocate more money to the Parks and Recreation Department?" To avoid leading or even irritating your source, ask neutral questions.

Also ask the interviewee one question at a time. Listen to journalists at press conferences jump up and ask two or three questions at a time. The source then chooses the one he or she wishes to answer and ignores the rest. That can happen in one-on-one interviews, too.

In situations where you have to ask embarrassing or awkward questions, Jeff Truesdell of *People* magazine suggests demonstrating empathy. "Say, 'I'm sorry I have to ask this,' or 'I can't believe I'm asking this but here goes,' or 'My editors will want to know'—editors in absentia make for great fall guys—or 'Let me play devil's advocate here,'" Truesdell suggests. "Acknowledge that there are unpleasant questions, apologize for asking, and then ask."

Sometimes the reporter's phrasing of a question unwittingly blocks a response. A reporter who was investigating possible job discrimination against women conducted several interviews before she told her city editor she didn't think the women with whom she talked were being frank with her. "When I ask them if they have ever been discriminated against, they always tell me no. But three times now during the course of the interviews, they have said things that indicate they have been. How do I get them to tell me about it?" she asked.

"Perhaps it's the way you are asking the question," the city editor replied. "When you ask the women whether they have ever been discriminated against, you are forcing them to answer yes or no. Don't be so blunt. Ask them if others with the same qualifications at work have advanced faster than they have. Ask if they are paid the same amount as men for the same work. Ask them what they think they would be doing today if they were male. Ask them if they know of any qualified women who were denied jobs."

The city editor was giving the reporter examples of both closed- and open-ended questions. Each has its specific strengths.

Open-Ended Questions

Open-ended questions allow the respondent some flexibility. Women may not respond frankly when asked whether they have ever been discriminated against. The question calls for a yes or no response. But an open-ended question such as "What would you be doing at work today if you were a man?" is not as personal. It does not sound as threatening to the respondent. In response to an open-ended question, the source often reveals more than he or she realizes or intends to.

A sportswriter who was interviewing a pro scout at a college football game wanted to know whom the scout was there to see. When the scout diplomatically declined to say, the reporter tried another approach. He asked a series of questions:

- "What kinds of qualities does a pro scout look for in an athlete?"
- "Do you think any of the players here today have those talents?"
- "Who would you put into that category?"

The reporter worked from the general to the specific until he had the information he wanted. Open-ended questions are less direct and less threatening. They are more exploratory and more flexible. However, if you want to know a person's biographical data, don't ask, "Can you tell me about yourself?" That question is too general. Phrase your questions to get information about specific times and places.

Closed-Ended Questions

Eventually, you need to close in on a subject, to pin down details, to get the respondent to be specific. **Closed-ended questions** are designed to elicit specific responses.

Instead of asking the mayor, "What did you think of the conference in Washington, D.C.?" you ask, "What did you learn in the session 'Funds You May Not Know Are Available'?" Instead of asking a previous employee to appraise the chancellor-designate's managerial abilities, you ask, "How well does she listen to the people who work for her?" "Do the people who work for her have specific job duties?" "Does she explain her decisions?"

A vague question invites a vague answer. By asking a specific question, you are more likely to get a specific answer. You are also communicating to your source that you have done your homework and that you are looking for precise details.

Knowing exactly when to ask a closed-ended question or when to be less specific is not something you can plan ahead of time. The type of information you are seeking and the chemistry between you and the source are the determining factors. You must make on-the-spot decisions. The important thing is to keep rephrasing the question until the source answers it adequately. Sports writer Gary Smith wrote in *Intimate Journalism*, "A lot of my reporting comes from asking a question three different ways. Sometimes the third go at it is what produces the nugget, but even if the answers aren't wonderful or the quotes usable, they can still confirm or correct my impressions."

Every reporter seeks anecdotes, and closed-ended questions help elicit them. "What is the funniest thing you've ever done?" "The weirdest?" "What's the saddest thing that ever happened to you?" When the source talks in generalities, ask a closed-ended question to get to specifics. "You say Mary is a practical joker. Can you think of an example of a practical joke she played on someone?" The answers to these types of questions yield the anecdotal nuggets that make your story readable.

Closed-Ended Questions	Open-Ended Questions
Do you like the proposal?	What are the strengths of the proposal? What are the weaknesses?
Did you have trouble coping when your child was in the car accident?	How did you cope after your child was in the car accident? Why did you attend counseling sessions?
Did you keep your promises to exercise today?	What was your exercise routine for today?
Did you give the theater teacher permission to stage that play?	What did you tell the theater teacher when she asked if her group could perform the play?
Do you use iChat in your work?	How do you use iChat in your work?

ESTABLISHING RAPPORT

The most basic requirement of any successful interview is a reasonable degree of trust between reporter and source. Usually, as a reporter you have to earn that trust. Wright Thompson, who worked for *The Kansas City Star* when he wrote this story and now works for ESPN, tells about the time he wanted to do a story about a former college football player named Ernest Blackwell, who had gone on a rampage in his neighborhood, shot a child and almost kicked another to death. He'd collapsed on a police gurney afterward and died en route to the hospital. No one could figure out what had happened. Media outlet after media outlet approached the family for an interview. All got turned down. Thompson tried a unique approach:

> When I called, I had a line. I told them I was going to talk to the cops and was going to do a story about Ernest. The police, I told them, would give me more than enough detail about the last five minutes of Ernest's life. Then I said, "I think there's a lot more to his life than the last five minutes. I think he deserves to be remembered for how he lived and not just how he died."

Thompson's reasoning won him the interview. His conclusion: "Have a plan. You must give someone a reason why it's better if they talk to you than if they don't."

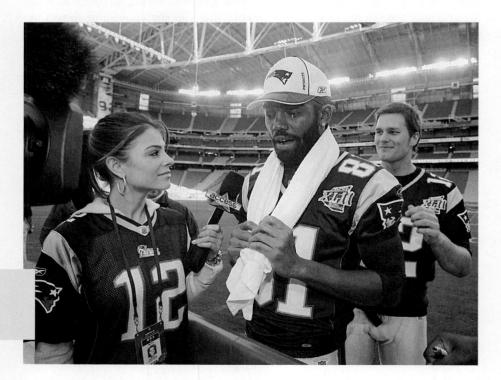

Establishing rapport with interview subjects helps a reporter get better story information.

Because he earned the trust of the family, he was able to develop the insights that allowed him to write this:

> Those who knew him wonder how Blackwell arrived on that day with so much rage in his heart, so much bad intent. Truth is, none of them could peer into the man's soul and see the hate that grew until it reached the breaking point.
>
> On Aug. 11, 2004, Blackwell could take no more.
>
> "Lord, why didn't I see the signs?" says his aunt Joyce Strong, who mostly raised Blackwell. "Why didn't I see he was reaching out for help? He must have been a ticking time bomb waiting to go off."

That's the payoff on the investment in building trust.

You probably won't have many assignments that difficult. It always helps, though, to have a plan. It also helps to have the honesty and empathy that lead strangers to be honest with you. Act like a human being.

Rapport—the relationship between the reporter and the source—is crucial to the success of the interview. It helps a reporter get better story information. The relationship is sometimes relaxed, sometimes strained. Often it is somewhere in between. The type of relationship you try to establish with your source is determined by the kind of story you are doing. Several approaches are possible.

Interview Approaches

For most news stories and personality profiles, the reporter can put the subject at ease by starting with small talk. Ask about a trophy, the plants or an engraved pen. Bring up something humorous you found during your research. Ask about something you know the source will want to talk about. If you think the subject might be skeptical about your knowledge of the field, open with a question that demonstrates your knowledge.

Rapport also depends on where you conduct the interview. Many people, especially those unaccustomed to being interviewed, feel more comfortable in their workplace. Go to them. Talk to the businessperson in the office, to the athlete in the locker room, to the conductor in the concert hall. However, if the source cannot relax at the workplace or is frequently interrupted, you may get a better interview elsewhere. Reporters have talked to politicians during car rides between campaign appearances. They've gone sailing with businesspeople and hunting with athletes. One student reporter doing a feature on a police chief spent a weekend with the chief, who was painting his home. To do a profile, which requires more than one interview, vary the location. New surroundings can make a difference.

There are times when the reporter would rather have the source edgy, nervous or even scared. When you are doing an investigation, you may want the key characters to feel uneasy.

> " I need to create what I call accelerated intimacy. We can't write the beautiful narrative stories that we all dream of unless we can get some things from the mouths of our sources. They must be comfortable enough to tell us *anything*. In journalism school, no one called the interactions between journalists and sources *relationships*, but that's what they are. "
>
> —Isabel Wilkerson, winner of the Pulitzer Prize for journalism

ON THE JOB
Relating to Your Subject

Scott Nishimura of the *Fort Worth Star-Telegram* has an unusual background for a newspaper reporter, and he takes advantage of it to get sources to talk.

"My wife and I own a small real estate business on the side," Nishimura says. "I found that being in business for myself made me a much more effective business reporter. I include that fact in my LinkedIn and Twitter profiles, and I usually figure out a way to get that into the initial conversation with new sources. That way, they know they're doing business with someone who knows more about business than your typical reporter."

Nishimura found his knowledge to be of particular help in dealing with small-business owners during his 20 years as a business reporter.

"By demonstrating that I understand their business, and by asking a series of very specific questions, I could often get business owners to disclose financial details they might not otherwise have provided.

"I also use LinkedIn to post some of my best work by embedding stories in blog posts and then linking to those posts from LinkedIn."

Nishimura is now the city hall reporter for his newspaper, but he borrowed the same tactic when he began covering his new beat. He considers it important to let news sources know that he understands the subjects about which he writes.

"I was a school and neighborhood volunteer for years, and people love dealing with me because they know I have context. They know that I understand what happens at city hall because it affects me as a citizen, too."

You may pretend you know more than you actually do. You want them to know that the material you have is substantive and serious. Seymour Hersh, a Pulitzer Prize–winning investigative reporter, uses this tactic. *Time* magazine once quoted a government official commenting on Hersh: "He wheedles, cajoles, pleads, threatens, asks a leading question, uses little tidbits as if he knew the whole story. When he finishes you feel like a wet rag."

In some cases, however, it is better even in an investigation to take a low-key approach. Let the source relax. Talk around the subject but gradually bring the discussion to the key issues. The surprise element may work in your favor.

So may the sympathetic approach. When the source is speaking, you may nod or punctuate the source's responses with comments such as "That's interesting." Sources who think you are sympathetic are more likely to volunteer information. Researchers have found, for instance, that a simple "mm-hmmm" affects the length of the answer interviewers get.

Other Practical Considerations

Where you sit in relation to the person you are interviewing can be important. Unless you deliberately are trying to make interviewees feel uncomfortable, do not sit directly in front of them. Permit your sources to establish eye contact if and when they wish.

Some people are even more disturbed by the way a reporter takes notes. A digital recorder ensures accuracy of quotes, but it makes many speakers self-conscious or nervous. If you have permission to use a recorder, place it in an inconspicuous spot and ignore it except to make sure it is working properly. Writing notes longhand may interfere with your ability to digest what is being said. But not taking any notes at all is risky. Only a few reporters can leave an interview and accurately write down what was said. Certainly no one can do it and reproduce direct quotes verbatim. You should learn shorthand or develop a note-taking system of your own.

Be sure that you address the people you are interviewing correctly. If you are unsure how they should be addressed—Mrs., Miss, Ms., Dr., Professor—ask them.

If you are interviewing someone from a culture or race different from your own, recognize and avoid your own stereotypes. Perhaps you are uncomfortable in the presence of an Islamic woman wearing a veil when she attends school in the U.S. Instead of letting your feelings influence your actions, respect her beliefs. As a reporter, take pride in your ability to move among people from all cultures. This requires that you read about cultural differences. It might help you to know that in Chinese society, people are generally uncomfortable with too much eye contact. Many Arabs consider it improper for a man to look into a woman's eyes. No one knows everything about every culture, but you can prepare for some situations, and you can also recognize what you don't know. These days, it is easy enough to do a quick search about specific cultural differences before you conduct an interview.

ENSURING ACCURACY AND FAIRNESS

Accuracy is a major problem in all interviews. Both the question and the answer may be ambiguous. You may not understand what is said. You may write it down incorrectly. You may not remember the context of the remarks. Your biases may interfere with the message.

Using a Recorder

The only way to be sure you capture the content of any interview with word-perfect accuracy is to record it. Careful listening is important, and taking good notes is essential. But using a recorder is the only way you can be certain you've got exactly what was said, both by the source and by you. That's important journalistically. As sources and audiences become increasingly skeptical, absolute accuracy adds to credibility and protects against complaints and even lawsuits.

Today's digital recorders are so small and so powerful that it's often possible to use them while they're in your pocket, purse or briefcase. However, there's seldom a need to be secretive. In fact, it's increasingly common for sophisticated sources to use their own recorders as a form of self-protection from reporters they may not trust. So the best approach usually is just to pull out your recorder, turn it on and place it in sight. If you do that as a matter of routine, chances are the source will take no notice. If

TIPS

Personal Pronouns for Transgender People

The *AP Stylebook* recommends using the pronoun (*he, she*) the person prefers. If you don't know the person's preference, use the pronoun that reflects the way the person lives publicly.

there is a question or complaint, explain the importance of accuracy and the benefit to both parties. Then get on with the interview.

Taking Notes

Knowing the background of your sources, having a comfortable relationship with them and keeping good notes are important elements of accuracy. All those were missing when a journalism student, two weeks into an internship at a major daily, interviewed the public information officer for a sheriff's department about criminal activity in and around a shelter for battered women. The reporter had never met the source. She took notes on her phone interview with the deputy and others in whatever notebook happened to be nearby. She didn't record the time, date or even the source. There were no notes showing context, just fragments of quotes, scrawled in nearly illegible handwriting.

After the story was published, the developer of the shelter sued. Questioned by attorneys, the deputy swore that the reporter misunderstood him and used some of his comments out of context. In several cases, he contended, she completed her fragmentary notes by putting her own words in his mouth. He testified that most reporters come to see him to get acquainted. Many call back to check his quotes on sensitive or complex stories. She did neither.

When the court ordered the reporter to produce and explain her notes, she had trouble reconstructing them. She had to admit on several occasions that she wasn't sure what the fragments meant.

The accuracy of your story is only as good as your notes. David Finkel, whose story on a family's TV-watching habits became a Pulitzer Prize finalist, took extra steps to be certain his material was accurate. Observing what his subjects were watching, he obtained transcripts of the shows so he could quote accurately from them. If he knew transcripts would not be available, he set his recorder near the TV to record the program.

Verifying Information

Reporters should do research after an interview to ascertain specific figures when a source provides an estimate. For example, if a restaurant owner says he runs one of 20 pizza parlors in town, check with the city business-license office to get the exact number.

When you finish your interview, go back over the key points in your notes to confirm them. Read back quotes to make sure that you have them right. Realize, too, that you will need to confirm some of the information you get from other, perhaps more authoritative, sources. And if your interview produces allegations against other people or organizations, you will need to talk to those named.

Some possibilities for making errors or introducing bias are unavoidable, but others are not. To ensure the most accurate and complete reporting possible, you should use all the techniques available to obtain a good interview, including observing and asking follow-up questions. Let's examine these and other techniques.

TIPS

Taking Notes

Here are some helpful guidelines for taking notes during an interview:

» Write the date, the place, and the interviewee's name at the top of the page.

» Develop a consistent shorthand. For example, always use "w/" to mean "with."

» Use a spiral-bound notebook with pages that are easy to turn and that lie flat.

» Make sure you have several working pens or sharpened pencils.

» Leave a wide margin so that you can annotate your writing later on.

» Look up at the interviewee frequently as you write.

» Ask for the spellings of names.

» Always take notes, even if you are using a digital recorder.

Observing

Some reporters look but do not see. The detail they miss may be the difference between a routine story and one that is a delight to read. Your powers of observation may enable you to discover a story beyond your source's words. Is the subject nervous? What kinds of questions are striking home? The mayor may deny that he is going to fire the police chief, but if you notice the chief's personnel file sitting on an adjacent worktable, you may have reason to continue the investigation.

Wright Thompson says, "It's all about the scenes. Don't just ask questions. Be an observer." Like any good writer, he offers an example to show what he means:

> I was doing a story about former Heisman Trophy winner Eric Crouch. It was almost exactly one year since he'd won the trophy, and that year had been tough for him. He'd quit pro football and had been forced to ask some hard questions about his life. As we sat in an Omaha bar, a clip of him running the football came on the television. One of the women at the table said, "You're on TV, Eric." I remember he looked up at the screen and spat, "That's not me, man." Then he took a shot of liquor. No amount of interviewing could breathe life into the idea that he had changed like that scene.

Asking Follow-Up Questions

If you understand what the source is saying, you can ask meaningful follow-up questions. There is nothing worse than briefing your city editor on the interview and having the editor ask you, "Well, did you ask . . . ?" Having to say no is embarrassing.

Even if you go into an interview armed with a list of questions, the most important questions will probably be the ones you ask in response to an answer. A reporter who was doing a story on bidding procedures was interviewing the mayor. The reporter asked how bid specifications were written. In the course of his reply, the mayor mentioned that the president of a construction firm had assured him the last bid specifications were adequate. The alert reporter picked up on the statement:

> "When did you talk to him?"
>   "About three weeks ago," the mayor said.
>   "That's before the specifications were published, wasn't it?"
>   "Yes, we asked him to look them over for us."
>   "Did he find anything wrong with the way they were written?"
>   "Oh, he changed a few minor things. Nothing important."
>   "Did officials of any other construction firms see the bid specifications before they were advertised?"
>   "No, he was the only one."

Gradually, on the basis of one offhand comment by the mayor, the reporter was able to piece together a solid story on the questionable relationship between the city and the construction firm.

There are three questions that are always useful. One is, "What did you mean by that?" The second is, "How do you know that?" and the last is, "Is there anything I haven't asked that I should?"

Using Other Techniques

Although most questions are designed to get information, some are asked as a delaying tactic. A reporter who is taking notes may fall behind. One good trick for catching up is just to say, "Hold on a second—let me get that" or "Say that again, please." Other questions are intended to encourage a longer response. "Go on with that" or "Tell me more about that" encourages the speaker to add more detail.

You don't have to be stalling for time to say you don't understand. Don't be embarrassed to admit you haven't grasped something. It is better to admit to one person you don't understand something than to advertise your ignorance in newsprint or on the airwaves in front of thousands.

Another device for making the source talk on is not a question at all; it is a pause. You are signaling the source that you expect more. But the lack of a response from you is much more ambiguous than "Tell me more about that." It may indicate that you were skeptical of what was just said, that you didn't understand, that the answer was inadequate or several other possibilities. The source will be forced to react.

ENDING THE INTERVIEW

There are two things you should always do when you finish your questions: Check key facts, figures and quotes, and then put away your pen or recorder but keep your ears open. You are not breaching any ethical rule if you continue to ask questions after you have put away your pen or turned off the recorder. Many dull interviews become interesting after they end. That's when some sources loosen up.

Quickly review your notes and check facts, especially dates, numbers, quotes, spellings and titles. Besides helping you get it right, this shows the source you are careful. If necessary, arrange a time when you can call to check other parts of the story or clear up questions you may have as you are writing. Researchers have found that more than half of direct quotations are inaccurate, even when the interview is recorded. That reflects an unacceptable sloppiness. Make sure you are the exception.

As a matter of courtesy, tell the source when the story might appear. You may even offer to send along an extra copy of the article when it's completed. And of course, thank the source for granting the interview in the first place.

> " Today one has the impression that the interviewer is not listening to what you say, nor does he think it important, because he believes that the tape recorder hears everything. But he's wrong; it doesn't hear the beating of the heart, which is the most important part of the interview. "
>
> —Gabriel García Márquez, Colombian writer and Nobel laureate

SUGGESTED READINGS

Adams, Sally, and Wynford Hicks. *Interviewing for Journalists*. 2nd ed. New York: Routledge, 2009. Adams and Hicks offer a useful description of interviewing techniques for journalists.

Kramer, Mark, and Wendy Call, eds. *Telling True Stories*. New York: Plume, 2007. This book contains excellent advice, including how to prepare for and conduct interviews.

Scanlan, Christopher, ed. *America's Best Newspaper Writing*. St. Petersburg, Fla.: Poynter Institute for Media Studies.

Reprints of winners of American Society of News Editors Distinguished Writing Awards and interviews with the writers make this an invaluable resource. It is published annually.

Sedorkin, Gail. *Interviewing: A Guide for Journalists and Writers*. 2nd ed. Crows Nest, New South Wales, Australia: Allen and Unwin, 2011. This is an excellent guide to interviewing skills for reporters and writers.

SUGGESTED WEBSITES

www.journalism.about.com/od/reporting/a/interviewing.htm
This site offers a discussion of basic journalism interviewing techniques.

www.poewar.com
The Writing Career Center offers advice on a variety of writers' concerns, including interviewing.

www.poynter.org/tag/interviewing
Various articles describe interviewing techniques for journalists.

EXERCISES

1. **Team project.** Your instructor will divide your class into teams to work on questions in preparation for an interview with a high-ranking official on your campus, such as the provost or chancellor. Brainstorm a list of issues that could be addressed in an interview. Choose an issue. Then prepare three open-ended and three closed-ended questions. As a class, rate the issues the teams have chosen in terms of relevance, timeliness and interest. Evaluate the questions. Which are effective, and why?

2. Learn to gather background on your sources. Write a memo of up to two pages about your state's senior U.S. senator. Concentrate on those details that allow you to focus on how the senator views health care issues. Indicate the sources of your information. Do an Internet search on the senator.

3. List five open-ended questions you would ask the senator. Then list five closed-ended questions you would ask.

4. Interview a student enrolled in your reporting class. Write a two- or three-page story focusing on one aspect of the

student's life. Ask your classmate to read the story and to mark errors of fact and perception. The instructor will read your story and the critique.

5. **Journalism blog.** In your blog, describe your experience completing Exercise 4. What did you learn about interviewing? Comment on the blog post of the classmate you partnered with. What can you add to each other's assessments of the exercise?

6. Interview a classmate about his or her hobbies. Then switch roles and do the interview again. Write a brief summary of what you learned, and list three additional questions you would ask if you had more time.

7. Interview a faculty or staff member at your college or university and write a profile of that person. Remember to include interviews with others who know the person.

5

Handling Quotations and Attributions

At the 2012 Olympics in London, nearly everyone expected 16-year-old gymnast McKayla Maroney to win a gold medal in the vault, especially after performing superbly on her first vault. On her second vault, however, Maroney and all who watched were shocked when she landed on her heels and her feet skidded out from under her.

In an interview after her fall, ESPN quoted Maroney as saying, "I already knew that I pretty much only had the silver medal. I really didn't deserve to win a gold medal if I fall on my butt. I was still happy with a silver, but it's still just sad."

What reporter could resist quoting those exact words of the young star? Not only are they colorful, but they also reveal a good deal about Maroney's character.

Direct quotes—the exact words that a source says or writes—add color and credibility to your story. By using a direct quote, you put your readers directly in touch with the speaker in your story. Like a handwritten letter, direct quotes are personal. Quotation marks, which always enclose a direct quote, signal to the reader that something special is coming. Direct quotes provide a story with a change of pace, a breath of fresh air.

As Paula LaRoque, former writing coach and assistant managing editor of *The Dallas Morning News*, says, "The right quotes, carefully selected and presented, enliven and humanize a story and help make it clear, credible, immediate and dramatic. Yet many quotations in journalism are dull, repetitive, ill-phrased, ungrammatical, nonsensical, self-serving or just plain dumb."

Now that's a quotation worth quoting!

Not everything people say is worth quoting. You need to learn what to quote directly, when to use partial quotes and when to paraphrase. You also must learn how and how often to attribute quotations and other information. Remember, though, that attributing a remark or some information does not excuse you from a possible libel suit. Finally, you want to be fair.

Being fair sometimes is difficult when sources do not want to be quoted. For that reason you also must learn how to deal with off-the-record quotes and background information.

In this chapter you will learn:

1. How to determine what is worth quoting directly.

2. How to ensure accuracy and fairness in quotations.

3. Whether, when and how to alter quotations.

4. When and how to attribute direct and indirect quotes.

5. How to handle both on- and off-the-record information.

McKayla Maroney watches the scoreboard after her disappointing finish on the vault in the 2012 Summer Olympics. Quotations from interviews after the event gave insight into her character.

WHAT TO QUOTE DIRECTLY

Crisp, succinct, meaningful **quotes** spice up any story. But you can overdo a good thing. Inexperienced reporters often tend to use too many direct quotations. Even many experienced public relations practitioners use too many quotes.

Remember the wonderful quote from McKayla Maroney at the beginning of this chapter? "I really didn't deserve to win a gold medal if I fall on my butt." Look at the quote used in a story on the official website for USA Gymnastics (USAgym.org):

> "It's really sad that I had to fall on that vault but I'm glad I won a silver medal."
>
> She added, "I know I can do better vaults but I also know I didn't deserve the gold medal because I fell on my second vault. It happens. It's gymnastics."

Which quote do you like better, this one or ESPN's? Which quote conveys more immediacy? More emotion?

You need direct quotes in your stories, but you also need to develop your skill in recognizing what is worth quoting directly. Let's look at the basic guidelines.

> ❝ I often quote myself. It adds spice to my conversation. ❞
>
> —George Bernard Shaw, playwright

Unique Material

A source sometimes tells you information you would not get in any other way. When you can say, "Ah, I never heard *that* before," you can be quite sure your readers would like to know exactly what the speaker said. Sometimes it is something surprising, something neither you nor your readers would have expected that person to say.

When singer Dolly Parton was asked how she felt about dumb-blonde jokes, she replied: "I'm not offended by all the dumb blonde jokes because I know I'm not dumb—and I also know that I'm not blond."

Use Good Judgment in Selecting Quotes

Striking statements like Parton's should be quoted, but not always. The *Arizona Daily Star* did a profile of a chef who writes a weekly column. Describing his food philosophy, the chef said, "I have a food philosophy, but it's a kind of an angry one. I'd eat a baby if you cooked it right. Yeah, that's pretty much it."

The *Star's* reader advocate wrote that at least a half dozen readers objected. Said one, "Shame on the chef for saying it, and shame on the *Star* for printing it."

Don't Use Direct Quotes for Straight Facts

There is no reason to place simple, factual material inside quotation marks. Here is an extract from a story about similarities in the careers of a father and son that needed no quotes at all:

> "My son was born on campus," says the elder Denney.
>
> "In fact, he was born in the same hospital that I met my wife," he says. Since that time, his son has earned his bachelor's degree "technically in agriculture with a major in biological science and conservation."

Although the quoted material is informative, it contains nothing particularly interesting, surprising, disturbing, new or even different.

Avoid quotes that provide statistics. You can usually make a clearer, more succinct presentation by paraphrasing and attributing the information to your source. Save quotes for reaction and interpretation.

Use Quotes That Move the Story Forward

A direct quotation should say something significant, and it should not simply repeat what has been said indirectly. It should move the story forward. Here's a passage from a *USA Today* story about a proposed law that would bar health-insurance companies,

TIPS

When to Use Direct Quotes

» Someone says something unique.

» Someone says something uniquely.

» Someone important says something important.

employers and managed-care plans from discriminating against people because of their genetic makeup:

> Fear of insurance discrimination based on the results of genetic tests has been on the rise for years. "It stops many people cold from getting tested," says Karen Clarke, a genetics counselor at Johns Hopkins University.

The quotation is useful, it is informative, and it moves the story forward.

Consider Using Dialogue to Tell Part of the Story

Sometimes spoken material is unique not because of individual remarks that are surprising or new but because of extended dialogue that can tell the story more effectively than writers can in their own words. Dialogue is not the same as a quotation. A quotation comes from a source speaking to the reporter. **Dialogue** occurs when two or more sources are speaking to one another.

Here's an example of how dialogue can move the story along and "show" rather than "tell." The story is about the restoration of old cars. A father is passing on a rare technique to his son:

> When the lead is smooth and the irregularities filled to his satisfaction, he reaches for his file.
>
> "How long has it been since you've done this?" his son asks.
>
> "It's been at least 20 years."
>
> "How do you tin it so it won't melt and all run off on the floor?"
>
> "Very carefully."
>
> Before the lesson is finished, a customer and two other shop workers have joined the group watching Larry at work. This is a skill few people know.
>
> "I don't like the way this lead melts," he says.
>
> "That's what it does when there's not enough tin?" his son asks.
>
> "Tin helps it stick."
>
> "Why do you pull the file instead of pushing it?"
>
> "So I can see better."
>
> "I would already have the fiberglass on and be done by now."
>
> "I know, but anything worthwhile you have to work for."

Notice the careful instruction and concerned advice from the father. His last sentence contains one of life's lessons: "Anything worthwhile you have to work for."

The Unique Expression

When you can say, "Ah, I've never heard it said *that* way before," you know you have something quotable. Be on the lookout for the clever, the colorful, the colloquial. For example, an elderly man talking about his organic garden said, "It's hard to tell people to watch what they eat. You eat health, you know."

A professor lecturing on graphic design said, "When you think it looks like a mistake, it is." The same professor once explained that elements in a design should not call attention to themselves: "You don't walk up to a beautiful painting in someone's home and say, 'That's a beautiful frame!'"

A computer trainer said to a reporter: "Teaching kids computers is like leading ducks to water. But teaching adults computers is like trying to teach chickens to swim."

Wendy Holden, the co-author of *Uggie, the Artist: My Story*, said about the Jack Russell terrier, "He was born to be a star. The fact he ended up being a dog is sort of by-the-by."

Sometimes something said uniquely is a colloquialism. Colloquialisms and regional usages can add color and life to your copy. A person from Louisiana might say, "I was just fixing to leave when the phone rang." In parts of the South you're apt to hear, "I might could do that." A person from around Lancaster, Pa., might "make the light out" when turning off the lights. In some parts of the U.S., people "redd up" the dishes after a meal, meaning that they wash them and put them away.

Important Quotes by Important People

If citizen Joe Smith says, "Something must be done about this teachers' strike," you might or might not consider it worth quoting. But if the mayor says the same words, many journalists would include the quote. Generally, reporters quote public officials or known personalities in their news stories (although not everything the famous say is worth quoting). Remember, prominence is an important property of news.

Quoting sources whom readers are likely to know lends authority, credibility and interest to your story. Presumably, a meteorologist knows something about the weather, a doctor about health, a chemistry professor about chemicals. However, it is unlikely that a television star knows a great deal about cameras, even if he or she makes commercials about cameras. Important, knowledgeable people are good sources for quotes even if what they say is not unique or said uniquely.

ACCURACY AND FAIRNESS IN DIRECT QUOTATIONS

The first obligation of any reporter is to be accurate. You must learn how to get the exact words of the source.

It's not easy.

Scribbled notes from interviews, press conferences and meetings are often difficult to decipher and interpret. A study by Adrienne Lehrer, now professor emeritus of linguistics at the University of Arizona, found that only 13 of 98 quotations taken from Arizona newspapers proved to be verbatim when compared to recordings. Only twice, however, were the meanings of the nonverbatim quotes considered inaccurate. Your passion for accuracy should compel you to get and record the exact words of your sources. Only then can you decide which words to put between quotation marks.

Ads Put Obese People in Spotlight

By Bruce Horovitz
USA Today, Oct. 4, 2012

Obese people are showing up in the very place that's mostly excluded them for decades: ads.

Some of the nation's largest brands—from Nike to Subway to Blue Cross Blue Shield—are featuring images of obese folks in their advertising in a bid to change consumer behavior. Obesity is considered to be anything 20% or more over ideal weight.

The move comes at a time two in three adults are overweight or obese, and diseases caused by obesity cost Americans $145 billion last year. In the past, obese folks in ads were often the butts of jokes. Now, they're increasingly visual images for change.

Why is it now acceptable to show obesity? "More of us are overweight, so it's a shared problem," says Valerie Folkes, marketing professor at University of Southern California.

It's a generational thing, too, says brand consultant Erich Joachimsthaler. "The new generation doesn't see (obese people) as different. There is a new, democratic world view: Everyone can be a star."

Among those showing obesity:

• **Blue Cross Blue Shield of Minnesota.** The health provider has two new ads with obese actors. In one, an obese father with a tray full of fast food thinks twice when he overhears his large son arguing with a big friend over whose father can eat more. "We want to encourage folks to make healthier choices," says Marc Manley, chief prevention officer.

• **Nike.** It launched an ad this summer showing an obese runner jogging. "It's not just championship athletes that aspire to push their limits," spokesman KeJuan Wilkins says.

• **Subway.** In March, the sandwich chain celebrates the 15th anniversary of Jared as spokesman. The ads feature photos of him at 425 pounds. "It's hard to lose the weight, but it's even harder to keep it off," says Tony Pace, head of Subway's marketing arm.

Marketers must avoid stereotypes, warns James Zervios of the Obesity Action Coalition. "So far, they're staying on the positive side of the line, but it's easy to cross over."

Annotations (left margin):

Note that all the attributions are in the present tense, which gives a sense of immediacy.

The different point of view expressed here is worth a direct quote.

This is not a new thought, but it's important to Subway's marketing.

Annotations (right margin):

This strong quote from an authority figure is nonthreatening and inviting.

This acceptable, if unexciting, quote is from an authority figure.

A more colorful and specific quote: It's important that we hear directly from industry people.

This is a good thought that makes for an excellent summary.

This story by *USA Today* marketing reporter Bruce Horovitz uses good quotations and excellent attributions.

Be sure to check the policy of your employer. Chances are, the policy is similar to that of *The Washington Post*: "When we put a source's words inside quotation marks, those exact words should have been uttered in precisely that form."

But no one expects reporters to insert every "huh" or "ya know," and there is almost never cause to embarrass anyone with few English skills.

Radio and television news editors can cut in and out of quotes, and they can certainly insert them out of context. Doing so is not just inaccurate because it distorts the meaning of what the source has said; it is also unethical.

Verification

When someone important says something important but perhaps false, putting the material in quotes does not relieve you of the responsibility for the inaccuracies. Citizens, officials and candidates for office often say things that may be partially true or altogether untrue and perhaps even libelous. (See Chapter 21 for more on libel.) Quotations need verification, like any other information you gather.

In the interest of balance, fairness and objectivity, many papers leave out, correct or point out the errors and inconsistencies in quotations. They do this in the article itself or in an accompanying story.

If candidate Joe Harkness says that his opponent, Jim McGown, is a member of the Ku Klux Klan, you should check before you print the charge. Good reporters don't stop looking and checking just because someone gives them some information. Look for yourself. Prisoners might have an altogether different account of a riot from the one the prison officials give you. Your story will not be complete unless you talk to all sides.

Quoting from Email, Social Media, the Internet and Chat Rooms

When you quote from email you have received personally, you can usually be sure the sender has written those words. If you have doubts, be sure to check with your correspondent. It's also a good idea to let readers know that you obtained the quote through email and did not speak with the source in person.

If you get a quote from the Web, you need to be much more careful. Try to verify the quote with the source, but if you can't do that, at least be sure to tell readers that the quote comes from the Web, and then cite the URL (Internet address).

Reading what people are saying in chat rooms, blogs and tweets can be useful to reporters. However, quoting what people write in these forums is unwise because some statements might be unverified and even libelous. Nevertheless, if you have verified the information—and identified the person who is saying it—and if you specifically state where you obtained the information, you might on occasion use such a quote. Identifying the person might well be impossible, though, because some people use screen names, aliases or pseudonyms on the Internet.

> " I think of quotes as spices. Spices in themselves have no nutritional value. They make nutritious things taste better, but, like spices, quotes should be used sparingly. "
>
> —Isabel Wilkerson, Pulitzer Prize–winning reporter at *The Washington Post*, quoted in *A Writer's Coach*

VideoCentral

bedfordstmartins.com /newsreporting

Watch **"Computer Assisted Reporting."**

- Computers offer research possibilities—but also challenges. What should journalists be cautious about?

- What experiences have you had using computers for research? Have you found information that would have been hard to locate by other methods?

Although quotes from experts and public figures are generally used to strengthen a story's authority, quotes from ordinary citizens with unique experience in a newsworthy event may also add credibility.

Using Someone Else's Direct Quotations

If you use a direct quotation that you did not personally get from a source, always indicate your source for the quote. Jessica Heslam wrote on BostonHerald.com that a *Boston Herald* review of WBZ-TV political analyst Jon Keller's book *The Bluest State* revealed "almost three dozen instances of direct quotes and other material lifted from numerous newspaper articles without any attribution."

Don't be tempted to use direct quotes you find in news releases. Don't be lazy; get your own quotes. Sources are much less likely to say things that are self-serving if they are talking to a journalist rather than a public relations person.

The Public Relations Society of America doesn't mind if you use material from a news release without attribution. Gerard Corbett, chair and CEO of PRSA, says doing so is not plagiarism, but he does recommend attribution when reporters use direct quotes, facts or figures from releases.

The Kansas City Star obviously disagrees about a reporter using material from news releases. The paper fired 32-year *Star* reporter Steve Penn for using news release materials in his columns dating back four years. Penn is suing McClatchy Co., owner of the newspaper. He says this practice was always OK at *The Star*, and he was not notified of a change in policy.

Practicing Prepublication Review

A decade ago, you would not have had a city editor tell you to check the accuracy of your direct quotations with your source. Today, it is standard practice on many newspapers. Steve Weinberg, a former Missouri School of Journalism professor and former head of Investigative Reporters and Editors, calls it PPR—prepublication review.

Weinberg states candidly that it is not sensitivity to the feelings of his sources that motivates him to support the use of PPR. Rather, he insists that prepublication review loosens the tongues of tight-lipped sources and gets their statements on the record. Prepublication review extends also to checking the facts. Most professional journalists insist it does not make them feel compromised or make them surrender control over their stories or appear as "obsequious lapdogs." *New York Times* Associate Managing Editor for Standards Philip B. Corbett used those words and assured readers they did not apply to reporters at *The New York Times*.

> " When you see yourself quoted in print and you're sorry you said it, it suddenly becomes a misquotation. "
>
> —Dr. Laurence J. Peter, author of *Peter's Quotations* and *The Peter Principle*

The fact is, however, that too many times journalists get direct quotes wrong. Craig Silverman, an award-winning journalist and author and founder of Regret the Error, a blog that reports on media errors and corrections, has reported on mangled direct quotations from the past and the present. No paper is immune, and neither is history. He writes that while doing research for his book, *Regret the Error: How Media Mistakes Pollute the Press and Imperil Free Speech*, he found that William Randolph Hearst did not say, "You furnish the pictures; I'll furnish the war"; President Lyndon Johnson did not say, "If I've lost Cronkite, I've lost Middle America"; and Vice President Al Gore "sure as hell" never claimed to have invented the Internet.

If you Google "Wikimedia: misquotations," you will find a list of 89 "misattributed, unsourced, unverified or other best guesses." You will also find a list of people who are most commonly misquoted. The name on top of the list? You guessed it. Yogi Berra.

Journalist Philip Weiss offers another reason why more journalists are practicing prepublication review: Reporters are often the subjects of stories. "They have had a taste of their own medicine and they don't like it."

Another reason for prepublication review is that it serves as a defense against libel. Jurors are less likely to find "reckless disregard for the truth" in an article that the source reviewed.

But what happens when sources want to change a quote? Weinberg says he makes it clear that the source is checking only for accuracy. He will consider comments about interpretation, phrasing or tone, but he retains the right to change or not change the quotes.

And what happens if someone denies saying something that is in a direct quote? That possibility is why you need to have good notes, Weinberg says, even if they are in shorthand. Having the interview on tape is even better.

The issue of quote approval is far from settled. In 2012, Poynter reported that *The New York Times*, *The Washington Post*, Bloomberg and Reuters had all agreed to let politicians and campaigns have prior approval on quotations.

Getting good quotes in a television interview takes skill and practice.

But policies can change in a hurry. Just two months later, *New York Times* Executive Editor Jill Abramson wrote a memo to her staff that said:

> So starting now (Sept. 20, 2012), we want to draw a clear line on this. Citing *Times* policy, reporters should say no if a source demands, as a condition of an interview, that quotes be submitted afterwards to the source or a press aide to review, approve or edit.

Note the words "review, approve or edit." What could be wrong with checking the accuracy of a quote? *The Huffington Post* admits that at times it allows sources to edit its quotes. Does "edit" mean change the wording or change the meaning? It surely means something different from checking the accuracy. The Associated Press, McClatchy Co. and *National Journal* have banned checking quotations.

Why? You certainly need to check the accuracy of the facts in your story. Doesn't it make sense to check the accuracy of the quotations? A simple reading of the quotes to the source can accomplish that.

That's a far cry from what *Washington Post* higher education reporter Daniel de Vise did when University of Texas officials were unhappy with his first draft of a story. An email accompanying his second draft included the words, "I'd like to know of any phrases in the piece that you think are too harsh or over-hyped. . . . Everything here is negotiable."

Patrick B. Pexton, ombudsman for *The Washington Post*, writes that de Vise made a mistake. "He forgot that *Post* reporters write for readers, not for sources."

We all need to remember that we write for our readers.

ALTERING QUOTATIONS

By now you realize that although you should use direct quotations, they present many challenges and problems. Though there is no set number you should strive to include, a story with no quotes often lacks life and substance. Still, including lengthy quotes indiscriminately is a sign that you haven't really digested the material for your audience. Instead of quoting someone at length, look for the effective kernel within a long quotation.

Paraphrasing Quotes

Some quotations need verification, others need clarification. Do not quote someone unless you are sure of what that person means. "But that's what the man said" is not a sufficient reason (or excuse) for using an ambiguous quote. It is much better to skip a quotation altogether than to confuse the reader.

The best way to avoid confusing or wordy quotes is to paraphrase. In a **paraphrase** you use your own words to communicate the speaker's meaning. As a reporter, you must have confidence that you will sometimes be able to convey that meaning in fewer words and in better language than the speaker did. Digesting, condensing and clarifying quotes take more effort than simply repeating them word for word. Here is a quote that could be cut drastically:

> "When I first started singing lessons I assumed I would be a public school teacher and maybe, if I was good enough, a voice teacher," he said. "When I graduated from the university, I still thought I would be a teacher, and I wanted to teach."

A paraphrase conveys the meaning more succinctly:

> When he first started singing lessons, and even after he graduated from the university, he wanted to be a public school voice teacher.

Using Partial Quotes

It is much better to paraphrase or to use full quotes than to use fragmentary or partial quotes. Partial quotes often make for choppy, interrupted sentences. Some editors would have you avoid these "orphan quotes" almost altogether. Here is an example of the overuse of partial quotes:

> The mayor said citizens should "turn off" unnecessary lights and "turn down" thermostats "to 65 degrees."

The sentence would be better with no quotation marks at all. Taking out the quotation marks would turn this sentence into an indirect quotation. In an indirect quotation, the reporter uses words and phrases of the speaker's language and includes an

TIPS

Getting Accurate Quotes

» Use a digital recorder during interviews, and be sure the interviewee knows you are using it.

» Develop a consistent short-hand method for note taking so you can reliably read your own notes.

» Check your written quotes against any available video of the situation.

» Call the source to verify the exact wording of any quote you're unsure of.

attribution but doesn't use quotation marks. Indirect quotations need to meet the same test for accuracy that direct quotations require.

If a particular phrase has special significance or meaning, a partial quote may be justifiable. Sometimes you might want to put a word or phrase in quotation marks to indicate that this was precisely what the speaker said. Look at this use of a one-word quote in a story about genetic engineering in *The Atlantic Monthly*:

> By all but eliminating agricultural erosion and runoff—
> so Brian Noyes, the local conservation-district man-
> ager, told me—continuous no-till could "revolution-
> ize" the area's water quality.

The writer thought it important that readers know that "revolutionize" was not his word but the word of his source. And he was right. "Revolutionize" is a strong word.

When you do use partial quotes, do not put quotation marks around something the speaker could not have said. Suppose a speaker told a student audience at a university, "I am pleased and thrilled with your attendance here tonight." It would be incorrect to write the following:

> **The speaker said she was "pleased and thrilled with the students' attendance."**

Partial quotes often contain an ellipsis (three periods) to tell the reader that some of the words of the quote are missing. For example:

> **"I have come here tonight . . . and I have crossed state lines . . . to conspire against the government."**

This practice at times might be justifiable, but you should not keep the reader guessing about what is missing. Sometimes the speaker's actual meaning is distorted when certain words are dropped. If a critic writes about a three-act play, "A great hit—except for the first three acts," an ad that picks up only the first part of that quote is guilty of misrepresentation. A journalist who uses the technique to distort the message is no less guilty.

Capturing Dialect or Accent

Using colorful or colloquial expressions helps the writer capture a person in a particular environment. The same can be true when you write the way people talk:

> **"Are you gonna go?" he asked.**
> **"No, I'm not goin'," she replied.**

In everyday speech hardly anyone enunciates perfectly. To do so would sound affected. In fiction, therefore, it is common to use spellings that match speech. But when conversation is written down in newspaper reporting, readers expect correct, full spellings. Not only is correct spelling easier to read, it is also less difficult to write. Capturing dialect consistently is difficult, as these passages from a story about a Hollywood actress illustrate:

> "Boy, it's hot out theah," she started. "I could sure use a
> nice cold beer. How about it, uh? Wanta go get a couple
> beers?"

If she said "theah," wouldn't she also say "beeah"? Perhaps she said, "How 'bout it, uh?" And if she said "wanta," maybe she also said "geta."

In another passage, the writer has the actress speaking "straight" English:

> "Would you believe I used to dress like that all the time?
> Dates didn't want to be seen with me. I was always
> being asked to change clothes before going out."

It is unlikely she is that inconsistent in her speech.

The writer of this story tried to show us something of the character of the actress. If he wanted to convey her speech patterns, he should have either been consistent or simply reported that she talked the same off the set as on it.

Sometimes when a newspaper attempts to quote someone saying something uniquely, it betrays a bias. A Southern politician is more likely to have his quote spelled phonetically than an Eastern politician who says "idee-er" and "Cuber."

However, you should not make everyone's speech the same. Barbara King Lord, former director of editorial training for the Associated Press, laments "our frequent inability to write other than insipid speech" and "our tendency to homogenize the day-to-day speech patterns of the heterogeneous people we write about." She acknowledges that writers worry about exposing to ridicule the immigrant's halting or perhaps unconventional speech while the stockbroker's speech appears flawless.

> " The surest way to make a monkey of a man is to quote him. "
>
> —Robert Benchley, humorist

Lord calls the argument specious. Of course, people should not be exposed to ridicule through their speech. "The point here," she says, "is simply that when the writer's intention in writing dialects, quaint expressions, nonconventional grammar, flowery or showy speech, or the Queen's English is to make a person human, that intention is not only acceptable, it's desirable."

The only way you can make people human is to listen to them. Lord says reporters and writers usually hear but rarely listen. She advises reporters to "listen for expressions, turns of phrase, idiosyncratic talk," and to work these into their stories.

J.R. Moehringer of the *Los Angeles Times* did this in his Pulitzer Prize–winning article:

> "No white man gonna tell me not to march," Lucy says,
> jutting her chin. "Only make me march harder."

Here the actual speech makes the speaker's determination and passion all the more evident.

You must be especially careful when quoting people for whom English is a second language. Nearly any attempt to quote nonfluent speakers exactly will be looked upon as making fun of their English. Better that you paraphrase their comments or, as some would advise, make them speak good English. Once again, however, if you have audio from baseball star Albert Pujols on your website and have the same quotes in perfect, fluent English in the written text, many would see the discrepancy as a serious problem. Others would say that you are hurting the uniqueness and character of the great slugger, who was born in the Dominican Republic. These problems are as old as radio and television, but convergence of the media has increased their frequency.

Mixing and Matching Questions and Answers

Writers often agonize over whether they must use quotations in the exact order in which the speaker said them.

The primary questions you must ask yourself are these: Why am I changing the order? Am I being fair? Am I distorting the meaning? Am I putting quotes together that change what the speaker intended to say?

Here are two versions of an emotional outburst in a Kansas City Chiefs' locker room after the Chiefs were defeated by Baltimore in 2012 and some Chiefs fans had cheered when quarterback Matt Cassel was knocked unconscious and suffered a concussion.

"It's 100 percent sickening," Chiefs tackle Eric Winston said. "I've never, ever—and I've been in some rough times on some rough teams—I've never been more embarrassed in my life to play football than at that moment right there. I get emotional about it because these guys, they work their butts off. Matt Cassel hasn't done anything to you people.

"Hey, if he's not the best quarterback, he's not the best quarterback, and that's OK, but he's a person," Winston continued, the big offensive lineman's voice slowly rising. "And he got knocked out in a game and we've got 70,000 people cheering that he got knocked out."

Here's another version of Winston's words in the locker room:

"But when you cheer, when you cheer somebody getting knocked out, I don't care who it is, and it just so happened to be Matt Cassel—it's sickening. It's 100 percent sickening. I've been in some rough times on some rough teams, I've never been more embarrassed in my life to play football than in that moment right there.

"I get emotional about it because these guys, they work their butts off. Matt Cassel hasn't done anything to you people, hasn't done anything to you people. Hasn't done anything to the media writers that kill him, hasn't done anything wrong to the people that come out here and cheer him. Hey, if he's not the best quarterback then he's not the best quarterback and that's OK. But he's a person. And he got knocked out in a game and we have 70,000 people cheering that he got knocked out?"

It's obvious that both of these quotes cannot be correct. Neither of them is exact. Other print versions of Winston's words were equally misquoted and out of order. Does it matter?

It should.

By October 2012, more than 80,000 fans heard (and saw) exactly what Winston said on YouTube. In fairness to Winston, he later apologized by acknowledging that he knew that not all 70,000 fans cheered when Cassel was knocked unconscious.

Correcting Grammar in Quotes

Perhaps the most perplexing problem tied to the proper handling of direct quotations is this: When should you correct grammatical errors in a direct quotation? Should you expect people in news conferences or during informal interviews to speak perfect English?

The Case for Correcting Grammar

It is accepted practice at many newspapers to correct mistakes in grammar and to convey a person's remarks in complete sentences. None of us regularly speaks in perfect, grammatical sentences. But if we were writing down our remarks, presumably we would write in grammatically correct English.

Reporters are expected to use standard American written English.

» Standard—News audiences expect to read or hear the most widely and generally accepted English.
» American—Some words have different spellings and meanings in England, Australia and other English-speaking countries.
» Written—Admittedly, people often use words and expressions while speaking that they do not use when writing.

Reporters and editors differ widely on when or even whether to correct quotes. A reporter for the *Rocky Mountain News* quoted an attorney as saying, "Her and John gave each other things they needed and couldn't get anyplace else." The reporter said the quote was accurate but, on second thought, said it might have been better to correct the grammar to "She and John" in the written account.

The Case Against Correcting Grammar

You are most likely to find direct quotations with grammatical errors in the sports pages of daily newspapers. Nevertheless, often you can read an entire newspaper sports section and not find a single grammatical error in a direct quote.

Washington Post reporter Howard Bryant quoted Clinton Portis, then playing for the Washington Redskins, as saying: "I don't know how anybody feels. I don't know how anybody's thinking. I don't know what anyone else is going through. The only thing I know is what's going on in Clinton Portis's life." *Post* columnist Mike Wise quoted Portis as saying: "I don't know how nobody feel, I don't know what nobody think, I don't know what nobody doing, the only thing I know is what's going on in Clinton Portis's life."

Bryant, an African-American then working with ESPN, did not agree with the *Post*'s policy of not changing quotes, a policy that, by the way, he said he never heard of. But Bryant did say, "I am totally convinced—along racial, class and cultural lines—that when it comes to white players from the South, reporters instinctively clean up their language."

Most papers have no written policy on correcting grammatical errors in direct quotations. Because so many variables are involved, these matters are handled on a case-by-case basis. Some argue you should sacrifice a bit of accuracy in the interest of promoting proper English—except for elected officials and public figures.

On the subject of correcting grammar in direct quotations, read what AP says under "Quotations in the News":

> Never alter quotations even to correct minor grammatical errors or word usage. Casual minor tongue slips may be removed by using ellipses but even that should be done with extreme caution. If there is a question about a quote, either don't use it or ask the speaker to clarify.

In this age of convergence, print reporters might also have shot video, and even if they haven't, they know someone has. Correcting quotations is even more unwise for radio and television reporters. Writers and editors for print should remember that the quotation they use might have been heard by millions of people on radio or television. Changing the quote even slightly might make viewers and listeners question the credibility of print reports. Readers might also ask why print writers feel the need to act as press agents who strive to make their subjects look good.

This applies to celebrities of all kinds (actors, sports figures), but it might also apply to political candidates and elected officials. At least, some argue, news agencies should have some consistency. If a reporter quotes a farmer using incorrect grammar, then should the same be done for the mayor or for a college professor?

Removing Redundancies

Another question reporters deal with is whether to remove redundancies and other irrelevant material by using ellipses. Again, there is no agreement in the industry. For most reporters and editors, the answer to the problem of correcting quotes is to take out the quotation marks and to paraphrase. Sometimes you can just remove a phrase or a sentence. However, when you do that, you sometimes lose a lot. The value of quotes often lies in their richness and uniqueness.

When the Columbia *Missourian* quoted University of Missouri basketball star Keon Lawrence after a winning game, it dropped a sentence:

> "That felt good," Keon Lawrence said. "I look forward to doing that again."

The *Columbia Daily Tribune* wrote it this way:

> "Oh, that felt good," Lawrence said a few minutes after the game that hardly anyone thought the Tigers could

win. "I didn't never do that. I look forward to doing
that again."

Which version do you like better? Which version would you have written?

Deleting Obscenity, Profanity and Vulgarity

Many news organizations never allow some things people say to be printed or broadcast—even if they are said uniquely. Obscenities (words usually referring to sexual
parts or functions), profanities (words used irreverently to refer to a deity or to beings
people regard as divine) and vulgarities (words referring to excretory matters) are usually deleted or bleeped unless they are essential to the story. Even at major newspapers, policy often demands that an obscenity, for example, be used only with the
approval of a top editor.

Of course, there are legitimate reasons to use proper sex-related terms in health
stories and in some crime stories, including child molestation stories.

News stories about sexual assaults or accusations sometimes contain words such
as these, especially if those involved are noted celebrities or politicians.

Obviously, words such as "God" and "Jesus Christ" used in discussions of religion
have always been acceptable to most people.

Nevertheless, the rules are different for what some call "swear" words in direct
quotation. Some papers follow *The Associated Press Stylebook* rule: "If a full quote
that contains an obscenity, profanity or vulgarity cannot be dropped but there is no
compelling reason for the offensive language, replace the letters of the offensive word
with hyphens, using only an initial letter."

News is likely to reflect the sensibilities of its audience. Like it or not, language
that was once considered vulgar in polite society is now tolerated more widely.

Of course, the Federal Communications Commission regulates the content of
radio and television (except for cable) and can still fine a station or suspend its license
for indecency. Fining is rare, but audiences are quick to let a station know that it has
gone too far.

Individuals and advocacy groups try to curtail the use of profanity in the media.
One such group is the Parents Television Council, a U.S.-based advocacy group
founded in 1995 by conservative activist L. Brent Bozell III. This group's primary
mission is to list television programs and other entertainment products it deems
harmful to children. Among other measures, it counts the times profanity is used on
a program.

Researchers from the University of Tennessee and Florida State University have
kept track of the rapid rise of words such as "jackass" and "sucks." *New York Times*
writer Edward Wyatt quotes Timothy Jay, a psychology professor at the Massachusetts
College of Liberal Arts, as saying, "Vulgar slang has a way of waxing and waning,
where we become desensitized to a word's earlier meanings."

At times you might wish to use vulgarities to show the intensity of someone's
anger, terror, frustration or bitterness. Few inside the news media condone the casual,
gratuitous use of vulgarities, however.

And neither do most readers and listeners.

Avoiding Made-Up Quotes

Fabricating a direct quote, even from general things that a source has said or from what the source might say if given the chance, is never acceptable. Even seasoned reporters are sometimes tempted to put quotation marks around words that their sources "meant to say," or to clarify or simplify a quote. They reason that it's more important to have a clear and concise quote for the reader than to be a slave to the verbose and unclear words of the source. That's bad reasoning. It's better to paraphrase.

Even worse is fabricating a quote that makes a source look bad or that is defamatory or perhaps even libelous. Doing so can result in a lawsuit. In 1991, in Masson v. Malcolm, the U.S. Supreme Court ruled that suits regarding quotations can proceed to trial if the altered quote "results in a material change in the meaning conveyed by the statement."

Libel or no libel, your credibility as a reporter demands that you be scrupulously exact when you place people's words inside quotation marks. When in doubt, paraphrase.

ATTRIBUTING DIRECT AND INDIRECT QUOTES

Now that you've learned some of the complexities of using quotations, let's take a look at when and how to attribute them to a source.

When to Attribute

Attribution involves giving the name of, and sometimes other identifying information about, the source of a direct quotation, an indirect quotation or paraphrased material. You should almost always attribute direct quotes—with some exceptions. You would not, for example, attribute a quotation to a 7-year-old who witnessed a gang shooting. You might not wish to attribute a quote to someone who saw a homicide suspect with the victim. To do so in either case could put the source in danger.

You need a good reason to allow an entire paragraph of direct quotations to stand without an attribution. However, if you are quoting from a speech, an interview or a press conference and only the speaker is mentioned in the story, it might be excessive to put an attribution in every paragraph.

Ordinarily you should attribute **indirect quotations**. You should usually have a source for the information you write, and when you do, attribute the information to that source. The source can be a person or a written document. However, there are exceptions.

If you are a witness to damages or injuries, do not name yourself as a source in the story. Attribute this information to the police or to other authorities. But you do not have to attribute the totally obvious. If you are on the scene of an accident and can see that three people were involved, you do not have to write, "'Three people were involved in the accident,' Officer Osbord said." If you are unsure of the information or if there are conclusions or generalities involved, your editor probably will want you to attribute the information to an official or a witness. Avoid, however, attributing factual statements to "officials" or "authorities" or "sources." "Such constructions," writes journalist Jack Hart, "suggest that we are controlled by form and that we have forgotten about function."

If you are quoting from an interview conducted by someone other than yourself, be sure to note that. Do not claim that you obtained the quote yourself by writing, "In an interview, Smith said. . . ." That would make it seem as though you conducted the interview.

Not everyone agrees. Well-known journalist and commentator Fareed Zakaria, who was found guilty of plagiarism, was also found guilty of not attributing sources. In one case he justified his actions by saying that his book was "not an academic work where everything has to be acknowledged and footnoted." He did not wish to "interrupt the flow for the reader."

Zakaria says he feels the same way about attributing quotes from other people's interviews.

He's wrong.

Hart pleads for common sense regarding attributions. "Let's save them for direct quotations or paraphrased quotes laced with opinion," he writes. "Or for assertions likely to be especially sensitive. Or controversial." He says we should attribute only "if it matters."

This is good advice for the veteran. Nevertheless, although it is possible to attribute too often and although you do not always need to attribute, when you have doubts, include an attribution.

That goes for attributing anonymous sources, too. Even though you should seldom use them, you must attribute them. Try to preserve your credibility by giving as much information as you can about the sources without revealing their names. For example, you might report "a source close to the chancellor said." For the second reference to the same source, use "the anonymous source said."

Whether we like them or not, anonymous sources are common, even in the best of newspapers. The figure "Using Anonymous Sources" (page 100) shows a few paragraphs from an Associated Press story published in the *Columbia Daily Tribune*. The attributions—all anonymous—are highlighted in bold.

Notice how many quotes are attributed to a "criminal complaint" without really saying exactly who was responsible for filing the complaint. Notice also the attribution "family members." The reporter had no reason to name them and invade their privacy.

Sometimes, as in stories about crime victims, you might have to change someone's name and follow the pseudonym with "not her real name" in parentheses to protect the source's privacy or to avoid endangering the source's life or family.

How to Attribute

In composition and creative writing classes, you may have been told to avoid repeating the same word. You probably picked up your thesaurus to look for a synonym for "to say," a colorless verb. Without much research you may have found 100 or more

TIPS

Attribution Not Needed

You need not attribute information to a source if you are a witness or if the information:

» Is a matter of public record.

» Is generally known.

» Is available from several sources.

» Is easily verifiable.

» Makes no assumptions.

» Contains no opinions.

» Is noncontroversial.

ANNOTATED MODEL   Using Anonymous Sources

Terror Sting Thwarts Car Bomb Attempt
Attack was planned on Federal Reserve.

NEW YORK (AP)—A Bangladeshi man snared in an FBI terror sting considered targeting President Barack Obama and the New York City Stock Exchange before settling on a car bomb attack on the Federal Reserve, just blocks from the World Trade Center site, a law enforcement official told The Associated Press today.

The official, who was not authorized to speak publicly about the investigation and talked to the AP on condition of anonymity, stressed that the suspect never got beyond the discussion stage in considering an attack on the president.

In a September meeting with an undercover agent posing as a fellow jihadist, Quazi Mohammad Rezwanul Ahsan Nafis explained he chose the Federal Reserve as his target "for operational reasons," according to a criminal complaint. Nafis also indicated he knew that choice would "cause a large number of civilian casualties, including women and children," the complaint said.

The bomb was fake, but authorities said that Nafis' admiration of Osama bin Laden and aspirations for martyrdom were not.

FBI agents grabbed the 21-year-old Nafis—armed with a cellphone he believed was rigged as a detonator—after he made several attempts to blow up a fake 1,000-pound bomb inside a vehicle parked next to the Federal Reserve yesterday in lower Manhattan, the complaint said. . . .

Nafis is a banker's son from a middle-class neighborhood, and family members said today that they were stunned by his arrest. . . .

The reporter states the reason for the source's anonymity.

The criminal complaint is a matter of public record.

The word "authorities" tells the reader the information was confirmed with more than one source.

The reporter preserves the sources' privacy.

Sources can be anonymous for a number of reasons. Explaining those reasons improves the credibility of the story.

substitutes. None of them is wrong. Indeed, writers might search long for the exact word they need to convey a particular nuance of meaning. For example:

> The presidential candidate announced the choice of a running mate.

> The arrested man divulged the names of his accomplices.

> The judge pronounced sentence.

At other times, in the interest of precise and lively writing, you might write:

"I'll get you for that," she whispered.

"I object!" he shouted.

Nevertheless, reporters and editors prefer forms of "to say" in most instances, even if these are repeated throughout a story. And there are good reasons for this word choice. "Said" is unobtrusive. Rather than appearing tiresome and repetitious, it hides in the news columns and calls no attention to itself. "Said" is also neutral. It has no connotations. To use the word "said" is to be objective.

Some of the synonyms for "said" sound innocent enough, but be careful. If you report that a city official "claimed" or "maintained" or "contended," you are implying that you do not quite believe what the official said. The word "said" is the solution to your problem. If you have evidence that what the official said is incorrect, you should include the evidence or the correct information in your story.

In some newspaper accounts of labor negotiations, company officials always "ask" and labor leaders always "demand." "Demanding" sounds harsh and unreasonable, but "asking" sounds calm and reasonable. A reporter who uses these words in this context is taking an editorial stand—consciously or unconsciously.

Other words you may be tempted to use as a substitute for "said" are simply unacceptable because they represent improper usage. For example:

"You don't really mean that," he winked.
"Of course I do," she grinned.
"But what if someone heard you say that?" he frowned.
"Oh, you are a fool," she laughed.

You cannot "wink" a word. Similarly, it is impossible to "grin," "frown" or "laugh" words. But you might want to say this:

"Not again," he said, moaning.
"I'm afraid so," she said with a grin.

This usage is correct. Words like "moaning" or phrases like "with a grin" sometimes are needed to convey the speaker's meaning, but often they are not necessary or even helpful.

Learning the correct words for attribution is the first step. Here are some other guidelines to follow when attributing quotations:

» **If a direct quote is more than one sentence long, place the attribution at the end of the first sentence.** This placement makes the copy flow better and doesn't keep the reader in the dark about the attribution for too long. For example:

"The car overturned at least three times," the police officer said. "None of the four passengers was hurt. Luckily, the car did not explode into flames."

That one attribution is adequate. It would be redundant to write the following:

"The car overturned at least three times," the police officer said. "None of the four passengers was hurt," he added. "Luckily, the car did not explode into flames," he continued.

Nor should you write this:

"The car overturned at least three times. None of the four passengers was hurt. Luckily, the car did not explode into flames," the police officer said.

Although you should not keep the reader wondering who is being quoted, in most cases you should avoid placing the attribution at the beginning of a quote. Do not write the following:

The police officer said: "The car overturned at least three times. None of the four passengers was hurt. Luckily, the car did not explode into flames."

» **If direct quotes from two different speakers follow one another, start the second with its attribution.** This placement avoids confusion for the reader:

"The driver must not have seen the curve," an eyewitness said. "Once the car left the road, all I saw was a cloud of dust."

    The police officer said: "The car overturned at least three times. None of the four passengers was hurt. Luckily, the car did not explode into flames."

Notice that when an attribution precedes a direct quotation that is more than one sentence long, wire service style requires that a colon follow the attribution.

» **Separate partial quotes and complete quotes.** Avoid constructions like this one:

The mayor said the time had come "to turn off some lights. We all must do something to conserve electricity."

The correct form is to separate partial quotes and complete quotes:

The time has come "to turn off some lights," the mayor said. "We all must do something to conserve electricity."

» **The first time you attribute a direct or an indirect quote, identify the speaker fully.** How fully depends on how well the speaker is known to the readers. In Springfield, Ill., it is sufficient to identify the mayor simply as Mayor Houston. But if a story in the *Chicago Tribune* refers to the mayor of Springfield, the first reference should be "J. Michael Houston, mayor of Springfield"—unless the dateline for the story is Springfield.

» **Attribute direct quotes to only one person.** For example, don't do the following:

"Flames were shooting out everywhere," witnesses said.

If indeed any witnesses made statements like this, all you have to do is eliminate the quotation marks to turn this into an indirect quotation. For example:

Several witnesses said that flames were shooting out everywhere.

He Said, She Said—Punctuating Direct Quotations

"Always put the comma inside quotation marks," she said. Then she added, "The same goes for the period."

"Does the same rule apply for the question mark?" he asked.

"Only if the entire statement is a question," she replied, "and never add a comma after a question mark. Also, be sure to lowercase the first word of a continuing quote that follows an attribution and a comma.

"However, you must capitalize the first word of a new sentence after an attribution," she continued.

"Do not forget to open and close the sentence with quotation marks."

"Why are there no quotation marks after the word 'comma' at the end of the third paragraph?" he asked.

"Because the same person is speaking at the beginning of the next paragraph," she said. "Notice that the new paragraph does open with quotation marks. Note, too, that a quote inside a quotation needs single quotation marks, as around the word 'comma' in the paragraph above."

» **Do not make up a source. Never attribute a statement to "a witness" unless your source is indeed that witness.** At times you might ask a witness to confirm what you have seen, but never invent quotes for anonymous witnesses. Inventing witnesses and making up quotes is dishonest, inaccurate and inexcusable.

» **In stories covering past news events, use the past tense in attributions, and use it throughout the story.** However, features and other stories that do not report on news events might be more effective if the attributions are consistently given in the present tense (see "Using Quotes Effectively," page 86, for example). In a feature story like a personality profile, when it is safe to assume that what the person once said, he or she would still say, you might use the present tense. For example, when you write, "'I like being mayor,' she says," you are indicating that the mayor still enjoys her job.

» **Ordinarily, place the noun or pronoun before the verb in attributions:**

"Everything is under control," the sheriff said.

However, if you must identify a person by including a long title, it is better to begin the attribution with the verb:

"I enjoy the challenge," says Janet Berry, associate dean for graduate studies and research.

Attributing Written Sources

Do not use the word "says" when quoting from written sources. You might be general at times and write, "As *Time* magazine reported last week . . ." or "According to *Time* magazine. . . ." When you know the author of the piece, you might wish to include it: "As Katha Pollitt wrote in the Sept. 21, 2009, issue of *The Nation*. . . ." For a report, survey or study cited in a news story, it's usually enough to identify the authors, the date of publication and the name of the journal or the issuing agency. (For guidance on avoiding unintentional plagiarism, see Chapter 22.)

HANDLING ON- AND OFF-THE-RECORD INFORMATION

Your job would be easy if all of your sources wished to be "on the record."

Some sources do not want to be named for sound reasons. You must learn to use professional judgment in handling the material they give you. If you agree to accept their information, you must honor their request to remain off the record. Breaching that confidence destroys trust and credibility and may get you in trouble with the law. But it is your obligation to take the information elsewhere to confirm it and get it on the record.

Anonymous sources helped *The New York Times* report the Bush administration's extralegal bugging of international communications. But another *Times* front-page story based on anonymous sources suggesting Sen. John McCain had an extramarital affair with a lobbyist was a great embarrassment.

Problems with Anonymous Sources

Not naming sources is dangerous for three important reasons. First, such information lacks credibility and makes the reporter and the newspaper suspect. Why should readers believe writers who won't cite the sources of their information? Who is to say that the writers didn't simply make things up to suit their stories?

Second, the source might be lying. He or she might be out to discredit someone or might be floating a trial balloon, that is, testing public reaction on some issue or event. Skilled diplomats and politicians know how to use reporters to take the temperature of public opinion. If the public reacts negatively, the sources will not proceed with whatever plans they leaked to the press. In such cases the press has been used—and it has become less credible.

Finally, once you have promised anonymity to a source, you might not change your mind without risking a breach-of-contract suit. In 1991, the U.S. Supreme Court ruled 5-4 in Cohen v. Cowles Media Co. that the First Amendment does not prevent news sources from suing the press for breach of contract when the press makes confidential sources public. That's why at papers such as *The Miami Herald* only a senior editor has authority to commit the paper to a pledge of confidentiality.

The New York Times' **Policy on the Use of Anonymous Sources**

" The policy requires that at least one editor know the identity of every source. Anonymous sources cannot be used when on-the-record sources are readily available. They must have direct knowledge of the information they are imparting; they cannot use the cloak of anonymity for personal or partisan attack; they cannot be used for trivial comment or to make an unremarkable comment seem more important than it is. "

—From "Culling the Anonymous Sources" by Clark Hoyt, former public editor, *The New York Times*

ON THE JOB
Off the Record

T.J. Quinn spent 16 years as a news and sports writer—eight at the New York *Daily News*—before moving to ESPN in 2007. As a reporter for the network's investigative/enterprise unit, most of his work is "cross-platform," with versions of the same stories appearing on television, ESPN.com and ESPN radio. His long-form stories appear primarily on the show "Outside the Lines," for which he is a backup anchor. Quinn's work also appears on "Sports-Center" and other ESPN news platforms, and he works as an adjunct professor at the Columbia University Graduate School of Journalism.

He finds that investigative work requires a lot of off-the-record and not-for-attribution interviews. "Be careful," he says. "Don't be too eager to grant sources anonymity unless they truly won't speak to you otherwise." After a not-for-attribution conversation, he usually asks sources whether they would be comfortable saying the same thing on the record. "They often are," Quinn says.

"If you do go off the record, be absolutely clear about what is on and what is off, and if you agree to stay off the record, respect it," Quinn says. "You'll have no credibility if you don't."

Disagreement About Terminology

Some reporters make these distinctions regarding sources and attribution:

- » **Off the record.** You may not use the information.
- » **Not for attribution.** You may use the information but with no reference as to its source.
- » **Background.** You may use it with a general title for a source (for example, "a White House aide said").
- » **Deep background.** You may use the information, but you may not indicate any source.

By no means is there agreement on these terms. For most people "off the record" means not for attribution. For some it means that you cannot use the information in any way. Some find no difference between "background" and "deep background." Journalists are vague about the meaning of the terms, and so are sources. Your obligation is to make sure you and your sources understand each other. Set the ground rules ahead of time. Clarify your terms.

Be careful not to allow a speaker to suddenly claim something is off the record. Sometimes in the middle of an interview a source will see you taking notes and try to change the rules: "Oh, I meant to tell you, that last example was off the record." With all the tact you can muster, try, without losing the source altogether, to change the person's mind. At least, tell the person to try to avoid doing that for the rest of the interview.

TIPS

Three Reasons to Avoid Anonymous Sources

- » You damage your credibility.
- » Your source may be lying or floating a trial balloon.
- » You may be sued if you later reveal your source.

Background Interviews

If a city manager or police chief wishes to have a background session with you, unless it is against newspaper policy, you should not refuse. Often these officials are trying to be as open as they can under certain circumstances. Without such background sessions the task of reporting complex issues intelligently is nearly impossible. But you must be aware that you are hearing only one point of view and that the information may be self-serving.

Some sources make a habit of saying everything is off the record and of giving commonplace information in background sessions. Although you should not quote a source who asks to remain off the record, you may use the information if one or more of the following is true:

» The information is a matter of public record.
» It is generally known.
» It is available from several sources.
» You are a witness.

So as not to lose credibility with your source, it's a good idea to make it clear that you plan to use the information for one or more of the preceding reasons.

Remember these two important points:

» When possible, set the ground rules with your sources ahead of time.
» Know your newspaper's policy regarding these matters.

Knowing when and how to attribute background information is an art you should continue to develop as a reporter.

SUGGESTED READINGS

Brooks, Brian S., James L. Pinson and Jean Gaddy Wilson. *Working with Words: A Handbook for Media Writers and Editors*. 8th ed. New York: Bedford/St. Martin's, 2013. The section on quotations is excellent and follows Associated Press style.

Callihan, E.L. *Grammar for Journalists*. Rev. ed. Radnor, Pa.: Chilton, 1979. This classic text contains a good section on how to punctuate, attribute and handle quotations.

Germer, Fawn. "Are Quotes Sacred?" *American Journalism Review* (September 1995): 34–37. This article presents views from all sides on whether and when to change quotes.

Hart, Jack. "Giving Credit When Credit Isn't Due." *Editor & Publisher* (Sept. 11, 1993): 2. Hart warns against useless attribution.

King, Barbara. "There's Real Power in Common Speech." *Ottaway News Extra*, no. 137 (Winter 1989): 8, 16. The author presents an excellent discussion on using real quotes from real people.

LaRoque, Paula. "People Are Using Quotes More Often — But in Many Cases They Shouldn't Be." *Quill* (March 1, 2004): 32. LaRoque, an excellent writer, writing coach and teacher, provides good advice.

Stein, M.L. "9th Circuit: It's OK to Make Up Quotes." *Editor & Publisher* (Aug. 12, 1989): 16, 30. This article reports reactions from the press and lawyers to the court decision allowing quotes that are not verbatim.

Stimson, William. "Two Schools on Quoting Confuse the Reader." *Journalism Educator* 49, no. 4 (Winter 1995): 69–73. Strong arguments against cleaning up quotes are presented in this article.

Stoltzfus, Duane. "Partial Pre-publication Review Gaining Favor at Newspapers." *Newspaper Research Journal* 27, no. 4 (Fall 2006): 23–37. A practice long thought unconscionable among journalists gains acceptance.

Weinberg, Steve. "So What's Wrong with Pre-publication Review?" *Quill* (May 1990): 26–28. Weinberg answers objections to prepublication review.

Weinberg, Steve. "Thou Shalt Not Concoct Thy Quote." *Fineline* (July/August 1991): 3–4. In this article, Weinberg presents reasons for allowing sources to review quotations before publication.

Weiss, Philip. "Who Gets Quote Approval?" *Columbia Journalism Review* (May/June 1991): 52–54. Weiss discusses the growing practice of allowing sources to check quotations before publication.

SUGGESTED WEBSITES

http://owl.english.purdue.edu/owl/resource/577/1
This site provides an excellent, succinct summary of the rules for using quotation marks.

http://journalism.about.com/od/writing/a/attribution.htm
This page provides an excellent discussion of attribution, including on- and off-the-record attribution and deep background.

EXERCISES

1. **Team project.** Get together with three other classmates. Each of you should interview a different news reporter or editor working in print, radio or television about his or her policies for handling sources regarding the following types of information:

   a. Off the record
   b. Not for attribution
   c. Background
   d. Deep background

   Then compare what the interviewees said. Which policy or policies seem the most reasonable and effective?

2. Rewrite the following story. Pay special attention to the use of quotations and attribution. Note the sensitive nature of some of the quotations. Delete or paraphrase when you think it's necessary.

   > Christopher O'Reilly is a remarkably happy young man, despite a bout with meningitis eight years ago that has left him paralyzed and brain-damaged.

"I am happy," O'Reilly commented, as he puffed a cigarette. He has much to be happy about. Physical therapy has hastened his recovery since the day he awoke from a 10-week-long coma. He has lived to celebrate his 26th birthday.

"I had a helluva birthday," he said. "I seen several friends. I had big cake," he added slowly.

He lives in a house with his mother and stepfather in the rolling, green countryside near Springfield.

O'Reilly's withered legs are curled beneath him now, and his right arm is mostly paralyzed, but he can do pull-ups with his left arm. He can see and hear.

"When he came back, he wasn't worth a damn," his mother said. "The hack doctors told me he would be a vegetable all his life," she claimed.

"He couldn't talk; he could only blink. And he drooled a lot," she smiled.

Now, Chris is able to respond in incomplete sentences to questions and can carry on slow communication. "He don't talk good, but he talks," his mother commented.

It all began when he stole a neighbor's Rototiller. His probation was revoked, and he found himself in the medium-security prison in Springfield. Then came "inadequate medical treatment" in the prison system. O'Reilly's family argued that he received punishment beyond what the Eighth Amendment of the U.S. Constitution calls "cruel and unusual."

"Those prison officials were vicious," they said.

As a result, he was awarded $250,000 from the state, the largest legal settlement in federal court in 10 years. "That sounds like a lot of money. But it really isn't, you know, when you consider what happened and when you consider the worth of a human life, and the way they treated him and all, we thought we should get at least a million," his mother remarked.

O'Reilly contracted the infection of the brain after sleeping "on the concrete floor" of a confinement cell, his mother maintained. He had been placed in solitary confinement because he would not clean his cell. The disease went undiagnosed for eight days, leaving him paralyzed and brain-damaged, she said.

Now O'Reilly likes watching television. "I like TV," he grinned. "And smoking."

His mother said she "never gives up hope" that "one day" her son will "come out of it."

3. Read the following passage by writer and artist John Gerstner. Write a brief story covering what Gerstner said, and use three—and only three—direct quotes.

I believe a magazine should be everything you would like your mate to be: intelligent, adventurous, stimulating, candid, helpful, spirited, nice to look at and full of surprises. I believe a magazine should feast the eye as well as feed the mind. Leafing through a magazine should be an aesthetic as well as an intellectual experience. Each page should be a synthesis of ideas, concepts, words, photographs, illustrations and graphic design that arrests, intrigues and instantly communicates . . . not only the subject of the article but also some of its nuances as well—no small trick.

I believe a magazine should continually evolve and take risks. About the time a winning formula is found is about the time a new one needs formulating. The best magazines stretch themselves in every issue and surprise both readers and staff.

I believe a magazine should be a team project. No editor is an island, nor should want to be. The editor's job is to set the course and the standard. After that it's a matter of squeezing every ounce of creativity out of himself or herself and others and "arguing, procuring, tinkering and sending things back," as one magazine editor put it. And no editor or publisher should ever underestimate the role human chemistry and magic play in putting out a successful magazine.

Finally, I believe the magazine is one of journalism's highest and noblest forms. The magazine format demands not just good reporting and writing but good communicating, which entails visual as well as verbal sophistication. The best magazines move minds, raise sights and spirits, and make waves to break on distant shores. They aspire to—and sometimes achieve—the level of art.

4. Attend a meeting, a press conference or a speech, and record it. While there, write down the quotes you would use if you were writing the story for your local newspaper. Then listen to the recording, and check the accuracy of your written quotations.

5. **Journalism blog.** Write a blog post explaining when you would feel justified in using an anonymous source. Give examples to support your reasons. If possible, link to one or two news stories that reflect your thinking.

6. Engage a classmate in a half-hour interview about his or her life. Write a story based on the interview, using as many direct quotes as you think are fitting. Then check the accuracy of the quotations with your classmate.

7. Find a story in the sports section of a newspaper, and try to change all or most of the attributions to the present tense. How does this change affect the impact of the story?

6

Gathering and Verifying Information

DURING THE SYRIAN UPRISINGS of 2012 and 2013, brave citizen journalists often risked their lives to chronicle a crackdown on dissidents by the government of President Bashar al-Assad. The images of police and military attacks on civilians frequently made their way to YouTube and Facebook, giving the outside world a glimpse of what was transpiring in a brutal dictatorship. Because the regime had blocked outside reporters from entering the country, reports from these citizen journalists were one of the few ways the world could learn about what was happening.

As brutal as the recent attacks were, according to veteran Middle East journalists they were nothing compared to the 1982 massacre of more than 10,000 protesters over a period of three weeks by the same Syrian government. Arguably, social media reporting led the regime to be more restrained 30 years later.

Tweets from both seasoned journalists and citizen reporters keep us informed of developments worldwide. We trust that most of those reports are accurate, but some are not, perhaps because of the confusion of the moment. And just how accurate were those photos coming from Syria? Were they authentic or doctored?

Social media did help some people get the latest news headlines and weather warnings during Hurricane Sandy, which struck the East Coast in 2012. They also helped friends and families stay in touch. Lamar Graham, chief content officer of NJ.com and a former editor of *Parade* magazine, was working hard in New Jersey to cover the storm while his family back in Manhattan hunkered down to survive it. He learned they were safe only when a friend of the family sent him a text of reassurance hours after the storm hit. It was a story akin to those of thousands of others affected by Sandy. Still, while social media offer benefits—getting quick news updates and keeping in touch with loved ones among them—they also have a dark side: Being first with the news is not a good thing when the report is false.

The role of social media in mainstream reporting continues to evolve. Most journalists, even citizen journalists, don't want to report erroneous information, but it's easy for those who want to deceive to doctor photos and put out false reports. For journalists, the need to get breaking news quickly to readers and viewers makes it tempting to put out news that has not been verified. Speed has always been important in journalism, and in the era of Facebook and Twitter, it counts more than ever. But so does accuracy.

In this chapter you will learn:

1. How to ensure accuracy in information gathering through the disciplines of multiple sources and verification.

2. How to find and evaluate information from online sources.

3. How to use traditional sources of information to check facts.

What social media do is useful—they almost always report the news first—but what matters even more is sorting through the mass of information, verifying it and making sense of what happened. That's what professional journalists do. It's their job to separate fact from fiction, the good information from the bad. Call this "curating" if you wish. Most journalists simply call it good journalism.

In this chapter, we'll explore the process of not only finding information on the Web, on social media and elsewhere, but also getting it right.

ACCURATE INFORMATION: THE BASIS OF A GOOD STORY

Ask any editor whether a reporter can be a good writer without being good at information gathering, and you're likely to hear a resounding "No!" That's because good writing depends on good reporting. Reporting isn't good unless it is thorough and accurate. To ensure reports are thorough and accurate, journalists employ two main techniques: the discipline of multiple sources and the discipline of verification.

The Discipline of Multiple Sources

Good writing is of course important, as we explore in other chapters, but the quality of writing depends in large part on good fact gathering, which we call good reporting. It's impossible to write a great story without first doing a great job of reporting. Gathering information requires skilled interviewing, as discussed in Chapter 4. It also requires knowing how to use the many sources of information readily available. Make no mistake about it: There are hundreds of places to find information.

bedfordstmartins.com /newsreporting

Watch **"The Objectivity Myth."**

- Is objectivity a myth? Why is it in such great demand? What effect does the goal of being objective have on journalists?

- Do you agree that there is something more "true" in the satire of *The Daily Show* than in major newspapers or on network television? Explain.

Good reporters know that the worst kind of news story is one with a single source. Rarely is such a story worth publishing. Even a personality profile should be based on more than just an interview with the subject. To get a fuller perspective, the journalist also needs to talk with individuals who know the subject. Gathering information from several sources is one of the keys to good writing and good communication. It's also the best way to ensure accuracy because when several sources are used, information is more likely to be verified. When additional sources are checked and cross-checked, the chances of a story being accurate improve greatly.

Imagine how many sources the reporters for the *Milwaukee Journal Sentinel* used in their award-winning series about how the federal government allowed chemical manufacturers to influence the approval of potentially harmful substances in everyday products. Even in the short excerpt from the multipart series, shown in "Integrating Multiple Sources into a Story," it's evident that the reporters used dozens of sources, including peer-reviewed research journals that most reporters seldom touch. Such reporting requires analyzing thousands of pages of data, poring over online and paper records, interviewing dozens of people, and checking, cross-checking and rechecking. Such reporting is both time-consuming and tedious, but work of this sort is exactly what journalists must do as they act as watchdogs over the actions of government agencies and others. Getting it right is of paramount importance.

ANNOTATED MODEL   Integrating Multiple Sources into a Story

Chemical Fallout: Bisphenol A Is in You

By Susanne Rust, Cary Spivak and Meg Kissinger
Milwaukee Journal Sentinel

For more than a decade, the federal government and chemical-makers have assured the public that a hormone-mimicking compound found in baby bottles, aluminum cans and hundreds of other household products is safe. But a *Journal Sentinel* investigation found that these promises are based on outdated, incomplete government studies and research heavily funded by the chemical industry.

The lead hints at the large number of sources the journalists consulted to counter safety claims.

Here the article gets specific about the wide scope of the newspaper's research.

In the first analysis of its kind by a newspaper, the *Journal Sentinel* reviewed 258 scientific studies of the chemical bisphenol A, a compound detected in the urine of 93 percent of Americans recently tested. An overwhelming majority of these studies show that the chemical is harmful—causing breast cancer, testicular cancer, diabetes, hyperactivity, obesity, low sperm counts, miscarriage and a host of other reproductive failures in laboratory animals.

The article summarizes the main findings regarding health hazards.

Studies paid for by the chemical industry are much less likely to find damaging effects or disease.

U.S. regulators so far have sided with industry by minimizing concern about the compound's safety.

The report outlines the most recent finding of toxicity in the chemical compound.

Last week, a panel commissioned by the National Toxicology Program released a report finding bisphenol A to be of some concern for fetuses and small children. It found that adults have almost nothing to worry about.

Its recommendations could be used by the U.S. Environmental Protection Agency and other regulators to assess federal policies on how much bisphenol A is safe and may have huge ramifications for the multibillion-dollar chemical industry.

The story hints at a possible government change of position and its impact on the chemical industry.

The panel said it considered more than 700 studies by university scientists, government researchers and industry-funded chemists. It picked the work it felt was best and threw out the rest.

The newspaper's investigation finds fault with previous claims of safety.

The *Journal Sentinel* found that panel members gave more weight to industry-funded studies and more leeway to industry-funded researchers.

• The panel rejected academic studies that found harm—citing inadequate methods. But the panel accepted industry-funded studies using the same methods that concluded the chemical does not pose risks.

Faulty methodology in government studies is reported.

(continued)

Using summaries, bulleted lists and quotes, the writers integrated research from a range of sources seamlessly into the story.

Integrating Multiple Sources into a Story *(continued)*

• The panel missed dozens of studies publicly available that the *Journal Sentinel* found online using a medical research Internet search engine. The studies the panel considered were chosen, in part, by a consultant with links to firms that made bisphenol A.

More reliable university research differs with federal conclusions.

• More and more university researchers and foreign governments are finding that bisphenol A can do serious damage in small doses. But the panel rejected studies mostly submitted by university and international government scientists that looked at the impact at these levels.

• The panel accepted a Korean study translated by the chemical industry's trade group that found bisphenol A to be safe. It also accepted two studies that were not subjected to any peer review—the gold standard of scientific credibility. Both studies were funded by General Electric Co., which made bisphenol A until it sold its plastics division earlier this year.

"This undermines the government's authority," said David Rosner, professor of history and public health at Columbia University. "It makes you think twice about accepting their conclusions."

An expert finds fault with the government position.

Panel chairman Robert Chapin, a toxicologist who works for Pfizer Inc., the pharmaceutical giant, defended his group's work.

The chairman of the government panel defends his group's work.

"We didn't flippin' care who does the study," said Chapin, who worked as a government scientist for 18 years before joining Pfizer.

If the studies followed good laboratory practices and were backed with strong data, they were accepted, Chapin said. . . .

The Discipline of Verification

Journalists, when operating as they should, follow the same investigative system employed by scientists. They develop a hypothesis and then seek facts to support or reject it. In the 20th century, journalists developed the concept of objectivity—an elusive idea that was often misinterpreted.

As Philip Meyer of the University of North Carolina suggests to journalists Bill Kovach and Tom Rosenstiel in *The Elements of Journalism*: "I think (the) connection between journalism and science ought to emphasize objectivity of method. That's what scientific method is—our humanity, our subjective impulses . . . directed toward deciding what to investigate by objective means."

What objectivity isn't, Kovach and Rosenstiel argue, is blind loyalty to the concepts of fairness and balance. Fairness, they argue, can be misunderstood if it is seen as a goal unto itself. Fairness should mean that a journalist is fair to the facts and to the public's understanding of them. It should not mean, "Am I being fair to my sources, so that none of them will be unhappy?" or "Does my story seem fair?" Those are subjective judgments that lead the journalist away from the task of independent verification.

Similarly, balance should not mean that it's necessary to get an equal number of scientists speaking on each side of the global-warming debate, for example, if an overwhelming number of scientists in fact believe that global warming is a reality.

Kovach and Rosenstiel argue that sharpening the meaning of verification and resisting the temptation to simplify it are essential to improving the credibility of what journalists write. So, while citizen journalists may rush to get out information quickly on Twitter and Facebook without much regard for accuracy, professional journalists seek to get it right—while also producing news as quickly as possible.

The journalistic process of layered editing also helps get facts right. At a good newspaper, magazine, radio or television station, or website, once the reporter writes a story, it may be subjected to extensive review by several editors. Each may find facts to correct or language to clarify in the quest for a story that is as compelling—and accurate—as possible. Thus, as a story flows through the editorial process (see Figure 6.1), the goal is to make it as nearly perfect as possible.

Editors talk about the need to look at a story on both the micro and macro levels. *Microediting* is the process of paying attention to detail:

» Are the facts correct?
» Are the names spelled correctly?
» Is the grammar sound?

Macroediting, on the other hand, looks at the big picture:

» Will readers understand this?
» Are there unanswered questions or inconsistencies in the story?
» Does this agree with what I know from previous stories on the subject?

All of this, and much more, goes into the editorial process of verification. In the end, the goal is to get the story right.

As they strive to get it right, journalists use all types of sources, including interviews, source documents and a variety of other sources ranging from the obvious, such as a Google search, to online sites, computer databases and traditional sources like printed almanacs and encyclopedias. Good reporters make frequent use of all these sources.

ONLINE SOURCES OF INFORMATION

Reporters and editors today have a wealth of information available at their fingertips. In addition to making raw data available, computers help reporters organize and analyze information.

INDIVIDUAL	ACTION
Reporter	Gathers facts, writes story, verifies its accuracy, forwards to city editor.
City Editor*	Edits story, returns to reporter for changes or additional detail (if necessary), forwards story to news editor.
News Editor*	Decides on placement of story in newspaper, forwards story to copy desk chief for implementation of instructions.
Copy Desk Chief	Prepares page dummy that determines story's length, setting and headline size, forwards to copy editor. At some large newspapers, a separate design desk may play this role.
Copy Editor	Polishes writing of story, checks for missing or inaccurate detail, writes headline, returns to copy desk chief for final check.
Copy Desk Chief	Verifies that story is trimmed as necessary and that correct headline is written, transmits story to typesetting equipment.

* Or assistant

Note: At any point in the process, a story may be returned to an earlier editor for clarification, amplification or rewriting.

FIGURE 6.1

Editing and producing a newspaper is a fast-paced and complex process in which editors at different levels review stories. Shown here is a typical copy-flow pattern for a daily newspaper.

From the news library in your local office to national databases of published newspaper, magazine, radio and television stories, the amount of online information is staggering. Primary sources of online information include the following:

» The news archive, or morgue, maintained digitally by your own publication, radio or television station or website. When you're hired, one of the first things you must do is learn to use your organization's archive. The background material you find there will help you provide context for the stories you cover.

» Search engines (Google, Bing, Yahoo, Blekko, DuckDuckGo). Anyone can use Google, right? Well, learning to use search engines wisely is important to a journalist. Some of the tools we use to search the Web have as a main purpose to sell advertising. Page-rank algorithms and filters that personalize search results can yield misleading material. In Google, Bing and Yahoo, search results are ranked based not on quality but on several factors related to audience targeting. These three search engines filter information and rank their results accordingly. A couple of newer search engines, Blekko and DuckDuckGo, claim not to filter or personalize results.

» News sites, social media and content aggregators (USAToday.com, NYTimes .com, msnbc.com, CNN.com, Yahoo News, Google News).

» Other sites on the Web. Millions of organizations maintain websites with useful information.

» Mobile apps (applications for mobile phones and tablets). News apps are available for *The New York Times*, the Associated Press, NPR, CNN, Reuters and Newsy.

» Commercial database services (Factiva, LexisNexis, NewsBank, ProQuest and others).

» Government databases (city, county, state and federal).

» Special-interest databases (those created by organizations with a cause).

» Custom databases and spreadsheets.

Let's explore the usefulness of some of these.

News Archives: The Place to Start

Digital archives are a marvel that good reporters and editors have learned to cherish. Before they were available, doing research for a story was a laborious process that involved a trip to the newspaper, magazine or television station library to sift through hundreds or even thousands of tattered, yellowed clippings or old scripts. Too often, clippings and scripts had disappeared, were misfiled or had been misplaced, which made such research a hit-or-miss proposition. Despite those shortcomings, the library was considered a valuable asset. Reporters were routinely admonished to check there first.

You still hear that advice in newsrooms today, but most of today's news libraries are online. This almost ensures that an item will not disappear and will be easy to locate. Typically, you can do a check of the archive from your own computer, sometimes even from a remote location. This makes it easier than ever to do good background work on a story. Your ability to search online databases is limited only by your skill with search techniques and your access to the databases you need.

Digital news archives are full-text databases. All words in the database have been indexed and are searchable. Such capability gives you great flexibility in structuring searches using Boolean search commands. Boolean operators such as AND, OR and NOT allow you to structure the search to find the material most closely related to the subject being researched. For example, if you are interested in finding articles in Factiva on former South African President Nelson Mandela's visits to the U.S., you might issue this command on the search line:

Mandela AND U.S.

That search command pulls all articles in which both "Mandela" and "U.S." appear, generating almost 40,000 hits. Obviously, that's too many. You need to narrow your search. Try:

Mandela SAME U.S.

That search generates more than 8,000 articles in which both terms appear in the same paragraph. You can then narrow further:

Mandela w/3 U.S.

That command asks for the Mandela-U.S. combination occurring within three words of one another. This yields more than 400 articles, closer to a manageable number. The next step is to narrow by date, region or source to find what you really need.

There are limitations. Some digital archives do not allow you to see photos, nor can you see articles as they appeared in the newspaper or magazine. PressDisplay .com, however, provides PDF files of thousands of newspapers from about 100 countries. (A **PDF file** preserves the formatting of the original document.) Some radio and television stations, including NPR and PBS, have podcasts or vodcasts—downloadable audio or video files—stored on their websites. Factiva also contains audio and video interviews and news clips along with transcripts.

Search Engines

Google is the first stop for many journalists. Indeed, Google and other search engines, such as Yahoo, Bing, Blekko and DuckDuckGo, can be helpful journalistic tools. The key to using them successfully is recognizing whether the information contained on the website to which the search takes you is accurate and therefore usable. Journalists also need to be aware that many search engines like Google, Yahoo and Bing filter information, personalizing it based on the information that they have gathered about the user's previous searches and online purchase history. Good journalists supplement these well-known search engines with newer ones that do not filter, like DuckDuckGo.

Blekko uses crowdsourcing to identify trusted sites, and users can employ slashes (/) to filter results. Typing "/conservative" after a search term yields sites written by right-leaning publications; "/liberal" yields left-leaning sources, for example.

Information from well-known sites may be reliable; information from websites advocating a cause may not be. Be wary of Wikipedia, a user-written and user-edited social encyclopedia. Although much of the information on Wikipedia is excellent, anyone can enter erroneous information into it. Errors or misrepresentations are usually corrected quickly by others, but beware of depending on information from only that source. We discuss how to evaluate such information later in this chapter.

News Sites, Social Media and Content Aggregators

Some might consider it strange to think of news websites, social media and content aggregators as useful sources of information for reporters. Don't tell that to the reporters who use them.

Such sites are accessible to anyone with a computer and an Internet connection. News sites are those published by established media outlets such as *The New York Times*, Microsoft's MSN and CNN.

While mainstream media offer blogs, those found on blog sites such as Google's Blogger or WordPress are usually classified as social media. In part, they are different because their writers answer only to themselves, not to editors. Social media also include Twitter, Facebook and other "friending" sites. Twitter has become so important to journalists that it now has its own journalism and news manager. Many journalists now "tweet their beat." They tweet events live and seek to grow followers for their company's website. Twitter is just one of the social media tools that journalists use to increase "engagement" with their audience.

Not only do journalists often learn about breaking news—such as airplane crashes, fires and shootings—from tweets, but they also communicate with readers through social media. They post links to their stories on Facebook, and they ask Twitter readers to suggest story ideas and sources.

The most popular content aggregators include Yahoo News, Google News and Newsy.com. An aggregator is a website that summarizes a story and links to the originating media for the full report. Newsy does so with the additional benefit of video.

Commercial Database Services

Commercial databases make it easy to see what has been written about a subject in other newspapers and magazines. But there are potential problems with using excerpts from those stories:

» **Copyright laws must be obeyed.** Take care not to use too much material without obtaining permission.
» **Not all articles that appeared in a newspaper can be found in a database.** Wire-service and market reports, death notices, box scores, social announcements and items written by freelancers often are excluded.

VideoCentral ▶

Jeff Goodby

bedfordstmartins.com /newsreporting

Watch **"Media Effects Research."**

- Why are media researchers so concerned with the effects of marketing on children? Is it a useful focus? Explain.

- How useful could media research be for bloggers and other Web journalists? Why?

» **Publication doesn't ensure accuracy.** History is littered with incidents of newspapers quoting each other's inaccuracies.
» **The reporter might not be credible.** The reporter who wrote the story may not have any real knowledge of the subject matter. Using information from that reporter may introduce an inaccuracy into your story.
» **Databases aren't infallible.** The information is entered by humans, who are susceptible to mistakes. Also, databases are occasionally doctored in an attempt to prove a position or promote a cause.

On many topics, searching your own digital archive will not be sufficient. If U.S. Rep. Michele Bachmann is making her first appearance in your community, your archive probably won't help; little will have been written about her in your city. It probably will be much more useful to search the Web or commercial databases for articles published both in Minnesota, where she resides, and nationally, because she was a candidate for the Republican presidential nomination. This research will arm you with questions to ask about recent events. In such situations, the national commercial databases are invaluable.

The three leading commercial database services are Factiva (see Figure 6.2), NewsBank and ProQuest Newsstand, all of which provide full-text access. If your employer does not subscribe to any of these, see if your local library does. Of course, while you are a student, you have access to many databases through your school's library.

Government Databases

For years, government agencies have maintained large databases of information as a means of managing the public's business. These databases cover almost every conceivable service that government offers, from airplane registration and maintenance records to census data to local court records. They are maintained not only by the federal and state governments but also by even the smallest of city and county agencies.

Now, any reporter with a computer and training can find stories in the numbers. Among the reporters taking advantage of the technology is Penny Loeb, now of ProPublica.org. When she worked for *New York Newsday*, she used a computer analysis of tax and property records to reveal an astounding story: New York City owed $275 million to taxpayers as a result of overpayments on real estate, water and sewer taxes. To get that story, Loeb had to analyze millions of computer records. Doing that by hand would have consumed a lifetime, but with the assistance of a computer, she accomplished the task in a matter of weeks. Still, Loeb cautions against expecting instant stories:

> Don't just (use a computer) and expect a great story. You need a tip that there is a problem that computerized data can confirm. Or you may have seen a problem occur repeatedly, such as sentencing discrimination. The computer can quantify the scope.

FACTIVA®

Simple Search

Simple Search offers a straightforward approach to searching. Similar to searching the Web, just type a few words or phrases into the free-text box to retrieve high-quality, relevant results.

Simple Search also includes a Discovery Pane, powered by Dow Jones Intelligent Indexing™. The Discovery Pane provides a visualization of search results, allowing you to quickly analyze and refine your search.

Start Your Search with Keywords

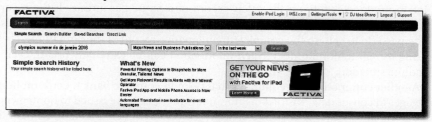

1. In the text box, enter your keyword just like you would in a free Web search engine.
2. Use the sources drop-down menu to focus your search to a specific content type, a Factiva source group, a personal source list, or a group source list created by your Administrator.
3. Use the date drop-down menu to expand or narrow your date range. You can search news as recent as today, or the full Factiva archive.
4. Click Search.

Start Your Search Using Simple Search History

Your last 10 searches from the Simple Search interface will be saved automatically. Click any search one time to instantly run the search again for the latest results. You can clear your Simple Search history by clicking the Clear link.

FIGURE 6.2

Factiva, owned by Dow Jones & Co., the parent company of *The Wall Street Journal*, allows subscribers to perform in-depth research on "more than 35,000 global news and information sources from 200 countries in 28 languages," according to www.dowjones.com.

Analyses of this type usually are done with relational database programs. **Relational database programs**, unlike simpler **flat-file databases**, permit you to compare one set of data to another. A classic example would be to compare a database of a state's licensed school-bus drivers to another database of the state's drunken-driving convictions. The result would be a list of school-bus drivers found guilty of such offenses.

After the introduction of this technology, investigative reporters were among the first to use it. Reporters can use database programs in their day-to-day work just as easily. For example, you might want to analyze federal records on airplane maintenance to produce a story on the safety record of a particular airline. If the records are maintained in an easily accessible format, the next time an airplane crashes it will be possible to call up the complete maintenance record of the aircraft merely by entering its registration number. Such information can be extremely useful, even in a deadline situation.

Another common use of computers has been to compare bank records on home mortgages to census data. By tracking how many mortgages are issued to homeowners in predominantly black or Hispanic areas, reporters have been able to document the practice of *redlining*, through which banks make it difficult or impossible for minorities to obtain loans.

Again, such records are useful even after the investigation is complete. Access to driver's license records, census data, bank records and other forms of data can be used daily to produce news stories, charts, maps and other graphic devices. Numbers can be valuable in helping to tell a story. They can be particularly effective as the basis for charts that illustrate the impact of the numbers.

Special-Interest Databases

Numerous special-interest groups have discovered the usefulness of placing information in computerized databases, and they are eager to introduce journalists to that information. Some of their material may be quite useful; indeed, it may be unobtainable from other sources. For instance, OpenSecrets.org has databases on campaign contributors that list who is spending what to lobby to whom, among other things. It has proved to be a credible source for news organizations. But other special-interest databases are designed to promote a particular perspective on a topic. Check the "About Us" link, and do a Web search to see how often the group's material appears in other media.

Custom Databases

Journalists Tracy Weber, Charles Ornstein and Maloy Moore had reason to believe the California Board of Registered Nursing was failing in its duty to ensure that nurses are competent, sober and law-abiding. To find out for sure, they had to build their own analysis tool.

ON THE JOB

The Challenges of Editing for the Web

Eric Ulken is among the journalists who have embraced the digital technologies that are changing journalism. After earning bachelor's and master's degrees, Ulken worked as a news producer at NOLA.com, the website of *The (New Orleans) Times-Picayune*, as well as at *The Columbus Dispatch* and the *Los Angeles Times*. Now he is assistant managing editor–digital at *The Seattle Times*.

Ulken urges would-be journalists to embrace the Web and to think not just about writing jobs but also about editing:

If you take a newspaper job today, chances are much of the work you do won't be for a newspaper at all, but rather for a website. Newsrooms are reorganizing to meet new challenges as their online editions grow in importance. It's still unclear how many duties copy editors ultimately will juggle, but their new responsibilities certainly transcend the traditional role. (Meanwhile, newspaper gigs aren't the only game in town: Broadcast and online-only sites are hiring more copy editors as their Web operations grow.)

In addition to learning basic copy editing skills (which never go out of style), here's how you can prepare yourself:

- Learn how to use content management systems. News organizations use a variety of online content platforms, but there are similarities among them. The simplest content management systems are blogging tools such as WordPress. Learning how they work will help you pick up more complex systems much faster.
- Understand how users find news on the Web. Many come to your site from search engines and aggregator sites such as Google News, which is one reason why Web headlines, optimized for search, are so important.
- Understand audio and video. It's less important to know how to edit in Final Cut Pro than it is to be able to identify what's missing from a multimedia package.
- Be flexible and make an effort to adapt to new technologies. Don't assume that the rules as you've learned them are immutable — even when it comes to style and usage: Technology and indeed language are always evolving.
- Use the Web constantly. The best way to learn how to produce great content for the Web is to experience great content on the Web.

To answer the question I know you're asking: Yes, you'll probably end up doing more work, and doing it faster, than previous generations of copy editors have done. But on the plus side, the greater variety of tasks should keep the routine from getting old.

Using a database manager, they entered and analyzed all the accusations filed and all the disciplinary actions taken by the board between 2002 and 2008. The printouts involved more than 2,000 nurses.

The team, representing the online news organization ProPublica and the *Los Angeles Times*, described the task as an enormous amount of work. But in the end, the database enabled the reporters not only to flag the best cases to use as examples but also to highlight a number of weaknesses in the board's oversight. Among the problems they uncovered were nurses involved in multiple disciplinary cases and those with multiple criminal convictions.

Evaluating Internet Sources

Journalists always have had to differentiate carefully between fact and fiction on the Web. Lately, however, they have also assumed the task of curating citizen contributions, particularly when citizens are the first to break the news. For instance, after a police officer was shot at Virginia Tech University in late 2011, many media outlets passed along tweets from the editor of the college paper. They determined that the student journalist was a reliable source.

Student editor Zach Crizer told Poynter.org that the college paper monitored tweets from students after the shooting. "For the most part, unless it was something completely unfounded or crazy, we'd try to react and investigate the tweets being sent to us. We wanted to confirm or deny information, and attempt to answer questions if we could."

Evaluating Web sources is not a guessing game. You won't always be correct in your assessment of a website's credibility, but you can dramatically improve your chances.

Journalists have developed methods of gathering and editing news that help ensure, though they don't guarantee, accuracy. Those methods are described in several other chapters in this book. The Web presents its own problems and solutions. How do you differentiate between a credible website and one that has a hidden agenda? Wikipedia is more popular than reputable print encyclopedias, but is it as credible? How do you know if a tweet or a Facebook posting is true? The answer lies in the discipline of verification.

A traditional method of verification relies on the journalistic process of layered editing. At most news media, print and digital, once the reporter writes a story, it is subject to extensive review by one or more editors. Each may find reporting inadequacies, facts to correct or language to clarify. Individual bloggers and those who post on social media outlets aren't edited. That's why curating and editing news posted on social media have become important new functions in newsrooms.

The Web is a great resource for reporters, but determining the credibility of online information can be problematic. If the source is a respected media organization such as *The New York Times* or *The Washington Post*, chances are the information is solid. But if the information was published by an organization promoting a cause, there is ample reason to be wary.

Stan Ketterer, a journalist and journalism professor, tells reporters to evaluate information on the Web by following the same standard journalistic practices that they would use for assessing the credibility and accuracy of any other type of information:

» **Before using information from a website in a story, verify it with a source.** There are exceptions to this rule, including taking information from a highly credible government site like the U.S. Census Bureau. Sometimes you can't contact the source on a breaking story because of time constraints. An editor must clear all exceptions.

The project had immediate impact. The day after their first story ran, California's governor replaced a majority of the nursing board's members. A day later, the board's longtime executive officer resigned.

TRADITIONAL SOURCES OF INFORMATION

Accessing information through computerized sources is quick and easy, but more traditional reference sources also are valuable. In some cases, the sources listed in this section cannot be found on computers.

» **In most cases, information taken directly from the Web and used in a story must be attributed.** If you have verified the information on a website with a source, you can use the organization in the attribution, for example, "according to the EPA" or "EPA figures show." If you cannot verify the information after trying repeatedly, attribute unverified information to the website—for example, "according to the Voice of America's website." Consult your editor before using unverified information.

» **If you have doubts about the accuracy of the information and you cannot reach the source, get it from another source, such as a book or another person.** When in doubt, omit the information.

» **Check the extension on the site's Web address to get clues as to the nature of the organization and the likely slant of the information.** The most common extensions used in the U.S. are *.gov* (government), *.edu* (education), *.com* (commercial), *.mil* (military), *.org* (not-for-profit organization) and *.net* (Internet administration). Most government and military sites have credible and accurate information. In many cases, you can take the information directly from the site and attribute it to the organization. But consult your editor until you get to know these sites.

» **Treat the sites of colleges and universities as you would other sites.** If college and university sites have source documents, such as the Constitution, attribute the information to the source document. But beware. Personal home pages can have

.edu extensions, and the information on them is not always credible.

» **In almost all cases, do not use information directly from the websites of commercial and not-for-profit organizations without verification.**

» **Check the date when the site was last updated.** The date generally appears at the top or bottom of the first page of the site. Although a recent date does not ensure that the information is current, it does indicate that the organization is paying close attention to the site. If no date appears, if the site has not been updated for a while or if it was created some time ago, do not use the information unless you verify it with a source.

» **Check to see if the website is what it appears to be.** The www.martinlutherking.org website was registered in 1999, but if you search its domain registration (whois.net), you'll find it is registered to a white supremacy organization, not the King family. The site ranks high in search results based on its longevity on the Web, its domain name (which includes Martin Luther King's name) and external links to the site. It has not been endorsed by the King family, and in fact, family members have tried many times to have the site removed. However, the domain was registered legitimately, and copyright doesn't protect website domain names. This is an excellent example of poor-quality or fraudulent sites ranking high in search results.

The Traditional Newsroom Library

Every working reporter gets this advice from an editor early in his or her career: Check the morgue. The morgue, or newsroom library, is often more than a digital archive. Indeed, at most publications and some broadcast stations it's also a physical place with a real librarian. We list it here because many such libraries house bound volumes of old printed editions and clippings of news stories that predate the publication's digital archive. The digital archive is usually the first stop for a reporter on any kind of assignment, but the traditional library also may be of great help, particularly when a reporter needs to understand the historical background of a story.

Covering a speech? Look up background information on the speaker. Covering a sports event? What are the teams' records? Who are the coaches? What's the history of the rivalry? Reporters answer questions like these, and many others, by checking the library, both the digital and analog versions.

One other note on the print or broadcast archive: Here you can find photos of a speaker or coach you haven't met. You'll also find historic photos. A contemporary photo might help you recognize that person for a possible one-on-one interview before the speech or game begins. An old photo may show readers a sports hero who set a record decades ago.

Other Traditional Sources

Traditional sources of information—such as reference books, dictionaries and encyclopedias—still play an important role in the production of the daily news product. Good reporters and editors make a habit of checking every verifiable fact. Here is a list of commonly used references. An increasing number of these are now available online, as noted below, but some are still available only in print form.

» **City directories.** You can find these directories, not to be confused with telephone books, in most cities. They provide the same information as a telephone book but also may include information on the occupations of citizens and the owners or managers of businesses. Useful street indexes provide information on the names of next-door neighbors. City directories usually are found in print form only.

» **Local and area telephone directories.** Use telephone books for verifying the spelling of names and addresses. They usually are reliable, but they are not infallible. Remember that people move and have similar names. Almost all landline telephone numbers in North America are now listed on various Web-based services, including Switchboard.com.

» **Maps of the city, county, state, nation and world.** Local maps usually are posted in the newsroom. Google Maps and Google's street views can help direct you around town. So can MapQuest.com.

» **State manuals.** Each state government publishes a directory that provides useful information on various government agencies. These directories, most of which are online, sometimes list the salaries of state employees.

» *Bartlett's Familiar Quotations* (Little, Brown). This writing resource is now available for free at Bartleby.com.

» *Congressional Directory* (Government Printing Office). The directory provides profiles of members of Congress. It's available at www.congress.org/congressorg /directory/congdir.tt.

» *Congressional Record* (Government Printing Office). The complete proceedings of the U.S. House and Senate are published in the *Congressional Record*. The *Record* is available at Congress.gov and at www.memory.loc.gov/ammem /amlaw/lwcr.html.

- » *Dictionary of American Biography* (Scribner's). There are several such biography sources, and this one lists famous deceased people up through 1995. There is no comparable online source for biographies of living people. LexisNexis has a "research people" function that provides biographies from newspapers, magazines and biographical directories.
- » *Facts on File World News Digest* (Facts on File Inc.). The digest is a weekly compilation of news from metropolitan newspapers.
- » *Guinness Book of World Records* (Guinness Superlatives). World records in countless categories are listed here. These are also available online at www .guinnessworldrecords.com.
- » *InfoPlease Almanac.* This resource includes biographies and almanac information. It is available at www.infoplease.com.
- » *National Trade and Professional Associations of the United States* (Columbia Books). USA.gov has an online directory of trade associations at www.usa.gov /directory/tradeassc/index.shtml.
- » *Readers' Guide to Periodical Literature* (EBSCO). This index to magazine articles on a host of subjects is available online for a fee.
- » *Webster's Biographical Dictionary* (Merriam-Webster). This dictionary is a good resource for historical biographical information.
- » *Webster's New World College Dictionary*, Fourth Edition (Wiley). This is the primary reference dictionary recommended by both the Associated Press and United Press International.
- » *Webster's Third New International Dictionary* (Merriam-Webster). AP and UPI recommend this edition of the unabridged dictionary as a backup to *Webster's New World Dictionary*.
- » *Who's Who* (St. Martin's). This resource contains international listings.
- » *Who's Who in America* (Marquis). A biennial publication, this resource is reliable for current biographies.
- » *World Almanac and Book of Facts* (Newspaper Enterprise Association). This almanac is published annually.

These useful publications, and many others like them, enable reporters to verify data and to avoid the embarrassment caused by errors in print. Traditional printed sources of information include government records, business documents, pamphlets published by government and nongovernment agencies, books, newspapers and magazines.

Be careful when using material from a source with which you are not familiar. Some publications come from biased sources promoting a cause. It's the reporter's job to determine whether the information is unbiased and reliable. A good way to do that is to balance information from one source with information from another source with an opposing viewpoint. It may not always be possible for you to determine who's correct. Ensuring balance between two viewpoints is the next best thing.

SUGGESTED READINGS

Associated Press Stylebook and Briefing on Media Law. New York: Associated Press, 2013. This is the definitive work on stylistic matters in journalistic writing. It is also available as an online subscription.

Brooks, Brian S., James L. Pinson and Jean Gaddy Wilson. *Working with Words: A Handbook for Media Writers and Editors*. 8th ed. New York: Bedford/St. Martin's, 2013. This is a definitive work on the correct use of language in journalistic writing and editing.

Callahan, Christopher, and Leslie-Jean Thornton. *A Journalist's Guide to the Internet: The Net as a Reporting Tool*. Boston: Allyn and Bacon, 2007. This is a useful guide to using the Internet as a reporting resource.

Houston, Brant. *Computer-Assisted Reporting: A Practical Guide*. New York: Bedford/St. Martin's, 2003. This excellent introduction to computer-assisted reporting was written by the former executive director of Investigative Reporters and Editors.

IRE Journal. This monthly magazine is available from Investigative Reporters and Editors in Columbia, Mo. It offers regular articles on the use of computers in the news-gathering process.

Schlein, Alan M. *Find It Online: The Complete Guide to Online Research*. Edited by Peter Weber and J.J. Newby. Tempe, Ariz.: BRB Publications, 2004. This book offers basic information on the use of Web resources.

SUGGESTED WEBSITES

www.bedfordstmartins.com/newscentral
When you visit News Central, you will find up-to-the-moment RSS feeds, research links and exercises to help you improve your grammar and AP style usage. In addition, the site's Video-Central: Journalism section hosts videos highlighted in this chapter as well as additional clips of leading professionals discussing important media trends.

www.ire.org
Investigative Reporters and Editors maintains an excellent website for anyone interested in investigative reporting.

www.journalism.org
Select "JTools" under "Journalism Resources" to find numerous suggestions for journalists and students.

www.nicar.org
The National Institute for Computer-Assisted Reporting conducts seminars for reporters on data analysis with computers. NICAR is a program of Investigative Reporters and Editors.

EXERCISES

1. **Team project.** Do an Internet search on a story from your local newspaper. Write a post for your blog explaining how the story could be improved or describing new angles the reporter could explore. List all your sources, or use hyperlinks.

2. If you needed to determine where Apple Inc. is located and the name of its chief financial officer, where would you look? What other sources of information about the company are available?

3. **Journalism blog.** On your blog, post a one-page biographical sketch of your congressional representative, based on information from your library or a database. Send a tweet

or a short email to your classmates highlighting a recent important action by the representative.

4. Using the Internet, find the following information:
   The census of Rhode Island (or your home state) in 2010.
   The size of Rwanda in land area.
   The latest grant awards by the U.S. Department of Education.
   The names of universities in Norway that provide information online for the general public.
   The name of a website that contains the complete works of Shakespeare.
   The name of a website that contains federal campaign contribution data.

5. Compile a background dossier on Lance Armstrong, the former Tour de France cycling winner who was stripped of his titles in 2012 as a result of a doping scandal.

6. Go to Google News and attempt to determine where the top three stories originated. Are any of them from the wire services or newspapers?

United States/Canada change your location ▼ | site map | conta

Search

Get Involved **About Us** **Where We Build** **Support Habitat** **Shop** **Stories & Multimedia**

Home

🐦 Tweet ⟨0⟩   f Like ⟨0⟩   🖳 Email   ✉ Print

World Water Day event to address global need for water and sanitation

ATLANTA (March 22, 2013) – To commemorate World Water Day, CARE; the Center for Global Safe Water at Emory's Rollins School of Public Health; the Centers for Disease Control and Prevention; the Task Force for Global Health; and Habitat for Humanity will host "Water, Sanitation and Hygiene: Transforming Lives." The event will be held on April 9, 2013, from 5 - 7 p.m. in the Claudia Nance Rollins Auditorium at the Rollins School of Public Health at Emory University.

"Water, Sanitation and Hygiene: Transforming Lives" will address the global concerns for water and sanitation needs, and the responsibilities of communities to provide it. It will feature a panel discussion moderated by Jeffrey Koplan, M.D., M.P.H., vice president for Global Health at Emory and former director of the CDC. Panelists include Robert Tauxe, M.D., M.P.H., deputy director of the Division of Foodborne, Waterborne and Environmental Diseases at CDC; Christine Moe, Ph.D., director of the Center for Global Safe Water at Emory's Rollins School of Public Health; and David Addiss, M.D., M.P.H., director of the Children Without Worms program at the Task Force for Global Health.

Safe water and sanitation are at the heart of reducing poverty. They are essential to preventing childhood mortality and morbidity, and for increasing food security. Nearly 2.5 billion people are without access to adequate toilets, and 800 million people lack a safe source of drinking water. The World Health Organization reports that diarrheal disease – primarily caused by drinking unsafe water or lack of good hygiene – kills more children every year than AIDS, malaria and measles combined.

"The U.S. made significant investments in providing safe water and adequate sanitation throughout the country in the early 1900s, which dramatically improved the health of all Americans," says Michael Beach, Ph.D., associate director for Healthy Water in the National Center for Emerging and Zoonotic Infectious Diseases at CDC. "The tremendous benefits resulting from those investments show how important it is for us to commit to working with developing countries around the world to support their efforts in providing safe water and adequate sanitation to their populations. We must help them prevent the same devastating diseases, like cholera and typhoid, that have now become history in more developed countries."

Lack of access to safe water and sanitation also disproportionately affects the health and safety of women and girls.

"CARE operates on the belief that poor girls and women hold the key to ending poverty. With the proper resources, they are able to transform lives and create positive change in their communities," says Helene Gayle, president and CEO of CARE USA. "This is why CARE has partnered with other organizations to improve water and sanitation."

Besides helping to reduce disease burden and improve gender equality, innovation in safe water and sanitation contributes to improved living and economic conditions and supports the growth of national and regional economies.

Finding the News in News Releases

THIS HEADLINE on a 2012 **news release** might have drawn some attention:

> Planners seek questions for next week's Child Sexual Abuse Conference

Readers' interest probably jumped when they saw the dateline, "University Park, Pa." The lead read:

> Organizers of Penn State's first national conference on the topic of child sexual abuse are seeking questions in advance from attendees and online viewers tuning in for live-streamed sessions.

The release informs readers that the conference was sold out and that it would feature several nationally recognized experts in child-abuse prevention and treatment. Questions could be emailed or sent by Twitter.

The news about this conference might not have been as notable had it come from another university. But coming from Penn State not long after the assistant football coach Jerry Sandusky sex scandal that got revered head coach Joe Paterno and president Graham Spanier and others fired, this release probably garnered a lot of attention.

In this chapter you will learn:

1. How to explain the importance of news releases.

2. How to recognize the types of news releases.

3. How to deal with news releases.

4. How to rewrite a news release.

THE IMPORTANCE OF NEWS RELEASES

Reporters do not go out and dig up all the stories they write. Many stories, like the one above, come to them. They are mailed, emailed, telephoned, sent via Twitter or another social networking service, faxed or hand-delivered by people who want to get something in "the news." They come from people or offices with different titles: press agents, press secretaries, public relations departments, public information offices, community relations bureaus and publicity offices. The people who write these stories call them news releases, press releases, or handouts. They are well-attuned to the social media and use Facebook, LinkedIn and other such sites to spread their messages.

Because good publicity is so important, private individuals, corporations and government agencies spend a great deal of money to obtain it. Much of the money pays the salaries of skilled and experienced personnel, many of whom have gained valuable experience working in the news business. Part of their job is to write news releases that newspapers, radio and television stations, websites and syndicated public relations wire services will use and that will appear on websites perhaps throughout the world. PR Newswire, for example, says it issues more than 1,000 news releases every day.

You might very well want to be among the people who write news releases and who get out the news in a whole number of ways for universities, corporations and organizations of all kinds. You might be seeking a career in public relations or advertising, but your journalism department wisely has you begin by studying news and news writing. Only by studying news and how news organizations handle news will you be successful in public relations or in offices of public information. Knowing how reporters are taught to deal with news releases will help you write better releases. Studying news also will help you enormously in the advertising world.

Skilled public relations or public information practitioners know how to write news stories, and they apply all the principles of good news writing in their news releases. A good news release meets the criteria for a good news story.

Nevertheless, as PR professionals know, news releases are not intended to take the place of reporters. In *On Deadline: Managing Media Relations*, Carole Howard, formerly with *Reader's Digest*, and Wilma Mathews, formerly with AT&T and Arizona State University, write that news releases simply acquaint an editor with the basic facts of potential stories. Those who write news releases accept that their carefully crafted sentences will be checked and rewritten by reporters.

As a reporter, you must recognize that news releases, regardless of how they are delivered, are both a help and a hindrance to news agencies of all kinds. They are a help because without them, news organizations would need many more reporters. They are a hindrance because they often contain incomplete, self-serving or even incorrect information. Because they are intended to promote the interests and favorable reputation of the individuals and organizations that disseminate them, news releases, by their very nature, are not objective.

Nevertheless, wise editors do not discard news releases without reading them. These editors often give them to reporters, often the newest ones, as sources for stories.

When your editor hands you a news release, you are expected to know what to do with it, regardless of which of the media you are employed in. You must be able to recognize the news in the release and apply all that you have learned about news values. The release may lead you to a good story. Your resourcefulness may improve your chances of being assigned to bigger things.

TYPES OF NEWS RELEASES

After you have read a number of news releases, you will notice that generally they fall into three categories:

» Announcements of coming events or of personnel matters: new hires, promotions, retirements and the like.
» Information about a cause.
» Information that is meant to build someone's or some organization's image.

Recognizing the types and purposes of news releases (and recognizing that some are hybrids and serve more than one purpose) will help you determine how to rewrite them.

Announcement Releases

Organizations use the news media to tell their members and the public about coming events. For example:

> The Camera Club will have a special meeting at Wyatt's Cafeteria at 7 p.m. on Wednesday, March 20. Marvin Miller will present a slide program on "Yellowstone in Winter." All interested persons are invited to attend.

Although the release promotes the Camera Club, it also serves as a public service announcement. Community newspapers and websites that offer such announcements are serving their readers. They might choose to present the information in a calendar of coming events.

Here is another example:

> The first reception of the new season of the Springfield Art League will be on Sunday, Sept. 8, 3 to 5 p.m. in the Fine Arts Building.
> Included in the exhibition will be paintings, serigraphs, sculpture, batiks, weaving, pottery and jewelry, all created by Art League members who, throughout the summer, have been preparing works for this opening exhibit of the season.
> The event also will feature local member-artists' state fair entries, thus giving all who could not get to the fair the opportunity to see these works.
> The exhibition continues to Friday, Sept. 13. All gallery events and exhibitions are free.

Other news releases concern appointments, promotions, new hires and retirements. The announcement of an appointment may read like this:

> James McAlester, internationally known rural sociologist at Springfield University, has been appointed to the board of directors of Bread for the World, according to William Coburn, executive director of the humanitarian organization.
> McAlester attended his first board meeting Jan. 22 in New York City. He has been on the university faculty since 1999. Prior to that, he served as the Ford Foundation representative in India for 17 years.
> The 19,000-member Bread for the World organization is a "broad-based interdenominational movement of Christian citizens who advocate government policies that address the basic causes of hunger in the world," says Coburn.

VideoCentral

Jonathan Adelstein

bedfordstmartins.com /newsreporting

Watch **"Filling the News Hole: Video News Releases."**

- How might a video news release interview differ from an interview conducted by a journalist?

- Would you want to see video news releases on televised news broadcasts? What rules should television news stations follow when airing a video news release?

ON THE JOB

Reading News Releases: Sweat the Small Print

Formerly the Associated Press bureau chief in Baghdad, Iraq, **Lara Jakes** is now an AP national security writer based in Washington, D.C. She previously served as a military, legal and counterterrorism writer for AP's Washington bureau. Then and now, hundreds of news releases and transcripts of briefings from around the world cross her desk every week. While it's impossible to scrutinize them all, Jakes files away for future reading those that seem interesting but that don't require a spot—that is, immediate—story.

On a quiet day in her Justice Department press room office in 2008, Jakes went back to a release handed out weeks earlier about new penalties for fraud, waste and abuse in government contracts. Attached to the release was the language of regulations outlining the kinds of abuses that would be prosecuted. And buried within that language was a multibillion-dollar loophole that specifically exempted penalties for overseas government work by private companies—despite U.S. contracts in Iraq and Afghanistan that had cost taxpayers more than $102 billion over five years.

None of the other Justice Department reporters who had gotten the release had written about the exemption, and at first Jakes assumed she had misread or misunderstood the small print in the rules' language.

"So I called the prosecutor who was in charge of the program," Jakes says. "He somewhat sheepishly agreed there was a major loophole in the regulations and blamed the White House (under President George W. Bush) for the wording of the new rules."

Jakes' stories caught the attention of Congress, sparking House of Representatives hearings and an investigation into how the loophole was quietly slipped into rules that were supposed to punish abusive contractors. One congressman called it an "egregious and flagrant disregard of taxpayer rights." Five months later, Congress passed a law to close the loophole and force stricter oversight of overseas contracts.

According to Jakes, Justice Department prosecutors later jokingly referred to the rules that closed the loophole as "L.J.'s law." Jakes says it was one of those stories that just seemed too good to be true—especially since it was initially handed over in a press release.

"I would have never found it if I'd not read the text of the regulations," Jakes says. The prosecutor who confirmed that the loophole was in the rules seemed surprised only that she'd found it—not that it was there. "It was almost like they were daring us to not read the release or pay attention to what was going on," Jakes says.

The moral: Sweat the fine print—even in news releases.

The occasion is the appointment of McAlester, but the release also describes the purpose of the Bread for the World organization. By educating readers about the organization's purpose, the writer hopes to publicize its cause.

Companies often send releases when an employee has been promoted. For example:

James B. Withers Jr. was named senior vice president in charge of sales of the J.B. Withers Co., it was announced Tuesday.

Withers, who has been with the company in the sales division for two years, will head a sales force of 23 people.

"We are sure Jim can do the job," James B. Withers Sr., company president, said. "He brings intelligence and enthusiasm to the job. We're pleased he has decided to stay with the company."

Founded in 1936, the J.B. Withers Co. is the country's second-largest manufacturer of dog and cat collars.

A release like this one is an attempt by the company to get its name before the public and to create employee goodwill. Written in the form of an announcement, it is an attempt at free publicity.

Cause-Promoting Releases

News releases in this category seek to further a cause. Some of these releases come from organizations whose worthwhile causes are in need of funds or volunteers. The letter reprinted here is from a county chairman of the American Heart Association to the editor of a newspaper. It is not written in the form of a release, but its effect is meant to be the same:

> The alumnae and collegiate members of the Alpha Phi Sorority have just completed their annual Alpha Phi "Helping Hearts" lollipop sale. This year Valerie Knight, project chairwoman, led sorority members to achieve record-breaking sales. The lollipop sale is a national project of the Alpha Phi Sorority.
>
> Sunday, March 5, Valerie Knight presented a check for $1,800 to the American Heart Association, Shelby County Unit. The contribution was presented during a reception at the Alpha Phi house. This contribution is an important part of the annual fundraising campaign of the American Heart Association.

Heads of organizations attempt to alert the public to their message in any way they can. Any release, notice or letter they can get into the media for free leaves money for the cause that they represent.

Image-Building Releases

Another kind of news release serves to build up the image of a person or organization. Politicians seeking to be elected or re-elected desire as much free publicity as they can get. For example:

> James M. Merlin, honorary chairman of the board and director of Merlin Corp., has been named honorary chairman of the Finance Committee, which will seek citywide financial support for the campaign to elect Hong Xiang as Springfield's next mayor.
>
> Merlin, a well-known civic leader and philanthropist, termed the election of Xiang "one of the most important and far-reaching decisions the voters of Springfield will make in a long time. The city's financial crisis can only be solved through the kind of economic leadership Xiang has demonstrated the past 10 years as 1st Ward councilperson."

The appointment of Merlin as honorary chairman serves only to promote the image of the candidate. The quote is self-serving.

Organizations and government agencies at all levels often try to build their public image. Many of them persuade local mayors to proclaim a day or a week of recognition for their group, as in the following:

> Mayor Juanita Williams has proclaimed Saturday, May 11, as Fire Service Recognition Day. The Springfield Fire Department in conjunction with the University Fire Service Training Division is sponsoring a demonstration of the fire apparatus and equipment at the Springfield Fire Training Center. The displays are from 10 a.m. to 5 p.m. at 700 Bear Blvd. All citizens are urged to attend the display or visit their neighborhood fire station on May 11.
>
> Our PRODUCT is your SAFETY.

An editor who hands you a release like this has probably decided that it is worth using in some form. The rest is up to you.

HANDLING NEWS RELEASES

Regardless of the type of news release, be sure to read the information that appears at the top (see Figure 7.1). All that information might be useful to you. Even so, many news releases leave unanswered questions. You will probably want to contact people other than the director of information or even the contact person if you have doubts about some of the data given. But for routine accuracy checks, the people listed on

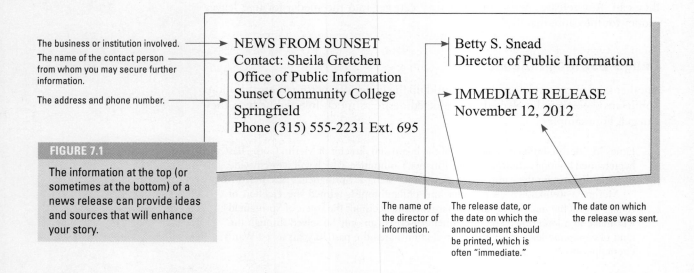

The business or institution involved.

The name of the contact person from whom you may secure further information.

The address and phone number.

NEWS FROM SUNSET
Contact: Sheila Gretchen
Office of Public Information
Sunset Community College
Springfield
Phone (315) 555-2231 Ext. 695

Betty S. Snead
Director of Public Information

IMMEDIATE RELEASE
November 12, 2012

FIGURE 7.1

The information at the top (or sometimes at the bottom) of a news release can provide ideas and sources that will enhance your story.

The name of the director of information.

The release date, or the date on which the announcement should be printed, which is often "immediate."

The date on which the release was sent.

the release can do the job. They might lead you to other helpful sources, too. Sometimes you might have sources of your own. And sometimes you might uncover the real story only from people who are neither connected to nor recommended by the director of information.

You might have to consult your editor regarding the release date. As a courtesy, most news media honor release dates. However, sometimes waiting would render the information useless. Also, once a release is public knowledge, editors feel justified in releasing whatever information it contains, even prior to the suggested release date. A release date is broken for all when it is broken by one.

Rewriting an Announcement Release

Sometimes directors of information want nothing more than a listing on the record or calendar page of a newspaper or news site. Here is an example of an announcement release:

> FOR THE CALENDAR
> Elisabeth Bertke, quiltmaker and designer from Salem, Massachusetts, will discuss her work at 7:00 o'clock P.M. Tues., February 7, in Charters Auditorium, Hampton College. Two quilts designed and constructed by Bertke are included in the exhibit "The New American Quilt," currently on display at the Smith Art Gallery.
> "This is an exciting display," Betty Martin, president of the Smith Art Gallery board of directors, said. "You simply can't afford to miss it."

This simple release may go directly to the news desk or to a special calendar editor.

If it is given to you, rewrite it. Some news organizations insist that you rewrite every news release if for no other reason than to avoid the embarrassment of running the same story as a competing news outlet. For some, it is a matter of integrity and professionalism.

After reading carefully through the release, check all the facts. Confirm the spelling of Bertke's name, and see if there is an apostrophe in "Charters Auditorium." The Smith Gallery may or may not be on the Hampton campus.

Next, if time allows, do some additional reporting. Call the gallery to ask how long the exhibit will be there. Are quilts made by local people included in the exhibit? Perhaps your questions will lead to a feature story on local quilting.

Then do your rewrite. Drop Martin's quotation: It is self-serving and promotional. But you might call Martin, Bertke or someone else connected to the event to try for a better quote. Reread your story to make sure the lead works and the writing is tight and clear.

Finally, correct any violations of AP style. In the preceding example:

» A hyphen should be inserted in "quilt-maker."
» "Massachusetts" should be abbreviated "Mass."
» "7:00 o'clock P.M." should be "7 p.m."

» "Tues." should be spelled out "Tuesday."
» "February" should be abbreviated "Feb."

Avoid relying on the copy desk to do your work if the rewrite is given to you.

Here is another example of an announcement release:

> Mr. Richard G. Hernandez has been selected as the Outstanding Biology Teacher of the Year by the National Association of Biology Teachers. He was previously selected as Nevada Science Educator of the Year.
>
> As an outstanding representative of good high-school biology teaching Hernandez will receive a certificate and a series 50 binocular microscope with an engraved citation. Hernandez has been teaching at Hickman High School since 1980.

The story is far from earthshaking, but the honor is statewide. In large markets the release might not get much **play**. Smaller markets, however, will use it and perhaps enlarge upon it.

A first reading of the release tells you that it is wordy and leaves many questions unanswered. Hernandez might be an interesting fellow, but the release tells us little about him. You should approach this release in the same way you approach any news release: Finish the reporting, and then rewrite it. News style demands a new lead to the release:

> A Hickman High School science teacher has been named Outstanding Biology Teacher of the Year by the National Association of Biology Teachers.
>
> Richard G. Hernandez, a Hickman teacher since 1980, will receive a certificate and a series 50 binocular microscope with an engraved citation.
>
> Previously selected as Nevada Science Educator of the Year, Hernandez . . .

There the story runs out of information. You need to ask the following questions:

» Age?
» Degrees from where?
» Local address?
» Spouse? Family?
» Annual award? One teacher selected from each state?
» Any previous Hickman winners? Any from local high schools?
» Year he received Nevada Science Educator award?
» Nominated for the award by whom?
» Date and place of bestowal? Public ceremony?
» Value of series 50 binocular microscope?

Then call Hernandez, and find out how he feels about the award. Talk to the principal, to fellow teachers and to some of Hernandez's students. Good quotations will spice up your story. The length of the story will ultimately depend on how much space your editor wishes to give it.

Rewriting a Cause-Promoting Release

News media generally cooperate with causes that are community-oriented. News releases like the following get attention:

> A free tax clinic for low-income persons and senior citizens will be held on Feb. 9 and 10 in Springfield.
>
> The clinic is sponsored by the Central State Counties' Human Development Corporation with the Accounting Department of the Springfield University College of Business.
>
> Senior and graduate accounting students under the direct supervision of accounting faculty members will work with each taxpayer to help that taxpayer complete accurately his or her tax return.
>
> The Human Development Corporation encourages persons especially to use the clinic who may be eligible for senior citizens' credits or other credits.
>
> This is the fifth year the clinic has operated in Shelby County. Last year more than 275 persons in the eight counties served were assisted.
>
> For information regarding the location of the clinics and to make an appointment, contact the Shelby County Human Development Corporation, 600 E. Broadway, Room 103, Springfield, 555-8376.

Again, you need more information. To begin with, you need to know more about the Human Development Corp. A background paragraph on its origins, where it gets its money and its other areas of concern will put the story into context.

The release is unclear about who is eligible. What must an applicant's income be? How old must the person be? Also, you must find out the exact locations of the clinics.

Once you have answers to all your questions, dig for some human interest. Talk to a participating faculty member and to students who helped before and will help again. Then talk to some people who were helped in the past and to some who will come for help. In addition, you must talk to those in charge of the joint effort.

Because activities like these are in the public interest, media outlets will give them some news play. News outlets will be more critical with releases that are merely self-serving.

Rewriting an Image-Building Release

The following is a typical release from a politician:

> Sen. John Choi said today that nearly $400,000 in grants have been given final approval by two departments of the state government for interlocking improvements in Springfield and Lincoln County.
>
> Choi said, "This is something I have been working on for this past year. It is a chance to show that state agencies are interested in communities. It also demonstrates that two agencies can work together to produce a coordinated, workable solution to improve a blighted area in Springfield."

The grants, Choi said, come from the State Bureau of Outdoor Recreation—$247,000 for purchasing Baltimore and Ohio railroad rights-of-way and developing a strip park—and the Department of Housing and Urban Development—$150,000 for planning the Flat Branch area. The second grant also stipulates that part of the money be used to coordinate the two projects: the B&O strip park and the Flat Branch redevelopment.

"I think residents of Springfield and Lincoln County will have a chance to help out in the planning of these two facilities. I hope this means the entire community will express opinions and come to a conclusion that will see these projects become a reality in the next two years."

The first three words of the release show just who is being served by the release. A Springfield reporter might write the lead this way to serve the reader instead:

Springfield and Lincoln County will receive nearly $400,000 in state grants to fund the B&O strip park and the Flat Branch redevelopment project, Sen. John Choi said today.

The second paragraph of the release, a long quote from the senator with no news value, should be eliminated. It's likely that he did not say those words at all; his press agent probably wrote them. If you want a quote from the senator, call him and talk to him yourself.

The second paragraph of your story should indicate the source of the funding. Of course, you will have to check these figures, as well as all other figures in the news release, with independent sources.

The grants come from two state agencies. The State Bureau of Outdoor Recreation granted $247,000 for purchasing the Baltimore & Ohio Railroad rights-of-way and for developing a strip park, and the Department of Housing and Urban Development granted $150,000 for planning the Flat Branch area. The second grant also stipulates that part of the money be used to coordinate the two projects.

You could shorten Choi's last quote with a paraphrase, retaining only Choi's essential point:

Choi said he hoped Springfield and Lincoln County residents would have a chance to help plan the two projects. "I hope this means the entire community will express opinions and come to a conclusion that will see these projects become a reality in the next two years."

Like many news releases of this kind, this announcement would trigger other news stories in the local media. This story would call for local reactions from city and county officials and from local residents. The editor might assign several stories on the matter.

REWRITING A NEWS RELEASE — AN EXAMPLE

Sometimes a news release can lead to an interesting story with broad implications for the community, even if the actual release is self-serving — or misleading. Suppose you were given the following news release.

NEWS RELEASE
Springfield Community Teachers Association
Lillian A. Briggs, President
Contact:
    Tom Monnin, SCTA Salary Committee Chairman
Phone:
    555-555-6794 (Central High School)
    555-555-2975 (home)

For Immediate Release

Springfield — Police officers and firefighters in Springfield earn a greater starting salary than Springfield teachers, as discovered in a recent survey by the Springfield Community Teachers Association. According to their research, a new teacher in the Springfield public school system makes $40,000, while a firefighter starts at $40,725, $725 more than a new teacher. "This is a shameful situation for an educational community," said Tom Monnin, SCTA Salary Committee chairman.

The statistics gathered by the SCTA Salary Committee indicate that police officers with a bachelor's degree make $42,758. A dogcatcher with no college education earns just $6,536 less a year than a beginning teacher. Following is a comparison of starting salaries of some Springfield city employees and of public school teachers for the school year:

Occupation	Starting Salary
Police officer with bachelor's degree	$42,758
Firefighter with bachelor's degree	40,725
Meter reader	32,402
Animal control officer	33,464
Bus operator	32,402
Teacher with bachelor's degree	40,000

"Springfield teachers do not think city employees are overpaid but that teachers are underpaid," Monnin said.

Even though teachers work under a 9¼-month contract, the workweek is not 40 hours. When the hours for preparing and grading, attending sports events, musical concerts, dances, other after-school activities and PTA meetings are considered, a teacher's workweek is much longer than 40 hours. Summer break is used by many teachers for advanced preparation at the university, at their own expense.

The SCTA Salary Committee will present the salary proposal at the next meeting of the Springfield Board of Education.

The SCTA represents approximately 523 members in the public school system.

TIPS

How to Rewrite a News Release

» Carefully read the news release, including the information at the top of the release form.

» Check for accuracy and fairness. Question missing information. Verify any spellings or information you have doubts about.

» Fill in missing information with your own reporting — research and interviews.

» Call the news release contact person. Watch for self-serving quotations and information.

» Write the story. Make sure your lead is strong, tighten the copy and check for AP style.

» Look for other possible news stories — local angles, reactions and the like — triggered by the release.

Read the News Release Carefully

Your first task is to read the release, including the information at the top of the form, closely a couple of times, making notes in the margin about items that stand out for you. For example, the second paragraph cleverly suggests that dogcatchers make nearly as much money as teachers do, but you notice it speaks only of starting salaries. The more you read the release, the more uncomfortable you start to feel with it. No one can blame teachers for wanting more money, but there are other factors to consider.

Check for Accuracy and Fairness

You should ask yourself what information is missing and what other viewpoints need to be considered. For example, you might wonder, What about working conditions? Teachers in Springfield's schools certainly don't have to put their lives on the line the way police officers and firefighters do. And most people do not want to spend their lives chasing stray dogs.

Take special care when news releases cite studies, polls or surveys. Check the source of the figures for accuracy and possible bias. If you can't confirm the figures and their reliability, don't use them.

The fact that teachers work for a little more than nine months a year is down in the fourth paragraph. The release fails to mention a two-week break over Christmas and a week off in the spring semester. Most police officers and firefighters get two weeks off per year.

Is the release trying to suggest that because teachers actually spend more than 40 hours a week working, they should not have to work more than 9¼ months? Not all teachers spend their summers going to school. You probably know several who have summer jobs or who take long vacations.

Do Additional Research and Interviews

Before you turn in a rewrite of this release, you have a lot of checking to do. But you also decide to go beyond checking to do some of your own reporting.

You begin by calling the city of Springfield's personnel office. The person answering the phone refers you to the department's website. Here you can gather all of the salary information you need, but you still have some questions. You call the personnel office again. When asked about the $40,725 starting salary of a firefighter, the personnel officer replies: "You wouldn't begin at that salary. Everyone is hired at $39,225 for a trial period of at least six months. If you work out OK, you might jump up to $40,725. Again, there are a lot of considerations besides the college degree."

Now you know you are on to something. Comparing starting salaries is one thing. But how much can a person eventually earn in a position?

You then ask about the starting salary for a police officer. "Yes," the director of personnel says, "$42,758 is the beginning salary for a police officer with a B.S. degree."

You then ask whether anyone with a B.S. degree can get hired at that salary.

"Most people wouldn't stand a chance of being hired," he says. "We have more than 100 applicants for every position, so we can be quite choosy. Unless a person has had some real experience as a police officer, I don't think he or she would make it."

Further questioning reveals that a top salary for a police officer is $54,712 after six years of service.

You also find the website of the Springfield public school system and check its salary schedule for teachers. Then you call a high school teacher. You ask her if she has to put in more than 40 hours a week at her job.

"Oh, yes," she says. "I teach a section of English composition, and I have a lot of papers to grade. I used to spend a lot of evenings preparing for classes, but once you've taught a course, it gets easier. And then I have to go to all those football games and basketball games."

You discover that she is indeed required to attend the games, but only because she is in charge of the cheerleaders. When you express sympathy, the teacher replies, "No, I really don't mind. After all, I get $3,500 a year extra for being in charge of the cheerleaders."

You then learn from someone at the Springfield Schools' personnel office that quite a few teachers receive compensation for after-school activities — coaching, directing plays and musical activities, advising the staffs of the school newspaper and senior yearbook, and chaperoning dances. Teachers sponsoring class and club activities can earn from $1,000 to $4,000; a sponsor of the pep squad can earn up to $2,300. The top teacher's salary without any of these extras is $67,214.

You note that top pay for a city dogcatcher is $37,626, so you think it might be interesting to interview one. You find Luis Gonzalez, an animal control officer. It doesn't take much prodding to get Gonzalez to talk. "I sure wish I got summers off like those teachers," he says. "I got nothing against teachers. But most of them make more money than I'll ever make. . . . Besides, students don't bite many teachers."

Get Back to the News Release Contact with Questions

Now you are ready to call Tom Monnin, the man whose name is on the release, for additional information. Here's how your interview might go:

Q: Is it fair to compare a new teacher's salary with a new police officer's salary when the top pay for a police officer is $54,712 and the top teacher's salary is $67,214?

A: Well, it takes 17 years for a teacher with a master's degree plus 75 hours of continuing education classes to reach that top salary. A teacher with a bachelor's degree can make $54,219 after 11 years of teaching.

Q: What about summers off and other vacations?

A: I figure I work a 60-hour week. That means I work fifty-one 40-hour weeks a year.

Q: Aren't teachers paid extra for after-school activities?
A: Many are paid. But not all of them are, and there are many activities we do feel the responsibility to attend.

Q: Teachers don't have to put their lives on the line the way police and fire officials and even dogcatchers do. Isn't that a factor?
A: It's debatable who has to put their lives on the line. We're not as bad off as some schools, but we often have to restrain students physically. We read about school shootings all of the time, and we can't help but wonder when that will happen here.

Write the Story

You've checked for accuracy, found out the important facts, and taken all the viewpoints into account. Only now are you ready to write the story. Write a lead that communicates the news, make sure your writing is tight, and check for AP style.

The annotated model on page 145 shows one possible story resulting from the news release. This story does with a news release what you should do with many of them. You should not be satisfied with the way the news release was written or with the information it contains. By asking some important questions, you can often put together an informative and more accurate story. Without saying that the news release was dishonest or misleading, a good reporter can correct or clarify some of the information it contains. Here, the plight of the teacher is told clearly and objectively, but it is placed in a much better perspective than that of the news release.

Like many news releases, this one was the basis for a story the news outlet otherwise would not have had. That is why editors pay attention to news releases and why reporters look for the real story.

ANNOTATED MODEL   **Integrating News Release Information**

The Springfield Community Teachers Association said Tuesday that new police officers can earn over $2,000 more than new teachers. ← Lead gives SCTA claim.

Info from research adds a differing point of view. → What the teachers did not say was that a teacher eventually can earn $12,502 more a year than a police officer can.

The SCTA statement was included with a survey that lists starting teachers' salaries at $40,000. Other figures listed as starting salaries are these: police officer with a bachelor's degree, $42,758; animal control officer, $33,464; meter reader, $32,402; bus operator, $32,402. ← Incorrect info about firefighters' starting salary is omitted.

Quotes from news release give teachers' point of view. → "This is a shameful situation for an educational community," said Tom Monnin, the SCTA Salary Committee chairman. "Springfield teachers do not think city employees are overpaid but that teachers are underpaid."

The association officers said that even though teachers work under a nine-month contract, extracurricular activities extend the workweek beyond 40 hours. Summer break, they said, is used for advanced study at the teachers' own expense. ← Info from the release is paraphrased and attributed to association officers.

Source of quote from interview is included. → "I figure I work a 60-hour week," Monnin said in an interview. "That means I work 51 40-hour weeks a year."

Some extracurricular activities, such as coaching, directing plays and supervising cheerleaders, earn extra compensation. ← Common knowledge is confirmed by two sources.

Quote clarifies info in earlier paragraphs. → Teachers are not compelled to attend after-school functions, but "we do feel the responsibility to attend," Monnin said.

Teachers also feel compelled to continue their education. Top pay for a teacher with only a bachelor's degree is $54,219 after 11 years of teaching. A teacher with a master's degree plus 75 hours of classes can earn $67,214 after 17 years of teaching. ← Facts verified by government sources are common knowledge.

Paraphrased opinion is attributed to source. → A police officer with a bachelor's degree can reach a top salary of $54,712 after six years of police work. But a person with a bachelor's degree and no police work experience is not likely to be hired, said Phil James, the Springfield director of personnel. James also said all firefighters are hired at $39,225. If a person has a bachelor's degree and stays on, he or she could make $40,725 after a six-month trial period.

Top pay for a dogcatcher is $37,626. "I sure wish I got summers off like those teachers," Luis Gonzalez, an animal control officer, said. "I got nothing against teachers. But most of them make more money than I'll ever make. . . . Besides, students don't bite many teachers." ← Quote adds color to the story.

The "so what" appears at the end. → The SCTA Salary Committee will present its salary proposal at the next meeting of the Springfield Board of Education.

Journalists can do their own research to build a story prompted by a news release.

SUGGESTED READINGS

Bivins, Thomas H. *Public Relations Writing: The Essentials of Style and Format.* 4th ed. Lincolnwood, Ill.: NTC/Contemporary Publishing Group, 1999. This book explains how public relations professionals approach a wide variety of writing tasks.

Howard, Carole, and Wilma Mathews. *On Deadline: Managing Media Relations.* 5th ed. Prospect Heights, Ill.: Waveland Press, 2013. This practical book offers suggestions on how organizations should deal with the news media.

Wilcox, Dennis L., and Lawrence W. Nolte. *Public Relations Writing and Media Techniques.* 6th ed. New York: HarperCollins, 2008. The authors cover the writing, production and distribution of a variety of public relations materials.

SUGGESTED WEBSITES

www.pressflash.com/resources_anatomy.php
On this website for a news release distribution service, you will find a terse description of a good news release.

http://press-release-writing.com/10-essential-tips-for-writing-press-releases
These 10 essential tips for writing news releases demonstrate how serious professionals approach this type of writing.

http://prwatch.org
This website is run by the nonprofit Center for Media and Democracy. According to the website, CMD "strengthens participatory democracy by investigating and exposing public relations spin and propaganda, and by promoting literacy and citizen journalism."

EXERCISES

1. **Team project.** Your professor will divide the class into groups of three. Read the following release. Then have each person in your group interview three households and ask these questions:

   a. When did you last change the batteries in your smoke alarms and carbon monoxide detectors?

   b. Do you test your smoke alarms monthly?

   c. Do you replace them every 10 years?

   d. Do you and those you live with have an evacuation plan in case of a fire?

   Set a time for your group to meet and to discuss your findings. Do you think you have a news story?

   SPRINGFIELD FIRE DEPARTMENT
   News Release
   For Immediate Release
   Reminder: Change Smoke Alarm Batteries and Clocks

   The Springfield Fire Department is reminding residents to change the batteries in their smoke alarms and carbon monoxide detectors when they turn their clocks back this weekend.

   Working smoke alarms cut in half the risk of dying in a home fire, yet Springfield Fire Department data shows less than half of Springfield homes have a working smoke alarm. Worn or missing batteries are the most common cause of a smoke alarm or carbon monoxide detector malfunction. Changing the batteries is one of the simplest, most effective ways to prevent tragic deaths and injuries.

   In addition to changing the batteries, smoke alarms should be tested monthly and replaced at least every 10 years.

   This weekend also serves as an ideal time for families to review their home evacuation plans. All family members should plan two ways to escape from each room and practice escape routes with the entire family at least twice a year.

   For information on how you can receive a free smoke alarm, call the Springfield Fire Department at 864-1500.

   Media Only: For more information, contact: Fire and Life Safety Educator Cara Restelli Erwin.

2. **Journalism blog.** Write a 300-word blog, aimed at journalism students, about dealing with news releases. Include questions a reporter must ask and all the things a reporter must check. Read your classmates' blogs and post comments on their ideas.

3. Read each of the following news releases. First, indicate the type of news release it is. Second, list questions you would have if you were to rewrite it, including the facts you would check and the sources you would turn to for the answers. Third, suggest ideas for visuals or videos that would accompany a Web story. Finally, correct all departures from Associated Press style rules.

   a. NEWS RELEASE
   For Further Information Contact:
   Humane Society of Missouri Media Center
   314-802-5712

   Humane Society of Missouri Confirms: Guilty Pleas Entered in Federal Court to Charges from Largest Dog Fighting Raid and Rescue in U.S. History
   Photos and Video of Dogs at Rescue Sites and Emergency Shelter Now Available

St. Louis, MO, September 14, 2013—The Humane Society of Missouri today confirms guilty pleas have been entered in connection to the July 8, 2013 multi-state federal dog fighting raid that resulted in the rescue of more than 500 fighting dogs. Federal agents made 26 arrests and dogs were rescued in 8 states.

This rescue operation is the largest dog fighting raid in U.S. history. The Humane Society of Missouri participated in the 18-month investigation and led the subsequent rescue and shelter operations, working in partnership with the Federal Bureau of Investigation, the Missouri State Highway Patrol, the United States Department of Agriculture's Office of the Inspector General, the U.S. Marshals Service and the United States Attorney.

Four eastern Missouri men, Robert Hackman of Foley, Teddy Kiriakidis of Leasburg, Ronald Creech of Leslie and Michael Morgan of Hannibal pled guilty today in U.S. District Court in St. Louis to charges connected to the dog fighting raid. Another man arrested in connection with the dog fighting raid, Jack Ruppel of Eldon, pled guilty to charges on September 4 in federal court in Jefferson City.

"We can confirm that five of the individuals charged with this gruesome form of animal abuse are being brought to justice," said Kathy Warnick, president of the Humane Society of Missouri. "Today's guilty pleas raise awareness that dog fighting is unacceptable, inhumane and illegal and will not be tolerated. The unprecedented scale of this investigation and rescue operation should alert the entire nation to what a horrible crime dog fighting is and what a dangerous and serious affect it can have on animals and communities.

Warnick continued, "We sincerely hope these guilty pleas will result in sentencing that sends the message that this form of animal abuse will no longer be tolerated. Humane Society of Missouri staff and our many partners have selflessly sacrificed much of their personal lives in the pursuit of this investigation and the care of these dogs. We fervently desire that this historic effort marks the beginning of the end to dog fighting in the United States."

"This was the largest dog fighting raid in U.S. history, but it will not be the last," warned Michael Kaste, Assistant Special Agent in Charge of the FBI in St. Louis. "This case sets precedents for the FBI along with our local, state and federal partners to aggressively root out underground dog fighting rings where people have absolutely no qualms about torturing man's best friend for money and entertainment."

b. NEWS RELEASE

The teaching faculty, administration and staff of The South Shore Country Day School formally began the school year Friday, August 30, with an all day workshop on curriculum planning.

This year, the School will be involved in a year long task of self evaluation. All aspects of the School's curriculum and student life will be considered and a new five year, long range plan for the curriculum will be written. The School's last major plan was constructed in 1994.

The evaluation process is designed to keep curriculum consistent with the School's educational philosophy and statement of mission. It will identify problems, strengths, and opportunities for expansion. At various stages of the process, all constituencies of the School will have an opportunity to express concerns and opinions. By the end of the school year, a new plan will be ready for integration and implementation by the School's administration.

William R. Lopez, Chairman of the School's Board of Trustees, spoke to the faculty about the upcoming project and the need to change. "We will attempt to make the current school better; we will not be creating a new school," he said.

Thomas B. Lang, the School's headmaster, emphasized the importance of total faculty participation in the formulation and execution of the mission statement. "We're all in this together," Lang said. "Curriculum is the sum of all the parts. No one teaches in a vacuum."

Among topics discussed at the workshop were: the importance of academic excellence; student social service; a need for diversity within the student body; the importance of educating the whole child; providing increased opportunity for students to participate in a variety of academic and nonacademic projects; and the ethical considerations in the School.

4. Assume you are a reporter for the Springfield paper. Rewrite the following release. Your instructor will be your news source for any questions you have.

NEWS RELEASE

Nearly 11,000 seat belt violation warnings were issued to motorists by the State Highway Patrol during the first month the new seat belt law was in effect.

Colonel Howard J. Hoffman, Superintendent of the State Highway Patrol, reported today that 10,908 warnings were issued to motorists in passenger vehicles for not wearing their seat belts as required by State Law.

Colonel Hoffman also noted that during this same reporting period, 50 persons were killed in traffic accidents investigated by the Highway Patrol. Only two of the persons killed in these mishaps were found to be wearing seat belts.

"The value of wearing a seat belt cannot be overemphasized," Hoffman said. "We don't know how many of these investigated traffic deaths could have been avoided by the use of seat belts. It is known, however, that seat belts have saved lives and prevented serious injuries to others. We will continue to vigorously enforce the State seat belt law and hopefully more and more motorists will make it a habit to buckle their seat belts."

5. Assume you are the editor of a news website. Write a memo to the staff explaining why you read every news release.

Reporting with Numbers

NUMBERS SURROUND US. They inform us, explain things and sometimes confuse us. As a journalist whose job it is to inform and not confuse, you need to understand how to use numbers. You need to understand those numbers whether you are reporting on your local school board's spending or on the national debt. Reporter Craig Harris dived into the numbers when he investigated Arizona's public pension system. After interviewing scores of people and analyzing the numbers, he reported to *The Arizona Republic*'s readers:

> Even as local governments and the state are slashing budgets, Arizonans are propping up public-pension systems that allow civil servants to retire in their 50s, receive annuities that can exceed $100,000 a year, and collect pensions while staying on the same job, *The Arizona Republic* has found.
>
> Over the past decade, government agencies have been forced to pour billions of dollars into the state's six pension systems to keep pace with continual benefit enhancements. The added cost of these enhancements has been largely borne by taxpayers as pension investments eroded amid stock-market declines.

The eight-part series revealed that several public-employee pension plans had grown unchecked over the years. Some employees were making more on pension than they did when they were working, and even those convicted of crimes continued getting their pensions. Harris built the series, in part, on the numbers:

> The tab for local governments and the state to run these systems grew 448 percent over the past 10 years to $1.39 billion annually, according to a *Republic* analysis of the benefits paid to more than 111,000 retired public employees. In many cases, taxpayer contributions to the pension funds far exceed workers' contributions. In fact, most employees earn all their contributions back within three to four years of retiring.

As a result of the series, all the state pension plans changed or considered changing their rules (see Figure 8.1, page 150).

This chapter covers the basics that will help you deal with numbers correctly in daily stories.

In this chapter you will learn:

1. How to put numbers in context by using proportion.

2. How to report on simple and compound interest.

3. How to understand and report on inflation.

4. How to figure and report on taxes.

5. How to read and report on budgets.

6. How to translate financial reports.

7. How to figure currency exchanges.

8. How to combine words and numbers.

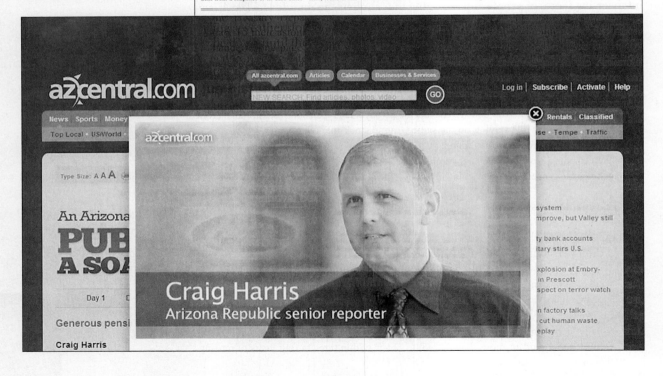

CARL EDWARDS WINS RACE AT PIR

CARDS GET POUNDED BY DIVISION RIVAL SEATTLE
SPORTS, C1

THE ARIZONA REPUBLIC

azcentral.com

75¢ Metro Phoenix Area
$1.00 Outside the Metro Phoenix Area

MONDAY, NOVEMBER 15, 2010

Generous pension benefits

Elected officials' plan is uncommon among government employees

By Craig Harris
THE ARIZONA REPUBLIC

There was a move in 2002 when Jane Dee Hull was Arizona's governor to raise her $95,000 salary because it was among the lowest of the nation's governors.

The raise never materialized. But thanks to a generous pension system for Arizona's elected officials, Hull now makes more in her golden years than when she served in office.

The generosity of that system is evident from a snapshot of its cost. Since 2000, the amount of public funding needed to maintain the elected officials' retirement system has increased by 325 percent, from $4.1 million to $17.5 million a year, according to records obtained by *The Arizona Republic*.

Contributing factors: regular cost-of-living increases that outpaced inflation and the pension's investment losses.

The average annual pension for a former elected official is $40,069. The highest is $216,424.

The Republic, as part of an investigation into the state's public-pension systems, found at least 43 elected officials of the 500 who retired since 2000 earn more from their state pensions than when they served in office.

Three-fourths of those 43 officials are judges who, depending on the Arizona county, run for election or are retained by voters. They are enticed to leave the bench after 20 years because they, and other elected officials, are able to retire on a pension that pays them 80 percent of their final annual salary in the first year alone, before any cost-of-living adjustments kick in.

See **PENSIONS** Page A10

REPUBLIC INVESTIGATION   **$1.39 billion**

PUBLIC PENSIONS: A SOARING BURDEN

In this eight-day series, *The Republic* examines the cost of Arizona's public-pension systems, the factors behind the rising expense and what can be done to rein it in.

Part 2 today: Elected officials' pensions.

Online: Search a database of pensions for retired elected officials and read more on this project at **watchdog.azcentral.com**.

PROPORTION

One of the most important services journalists perform for their readers is to give **proportion** to numbers in the news—explaining things relative to the size or the magnitude of the whole. A municipal budget that is going up by $500,000 would be a windfall for a small town in New Hampshire but a minor adjustment for a metropolis such as New York, Chicago or Minneapolis. At the state level in 2009, New York Gov. David A. Paterson proposed cutting $5 billion to try to balance the state budget. That proposed cut would cover the combined state budgets of Alabama, Alaska, Colorado, Indiana and Mississippi.

Other figures might mean a lot or a little, depending on the context. If you know little or nothing about baseball, you might think that Babe Ruth's career batting average of .342—34.2 hits for every 100 times at bat—indicates that Ruth wasn't a good hitter. After all, he failed almost two out of three times at bat. But when you look at the context—other players' averages—you realize that Ruth was exceptional. For instance, in 2012, no major league players had a higher average than Ruth's career average.

Percentages and Percentage Change

Percentages are basic building blocks used to explain proportion. Batting averages explain the number of hits compared with the number of times at bat. The political strength of a public official is partly reflected in the percentage of votes won at the polls. Stories about budgets, taxes, wages, retail sales, schools, health care and the environment all are explained with percentages.

To calculate a percentage, take the portion that you want to measure, divide it by the whole and then move the decimal two places to the right. For example, suppose you want to know what portion of the city's budget is allocated to police services. Divide the police budget by the city budget, move the decimal point two places to the right, and you get the percentage of the budget that pays for police services.

> **To calculate a percentage:**
>
> **Step 1**   Portion (police budget) ÷ whole (city budget) = .xxx
> $30,000,000 ÷ $120,000,000 = .25
>
> **Step 2**   Move the decimal point two places to the right: 25%

Precision in the use of numbers requires that you ask some basic questions. Reporters need to be careful of percentages that might be misleading or that tell only part of a story.

Populations, Samples and Margins of Error

If someone is giving you percentages, you must ask what **population** the figures are based on. For instance, suppose a juvenile officer tells you that 70 percent of the juvenile offenders do not have to return to his program. Your first question should

TIPS

To Calculate a Percentage

» Portion ÷ whole = .xxx.

» Move decimal point two places to the right: .xxx = xx.x percent.

be, "What population was used to figure the percentage?" Was it all the juveniles in the program during the last calendar year? If so, perhaps the success rate is high because the period being measured isn't long enough to take less successful years into account. And how has your source counted juveniles who are old enough now to be certified as adults? How does he account for juveniles who may have committed a crime in another jurisdiction?

The officer might explain that the figure is based on a sample of the population in the program over 10 years. A **sample** is a small number of people picked at random to represent the population as a whole. Using common statistical tables, researchers draw a sample of the names of all juveniles who were in the program over 10 years and contact them. From those contacts, they can determine the success rate of the program. If the figure is based on a scientific sampling like the one just described, there will also be a **margin of error**, which will be expressed as "plus or minus *x* points." Say that the margin of error for this sample is 4. That means that the success rate for the juvenile offender program is between 66 and 74 percent.

The base on which a percentage is calculated is significant. Say a colleague is making $40,000, and you make $30,000. The salary is the base. Your employer decides to give your colleague a 4 percent increase and to give you a 5 percent increase. Before you begin feeling too good about your raise, consider that your colleague's raise is $1,600, and yours is $1,500. Your colleague won a bigger raise, and the gap between the two of you grew. Hence, if you have different bases on which to figure the percentages, the comparisons are invalid.

In one investigative report, the *St. Louis Post-Dispatch* recognized it had percentages with different bases, and it handled them correctly. The newspaper examined repeat drunken-driving offenders in seven jurisdictions in its circulation area. In Missouri, drivers convicted two times of driving while intoxicated are supposed to be charged with a felony on the third offense. In reporting on the results, the reporters carefully gave the percentages and the base for each jurisdiction. That was important because the base ranged from seven cases in the city of St. Louis to 120 in St. Louis County. The percentages of cases handled correctly ranged from 29 to 51 percent.

Percentage Change and Percentage Points

Confusion often occurs when people talk about the difference between two percentage figures. For example, say the mayor won the election with 55 percent of the vote and had only one opponent, who received 45 percent. The mayor won by a margin of 10 **percentage points**. The percentage points, in this case, equal the difference between 55 and 45. However, the mayor won 22 percent more votes (10 divided by 45 equals .22). Because the 55 and 45 percentages are based on the same whole number—in this case, the total number of votes cast—the percentages can be compared. But if you compare the percentage of a city budget devoted to law enforcement in consecutive years, you will need to include the actual dollar amounts with the percentages because total spending probably changed from one year to the next.

Another important aspect of percentages is the concept of **percentage change**. This number explains how much something goes up or down. In the city budget

TIPS

To Calculate Percentage Change

» (New number) – (old number) = change.

» Change ÷ old number = .xxx.

» Move decimal point two places to right: .xxx = xx.x percent.

» Percentage change can be a positive or a negative number.

summary shown in Figure 8.2 (page 161), for example, look under "Appropriations" and then under "Revised Fiscal Year 2012." Total spending in 2012 was $18,654,563. The proposed budget for 2013 ("Adopted Fiscal Year 2013") is $19,570,518. What is the percentage increase? You find a percentage change by dividing the increase or decrease by the old budget.

To calculate a percentage change:

Step 1 Find the change.
$19,570,518 − $18,654,563 = $915,955 (increase)

Step 2 Change ÷ base amount = .xxx
$915,955 ÷ $18,654,563 = .049

Step 3 Move the decimal point two places to the right: 4.9 percent

Rounded off, this is a 5 percent increase in spending.

If the 2013 budget is increased 4.9 percent again in the following year, that will be a $958,955 increase, or $43,000 more, because of the bigger base.

When changes are large, sometimes it is better to translate the numbers into plain words rather than using a percentage figure. In New York, for instance, that proposed $5 billion cut in the state budget amounted to about $256 per resident of the state.

Averages and Medians

Averages and medians are numbers that can be used to describe a general trend. For any given set of numbers, the average and the median might be quite close, or they might be quite different. Depending on what you are trying to explain, it might be important to use one instead of the other or to use both.

The **average**—more technically called the *arithmetic mean*—is the number you obtain when you add a list of figures and then divide the total by the number of figures in the list. The **median** is the midpoint of the list—half the figures fall above it, and half the figures fall below it.

To calculate an average:

Step 1 Add the figures.

Step 2 Divide the total by the number of figures:
Total ÷ number of figures = average

To find the median:

Step 1 Arrange the figures in rank order.

Step 2 Identify the figure midway between the highest and lowest numbers. That figure is the median.

Note: When you have an even number of figures, the median is the average of the two middle figures.

"Average" Can Mean Different Things to Different People

Although most people understand "average" to refer to "arithmetic mean," the word is sometimes used for other types of statistical results, including "median" and "mode."

In reporting statistics, be certain you know the "average" involved. All of the following are averages.

» **Mean.** The arithmetic average, found by adding all the figures in a set of data and dividing by the number of figures. The mean of 2, 4 and 9 is 5 (2 + 4 + 9 = 15; 15 ÷ 3 = 5).

» **Median.** The middle value in a set of figures. If there is no middle value because there is an even number of figures, average the two middle numbers. The median of 2, 4 and 9 is 4. The medians of 5, 7, 9 and 11 and of 3, 7, 9 and 15 both are 8 (7 + 9 = 16; 16 ÷ 2 = 8).

» **Mode.** The most frequent value in a set of figures. The mode of 2, 5, 5, 5, 15 and 23 is 5.

As a general rule, you are safe using averages when there are no large gaps among the numbers. If you took an average of 1, 4, 12, 22, 31, 89 and 104, you would get 37.6. The average distorts the numbers because the average is higher than five of the seven numbers. The mean, or midpoint, is 22. On the other hand, if you had numbers ranging from 1 to 104 and the numbers were distributed evenly within that range, the average would be an accurate reading.

Rates

A **rate** is used to make fair comparisons among different populations. One example of a rate comparison is *per capita*, or per person, spending, such as for school funding. Even though a big-city school budget looks incredibly large to someone in a small community, the money has to stretch over more students than it would in a smaller district. As a result, spending per capita provides a better comparison between districts with different enrollments. Suppose your school district (district A) has 1,000 students and spends $2 million. You want to compare spending in your district with spending in district B, which has 1,500 students and a budget of $3 million. You would use the following formula to calculate per capita spending.

TIPS

To Calculate per Capita Spending

Divide the budget by the number of people:

» Budget ÷ population = per capita spending.

To calculate per capita spending:

Budget in dollars ÷ number of people = dollar amount per capita
District A: $2,000,000 ÷ 1,000 = $2,000 per capita
District B: $3,000,000 ÷ 1,500 = $2,000 per capita

School district B spends $1 million more a year than district A, but both districts spend the same amount per pupil.

To compare crime incidents or spending amounts among municipalities with varying populations, use per capita figures.

When Averages Distort

Take a set of scores from a final exam in a class of 15 students. The students scored 95, 94, 92, 86, 85, 84, 75, 75, 65, 64, 63, 62, 62, 62 and 62. Both the average (that is, the arithmetic mean) and the median are 75.

The picture can look quite different when the figures bunch at one end of the scale. Consider this example from professional baseball:

In 2009 the Chicago Cubs had a payroll of $134.8 million. With a range of salaries from $400,000 to $18.6 million, the median income was $2.2 million. However, the average, or mean, was $5.4 million ($134,809,000 ÷ 25 players).

INTEREST AND COMPOUNDING

Interest is a financial factor in just about everyone's life. Consumers pay interest on home mortgages, car loans and credit card balances. Individuals and businesses earn interest when they deposit money in a financial institution or make a loan. Federal regulations require the interest rates charged by or paid by most institutions to be expressed as an **annual percentage rate (APR)**, so that interest rates are comparable from one institution to another.

There are two types of interest: simple and compound. **Simple interest** is interest that is paid on the **principal**, the amount borrowed. It is calculated by multiplying the amount of the loan by the annual percentage rate.

Suppose a student borrows $1,000 from her grandfather at a 5 percent annual rate to help cover college expenses. She needs only a one-year loan, so the cost is figured as simple interest.

To calculate simple interest:

Multiply the principal by the interest rate.
$1,000 × .05 = $50

To find the amount the student will repay her grandfather at the end of the year, add the principal to the interest. The student will owe $1,050.

If the loan is made over a period longer than a year, the borrower pays **compound interest**. Compound interest is interest paid on the total of the principal and the interest that already has accrued.

Suppose the student borrows $1,000 at an annual percentage rate of 5 percent and pays her grandfather back four years later, after graduation. She owes 5 percent annual interest for each year of the loan. But because she has the loan for four years, each year she owes not only simple interest on the principal but also interest on the interest that accrues each year.

At the end of year 1, she owes $1,050. To see how much she will owe at the end of year 2, she has to calculate 5 percent interest on $1,050: $1,050 × .05 = $52.50.

TIPS

To Calculate Simple Interest and Total Amount Owed

» Express the interest rate as a decimal by moving the decimal point two places to the left.

» Multiply the principal by the interest rate:

$1,000 × .05 = $50

» Add the principal to the interest owed:

$1,000 + $50 = $1,050

The same result can be obtained another way.

» Multiply the principal by 1 plus the interest rate expressed as a decimal:

$1,000 × 1.05 = $1,050

TIPS

To Calculate Compound Interest

» Add 1 to the interest rate expressed as a decimal:

1 + .05 = 1.05

» Using a calculator, multiply the principal by $(1.05)^n$ (the superscript n represents the number of years of the loan).

The result is the total amount owed.

Here is how to calculate the interest for all four years. (Note that 1.05 is used instead of .05 to produce a running total: principal and interest. If you multiply 1,000 by 1.05, you get 1,050; if instead you multiply 1,000 by .05, you get 50, which you then have to add to 1,000 to get the principal and interest.)

$$\$1,000 \times 1.05 \times 1.05 \times 1.05 \times 1.05 = \$1,215.51$$

Because most consumers pay off student loans, car loans, mortgages and credit card debt over a period of time, and because interest is compounded more often than once a year, calculations usually are far more complicated than those in the example. Many financial websites and computer programs offer calculators for computing interest. Simply search for calculators.

Student loans taken out through federal programs administered by banks, credit unions and universities are a prime example of more complicated transactions. Suppose a student has a $5,000 guaranteed student loan with an interest rate of 8 percent per year. After finishing school, the student has 10 years to repay, and each year she pays 8 percent interest on the amount of the original principal that is left unpaid. If the student makes the minimum payment of $65 on time each month for the 10-year life of the loan, she will pay the bank a total of $7,800. She pays $2,800 in interest on top of the original principal of $5,000. If she does not pay the balance down each month, the interest she owes will be even higher.

Consumers get the benefits of compounding when they put money in interest-bearing accounts, because their interest compounds. The same effect takes place when people make good investments in the stock market, where earnings are compounded when they are reinvested.

INFLATION

Inflation is an increase in the cost of living over time. Because prices rise over time, wages and budgets also have to increase to keep up with inflation. A worker who receives a 2 percent pay increase each year will have the same buying power each year if inflation rises at 2 percent. Because of inflation, reporters must use a few simple computations to make fair comparisons between dollar amounts from different years.

Let's say the teachers in your local school district are negotiating for a new contract. They claim that their pay is not keeping pace with inflation. You know that the starting salary for a teacher in 2002 was $40,000 and that the starting salary in 2012 was $48,000. To determine whether the teachers' claim is true, you convert 2002 dollars to 2012 dollars. You will find that the starting salary in 2012 would have been $51,681 if the district had been keeping up with inflation. In other words, in constant dollars, first-year teachers earned $3,681 less in 2012 than they earned in 2002. (Numbers that are adjusted for inflation are called *constant*, or *real*, *dollars*. Numbers that are not adjusted for inflation are called *nominal*, or *current*, *dollars*.)

The most common tool used to adjust for inflation is the Consumer Price Index, which is reported each month by the U.S. Bureau of Labor Statistics, an agency of the Labor Department. You can get current CPI numbers on the Web at www.bls.gov/cpi.

TAXES

Reporters not only pay taxes, but also have to report on them. Governments collect taxes in a variety of ways, but the three major categories are sales taxes, income taxes and property taxes. Tax rates are expressed as percentages.

Sales Taxes

State, county and municipal governments can levy sales taxes on various goods and services. Sales taxes—also known as *excise taxes*—are the simplest to figure out.

To figure a sales tax, multiply the price of an item by the sales tax rate. Add the result to the original price to obtain the total cost.

Take the example of a student buying an $1,800 computer before beginning school at the University of Florida. If he shops in his home state of Delaware, he will pay no state sales tax. If he buys the computer after arriving in Florida, where the state sales tax is 6 percent, he will pay a state sales tax of $108 and another $13.50 in county sales tax, for a total of $1,921.50.

Sales taxes are an excellent way for you to track sales in your city, county or state. The appropriate government unit—a finance or comptroller's office, for instance—will have sales tax revenues, which are a direct reflection of sales and, therefore, an excellent resource for reporting on the economy in your area.

Income Taxes

Governments tax your income to support such services as building roads, running schools, registering people to vote and encouraging businesses to grow. Income taxes are paid to the federal government, to most state governments, and to some municipalities.

Calculating income taxes can be tricky because many factors affect the amount of income that is subject to the tax. For that reason, the only way to figure a person's income tax is to consult the actual numbers and follow tables published by the Internal Revenue Service (www.irs.gov) or the state department of taxation.

Governments use tax incentives to encourage people to undertake certain types of economic activities, such as buying a home, saving for retirement, and investing in business ventures. By giving people and businesses tax deductions, the government reduces the amount of income that is taxable.

A tax deduction is worth the tax rate times the amount of the tax deduction. The most common tax deduction is for the interest people pay on their home loans.

ON THE JOB
Working with Numbers

From city budgets to election results to the economic meltdown, today's important stories frequently involve numbers. Too often, unfortunately, reporters avoid them or leave their interpretation to officials.

But understanding how to interpret and present numbers in a news story can make a big difference. As the computer-assisted reporting editor for three newspapers and as training director for Investigative Reporters and Editors, **Jennifer LaFleur** saw that reporters who had these skills were able to break important stories. For instance, at *The Dallas Morning News*, math skills led education reporters to uncover millions of dollars in misspending in the Dallas Independent School District. At ProPublica—the non-profit investigative newsroom where she now works—many of LaFleur's first stories involved the nation's economic crisis and the nearly $800 billion federal stimulus

package. ProPublica reporters have used math skills to uncover problems in banking and campaign finance.

Over the years, LaFleur has noticed these common problems:

» Love for the superlative leads some reporters to use phrases such as "Texas has the most hunting accidents" or "California has the most cars"

without putting them in perspective. Big states have lots of everything, so the numbers should be adjusted for the population.

» Things cost more today than in the past, but too often reporters fail to adjust the figures for inflation. A 1950 dollar was not what it is today.

» In striving for precision, some reporters give readers a false message. A poll of just 400 people can't be that precise, so we shouldn't report that 43.25 percent of respondents said something.

"In a time when every reporter is asked to do more, no reporter should be without the basic skills to interpret the numbers they run across every day," LaFleur says. "They should know how to compute a percent change, percent of total and per capita and know what all those things mean."

Tax deductions are worth more to people with higher incomes. Take the example of two families who own homes. Both pay $2,500 in interest on their home mortgage in a year, the cost of which is deductible for people who itemize deductions on their income tax forms. The lower-income family is in the lowest federal income tax bracket, in which the tax rate is 10 percent, so that family saves $250 on its tax bill ($2,500 × .10 = $250). The higher-income family, which is in the federal income tax bracket of 33 percent, saves $825 on its tax bill ($2,500 × .33 = $825). In fact, the family in the 33 percent tax bracket probably owns a more expensive home and probably pays much more than $2,500 in mortgage interest a year. The impact is that the family saves even more on its income tax.

Income tax rates are based on your *adjusted gross income*. For example, if you are single and make between $8,350 and $8,400 after deductions, you will pay $838, or 10 percent. If you make between $40,000 and $40,050 after deductions—enough to move you into the 15 percent bracket—you will pay $6,036.

Property Taxes

City and county governments collect property taxes. When people talk about property taxes, they usually mean taxes on the value of houses, buildings and land. In some places, people also are taxed each year on the value of their cars, boats and other personal property.

The two key factors in property taxes are the assessed value and the millage rate. The **assessed value** is the amount that a government appraiser determines a piece of property is worth. The **millage rate**—the rate per thousand dollars—is the tax rate determined by the government.

To calculate property taxes:

Step 1 Divide the assessed value by 1,000.
$140,000 ÷ 1,000 = 140

Step 2 Multiply the result by the millage rate.
140 × 2.25 = $315 in taxes

Counties and cities hire professional appraisers to assess the values of land and buildings in their jurisdiction, and typically their assessments have been far lower than the actual market value of the property. Because of abuses and public confusion, most states in recent years have ordered revaluations to bring assessments into line with market values, and they have adjusted millage rates accordingly, though assessments can vary widely from appraiser to appraiser.

Appraisals are based on complicated formulas that take into account the size, location and condition of the property. Still, the government may say your house is worth $160,000, even if you know you could sell it for $180,000.

When you are reporting tax rate changes, you should find out how they affect houses in different value brackets to help explain the impact. By talking to the assessor or tax collector, you should be able to report, for instance, that the taxes for a house valued at $140,000 would be $315 and that taxes for a house valued at $250,000 would be $562.50.

BUDGETS

The budget is the blueprint that guides the operation of any organization, and a reporter must learn to read a budget just as a carpenter must learn to read a set of blueprints. It's not as difficult as it appears at first glance.

In many cases today, you'll be able to get the budget (and other financial information as well) for your city or school district in an electronic file. You might also be able to view it on a local website, but you probably cannot download that file into a spreadsheet database. However, once you have the budget in an electronic file, you can create your own spreadsheet and perform analyses that not long ago were only in the power of the institution's budget director. This is one of many ways the computer has become an essential newsroom tool. However, with a computer or without, first you need to know the basics of budgeting.

Budget Basics

Every budget, whether it's your personal budget or the budget of the U.S. government, has two basic parts—*revenues* (income) and *expenditures* (outgo). Commercial enterprises earn their income primarily from sales; not-for-profit organizations depend heavily on contributions from public funding and private donors. Government revenues come from sources such as taxes, fees and service charges, and payments from other agencies (such as state aid to schools). The budget usually shows, in dollar amounts and percentages, the sources of the organization's money. Expenditures go for such items as staff salaries, supplies, utility bills, construction and maintenance of facilities, and insurance. Expenditures usually are listed either by line or by program. The difference is this: A **line-item budget** shows a separate line for each expenditure, such as "Salary of police chief—$150,000." A **program budget** provides less detail but shows more clearly what each activity of the agency costs—for example, "Burglary prevention program—$250,000."

Finding Stories in Budget Changes, Trends and Comparisons

Now let's see what kinds of stories budgets might yield and where to look for those stories. Take a minute to scan Figure 8.2, a summary page from the annual budget of a small city. You can apply the skills of reading a city's annual budget to similar accounting documents on other beats—for example, annual reports of businesses and not-for-profit organizations.

The most important budget stories usually deal with changes, trends and comparisons. Budget figures change every year. Generally, as costs increase, so do budgets. But look under "Department Expenditures" in our sample budget (Figure 8.2) at the line for the parks and recreation department. There's a decrease between Revised Fiscal Year 2012 and Adopted Fiscal Year 2013. Why? The summary page doesn't tell you, so you'll have to look further. Sometimes that information will be in the detail pages; other times, you'll have to ask the department director. You might discover, for example, that the drop resulted from a proposal by the city staff to halt funding of a summer employment program for teenagers. That's a story.

Another change that may be newsworthy is the increase in the police department budget. In 2012 the budget was $4,007,593, and the budget adopted for 2013 is $4,375,336. In this case, it turned out that most of the increase was going to pay for an administrative reorganization that would add new positions at the top of the department. The patrol division was actually being reduced. Another story.

Look again at the police department line. Follow it back to Actual Fiscal Year 2011, and you'll see that the increase the year before was even bigger. In two years, the expenditures for police increased by nearly one-third, from $3.3 million actually

General Fund — Summary

Purpose

The General Fund is used to finance and account for a large portion of the current operation expenditures and capital outlays of city government. The General Fund is one of the largest and most important of the city's funds because most governmental programs (Police, Fire, Public Works, Parks and Recreation, and so on) are generally financed wholly or partially from it. The General Fund has a greater number and variety of revenue sources than any other fund, and its resources normally finance a wider range of activities.

APPROPRIATIONS

	Actual Fiscal Year 2011	Budget Fiscal Year 2012	Revised Fiscal Year 2012	Adopted Fiscal Year 2013
Personnel services	$9,500,353	$11,306,619	$11,245,394	$12,212,336
Materials and supplies	1,490,573	1,787,220	1,794,362	1,986,551
Training and schools	93,942	150,517	170,475	219,455
Utilities	606,125	649,606	652,094	722,785
Services	1,618,525	1,865,283	1,933,300	2,254,983
Insurance and miscellaneous	1,792,366	1,556,911	1,783,700	1,614,265
Total operating	15,101,884	17,316,156	17,579,325	19,010,375
Capital additions	561,145	1,123,543	875,238	460,143
Total operating and capital	15,663,029	18,439,699	18,454,563	19,470,518
Contingency	—	200,000	200,000	100,000
Total	$15,663,029	$18,639,699	$18,654,563	$19,570,518

DEPARTMENT EXPENDITURES

	Actual Fiscal Year 2011	Budget Fiscal Year 2012	Revised Fiscal Year 2012	Adopted Fiscal Year 2013
City Council	$75,144	$105,207	$90,457	$84,235
City Clerk	61,281	70,778	74,444	91,867
City Manager	155,992	181,219	179,125	192,900
Municipal Court	164,631	196,389	175,019	181,462
Personnel	143,366	197,844	186,247	203,020
Law Department	198,296	266,819	248,170	288,550
Planning and Community Development	295,509	377,126	360,272	405,870
Finance Department	893,344	940,450	983,342	1,212,234
Fire Department	2,837,744	3,421,112	3,257,356	3,694,333

(continued)

FIGURE 8.2

Summary page of a typical city budget

DEPARTMENT EXPENDITURES

	Actual Fiscal Year 2011	Budget Fiscal Year 2012	Revised Fiscal Year 2012	Adopted Fiscal Year 2013
Police Department	3,300,472	4,007,593	4,139,085	4,375,336
Health	1,033,188	1,179,243	1,157,607	1,293,362
Community Services	50,882	74,952	74,758	78,673
Energy Management	—	—	54,925	66,191
Public Works	2,838,605	3,374,152	3,381,044	3,509,979
Parks and Recreation	1,218,221	1,367,143	1,400,334	1,337,682
Communications and Information Services	532,153	730,129	742,835	715,324
City General	1,864,200	1,949,543	1,949,543	1,739,500
Total Department Expenditures	15,663,028	18,439,699	18,454,563	19,470,518
Contingency	—	200,000	200,000	100,000
Total	**$15,663,028**	**$18,639,699**	**$18,654,563**	**$19,570,518**

TIPS

Some Guidelines for Reporting Numbers

» Cite sources for all statistics.

» Use numbers judiciously for maximum impact.

» Long lists of figures are difficult to read in paragraph form. Put them in charts and graphs when appropriate.

» Graphs sometimes include estimates. If you use figures from a graph, make sure they are precise.

» Round off large numbers in most cases. For example, use $1.5 million rather than $1,489,789.

» Always double-check your math, and verify any statistics a source gives you.

» Be especially careful with handwritten numbers. It is easy to drop or transpose figures in your notes. Write neatly; when you read your notes, you'll want to be able to tell a 1 from a 7.

» If you don't understand the figures, get an explanation.

spent in 2011 to nearly $4.4 million budgeted for 2013. That's an interesting trend. The same pattern holds true for the fire department. More checking is in order. With copies of previous budgets, you can see how far back the growth trend runs. You can also get statistics on crimes and fires from the individual departments. Are the budget-makers responding to a demonstrated need for more protection, or is something else at work behind the scenes?

More generally, you can trace patterns in the growth of city services and city taxes, and you can compare those with changes in population. Are the rates of change comparable? Is population growth outstripping growth in services? Are residents paying more per capita for city services than they paid five or 10 years ago? More good story possibilities.

Another kind of comparison can be useful to your readers. How does your city government compare in cost and services with the governments of comparable cities? Some professional organizations have recommended levels of service—such as the number of police officers or firefighters per 1,000 inhabitants—that can help you help your readers assess how well they're being governed.

The same guidelines can be applied to the analysis of any budget. The numbers will be different, as will the department names, but the structures will be much the same. Whether you're covering the school board or the statehouse, look for changes, trends and comparisons.

FINANCIAL REPORTS

Another document that is vital to understanding the finances of local government or of any organization is the annual financial report. The report explains the organization's

Lies, Damned Lies and Statistics

Get your facts first, and then you can distort them as much as you please.

— Mark Twain

Here are some of the ways statistics can deceive:

» **Bias can influence the credibility of a survey.** For example, a national survey on sexual behavior indicated that 1 percent of 3,321 men questioned said they were gay, compared with the 10 percent commonly accepted as constituting the gay population. When reporting the survey results, *Time* magazine pointed out that people might be reluctant to discuss their sexual orientation with a "clipboard-bearing stranger."

» **One year does not a trend make.** A large increase in the number of rapes merits a story, but it might represent a fluctuation rather than a trend. Depending on the subject matter, you need to study at least five to 10 years of data to determine whether there is a significant shift.

» **The way organizations compile figures can differ, and that can distort comparisons.** The Scripps Howard investigation of sudden infant deaths, for example, found what one expert called a "deeply muddled approach" of wide variations in reporting from one state to the next, distorting real results and making accurate comparisons impossible. Jurisdictions with inadequately trained medical examiners report many times as many "unexplained" deaths as do jurisdictions with more rigorous standards. Inadequately trained journalists unknowingly spread misinformation.

» **Conclusions that sound credible might not hold up under the scrutiny of cause and effect.** Advocacy groups that call for less violence on television say studies show TV violence causes violence in children. They cite research at Yale University showing that prolonged viewing of violent programs is associated with aggressive behavior among children. But the association could be that children who tend to be aggressive watch more violent programming, not the other way around.

financial status at the end of a fiscal year, which often is not the same as the end of the calendar year. (For example, a fiscal year might end on June 30.) In the report you will find an accounting of all the income the organization received during the year from taxes, fees, state and federal grants, and other sources. You'll also find status reports on all the organization's operating funds, such as its capital improvement fund, its debt-service fund and its general fund.

Making sense of a financial report, like understanding a budget, isn't as hard as it may look. For one thing, the financial officer usually includes a narrative that highlights the most important points, at least from his or her viewpoint. But you should dig beyond the narrative and examine the numbers for yourself. The single most important section of the report is the statement of revenues, expenditures and changes, which provides important measures of the organization's financial health. Depending on the comprehensiveness of the statement, you may have to refer to the budget document as well. You can check:

» Actual revenue received compared with budgeted revenue.
» Actual spending compared with budgeted spending.
» Actual spending compared with actual revenue.
» Changes in balances available for spending in years to come.

**bedfordstmartins.com
/newsreporting**

Watch **"Freedom of
Information."**

- What effect might freedom
  of information laws
  have on using statistical
  information?

- Should governments ever
  be allowed to keep secrets
  from the public? Explain.

The guidelines offered here should help you shape your questions and understand the answers. With financial statements, as with budgets, look for changes, trends and comparisons, and ask for explanations.

MIXING NUMBERS AND WORDS

Whatever the story and whatever the subject, you probably can use numbers to clarify issues for readers and viewers. All too often, however, numbers are used in ways that muddy the water. Many journalists have some trepidation about working with numbers, and they create confusion unwittingly when they work with the volatile mixture of numbers and words.

Jennifer LaFleur (see the "On the Job" box in this chapter) says she has seen numerous reports from government agencies with math errors that a quick double check by a reporter would find. "Reporters background-check sources. They verify anecdotes with documents. But seldom do we double-check numbers," she reminds us.

One website that does check numbers regularly is PolitiFact.com. During the presidential campaign in 2012, President Barack Obama said during a debate that unemployment among veterans was lower than the rate among the general population. "It was higher (than the general population rate) when I came into office," he added.

PolitiFact compared the unemployment rate of veterans with that of the general population. Reporters confirmed that the unemployment rate for veterans had fallen from 7.4 percent in 2009 to 6.7 percent in 2012. During the same period, the rate for the general population had stayed at 7.8 percent. By looking at the numbers, PolitiFact was able to confirm that the president was right about the veterans' rate being lower than that of the general population in 2012. However, he was wrong when he said it was higher than the rate for the general population in 2009.

Sometimes, journalists encourage misunderstandings by describing large increases in percentage terms. For example, when gasoline prices increased from about \$2 to nearly \$4 a gallon, some in the media reported, accurately, that the price had doubled. Others, however, incorrectly called it a 200 percent increase instead of a 100 percent increase: $\$2 + (100\% \times \$2) = \$4$.

Another trouble spot for mixing numbers and words occurs when reporters calculate how much larger or more expensive something is. For example, a class that grew from 20 students to 100 students is five times bigger than it was ($5 \times 20 = 100$), but it has four times as many students as it had before: $(4 \times 20) + 20 = 100$.

The lesson to be learned from these examples is not to avoid numbers, but rather to use great care to ensure accuracy. Picking the right numbers to use and using them wisely will help your news stories have the biggest impact.

SUGGESTED READINGS

Blastland, Michael, and Andrew Dilnot. *The Commonsense Guide to Understanding Numbers in the News, in Politics, and in Life*. New York: Penguin, 2009. You can laugh as you learn more about handling numbers.

Cohen, Sarah. *Numbers in the Newsroom: Using Math and Statistics in News*. Columbia, Mo.: Investigative Reporters and Editors, 2001. This book includes helpful, readable information on how to do basic math, graphs and polls.

Cuzzort, R.P., and James S. Vrettos. *The Elementary Forms of Statistical Reason*. New York: St. Martin's Press, 1996. Non-mathematicians in the humanities and social sciences who must work with statistics will appreciate this basic guide.

Meyer, Philip. *Precision Journalism: A Reporter's Introduction to Social Science Methods*. 4th ed. Lanham, Md.: Rowman and

Littlefield, 2002. This step-by-step guide explains how to use social science research methods in news reporting.

Paulos, John Allen. *A Mathematician Reads the Newspaper*. New York: Anchor Books, 1997. Structured like the morning paper, this book investigates the mathematical angles of stories in the news and offers novel perspectives, questions and ideas.

SUGGESTED WEBSITES

www.bls.gov/data/inflation_calculator.htm
The Bureau of Labor Statistics has a calculator that enables you to adjust dollar amounts for inflation. In addition, the website provides Consumer Price Index information for the entire nation, broken down by region and type of spending.

www.math.temple.edu/~paulos
John Allen Paulos, a professor at Temple University, is the author of *Innumeracy: Mathematical Illiteracy and Its Consequences*. At this site you can read more from the master of numbers.

www.minneapolisfed.org
The Federal Reserve Bank of Minneapolis maintains a great website that helps you calculate inflation. It also has clear and

simple explanations of how inflation is calculated and how to use the Consumer Price Index.

www.robertniles.com/stats
Robert Niles, who worked at newspaper Internet sites in Denver and Los Angeles, is a self-described "math and computer geek." His explanations of statistics are simple and clear.

www.bankrate.com
Bankrate offers calculators to figure everything from interest rates to currency conversions.

EXERCISES

1. **Team project.** Your instructor will divide the class into two teams to examine crime on your campus and compare it with crime on other campuses. The Clery Act requires colleges and universities to publicly report crimes that occur on campus. Many schools post the data on their websites. One team should get the crime report and student enrollment figures for your campus. A second team should search the Web for crime statistics for comparable campuses and should obtain the student enrollment for each of those campuses. Take the figures for six of the crime categories and calculate the crimes per capita for each of the schools. As a class, discuss the stories that could grow out of these comparisons.

2. Your local school board sets the tax rate at $3.33 per thousand valuation, up from $3.21. Explain to readers the impact on a typical home.

3. Find a national survey released by any of the national media or by one of the major polling firms, such as Gallup. Report the margin of error and whether the main results are within that margin or exceed it.

4. The federal minimum wage began in 1938 at 25 cents. In 1968, it was $1.60. Calculate how much 25 cents in 1938 is worth today and what $1.60 in 1968 is worth today. Compare those numbers with the present minimum wage. Suggest a story idea based on the result. (Consult

   www.dol.gov/whd/minimumwage.htm for the current federal minimum wage and www.dol.gov/whd/minwage /america.htm for the current state minimum wages.)

5. If one candidate gets 48 percent of the vote and another gets 52 percent, what is the percentage difference? What is the difference in percentage points?

6. Get a copy of your city or university budget, and come up with five questions that a reporter should ask about the changes, patterns and trends that the budget suggests. The budget may be available on the Internet.

7. If a city budgets $186,247 for personnel one year and $203,020 the next, what is the percentage increase?

8. A city of 219,000 had 103 murders last year. Another city of 88,812 in the same state had 48 murders. How many murders were there per 1,000 residents in each city?

9. **Journalism blog.** Find out how much your college charged for tuition in 1996, 2006 and 2012. Adjust those numbers for inflation so they can be compared. (Use an inflation calculator like the one at www.minneapolisfed.org.) Write a blog post about the cost of going to college, and use figures adjusted for inflation. Remember to keep your reader in mind. Are you writing for students? Parents? University officials? All of these?

9

The Boston Globe

TUESDAY, APRIL 16, 2013

Marathon terror

The Inverted Pyramid

THE INVERTED PYRAMID—a news story structure that places all the important information in the first paragraph—has been used to write the "first draft of history" in the U.S. for generations. Here is the Associated Press lead on the first use of the atomic bomb in 1945:

> An atomic bomb, hailed as the most destructive force in history and as the greatest achievement of organized science, has been loosed upon Japan.

Twenty-four years later, here is how the AP started its story of the first moon landing:

> Man came to the moon and walked its dead surface Sunday.

And in 2012, when Hurricane Sandy smashed into the East Coast, the AP again used the inverted pyramid:

> NEW YORK (AP)—Stripped of its bustle and mostly cut off from the world, New York was left wondering Tuesday when its particular way of life—carried by subway, lit by skyline and powered by 24-hour deli—would return.
>
> Mayor Michael Bloomberg and the power company said it could be the weekend before the lights come on for hundreds of thousands of people plunged into darkness by what was once Hurricane Sandy.
>
> Bloomberg said it could also be four or five days before the subway, which suffered the worst damage in its 108-year history, is running again. All 10 of the tunnels that carry New Yorkers under the East River were flooded.

The lead reporting the moonwalk would work within Twitter's 140-character restriction. In fact, citizens who are suddenly thrust into reporting what's happening around them are tweeting inverted pyramid style. Twitter's limitation on the length of tweets neatly reflects the goal of the traditional inverted pyramid news lead: Report the most important news succinctly.

In this chapter you will learn:

1. Why the inverted pyramid story is important.

2. How to translate news values into leads.

3. How to create variations on the inverted pyramid lead.

4. How to organize a story using the inverted pyramid.

5. How to use the inverted pyramid across media platforms.

6. How to improve your accuracy.

With that goal, citizen journalists have joined specialized financial news services such as Bloomberg News, which relies on the inverted pyramid. So do newspapers, despite many editors' encouragement of new writing forms. So do radio, television, the Internet and newsletters. Businesspeople often use the inverted pyramid in company memos so their bosses don't have to read to the end to find the main point. Public relations professionals use it in news releases to get the attention of news editors.

IMPORTANCE OF THE INVERTED PYRAMID STORY

Frequently misdiagnosed as dying, the inverted pyramid has more lives than a cat— perhaps because the more people try to speed up the dissemination of information, the more valuable the inverted pyramid becomes. In the inverted pyramid, information is arranged from most important to least important. The king in *Alice in Wonderland* would never succeed in the electronic news service business. When asked where to start a story, he replied, "Begin at the beginning and go on till you come to the end; then stop." Reporters, however, often begin a story at its end.

> " Because a story is important, it doesn't follow that it must be long. "
> — Stanley Walker, city editor

Subscribers to financial services such as Reuters, Dow Jones Factiva and Bloomberg, for instance, react instantly to news about the financial markets to get an edge over other investors. They don't want narration; they want news. This is a typical Bloomberg lead:

> California home prices rose 25 percent in the 12 months through November, the most in eight years, as demand rose in expensive coastal areas, the state Realtors group said.

Many newspaper readers, on average, spend 15 to 25 minutes a day reading the paper. Online readers, who skip around sites as if they were walking barefoot on a hot stove, spend even less time. Both prefer short stories with the news on top. If a reporter were to write an account of a car accident by starting when the driver left the house, many readers would never read far enough to learn that the driver and a passenger had been killed. Instead, such a story starts with its climax:

> Two people died Thursday when a backhoe fell off a truck's flatbed and sliced the top off an oncoming vehicle near Fairchild Air Force Base.

In the inverted pyramid, the lead, which can consist of one or two paragraphs, sits atop other paragraphs arranged in descending order of importance. These paragraphs explain and provide evidence to support the lead. That's why print editors can quickly shorten a story by cutting from the bottom; the paragraphs at the end are the least important. On the Internet, as you will learn in Chapter 12, space is not a consideration, but readers' time is. That's why the same inverted pyramid that is

When exiled Syrian opposition members met in Turkey to demand the resignation of Syrian President Bashar Assad, the *Los Angeles Times* reported the news in an inverted pyramid news story.

used in newspapers is the most common story structure found on such news websites as CNN.com, msnbc.com, CBSNews.com and ABCNews.com. For instance, CNN used the inverted pyramid to report the release of journalists:

> An NBC reporter and his crew spoke Tuesday of their overwhelming relief after being freed from kidnappers in Syria who kept them bound, blindfolded and repeatedly threatened to kill them during a five-day ordeal.
>
> Speaking from Turkey, Richard Engel described on NBC's "Today" show how he and his crew were seized by a group of masked, heavily armed men shortly after crossing into northwest Syria from Turkey on Thursday.

The inverted pyramid does have some shortcomings. Although it delivers the most important news first, it does not encourage people to read the entire story. Stories stop; they don't end. There is no suspense. In a Poynter Institute study, researchers found that half of the 25 percent of readers who started a story dropped out midway through. Interest in an inverted pyramid story diminishes as the story progresses. But the way people use it attests to its value as a quick form of information delivery. Readers can leave a story whenever their needs are met, not when the writer finishes the story. In an age when time is golden, the inverted pyramid still offers value.

The day when the inverted pyramid is relegated to journalism history is not yet here and probably never will be. Perhaps 80 percent of the stories in today's newspapers and almost 100 percent of the stories on news services for target audiences such as the financial community are written in the inverted pyramid form. That's changing,

TIPS

The Inverted Pyramid

» Requires the writer to rank the importance of information.

» Puts the most important information first.

» Arranges the paragraphs in descending order of importance.

but it's changing slowly. Some of the new media highlight other forms of writing, such as narratives and essays. Still, as long as newspaper, electronic and television journalists continue to emphasize the quick, direct, simple approach to communications, the inverted pyramid and its variations will have a role.

There are many other ways to structure a news story. You will learn about some of the options in Chapter 11. However, before you explore the alternatives, you should master the inverted pyramid. As you do, you will master the art of making news judgments. The inverted pyramid requires you to identify and rank the most newsworthy elements in each story. This is important work. No matter what kinds of stories you write—whether obituaries, accidents, speeches, press conferences, fires or meetings—you will be required to use the skills you learn here.

FINDING THE LEAD

To determine a **lead**—a simple, clear statement consisting of the first paragraph or two of a news story—you must first recognize what goes into one. As you read in Chapter 1, you begin by determining the story's relevance, usefulness and interest for readers. One way to measure these standards is to ask "So what?" or "Who cares?" So what if there's a car accident downtown? If it's one of hundreds a month, it may not be news. Any holdup in a community of 5,000 may be news because the "so what" is that holdups are uncommon and some residents probably know the victim. It's unlikely newspapers, radio or television stations would report the holdup in a metropolitan area where holdups are common. But if the holdup appears to be part of a pattern or if someone is killed, the story becomes more significant. One holdup may not be news, but a holdup that authorities believe is one of many committed by the same person may be news. The "so what" is that if the police catch this robber, they stop a crime spree.

To determine the "so what," you have to answer six basic questions: who, what, where, when, why and how. The information from every event you witness and every story you hear can be reduced to answers to these six questions. If the answers add up to a significant "so what," you have a story. Consider this example of an incoming call at fire headquarters.

> "Fire Department," the dispatcher answers.
> "Hello. At about 10 o'clock, I was lying on my bed watching TV and smoking," the voice says. "I must have fallen asleep about 10:30 because that's when the football game was over. Anyway, I woke up just now, and my bedroom is on fire. . . ."

That dialogue isn't informative or convincing. More likely, our sleepy television viewer awoke in a smoke-filled room, grabbed his cellphone and punched in 9-1-1. The conversation with the dispatcher would more likely have gone like this:

"9-1-1 call center."

"FIRE!" a voice at the other end yells.

"Where?" the dispatcher asks.

"At 1705 W. Haven St."

When fire is licking at their heels, even nonjournalists know the lead. How the fire started is not important to the dispatcher; that a house is burning—and where that house is located—is.

The journalist must go through essentially the same process to determine the lead. Just as the caller served himself and the fire department, reporters must serve their readers. What is most important to them?

After the fire is over, there is much information a reporter must gather. Among the questions you would routinely ask are these:

» When did it start?
» When was it reported?
» Who reported it?
» How was it reported?
» How long did it take the fire department to respond?
» How long did it take to extinguish the fire?
» How many fires this year have been attributed to smoking in bed?
» How does that compare with figures from previous years?
» Were there any injuries or deaths?
» What was the damage?
» Who owned the house?
» Did the occupant or owner have insurance on the house?
» Will charges be filed against the smoker?
» Was there anything unusual about this case?
» Who cares?

With this information in hand, you can begin to write the story.

Writing the Inverted Pyramid Lead

Start by looking over your notes.

Who? The owner, a smoker, Henry Smith, 29. The age is important. Along with other personal information, such as address and occupation, the age differentiates the subject from other Henry Smiths in the readership area.

What? Fire caused damage estimated by the fire chief at $2,500.

Where? 1705 W. Haven St.

When? The call was received at 10:55 p.m., Tuesday. Firefighters from Station 19 arrived at the scene at 11:04. The fire was extinguished by 11:30. Those times are important to gather even if you don't use them. They show whether the fire department responded quickly.

Why? The fire was started by carelessness on the part of Smith, according to Fire Chief Bill Malone.

How? Smith told fire officials that he fell asleep in bed while he was smoking a cigarette.

If you had asked other questions, you might have learned more from the fire department:

» This was the eighth fire this year caused by smoking in bed.
» All last year there were four such fires.
» Smith said he had insurance.
» The fire chief said no charges would be filed against Smith.
» It was the first fire at this house.
» Smith was not injured.

Have you figured out the "so what"?

Assume your city editor has suggested you hold the story to about six paragraphs. Your first step is to rank the information in descending order of importance. There are lots of fires in this town, but eight this year have been caused by smoking in bed. Perhaps that's the most important thing about this story. You begin to type:

> A fire started by a careless smoker caused an estimated $2,500 in damage to a home Tuesday.

Only 17 words. You should try to hold every lead to fewer than 25 words unless you use more than one sentence. Maybe it's too brief, though. Have you left anything out? Maybe you should include the time element—to give the story a sense of immediacy. Readers would also want to know where the fire occurred. Is it near their house? Is it someone they know? You rewrite:

> A Tuesday night fire started by a careless smoker caused an estimated $2,500 in damage to a home at 1705 W. Haven St.

Just then the city editor walks by and glances over your shoulder. "Who said it was a careless smoker?" she asks. "Stay out of the story."

You realize you have committed a basic error in news writing: You have allowed an unattributed opinion to slip into the story. You have two choices. You can attribute the "careless smoker" information to the fire chief in the lead, or you can omit it. You choose to rewrite by attributing the opinion. You also revise your sentence to emphasize the cause instead of the damage. You write:

> Fire that caused an estimated $2,500 in damage to a home at 1705 W. Haven St. Tuesday was caused by smoking in bed, Fire Chief Bill Malone said.

Now 28 words have answered the questions "what" (a fire), "where" (1705 W. Haven St.), "when" (Tuesday) and "how" (smoking in bed). And the opinion is attributed. But you have not answered "who" and "why." You continue, still ranking the information in descending order of importance.

> The owner of the home, Henry Smith, 29, said he fell asleep in bed while smoking a cigarette. When he awoke about 30 minutes later, smoke had filled the room.
>
> Firefighters arrived nine minutes after receiving the call. It took them about 26 minutes to extinguish the fire, which was confined to the bedroom of the one-story house.
>
> According to Chief Malone, careless smokers have caused eight fires this year. Smith, who was not injured, said the house was insured.

You take the story to the city editor, who reads through the copy quickly. As you watch, she changes the lead to emphasize the "so what." The lead now reads:

> A smoker who fell asleep in bed ignited a fire that caused minor damage to his home on West Haven Street Tuesday, Fire Chief Bill Malone said. It was the city's eighth fire caused by smokers, twice as many as occurred all last year.

The lead is 44 words, but it is broken into two sentences, which makes it more readable. The importance of the "so what" changed the direction of the story. The fire was minor; there were no injuries. However, the increase in the number of fires smokers caused may force the fire department to start a public safety campaign against careless smoking. The city editor continues:

> The owner of the home, Henry Smith, 29, of 1705 W. Haven St., said he fell asleep in bed while smoking a cigarette. When he awoke about 30 minutes later, smoke had filled the room.

Too many numbers bog down a lead. Focus on the impact of the figures in the lead, and provide details later in the story.

When the editor checks the telephone listings and the city directory, she uncovers a serious problem. Both the telephone listings and the city directory give the man who lives at 1705 W. Haven St. as Henry Smyth: S-m-y-t-h. City directories, telephone lists and other sources can be wrong. But at least they can alert you to possible errors. Confirm spellings by going to the original source, in this case, Mr. Smyth.

Never put a name in a story without checking the spelling, even when the source tells you his name is Smith.

Look at the annotated model "A Sample Inverted Pyramid Story" on page 175 to see the completed fire story. There are several lessons you can learn from this example:

» Always check names.
» Keep the lead short, usually fewer than 25 words, unless you use two sentences.
» Attribute opinion. (Smoking in bed is a fact. That it was careless is an opinion.)
» Find out the who, what, where, when, why and how. However, if any of these elements have no bearing on the story, they may be omitted.

TIPS

When Writing the Lead, Remember

» Always check names.
» Keep the lead to fewer than 25 words.
» Attribute opinion.
» Find out the who, what, where, when, why and how.
» Tell readers what the news means to them.
» Gather basic information even if it's routine.

» Write a sentence or paragraph telling readers what the news means to them.
» Report information basic to the story even if it is routine. Not everything you learn is important enough to be reported, but you'll never know unless you gather the information.

When you are learning to write an inverted pyramid story, the process is deliberate. You'll check your notes to be certain you have the six basic questions answered. Eventually, though, you will mentally check off those questions quickly. Of course, you will not always be able to find answers immediately to "how" and "why." Sometimes, experts need time to analyze accidents, crimes, fires, and so on.

After you've checked your notes, ask yourself, "What else do readers need to know?" Using the news values of relevance, usefulness and interest and figuring out the "so what," decide which answers are the most important so you can put them in the lead. The rest go in the second and third paragraphs. In the Annotated Model, the news values and "so what" are these:

> " Writing is easy; all you do is sit staring at a blank sheet of paper until the drops of blood form on your forehead. "
>
> —Gene Fowler, author

Relevance	Eight similar fires are more relevant than one minor fire.
Usefulness	Highlighting the number of fires also establishes usefulness by pointing out the bigger problem.
Interest	Multiple fires attract more interest than one minor one.
The "so what"	One minor fire lacks impact, but the fact that eight fires this year were caused by smoking suggests a public safety problem.

In what order are the key questions answered in the fire story? What does that order say about news values?

Emphasizing Different News Values

In the lead reporting the house fire, the "what" (fire) is of secondary importance to the "how" (how the fire started). A slightly different set of facts would affect the news value of the elements and, consequently, your lead. For instance, if Smyth turned out to have been a convicted arsonist, you would probably emphasize that bizarre twist to the story:

> A convicted arsonist awoke Tuesday to find that his bedroom was filled with smoke. He escaped and later said that he had fallen asleep while smoking.
> Henry Smyth, 29, who served a three-year term for . . .

That lead emphasizes the news value of novelty. If Smyth were the mayor, you would emphasize prominence:

> Mayor Henry Smyth escaped injury Tuesday when he awoke to find his bedroom filled with smoke. Smyth said he had fallen asleep while smoking in bed.

ANNOTATED MODEL   **A Sample Inverted Pyramid Story**

The identification of "who" is delayed until the next paragraph because the person is not someone readers would recognize and because his name would make the lead unnecessarily long. Also in the lead are the "what," "when," "how" and, most significantly here, the "so what."

The performance of the fire department is monitored.

> A smoker who fell asleep in bed ignited a fire that caused minor damage to his home on West Haven Street Tuesday, Fire Chief Bill Malone said. It was the city's eighth fire caused by smokers, twice as many as occurred all last year.

The owner of the home, Henry Smyth, 29, of 1705 W. Haven St., said he fell asleep in bed while smoking a cigarette. When he awoke about 30 minutes later, smoke had filled the room. — The "who" is identified. More details on the "how" are given.

> The fire department, which received the call at 10:55 p.m., had the fire out by 11:30.

Malone said the damage, estimated at $2,500, was confined to the bedroom. The house was insured. — Details on the "so what" are given. The impact question is answered with the possible campaign.

Careless smokers caused only four fires last year in the city. Malone said that he is considering a public awareness campaign to try to alert smokers to the hazards. Those four fires caused total damages of $43,000. This year, fires started by careless smoking have caused total damages of $102,500, Malone said.

Least important: If someone else had been endangered and charges had been filed, this information would move higher in the story.

> No charges will be filed against Smyth because no one other than the smoker was endangered, Malone said.

The inverted pyramid structure dictates that the most important information goes in the lead paragraphs. It is the job of the writer and the editor to decide what that information is.

What, So What and What's Next

You know that the answer to "what" is often the lead. The preceding example also illustrates the "so what" factor in news. A $2,500 fire is not news to many people in large communities where there are dozens of fires daily. Even if you crafted a tightly written story about it, your editor probably would not want to print or broadcast it.

In small communities, the story would have more impact because there are fewer fires and because a larger proportion of the community is likely to know the victim.

The "so what" factor grows more important as you add other information. If the fire occurred during a fire-safety campaign, the "so what" would be the need for fire safety even in a community where awareness of the problem had already been heightened. If the fire involved a convicted arsonist or the mayor, the "so what" would be stronger. Oddity or well-known people increase the value of a story. If someone had been injured or if the damage had been $1.2 million instead of $2,500, the "so what" factor might even push the story into the metropolitan press. As discussed, once you have answered all six of the basic questions, it's important to ask yourself what the answers mean to the reader. That answer is your "so what" factor.

In many stories, it is also important to answer the question "What's next?" The city council had its first reading of its budget bill. What's next? *Members will vote on it next month.* Jones was arrested Monday on suspicion of passing bad checks. What's next? *The prosecuting attorney will decide whether there is enough evidence to file charges.*

A reader in a focus group once told researchers that she just wants to be told "what," "so what" and "what's next." That's a good guideline for all journalists to remember.

VARIATIONS ON THE INVERTED PYRAMID LEAD

No journalist relies on formulas to write inverted pyramid leads, but you may find it useful, especially in the beginning, to learn some typical types of leads. The labels in the following sections are arbitrary, but the approaches are not.

The "You" Lead

Regardless of which of these leads journalists use, they are trying to emphasize the relevance of the news to the audience. One good way to highlight the relevance is to speak directly to readers by using "you." This informal, second-person lead—the **"you" lead**—allows the writer to tell readers why they should care. For instance:

> You will find the lowest rates in two years if you are buying a home.
>   Most Springfield banks yesterday lowered the 15-year loan rate to 2.85 percent, down from 3.9 percent a year ago.

Readers want to know what's in it for them. The traditional approach is less direct:

> The real estate mortgage rate hit a two-year low yesterday.

As with any kind of lead, you can overdo the "you" lead. You don't need to write "You have another choice in the student president's race." Just tell readers who will be running. However, you may use those words in writing for radio or television news as a setup for the story to come. And in tweets and on Facebook, where you are talking to readers one-on-one, "you" is usually appropriate.

The Immediate-Identification Lead

In the **immediate-identification lead**, one of the most important facts is "who," or the prominence of the key actor. Reporters often use this approach when someone important or well-known is making news. Consider the following example:

NEW YORK (AP)—Lady Gaga is donating $1 million to the Red Cross to aid those affected by Superstorm Sandy.

If Lady Gaga were not well-known, the lead probably would have said that a New York–born singer was donating the money. Names make news.

When writing for your campus newspaper or your local newspaper, you would use names in the lead that are known locally but not necessarily nationally. The name of your student body president, the chancellor, the mayor or an entertainer who has a local following would logically appear in the lead. None of these names would be used in a newspaper 50 miles away.

In small communities, names almost always make news. The "who" involved in an accident is usually in the lead. In larger communities, names are not as recognizable. As a rule, if the person's name or position is well-known, it should appear in the lead.

> " Language is a very difficult thing to put into words. "
>
> —Voltaire, philosopher

The Delayed-Identification Lead

Usually a reporter uses a **delayed-identification lead** because the person or organization involved has little name recognition among readers. Thus, in fairly large cities, an accident is usually reported like this:

MADISON, Wis.—A 39-year-old carpenter was killed today in a two-car collision two blocks from his home.

William Domonske of 205 W. Oak St. died at the scene. Mary Craig, 21, of 204 Maple Ave., and Rebecca Roets, 12, of 207 Maple Ave., were taken to Mercy Hospital with injuries.

However, in a smaller community, names almost always make news. Unless a name is nationally recognized, it often appears in the second paragraph:

LOS ANGELES (AP)—A Southern California insurance broker was arrested Wednesday on allegations he overcharged Tom Hanks, musician Andy Summers and others hundreds of thousands of dollars for insurance premiums.

Jerry B. Goldman, who was arrested at his Thousand Oaks home, remained jailed Wednesday, U.S. attorney's spokesman Thom Mrozek said.

This example demonstrates two things. The name Jerry B. Goldman was not widely known, so his identification was delayed until the second paragraph. However, note that the writer worked two entertainers' names into the lead to attract attention.

A Case Study of Leads

Tina Macias (see the "On the Job" box in this chapter) covered the news of a school bus driver who was charged with driving while intoxicated. Of course, her stories for *The Daily Advertiser* in Lafayette, La., went into detail, but if you read nothing but the leads, you can follow the essential news. She also posted messages on Twitter while at the school board meeting ("The 3-day suspension for bus driver Kenny Mire approved w/out debate. The policy has been pulled and is about to be debated."). The leads from her series of articles appear below. Leads 3 and 4 begin two stories from the same meeting.

Lead from Story 1
The Lafayette Parish School Board at its meeting tonight could approve a new policy that outlines how to discipline bus drivers if they are charged with drunken driving off duty.

Lead from Story 2
The Lafayette Parish School Bus Drivers Association is "behind the superintendent 100 percent" when it comes to a new policy set to be debated tonight.

Lead from Story 3
The Lafayette Parish School Board tonight voted to suspend bus driver Kenny Joseph Mire for three days without pay.

Lead from Story 4
The Lafayette Parish School Board tonight unanimously approved a new policy that addresses how to discipline bus drivers who are arrested for drunken driving off duty.

Lead from Story 5
Bus drivers who are charged with drug- or alcohol-related driving incidents will be suspended with pay until a substance-abuse professional deems them capable of returning to work, according to a policy unanimously approved by the Lafayette Parish School Board on Wednesday.

The new policy puts Lafayette Parish more in line with several other Louisiana school systems.

The Summary Lead

Reporters dealing with several important elements may choose to sum up what happened in a **summary lead** rather than highlighting a specific action. This is one of the few times when a general statement is preferable to specifics.

The Associated Press wrote scores of stories as Hurricane Sandy moved up the East Coast of the U.S. in November 2012. When the worst was over, the AP wrote a summary lead rather than focusing on one impact from the storm:

> Death blew in on the superstorm's wild winds and sea water torrents, claiming 90-year-olds and children with capriciously toppling trees, taking tall-ship adventurers in mountainous Atlantic waves and average folks just trying to deal with a freakish snowstorm. It felled both heroes rushing into harm's way and, ironically, people simply following advice to play it safe at home.

> At least 72 died as the shape-shifting hurricane and
> winter storm ravaged the eastern U.S., and searchers
> continued looking for victims Wednesday.

Likewise, if a city council rewrites city ordinances, unless one of the changes is of overriding importance, most reporters will use a summary lead:

> MOLINE, Ill.—The City Council replaced the city's
> 75-year-old municipal code with a revised version
> Tuesday night.

Summary leads do not appear only in reports of board meetings. A Spokane, Wash., reporter used a summary lead to report a neighborhood dispute:

> An Idaho farmer's fence apparently was cut last week.
> It set off a chain of events Friday night that landed three
> people in the hospital, killed a cow and totaled a vehicle
> in the eastern Spokane Valley.

The basic question you must answer is whether the whole of the action is more important than any of its parts. If the answer is yes, use a summary lead.

The Multiple-Element Lead

In some stories, choosing one theme for the lead is too restrictive. In such cases, you can choose a **multiple-element lead** to work more information into the first paragraph. But you should write the lead within the confines of a clear, simple sentence or sentences. Consider this example:

> PORTLAND, Ore.—The City Council Tuesday
> ordered three department heads fired, established an
> administrative review board and said it would begin to
> monitor the work habits of administrators.

Notice that the actions are parallel, as is the construction of the verb phrases within the sentence. Parallel structures also characterize the following news extract, which presents a visual picture of the scene of a tragedy:

> BAY CITY, Mich.—A flash fire that swept through a
> landmark downtown hotel Saturday killed at least 12
> persons, injured 60 more and forced scores of residents
> to leap from windows and the roof in near-zero cold.

We are told what happened, where it happened and how many were killed and injured.

ON THE JOB

Inverted Pyramid—A Basic Tool

Tina Macias is an investigative producer at KATC-TV 3 in Lafayette, La. Before she made the jump to TV, she spent nearly five years as a reporter at *The Daily Advertiser* in Lafayette. Macias' time was split between writing human interest stories and breaking news.

Despite all the changes in the industry, she believes the inverted pyramid format still is an essential tool, especially in this 24-hour news age.

Macias says the easiest and most efficient way to organize breaking news on the Web is with the inverted pyramid. Only months out of school, she found herself covering hurricanes. Her job was to get information quickly and put it online and then follow with print stories. Most of the information about school closings, food stamps, curfews and power outages appeared on the Web in

the inverted pyramid format. This story was put online the Friday before Labor Day when Hurricane Gustav made landfall:

> With Hurricane Gustav edging toward the Gulf, and projections showing Acadiana in its path, public and private schools are preparing for the worst.

> One day before she arrived at work, a colleague had reported the bare details of

a school bus accident that morning. Macias' job was to update the story.

"As I started to make my phone calls, I thought about the vital information and how I could easily organize it," she says. She produced this inverted pyramid lead:

> Nine people, including eight children, were transported to a local hospital Monday morning after a black Impala plowed into the side of a Lafayette Parish school bus.

> All were transported for minor or moderate injuries and complaints.

Though then a rookie reporter, Macias was able to be productive immediately, in part because of two internships she held while attending journalism school. Now she is used to covering news quickly for both the Web and print.

Some multiple-element leads consist of two paragraphs. This occurs when the reporter decides that several elements need prominent display. For example:

> The Board of Education Tuesday night voted to lower the tax rate 12 cents per $100 valuation. Members then approved a budget $150,000 less than last year's and instructed the superintendent to decrease the staff by 25 people.
>
> The board also approved a set of student-conduct rules, which include a provision that students with three or more unexcused absences a year will be suspended for a week.

This story, too, could emphasize the "so what" while retaining the multiple elements:

> The Board of Education lowered your real estate taxes Tuesday. Members also approved a budget $150,000 less than last year's and instructed the superintendent to decrease the staff by 25 people.

Simpler leads are preferable. But a multiple-element lead is one of your options. Use it sparingly.

Many newspapers are using graphic devices to take the place of multiple-element leads. They use summary boxes to list other actions. Because the box appears under the headline in type larger than the text, it serves as a graphic summary for the reader who is scanning the page. The box frees the writer from trying to jam too many details into the first few paragraphs. On the Web, such lists are even more common. When Instagram announced that it could sell the photos people post on the site, CNN included four related points in its Story Highlights list to the left of the lead (see Figure 9.1).

Instagram backtracks after user privacy revolt

 By **Doug Gross**, CNN
updated 6:53 AM EST, Wed December 19, 2012 | Filed under: Social Media

GETTY IMAGES

Click to play

Can Instagram sell your photos?

STORY HIGHLIGHTS

- NEW: Instagram backtracks on controversial privacy language
- Language appeared to let the app sell users' images for advertising
- Facebook CEO Mark Zuckerberg's wedding photographer called it unfair
- NEW: Instagram co-founder: "It is not our intention to sell your photos"

(CNN) -- Faced with a loud and angry backlash from some of its most active users, photo-sharing app Instagram backtracked Tuesday on new language that appeared to give the company ownership of their images.

"The language we proposed ... raised question about whether your photos can be part of an advertisement," Instagram co-founder Kevin Systrom wrote in a blog post. "We do not have plans for anything like this and because of that we're going to remove the language that raised the question."

FIGURE 9.1

A list, such as CNN's Story Highlights on the left, allows the writer to simplify the lead.

Another approach is to break the coverage of a single event into a main story and a shorter story called a **sidebar**. This approach offers the advantage of presenting the information in short, palatable bites. It also allows the writer to elevate more actions into lead positions. Researchers have found that breaking stories into small segments increases readers' comprehension and retention. For instance, in the Board of Education lead above, the angle about the superintendent's having to decrease staff could be spun off into a short sidebar.

On the Web, there is an additional advantage. The more stories with separate headlines, the better chance you have to increase the **click-through rate**, the measurement of how many people open the stories.

> " The lead should be a promise of great things to come, and the promise should be fulfilled. "
> —Stanley Walker, city editor

Danger Signals

Here are some leads that understandably raise red flags to editors:

» **Question leads.** Readers don't know the subject, don't know why they are being asked a question and probably couldn't care less. So the next time you are writing a weather story and are tempted to begin with "So, how hot was it yesterday?" lie down until the temptation passes. Either tell readers the temperature or open with an anecdote of a specific roofer sweating on the job. That's showing how hot it is.

» **Leads that say what might happen or what might have happened.** News organizations try to report what happened. Stay away from leads like this: "Springfield residents might be looking forward to warmer weather." Or they might not. Talk to people. Don't speculate.

» **Leads that overreach.** Report what you know. You might think it's harmless to write, "Springfield residents warmly greeted spring yesterday," but you don't know that all Springfield residents were happy about it. Maybe the guy who runs a snow-removal business would rather see winter last longer.

Leads with Flair

Although the inverted pyramid tells readers the news first and fast, not all stories begin with the most important statement. When the news value you want to emphasize is novelty, often the lead is unusual.

CASTLE SHANNON, Pa. (AP)—This deer wasn't caught in the headlights. It was called on the carpet.

A Pittsburgh-area carpeting store has been cleaning up after the wild animal smashed into the store and ran amok Tuesday.

A less imaginative writer might have written:

> A deer ran through the window of a Pittsburgh-area car-
> peting store Tuesday.

That approach is like slapping a generic label on a Mercedes-Benz. The inverted pyramid approach is not so rigid that it doesn't permit fun and flair.

STORY ORGANIZATION

Like a theater marquee, the lead is an attention-getter. Sometimes the movie doesn't fulfill the promises of the marquee; sometimes the story doesn't fulfill the promises of the lead. In either case, the customer is dissatisfied.

The inverted pyramid helps you put information in logical order. It forces you to rank, in order of importance, the information you will present.

The One-Subject Story

As we have seen in this chapter, constructing an inverted pyramid news story involves a series of judgments based on classic news values and the specific news outlet. A fire or an accident in a small community is bigger news than a fire or an accident in another, larger area. Earlier events will also influence how you write a story.

The annotated model "A Single-Subject Inverted Pyramid Story" on page 184 shows a story about the arrest of a suspect in an assault case. Police say drugs were involved. If there had been a string of assaults or a pattern of drug-related violence, the writer probably would have emphasized different aspects of the story. For instance, the writer could have emphasized the suspect's criminal record with this lead:

> A Columbia man who was convicted of assault three
> times was arrested again Thursday night for an attack
> on his girlfriend.

The Memo-Structure Story

The memo structure (as illustrated in the annotated model on page 185) is one of many hybrids journalists are experimenting with as they transition to the Web. It is an effective way to organize information that has no narrative and few voices. You can use it to write an **advance** about upcoming meetings and to update developing stories. The categories can follow the standard who, what, where, when, why, how and so what, or you can create your own subject categories. Reporters can write memo-structure stories quickly, and readers can scan them quickly—a convenient feature for readers using a small-screen device such as a smartphone.

ANNOTATED MODEL   **A Single-Subject Inverted Pyramid Story**

Man Arrested in Attack, Charged with Child Endangerment

By Elizabeth Phillips
Columbia Missourian

The arrest, not the assault, is the latest development, so it is emphasized.

Police arrested a Columbia man in connection with an attack on his girl-friend Thursday night.

The lead gives "who," "what" and "when."

Details of the charges are in the second paragraph because the list is too long to put in the lead.

Darrell Vanness Johnson, 37, was arrested on suspicion of second-degree domestic assault, unlawful use of a weapon, felony possession of a controlled substance, misdemeanor possession of a controlled substance and endangering the welfare of a child at about 9 p.m. Thursday in the 1500 block of Greensboro Drive.

The name is not in the lead because most readers would not recognize it.

The writer adds details, attributed to the police, on how the assault occurred. This information includes the "why."

Johnson and his girlfriend began arguing over drugs Thursday evening, Columbia Police Sgt. Ken Hammond said. Johnson choked her and held a revolver to her head before she was able to escape and call 911 from a neighbor's house, Hammond said. Three children, two 9-year-olds and a 4-year-old, were in the home during the attack, Hammond said.

"Where" is identified. "When" is made more specific than in the lead.

This paragraph continues the chronology of the assault and capture.

When Columbia police arrived, Johnson was driving away from the Greensboro Drive home with the three children in the car, Hammond said. When police arrested Johnson, they found marijuana and cocaine, Hammond said.

Information about the children is pertinent because it adds to the "so what"—the children were also endangered.

The victim was taken to an area hospital by ambulance for treatment of bruises and scratches to the hands, neck and back, Hammond said. Her injuries were not life threatening.

The writer offers evidence of the injuries and attributes this information.

Now that the basic facts are established, the writer adds background on the suspect, attributed to a public safety website.

According to Missouri Case.net, Johnson has pleaded guilty to third-degree domestic assault three times in the past four years in Boone County Circuit Court, serving close to seven months in jail for those charges. He has also pleaded guilty to theft, first-degree trespass and second-degree property damage in Boone County Circuit Court, serving 75 days in Boone County Jail for the theft charge and receiving two years of unsupervised probation for the trespass and property damage charges.

Johnson violated his probation on the trespass and property damage charges and was scheduled to appear in Boone County Circuit Court for a probation violation hearing in December. He was charged with theft last October in Boone County Circuit Court.

Writer gives the "what's next."

He faces up to 40 years in prison and up to a year in jail in connection with the attack.

Copyright © 2006 Columbia Missourian

This typical one-subject story written in the inverted pyramid form features a delayed-identification lead.

ANNOTATED MODEL **A Memo-Structure Story**

Parks and Recreation, City Council Discuss Plans for Parks Tax

By Asif Lakhani
Columbia Missourian

The multiple-element lead gives basic facts—the "who," "what" and "when." → COLUMBIA—Earlier this month, Columbia voters approved the extension of the park sales tax. On Monday night, the Columbia City Council and the Parks and Recreation Department attended a work session where they discussed where the tax revenue would go.

Subheadings introduce the paragraphs. → **What happened:** Mike Hood, director of parks and recreation, presented a proposed five-year plan to council members. ← Subsequent paragraphs organize information by categories, not necessarily by importance.

Cost: During the next five years, the one-eighth-cent sales tax is expected to garner about $12 million for Columbia's parks. ← The writer has chosen categories that are relevant to the reader.

Timetable: The proposed plan divides projects into four categories: land acquisition and annual park funding, new facility and park development, improvements to existing parks, and trails and greenbelts. . . .

Projects: The five-year plan would be front-loaded with construction projects over a four-year fiscal period between 2011 and 2015, which would leave more room for land acquisition later on, Hood said. Most of the construction projects are listed under new facility and park development and improvements to existing parks. . . .

Comments: First Ward Councilman Paul Sturtz and Sixth Ward Councilwoman Barbara Hoppe voiced concern about front-loading the plan with construction. Both said land acquisition is more important because its value could increase over the next five years. . . .

The last paragraph wraps up the story. → **What's next:** The proposed plan now goes to the Parks and Recreation Commission. After, it will go to the City Council for consideration. The council plans to discuss the suggested land acquisition at an upcoming council meeting.

In a memo-structure story, subheads can reflect the answers to essential questions.

The Multiple-Element Story

Multiple-element stories are most commonly used in reporting on the proceedings of councils, boards, commissions, legislatures and courts. These bodies act on numerous subjects in one sitting. Frequently, their actions are unrelated, and more than one action is often important enough to merit attention in the story. You have four options:

1. **You can write more than one story.** This, of course, requires permission from your editor. There may not be enough space.
2. **You can write a story highlights list.** The list would be displayed along with the story either in print or on the Web. In it you would list the council's major actions or the court's decisions.
3. **You can write a multiple-element lead and story.** Your lead would list all the major actions at the board meeting. The remainder of the story would provide more detail about each action.
4. **You can write a single-element lead and cover the other elements further on in the story.** Your lead would focus on the element you believe readers would find most interesting, relevant and useful.

Let's go back to a multiple-element lead we saw earlier:

> The Board of Education Tuesday night voted to lower the tax rate 12 cents per $100 valuation. Members then approved a budget $150,000 less than last year's and instructed the superintendent to decrease the staff by 25 people.
>
> The board also approved a set of student-conduct rules, which include a provision that students with three or more unexcused absences a year will be suspended for a week.

Four newsworthy actions are mentioned in those two paragraphs: (1) changing the tax rate, (2) approving a budget, (3) cutting staff, (4) adopting student-conduct rules. In stories that deal with several important elements, the writer usually highlights the most important. When this is the case, it is important to summarize the other, lesser actions after the lead.

If you and your editor judge that changing the tax rate was more important than anything else that happened at the school board meeting, you would approach the story like this:

Lead	The Board of Education Tuesday night voted to lower the tax rate 12 cents per $100 valuation.
Support for lead	The new rate is $1.18 per $100 valuation. That means that if your property is assessed at $300,000, your school tax will be $3,540 next year.
Summary of other action	The board also approved a budget that is $150,000 less than last year's, instructed the superintendent to cut the staff by 25 and approved a set of rules governing student conduct.

Notice that the lead is followed by a paragraph that supports and enlarges upon the information in it before the summary paragraph appears. Whether you need a support paragraph before summarizing other action depends on how complete you are able to make the lead.

TIPS

Checklist for Assembling the Rest of the Inverted Pyramid

» Introduce additional important information you were not able to include in the lead.

» If possible, indicate the significance or "so what" factor.

» Elaborate on the information presented in the lead.

» Continue introducing new information in the order in which you have ranked it by importance.

» Develop the ideas in the same order in which you have introduced them.

» Generally, use only one new idea in each paragraph.

In every multiple-element story, the first two or three paragraphs determine the order of the rest of the story. To ensure the coherence of your story, you must describe the elements in the order in which you introduce them.

WRITING A STORY ACROSS MEDIA PLATFORMS

The inverted pyramid can serve you throughout the news reporting and writing process, from tweets to online updates. Most breaking news stories are first tweeted and then put on the Web before they are printed in a newspaper or broadcast on television. In fact, the story may never even be printed or broadcast.

The story in the annotated model "The Classic Inverted Pyramid Story" on page 188 appeared in print. Let's follow its progress from the first tweet to its final form.

Tweeting Breaking News

If you can write a lead, you can write a tweet. The limitation of 140 characters is not much of a problem for journalists. The lead on the accident story is only 95 characters. The difference between writing a lead and writing a tweet is that the journalist often does not know as many details when tweeting. A journalist at the scene of an accident might send this tweet:

> EMT crews are working 4-car accident on I-70 near Stadium Blvd. Exit Missouri 41 to avoid traffic backup.

After the reporter has had a chance to talk to an officer at the scene, she sends the next tweet:

> Police: 4 injured in accident on I-70 near Stadium Blvd. No IDs yet. Exit Missouri 41 to avoid traffic backup both directions.

Initial Online Story

When the reporter is able to get more information, she can post the first blast for online and mobile devices:

> Two people were killed and two others were injured today in a four-car accident on I-70 near Stadium Boulevard, Springfield police said.
>
> Names of the victims were being withheld pending notification of relatives. All four were state residents.
>
> The two injured were taken to Springfield Hospital.
>
> Authorities said a westbound Toyota pickup truck swerved across the median and collided with an Oldsmobile in the eastbound lane.

ANNOTATED MODEL   The Classic Inverted Pyramid Story

The lead identifies the "what," "where" and "when." The "so what" is that people were killed.

The second paragraph provides details to support the lead and answers "who."

This paragraph shows impact beyond deaths and injuries.

A four-vehicle accident on eastbound I-70 near Stadium Boulevard ended in two deaths on Sunday.

Barbara Jones, 41, of St. Louis died at the scene of the accident, and Juanita Doolan, 73, of St. Joseph died at University Hospital, according to a release from Springfield police. Two other people, William Doolan, 73, of St. Joseph and Theodore Amelung, 43, of Manchester, Mo., were injured in the accident.

Both lanes of traffic were closed on the eastbound side and limited to one lane on the westbound side as rescue workers cleared the scene.

Authorities said a westbound late-model Ford Taurus driven by Lan Wang of Springfield was traveling in the right lane, developed a tire problem and swerved into the passing lane. A Toyota pickup truck in the passing lane, driven by Jones, was forced over the grassy median along with the Taurus. The two vehicles entered eastbound traffic where the truck struck an Oldsmobile Delta 88, driven by Juanita Doolan, head on.

Wang and the one passenger in his car, Kenneth Kuo, 58, of Springfield, were not injured.

John Paul, a tractor-trailer driver on his way to Tennessee, said he had to swerve to miss the accident.

"I saw the red truck come across the median and hit the blue car," Paul said. "I just pulled over on the median and called 911."

Jones, who was wearing a seat belt, died at the scene, Officer Stan Williams said. Amelung, a passenger who had been in the truck, was out of the vehicle when authorities arrived, but it was unknown whether he was thrown from the truck or was pulled out by someone else, Williams said.

No charges have been filed, but the investigation continues.

The "how" is less important than the "what," "where" and "when," so it appears later in the story.

An eyewitness account adds sensory details that make the scene more vivid.

What's next? This would be higher if the driver, rather than a tire, appeared to be the cause of the accident.

Note how this story, typical of the inverted pyramid structure, delivers the most important news in the lead and provides less essential details toward the end. It also reflects more complete reporting than an earlier Web version.

Full Story with Ongoing Updates

The next version, shown in the annotated model above, would appear both in print and on the Web. Most publications post the story on the Web immediately, even before the newspaper is printed or the news report is aired. The next day, the reporter is able to update the Web version:

Two people injured in a four-car accident Sunday were released from Springfield Hospital today. The accident claimed the lives of two others.

William Doolan, 73, of St. Joseph, and Theodore
Amelung, 43, of Manchester, were released. Barbara
Jones, 41, of St. Louis, and Juanita Doolan, 73, of St.
Joseph, died as a result of the collision.

This new lead would replace the first three paragraphs of the existing story. In all versions for all platforms, it is essential to answer and rank the questions that are basic to any inverted pyramid story.

CHECKING ACCURACY AND ATTRIBUTIONS

All of us can improve our accuracy. Some improvement comes with experience, but most of the errors journalists make involve routine facts. In Chapter 4, you learned the importance of accurately capturing the words that you quote. Here are additional procedures you should use to produce more accurate stories.

These four habits will help you become more accurate:

1. **Go over your notes at the end of every interview.** Read back the quotes and the facts as you have written them down. Don't assume anything. As you read earlier in the chapter, if someone tells you his name is Smith, ask him how to spell it.

2. **Carefully check your story against your notes and the documents you have collected to be certain you didn't introduce any errors while writing.** We all make typing errors. We make errors because of background noise and commotion. If you recognize that you are not infallible, you will be a more accurate journalist.

3. **When sources give you facts, check them if possible.** During an interview, the mayor may tell you that the city has 50 police officers. Check with the police department. The mayor may have the number wrong.

4. **Do a prepublication check.** Some journalists object to prepublication checks because they believe it gives the source too much opportunity to argue over what they will print. Some are afraid sources may approach other media to get their version of the story out even before publication, but those situations are rare.

> Selecting the quotes isn't so hard; it's presenting them that causes the trouble. And the worst place to present them is at the beginning. Quote leads deserve their terrible reputation. Yet they still appear regularly in both print and broadcast journalism.
>
> "We can make three generalizations about quote leads. They're easy, lazy, and lousy. They have no context. The readers don't know who's speaking, why, or why it matters. Without context, even the best quotations are wasted."
>
> —Paula LaRocque, former assistant managing editor, *The Dallas Morning News*

In a study published in the *Newspaper Research Journal*, researcher Duane Stoltzfus found that more newspapers than formerly believed permitted their reporters to check stories or portions of stories with sources before publication. In all cases, sources are told that they are being asked to check the accuracy of the information. No journalist should cede authority for decisions about what goes in and what does not. But no journalist should be afraid to take every step possible to ensure accuracy. Some read back quotes; some read back facts gathered from that source. Some even describe information obtained from other sources. *USA Today*, among many other newspapers, permits its reporters to decide whether to check with sources before publication.

If your publication permits prepublication checks, you will do yourself and your profession a favor by performing them. Verify everything you intend to publish or broadcast. In the online world, where speed is king, verification often is sacrificed in the rush to be first. But being first and wrong is never right, as bloggers will tell you. In an effort to be transparent, some news sites put a note on stories that have been corrected.

SUGGESTED READINGS

Brooks, Brian S., James L. Pinson and Jean Gaddy Wilson. *Working with Words: A Handbook for Media Writers and Editors.* 8th ed. New York: Bedford/St. Martin's, 2013. This must-have book provides excellent coverage of grammar and word usage and has a strong chapter on "isms."

Gillman, Timothy. "The Problem of Long Leads in News and Sports Stories." *Newspaper Research Journal* (Fall 1994): 29–39. The researcher found that sentences in leads were longer than sentences in the rest of the story.

Kennedy, George. "Newspaper Accuracy: A New Approach." *Newspaper Research Journal* (Winter 1994): 55–61. The author suggests that journalists do prepublication accuracy checks with proper safeguards in place.

Maier, Scott R. "Accuracy Matters: A Cross-Market Assessment of Newspaper Error and Credibility." *Journalism and Mass Communications Quarterly* (Autumn 2005): 533–51. This study documents the error rates of journalists and the impact on credibility.

Stoltzfus, Duane. "Partial Pre-publication Review Gaining Favor at Newspapers." *Newspaper Research Journal* (Fall 2006): 23–37. The researcher surveyed the 50 largest newspapers to determine their policies toward prepublication review and found that the trend is to permit it.

SUGGESTED WEBSITES

www.poynter.org/category/latest-news/regret-the-error
Regret the Error, housed on the Poynter.org website, chronicles errors made in all media. It is valuable in that it shows that even professional reporters are fallible.

www.stateofthemedia.org
The Pew Research Center's Project for Excellence in Journalism produces an annual "State of the News Media" report that examines journalistic trends and economic trends.

www.public.wsu.edu/~brians/errors/index.html
Paul Brians, a professor of English at Washington State University, will answer your questions about the English language.

EXERCISES

1. **Team project.** Your professor will divide the class into teams. Read *The Widget Effect, 2009,* a study by the New Teacher Project, which is an organization founded by teachers in 1997 "to address the growing issues of teacher shortages and teacher quality throughout the country." The study reports that teachers are not interchangeable widgets. It can be downloaded at www.widgeteffect.org/downloads/TheWidgetEffect.pdf.

   As you read, annotate your copy of the study with questions and responses, including possible story ideas. Collaborate with your team members to choose four story ideas prompted by the study. Each team member should write a lead for one story idea. As a group, edit the leads to meet the requirements of an inverted pyramid lead. Your teacher may choose to have you report on the best story idea.

2. Identify the who, what, where, when, why and how, if they are present, in the following lead:

> The United Jewish Appeal is sponsoring its first-ever walkathon this morning in Springfield to raise money for the Soup Kitchen, a place where the hungry can eat free.

3. Here are four versions of the same lead. Which version answers more of the six questions basic to all stories? Which questions does it answer?

   a. What began 12 years ago with a federal staff investigation and led to hearings and a court fight culminates today with a Federal Trade Commission rule to prevent funeral home rip-offs.
   b. The nation's funeral home directors are required to offer detailed cost statements starting today, a service they say they are now ready to provide despite nearly a dozen years of debate over the idea.
   c. A new disclosure law going into effect today will make it easier for consumers to determine the cost of a funeral.
   d. Twelve years after first being proposed, a federal regulation goes into effect today to require funeral homes to provide an itemized list of services and materials they offer, along with the cost of each item, before a person agrees to any arrangements.

4. Rewrite two of the leads in exercise 3 as "you" leads. Which are better, the third-person or second-person leads? Why are they better?

5. From the following facts, write a tweet of 140 characters or fewer that you could send to tell the story and promote it for a website.

   Who: A nuclear weapon with a yield equivalent to 150,000 tons of TNT

   What: Detonated

   Where: 40 miles from a meeting of pacifists and 2,000 feet beneath the surface of Pahute Mesa in the Nevada desert

   When: Tuesday

   Why: To test the weapon

   How: Not applicable

   Other information: Department of Energy officials are the source; 450 physicians and peace activists were gathered to protest continued nuclear testing by the U.S.

6. **Journalism blog.** Collect three leads from different Internet news sites. Write a blog post in which you identify each type of lead used and determine what questions each lead answers and what questions it does not. Give your opinion of the effectiveness of each lead. Then review the blog post of at least one other classmate and post a comment in response.

7. From the following facts, write the first two paragraphs of a news article.

   Who: 40 passengers

   What: Evacuated from a Northwest Airlines jet, Flight 428

   Where: At the LaCrosse, Wis., Municipal Airport

   When: Monday following a flight from Minneapolis to LaCrosse

   Why: A landing tower employee spotted smoke near the wheels.

   How: Not applicable

   Other information: There was no fire or injuries; the smoke was caused by hydraulic fluids leaking onto hot landing brakes, according to Bob Gibbons, a Northwest spokesman.

8. Describe picture and information-graphic possibilities for the story in exercise 5.

9. Collect six leads from newspapers. Determine which basic questions are answered and which are not. Identify the kind of lead used.

10

Writing to Be Read

WHETHER YOU ARE WRITING a newspaper story, a television script, a news release or an article for a website, a good story told well is important to readers and viewers and to the financial success of your company. Many journalists are getting the message. When Hurricane Sandy bore down on the East Coast, *The (Newark, N.J.) Star-Ledger* positioned several reporters to observe the impact of the storm. They filed frequent reports, and just five days after the storm left, Amy Ellis Nutt combined her work with that of several other reporters to create a narrative report on the storm, starting 48 hours before it hit (see Figure 10.1). Until then, the news had been in pieces. These excerpts show you the big story:

In this chapter
you will learn:

1. How the skills of reporting make good writing possible.

2. How to add accurate, specific details.

3. How to write a coherent story.

4. How to write with conciseness and simplicity.

5. How to use correct and effective language.

6. How to use four narrative writing techniques: scenes, dialogue, anecdotes and foreshadowing.

The forecast has hovered like a Sword of Damocles over the state for days. Plenty of time to get ready—shore up windows, move possessions to second floors, purchase batteries and water. That's what New Jersey did last year, right before Irene hit. But this is different—a hurricane buddying with a nor'easter. Almost everyone believes the damage will be substantial and the pain, perhaps unprecedented. But few are prepared for the meteorological time bomb set to explode over New Jersey's coast, or the suddenness of a tidal surge that in the time it takes to watch a movie, will forever change the geography of the state. . . .

In Seaside Heights, Police Chief Thomas J. Boyd studies the forecast on the computer in his office, zeroing in on the radar predicting the storm's path.

"Follow the map, follow the map," he repeats to himself.

At this moment, with Sandy still only a swirl of color on a meteorologist's computer screen, few up and down New Jersey's 127-mile-long shore could mistake the Atlantic for a monster.

Twenty-four hours later, they will.

Although meteorologists record the first tropical storm-force winds in Cape May at 7 a.m. Sunday, by early afternoon, with Sandy still moving slowly north, there remains a slim possibility it still might skirt New Jersey and turn eastward. That's what Chief Boyd is counting on. But that door out to the east, away from land, is rapidly closing. . . .

When Chief Boyd sees the hurricane make an abrupt left-hand turn on the computer screen, he says to himself, "We're screwed." Immediately he begins calling in more officers and making arrangements to pull cruisers off the island—cars will be useless, and worse, 1-ton missiles in a flood.

The unthinkable is now the inevitable. A storm of historic proportions and intensity is rushing headlong toward one of the most densely populated coastlines in the world. Sixty-five million Americans, 9 million of them in New Jersey, are in her path. And those remaining on the barrier islands are in the bull's-eye.

Readers don't see this type of writing as often as they should, but when they do, they appreciate it. Readers on the website commented: "A fantastic piece of journalism"; "Superbly written"; "A vivid slice of the mayhem we all experienced in so many forms last week."

Stories help people, even those caught in the midst of a storm, make sense of events. Nutt expertly used chronology, built tension, created scenes and reached a resolution. That's the work of a narrative writer.

Writing to inform and entertain is as important for journalists as it is for novelists. Just because newspapers and broadcast reports are finished and gone in a day doesn't mean that we should accept a lower level of skill. Comparing the temporal nature of newspapers to a beach, syndicated columnist James Kilpatrick challenged writers: "If we write upon the sand, let us write as well as we can upon the sand before the waves come in."

If Kilpatrick's challenge to your pride is not enough, then the demands of readers and listeners—and of the editors and news directors who are hiring—should be. Editors are looking for those unusual people who can combine reporting and writing

48 hours: Before, during, and after Hurricane Sandy in Seaside Heights and Cape May

11 comments

By **Amy Ellis Nutt/The Star-Ledger**
on November 04, 2012 at 8:07 AM, updated November 09, 2012 at 4:24 PM

 Tweet 98   Like 337 Share 7   Foursquare   Email

Enlarge   Star-Ledger Staff
Tom Kowal, left, and Joe Rulli, owners of Joeys Pizza and Pasta, board up their restaurant on Long Beach Blvd as Hurricane Sandy makes its way toward Long Beach Island. They were prepared with their orange

Ancient mariners believed the tides were the angry breathing of a sea creature chained to the ocean floor.

In Cape May on Sunday morning, Oct. 28, with Hurricane Sandy still 300 miles from shore, the tides, instead, beckon surfers, riding wind-driven swells off the Ocean Street beach.

Just inland, residents and business owners take the usual precautions against an impending storm. At the Congress Hall, where Abraham Lincoln once stayed, workers

FIGURE 10.1

After reporting the news of Hurricane Sandy as it happened, reporter Amy Ellis Nutt went back and created a narrative story detailing the impact of the storm. After getting information in fragments, readers could now see the entire story in context.

talents. The journalist whose prose jerks around the page like a mouse trapped in a room with a cat has no future in the business. The American Society of News Editors has made the improvement of writing one of its principal long-range goals. Each year, it honors the reporting and writing of journalists in several categories. Some of them go on to win Pulitzer Prizes. Many well-known writers—among them Daniel Defoe, Mark Twain, Stephen Crane, Ernest Hemingway and Alex Haley—began their careers as journalists. At newspapers around the country today, small but growing numbers of journalists are producing literature daily as they deal with everything from traffic accidents to affairs of state. If you have respect for the language, an artist's imagination and the dedication to learn how to combine them, you, too, may produce literature.

We should all attempt to bring quality writing, wit and knowledge to our work. If we succeed, our work will be not only informative but also enjoyable, not only educational but also entertaining, and not only bought but also read.

GOOD WRITING BEGINS WITH GOOD REPORTING

It was not only Nutt who rode out the storm; nine colleagues were reporting simultaneously throughout the region. Her story, which opened this chapter, is a testament to the power of reporting and writing. (See the link to the full story at the end of this chapter.) Without the proper use of participant accounts, personal observation and detail, the best writer's stories land with a thud. Good writing begins with good reporting. You can settle for a dry police report, or you can go to the scene and gather details. In Chapter 9 we introduced you to this lead:

> Two people died Thursday when a backhoe fell off a truck's flatbed and sliced the top off an oncoming vehicle near Fairchild Air Force Base.

Now let's look at some of the detail writer Alison Boggs of *The (Spokane, Wash.) Spokesman-Review* collected by being there:

> The top of the Suburban, from about hood height, was shorn off by the backhoe's bucket. The front seats were forced backward, and the dashboard, roof and steering wheel were torn off.
>
> Parts of the car lay in a heap of crumpled metal and glass under the overpass. The silver Suburban was identifiable only by a 1983 owner's manual lying in the dirt nearby.
>
> Both victims wore seat belts, but in this case, that was irrelevant, (Sgt. Jeff) Sale said. Both suffered severe head injuries.
>
> Sleeping bags, a Coleman cooler and fishing equipment scattered on the highway and in the back of the Suburban suggested a camping trip. Unopened cans of Pepsi were jammed behind the front seat of the car.

Notice that the writer built every sentence on concrete detail. Good reporting makes good writing possible.

ON THE JOB
Setting the Hook in the Opening

Justin Heckert, who lives in Indianapolis and writes for national magazines such as *Sports Illustrated* and *Esquire*, believes one of the most important aspects of writing is the first few sentences of a story:

> The experience of reading and being hooked can be because of word play, or rhythm, or a particular style or device. I can recite the first sentences to some of my favorite stories. That's just how they stick with me.
>
> "The madness of an autumn prairie cold front coming through." That's Jonathan Franzen. "It was a pleasure to burn. It was a special pleasure to see things eaten, to see things blackened and changed." That's Ray Bradbury. "Aye, that face. There's a story about that face, you know. About what he was willing to do with it." That's Tom Junod. "Sometimes the silence gets inside of you." That's Gary Smith. "They don't count calories at Fausto's Fried Chicken." That's Wright Thompson. These books/stories are nowhere near me as I write this, but I can remember those sentences, and I know I got them right.

This idea has been a huge part of my own writing. I've done it, or tried to, in pretty much every single story I've ever written, be it a success or failure. A recent example: In 2009, I reported and wrote a story for *Men's Journal*. I was sitting on top of amazing material. I could've, honestly, probably just written it out like I was talking to a third grader, and it still would've been an interesting story. But after I talked to my editor and sat down to write it, I sweated forever about how to begin. I sat on the porch and thought about it. I thought about it driving the car. I thought about how to begin while I was watching a football game, before I was going to bed.

The story was about two people who had been pulled out to the sea and had treaded water for hours. The ocean has been written about more than anything since the beginning of time. It was hard to try and think of something new to say about it, to tie it in to the experience of this guy and his son, victims of the ocean, even though they didn't die. How this situation resolved itself is as esoteric as the nature of writing itself: It just came to me.

"The ocean at night is a terrible dream. There is nothing beyond the water except the profound discouragement of the sky, every black wave another singular misfortune." I had stared at the ocean for hours, had thought about how it affected the characters of the story, thought about everything they said about it. I knew it when the words appeared — they came to me the way ideas come to people, inexplicably. I think those are two good sentences. So did my editor. So have a lot of other people who read it. They were that important to me because I wanted them to hook the readers and then keep them with me.

ACCURATE, SPECIFIC DETAILS

Good writing is accurate when it is built on concrete details. When you use language to communicate those details precisely, you inform and entertain your readers.

Use Concrete Examples

For lawyers, the devil might be in the details, but for writers, clarity is in the details. Echoing your bureaucratic sources, you can write of infrastructures or facilities or learning pods. But try actually touching any of these. By contrast, you ride on a highway, sit in an arena and learn in a reading group.

Be specific. You might write that the speaker is big, but compared to what? Abstractions are ambiguous. To someone who is 6 feet tall, someone big might be 6 feet 6 inches tall. To someone who is 5 feet 2 inches tall, 6 feet is huge.

Note how the concrete details in the following lead from *The Boston Globe* about an employee who killed five co-workers make the story more interesting:

> He was an accountant who had a chip on his shoulder and a bayonet on his kitchen table. He lived with his parents across from a llama farm in a small beige house with a sign informing visitors: "Trespassers will be shot; survivors will be shot again."
>
> As dawn broke over Ledyard yesterday, Matthew Beck, 35, left his folks' home—across town from the casino—got in his car, and drove 1½ hours to his job at Connecticut Lottery headquarters. At some point, he strapped a bandolier of bullets across his chest, over his gray pin-striped shirt but concealed by a brown leather jacket. He carried a 9mm pistol and a knife.

Almost every sentence contains specific, concrete detail: "accountant," "bayonet," "across from a llama farm," and so on.

Nutt, whose story opens this chapter, packed specific, concrete details into her story to create this scene describing a harrowing ride during Hurricane Sandy:

> Boyd is in his truck with Fire Chief James Samarelli, who is at the wheel. They turn right onto Sampson Avenue and are nearly hit by a wooden lifeguard boat slicing through the floodwater. A wall of water is headed directly for them, bringing a second lifeguard boat. Samarelli jerks the truck to the right. A large piece of the boardwalk, ripped away by the waves, slams into the front of the flatbed truck. Boyd looks down at his suddenly cold feet. Seawater is rushing into the cab and a 6-foot-tall swell lifts the truck and begins pushing it sideways, into a telephone pole.

To be concrete, you must have facts. And you must describe those facts in a way that makes readers able to touch, feel or smell them. Lazy reporters create puffballs. Poke their stories, and you'll stick your finger clear through them. Instead of saying "some council members," say "five council members." Instead of writing that a business is "downsizing," report that 150 workers will lose their jobs. Avoid abstractions; covet concrete details.

Show, Don't Just Tell

As you chauffeur the reader through the scenes in your story, you can drive down the road or over the green-laced, rolling hills of Kentucky. You can report that a car hit a skunk, or you can convey the nauseating smell. A word here, a phrase there, and you can hear the plane ripping the tin roof off a house, smell the acrid stench of burning tires, feel the boxing glove's leather rasp against the skin. Good writing appeals to one or more of our five senses: sight, hearing, smell, taste and touch.

Reporting for *The Oregonian*, Steve Duin talked to voters standing in the rain while waiting to vote. He observed: "They arrived in wool hats and sweatpants, in Chuck Taylors and hospital scrubs, with borrowed umbrellas and voter guides and 18-month-olds in their arms."

> " There's a time to sow and a time to reap, but there's never a time for seasonal agricultural activities. "
> —Jack Cappon, Associated Press senior writer and writing coach

In addition to the years of anecdotal experience journalists have, there is also statistical support for the common advice to show rather than just tell. For instance, researchers constructed 10 sentences telling information and 10 showing information. College students were divided into two groups and asked to read one of the groups of sentences. Then they were asked to rate the sentences on such qualities as interesting-dull, clear-unclear and engaging-unengaging. The researchers concluded, "The experiment found strong evidence that, as many experts have implied, show sentences are seen as more interesting and engaging than tell sentences."

Writer Walt Harrington could simply have told readers that detective V.I. Smith picked up his notebook to leave on a call, but instead he showed us the detective's preparation:

> "Well, here we go," says V.I., in his smooth, lyrical baritone as he palms a radio, unconsciously pats his right breast coat pocket for evidence of his ID wallet, pats his left breast coat pocket for evidence of his notebook and heads out the door in his athlete's saunter, a stylized and liquid stroll, a modern cakewalk.

Readers can see and hear V.I. because the writer is showing, not telling.

A student writer used her sense of touch to gather information: "After 40 years of working outside, his skin is as leathery as an alligator's." Did she actually touch the farmer? "Yes," she says. "I kept looking at his skin. Finally, even though I was embarrassed, I asked him if I could touch his face. He laughed. 'You can tell I don't use no fancy lotions, can't you?'"

The writing is better because the reporters didn't just ask questions and record answers. They looked; they listened; they touched. Readers can see and feel along with the reporters.

Use Words Precisely

Words should mean exactly what you intend them to mean. You should never use "uninterested" when you mean "disinterested." Nor should you use "allude" for "refer," "presume" for "assume," "endeavor" for "try," "fewer" for "less," "farther" for "further." If you report that fire destroyed a house, you mean the home needs rebuilding, not repair. If you say firefighters donned oxygen masks to enter a burning building, you are either impugning their intelligence or revealing your ignorance. (Oxygen is dangerous around fire; firefighters use air tanks.) You can make the mayor "say," "declare," "claim" or "growl"—but only one is accurate.

COHERENCE

When you write coherently, your writing is understandable. Coherence is built by following a logical order, by matching the content to the appropriate sentence structure, by using the correct coordinating conjunctions and by guiding readers with transitions.

Decide on the Order of Elements

Chronology is the most easily understood of story structures. You start at the beginning and go to the end. The story that opens this chapter begins 48 hours before the storm hits and continues until the storm passes and the "sun makes a welcome appearance." (For more on story structure, see Chapter 11.) Journalists, however, often don't have the luxury of readers' time or publication space to use chronology. That's why it is important to outline a story, even if your outline merely lists the three or four points you expect to make. Your outline is your map. If you know where you are going, your readers will be able to follow.

Here's a list you might make about what happened at a city council meeting:

1. Approved one-way streets.
2. Raised parking fines.
3. Bought snowplows.
4. Agreed to study downtown parking facilities.
5. Hired audit firm.

To outline the story, first you rank the actions in order of importance. Then you decide whether to focus on one element or to write a summary lead or a multiple-element lead. (See Chapter 9 for more on leads.) Once you have done that, you add detail to your outline:

1. Single-element lead: one-way streets
2. Summary of other actions
   a. Parking fines
   b. Snowplows
   c. Parking study
   d. City audit
3. Support for lead
   a. The vote
   b. Jones quote
   c. Opposition
4. Support for other actions (in order introduced in second paragraph)
   a. Parking fines
      (i) Amount; (ii) reason; (iii) no opposition
   b. Snowplows
      (i) Cost; (ii) when delivered

TIPS

Writing a Coherent Story

» Create logical story structures.

» Express the relationship between ideas properly.

» Use language precisely.

» Use transitions.

c. Parking study
   (i) Define problem; (ii) when study is due; (iii) who will do it; (iv) Dehaven quote; (v) Chamber of Commerce request
d. City audit
   (i) Who will do it; (ii) cost; (iii) when due

Although outlining might take five minutes, it will save you much more time. The outline also creates a structure that flows logically from one idea to the next. Here's how you could start the story outlined above:

> The Springfield City Council voted Tuesday to make four streets in the downtown area one-way.
>
> The council also raised parking fines to $5, voted to buy two snowplows, ordered a study of downtown parking facilities and hired a firm to audit the city.
>
> Effective March 1, the four streets that will be one-way are . . .

Select the Proper Sentence Structure

Within each sentence, you must express the proper relationships between ideas. One way to do this is to think about your sentence structure. Simple sentences express one idea. Compound sentences express two or more ideas of equal importance. Complex sentences subordinate one idea to another. Here are some examples.

Simple   The mayor scolded the council.

Compound   The mayor scolded the council, and she insisted on a vote.

Compound sentences equate two or more ideas without commenting on them. Complex sentences allow you to show sequence and cause and effect, among other things:

Complex   After the mayor scolded the council, she insisted on a vote. (Shows sequence.)

Complex   Because the mayor was angry, she insisted on a vote. (Shows cause and effect.)

Both sentences are correct, but the meaning of each is slightly different.

Use the Precise Conjunction

Subordinating conjunctions—such as "if," "since," "while," "after" and "until"—each carry a different and precise meaning. Choose the subordinating conjunction that expresses the idea you want.

Coordinating conjunctions ("and," "or," "but," "for," "nor," "so," "yet") also require careful selection. Observe how the meaning changes with the conjunction in these examples:

> The mayor insisted that the council vote, and the members ignored her.

> The mayor insisted that the council vote, but the members ignored her.

The second example is more coherent because it expresses the council members' reaction more logically.

Use Transitions

Transitions are words, phrases, sentences or paragraphs that show the logical progression of the story structure and the ideas within the structure. Transitions are road signs directing readers through a story. The annotated model "Using Transitions" (see page 202) shows how transitions can be used in a story.

The reference to memory in the next example directs us from the first to the second paragraph:

> Mr. and Mrs. Lester Einbender are using their memory to project life as it might have been.
> *That memory* centers around a son named Michael, a rheumatic disease called lupus and a desire to honor one while conquering the other.

The use of the word "That" at the beginning of the second paragraph is subtle, but its impact is dramatic. If you wrote "A memory," you would not link the reader to the memory already mentioned. If you wrote "The memory," you would be more specific, but by writing "That memory," you point directly to the memory mentioned in the preceding paragraph. Because "a" is good only for general references, "a" is called an *indefinite modifier*. Because "the" is more specific, "the" is called a *definite modifier*. Because "that" is most specific, it is a *demonstrative adjective*; it demonstrates precisely the word or phrase to which you are referring when you couple it with the noun ("memory"). When you move from indefinite to definite modifier and then to demonstrative adjective, you climb the ladder of coherence.

> " But I obsess during writing to the point where I can lose sleep over the right word. "
>
> —Madeleine Blais, writer

Transitions help you achieve coherence, the logical connection of ideas. They guide you from one sentence to the next, from one paragraph to the next. Writers unfamiliar with transitions merely stack paragraphs, like pieces of wood, atop one another. Transitions keep the story, if not the woodpile, from falling apart.

ANNOTATED MODEL   Using Transitions

The first four paragraphs focus on Billman, which makes the story easy to follow. Billman's name or a pronoun links the paragraphs.

On a Monday afternoon, Dr. Glenn Billman pulled back from the autopsy he was performing on a dead girl and stared at the sight before him.

In his seven years at Children's Hospital, he had never seen anything like it. The girl's colon was severely hemorrhaged, ravaged by bacteria that normally lived in a cow's intestine.

Puzzled and quietly alarmed, Billman notified local health officials. It was the first indication that the lethal strain of bacteria E. coli 0157:H7 was on the loose.

"But" is a transition that shows the writer is introducing another angle.

But Billman didn't make his discovery at Children's Hospital in Seattle. He made it at Children's Hospital in San Diego, and he made it three weeks before the E. coli epidemic struck the Northwest, killing three children and sickening about 500 people.

In December, San Diego was hit by a small E. coli outbreak that killed the 6-year-old girl and made at least seven other people sick.

Time reference used as a transition: "It is now . . ." links the Northwest outbreak to the earlier San Diego outbreak ("In December . . .").

It is now being linked to the Seattle outbreak, but in its early stages, San Diego health officials were slow to recognize the crisis, and they have been sharply criticized for failing to notify the public about the E. coli death and illnesses.

"I really believe we need to be safe and not sorry, and the fact is, a girl died in San Diego," said San Diego County Supervisor Dianne Jacob. "I was outraged. The only way I found out was by reading it in the newspaper" after the Northwest outbreak.

Time references ("after the Northwest outbreak" and "When the first . . .") link these paragraphs.

When the first Washington cases were reported in mid-January, authorities there immediately queried neighboring states, including California, but were not told about the E. coli death of the San Diego girl. That information would have alerted them about the bacteria's severity and might have pointed them sooner to the source of the contamination.

The phrase "Like the patients here" links this paragraph to the preceding one.

Like the patients here, the San Diego girl had eaten a hamburger at a Jack in the Box restaurant days before she got sick and died. The seven other E. coli patients had all eaten hamburgers at fast-food restaurants, among them Jack in the Box.

The word "that" is a demonstrative adjective that points to the preceding paragraph.

That information was available in early January, according to Dr. Michele Ginsberg, San Diego County epidemiologist. She would not say how many of the seven patients had eaten at Jack in the Box.

"A variety of restaurants were mentioned," she said. "Naming any one of them would create public reaction and perhaps avoidance of those restaurants."

"That" again creates a transition from the preceding paragraph.

That reticence angers Jacob, the San Diego County supervisor. "I had a follow-up meeting with county health officials, and I have to tell you, very honestly, I was not pleased with their attitude," she said. . . .

Transitions, like road signs, help readers understand where they have been and where they are going.

Repeating a word or phrase also helps to keep the story from falling apart. In the preceding example, the writer used a demonstrative adjective and repeated a word. (Other demonstrative adjectives are "this," "these" and "those.")

Parallelism, repetition of a word or grammatical form, is another way to guide readers through a story. Writers frequently use parallelism to achieve coherence.

Writing about the complicated subject of nuclear-waste disposal in America, Donald Barlett and James Steele, then of *The Philadelphia Inquirer*, relied on parallelism for coherence and emphasis. Notice the parallel use of "They said . . ." to start sentences—and the repeated variations of "It cannot."

This assessment may prove overly optimistic. For perhaps in no other area of modern technology have so many experts in the government, industry and science been so wrong so many times over so many years as have those involved in radioactive waste.

They said, repeatedly, that radioactive waste could be handled like any other industrial refuse. It cannot.

They said that science had most of the answers, and was on the verge of getting the few it did not have, for dealing with radioactive waste permanently. It did not, and it does not.

They said that some of it could be buried in the ground, like garbage in a landfill, and that it would pose no health hazard because it would never move. It moved.

They said that liquid radioactive waste could be put in storage tanks, and that rigorous safety systems would immediately detect any leaks. The tanks leaked for weeks and no one noticed.

Barlett and Steele's use of parallelism sets up the story. In the following case, the writer repeated the word "waiting" for emphasis:

Realized or not, we live in constant anticipation. We're always waiting. Waiting to drive. Waiting to turn 21. Waiting for winter break. Waiting to graduate. Waiting for a significant other to come along.

Chronology and references to time provide other ways to tie a story together. Words and phrases such as "now," "since then" and "two days later" are invaluable in helping readers understand where they have been and where they are going. Chronology is important in everything from reports of automobile accidents (which car entered the intersection first?) to recaps of events that occurred over months or even hours, as in the Hurricane Sandy story at the beginning of this chapter.

CONCISENESS AND SIMPLICITY

Conciseness is a virtue, particularly in newspapers and broadcasting where space and time constraints are severe—as well as on Twitter and Facebook feeds. However, even when you write longer online stories, you have to respect readers' time. No one has unlimited time or attention to give you.

Be Concise

Being concise means saying what you need to say in as few words as possible. Some subjects require more details than others. Here are four ways to shorten your stories. (See also the annotated model "Editing for Conciseness" on page 205.)

1. **Eliminate some subject areas.** Always ask yourself whether all of the subjects need to be included. No doubt, your editor will have a more dispassionate view of what's needed than you will.
2. **Eliminate redundancies.** One way to achieve conciseness is to rid your sentences of cabooses, unneeded words or phrases that hitch themselves, like barnacles, onto other words. Delete the barnacles in italics: remand *back*; gather *together*; consensus *of opinion*; *totally* destroyed; *excess* verbiage; open *up*; fall *down*; my *own personal* favorite; strangled *to death*.
3. **Challenge intensive and qualifying adverbs.** Your job is to select the right word so you don't need two or more. Instead of "really unhappy," perhaps you mean "sad." Instead of "very cold," perhaps you mean "frigid." "Really" and "very" are examples of intensive adverbs. When you say "almost there," you are using a qualifying adverb. You might be near, or you might be a mile away. Be specific.
4. **Train yourself to value brevity.** Some of the most notable writing in history is brief: Lincoln's Gettysburg Address contains 272 words; the Ten Commandments, 297; and the American Declaration of Independence, 300.

You will use fewer words when you figure out what you want to say and then express it positively. Enter the following negatively phrased thicket of verbiage at your own risk:

The Missouri Gaming Commission has 30 days to appeal a judge's temporary order reversing the commission's decision not to grant a gaming license to a firm that wanted to dock a riverboat casino in Jefferson City.

The writer is lost in a maze of reversals of negative findings. The lead tries to cover too much territory. Express it in the positive and strip it to its essential information:

The state has 30 days to persuade a judge it should not have to license a firm that wants to open a riverboat casino in Jefferson City.

The writer of this sentence also failed to think clearly:

Amtrak, formally the National Passenger Railroad Corp., was created in 1970 to preserve declining passenger train service.

Does the writer really mean that Amtrak was created to preserve declining passenger train service?

ANNOTATED MODEL Editing for Conciseness

"Currently" is usually redundant because the verb tense implies it.

"With" is unnecessary.

The plural form gets around the wordy "his or her."

"Season" isn't required in either paragraph in this paragraph.

"Strong" and "too" are unnecessary intensifiers.

Bartholow is ~~currently~~ working on other projects, but he ~~has~~ plans to continue ~~with~~ his video game research. ~~In the future~~, he hopes to recruit female subjects—a difficult task because far fewer women than men play violent video games. He's also interested in examining how ~~a person's prior~~ *people's* gaming history affects ~~his or her~~ *their* response to a single exposure to a violent video game.

Pumpkins are everywhere ~~during the fall season~~ *in fall*. They ~~serve as a way to~~ help families and friends ~~to get closer~~ *bond* during the ~~holiday season~~ *holidays*. Whether you're ~~taking a trip~~ *traveling* to the local pumpkin patch ~~to search for the perfect pumpkin~~, or baking ~~up some delicious~~ treats ~~for people to enjoy~~, pumpkins are a ~~strong~~ reminder that comfort isn't ~~too~~ far away.

Change "has plans" to "plans" to strengthen the verb.

"In the future" is already implied in the verb.

No information is lost by eliminating "serve as a way to."

"Traveling" says "taking a trip" in one word.

"Up" is an unnecessary caboose on "baking." Treats are delicious. Whom else do you bake treats for?

To be concise, challenge every word or phrase you write. These examples show how to eliminate 36 of the 127 words. (The replacement words are in italics.)

Keep It Simple

The readers of one newspaper confronted the following one-sentence paragraph:

"Paradoxically, cancer-causing mutations often result from the repair of a cell by error-prone enzymes and not the 'carcinogenic' substance's damage to the cell," Abe Eisenstark, director of biological sciences at the university, said at a meeting of the Ad Hoc Council of Environmental Carcinogenesis Wednesday night at the Cancer Research Center.

> " Short is beautiful. Short and simple is more beautiful. Short, simple and interesting is most beautiful. "
>
> —Don Gibb, educator

If there is a message in those 53 words, it would take a copy editor, a lexicologist and a Nobel Prize–winning scientist to decipher it. The message simply is not clear. Although the sentence is not typical of newspaper writing, it is not unusual either.

The scientist is using the vocabulary of science, which is inappropriate for a general audience. The reporter should say, "I don't understand that exactly. Can you translate it for my readers?" The response may produce an understandable quote, but if it doesn't, paraphrase the statement and check back with your source to be sure you have paraphrased it accurately.

Too much of what is written is mumbo jumbo. For instance:

> Approximately 2 billion tons of sediment from land erosion enters our nation's waters every year. While industrial waste and sewage treatment plants receive a great deal of attention, according to the Department of Agriculture the No. 1 polluter of our waterways is "non-point" pollution.

The writer of that lead contributed some linguistic pollution of his own. The message may have been clear in his mind, but it is not clear in print. Here's another way to approach this story:

> Soil carried into the water by erosion, not industrial waste or sewage from treatment plants, is the No. 1 polluter of U.S. waterways, according to the Department of Agriculture.

One remedy for unclear writing is the short sentence. The following examples introduce the same subject:

> From measurements with high-precision laser beams bounced off reflectors left at three lunar sites by Apollo astronauts, plus one atop an unmanned Soviet lunar vehicle, scientists believe that the moon is still wobbling from a colossal meteorite impact 800 years ago.

> Scientists believe the moon is still wobbling from a colossal meteorite impact 800 years ago.

The writer of the first example drags the reader through some prickly underbrush full of prepositional phrases. The writer of the second has cleared the brush to expose the flowers.

CORRECT AND EFFECTIVE LANGUAGE

Writing to be read is not easy. Reporters become writers by the sweat of their brows. John Kenneth Galbraith, a best-selling author who was able to make economics understandable to the lay reader, commented on the difficulty of writing well. "There are days when the result is so bad that no fewer than five revisions are required," he wrote. "In contrast, when I'm inspired, only four revisions are needed."

Trying the techniques discussed in this chapter is the first step. Mastering them will be the result of repeated practice.

Figures of Speech

Good writers understand how to use literary devices known as figures of speech. Similes and metaphors, two common figures of speech, permit writers to show similarities and contrasts. *Similes* show similarities by comparing one thing to another, often using the word "like" or "as." Describing her roommate's reaction to the news that she was moving, one writer said, "She stared into space for a few moments, scowling, *as if she were squaring large numbers in her head.*" Writing about a high school girls' basketball coach, Madeleine Blais wrote, "At 6 feet 6 inches, Moyer looms over his players. With a thick cap of graying brown hair and bangs that flop down over his forehead, *he resembles a grizzly bear on spindly legs.*"

Metaphor is the first cousin of simile. A simile says one thing is *like* another, but a metaphor says one thing *is* another: "Michael is a lion with gazelle legs." A metaphor is a stronger analogy than a simile. Describing the radio personality and writer Garrison Keillor, a reporter once wrote, "And there he is. A sequoia in a room full of saplings." The metaphor works on two levels. Keillor is tall enough to tower over most others in the room. Because he is known internationally, his work towers over that of others, too.

With similes and metaphors, writers draw word pictures. These techniques turn the pages of a scrapbook of images in each reader's mind.

Careful Word Choice

Freedom in word choice is exhilarating when the result is a well-turned phrase. Here's how one student described the weather in fresh terms: "I rushed off the bus into a downpour of beaming sunlight." Here's Julie Sullivan of *The Spokesman-Review*: "Hand him a soapbox, he'll hand you a homily."

Freedom in word choice is dangerous when it results in nouns masquerading as verbs (*prioritize, impact, maximize*) or jargon masquerading as respectable English (*input, output, throughput*).

Precision, however, means more than knowing the etymology of a word; it means knowing exactly what you want to say. Instead of saying, "The City Council wants to locate the landfill three blocks from downtown," to be precise, you say, "Some members of the City Council . . ." or, better yet, "Five members of the City Council. . . ."

Precision also means using the conditional mood (*could, might, should, would*) when discussing proposals:

| Incorrect | The bill will make it illegal . . . |
| Correct | The bill would make it illegal . . . |

> " The real problem is that misplaced modifiers and similar glitches tend to distract readers. Introduce blunders to an otherwise smoothly flowing story and it's as though a drunk stumbled through a religious procession.
>
> "What's more, while those errors due to carelessness may not permanently damage the language, they can damage a paper's credibility. Botching a small job sows mistrust about the larger enterprise. "
>
> —Jack Cappon, Associated Press senior writer and writing coach

The use of "will" is imprecise because the legislation has not been passed. By using "would," you are saying, "If the legislature passes the bill, it would. . . ."

Bias-Free Language

Even when used innocently, sexist and racist language, besides being offensive and discriminatory, is imprecise. Doctors aren't always "he," nor are nurses always "she." Much of our language assumes people are male unless they are identified as female.

TIPS

Avoiding Carelessness in Word Choice

» Know precisely what you want to say.

» Use the conditional mood ("could," "might," "should," "would") when discussing proposals.

» Choose the correct sentence structure to communicate explicitly what you mean.

Precise writers avoid "policeman" ("police officer"), "ad man" ("advertising representative"), "assemblyman" ("assembly member") and "postman" ("postal worker"). In some situations, you can use the plural to eliminate the need for a gender-specific word: "Doctors treat their patients."

Check *The AP Stylebook* to see whether to identify a person's race or ethnicity. Then try to follow the person's own preference and be as specific as possible: "Asian-American" is acceptable but "Chinese-American" may be preferable. "Black" is acceptable for any nationality, but use "African-American" only for an American black person of African descent.

Some words, perfectly precise when used correctly, are imprecise when used in the wrong context. "Boy" is not interchangeable with "young man," and "girl" is not interchangeable with "young woman." Not all active retired people are "spry," which implies that the writer is surprised to find that the person is active. "Grandmotherly" fails when you describe people in their 40s who are grandmothers. It also fails when you use it indiscriminately. When Nancy Pelosi became the first female speaker of the U.S. House of Representatives, many accounts identified her as a grandmother. While it is true that she's a grandmother, accounts of new male leaders seldom mention that they are grandfathers. Pelosi's wardrobe also became a subject of stories, something seldom found in accounts of male leaders.

"Dumb," as in "deaf and dumb," is imprecise and derogatory. Instead, use "speech-impaired." When the terms are used in tandem, use "hearing-impaired and speech-impaired" for parallelism. Because alcoholism is a disease, use "recovering alcoholic" instead of "reformed alcoholic." "Handicapped" is imprecise; "disabled" is preferred.

The Associated Press recommends "gay" and "lesbian" and sometimes allows "homosexual" but does not permit "queer" and other derogatory terms. AP suggests consulting the National Lesbian and Gay Journalists Association (www.nlgja.org /Toolbox) for background on this issue. The battle over abortion extends to the terms used in news. One side wants to be described as "pro-life"; the other wants to be described as "pro-choice." The Associated Press prescribes the terms "anti-abortion" and "pro-abortion rights" in an attempt to be neutral.

Some dismiss this concern for language as overly zealous political correctness. That attitude implies that we are afraid to tell the truth. What is the truth about ethnic slang? The truth is that many words historically applied to groups of people were created in ignorance or hate or fear. During the world wars, American citizens of German descent were called "krauts" to depersonalize them. Over the years, pejorative terms have been applied to immigrants from Ireland, Poland, China and Africa. We see the same thing happening to more recent immigrants from Latin America, the Caribbean and the Middle East. The adjective "Muslim" is seldom seen or heard in news reports except to modify "terrorists" or "fundamentalists." As writers concerned with precision of the language, we should deal with people, not stereotypes.

Words are powerful. When used negatively, they define cultures, create second-class citizens and reveal stereotypical thinking. They also change the way people think about and treat others. Writers have the freedom to choose precisely the right word. That freedom can be both exhilarating and dangerous.

Correct Grammar and Punctuation

Far too often, grammar and punctuation errors obscure meaning. Consider this example:

> Watching his parents struggle in low-paying jobs, a college education looked desirable to him.

Because the participial phrase ("Watching . . .") is dangling, the sentence seems to mean that the college education did the watching. Write the sentence this way:

> Watching his parents struggle in low-paying jobs, he realized he wanted a college education.

No one who aspires to be a writer will succeed without knowing the rules of grammar. Dangling participles, subject-verb disagreement, pronoun-antecedent disagreement and misplaced modifiers are like enemy troops: They attack sentences and destroy their meaning, as the authors of a survey discovered.

The personnel director of an Inglewood, Calif., aerospace company had to fill out a government survey form that asked, among other things, "How many employees do you have, broken down by sex?" After considering the sentence for a few moments, she wrote, "Liquor is more of a problem with us."

Here are some typical errors and ways to correct them:

Pronoun-antecedent disagreement	Each of the boys brought *their* sleeping bags.
Correct	Each of the boys brought *his* sleeping bag.
Subject-verb disagreement	The *mayor* together with the city council *oppose* collective bargaining by the firefighters.
Correct	The *mayor* together with the city council *opposes* . . .
	The *mayor and city council oppose* . . .
Misplaced modifier	*Despite his size*, the coach said Jones would play forward.
Correct	The coach said that Jones, *despite his size*, would play forward.

Improper punctuation creates ambiguities at best and inaccuracies at worst. For instance:

> Giving birth to Cynthia five years earlier had been difficult for Mrs. Davenport and the two parents decided they were content with the family they had.

TIPS

Avoiding Sexism in Language

» Use a generic term ("flight attendant," "firefighter").

» Participate in the movement to drop feminine endings. (Use "comedian," "hero," "actor" and "poet" for both genders.)

» Make the subject plural. ("Reporters must not reveal their opinions.")

» Drop the gender-specific pronoun and replace it with an article. ("A reporter must not form *a* judgment.")

» Rewrite to eliminate the gender-specific pronoun. ("A reporter must not judge.")

» Write the sentence in the second person. ("You should not form *your* judgment.")

Without the required comma before "and," the sentence can easily be misunderstood. A person reading quickly misses the pause and sees this: "Giving birth to Cynthia had been difficult for Mrs. Davenport and the two parents." That's a lot of people in the delivery room. (For more examples of common grammar and punctuation errors, see Appendix 1.)

Most newspapers have two or three people who read each story to catch these and other errors. However, the writer's responsibility is to get it right in the first place.

THE TOOLS OF NARRATION

The tools of narration allow you to build interest in stories. When we use scenes, dialogue and anecdotes, we are using narrative tools that help make our stories as entertaining as they are interesting. In exposition, the writer clearly stands between the reader and the information: Journalists have sources, who tell them things. Journalists then tell the reader what they heard and saw. Scenes, dialogue and anecdotes allow the reader to see the action. If you also learn to tease this good stuff with foreshadowing, readers will be more likely to read it. But more about foreshadowing later.

Scenes

Gene Roberts, former managing editor of *The New York Times,* tells about his first job at a daily newspaper. His publisher, who was blind, had someone read the newspaper to him each morning. One day, the publisher called Roberts into his office and complained, "Roberts, I can't see your stories. Make me see."

> " The most important thing to any writing, and especially profile writing, is the telling detail. "
> —Jacqui Banaszynski, Pulitzer Prize winner

We should all try to make readers see, smell, feel, taste and hear. One way to do that is to write using scenes as much as possible. To write a scene, you have to be there. You need to capture the pertinent details. Think of yourself as a playwright, not as a narrator standing on a stage. Leave the stage and let your readers see the action and hear the dialogue. You can see and hear what is happening in the following excerpt. Put yourself in a theater watching the actors on stage:

She was in her office getting ready to attend a doctoral candidate's prospectus defense when the call came that would turn her life upside down. The surgeon told her she was very sorry, but it was invasive breast cancer.

"Am I going to die?" Carver asked her.

"Well, I certainly hope not," the surgeon said.

She hung up the phone in a daze but refused to go home. Somehow, she managed to get through the defense. Then she went to see her husband, Bill Horner, an MU political science professor. She walked into his office and shut the door. Horner knew before she had uttered a word.

A student reporter at South Dakota State University was on the farm to capture this opening scene:

"Don Sheber's leathery, cracked hands have been sculpted by decades of wresting a living from the earth." Use descriptive language to paint a vivid picture for readers and to bring a story to life.

Don Sheber's leathery, cracked hands have been sculpted by decades of wresting a living from the earth.

But this year, despite work that often stretches late into the evening, the moisture-starved soil has yielded little for Sheber and his family.

Sheber's hands tugged at the control levers on his John Deere combine last week as rotating blades harvested the thin stands of wheat that have grown to less than a foot high.

The writer allows the reader to visit Sheber on the farm. We can see and feel the farmer's hands. We can touch the John Deere combine and the stunted wheat.

To create such scenes, you must use all your senses to gather information, and your notebook should reflect that reporting. Along with the results of interviews, your notebook should bulge with details of sights and smells, sounds and textures. David Finkel, winner of the American Society of News Editors Distinguished Writing Award in 1986 and a Pulitzer Prize in 2006, says, "Anything that pertains to any sense I feel at any moment, I write down." Gather details indiscriminately. Later, you can discard those that are not germane. Because you were there, you can write the scene as if you were writing a play.

Because Bartholomew Sullivan of *The (Memphis) Commercial Appeal* was observing and listening closely at a trial, his readers were able to sit in the courtroom with him:

Helfrich banged an index finger on the rail of the jury box as he recalled Thursday's

testimony in which a string of Bowers's Jones County friends testified that he was a solid businessman, a Christian—"a gentleman." One of the witnesses was Nix, who called Bowers a "real, real nice man."

"They talk of gentlemen," Helfrich whispered. Then, shouting, he said: "These people don't have a gentle bone in their bodies. They were nightriders and henchmen. They attacked a sleeping family and destroyed all they owned."

Analyze the detail: the banging of an index finger, the whisper, the shout. We can see and we can hear.

By creating a scene, the writer transported us to the courtroom rather than just telling us what he saw.

Dialogue

The use of *dialogue*—conversation between two or more people, not including the reporter—allows the reporter to recede and the characters to take center stage. When you use quotations, you—the writer—are repeating for the reader what the source said, and the reader listens to you relating what was said. But when you use dialogue, you disappear, and the reader listens directly to the characters. Dialogue is a key element in creating scenes. Compare these examples:

During the public hearing, Henry Lathrop accused the council of wasting taxpayers' money. "If you don't stop voting for all this spending, I am going to circulate a recall petition and get you all kicked off the council," he said.

Mayor Margorie Gold told Lathrop he was free to do as he wished. "As for us," she said, "we will vote in the best interests of the city."

That is the traditional way of presenting quotations. The reporter uses quotes but also paraphrases some of what was said. That's telling readers instead of taking them to the council chambers and letting them listen. Here is how that account would sound handled as dialogue:

When Henry Lathrop spoke to the City Council during the public hearing, he pounded on the podium. "You folks are wasting taxpayers' money. If you don't stop voting for all this spending, I am going to circulate a recall petition and get you all kicked off the council."

Mayor Margorie Gold slammed her gavel on her desk.

"Mr. Lathrop," she said as she tried to control the anger in her voice. She looked at him directly. "You are free to do as you wish. As for us, we will vote in the best interests of the city."

At the hearing, Lathrop and Gold were speaking to each other. The second version captures the exchange without the intercession of the writer.

Here's another example of dialogue. This conversation took place between Cindy Martling, a rehabilitation nurse, and Mary Jo, a patient's wife, after Martling scolded the patient for feeling sorry for himself:

> She wandered around a bit, then saw Mary Jo standing in the hallway. The two women went to each other and embraced. "I'm sorry," Martling said through more tears. "I didn't mean to lose control. I hope I didn't offend you."
>
> "What you did was wonderful," Mary Jo said. "He needed to hear that. Dan is going to work through it, and we're all going to be OK."

Anecdotes

The ultimate treats, **anecdotes** are stories embedded in stories. They can be happy or sad, funny or serious. Whatever their tone, they should illustrate a point. Readers are likely to remember the anecdotes more readily than anything else in a story. You probably remember the stories that your professors tell regardless of whether you remember the rest of the lecture. Long after you've forgotten this chapter, you will probably remember some of the examples from it. Facts inform. Anecdotes inform and entertain.

> " If history were taught in the form of stories, it would never be forgotten. "
> —Rudyard Kipling, English writer

As befits something so valuable, anecdotes are hard to obtain. You can't get them by asking your source, "Got any good anecdotes?" But you can get them by asking for examples so you can re-create the scene. To do this, be alert to the possibilities that an anecdote might be lurking in the details. One reporter gathered this quote:

> "We had one of those coaching nights where we sat up until I don't know when trying to figure it out," Richardson says. "We refer to that as the red-letter day in Spartan football, and since that day, we are 33-15, with three district titles and a conference championship."

The editor pointed out to the reporter that if it was a red-letter day, the reporter should have asked more questions about that coaching meeting. He did, and he ended up with an anecdote about how the coaches figured out a new strategy that turned out to be successful.

Here's another example. Your source says: "Darren is like a one-man entertainment committee. He's always got something going on. And if nothing is going on, he'll hike up his pants really high and dance to the Jonas Brothers."

To turn this dry quote into an anecdote, you need to ask, "Can you give me an example of when he acted like an entertainment committee?" or "Tell me about the time he danced to the Jonas Brothers."

Some anecdotes come from phrasing questions in the superlative: "What's the funniest thing that ever happened to you while you were standing in front of an audience?" "What's the worst case you've ever seen come into this emergency room?" "People tell me Rodney is always the first one they call when they need help on a project. Has he ever helped you? Can you give me an example?"

When leading bankers were summoned to the Treasury Department to discuss the financial meltdown, journalists were not allowed in the meeting. Yet some were able to reconstruct the scene inside. Here's an anecdote set in a scene:

Drama Behind a $250 Billion Banking Deal

By Mark Landler and Eric Dash

WASHINGTON—The chief executives of the nine largest banks in the United States trooped into a gilded conference room at the Treasury Department at 3 p.m. Monday. To their astonishment, they were each handed a one-page document that said they agreed to sell shares to the government, then Treasury Secretary Henry M. Paulson Jr. said they must sign it before they left.

The chairman of JPMorgan Chase, Jamie Dimon, was receptive, saying he thought the deal looked pretty good once he ran the numbers through his head. The chairman of Wells Fargo, Richard M. Kovacevich, protested strongly that, unlike his New York rivals, his bank was not in trouble because of investments in exotic mortgages, and did not need a bailout, according to people briefed on the meeting.

But by 6:30, all nine chief executives had signed—setting in motion the largest government intervention in the American banking system since the Depression and retreating from the rescue plan Mr. Paulson had fought so hard to get through Congress only two weeks earlier.

Use anecdotes to entertain while you are informing. If the relevance of the anecdote to the larger story isn't obvious, tell in the transition into the anecdote or at the end of it.

Foreshadowing

Foreshadowing is the technique of giving hints about what's coming. Moviemakers tease you with the scenes they think will encourage you to buy a ticket. Broadcasters use foreshadowing to keep you from leaving during a commercial: "Coming up, there's a burglar prowling your neighborhood." Every lead foreshadows the story. The leads that not only tell but promise more good stuff to come are the most successful. Tom Koetting, then of *The Wichita Eagle*, spent nine months observing the recovery of a doctor who had nearly lost his life in a farm accident. He produced a story of about 100,000 words. The simple lead promised great things to come: "Daniel Calliendo Jr. had not expected to meet death this calmly."

A student at Florida A&M University used the same technique to invite readers to continue reading the story:

> A North Carolina family thought the worst was behind them when they were robbed Saturday morning at a gas station just off Interstate 95.
> The worst was yet to come.

The worst was yet to come. That's another way of saying, "Read on; the story gets even better."

In the next example, the long opening is packed with promises of great things to come:

> Deena Borman's relationship with her roommate, Teresa, during her freshman year in college had shattered long before the wine bottle.
>
> Weeks had gone by with Teresa drawing further and further away from Deena. Finally, after repeatedly hearing Teresa talk about suicide, Deena says, "I kept telling her how silly she was to want to die."
>
> That made Teresa angry, so she threw a full wine bottle at Deena. It shattered against the wall and broke open the simmering conflict between them. That was when Deena tried to find out what had gone wrong with Teresa's life, and that was when Teresa told Deena that she wanted to do something to get rid of her.
>
> And that was when Deena began to be scared of her own roommate.

The writer is promising a great story. What is wrong with Teresa? Does Teresa really try to hurt Deena? Does Deena really have something to be scared about? There is a promise of great things to come. Would you keep reading?

SUGGESTED READINGS

Hart, Jack. *A Writer's Coach: The Complete Guide to Writing Strategies That Work*. New York: Pantheon, 2006. This guide helps you understand the "how" and "why" of sentence, paragraph and story construction.

Kramer, Mark, and Wendy Call, eds. *Telling True Stories*. New York: Plume, 2007. This book offers the collected wisdom of many writers, gathered in short bits. You can jump around easily to pick out applicable bits of advice.

Osborn, Patricia. *How Grammar Works: A Self-Teaching Guide*. New York: John Wiley and Sons, 1999. This book will do for you what it promises: It will guide you, step by step, through the basics of English grammar. Its goal is to make you feel comfortable with grammar and the way words work.

Strunk, William, and E.B. White. *The Elements of Style*. 3rd ed. Boston: Allyn and Bacon, 1995. This little book practices what it preaches. For the beginner, it is a good primer; for the pro, it is a good review of writing rules and word meanings.

Tankard, James, and Laura Hendrickson. "Specificity, Imagery in Writing: Testing the Effects of 'Show, Don't Tell.'" *Newspaper Research Journal* (Winter/Spring 1996): 35–48. The authors found that participants in a test said that examples of "show" writing were more interesting and believable.

SUGGESTED WEBSITES

www.papyr.com/hypertextbooks/comp1/coherent.htm
Daniel Kies of the Department of English at the College of DuPage explains how to achieve coherence in your writing.

www.nieman.harvard.edu/narrative/home.aspx
The Nieman Foundation at Harvard has a "Narrative Digest" site that offers narrative stories and, often, interviews with writers.

www.nj.com/news/index.ssf/2012/11/48_hours_before_during_and_aft.html#
Go to this website to see the full version of the hurricane story that opens this chapter.

EXERCISES

1. **Team project.** Your instructor will divide the class into three groups. On the Internet, find at least three versions of the same news event written on the same day. Each group should compare the sentence lengths. Look for transitions. Find figures of speech and analogies. Which, in your opinion, is the most readable? The least readable? Why?

2. **Journalism blog.** In the following paragraph from earlier in this chapter, identify the concrete details and the similes. Evaluate what they add to your understanding of the scene. Then list and evaluate the verbs. Write a blog post about your analysis of the paragraph.

   > Boyd is in his truck with Fire Chief James Samarelli, who is at the wheel. They turn right onto Sampson Avenue and are nearly hit by a wooden lifeguard boat slicing through the floodwater. A wall of water is headed directly for them, bringing a second lifeguard boat. Samarelli jerks the truck to the right. A large piece of the boardwalk, ripped away by the waves, slams into the front of the flatbed truck. Boyd looks down at his suddenly cold feet. Seawater is rushing into the cab and a 6-foot-tall swell lifts the truck and begins pushing it sideways, into a telephone pole.

3. Choose precisely the right word:
   a. We need to (ensure, insure) a victory.
   b. Stop (annoying, irritating) your friend.
   c. The attorney won because she (refuted, responded to) the allegations.
   d. The prisoner was able to produce (mitigating, militating) evidence.

4. Rewrite Barlett and Steele's story on nuclear-waste disposal (p. 203) to take out the parallelism. Which version, the original or yours, is better? Why?

5. Punctuate the following sentences:
   a. Government officials have come under a newly enacted censorship system and several foreign speakers have been denied permission to enter the country.
   b. It was a Monday night and for the next two days he teetered between life and death.
   c. The council approved the manager's proposals and rejected a tax increase.

6. Use a simile to explain the following numbers:

   The student council's budget is $350,000. The university has 19,000 students. The local city budget is $3 million. The city has 70,000 residents.

7. Calculate the readability levels of a couple of paragraphs you have written and stories from *The New York Times* and the Associated Press. Compare the readability scores, and account for scoring differences and similarities. You can get the calculation at www.standards-schmandards.com /exhibits/rix.

11

Alternatives to the Inverted Pyramid

NEWSPAPERS, MAGAZINES AND WEBSITES publish some stories that are not suited for the inverted pyramid structure. Here's the opening to a story written as if it were a novel, except that it is all true.

In this chapter you will learn:

1. How to construct a chronology.

2. How to construct a news narrative story.

3. How to construct a focus structure story.

4. How to deliver information in service journalism formats.

Ill-Fated Train Ride Tears Indian Boy from Mother, Sparks 25-Year Worldwide Hunt for Home

By Kristen Gelineau and Ravi Nessman

KHANDWA, India — Saroo's eyes snapped open and everything was suddenly, horribly, wrong.

The 5-year-old's tiny body was still curled up on the hard wooden seat of the Indian train, just as it was when he'd drifted off to sleep. The rattle of the train was loud and steady, just as it always was when he rode home with his big brother, Guddu.

But Guddu was not there. And the alien landscape flashing past the window looked nothing like home.

Saroo's heart began to pound. The train car was empty. His brother should have been there, sweeping under the seats for loose change. Where was Guddu?

Where was Saroo?

It was 1987 and Saroo knew only that he was alone on the train.

Soon, he would find himself alone in the world. He wouldn't know for decades that this fateful train ride was setting into motion a chain of events both fantastic and horrific — events that would tear him away from his family and join him with a new one. Events that would spark the determined hunt of a mother for her son and a son for his mother, brought together only to realize that you can never really go home again.

In the beginning, though, all Saroo knew was that nothing was as it should be. "MA!" he screamed, wild with fear as he ran up and down the empty compartment, tears streaming down his face. "GUDDU!"

Only the relentless hum of the train answered his cries. Outside the window, the remains of his old life had faded into the distance. The train was thundering down the track toward a destination — and a destiny — unknown.

Fatima Munshi was frantic. When she returned to her cramped house after a hard day of work on a construction site, her two young sons still hadn't arrived. They should have been back hours earlier.

Fatima lived for her children. She had little else to live for. . . .

When night fell and her boys still weren't home, Fatima panicked. She took a neighbor she called Uncle Akbar to the station to look for them, but most of the trains had already come and gone. They searched the nearby market where the boys would beg. She went to the fountain where they liked to play.

By morning, her body felt like it was on fire. Her mind raced.

Maybe they had been kidnapped.

Maybe they were lost.

Maybe they were dead.

She had never been on a train before, but she and Uncle Akbar rode to Burhanpur and Bhusawal, asking police if they had seen her sons. She widened her search to bigger and further cities.

She cried and prayed for their safe return at the holy crypt of the Sufi Muslim saint Tekri Wale Baba. She approached another mystic said to channel the dead saint's spirit.

"There are no longer two flowers," he said. "One flower has fallen, the other has gone to a far off place. He doesn't remember where he is from. He will come back, but only after a long, long time."

She didn't believe him. Her boys were going to be fine.

Then she ran into a police officer she knew.

Guddu was dead, he said.

The boy had either fallen off the train or been pushed. Police took photos of the mangled but still identifiable body found by the tracks, and then cremated him.

Fatima fainted.

AP writers Gelineau and Nessman used chronology to reconstruct the story of a young boy's separation from his family and his search, which ended successfully 25 years later. In Chapter 9 you learned how to rank information from most important to least important. That inverted pyramid structure serves news, particularly breaking news, well. Other structures support other types of stories better. Like the standard formula for telling fairy tales, chronology works best when characters encounter complications in bringing the story to a resolution. Writers focus on the people involved in issues to tell important stories—health care, cancer research, prayer in schools—in an interesting and informative way.

If time, detail and space are available, consider the alternative structures we describe in this chapter and summarize in Figure 11.1 on pages 222–23. Whether you are writing about a car accident, the Boy Scouts' jamboree or the campaign for student government president, writing the story will be easier if you know how to use some of the alternative story forms: the chronology, news narrative, focus structure and service journalism formats.

CHRONOLOGY

Stories that work best as a chronology are those that have complications or tension and a resolution worth waiting for. Saroo Brierley was separated from his family. That's a complication. Fortunately, he ended up in an orphanage, was adopted by a family in Australia and grew up healthy and educated. But there was another complication. Brierley wondered about his family in India. So the next complication is how to find his family when he didn't know his Indian name or the city in which he lived. That part of the story reaches a resolution when he returns to India and finds his mother.

Complications are present even in events like meetings. When a city council faces a contentious issue, such as a proposed smoking ban in public places, you are presented with controversy (supporters and opponents testifying), tension (weighing health and economic interests) and a resolution (the vote). Time constraints and tradition often dictate an inverted pyramid structure. But you have other options:

» You could summarize the vote in a sidebar and use chronology to tell the story of the meeting.

» You could write an inverted pyramid version of the story for both the website and the newspaper and then write a chronological version for the Web to replace the earlier version.

» You might use news narrative (see the next section) to report the results and then move to chronology.

Where to Start

Oddly enough, when you use chronology, you don't have to begin at the beginning. Instead, you look for a key moment you can use in the lead to engage readers. To get started, writers often jot down a timeline. In the case of the council meeting, it might look like this:

7:00 p.m.	Opponents and supporters of the smoking ban begin testifying before the council.
	Jones, an opponent, angrily denounces the proposal.
	Smith, a supporter, relates a story about her cancer.
8:15	Council members begin debate.
	Mayor pounds the gavel to break up an out-of-control argument between two council members.
	Council member Rodriguez is nearly in tears as he urges the council to pass the ordinance.
	Council member Jackson says merchants will face financial ruin.
8:47	Solinski, a member of the audience, interrupts the debate and is escorted out of the chambers by city police. Several in the audience boo, but some cheer.
9:10	During a recess, no council members mingle with the public, which irritates several of those who are attending.
9:30	The council votes 5-4 in favor of the smoking ban. There are both jeers and cheers.

A Sample Outline

You could begin at the beginning of the timeline given above, with the chamber filling with members of the public, but this lead would not attract attention. You need a dramatic scene that captures emotion, is short and does not give away the outcome. The removal of a member of the audience has potential; so does the heated argument within the council.

News Story Structures

	Inverted Pyramid	Chronology
What is it?	The lead paragraphs have the most important information, and succeeding paragraphs give details in descending order of importance.	Starting at a particular point of interest, the paragraphs tell a story in chronological order.
When should it be used?	It's best used for hard news, where timeliness is essential and the reader wants to know the important facts right away.	It's good for reporting a detailed sequence of events in a story with controversy or tension and resolution, especially as a follow-up to a news story.
How is it structured?	**Traditional news lead** • Give who, what, when, where, why and how. • Frame the story. **Body: support paragraphs in descending order of importance** • Give additional details about the lead. • Summarize other significant actions or elements relevant to the lead. • Give the impact or effect of the event. • Give the "so what"—the story's importance to the reader. • Give background and history. • Describe relevant physical details. • Narrate relevant sequences of events. • Use quotations from relevant sources. • Give sources of additional information, including links to websites. **Ending** • End with the least significant information, *not* with a conclusion, summary or tie-back to the beginning. The story can be cut from the bottom up without compromising its effectiveness.	**Narrative lead** • Describe a dramatic point in the story. • Create narrative suspense with foreshadowing. **Nut paragraph** • Give the theme of the story. **Body: narrative support paragraphs** • Use foreshadowing. • Pick up story with a transition back to the beginning of the narrative. • Tell the story in chronological order, highlighting key events found in the timeline. • Describe relevant physical details. • Use narrative techniques like dialogue, flashback and foreshadowing. **Ending** • Give a conclusion to the story. • Resolve the tension or conflict in the story.

FIGURE 11.1

Different structures are useful for different types of news stories.

News Narrative

The story combines elements of inverted pyramid and chronology formats, with an emphasis on either news or narrative.

It's useful for stories where timeliness is somewhat important, but the hard news element is not prominent.

Narrative lead
- Open with an interesting scene or twist that teases the story.
  or

Traditional news lead
- Give who, what, when, where, why and how.

Support paragraphs
- Briefly add whatever helps the reader understand the story summarized in the lead.

Body: narrative support paragraphs
- Go back to the beginning, and tell the story in chronological order.

Ending
- Give a conclusion to the story.
- Resolve the tension or conflict in the story.

Focus Structure

The story follows one individual as a representative of a larger group.

It's useful for making complex or abstract stories meaningful to readers.

Narrative lead
- Introduce the subject and describe the person's problem.

Transition
- Create a bridge from the subject to the theme of the story.

Nut paragraph
- Give the theme of the story.

Support paragraphs
- Foreshadow.
- Give the "so what"—the story's importance to the reader.
- Give the "to be sure"—opposing perspectives.

Body: narrative and expository support paragraphs
- Interweave narrative about the subject with facts about the theme to tell the story.

Ending
- Conclude the story, with a summary or with a tie-back that refers to the beginning of the story.

Here is a typical outline for a story using chronology:

1. The lead (the scene with Rodriguez).
2. The nut (theme) paragraph.
3. Foreshadowing.
4. A transition back to the beginning of the meeting to pick up the story from that point.
5. The body, highlighting key events found in the timeline. (As with any news story, much of the action is left out; this is a news story, not a secretary's report.)
6. An ending that highlights the vote and the audience reaction.

The Nut Paragraph, Foreshadowing and the "To Be Sure"

Like the lead in an inverted pyramid story, a **nut paragraph** (or *nut graf*) is a paragraph that gives the theme of the story and summarizes the key facts. Unlike the lead in the inverted pyramid format, however, the nut paragraph is not the first paragraph in the story. For the council story, after the first (or lead) paragraph describing the scene with Rodriguez, the nut paragraph might look like this:

In a meeting filled with emotional, sometimes angry testimony, citizens and the City Council debated the proposed smoking ban for nearly three hours. Citizens urged—sometimes threatened—council members. The mayor pounded his gavel to bring the council to order several times when some members engaged in heated, personal arguments. In the end, council members voted on the landmark legislation amid jeers and cheers and then left through a back door.

From the beginning, it was clear that emotions were running high. . . .

The nut paragraph both defines the story and foreshadows the heated debate. Even though readers will know the results, many will want to read the blow-by-blow account. It also establishes the "so what": This is a divisive issue, involving landmark legislation, that people care about. Notice that the last line, "From the beginning . . . ," creates a transition back to the start of the story narrative.

In the story that opened this chapter, the nut paragraph and foreshadowing start in paragraph 5:

Where was Saroo?

It was 1987 and Saroo knew only that he was alone on the train.

Soon, he would find himself alone in the world. He wouldn't know for decades that this fateful train ride was setting into motion a chain of events both fantastic and horrific—events that would tear him away from his family and join him with a new one. Events that would spark the determined hunt of a mother for her son and a son for his mother, brought together only to realize that you can never really go home again.

In some stories, you might also need to include a **"to be sure" paragraph**. This paragraph, which gives opposing points of view, is a must when you are focusing on one side of an issue. Before the council vote, you could do a story about a restaurant shift from the perspective of a server. You could follow that with a story from the perspective of a smoker at a bar. In both cases, you would include a paragraph acknowledging that others disagree, especially if that opposing viewpoint is not included elsewhere in the story. For instance:

> Not everyone agrees with Megan Addison that smoking should be banned. Others, including smokers and business owners, believe that the proposal infringes on their right to smoke or to run their business as they please. But Addison and her fellow servers at the Sports Grill want to work in a smoke-free environment.

You do not need a "to be sure" paragraph in the council meeting story because all sides are represented in the debate.

The Ending

Stories written chronologically need strong endings. After the tearful reunion with his family, Saroo Brierley returned to Australia, where he had another family, a girlfriend and a job. His Indian mother wanted him to live in India. The resolution is not a simple, happy ending. Instead, both parties accept the separation reluctantly:

> Saroo doesn't want to overthink it. He wants to revel in the joy of their remarkable reunion. For him, it has been a miracle punctuated by a happy ending.
>
> "It's sort of taken a weight off my shoulders," he says. "Instead of going to bed at night and thinking, 'How is my family? Are they still alive?' I know in my head now I can let those questions rest."
>
> He hopes to visit India once or twice a year, but he cannot move back. He has other responsibilities, other family and a whole other life in Tasmania.
>
> He is Australian now.
>
> "This is where I live," he says. "When I come back, whether it's sooner or later, then we can start building our relationship again."
>
> Fatima is confused and frustrated.
>
> She doesn't want him to move back here, where there is nothing. But she wants to be with him. Maybe she can move to Australia, she says. She adds sternly that she would ban all girlfriends from his house.
>
> A few minutes later she softens. She couldn't really move away from her life here to an unfamiliar place where no one can talk with her, she says.
>
> At least, and at last, Saroo's return has brought her "mental peace," she says. She tries to understand that he has new parents, new expectations and a new life a world away.
>
> She just wants him to see her once in a while, to call her occasionally, even if they can only speak a few sentences to each other.
>
> "For the moment," she says, "it's enough for me that I went to him. And he called me Amma."
>
> Mother.

For both the hypothetical council story and the real story of the reunion, readers want to know the outcome of the narrative. In the council story, how did the meeting end? How heated was it? The reunion story was framed through the eyes of Saroo, searching for his mother, and Fatima, searching for her son. Readers read a chronology to the end because they want to know the conclusion of the story.

NEWS NARRATIVE

In Chapter 9, you saw examples of inverted pyramid stories that didn't have the news in the first paragraph (see "The 'You' Lead" and "Leads with Flair") but as soon as the writer teased the reader, the news lead appeared. Then the writer arranged the rest of the story in the traditional descending order of importance. Further modification, though, offers writers more choices. The **news narrative** structure combines the inverted pyramid and chronology. Here is an outline of its basic elements:

1. An opening with an interesting scene or twist that teases the story.
2. A traditional news lead.
3. Brief paragraphs that add whatever help readers need to understand the story summarized in the traditional lead.
4. A transition back to the beginning to tell the story in chronological order.

The "news" in "news narrative" implies that the story has a time element and that the story is not a feature. **Features**, sometimes called "soft stories," are those that can run nearly any time, such as a profile of a stamp collector, a story on a volunteer at the local food bank or an article about riding with a police officer for a shift. A story with a time element usually has to be tweeted, posted on the Web and published in the next issue of the newspaper. The "narrative" in "news narrative" means that you can use chronology, one of the most important tools of narrative writing. In the news narrative, you will often find other narrative tools, such as those discussed in Chapter 10: scenes, dialogue, anecdotes and foreshadowing.

News Narrative with News Emphasis

When the local sheriff's department broke an unusual burglary ring, Jane Meinhardt of the *St. Petersburg (Fla.) Times* elected to use the news narrative structure. In the annotated model "News Narrative with News Emphasis," you can read her story, which follows the outline above. Notice that the story is a news narrative with news emphasis. This format works well for news that is significant but not earth-shattering. You probably wouldn't use it to report during the first few hours or perhaps even the first couple of days after a major news event like a mass shooting. You need to be able to get all the details of how something happened to relate the chronology. Immediately following a disaster or other major event, the authorities

ANNOTATED MODEL   News Narrative with News Emphasis

The opening paragraphs set the scene with information that informs and is interesting.

PALM HARBOR—They carried knapsacks and bags to tote loot. They had a screwdriver to pry open doors and windows.

They used latex gloves.

They acted like professional criminals, but officials say they were teenage burglars coached and directed by a Palm Harbor woman whose son and daughter were part of her gang.

A traditional news lead gives "who," "what" and "when."

Pinellas County Sheriff's deputies arrested Rovana Sipe, two of her children and two other teens Wednesday after a series of home burglaries.

"She was the driver," said Sheriff's Sgt. Greg Tita. "She pointed out the houses. She's the one who said 'Do these.'"

The writer supports the lead with a quote.

The story continues with the breaking news for the next four paragraphs.

Sipe, 38, of 2333 State Road 584, was charged with two counts of being a principal in burglary. She was held Thursday in lieu of $20,000 bail.

Her daughter, Jackie Shifflet, 16, was charged with grand theft. Her son, Ryan Shifflet, 15, was charged with two counts of burglary.

Charles Ruhe, 17, of 1600 Ensley Ave., in Safety Harbor, and Charles Taylor, 16, of 348 Jeru Blvd. in Tarpon Springs, also were held on four counts of burglary each.

"They were very well-prepared to do burglaries, especially with the guidance they were given," Tita said. "We recovered thousands of dollars of stolen items. Anything that could be carried out, was."

The burglary ring unraveled Tuesday, Tita said. A Palm Harbor woman saw a large, yellow car driven by a woman drop off three boys, he said. The three went to the back of her house.

Now that the news has been established, instead of continuing to present the information in order of importance, the writer presents the rest of the story in chronological fashion. Note the important transition from inverted pyramid to chronology: "The burglary ring unraveled Tuesday, Tita said."

They put on gloves and started to pry open a window with a screwdriver, she said. When she tapped on a window, they ran.

She called 911. As she waited for deputies, other neighbors saw the boys walk through a nearby neighborhood carrying bags.

Deputies chased the boys and caught two. The third got into a large yellow car driven by a woman.

The bags contained jewelry, a shotgun and other items deputies say were taken from another house in the neighborhood.

Tita said the boys, later identified as Taylor and Ruhe, told detectives about other burglaries in Dunedin and Clearwater and who else was involved.

At Sipe's house, detectives found stolen VCRs, televisions, camcorders and other valuables. They arrested the other two teens and Sipe.

The story ends with a quote rather than a tie-back or summary.

"We're very familiar with this family and its criminal history," Tita said. "We have found stolen property at the house in the past and made juvenile arrests."

In news narratives with a news emphasis, the writer needs to establish the facts before giving the chronology. This format is associated with breaking news of significance, such as crime.

Source: Jane Meinhardt, "Mother Accused of Being Criminal Ringleader," *St. Petersburg Times,* Oct. 21, 1994.

don't have all the information, and the reporter might not have access to witnesses or documents.

News Narrative with Narrative Emphasis

When the news is less important, the news narrative structure is also useful, but the emphasis is on narrative rather than news. John Tully, a reporter for the Columbia *Missourian*, was asked to look for a story at a horse-riding competition one Sunday afternoon. Because most of the competitors were not from the newspaper's local area, reporting the results of the competition was not as important as finding a good story.

Tully knew nothing about horse-riding competitions, so he first found people who could explain the judging. He also asked people to suggest interesting competitors. A youth coordinator told him that Cara Walker was competing for the first time since her accident. After gathering more information from the coordinator, Tully found Walker and her mother—and a story that lent itself to news narrative. Through Tully's story (see the annotated model on page 229), readers learned that Walker, who had been seriously injured in a car accident, was able to recover enough to ride again. What they didn't find out until the end was that she won the competition. Because he had less news to report, Tully was able to go to the chronological format more quickly than Meinhardt. He used the outcome of the competition to reward readers who completed the story.

FOCUS STRUCTURE

For centuries, writers have used the focus structure to tell the story of an individual or a group that represents a bigger population. This approach allows the writer to make large institutions, complex issues and seven-digit numbers meaningful. Not many of us can understand—let alone explain—the marketing system for wheat, but we could more easily do so if we followed a crop of wheat from the time it was planted until a consumer bought a loaf of bread.

The Wall Street Journal knew that not many of us would be attracted to a story about the interaction between pesticides and prescription drugs. That's why a reporter focused on one person to tell a story of pesticide poisoning:

> Thomas Latimer used to be a vigorous, athletic man,
> a successful petroleum engineer with a bright future.
>   Then he mowed the lawn.

Does this opening make you want to read on?

In a quip attributed to him, the Soviet dictator Josef Stalin summed up the impact of focusing on a part of the whole: "A single death is a tragedy; a million deaths is a statistic." Think about that the next time you hear that a plane crash killed 300 people. Some events, such as mass shootings or earthquakes, are horrific enough to attract attention in and of themselves. However, when readers have digested the news, you can reach them again by creating a narrative told through the eyes of participants.

ANNOTATED MODEL   **News Narrative with Narrative Emphasis**

The first two paragraphs reveal the news of the injury and the twist that even though doctors were unsure, she recovered enough to compete. The horse show is the news event that generated the story. Note that the second paragraph reveals that she competed but only foreshadows how she did.

About five months ago, Cara Walker, 17, was lying in a hospital recovering from the spinal injury she received when she lost control of her car, rolled the vehicle and was thrown halfway through the side window.

Doctors weren't sure she would ever ride again. On Sunday, in a remarkable turnaround, Walker competed in the Midway Fall Classic Quarter Horse Show at the Midway Expo Center. The results were surprising.

Last July, Walker, a junior at Rock Bridge High School, was taking a lunch break from riding in preparation for the Fort Worth Invitational, where she qualified in five events. Driving with three passengers on a back road near Moberly, she rolled her car at 50 mph where the paved road turned to gravel without warning. Walker was the only one not wearing a seat belt. Her head and upper body smashed through the side window.

"Last July" is the transition to chronology after the news lead.

Fortunately, she was still in her riding boots. Her spurs got caught on the bar under the seat, which Walker says may have saved her life.

At the time of the accident, Walker was nationally ranked in the trail-riding event.

Note that there are no quotes to break the narrative flow. "My spurs got caught on the bar under my seat" and "She first started walking, and going to the mailbox wore her out" (paragraph 8) are paraphrased to stay in storytelling mode.

Doctors fused her neck in surgery. During the next couple of weeks, she was able to shed her full upper-body cast. Walker returned home to her parents and twin sisters two days after surgery, but her mother, Jane Walker, said doctors told her to stay away from her sport for a few months until she healed.

This background helps establish that she isn't just any rider and that she had more to lose in this accident than most riders.

For Walker, the top all-around youth rider in Missouri and the president of the American Quarter Horse Youth Association, the four months following the accident was her first time away from riding.

After returning home she worked to regain strength and mobility from the accident that initially left her right side paralyzed. She walked short distances. Going to the mailbox at the end of the driveway wore her out, her mother recalls.

The story has a surprise ending, which is possible in a chronology. In a straight news story, this would have been the lead.

Walker had to work almost every muscle in her body back into shape. After the accident, the family brought her 10-year-old quarter horse to their barn in Columbia. That motivated Walker to at first walk to the barn and then to start caring for the horse and eventually ride again.

Sunday, the rehabilitation was complete. With ramrod posture and strict horse control, she won first place in the horsemanship class.

In news narratives with a narrative emphasis, less space is devoted to the news, and more narrative techniques are used than in the inverted pyramid format. These types of narratives use fewer quotes and save important information for a strong ending.
Source: John Tully, "Horse Power," *Missourian*, Nov. 27, 2006.

Writing the Lead

Issues like health care, budget deficits and sexual harassment don't have much emotional appeal in the abstract. You make them relevant if you discuss the issue by focusing on someone affected by it. For instance, the college student who wrote the following story spoke to Karen Elliott, who willingly told her story to help others with the same disease. The key word is "story." You write articles about diseases; you write stories about people. The lead paragraphs focus on one person in an anecdote that shows her as a character we can relate to:

Karen Elliott, 44, remembers the phone call from Dr. Jonathen Roberts, a general surgeon, as if it had happened yesterday. Dr. Roberts' nurse called one afternoon two years ago and told Karen to hold the line. She froze. She had just had a biopsy on her right breast because of a new lump. It's never good news when the doctor calls at home. Dr. Roberts cut to the chase.

"You have atypical hyperplasia," he said.

Being a nurse, Karen knew exactly what he meant. No number of breast self-exams could have detected this. Atypical hyperplasia is a life-long condition characterized by abnormal cells. Affecting only 4 percent of the female population, it puts Karen and others at an increased risk for breast cancer. With her family history of the disease, her risk of breast cancer jumps sky-high.

Reporters working on local stories have just as many opportunities to apply this approach as those writing national and international stories. For example, instead of keeping score on the United Way fund drive, focus on the people who will benefit—or will fail to benefit—from the campaign. If the streets in your city jar your teeth when you drive, write about the problem from the point of view of a driver. If a disease is killing the trees in your city, concentrate on a homeowner who has lost several. The focus structure offers the writer a powerful method of reducing institutions, statistics and cosmic issues to a level that readers can relate to and understand.

Advertising agencies use the technique, too. That's why instead of being solicited for money to help the poor and starving, you are asked to support one child for only pennies a day. The technique gives poverty and hunger a face. A starving population is an abstraction; one starving child is a tragedy.

Writing the Setup

Once you've completed the opening, you must finish the setup to the story. The **setup** consists of the transition to the nut paragraph, foreshadowing, the "so what" and the "to be sure." Let's look at each of these elements.

The Transition and the Nut Paragraph

When you open with a scene or an anecdote, you must construct a transition that explicitly makes the connection to the nut, or theme, paragraph. "Explicitly" is the key word. If you fail to help readers understand the point of the opening, however interesting it is, you risk losing them. The transition in this example is in italics:

Anita Poore hit the rough pavement of the parking lot with a thud. She had never felt such intense, stabbing pain and could barely lift her heavy head. When she reached for the car door, a police officer stared at her and asked her husband, "Is she drunk?" A wave of nausea swept over her, and she vomited.

"That's it. Get her out of here!" the officer demanded.

Poore was not drunk. She avoided jail, but she faces a life sentence of pain.

Now 25, she has suffered migraine headaches since she was in seventh grade.

Not that it is much comfort, but she's not alone. Health officials estimate that Americans miss 157 million workdays a year because of migraines and spend more than $2 million a year on over-the-counter painkillers for migraine, tension and cluster headaches. Researchers haven't found a cure, but they have found methods to lessen the pain.

The italicized transition explicitly places Anita Poore among those who miss work, buy painkillers and are waiting for a cure. The material that follows the transition is the theme.

Let's return to the story of Karen Elliott, who was diagnosed with atypical hyperplasia. Here is the nut paragraph, the part of the story that states the theme:

What Karen didn't know was that her pleasant life in New Bloomfield would become a roller coaster of ups and downs for the next two years, a ride that nearly destroyed her. Her husband of 19 years, Bob, and their two children, Bethany, 6, and Jordan, 8, could only watch as she struggled with the decision of whether to voluntarily have her breasts removed because Karen, and only Karen, could make that choice.

This is where the writer tells readers what the story is about—in this case, Karen's struggle with her decision. There are many other themes the writer could have pursued.

The nut paragraph, says Jacqui Banaszynski, Pulitzer Prize–winning writer, "is like a secret decoder ring—it lets the hapless reader know what your story is about and why they should read it." When you have involved the reader and successfully written the explicit transition to the nut paragraph, you are ready to build the rest of the setup.

Foreshadowing

Foreshadowing can be done in a single line: "The killing started early and ended late." Or you can foreshadow events over several paragraphs. The goal is to assure readers they will be rewarded if they continue reading.

This is what Erik Larson of *The Wall Street Journal* promised readers of his fire investigation story:

And so began what may well be the most intensive scientific investigation in the history of arson—not a whodunit, exactly, but a whatdunit. So far the inquiry has taken

Seattle investigators places arson squads don't typically go, even to the Navy's weapons-testing grounds at China Lake in California. Along the way, the investigation has attracted a team of scientists who, likewise ensnared by the "Twilight Zone" nature of the mystery, volunteered time and equipment. At one point the investigators themselves torched a large building just to test a suspected fuel.

The "So What"

The "so what" tells readers explicitly why they should care. Thomas Latimer was poisoned when he mowed his lawn. Karen Elliott has to decide whether to have surgery. Anita Poore almost got arrested for having a migraine headache. Interesting, but so what? Reporters and editors know the "so what" or they wouldn't spend time on the story. Too often, however, they fail to tell it to readers. Latimer's story is interesting, but it's much more important because the writer added the "so what" (in italics):

The makers of the pesticide, diazinon, and of Tagamet firmly deny that their products had anything to do with Mr. Latimer's condition. The pesticide maker says he doesn't even believe he was exposed to its product. And in fact, Mr. Latimer lost a lawsuit he filed against the companies. *Even so, the case intrigues scientists and regulators because it illustrates the need for better understanding of the complex interactions between such everyday chemicals as pesticides and prescription drugs.*

Neither the Food and Drug Administration nor the Environmental Protection Agency conducts routine tests for such interactions. Indeed, the EPA doesn't even evaluate the synergy of two or more pesticides commonly used together. "We have not developed ways to test any of that," says an EPA spokesman. "We don't know how to do it." And a new congressional report says the FDA lacks both the resources and the enforcement powers to protect Americans from all kinds of poisons.

The "so what" is the impact—the relevance—for people who have no warning that pesticides and prescription drugs may interact to poison them.

In other cases, the "so what" may be included in the theme statement. Let's look at the migraine story again:

[1] Not that it is much comfort, but she's not alone.

[2] Health officials estimate that Americans miss 157 million workdays a year because of migraines and spend more than $2 million a year on over-the-counter painkillers for migraine, tension and cluster headaches.

[3] Researchers haven't found a cure, but they have found methods to lessen the pain.

Sentence 1 is the transition. Sentence 2 is the "so what." The reporter is writing about Anita Poore, but the problem is widespread. Sentence 3 is the theme, which includes foreshadowing. The search for a cure, and the intermediate discovery of ways to lessen the pain, will be the focus of the story. The "so what" establishes the dimensions of the problem. When you define the "so what," you are establishing the story's impact.

Types of Journalistic Writing

News Writing

» News stories emphasize facts and current events.
» Timeliness is especially important.
» Typical news stories cover government, politics, international events, disasters, crime, important breakthroughs in science and medicine, and sports.

Feature (Soft News) Writing

» Feature stories go into depth about a generally newsworthy situation or person.
» Timeliness is relevant but not critical.
» Typical feature stories are profiles, day-in-the-life stories, how-to stories, and background stories.

The "To Be Sure"

To maintain an evenhanded approach, writers must acknowledge that there are two or more sides to a story. We call this the "to be sure," as in "to be sure, there are other opinions." We've seen in the pesticide story that the drug and pesticide makers "firmly deny that their products had anything to do with Mr. Latimer's condition." We see the technique again in an article about the impact of gambling on Tunica, Miss. Writer Jenny Deam opens with a scene in the mayor's store. The mayor says gambling is the best thing that ever happened to the town. At the front counter, a woman is asking for the $85 back she paid on furniture last week because she lost her grocery money gambling. What comes next is a combination theme and "to be sure" statement, highlighted in italics:

And so is the paradox of this tiny Mississippi Delta county, now that the casinos have come to call.

On the one hand, unemployment in a place the Rev. Jesse Jackson once called "America's Ethiopia" has dropped from nearly 24 percent to a low last fall of 5 percent. Anyone who wants a job has one with the casinos. There are more jobs than people to fill them. In a county of about 8,100 people, the number of food stamp recipients fell from 4,218 before the casinos to 2,907 now.

But there is another side. New problems never before seen.

Since the first casino opened in 1992, the number of DUI arrests has skyrocketed by 400 percent. U.S. Highway 61 leading to Memphis is constantly jammed. On a busy weekend as many as 28,000 cars head toward the nine casinos now open. The criminal court system is just as overloaded. In 1992, there were 1,500 cases filed. A year later, 2,400. As of last month there had already been 6,800 cases filed for this year.

"Well," says the mayor, "it's just like anything else in life: You got to take the evil with the good."

The story of Tunica's economic rebirth had been told before. This story focused on the problems that inevitably follow gambling. To be sure, there are benefits, but this story also examined the costs.

Now that you have constructed the setup, you are ready to enter the body of the story.

ON THE JOB
Tips for Writing

Wright Thompson, a senior writer at *ESPN The Magazine*, concentrates on long-form stories built around characters, complications and resolutions in both print and television documentaries. This is how he describes his approach:

In his book *Writing for Story*, Jon Franklin details the most important element in storytelling: conflict and resolution. Every story has characters, is laced through with a strong sense of place, and the character faces a challenge that reveals something. That's such a standard definition that now that I've typed it, I'm sure it's stolen from somewhere. It's that essential and universal. There must be conflict, and there must be resolution. So how do you turn the theory of characters facing challenges into an actual story?

For me, it's through religious and detailed outlining, whether you're doing a 10,000-word profile for print or an hour-long documentary for television. Stories are all about arc, and when there are multiple and supportive arcs in a story, it has more muscle and driving force. So when you're outlining, make sure you see that your story moves with determined but steady pace. Figure out the micro arc of chronology, and the macro arc of understanding. We go from, say, Monday to Tuesday, or 1980 to 2012, while we are also going from nothing to something, mystery to knowledge, light to dark.

Remember to ask a question in the beginning that is answered at the end. Use scenes as the engine of a story. Use backstory as the mechanism to give the action meaning, not as the story itself. Remember, the facts are the tool for the job, not the job itself.

When I'm outlining, thinking about these principles of asking a question and answering it, and about scenes, I start by reading through the notes with a pen and a highlighter. I do this once or twice. Then I transfer these notes to note cards, laying them out so I can see them visually, and see the story start to take shape. I read and reread the cards. Then when I know where everything goes, I begin to write, hopefully without notes. I want to know the story, know the scenes and the characters and the setting, know the conflict and the resolution, and just relax and tell a story.

Writing the Body

Think of readers as people antsy to do something else. To maintain their interest, offer them frequent examples to support your main points. Use anecdotes, scenes and dialogue to move the story line. Mix *exposition* (the facts) with narration (the story line). Let's return to Karen Elliott, who just learned that she has atypical hyperplasia. The writer, Tina Smithers, has been dealing in exposition for a few paragraphs, so she shares an anecdote set in the following scene to keep the readers' interest:

Karen was walking downstairs to get the beach ball out of the summer box for Bethany's Hawaiian swim party at Kindercare. Suddenly, Karen fainted and fell down the stairs. She knew she had broken something. Coming to, she blindly made her way upstairs and lay on the bed.

"The cat was staring me in the eyes," she mumbled as Bob, fresh from the shower, grabbed ice and a pillow.

Karen noticed Bethany crying in the doorway. At this point, Karen realized she had been shouting, "Call 9-1-1! Call 9-1-1!" She didn't want her daughter to see her lose control. She quieted down and told Bethany to come to her bed.

"It's okay, honey. Mommy broke her arm, but they'll be over soon to fix it." Later, in the ambulance, one of the paramedics tried to cut off her yellow Tommy Hilfiger sweater.

"It's brand new," Karen shouted. "Can't you pull it off?"

They gave one small yank, and Karen immediately changed her mind. Every bump along the way was agonizing. Karen pleaded for more morphine. Her wrist, it turned out, was broken in 20 places.

Writing the Ending

As in the chronology structure, you need a strong ending in the focus structure. The difference is that in chronology, you end with the resolution or outcome. In the focus structure, one device is the **tie-back**, a reference to something that appears at or near the beginning of the story. Here is the lead from a *Wall Street Journal* story:

> ETHEL, Mo.—Kristin Gall can't look at an old tractor without wondering about the lives it's rolled through. "There's a story behind every one if you can find it," says the 36-year-old farmer. In 2000, he began trying to track down one that belonged to his late grandfather.
>
> By then, Leonard Gall had been dead for 11 years and the tractor had been gone from the family for nearly twice that long. But Kristin Gall's memories were stirred after he stumbled across a tattered notebook in which his grandfather had jotted down the vehicle's serial number, along with the dates of each oil change.

The story goes on to detail Gall's successful search. It even mentions, high in the story, that his grandfather sometimes bought his grandchildren pedal-driven toy tractors. The story ends with this tie-back to the lead and that anecdote:

> Mr. Gall's hopes are clearer. Aiming to keep his grandfather's tractor in the family for at least one more generation, he revived a tradition his grandfather started: He bought his toddler son a pedal-driven 1206 for Christmas this year.

The goal in the focus structure is to summarize the theme of the story or tie back to the top of the story. Anecdotes, dialogue, scenes and good quotes can all end the story. Don't just stop writing; construct an ending.

SERVICE JOURNALISM

In Chapter 1, you read that one of the criteria for news is usefulness. Many, if not most, magazines you find on the racks appeal to readers by presenting information they might find useful. More than that, they attempt to present this useful information in the most usable way. This approach to presenting information has been called **service journalism**. You often see it labeled "news you can use." One way to think of this is "refrigerator journalism," information presented in such a way that people can cut it out and put it on their refrigerator or bulletin board. (See Figure 11.2, pages 236–37.)

When Hurricane Sandy combined with a winter storm to hit parts of the East Coast, news media across the region used Twitter to send information about where to

Service Journalism

In today's digital world, in-a-hurry readers want practical information presented in the most efficient and effective way.

What this means is that you must think not just of a message—the words. You also must think of how those words will appear on the page or screen—the presentation.

• • • • • • • • • • • • • • • • • • • •

Basics

Service journalism is:

• **Useful.** You must inform people, but if you also find ways to demonstrate how your audience can use the information, you will be more successful. Emphasize WIIFM: "What's in it for me?" See how often you can get "you" in the first sentence of your copy.

• **Usable.** Whenever you can, make a list. Lists get more attention and are better understood and more easily retained. You don't have to write sentences. "Tips" is a magical word.

• **Used.** People stop paying attention to information they never use. You should be able to prove that your audience acts on information. To get people to respond, promise them something. Offer a prize; give them something free.

• *Refrigerator Journalism* •

10 tips to serve audiences today

1. **Save them time.**
2. **Help them make more money, save money or get something free.**
3. **Address different levels of news interest.**
4. **Address niche audiences more effectively.**
5. **Become more personally useful.**
6. **Make information more immediately usable.**
7. **Become more accessible.** Give people your name, phone number, fax number, Web address and email address.
8. **Become easier to use.** Learn to layer the news, use cross-references and links, put things in the same place, color-code, tell people where to find things, use page numbers on contents blurbs, use glossaries and show readers where to find more information.
9. **Make effective use of visuals and graphics.** Use photos, videos, slide presentations, interactive graphics, maps, cartoons, comics and other visuals.
10. **Become more engaging and interactive.** Use contests, quizzes, crosswords, games. People remember better if they do something. Give awards to those who send in answers. Give a coffee mug to the person with the best tip or post of the month.

FIGURE 11.2

Employing the common presentation devices of service journalism, such as boxes and sidebars, this example shows how to highlight information so readers can easily find it and use it.

Refrigerator journalism—giving people printouts they can post in a handy place — invites access and participation.

Other Devices of Service Journalism

1. Use blurbs. After a title and before the article begins, write a summary/contents/benefit blurb. David Ogilvy says no one will read the small type without knowing the benefit upfront. Use the same benefit blurb in a table of contents or menu or briefs column. The best word in a benefit blurb is "how." How to, how you, how I do something. Be personal. Use people in your messages. Also, use internal blurbs, little summaries, pull quotes and tips to tease and coax readers into the story.

2. Use subheads. Before you write, outline. Put the main points of the outline into the copy. Perhaps a better word than subhead is "entry point." Let readers enter the copy where they find something interesting.

3. Have a FAQ page or question-and-answer column. A Q&A format allows readers to skip over things they already know or are not interested in.

4. Repeat things in different ways for different people. Don't be afraid to say something in a box or a graphic that you have said elsewhere. Reinforcing a message aids retention.

5. Think more visually. Include pictures and graphics that contain information and are not purely decorative. Remember, being effective and efficient is the only thing that matters. We used to write articles and then look for graphics or photos to enhance the message. Now we put the information in the graphic (where it will get more attention and have more impact) and write a story to enhance the graphic.

"Never be above a gimmick."
—Dave Orman, ARCO

The power of the box

When you can, put some information in a box. Like lists, boxes or sidebars (1) get more attention, (2) increase comprehension, and (3) aid retention. On the Web, these kinds of boxes can be linked from the main story:

1. **A reference box.** "For more information, see, read, call, click . . ."

2. **A note box.** Take notes from your articles as if you were studying for an exam. Give them to your readers to complement your message.

3. **A glossary box.** Put unfamiliar or technical terms in a glossary box. Use color or another graphic treatment to indicate which words are defined. Also, teach your audience how to pronounce difficult words.

4. **A bio box.** When you need to say something about where a person lived, went to school and worked, put this information in a box or on a separate linked Web page so that your main story is not interrupted.

The 4 goals of the service journalist:

In a nutshell

1. Attention
2. Comprehension
3. Retention
4. Action

PR Tip

Newspapers, magazines, newsletters and websites are doing more and more service journalism. "News You Can Use" and "Tips & Tactics" have become familiar heads. Both newspapers and magazines are becoming more visual. Yet most news releases sent out by PR professionals look the same as they did five and 50 years ago. Why not try refrigerator journalism techniques in your next news release, whether it's sent by mail or digitally?

VideoCentral ▶

Ernie Rideout

**bedfordstmartins.com
/newsreporting**

Watch **"Narrowcasting
in Magazines."**

- Which magazines are good
  examples of narrowcasting?
  Why? Do you consider these
  magazines successful?

- What role might service
  journalism play in niche
  publications?

get shelter and supplies, posted how-to and where-to-go information on their websites and used service journalism techniques in their print products to help residents cope. The *Star-Gazette* in Elmira, N.Y., was typical in carrying news about help coming from the military and the Red Cross. A box on its front page listed ways readers could donate money and explained how to sign up for text alerts.

A pioneer in service journalism, James Autrey of the Meredith Corp., liked to call service journalism "action journalism." Its goal is to get readers to use the information. Magazine publishers know that people are more likely to resubscribe to a magazine if they do some of the things the magazine suggests they do.

All media produce service journalism. Many newspapers have sections dedicated to travel, food and entertainment. Providing tips on how to save money on travel is service journalism. A recipe is service journalism. Telling people when and where an upcoming event is and how much tickets are is service journalism. Front-page news stories, too, often contain elements of service journalism, even if it's just a box listing a sequence of events or directing readers to more information. Service journalism is even easier to do on the Web. You can provide links to lists, how-to information, time-date-place of events, and relevant websites.

In this textbook, you see examples of service journalism in the marginal elements that list the learning objectives for each chapter or that highlight important points. The techniques of service journalism require that you think about content and presentation even as you are reporting. Ask yourself, "What do readers need so they can act on this information?" The answer might range from a Web address to a phone or fax number to instructions on how to fix a lawnmower or make a loaf of bread. It might include directions on how to travel to a festival or information on where and when to buy tickets. As these examples illustrate, you move from simply talking about something to providing the information the reader needs to act on your story.

Much of the basic service journalism information can be presented as sidebars or lists or boxed material. Figure 11.2 uses common service journalism devices to present more information about this topic.

SUGGESTED READINGS

Franklin, Jon. *Writing for Story: Craft Secrets of Dramatic Nonfiction by a Two-Time Pulitzer Prize Winner*. New York: Plume, 1994. If you want to write nonfiction narratives, this book will show you the structure and explain all the elements.

Harrington, Walt, and Mike Sager, eds. *Next Wave: America's New Generation of Great Literary Journalists*. The Sager Group at Smashwords, 2012. E-book. This is a collection of literary journalism written by authors under 40. They are practicing what we describe in Chapters 10 and 11 of this textbook.

LaRocque, Paula. *The Book on Writing: The Ultimate Guide to Writing Well*. Oak Park, Ill.: Marion Street Press, 2003. This great book for new writers covers three main topics: mechanical and structural guidelines; creative elements of storytelling; and grammar, usage and punctuation.

Stewart, James B. *Follow the Story: How to Write Successful Nonfiction*. New York: Touchstone, 1998. Stewart, formerly of *The Wall Street Journal*, won a Pulitzer Prize in 1988 for his reporting on the stock market crash and insider trading. He uses his work to illustrate how to write narration.

SUGGESTED WEBSITES

www.gangrey.com
Gangrey compiles stories primarily written in narrative style, usually using chronology.

www.longreads.com
Longreads offers a selection of stories using the structures described in this chapter.

www.niemanstoryboard.org/2012/07/20/the-aps-kristen
-gelineau-ravi-nessman-and-mary-rajkumar-on-the-saroo
-brierley-saga
This is an interview with the writers and editor of the story of
Saroo Brierley, which opens this chapter. It also contains a link
to the complete story.

www.writersandeditors.com
This site offers everything from advice to freelancers to how-to
material for writers and editors to great links to related content.

EXERCISES

1. **Team project.** Your instructor will organize the class into
   four teams. Each team selects a different story structure to
   analyze and locates at least three stories using that structure.
   (The focus structure is often found in *The Wall Street Journal* and *USA Today*, among other publications.) Identify the
   elements of the setup. Find all the anecdotes. Identify any
   dialogue. Then discuss the impact of the story. How does
   the story structure suit, or not suit, the subject? Report your
   findings to the class.

2. From the first seven paragraphs of the following story,
   identify:

   a. The nut paragraph
   b. Foreshadowing
   c. How chronology is used

   ### Web Plays Incendiary Role in Ohio High School Rape Case
   By Matt Pearce, LATimes.com
   The two high school football players accused of rape will get
   their day in court. The city of Steubenville, Ohio, however,
   will have to fight some of its battles online, where news of
   the case began.

   It's the story of a horrifying accusation met with small-
   town side-taking and blown up into a national scandal.
   Trent Mays and Ma'lik Richmond, both 16, are accused of
   raping a drunk and unconscious 16-year-old girl at a party
   on the night of Aug. 11 while other partygoers tweeted and
   Instagrammed about the attack.

   On Aug. 14, the incident was reported to the Steubenville police, and on Aug. 22, the boys were arrested and
   charged. As they await trial, their attorneys have asserted
   their innocence, saying the girl was conscious enough to
   consent to sex.

   The viral nature of the news was not limited to tweets
   on the night of the incident. The high-profile criminal case
   spotlighted by social media has put not only the defendants
   on trial but the culture surrounding them. Some town residents have compared the attention to a public lynching;
   others have said that without the attention, nothing would
   have been done.

   Steubenville, a city of about 18,000 on the Ohio River,
   dotes on its Big Red high school sports teams.

   A blogger and a native of Steubenville, Alexandria God-
   dard, was among the first to flag the attack, saving screen

   shots from social media at the party and using students'
   names. Others have wondered why more students at the
   party weren't charged; the county sheriff said investigators
   interviewed 59 people and decided that only the two boys
   were responsible.

   But the scandal has entangled more than those two.
   Hacker collective Anonymous recently posted video of
   youths who were said to be Steubenville High School students and alumni joking about the rape victim. Someone
   also hacked and defaced a website dedicated to Steubenville High School athletics, drawing scorn and the promise
   of litigation.

3. **Journalism blog.** Write four to eight paragraphs about
   how you and your classmates learned to be reporters. Use
   narrative tools. For instance, re-create a scene from one
   of your classes. Provide the transition into the body of the
   story, and then stop. Invite your classmates to comment on
   your story—how closely does it match their recollection of
   events?

4. Attend a local school board or city council meeting, and
   write the story as either news narrative or chronology focusing on a key agenda item.

5. Using a chronology, write about eight paragraphs of a story
   about some aspect of your experience in your reporting
   class.

6. Create a news narrative opening for either a story based on
   your own reporting or an inverted pyramid story that has
   already been published.

7. Find two examples of service journalism in newspapers or
   magazines, and analyze them. Find an example of a story
   that would have benefited from service journalism techniques. Tell what you would have done to make the information more usable for readers.

8. Write the first two pages of a story describing an event in
   your life. Try to include as many parts of the setup as you
   can: scenes, dialogue, foreshadowing and the "so what"
   statement.

Writing News for the Web

WHEN HUNDREDS OF THOUSANDS of Egyptians flocked to Tahrir Square in 2011, they came determined to overthrow the government of President Hosni Mubarak. Through Facebook, organizers directed followers to Tahrir and other protest sites for the rallies. The word spread via Twitter, and massive demonstrations followed. The government figured out what was happening and, on Jan. 24, 2011, blocked access to the two websites.

That might have been the end of it, but Web-savvy Egyptians found a way to circumvent the blockage by using sites like HootSuite, which allowed them to reach Facebook and Twitter indirectly. As a result, the Egyptian uprising arguably became the first revolution engineered through social media, although scholars continue to debate the impact of those media.

Mubarak's elected successor, Mohamed Morsi, learned the power of social media during the 2011 revolution and began using Twitter to win favor with Egyptians. He collected a half million followers before issuing a decree in late 2012 giving himself what amounted to dictatorial powers. The online-inspired uprising began anew.

If the Egyptian uprisings were engineered in part on the Web, they also were well-covered there. On one day alone in late November 2012, the BBC website (BBC.co.uk) offered this:

» A story on the Egyptian Parliament rushing to complete a new constitution.
» An account of protesters in Tahrir Square insisting "we won't leave" until the Morsi decree is rescinded.
» A video of an Egyptian publisher talking about the power of the Tahrir protests.
» Another video of judges criticizing the Morsi decree.
» A story on inconsistencies in coverage of the events by the Egyptian state-owned media.
» A photo gallery of the protests.

All that was complemented with maps and graphics.

The longest story had fewer than 1,000 words, and it was broken up with subheads. Most of the other stories were approximately 500 words or fewer. As we'll see,

In this chapter you will learn:

1. Why the Web is a unique media form.
2. What readers expect from the digital media.
3. How to write for the Web.
4. How to write with search engines in mind.
5. How to write for blogs.
6. How to promote news on social media.

241

the BBC's coverage employed the best conventional wisdom about how to write for the Web.

Increasingly, journalists are realizing that writing, editing and packaging news for the Web is different from writing for print or broadcast. We'll explore those differences in this chapter.

THE WEB AS A UNIQUE MEDIA FORM

When it first appeared, Web journalism followed a familiar pattern—one established when radio began to yield to television. As television emerged as a major medium in the post–World War II era, news reports consisted almost entirely of someone sitting at a desk reading written-for-radio news. Similarly, when the Web appeared in the mid-1990s, media organizations quickly adopted it but merely regurgitated news written for traditional media, creating **shovelware**. Sites operated by legacy media—newspapers, magazines, radio and television—contained little more than that morning's stories, which had already appeared in print or on the air.

As the Web evolved, that began to change. News organizations started to write Web-exclusive, or at least Web-first, stories. Also, citizen journalism began to flourish and to challenge the dominance of traditional media in disseminating news. Anyone, it seemed, could now become a journalist or even a publisher.

Those developments have slowly led editors and publishers of legacy media to the conclusion that the Web is an entirely new medium that demands a fresh approach. In this age of consumer choice, people want information when they want it and how they want it. Traditional publishers have now embraced blogs, news alerts on social media networks such as Twitter and Facebook, and even citizen journalism itself.

Some readers receive the news on their smartphones, others on their desktop or tablet computers. Publishers have developed apps for smartphones and tablet computers. These devices put pressure on news disseminators to deliver breaking news instantly and in bursts. In addition, the news media now provide links to other sites, link people with two-way communication and provide not only text, photos and graphics but also audio and video on demand to users with high-speed connections.

When the Web first came along, no one knew how to make money with it, an essential ingredient in a country such as the U.S. in which most media are not state-supported. All that has changed. In 2012, global online advertising revenue was expected to exceed $486 billion worldwide. No other medium in recent years has experienced revenue growth even approaching that.

Just as writing for television evolved from its early iterations, so too is writing for the Web evolving. Most now recognize that writing for the Web is different from writing for television, magazines or newspapers. The Web is clearly a unique medium that requires a new approach, but that approach is still evolving as journalists learn new ways to communicate online. Let's look at the latest conventional wisdom on writing for the Web. (See Figure 12.1 for a comparison of print and digital media news stories.)

Comparison of Print and Digital Media Stories

	Print Stories	Web Stories
Audience	Communication is one-way: from writer to reader. All readers get the same stories.	Communication is two-way: Readers expect to be able to respond online through blogs, forums and so on. Readers customize their reading by using links and specifying preferences.
Structure	Inverted pyramid predominates, but writers use other structures too. All of a news event is covered in one major story.	Inverted pyramid, with the key facts up front, is standard; use of suspense is rare. Coverage is layered so that readers can choose how much of a story to read.
Style	Writers sometimes use literary techniques to enhance stories. Stories are mostly written paragraphs with some breakers.	Readers expect stories to be straightforward, crisp and clear, without much use of literary techniques. Writers use a lot of bullets and lists.
Length	Important stories may be lengthy to accommodate in-depth coverage.	Stories are usually short; additional info is "chunked" into linked sidebar stories that readers can click on if they want to know more.
Sidebars	Writers might add short sidebars on one aspect of a story; newspapers may print the text of a speech.	Stories provide links to past stories that are of possible interest and to information on other sites that readers might want.
Visual Appeal	Newspapers use photos, charts, graphs and drawings. Readers expect to see columns of print.	Websites use photos, charts, graphs and drawings, as well as audio, video and animation. Readers expect sites to be colorful, well-designed, interesting and easy to navigate.
Timeliness	Newspapers are published on a regular schedule, and writers have set deadlines for stories. Readers get news from one medium—the printed newspaper.	Websites are updated throughout the day, and breaking news is posted immediately. Readers get the news at any time on devices such as smartphones.

FIGURE 12.1

Writing for digital media is different in many respects from writing for print newspapers.

READERS' EXPECTATIONS OF THE DIGITAL MEDIA

Before you start to write for the Web, you need to understand readers' expectations of the medium. Even if you plan to work at a print newspaper or magazine, or at a radio or television station, you will need to know how to write for the Web. Every company has a website. At a growing number of newspapers, for example, journalists are being asked to turn in two versions of their stories, one for the newspaper and one for the paper's website.

To be sure, there are readers who want the stories as they appear in the newspaper and not rewritten in some other form. Those readers *want* shovelware because they want to know what other readers are seeing. Many worldwide readers of *The New York Times'* online edition undoubtedly want to see what the print readers have read. *The Times* and many other newspapers now produce downloadable PDF versions that look exactly like the print edition. So, there's a market for that. But most readers want stories tailored to take advantage of the Web's considerable power. They want links, and they want graphics, audio and even video to accompany the text.

To write effectively for the Web, you need to learn a unique way of thinking about writing. Let's begin with these realities about the nature of the Web and what readers expect online:

» Readers want the news right away.
» Readers want to have their say.
» Readers want multimedia variety.
» Readers want the news upfront.
» Readers want to customize content.
» The audience is international.
» Structure is all-important.

Readers Want the News Right Away

At the St. Paul *Pioneer Press*, all print reporters must file a Web story for TwinCities.com (see Figure 12.2) within 30 minutes after witnessing an event or learning about the news. Typically, this story is accompanied by Twitter news bulletins or Facebook posts designed to drive traffic to the story on the newspaper website.

One of the first expectations of Web-based journalism is immediacy. In the old days, newspapers printed several editions a day and occasionally came out with an "extra." Today, cyberspace has turned newspapers into 24-hour competitive news machines, and print-only reporters are rapidly becoming a disappearing species. Television reporters, too, post stories to their companies' websites throughout the day, and the stories they write for the website are much more like those of the newspaper reporter than those they write for the nightly newscast. Web-based journalism, like wire-service journalism, is all about getting out the story as quickly as possible. For today's journalist, the message is this: mobile and Web first, print and broadcast second. Readers expect to get the news as soon as it breaks.

Readers Want to Have Their Say

A major reason why legacy media are increasingly being abandoned in favor of digital media is that readers want to be more than passive consumers of news, which for the most part is what legacy media offer. Many Web users expect to be active participants in the discussion who propose their own take on the news, argue about the impact of the news with their peers and with writers, and perhaps even add significant information or perspective to the discussion. Indeed, some readers want to provide content by

VideoCentral ▶

Peggy Miles

bedfordstmartins.com /newsreporting

Watch **"Going Viral: Political Campaigns and Video."**

- Think of an example of a political video that went viral on the Internet. What effect did the video have on events at the time?

- If video images have been important since 1960, is being able to share them on the Internet really so significant? Explain.

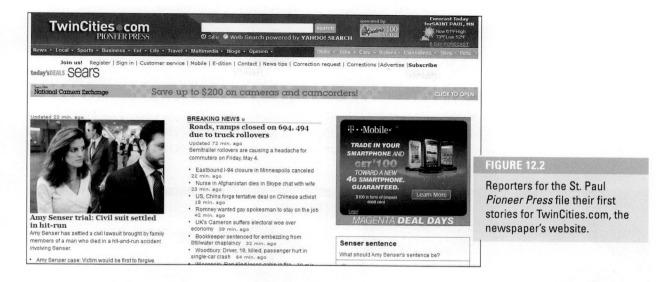

FIGURE 12.2

Reporters for the St. Paul *Pioneer Press* file their first stories for TwinCities.com, the newspaper's website.

sending in written accounts, photos or videos of things they have witnessed. Citizen journalism, as that phenomenon is called, is alive and well.

The one-way communication paths of the past are increasingly giving way to the two-way communication path the Web provides. Journalists must understand that changing dynamic and adjust to it.

Readers Want Multimedia Variety

The most successful writers understand that reading news on the Web is a much different experience compared with reading it in a newspaper or magazine. The best writers know that the Web excels when it presents news using a full spectrum of assets—not only text but also hyperlinks, photos, graphics, audio and video. Online readers expect more than text, and increasingly that's just what they're getting.

Writing for the digital media is about determining the best way to tell a story and then using a variety of media tools—text, audio, video, photographs and graphics—to deliver it. This requires an understanding of audio and video production and the use of information graphics. Even the staid *New York Times* recognizes that and delivers an incredible amount of multimedia on its website. So, too, do ESPN, CNN and a host of others. And slowly but surely, the way things are written and packaged for these websites is changing, too.

Writing for the Web also requires us to think about changes in the ways media messages are consumed. No longer is the Web something you navigate only on a desktop or laptop computer. Today's readers also use netbooks, smartphones, tablet computers and e-readers to consume news. These devices are sometimes more limited in capability than desktop computers and laptops and require journalists to consider how information can best be presented on them. Indeed, many media organizations have created applications for consuming news on smartphones and tablets, allowing material to be plucked from the Web and displayed in the ideal format for the smaller screens (see Figures 12.3 and 12.4). ESPN puts lots of effort into its widely read website. Predictably, video complements the text nicely.

Readers Want the News Upfront

On occasion, print journalists writing for newspapers and magazines build a story with a suspenseful ending. Online news writers, on the other hand, should keep no secrets from readers. With rare exception, they should not try to withhold information

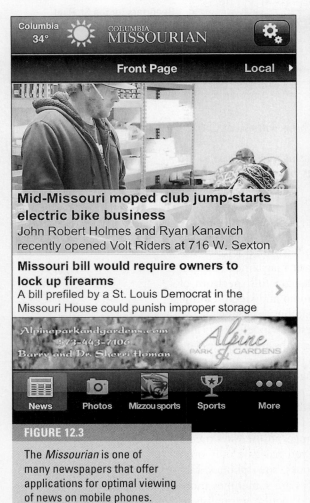

FIGURE 12.3

The *Missourian* is one of many newspapers that offer applications for optimal viewing of news on mobile phones.

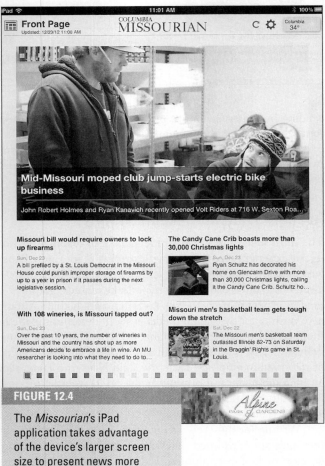

FIGURE 12.4

The *Missourian*'s iPad application takes advantage of the device's larger screen size to present news more attractively than on its mobile phone app.

until later in the story. When you're writing online, it's important to surrender control of the story's sequence to the reader.

In Chapter 9, you were introduced to the most traditional news writing form, the inverted pyramid, which places the most important information in the first paragraph. That technique is exactly what's needed for most Web stories because the lead is even more important in an online story than it is in print. It literally may be all that appears on the screen, and readers may have to click to get more of the story. In addition, for most search engines the lead will be the only information provided for the link to the story. It's smart to include keywords such as "Maine" and "governor" in the lead of a story concerning the Maine governor to help interested readers find it. The lead must nail the "what" or the "so what" to get the full attention of the reader. In fact, it is similar to the anchor's introduction to a television news story.

But as we learned in Chapter 11, even on the Web there is sometimes a place for writing formats other than the inverted pyramid. It would be difficult to argue that a superbly written eight-part series like *The Boston Globe's* 10-year retrospective on 9/11 should be condensed for the Web. Here's what we would suggest: For most daily news stories, write briefly in the inverted pyramid format for the website. But at the same time, don't be afraid to give online readers the full measure of your best newspaper or magazine writing.

Readers Want to Customize Content

On the Web, authors lose their "position of central authority," writes David Weinberger, author and editor of the *Journal of the Hyperlinked Organization,* a newsletter that considers the Web's effect on how business works. Every reader is different; every reader has different needs. Every reader, therefore, not only will select and choose what to read but also will choose a path that best meets those needs.

Think of ways to present different information for different people at different times. Unlike newspapers and magazines, which must decide how long to make a story, digital media should present information so that readers can choose the amount they need. Not many websites have mastered this concept, but it's important.

Note also that the reader is active, not passive. Steve Outing writes on Poynter.org:

> If I gave you an assignment to look at the content of 100 news Web sites, you'd probably find that 95 percent of them don't ever go beyond routine presentation of text, images and the occasional audio or video clip. It's still the rare few that craft content in such ways that go beyond what would be possible in print or broadcast. Rare is the story that uses online interactive techniques that help the user understand the story best by letting him or her interact with and manipulate elements of the story—to experience it, not just read about it.

Outing writes that good writing for the Web says to the reader, "Don't read—do!" It does this because it plays to the essential nature of the Web: It is interactive.

The Big Story: An Alternative Approach

At the start of this chapter, we examined the BBC website's coverage of the uprisings in Egypt, which told a complex story using multiple short stories, audio, video, still photographs and information graphics. All of it was teased on Facebook and Twitter in an attempt to drive readers to the coverage. For most stories, this is probably the most effective approach. But what if the story is even more complex, like *The Boston Globe*'s 10-year retrospective of 9/11, an eight-part series with multiple sidebars, video and information graphics?

Conventional wisdom holds that digital media users won't read long stories like those written by *The Globe*'s reporters, yet it made little sense to hack apart the terrific writing produced for the print edition. Editors at Boston.com, *The Globe*'s website, attempted to solve that problem by putting together an anchor page that led with a video, multiple hyperlinks, a series of photo packages, notable quotes to tease stories and finally links to the actual stories in the series. The anchor page was linked from the front page of Boston.com for days as the series unfolded.

The editors hoped that the video, picture packages and other material would convince readers to plunge into the text itself. While it's tough to tell if this worked, the approach seems to be a sensible one.

The Audience Is International

Few websites of U.S. media companies are bilingual or multilingual, but the fact is that many website users do not speak English, Spanish or French as a first language. Ideally, our websites would be multilingual, but hiring a large translation staff is usually too costly. Fortunately for the English-speaking world, English has become the most commonly used language in international commerce and interaction, so if a site must have only one language, English is usually the best choice.

Still, it's important to remember that the Web is a worldwide medium, not a local one. Writers can help users around the world understand their content by using plain language and avoiding colloquialisms. Simple writing also allows international users to more accurately run a story through online translation programs, such as Google Translate, and make sense of it.

With the growth of Spanish as a second language in the U.S., news outlets need to consider providing content in that language. In the southern tier of states, it's already essential.

Structure Is All-Important

Some who write online forget entirely about structure. That's a huge mistake. Even though Web stories have a unique structure, they still must be organized in a logical, coherent way. Digital media readers do not revel in chaos. Even though a story may appear on the screen as a mosaic, the way that mosaic is composed will attract readers, keep them and help them follow what for them is the most logical path.

Web writers should consider presenting information in layers (see annotated model on page 250). Remember: No two readers are alike. You can present the same information with different degrees of detail and support. It works like this:

Layer 1. Give readers a lead paragraph or several paragraphs—enough so they can understand the basic story. This first layer is information that is immediately available to readers. No action or effort is demanded of them.

Layer 2. Provide a way for readers to click to continue reading the story. Alternatively, readers should be able to easily access more information by moving the cursor or by scrolling.

Layer 3. Provide links to earlier stories on the same subject or to related written material.

Layer 4. Complement the story with video, photos, graphics or audio, or make the video or photo the centerpiece of the story and subordinate the text. This layer may require readers to click on a link that opens up still more information—perhaps audio, video or a source document.

When you write for print, you are concerned with continuity, with themes, with working in all aspects of the story while keeping the writing clear and coherent. When you write for the Web, you need not worry so much about the structure or flow of the whole piece but rather about the relationships of the layers and parts. It's all about understanding what readers want and helping them navigate from place to place to get the information they seek. It is important to offer clear entry and exit points.

Sometimes you may want to take readers down a path that branches into several other paths. Some call this technique *threading*. The story of a plane crash can lead to various threads: the airline and its safety record, the plane itself and the record of that type of plane, the place of the accident, the people involved, and so forth.

Don't be too concerned about repetition. Remember, readers choose what parts to read. Besides, a certain amount of repetition or of stating things in different ways, perhaps visually, increases retention. All readers—whether on the Web or elsewhere—process information differently.

So, because most people don't think linearly, writing done for the digital media is more in line with the way people think. It's even more in line with the way today's readers read. For the Web, break the story into short, digestible pieces. Rather than stringing together a long story and trying to get readers to read the whole thing in the order in which you present it, keep in mind that many readers don't want to read everything you have to tell them. You must give them choices and let them decide what to read and in what order.

The website of the BBC (BBC.co.uk) presents information for the Web in the most desirable way. The brevity of its stories, even in reporting a major event like the uprisings in Egypt, is ideal for a website. Perhaps the BBC's history of writing concisely for radio and television helps. Perhaps that's why readers increasingly favor television station websites over newspaper websites in many cities. Newspaper stories tend to be longer, and they too often are not tightened for the Web.

TIPS

Characteristics of Hypertext Links

Hypertext and hypermedia have the following characteristics:

» They present ideas nonsequentially.

» They follow the thought process.

» They allow users to choose individual pathways through the information.

» They allow information to transcend individual documents.

» They link text with pictures, audio and video.

—Andrew Bonime and Ken C. Pohlmann, *Writing for New Media*

ANNOTATED MODEL   **Layering Content on a Web Page**

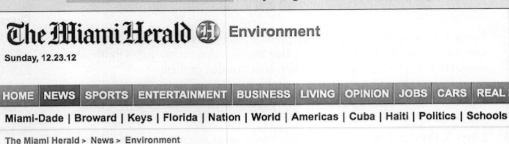

The Miami Herald 🅗 Environment

Sunday, 12.23.12

HOME | NEWS | SPORTS | ENTERTAINMENT | BUSINESS | LIVING | OPINION | JOBS | CARS | REAL

Miami-Dade | Broward | Keys | Florida | Nation | World | Americas | Cuba | Haiti | Politics | Schools

The Miami Herald > News > Environment

Posted on Saturday, 12.22.12   A A   🅾 Share 1   email   print   comment   reprints

Readers click on a link on the home page to get the full story and a photo, shown here.

The Everglades: Where the wildflowers are   👍 Like 1

The swamp is dotted with strange, beautiful varieties, each with its own story

Botanist Roger Hammer in the Pine Flatwoods of Big Cypress Preserve searches for wildflowers to update his book on Everglades wildflowers. Hammer has spent his life as a naturalist and recorder of wild Florida. TIM CHAPMAN / MIAMI HERALD STAFF

Fullsize 🔳 Buy Photo   ◀ previous | next ▶
Image 1 of 6

Readers can click on the photo gallery.

Related Content

Another link connects to additional photos.

- Wildflowers in the Everglades 🔲

MORE INFORMATION

Naturalist Roger Hammer, who lives in Homestead, has written four books, including guides to wildflowers in the Everglades and Florida Keys as well as a visitor guide to Everglades National Park and photo-essay book on iconic places and things in Florida. For more information on his work, go to www.rogerhammer.com.

A link to the subject's website gives the interested reader more info.

BY CURTIS MORGAN
CMORGAN@MIAMIHERALD.COM

They're so easy to miss in a landscape almost monotonously green.

But for naturalist Roger Hammer, it's the small, scattered drops of color that stand out among the slash pines and saw palmetto. Wildflowers. The vast Everglades is home to hundreds of them.

Some are spectacular but most are small and subtle. Some are fragrant, others poisonous. With the exception of a few big names — notably, the rare ghost orchid made famous in a best-selling book — many are largely unknown and unnoticed, at least outside a small group of scientists, enthusiasts and, unfortunately, poachers.

"The average person driving by has no idea of what is out here," said Hammer, as he hiked the northeastern corners of the Big Cypress National Preserve in an ongoing quest to find and photograph an exceptionally scarce yellow bloom called the Fakahatchee burmania.

If Hammer — a longtime Miami-Dade County parks naturalist and one of Florida's foremost authorities on native plants — hasn't seen an Everglades wildflower, then few other people in the

The Miami Herald uses layering to draw a reader into a story. Here, the photo and text are complemented by links to additional photos and an external link to the subject's own website.

Stories that require multiple continuous screens turn off many readers immediately. Many readers hate to scroll on screen. Some exit even before they get to the bottom of the screen. Few will take the time to read a lot of text in one clump. Note, of course, that this is not true of highly motivated readers who crave your information or sites like *Slate* magazine where readers expect long-form stories. It's important to know your audience and what it expects.

GUIDELINES FOR WRITING FOR THE WEB

Those who read the digital media are surfers or scanners, much more so than readers of print, perhaps because it takes 25 percent longer to read online than it does in print. Researchers Jakob Nielsen and John Morkes found that 79 percent of those they tested scanned a new page they came across; only 16 percent read the copy word for word.

Web expert Shel Holtz says you want readers to dive, not surf. Surfing is what frustrated readers do. Here are 10 ways to turn surfers into divers—or at least hold their attention long enough to get your message across.

Think Immediacy

Although you must make sure what you write is accurate, the Web can deliver news when it is brand-new, so speed in handling breaking news is essential. Writing for the Web is, in many ways, like writing for the wire services. Internet users now consume information the way wire-service subscribers do. Keeping readers with you means keeping them up-to-the-minute. You must expect to update breaking stories quickly and to add depth whenever it is available. But just because you can easily correct your mistakes does not mean you are allowed to make them. Columnist David Broder of *The Washington Post* warns that posting news quickly could sacrifice quality and damage credibility.

Save Readers Time

One thing most readers do not have is time. Whatever you can do to save readers time is worth *your* time. It's been said by various people in different ways since the philosopher Blaise Pascal first said it: "I would have written a shorter letter, but I did not have the time." For many stories, if not most, perhaps your chief concern should be this: Have I presented this information in such a way as to cost readers the least amount of time?

The best way to save readers time is to be clear. Choose the simple word. Vary the length of sentences, but keep them short. Write short paragraphs. Help readers. Emphasize key words by highlighting them.

Another reason to write simply, using simple words and simple sentences, is to enable the automated translation programs used by some search engines to translate the page. The simpler the words and sentences, the more likely it is that a foreign-language translation of the story will be accurate and understandable.

TIPS

Web Writing Guidelines in a Nutshell

» Get the news online fast.

» Write shorter stories, with subheads if necessary.

» Use sidebars to keep the main story short.

» Include keywords in your lead or introductory blurb.

» Add hyperlinks, still photographs and video.

» Design a visually appealing and well-organized package.

» Use social media to drive traffic to the website.

ON THE JOB
An Online Career

Since graduating from college, **Jenifer Langosch** has worked as a beat writer for MLB.com, covering the Pittsburgh Pirates and now the St. Louis Cardinals. Though the job revolves heavily around the six-month baseball season, it's a profession that essentially keeps her busy 12 months a year.

Langosch's responsibilities include covering every facet of the ballclub. In season, that includes writing game stories and feature stories, covering breaking news and updating fans on roster moves, injuries or implications of certain games or events.

While the demands do lessen a bit during baseball's offseason, she's still responsible for reporting on any news that involves the organization. There are trades and free agent acquisitions to cover, as well as season preview content to put out. She covers baseball's winter meetings every December and races to break news about player movement or personnel changes.

The job sends her to Jupiter, Fla., every winter to cover seven weeks of spring training. She also covers most of the team's road games, which means she lives away from St. Louis for much of the baseball season.

Working with MLB.com has afforded Langosch the opportunity to cover other Major League events, too. In her first six seasons with the company, she covered five All-Star games and multiple playoff series, including three World Series.

"It's hard to narrow down the things I like most about this job," Langosch says. "It's an ongoing challenge to immerse myself so heavily in knowing a team — its players, inner workings, management team, past and future — so that I can bring both a casual baseball fan and a know-it-all type all the information.

"The fact that I get to do so many different types of writing also appeals to me. Writing a game story is quite different from writing an in-depth feature story, which is quite different from writing a hard news article. On a weekly basis, I typically have to do all of these at one time or another. Doing so has really helped me develop different voices in my writing."

The chance to incorporate all forms of new media has also been a plus, further expanding her skill set.

"I run a blog on the site and interact with fans through Twitter. There are times where I take my own digital camera and digital camcorder on site to bring images to fans that way.

"Working with an online company has put me in a position to better weather the storm that the journalism industry finds itself in right now. While I still have a place for newspapers in my heart, my recommendation to anyone wanting to pursue a career in print journalism is to also explore online opportunities. It's the same job, just a different medium."

Langosch also urges would-be journalists to immerse themselves in all forms of journalism.

"Even if you're a writer, learn how to use a camera and camcorder. Find a way to allow social networking sites to help you better reach out and interact with readers. If you're interested in going into sports reporting, know ahead of time that your love of writing, not your love of sports, will sustain your interest in the profession long-term. Expect to work mostly nights and weekends, but also know that sports sometimes allows for the best storytelling."

Provide Information That's Quick and Easy to Get

The overall organization of your story must tell readers that they can get the information quickly and easily. Digital media readers have zero tolerance for confusion and no time at all to be led astray. It's too easy for them to click on something else.

Don't get carried away by your own eloquence. Be guided by what your readers want or need to know. Make it easy for them. Write short paragraphs with one idea per paragraph.

Think Both Verbally and Visually

In the past, writers for print thought little about how their stories were going to appear. Their job was to write the story—period. The designer's job was to make the story fit on the page in some meaningful way. Writers did not worry about headlines, subheads, summary quotes, photos, illustrations or anything but the story.

Television news writers know that they must write to the pictures. Good television has good video, so the visual medium tries to show rather than to tell. Words complement pictures and say what the pictures do not. Many times, of course, the writer does not make the pictures and is not responsible for getting them. But the writer still must consider the best way to tell the story, and sometimes visuals convey the story as no amount of text could possibly do.

As a Web journalist, you may or may not have to do it all by yourself, but you definitely must *think* both verbally and visually. From the outset, you must be concerned about the most effective and efficient way for the information to appear on the screen. You have to think not only about the organization of the page but also about ways to use graphics, to be interactive and to use online tools.

No one doubts that photos and graphics grab readers' attention. That's why you see icons and information graphics in magazines and newspapers, and that's why you must think, perhaps with the help of graphic designers, of ways to use graphic elements online.

Cut Your Copy

Most digital media readers simply will not read long stories. Even veteran computer users find reading on screen somewhat difficult, even unpleasant, says Jakob Nielsen. Studies contradict each other about people's aversion to scrolling, however. In the not-so-distant past, some experts advised getting the whole story on one screen. Because some screens are small, they advised not writing more than 20 lines of text. Now, because of the proliferation of larger and less-irritating screens, some readers are finding it easier and less frustrating to scroll for more information. But as home and office screens have grown larger, smaller screens on smartphones and tablets have also grown popular; scrolling is often necessary, but readers on the go may not want to scroll a dozen times to read a single news story. As in broadcast news writing, there's little room online to be cute or even literary. Be crisp and clear.

Use Lots of Lists and Bullets

Often you can cut copy by putting information into lists. Whenever possible, make a list. Lists get more attention and allow for better comprehension and more retention than ordinary sentences and paragraphs. (The Web-friendly memo-structure story format, illustrated in Chapter 9, has list-like features.) Bulleted or numbered lists are scannable. Readers can grasp them immediately. Think of information on the Web as a database. That's how people use their digital media. Besides, it's also quicker for the writer to make lists than to write paragraphs.

Mark Deuze and Christina Dimoudi of the Amsterdam School of Communications Research conclude from their study that Web-based journalism is really a fourth kind of journalism after print, radio and television. Its main characteristic is "empowering audiences as active participants in the daily news." Web journalists have "an interactive relationship with their audience" and a "strong element of audience orientation" and are "more aware of their publics and service function in society than their colleagues elsewhere."

Nielsen tested five versions of the same information for usability. Look first at the longest version, which he calls promotional writing, his control condition:

> Nebraska is filled with internationally recognized attractions that draw large crowds of people every year, without fail. Some of the most popular places were Fort Robinson State Park (355,000 visitors), Scotts Bluff National Monument (132,126 visitors), Arbor Lodge State Historical Park & Museum (100,000), Carhenge (85,598), Stuhr Museum of the Prairie Pioneer (60,002), and Buffalo Bill Ranch State Historical Park (28,446).

Now look at this same material in list form:

> In 1996, six of the most visited places in Nebraska were:
> - Fort Robinson State Park.
> - Scotts Bluff National Monument.
> - Arbor Lodge State Historical Park & Museum.
> - Carhenge.
> - Stuhr Museum of the Prairie Pioneer.
> - Buffalo Bill Ranch State Historical Park.

The list version of the information scored a 124 percent usability improvement over the longer version.

Write in Chunks

When you can't put material into lists, you can still organize it into chunks of information. Put information into sidebars or boxes. Readers will read more, not less, if you break up the information into small bites. Research has also shown that putting some information in a sidebar can give readers better comprehension of the subject. But the main objective here is to write for diverse readers who want to get only the information they want in the order in which they want it.

Think of your story as having parts. When writing a story for a newspaper, you need to think of ways to join the various parts of the story. You craft transitions carefully, and you may even add subheads. When writing a story for the digital media, use subheads if necessary. Better yet, make each segment a separate story. Be sure that

Producing Video for the Web

Website users expect multimedia presentation of news, particularly in the case of important news stories. Many Web producers are relatively new to video production and editing, so here are some tips for beginners:

» **Get instruction from someone who has professional video production skills.** You can learn a lot in a day or two.
» **Use good equipment.** You won't need cameras and microphones capable of producing a Hollywood movie or a CNN broadcast, but the quality of the equipment is still important.
» **Eliminate background noise as much as possible.** Some background sound is good for an on-site video, but don't record in an atmosphere where the background noise will drown out your message.
» **Use digital compression rates that are optimized for the Web.** For audio, use a sample rate of 22.5 Hz and 16-bit mono or stereo at 56 Kbps. For video, save the video in uncompressed AVI format for editing and then upload it to the Web in WMV or FLV format.

» **Employ search-engine optimization techniques so that your video can be found on the Web.** Use important keywords in metadata and even in the name of the file itself.
» **Use video to complement other material on your site.** Video is best used in conjunction with text, photos, information graphics, links and other material.
» **Keep videos short, no more than five minutes.**
» **Brand your videos with your logo, and make it easy for social media users to link to them.** Facebook and Twitter can drive plenty of traffic to your video and consequently to your website.
» **Consider allowing users to rate your video.** This, too, can drive more users to the video and to your site.

---

each part can stand on its own well enough to be comprehensible and to make your point. Again, remember the importance of a strong lead in the inverted pyramid form.

Use Hyperlinks

To understand the Web, think of a spider web. The Web, says David Weinberger, is a place where we go to connect. Users of the Internet like to feel connected. If you want them to read your copy and come back for more, you must satisfy and enhance that sense of connection.

Nielsen argues that websites must employ scannable text using these elements:

» Highlighted key words, including hypertext links.
» Meaningful subheads.
» Bulleted lists.
» One idea per paragraph.
» Half the word count of conventional writing.

Being connected means being interactive. Web users want to be actively involved in what they are reading. They are not passive observers. Like video game players, they want to be in control of where they are going and how they get there. Both individual stories and whole pages must be internally and externally interactive.

Internal Connections

The most challenging and necessary aspect of writing for the Web is making the copy interactive. You begin that process by streamlining your copy and not including everything. Create **hyperlinks** that allow readers to access information elsewhere on your site or even on another site.

One of the most perplexing problems writers face is deciding when to include the definition of a word. Will you insult some readers by defining a term they know? Will you leave others behind if you do not define the term? A similar problem is whether to tell who a person is. Many readers may wonder how stupid you think they are for telling them that actor Arnold Schwarzenegger was the Republican governor of California. Other readers may need or want that information.

The Web writer can simply make the word or name a hyperlink to a different page. Readers need only click on a hyperlinked word to find its meaning or to read more about it. No longer do writers have to write, "For more information, see. . . ." Academic writers use footnotes. Hypertext and hypermedia, linking readers to audio, video and pictures, are much more convenient.

Other techniques can also save space while reducing visual clutter on the screen. Some sites display information only when an interested reader rolls the cursor over an item on the page.

Writing concisely has never been easier. You can stick to the essentials and link to the rest. A story about a homicide can link to a map of where the crime took place, to a chart showing the number of homicides this year as compared with last year, to a piece about friends of the victim, to information about violent crimes nationally, and so forth.

Remember, too, that unlike the newspaper, where you may be short of space, and unlike radio and television, where you may be short of time, online you have unlimited space and time to run photos and aspects of stories that could be of real interest to some readers. Sports fans, for example, would probably enjoy seeing a whole gallery of photos from Saturday's championship game, and they would enjoy reading interviews with the stars of the game.

> " We have derived three main content-oriented conclusions from our four years of Web usability studies:
>
> » Users do not read on the Web; instead they scan the pages, trying to pick out a few sentences or even parts of sentences to get the information they want.
>
> » Users do not like long, scrolling pages; they prefer the text to be short and to the point.
>
> » Users detest anything that seems like marketing fluff or overly hyped language ('marketese') and prefer factual information. "
>
> —John Morkes and Jakob Nielsen,
> "Concise, Scannable, and Objective: How
> to Write for the Web," nngroup.com

External Connections

Don't forget the power of hyperlinks to different websites. Academic writers include bibliographies. Print journalists often identify sources in their stories. Other writers simply say to readers: "That's all I know about the subject, I'm not going to tell you where I obtained my information, and I'm not telling you where you can find more information." Hypertext and hypermedia have changed all that. Readers now expect hyperlinks to source material, and you should provide them when writing for the digital media.

Obviously, you are not expected to lead readers away from your site to a competitor's, especially on a breaking story. Nevertheless, readers will come to rely on your site to help them find more information about subjects that interest them greatly. And many news sites post supporting documents to buttress their stories.

The New York Times made terrific use of an external hyperlink when it reported on the death of singer Etta James on its website. It provided a link to a YouTube version of James' hit song "At Last," with the lyrics of the tune superimposed on a photo of James. Even those not familiar with her music were able to hear a sample of her talent.

To find appropriate external hyperlinks, you need to know how to use search engines like Yahoo and Google. Google News is a master of providing links galore for readers to peruse.

Give Readers a Chance to Talk Back

A big part of providing interactive content is allowing readers to talk back. The Web has leveled the playing field. Everyone can be an owner or a publisher. Everyone feels the right, and often the need, to talk back—if not to the writer of the piece, then to other readers in **chat rooms** (computer applications that allow users to communicate with one another in real time) or blogs. The wonderful thing about allowing readers to talk back is that they do. When they do, they will revisit the site again and again. Web readers want to be part of the process. Readers love it when newspapers like *The Miami Herald* include the reporter's email address in the byline, and many of them respond.

Never has it been easier to find out what is on the minds of your readers. Print and broadcast have mainly been forms of one-way communication. Now, not only can you get opinions easily and quickly, but you also can incorporate them into your story or include hyperlinks to them. Letters to the editor have always been among the best-read sections in newspapers and magazines. Many readers, especially those reading on the Web, not only want to express their own opinions but love to read the opinions of others. Be sure, however, that you use the same strict standards for publishing others' remarks on your website that you use for publishing in your newspaper or magazine. Even email polls can and have been flooded by advocacy groups. Reporting their results can be meaningless, misleading and certainly unprofessional unless the polls are monitored carefully.

Don't Forget the Human Touch

Veteran correspondent Helen Thomas told a convention of newspaper interactive editors, "I do hope the human touch remains in the robotic scheme of things. Human beings still count." Remember, people make the news. Facts are just facts unless you relate them to people.

The 3-2-2-1 Format

After spending 25 years as a professional newsman, the last four of those as a general manager, Associate Professor Clyde Bentley now teaches classes in online journalism. In one class, students take stories from the newspaper and rewrite them for use online. Bentley calls students online "producers" rather than reporters.

"I was surprised at the resistance my students had to changing the copy of reporters," Bentley says. "They preferred the 'shovelware' concept so they would not tamper with the prose of their friends."

In frustration, he instituted what he called a "3-2-2-1 format." "It was a way to force my young journalists to take on a new process," he says.

Here's what the numbers mean.

3 Subheads

By inserting three subheads, the producers "chunk" the story into four pieces. "This is easier to read than one long, scrollable piece of text," Bentley says. The subdivisions can be as simple as "who, what, when. . . ."

2 External Links

These links direct readers to further information posted outside the story. "For instance, in a story about the local dog pound, we might have external links to the ASPCA and the American Kennel Club."

2 Internal Links

These explanatory links are tied to text within the story. "In the pound story," Bentley explains, "the word 'Doberman' might be a link that takes one to a breeder's site that explains the Doberman pinscher."

1 Photo or Graphic Not Available in the Print Edition

Print publications limit art primarily because of space limitations. There are no such limits on the Web. "If a photographer shoots 20 shots, we can run more than one," Bentley says. "More commonly, however, the producers insert mug shots of people mentioned in the story. There is no reason not to run mugs of everyone who is mentioned in a story."

A word of caution: Including email addresses on the Web leaves you vulnerable to spammers and others who use a program called an "email siphon" to collect contact information. Putting your email address in a news story or magazine article can subject you to a deluge of spam. Rather than giving your permanent personal address, include in your stories a different address that you change from time to time.

WRITING WITH SEARCH ENGINES IN MIND

It's almost impossible to overemphasize one major consideration in writing for the digital media: If your online story cannot be found, it won't be read. That's why editors of websites place great emphasis on *search-engine optimization*, the process of making sure your story will be found when someone searches for its topic on sites such as Google or Yahoo. Generally, the better job you do getting keywords into the lead, the more likely your story will appear near the top of the search results for that topic.

In fact, search engines are more likely to rank the story higher if those keywords are repeated in the headline and in the first couple of paragraphs—something newspaper and magazine editors often try to avoid. How does that work with a story in which the lead obviously was not written with search-engine optimization in mind? A good solution is to place a summary blurb at the top of the Web story for indexing purposes.

Another way to accomplish the same thing is to craft a lead in the form of an extended headline, followed by two or three statements that also read as headlines. If you hyperlink the headlines, readers can click on them to read the full version of the story on another page within the website.

Newspapers and magazines are notorious for writing baseball stories that never mention the word "baseball" and hockey stories that never use the word "hockey." That's not a problem if users search for the team name, such as Atlanta Braves. They'll find your story even if it doesn't include the word "baseball." But what if users search for "baseball"? Your story will not be found unless it contains metadata—that is, tagging information—that includes that search term. Understanding how search engines work is the key to making sure that all possible search terms appear either in the metadata accompanying the story or in the story itself.

Remember, again, that search engines are more likely to rank your story higher if keywords are repeated in the headline and in the first couple of paragraphs. Making these search-engine-specific changes may require some extra attention at newspapers and magazines that try not to repeat words in the headline and lead.

Many websites have protocols for ensuring that the proper keywords are used, and several companies now offer services that ensure content is optimized for search engines. These services can be a wise investment for any site looking to increase its readership.

WRITING FOR BLOGS

Blog entries range from short, inverted pyramid stories, often written quickly by beat reporters, to essays. Whereas traditional journalism is formal, blogging is informal. Whereas traditional journalism is dispassionate, much of blogging is passionate. Whereas traditional journalism is third person ("he," "she," "they"), much of blogging is first person ("I," "we"). Whereas much of traditional writing is vetted by layers of editors, much of blogging goes straight from the writer to the reader.

Wide-Ranging Subject Matter

Political and sports bloggers capture a disproportionate amount of the attention, but there are respected bloggers, some of them independent, most of them working for startups or the traditional media, who blog on everything from travel to technology. Even some heads of companies are blogging, and public relations professionals are doing it on behalf of their companies or organizations. The best blogs are conversational, based in specifics, full of comparisons, explanations, turns of phrase and links. While some Web writers do not distinguish between fact and fiction, professional journalists must be meticulous about the facts in their blogs. Here are a few examples of good blogging.

First, a blog about blogging by David Carr from the "Media Decoder" blog (http://mediadecoder.blogs.nytimes.com). It's conversational, it's based in fact and it's to the point.

> Academics and Web thinkers have spent a lot of time jawboning about whether a blogger fits the definition of a journalist. It's an endless discussion, but this week in Oregon, the debate turned costly for one blogger.
>
> Crystal Cox, a Montanan who calls herself an investigative blogger and produces several blogs about the law, was sued in January by the investment firm Obsidian Finance Group over several opinionated blog posts that were highly critical of Obsidian and its co-founder Kevin Padrick. The firm sought $10 million in damages. Although the judge threw out several of the firm's claims, he ruled against her on a single post and ordered her to pay $2.5 million in damages.

A popular blog topic is parenting. Here's an autobiographical excerpt from the blog of a father who shares the tribulations of raising five children, including twin boys (www.stuffboysdo.com). He appropriately uses first person, and he has a distinctive sense of humor. Because the blog is his own, the author doesn't have to reflect an institution or its voice. By sharing his experiences, he is providing a measure of service journalism, helping other parents who encounter similar problems.

> Hi, my name is Tony and I am a survivor of boys. So far. I live in the Florida panhandle with my gorgeous wife and our five children. Two of them are not boys, which is fortunate, because it means there is a slight chance I will survive the next 15 years and become an author and standup comedian, fueled solely by brilliant material provided by the boys. For now, I work as a video producer and write this blog. And try to survive the boys.

In the *New York Times* blog "The Lede" (http://thelede.blogs.nytimes.com), Jere Longman wrote a personal essay for readers:

> EUNICE, La.—The electricity has been out since Hurricane Gustav blew through the Cajun prairie, but I still flick the light switch every time I walk into the kitchen or the bathroom.
>
> My father, who is 76, has been shaving in a pail under the carport and making his coffee on the barbecue pit. "I'd walk a mile for a Camel and a mile for a cup of coffee," he said.

Professional Standards

Dan Steinberg, who is a full-time sports blogger for *The Washington Post*, has two gripes about blogs. In an interview with *Gelf* magazine (GelfMagazine.com), he says bloggers shouldn't steal good stuff from journalists who are doing the reporting. He also chafes at the traditional restrictions of taste imposed upon him by his newspaper. Steinberg, a former beat reporter, spends a lot of time in locker rooms. He would like to reflect some of the off-color talk, but his editors impose the same standards on his blog as they do on the rest of the paper.

Other bloggers have more freedom. Steinberg is one of the few journalists working for the traditional media who are full-time bloggers. Most are beat reporters who drop news tidbits or humorous observations into a blog about their beats. *The New York Times*, for instance, offers more than 60 blogs, all written by staff writers or columnists. Some bloggers are primarily mini-aggregators. They monitor the Web for news of whatever specialty they cover and provide the links for readers. From bursts to full-blown essays, bloggers use a variety of writing styles. There may not be rules or even best practices, but there are two worthwhile guidelines: Be interesting, and be accurate.

PROMOTING NEWS ON FACEBOOK AND TWITTER

Most journalists today are asked to promote their stories on social media such as Facebook and Twitter. For example, before or after a writer's article goes live on the website, he or she tweets followers with a tease or link to the piece. This helps drive traffic to the news organization's website, enabling the organization to charge more for advertising on the site.

Facebook is used in a similar way. Many newspapers, magazines, and radio and television stations have Facebook sites on which reporters post links to their stories and readers comment on them. Facebook Subscribe allows readers to subscribe to the public updates of a journalist on Facebook without having to add that journalist as a friend. Both *The New York Times* and *The Washington Post* are heavy users of this service.

Journalists use Twitter primarily to promote their stories, according to a Pew Research Center study, much like television anchors use teases before they break for commercials: "After the break, we'll find out when the snowstorm will arrive." An effective tease gives enough information to pique the reader's interest but does not give away the key elements of the story.

A good example can be found in this tweet from Journalism Buzz: "31% of digital ads not seen by consumers." That's a significant fact, but there is a lot of context missing. In contrast, JournoResources tweeted, "Useful background report on #Iran-US tensions." There is no tease, no reason to follow the link other than that the report is "useful."

Journalists also use Twitter to solicit reader suggestions, to talk about the process of news gathering and to break news before they are able to write even a short story for the Web.

Because tweets don't go through the editing process, it is important that you reread and edit your own tweet before sending it. Journalists who send tweets with spelling, grammar and factual errors are damaging their reputations and those of their employers.

Writing at Poynter.org, Jeff Sonderman reported on research by Dan Zarrella, who studied thousands of tweets to determine what led to the highest click-through rates. Zarrella's advice:

» Write between 120 and 130 characters.
» Place links about a quarter of the way through the tweet (not always at the end).
» Tweet only once or twice an hour.

Zarrella also confirmed earlier research that advised using more verbs and determined that tweets are most effective at night or on weekends.

TOMORROW'S READERS

Print has been around for centuries, and we are still figuring out ways to use it effectively. In contrast, writing for the digital media is relatively new, and both writers and readers are still learning the most effective uses of the newest media. Like all good journalists, those who write for the Web must be students of writing. Writing for the Web is more about showing than telling. Good writing allows the audience to experience rather than witness, to actively participate rather than be passive, to do rather than merely read. Never before have writers been more challenged.

SUGGESTED READINGS

Craig, Richard. *Online Journalism: Reporting, Writing, and Editing for New Media*. Stamford, Conn.: Wadsworth-Thomson Learning, 2004. This book is a comprehensive source of information about writing for the Web.

Foust, James C. *Online Journalism: Principles and Practices of News for the Web*. Scottsdale, Ariz.: Holcomb Hathaway, 2011. This is an excellent book on writing for the Web.

Friend, Cecilia, and Jane Singer. *Online Journalism Ethics: Traditions and Transitions*. Armonk, N.Y.: M.E. Sharpe, 2007. Friend and Singer have written an excellent treatise on the ethics of online sites.

Morkes, John, and Jakob Nielsen. "Concise, Scannable, and Objective: How to Write for the Web." Available from http://www.nngroup.com/articles/concise-scannable-and-objective-how-to-write-for-the-web. This article contains a wonderful summary of the authors' research regarding effective online writing.

Nielsen, Jakob. "How Users Read on the Web." Available from www.nngroup.com/articles/how-users-read-on-the-web. Nielsen offers practical advice, including research, on the usability of online copy.

SUGGESTED WEBSITES

www.bedfordstmartins.com/newscentral

When you visit News Central, you will find up-to-the-moment RSS feeds, research links and exercises to help you improve your grammar and AP style usage. In addition, the site's Video-Central: Journalism section hosts the videos highlighted in this chapter as well as additional clips of leading professionals discussing important media trends.

www.espn.go.com

ESPN.com, one of the best sites on the Web, is probably the most extensive Internet site for sports fans. It was an early leader in the use of audio and video.

www.mercurynews.com

MercuryNews.com, one of the first comprehensive local news websites, includes area news courtesy of the *San Jose Mercury News*.

www.miamiherald.com

Like many daily newspapers, *The Miami Herald*'s online edition includes most of the stories from its print edition, along with additional online-only posts.

www.newsy.com

This innovative, video-heavy site compares the coverage of major stories by various media around the world.

www.nng.com

This is expert Jakob Nielsen's site. You won't find anyone more knowledgeable and up-to-date on the research in the field of online writing than Nielsen.

http://tv.msnbc.com

This companion site to the cable news channel offers a wealth of news resources. Its opinions section includes, among other things, links to top stories; stories from *Slate*, another Microsoft website; and opinion pieces and blogs by pundits and journalists.

EXERCISES

1. **Team project.** Your instructor will divide the class into teams. With your team, select five newspaper or magazine websites. Each team member should read at least three articles on a specific site, evaluating how well the articles illustrate the 10 guidelines for online writing covered in this chapter. When the team reassembles, discuss your results. Rank the websites in terms of how good a job they do of using online writing techniques. Share your conclusions with the class.

2. Visit your local newspaper or television station and interview journalists who do the news online. Find out how they were trained and what major challenges they face.

3. Your instructor will assign you a newspaper story. Rewrite it for online use, and indicate any hyperlinks that you might include.

4. **Journalism blog.** Choose a major national story from a recent newspaper or newsmagazine. Then visit two newspaper websites and compare their treatment of the story. Write a 300-word critique of the online writing techniques that the websites used. Post the critique on your blog, and send a tweet to your classmates inviting them to comment on your post.

5. Find a website that does a good job of linking readers to original source material. Evaluate the use of that technique, and explain why it works for the website.

6. Go to the BBC website (**BBC.co.uk**) and choose one of the major stories of the day. In a one-page memo, outline how the BBC took advantage of different media types to tell the story.

7. List five differences in how information is conveyed in a newspaper vs. how it is conveyed on a website.

13

Writing News for Radio and Television

In this chapter you will learn:

1. What radio and television do best.

2. How the selection criteria for radio and television news differ from those of print news.

3. How to write radio and television news.

4. How social media can supplement radio and television content.

5. How to prepare radio and television news copy.

INAUGURATIONS of U.S. presidents are required by the Constitution, but they are made for television.

The first president to have his inaugural oath broadcast nationally on radio was Calvin Coolidge in 1925. Harry S. Truman's inauguration in 1949 was the first to be carried on television. Since then, the quadrennial event has become a major viewing experience. When Barack Obama took the oath in 2013, 20.6 million watched on television.

The 20th Amendment to the Constitution, ratified in 1933, says: "The terms of the President and the Vice President shall end at noon on the 20th day of January." So President Obama was sworn in for his second term by Chief Justice John Roberts in a private ceremony in the Blue Room of the White House on Sunday, Jan. 20. Family members and a small pool of reporters were there to witness it, and a television camera carried the scene to the world. It took less than five minutes.

Still, when President Obama took the oath again on Jan. 21, the ceremony itself was only part of what television showed viewers. A cheering crowd lined the streets to watch the usual inaugural parade, and television viewers had warm, close-up views that the chilled crowd strained to see.

Viewers also peeked in on the two inaugural balls to see the president and vice president and their wives. Few people saw President George Washington and his wife dance at the first inaugural ball, but millions watched President Obama and the first lady dance. Television commentators couldn't stop talking about Michelle Obama's red chiffon and velvet gown, designed by Jason Wu.

Radio and television are at their best when they bring to the world instant news, usually of crises such as floods, hurricanes, mass murders and serious accidents. But they are also useful in helping to solidify and bring together the people of a democracy.

Radio and television play a critical role in getting accurate information to the public when time is of the essence—warning folks of the coming dangers, helping them prepare and get to safety and connecting them with aid after the immediate crisis is past. But perhaps just as crucial is their role in helping the nation take a breath and feel good about itself. It was President George H.W. Bush who said at his inauguration, "We meet on democracy's front porch." Why did we go through the time and expense of a second inauguration? President Obama had already been sworn in as president. Author Sally Quinn explains, "We want to see the flags wave and the bands play, the parades march along and the leader of the free world standing before our Capitol dome."

Television and online media help us do that.

WHAT RADIO AND TELEVISION DO BEST

During major news events, radio and television newscasters repeat their reports and update their audiences as the news develops. If you tune in to CNN, not only do you see what's happening and listen to commentary, you also see additional headlines streaming below the picture on a ticker. You can pay attention to the news you are most interested in, and you feel as if you are witnessing history.

Of course, much of the time, journalists must write and report news after it has occurred. Many, if not most, radio and television stations provide at least some news that is written by journalists working for the wire services, such as the Associated Press or Reuters.

In addition, radio and television journalists might publish updates all day leading up to news broadcasts, using new media sources like Twitter, Facebook and YouTube. They also often produce news for podcasts, blogs or wikis. And some have found ways to take content that used to be available only online and merge it with traditional newscasts. Information and reactions posted on social media are often shared during newscasts.

Even if your primary emphasis is not radio or television news, you will probably find yourself producing content that involves the use of audio and video. And if you are writing for radio or television news, almost certainly you will be required to contribute to the station's website.

Radio and television stations have expanded their news operations to give background for stories they don't have time to air. Rather than interrupt programming with new facts about a developing story, they often send listeners and viewers to their websites. CNN and MSNBC, for example, often do that and use instantaneous tools to reach their audiences quickly. Tools such as email, text messaging, RSS feeds, Twitter, Facebook and mobile applications offer a "push" method of delivering the news. Audiences do not have to go to the news operation on television or a website to be informed. The information can come to them.

CRITERIA FOR SELECTING RADIO AND TELEVISION NEWS

Four criteria specifically distinguish the selection of radio and television news from that of print news: timeliness, emphasis on information rather than explanation, audio or visual impact, and emphasis on people rather than concepts.

Timeliness

The radio and television news writer emphasizes one criterion of news value more than any other: timeliness. *When* something happened often determines whether a news item will be used in a newscast. The breaking story receives top priority.

Radio and television news "goes to press" many times a day. If an event is significant enough, regular programming can be interrupted.

The sense of immediacy influences everything in radio news, from what is reported to how it is reported. Often this is true of television news as well. Even when radio and television air documentaries or in-depth segments, the producers typically try to infuse the program with a sense of urgency, a strong feeling of the present, an emphasis on what's happening now. With the help of websites, broadcast and cable radio and television newsrooms can go live online with extended newscasts using streaming audio or video services.

Information Rather Than Explanation

Because airtime is so precious, radio and television reporters are generally more concerned with information than with explanation. Most stories must be told in 20 to 30 seconds; rarely does a story run longer than two minutes. A minute of news read aloud is only 15 lines of copy, or about 170 to 180 words. After you subtract time for commercials, a half-hour newscast has only 22 minutes of news, which equates to about one-half of the front page of a newspaper.

Although radio and television news writers should never assume that their audience knows anything about a story, they often have to assume that listeners or viewers will turn to newspapers, newsmagazines or the Internet for further background and details. Often newscasts remind viewers to go to the station's website to expand their view of the story and get an extra perspective without relying on a different news outlet.

Because of their relatively low production costs, newsmagazine formats such as *60 Minutes*, *20/20* and *Dateline NBC* continue to be successful. These programs represent a somewhat different challenge to television news writers, but even so, writing for a newsmagazine format resembles writing for television news.

Audio or Visual Impact

Some news is selected for radio because a reporter has recorded an on-the-scene audio report. Some news is selected for television because it is visually appealing or exciting. For this reason, news of an accident or fire that might get attention only in the records column of a newspaper might get important play on a television newscast. If a television crew returns with good pictures of an event, that event often receives prominent placement in the next newscast.

Whether you work for a news organization, for a public relations firm or in organizational communications, you might have to decide which of the media will best carry your messages and attract the most attention from your audience. You can also decide to use several media to send out your message.

Emphasis on People

Radio and television tell the news through people more often than print does. Radio and television writers follow the classic focus structure formula of making a problem come alive by finding someone who is dealing with the problem and showing the audience how he or she is doing. (See Chapter 11 for more on the focus structure.) That "someone" can be a representative person or family, a person affected by the story or a chief player. Thus, rather than using abstract concepts, television in particular humanizes the story. You can't shoot video of an issue, but you can show the impact that the issue has on people. When Don Hewitt, legendary creator of *60 Minutes*, was once asked why he didn't do a segment on AIDS, his response was quick and simple: "AIDS is not a story; it's an issue."

WRITING RADIO AND TELEVISION NEWS

Radio and television news writing emphasizes certain characteristics that newspaper and online news writing do not, and story structure may vary.

Characteristics of Radio and Television News Writing

Because of the focus on timeliness, radio and television news writers, like journalists writing for digital media, must emphasize immediacy and try to write conversationally, tightly and clearly.

Immediacy

Radio and television news writers achieve a sense of immediacy in part by using the present tense as much as possible. Note the use of present, present progressive and present perfect tense (italicized) in this Associated Press story.

GREENVILLE, S.C. (AP)—Sheriffs in five South Carolina counties *are offering* people a chance to turn in explosives, no questions asked.

Officials in Abbeville, Anderson, Greenville, Oconee and Pickens counties *have set* aside this week as Explosives Amnesty Week.

People in those areas *can call* their sheriff's office to have any explosives, ammunition, weapons, bomb materials or military ordnance removed from their property. Certified bomb technicians will respond to remove and destroy the hazardous materials.

Dispatchers will request information about the materials to be collected, including the address where the materials *are stored*.

Callers *aren't* required to give their names and no criminal charges related to hazardous materials reported or collected will be filed against people who *participate*.

Checklist for Writing Radio and Television News

Does My Writing Have Immediacy?

» Uses the present, present prefect and present progressive tenses.

» Includes the time element if the lead uses the past tense.

» In a follow-up story, leads with a new development or a new fact.

Does My Writing Feature a Conversational Style?

» Uses simple, short sentences instead of complex sentences.

» Uses active, rather than passive, verbs.

» Avoids contractions that could be misunderstood.

» Uses fragments sparingly and with effect.

» Doesn't use slang, colloquialisms or vulgar or off-color expressions.

» Uses correct grammar.

Does My Writing Employ Tight Phrasing?

» Uses as few words as possible.

» Uses few adjectives and adverbs.

» Includes carefully selected facts.

Does My Writing Have Clarity?

» Uses familiar words — not jargon or technical terms.

» Avoids unnecessary or confusing synonyms.

» Repeats words or phrases for greater comprehension.

» Avoids foreign words and phrases.

» Avoids phrases like "the former" and "the latter."

» Repeats proper names rather than uses pronouns.

» Keeps the subject close to the verb, without many intervening words.

» Avoids clever figures of speech.

» Avoids lists of numbers.

» Breaks down statistics so they are understandable.

For accuracy, the past tense is sometimes necessary. But radio and television writers like to use the progressive form of the verb ("are offering") to show continuing action, and the present perfect tense ("have set") more than the past tense because the present perfect indicates past action that is continuing (see the annotated model "Use of Verb Tenses in a TV Story" on page 270).

Sometimes reporters stress immediacy by saying, "just minutes ago" or, on a morning newscast, "this morning." If there is no danger of inaccuracy or deceit, though, you can omit references to time. For example, if something happened yesterday, you might report it like this:

The latest rash of fires in southern California is under control.

But if you use the past tense in a lead, you should include the time element:

The legislature sent a welfare reform bill to the governor late last night. It finished just in time before the spring recess.

The best way to avoid the past tense is to avoid yesterday's story. You can do that by updating yesterday's story. By leading with a new development or a new fact, you might be able to use the present tense.

Remember, radio and television newscasts are "live." Your copy must convey that important characteristic.

ANNOTATED MODEL   Use of Verb Tenses in a TV Story

Present and Present Perfect Tenses

The lead is in the present progressive tense ("are investigating"). The reporter wants to indicate the investigation is continuing.

The attribution "says" is in the present tense to make the report more alive and current. "Getting" is a present participle, again signifying continuing action.

"Reports" and "do not believe" are again in the present tense, even though the event happened in the past.

"Are looking" is present progressive, indicating continuing action. "Is" indicates the man is still a person of interest.

"Do not believe" is a form of the present emphatic, again indicating continuing action.

Police: Jefferson City Couple Found Shot to Death

JEFFERSON CITY, Mo. (AP)—Jefferson City police **are investigating** the shooting deaths of a man and woman.

Jefferson City police Capt. Michael Smith **says** police went to an apartment complex about 3:30 a.m. Monday after **getting** calls from neighbors.

KRCG **reports** that police **do not believe** anyone other than the couple **was** in the apartment.

Police **are looking** for a man who **is** a person of interest in the case.

Authorities **do not believe** the killings **were** drug- or gang-related.

Past Tense

"Was" is simple past tense. No one is presently in the apartment.

"Were" is past tense, indicating that the killings took place in the past.

To convey a sense of immediacy, radio and television news writers use the present or present perfect tense whenever possible.

Conversational Style

Although "write the way you talk" is questionable advice for most kinds of writing, it is an imperative for radio and television news writing. "Read your copy aloud" is good advice for most kinds of writing; for radio and television news writing, that's what it's all about.

Write so that your copy *sounds* good. Use simple, short sentences, written with transitive verbs in the active voice. Transitive verbs do things to things; they demand an object. People rarely use verbs in the passive voice when they talk; it usually sounds cumbersome and awkward. You don't say, "Guess what I was just told by somebody." "Was told" here is in the passive voice; the subject is being acted upon. The preposition "by" also tells you the verb is in the passive voice. "Guess what somebody just told me" is active and more natural, less wordy and stronger. "Told" is in the active voice; the subject is doing the acting.

Because casual speech contains contractions, an occasional contraction is OK as long as your pronunciation is clear. But remember that the negative "not" is more clearly understood when you use the whole word rather than a contraction.

> " Good television journalism presents news in the most attractive and lucid form yet devised by man. "
>
> — Bill Small, author, veteran broadcaster, former president of CBS News

Conversational style also permits the use of occasional fragments. Sentences are sometimes strung together loosely with dashes. They sometimes begin with the conjunction "and" or "but," as in the following example:

> BEAVER FALLS, Pa. (AP)—Police do not plan to cite the drivers of a truck and school bus that crashed in western Pennsylvania.
>
> But only because neither vehicle had a driver when they wrecked.

Writing in conversational style does not mean that you may use slang, colloquialisms or incorrect grammar. Nor does it mean that you may use vulgar or off-color expressions. Remember that your audience includes people of all ages, backgrounds and sensitivities.

Tight Phrasing

You must learn to write in a conversational style without being wordy. This means you must condense. Use few adjectives and adverbs. Reduce the use of the passive voice to save a couple of words. Make each word count.

Keeping it short means selecting facts carefully because often you don't have time for the whole story. Radio and television newscasters want good, tight writing that is easy to follow. Let's examine how a wire story written for newspapers can be condensed for radio and television. Look at this Associated Press newspaper wire story.

> JEFFERSON CITY, Mo. (AP)—A Florida telemarketer and his company are temporarily barred from making solicitation calls to Missourians on the state's no-call list.
>
> Attorney General Chris Koster said in a release Monday that his office had obtained a temporary restraining order that prohibits the telemarketer, Christian Serna, and his company, All in One Service, from making any further solicitation calls to Missourians on the no-call list.
>
> Koster says he's seeking a $5,000 fine for each violation, costs of the investigation and prosecution, and all court costs.
>
> The company is accused of making solicitation calls to consumers claiming the company could reduce customers' credit card interest rates. Koster's office says thousands of phone calls were made to consumers on the no-call list.

The print story has 121 words. Here's how it appeared on the Associated Press broadcast wire in its entirety:

> JEFFERSON CITY, Mo. (AP)—A Florida telemarketer and his company are temporarily barred from making calls to Missouri residents on the state's no-call list. Attorney General Chris Koster says a temporary restraining order has been obtained against Christian Serna and All in One Service. Koster says he's seeking a $5,000 fine for each violation.

The broadcast version has just 53 words. Listeners are given just the bare facts. They must turn to print or online news sources for the details, and more and more, newscasts send their audiences to the station's website for additional content. One newspaper story is often the same length as two or three newscast stories. An online story can be and often is much longer than a newscast story and a newspaper story.

In radio and television news, tight writing is important even when time is available. Broadcast writers usually strive to waste no words, even in documentaries, which provide in-depth coverage of events.

Clarity

Unlike readers, radio and television news audiences can't go back over the copy. They see or hear it only once, and their attention waxes and wanes. So you must be clear and precise.

Write simply, in short sentences filled with nickel-and-dime words. Don't look for synonyms. Don't be afraid to repeat words or phrases. Oral communication needs reinforcement. Avoid foreign words and phrases. Avoid phrases like "the former" and "the latter." Repeat proper names in the story rather than use pronouns. The listener can easily forget the name of the person to whom the pronoun refers.

> " Short words are best, and old words, when short, are best of all. "
>
> —Winston Churchill, British politician

When you are tempted to write a dependent clause in a sentence, make it an independent clause instead. Keep the subject close to the verb. Close the gap between the doer and the activity. This version doesn't do that:

> A man flagged down a Highway Patrol officer near Braden, Tenn., today and told him a convict was hiding in his house. The prisoner, one of five who escaped from the Fort Pillow Prison on Saturday, surrendered peacefully.

The second sentence contains 12 words between the subject, "prisoner," and the main verb, "surrendered." By the time the broadcaster reaches the verb, many listeners will have forgotten what the subject was. The story is easier to understand when written this way:

> A man flagged down a Highway Patrol officer near Braden, Tenn., today and told him a convict was hiding in his house. The prisoner surrendered peacefully. He's one of five who escaped from the Fort Pillow Prison on Saturday.

The third sentence is still a complex sentence ("who escaped . . ." is the dependent clause), but it is more easily understood than the original version.

Clarity also requires that you resist a clever turn of phrase. Viewers and listeners are probably intelligent enough to understand it, but a good figure of speech takes time to savor. If listeners pause to savor it, they will not hear what follows. For that reason, clever columnists often fail as radio commentators.

Even more dangerous than figures of speech are numbers. Don't barrage the listener or viewer with a series of numbers. If you must use statistics, break them down so that they are understandable. For example, it is better to say that one of every four Americans smokes than to say there are 46 million smokers in the United States. You might be tempted to say how many billions of dollars a federal program will cost, but you will help listeners understand if you say that the program will cost the average wage earner $73 for each of the next five years. Television reporters often supply an on-air graphic illustrating the data given orally to help the audience understand the information.

Story Structure

Writers must craft radio and television leads somewhat differently from the way they cast print and online leads. They also must construct special introductions and conclusions to video or audio segments and synchronize their words with taped segments.

Writing the Radio and Television Lead

Like newspaper reporters, radio and television reporters must grab the attention of their audience. Much of what you learned in Chapter 9 applies to radio and television leads. But be aware that people tend to be doing other things when listening to radio or watching television, so you must strive to attract their attention in different ways.

One way is by preparing your audience for what is to come. You cue listeners to make sure they are tuned in. You introduce the story with a general statement, something that will pique the interest of the audience; then you go to the specifics. For example:

General statement	Things are far from settled for Springfield's teacher strike.
Specifics	School officials and union representatives did not agree on a contract yesterday. They will not meet again for at least a week.

Sometimes the opening sentence will cover a number of news items:

There were several accidents in the Springfield vicinity today.

"Cuing in" is only one method of opening a radio or television story. Other leads go immediately into the "what" and the "who," the "where" and the "when." In radio or television news, the "what" is most important, followed by "who" did the "what." The time and place may be included in the lead, but seldom is the "why" or the "how." If time permits, the "why" and the "how" may come later in the story, but often they are omitted.

The first words of the lead are the most important. Don't keep the listener guessing as to what the story is about. Don't begin with a dependent clause or with a prepositional phrase, as in this example:

In strong and urgent language, New Mexico Gov. Susana Martinez Wednesday asked her administration to remove language about "forcible rape" from a new state policy.

The opening words are meaningless without what comes later. The listener may not know what you are talking about. Here is a better way to introduce this story:

> New Mexico Gov. Susana Martinez strongly urged her administration to remove language about "forcible rape" from a new state policy Wednesday.

Be sure to "tee up," or identify, an unfamiliar name to prepare listeners for a name they otherwise may miss. Do it this way:

> *Veteran Kansas City, Kan., businessman and civic leader* Kenneth Durban died yesterday in a nursing home at age 83.

Don't mislead. The opening words must set the proper tone and mood for the story. Attract attention; tease a little. Answer questions, but don't ask them. Lead the listener into your story.

Writing Lead-Ins and Wrap-Ups

Radio and television journalists must learn how to write a **lead-in** that introduces a taped excerpt from a news source or from another reporter. The functions of a lead-in are twofold: to set the scene by briefly telling the "where," the "when" and sometimes the "what," and to identify the source or reporter. The lead-in should contain something substantive. Here's an example:

> A grand jury has decided not to charge a Springfield teenager in the killing of his father. Jan Morrow reports the panel believes the death was an accident.

Lead-ins should generate interest. Sometimes several sentences are used to provide background, as in the following:

> It's a long comeback, indeed, and a slow one at that. But some economists continue to be optimistic about the future. Here's a report from Bill McKinney.

Be careful not to include in the lead-in what is in the story. Just as a headline should not steal word-for-word the lead of a newspaper story, the lead-in should not rob the opening words of the correspondent. The writer must know the contents of the audio report in order to write a proper lead-in.

After the recorded report, you may want to wrap up the story before going on to the next item. The **wrap-up** is especially important in radio copy because there are no visuals to identify the person just heard. If the story reported by Evelyn Turner was about a meeting to settle a strike, you might wrap up Turner's report by adding information:

> Turner reports negotiations will resume tomorrow.

A wrap-up like this gives the story an ending and clearly separates it from the next story.

Christiane Amanpour is CNN's chief international correspondent and host of CNN International's nightly interview program. She also serves as global affairs anchor of ABC News. Her authoritative reports from around the world have informed millions.

Writing to the Video

Writing for a video report begins with the selection of the subject and deciding how it is to be shot. The writing continues through the editing process and is done with the pictures clearly in mind.

Words and pictures must be complementary, never interfering with each other, never ignoring each other. Your first responsibility is to relate the words to the pictures. If you do not, viewers will not get the message because they will be wondering what the pictures are about.

There is a danger, however, in sticking too closely to the pictures by pointing out the obvious in a blow-by-blow account. You need to avoid both extremes and use what Russ Bensley, formerly of CBS News, calls the "hit-and-run technique." This means that at the beginning of a scene or when a scene changes, you must tell the viewer where you are or what is happening. Once you are into the scene, the script may be more general and less closely tied to the pictures.

Suppose the report concerns the continuation of a hospital workers' strike and the opening scene shows picketers outside the hospital. You can explain the tape by saying:

> Union members are still picketing Mercy Hospital today as the hospital workers' strike enters its third week.

Viewers now know three things that are not obvious on the video: who is picketing, where and how long they've been picketing. If the video switches to people sitting around a table negotiating, you must again set the scene for viewers:

Meanwhile, hospital administrators and union leaders are continuing their meetings — apparently without success.

Once you have related the words to the pictures, you may add other details of the strike. Not only must you comment on the video, but you must complete it as well. Part of completing it is giving the report a wrap-up or a strong ending. Don't be cute and don't be obvious, but give the story an ending. Here's one possible ending for the strike story:

Strikers, administrators, patients and their families agree on one sure effect of the strike — it's a bad time to be sick.

USING SOCIAL MEDIA IN RADIO AND TELEVISION

A growing number of newsrooms are finding ways to merge the traditional "small-screen" delivery of news via television with the even smaller screens of computers and smartphones. This technique, called "two-screen viewing" or "three-screen viewing," presents an opportunity for broadcast outlets to deliver additional news content.

Blending Online with On-Air

NBC News teamed up with Facebook and the Sunday morning show *Meet the Press* to enhance its coverage of a 2012 Republican primary debate. The network gathered questions for the debate from Facebook and encouraged real-time participation through the *Meet the Press* mobile website. During an earlier debate, Fox News encouraged viewers to use Twitter to share their opinions. Viewers were asked to add "#answer" or "#dodge" hashtags to their tweets so the network could gauge how Twitter users felt about the candidates' comments during the debate.

> " Writing a silence is as important as writing words. We don't rely on video enough. "
>
> —John Hart, prize-winning TV newsanchor

Along with real-time sharing during a live broadcast, radio and television newsrooms use social media as a way to crowd-source (collaborate with the audience) and gather additional perspectives on daily and long-term projects. The "second screen" is growing as a way to maintain and increase audience involvement. A Seattle television station, KOMO-TV, broadcasts its newscasts in the traditional way along with live streams online and on mobile devices. National Public Radio has a customized iPhone application that allows listeners to create their own radio program or to listen to affiliate stations across the country.

A well-known broadcast industry blog, Lost Remote (lostremote.com), has a section specifically focused on second-screen applications, which enable broadcast brands to extend their reach to people who use digital devices.

As news consumers continue to explore new places to learn about the news, it is increasingly important for all journalists to think about sharing news across many different platforms, no matter for what type of newsroom they work.

ON THE JOB

Writing News for Radio, Television and More

Award-winning reporter and anchor **Victoria Lim** works for Bright House Sports Network in Tampa, Fla. She previously worked for KYW (CBS) in Philadelphia, WWMT (CBS) in Kalamazoo, Mich., and WFLA (NBC) in Tampa. She earned her way through Temple University by working for television and radio newsrooms in the Philadelphia area.

For 11 years, Lim was a consumer and investigative journalist at WFLA-TV, *The Tampa Tribune* and www.tbo.com, where she honed her skills as a beat reporter. She earned many regional awards from the Society of Professional Journalists and a national Emmy award for her coverage of the 2007 hurricane season.

Lim says making yourself credible while building a beat is incredibly important, especially when you need sources and experts to help you with challenging investigative stories. Building credibility takes more than phone calls or emails. It requires spending time getting to know your sources in person.

You must show your sources that you can be trusted, Lim says. It can take years to earn their trust, but once you do, it spreads. She explains that once one source trusts you, he or she will be willing to refer you to additional sources. Trust, and contacts, can build exponentially from there.

Lim's advice to future journalists: Don't be afraid to try everything, and do a great job. To her, cross-platform journalism helps reporters become better critical thinkers.

"It's so easy to report the news when you're just dealing with one platform," she explains. "But it takes a higher degree of critical thinking to deliver the news across multiple platforms."

Lim tells new journalists that consuming news across platforms will help them understand what makes each element different and worth consuming.

Her last tip: Take risks.

"Journalism is really such an experimental playground," she says. "There are constantly new storytelling methods being implemented. This means if we want to provide more information, we must use more critical thinking to do so."

Guidelines for Using Social Media

When a newsroom gathers content from viewers and social media, it must follow three strict guidelines:

1. All information gathered from social media must be verified before being published.
2. All information gathered by reporters should be shared online and on social media before the newscasts. The only information held for newscasts is investigative reporting.
3. Video and photos must be submitted through a part of the website where the users agree to share the content with the newsroom. Submissions must include contact information in case the newsroom needs additional information about the content.

You can expect to encounter innovations like KOMO's when you enter the new world of digital and social media. Newsrooms across the country continue to look for innovative ways to merge the old with the new.

ON THE JOB
Be Ready to Meet the Challenge

Whether she's in the control room calling the shots or digging through documents for an investigative piece, **Michelle Flandreau** has a passion for visual storytelling, organization and in-depth journalism.

After graduating with a degree in broadcast journalism, she began her career as a producer at WBIR, the NBC affiliate in Knoxville, Tenn. Flandreau produces the weekday 5 p.m. newscast and serves as the producer for WBIR's investigative team.

"Each day is a different challenge, but that's what keeps me coming back," Flandreau says. "As the newscast producer for *10 News at Five*, I help shape what stories we cover and how we cover them. I organize the content within the show and think of creative ways we can break the newscast

mold. I'm in the control room during the newscast to make sure everything goes smoothly. And, of course, there's a lot of writing!"

After a few months at WBIR, her career expanded when she became producer of the investigative team. "My news director approached me about launching an

investigative unit at our station. I had a background in computer-assisted reporting but had never done anything quite like this. However, I knew I was ready for the challenge. We dived right in, and I have learned so much through the process."

"One of the stories I'm most proud of was a five-month investigation into a local tourism nonprofit funded primarily by taxpayer dollars. We uncovered legal questions surrounding the president and CEO's employment contract. Our reporting ultimately led to a company reorganization that saved thousands in taxpayer dollars."

She says she believes one of the most gratifying things about journalism is knowing your work can have a tremendous impact.

PREPARING RADIO AND TELEVISION NEWS COPY

In preparing copy to be read by a newscaster, your goals are to make the copy easy for the newscaster to read and easy for the audience to understand.

Format

Most radio and television news editors want triple-spaced copy. Leave two to three inches at the top of the page and one to two inches at the bottom.

In radio copy, the portion read live is separated from any prerecorded elements (see Figure 13.1). Quotes are italicized. Each story starts on a separate piece of paper. That way, the order of the stories can be rearranged, and stories can be added or dropped easily. If a story goes more than one page, "MORE" is written in parentheses at the bottom of the page.

Television copy is typed in a column on the right half of the page (see Figure 13.2). Each line averages four words, and newscasters average 40 lines per minute. The left side of the copy is for audio or video information. This information, which is not read by the newscaster, is usually typed in all caps. The copy that is read generally appears in all caps as well.

Date	Slug	Reporter's name

09/06/12   SOBOCO0906a   Ryan Schmidt

The Southern Boone County Library in Ashland will move to a new location next fall, pending the approval of the Daniel Boone Regional Library board. KBIA's Ryan Schmidt tells us why officials say they need a new library, and how they will use the new space.

SOBOCO0906a   TRT 1:06   SOC

Daniel Boone Regional Library System associate director Elinor (ELEANOR) Barrett says the library in Ashland is outgrowing the current building.

Barrett0906a   TRT: 20   OC: *"five years or so."*

"Based on the population growth in the Southern Boone area, as well as the size of collection that we need to have to adequately serve that population, we need to increase the space that will be available to us, over the course of the next five years or so."

Barrett thinks library goers will appreciate the new multipurpose room included in the plan. . . .

Prerecorded elements are separated from live portions.

Quotations are typed in italics.

FIGURE 13.1

In this radio copy, the name Elinor is also spelled ELEANOR, in case the announcer is unfamiliar with the first, less common spelling.

In television copy, the stories and pages are numbered, and each story starts on a separate page. Never hyphenate words at the end of a line, and end each page with a complete sentence or, if possible, with a complete paragraph. Then if the next page should be missing in the middle of a newscast, the newscaster could at least end with a complete sentence or paragraph.

Most newsrooms use a computer system that helps with the formatting of scripts.

At most stations, copy is prepared for a **teleprompter**, an electronic device that projects the copy over the camera lens in the studio so the newscaster can read it while appearing to look straight into the camera.

Stations vary with scripting basics. Generally, the newscast producer determines the **slug**, or identifying name, for a story and its placement. Some producers insist that the slug contain the time of the broadcast to keep track of content when multiple newscasts are in production at the same time. Newsroom computer systems help number the pages and can estimate how long a script might run on the air on the basis of an anchor's read rate.

Names and Titles

In radio and television style, well-known names are not given in full, even on first reference. Don't use middle initials unless they are a widely recognized part of someone's name (Edward R. Murrow) or unless they are necessary to distinguish two

Story slug   Time of broadcast, reporter

A15.5 - 1 V-5 ENERGY...   **15:44:31, Reporter Name**
CAM: 4   ((JIM ON CAM))
                                                          FOR LOCAL
ON CAM means live on   BUSINESSES, SAVING
camera with microphone.   ENERGY ACTUALLY
                                                     MEANS MAKING MORE
                                                     MONEY.
TAKE VO means take   TAKE VO   ((TAKE VO))
video while anchor   *CG [1] 2LINE:PROVIDENCE   A FORUM IN
reads. (VO stands for   ROAD|COLUMBIA   COLUMBIA TODAY SOLD
"voice over.")   THIS MESSAGE TO
                                                     BUSINESS OWNERS.
CG indicates title to be   THE ENERGIZE
shown over video.   MISSOURI INDUSTRIES
                                                     FORUM ATTRACTED
                                                     NINETY PEOPLE FROM
                                                     BOTH IN-STATE AND
                                                     OUT-OF-STATE.
                                                          THE BIGGEST
                                                     QUESTIONS WERE
                                                     ABOUT NEW
                                                     TECHNOLOGY, FUNDING
                                                     OPPORTUNITIES AND
                                                     AVAILABLE
                                                     RESOURCES.

A16.5 - 1 S/V-5 ENERGY...   **15:45:18, Reporter Name**
TAKE SOT means sound   TAKE SOT   ((TAKE SOT))
should be taken in full.   RUNS=7   "HAVING AN
(SOT is short for "sound   *CG [1] 2LINE:GERALD   ACCESS TO THE
on tape," though now   WELK|BUSINESS MANAGER INFORMATION AND
most TV stations use   1-7   WHERE TO FIND THINGS,
digital rather than   I THINK THAT'S THE
rolling videotape.)   BIGGEST THING."
                                                     ((JIM/VO))
RUNS=7 means sound   VO RESUMES   THE MISSOURI
runs seven seconds.   DEPARTMENT OF
                                                     NATURAL RESOURCES
1-7 means title is to be   AND THE U.S.
shown for seven seconds   DEPARTMENT OF
after story begins.   ENERGY CO-HOSTED
                                                     THE FORUM.

FIGURE 13.2

Television copy is typed in two
columns—one for text to be read
and the other for audio and video
directions.

people with the same first and last names, as with former Presidents George W. Bush and George H.W. Bush.

Titles should always precede names so that listeners are better prepared to hear the name. When you use titles, give only the last name. For example, you would say Federal Reserve Chairman Bernanke, not Federal Reserve Chairman Ben S. Bernanke, and Justice Ginsburg, not Justice Ruth Bader Ginsburg.

Pronunciation

You must help the newscaster pronounce the names of people and places correctly. To do this, write out difficult names phonetically in parentheses. Many stations have their own handbooks, the Associated Press offers a pronunciation guide for names that are currently in the news, and a growing number of websites offer audio pronunciation examples. Look up difficult names in unabridged dictionaries. If you don't find the name there, call the person's office or the consulate or embassy. If the name is of a U.S. town, try calling someone in that town. There is no rhyme or reason to the way some people pronounce their names or to the way some place names are pronounced. Never assume. Never guess. Find out. Here's an example of how to write out difficult names:

> ZAMBOANGA, Philippines (AP)—There's been another deadly bombing in the Philippines.
> A bomb exploded near a Roman Catholic church in the southern city of Zamboanga (zahm-BWAHNG-gah), killing one person and injuring 12.

Perhaps most people would know how to pronounce Lima (LEE-mah), Peru, but not everyone would correctly pronounce Lima (LIE-mah), Ohio. You must note the difference between NEW-erk, N.J., and new-ARK, Del., both spelled "Newark." And who would guess that Pago Pago is pronounced PAHNG-oh PAHNG-oh?

Abbreviations

Generally, do not use abbreviations in your copy. It is easier to read a written-out word than an abbreviation. Do not abbreviate the names of states, countries, months, days of the week or military titles. You may, however, use the abbreviations "Dr.," "Mr.," "Mrs." and "Ms.," and "a.m." and "p.m."

When you do abbreviate, use hyphens instead of periods to prevent the newscaster from mistaking the final period in the abbreviation for the period at the end of the sentence. You may abbreviate "United States" when you use it as a noun or adjective; "U-S" would be the correct form. If an abbreviation is well-known—"U-N," "G-O-P," "F-B-I"—you may use it. Hyphens are not used in acronyms like "NATO" and "HUD" that are pronounced as one word.

Symbols and Numbers

Do not use symbols — not even $, % and # (for number) — in your copy because newscasters can read a word more easily than a symbol.

Numbers can also be a problem. As in newspaper style, write out numbers one through nine. Also write out eleven, because 11 might not be easily recognized as a number. Use figures for 10 and from 12 to 999, but write out the words "thousand," "million" and "billion" — for example, "3,800,000" becomes "three million, 800 thousand." Write out fractions ("two-and-a-half million dollars") and decimals ("three-point-two percent").

Some stations have exceptions. Figures often are used to give the time ("3:20 a.m."), sports scores ("ahead 5 to 2") and statistics, market reports ("an increase in the Dow Jones industrial average of 2-point-8 points") and addresses ("3-0-0-2 Grand Street").

Ordinarily, you may round off big numbers. Thus, for 48.3 write "nearly half." But when dealing with human beings, don't say "more than one hundred" if you know that 104 people died in an earthquake; be precise.

Use "st," "nd," "rd" and "th" after dates: August 1st, September 2nd, October 3rd, November 4th. Make the year easy to pronounce by using numerals: June 9th, 1973.

Quotations and Attributions

Because it is difficult and awkward to indicate to listeners which words are being quoted, use indirect quotes or a paraphrase instead of direct quotations.

If it is important for listeners to know the exact words of a quotation (as when the quoted words are startling, uncomplimentary or possibly libelous), introduce the quote by saying "in his words," "with these words," "what she called" or "he put it this way." Most writers prefer to avoid the formal "quote" and "unquote," though "quote" is used more often than "unquote." Here's an example:

In Smith's words, quote, "There is no way to undo the harm done."

When you must use a direct quotation, the attribution should always precede the quotation. Because listeners cannot see the quotation marks, they will have no way of knowing the words are a direct quote. If by chance they do recognize the words as a quote, they will have no idea who is being quoted. For the same reason, the attribution should precede an indirect quote as well.

If you must use a direct quotation, keep it short. If it is important to use all of a long quote, use a video of the person saying it. If you wish to use a quote of more than one sentence, break it up with phrases such as "Smith went on to say" or "and still quoting the senator." For television, put a longer or more complicated quote on a full-screen graphic display as it is read.

Punctuation

In radio and television copy, less punctuation is best. The one exception is the comma. Commas help the newscaster pause at appropriate places. Use commas, for example, after introductory phrases referring to time and place, as in these examples:

> In Paris, three Americans on holiday met their death today when their car over-
> turned and caught fire.

> Last August, beef prices reached an all-time low.

Sometimes three periods are used in place of a comma. Three periods also take the place of parentheses and the semicolon. They signal a pause and are easily visible. The same is true of the dash—typed as two hyphens in most word-processing programs. Note the dash in the following example:

> But the judge grumbled about the news coverage, and most prospective jurors
> agreed—saying the news coverage has been prone to overstatement, sensation-
> alism and errors.

To make the copy easier to read, add hyphens to some words even when the dictionary and Associated Press do not use them: "anti-discrimination," "co-equal," "non-aggression."

Stations vary in writing style and in the preparation of copy. But if you learn the guidelines presented here, you will be well-prepared to work in radio or television. Differences will be small, and you will adapt to them easily.

SUGGESTED READINGS

Bliss, Edward, Jr., and James L. Hoyt. *Writing News for Broadcast*. 3rd ed. New York: Columbia Univ. Press, 1994. This classic text, often called the Strunk and White of broadcast news writing, excels in good writing and sets a superb example for students to do the same.

Block, Mervin. *Writing Broadcast News: Shorter, Sharper, Stronger*. 3rd ed. Washington, D.C.: CQ Press, 2010. This excellent book was written by a former network news writer.

Freedman, Wayne. *It Takes More Than Good Looks to Succeed at Television News Reporting*. Chicago: Bonus Books, 2003. Freedman has been called "the best local TV news feature reporter in the country." His book is packed with practical, down-to-earth advice.

Schultz, Brad. *Broadcast News Producing*. Thousand Oaks, Calif.: Sage, 2004. This text teaches how to put together a newscast.

Wenger, Deborah Halpert, and Deborah Potter. *Advancing the Story: Broadcast Journalism in a Multimedia World*. 2nd ed. Washington, D.C.: CQ Press, 2011. This text continues to be updated online.

White, Ted, and Frank Barnas. *Broadcast News Writing, Reporting, and Producing*. 5th ed. Boston: Focal Press, 2010. This is the best book on all aspects of broadcast news writing.

SUGGESTED WEBSITES

www.advancingthestory.com
Be sure to check out this excellent website.

www.bedfordstmartins.com/newscentral
When you visit News Central, you will find up-to-the-moment RSS feeds, research links and exercises to help you improve your grammar and AP style usage. In addition, the site's Video-Central: Journalism section hosts the videos highlighted in this chapter as well as additional clips of leading professionals discussing important media trends.

www.nab.org
The website of the National Association of Broadcasters is a wonderful resource for all kinds of radio- and TV-related information. It includes a career center.

www.newscript.com
This site's purpose is to help radio journalists improve their skills as writers and anchors.

www.rtdna.org
The Radio Television Digital News Association promotes excellence in electronic journalism through research, education and professional training. The site features excellent reports and useful links.

www.rtdna.org/article/social_media_blogging_guidelines
This RTDNA site will help you answer questions about sharing user-generated content. It offers detailed guidelines for newsrooms and journalists to follow when considering the use of social media.

EXERCISES

1. **Team project.** Your instructor will divide your class into five groups. Each group will watch a local evening television newscast on ABC, CBS, NBC, FOX or PBS. With the members of your group, make a simple list of the news stories. Then find those stories in the next day's print-edition newspaper, and compare the coverage. Be prepared for a good class discussion.

2. **Journalism blog.** Write a blog post about a complicated local news event. Then boil down the issue and write a 45-second television piece to present in front of your class. Finally, write a tweet that teases the story in 140 characters or fewer.

3. Check to see if the following AP story, written for broadcast, follows acceptable broadcast style. Is it technically correct? Does it emphasize immediacy? Change the copy where you think it's necessary.

California Woman Wants Roadside Memorial to Honor Fish
IRVINE, Calif. (AP)—Animal activists want a California roadside memorial sign to honor fish killed during a container truck crash.

People for the Ethical Treatment of Animals volunteer Dina Kourda told Irvine's street maintenance chief the sign would remind drivers that fish value their lives and feel pain.

About 1,600 pounds of saltwater bass died on Oct. 11 when the truck hauling them to market got into a three-way crash.

The *Los Angeles Times* says Kourda's letter acknowledges roadside memorials traditionally honor humans, but she hopes an exception will be made.

Irvine spokesman Craig Reem says there won't be a fish memorial.

4. Rewrite the following AP newspaper story in broadcast writing style. Assume that the news is current.

Scientist Appears in Court in Secrets Case
By Devlin Barrett and Pete Yost, Associated Press
WASHINGTON (AP)—A scientist who allegedly tried to sell classified secrets to Israel had worked on the U.S. government's Star Wars missile shield program, and the Justice Department declared Tuesday that he had tried to share some of the nation's most guarded secrets.

Arrested in an FBI sting operation, Stewart David Nozette was jailed without bond and accused in a criminal complaint of two counts of attempting to communicate, deliver and transmit classified information.

A former colleague of Nozette says the scientist worked on the Reagan administration's Star Wars missile shield program.

In an interview, Scott Hubbard said that a scientist arrested in an FBI sting, Stewart David Nozette, was primarily a technical defense expert working on the Reagan-era effort formally named the Strategic Defense Initiative.

"This was leading edge, Department of Defense national security work," said Hubbard, a professor of aerospace at Stanford University who worked for 20 years at NASA. Hubbard said Nozette worked on the Star Wars project at the Energy Department's Lawrence Livermore National Laboratory.

At Energy, Nozette held a special security clearance equivalent to the Defense Department's top secret and "critical nuclear weapon design information" clearances. DOE clearances apply to access to information specifically relating to atomic or nuclear-related materials.

Nozette more recently developed the Clementine bistatic radar experiment that is credited with discovering water on the south pole of the moon. A leader in recent lunar exploration work, Nozette was arrested Monday and charged in a criminal complaint with attempting to communicate, deliver and transmit classified information, the Justice Department said.

Hubbard said that the Clementine project Nozette worked on in the 1990s was essentially a non-military application of Star Wars technology. Nozette also worked for the White House's National Space Council in 1989 and 1990.

5. Write a couple of paragraphs explaining how learning to write for radio and television makes you a better writer for print.

14

Covering a Beat

In this chapter you will learn:

1. Basic principles for covering any beat.

2. How to use social media in covering beat stories.

3. How to apply the basic principles to some of the most common beats.

DAVID NAKAMURA'S BEAT is a little unusual. He and the swarm of reporters who compete with him seldom get a chance to talk with their most important source. He spends much of his workday in a cramped, crowded room filing tweets about developments his colleagues back in *The Washington Post* newsroom could watch live online. His most important stories often rely on unnamed aides and outside experts. The frustrations are many, and the opportunities for originality few. Yet you couldn't get him to trade places. He explains: "Covering the White House is an exhausting and all-consuming beat that requires immense energy and enthusiasm—and an equal amount of patience. In some ways, every beat I've had has helped prepare me for this job, but in other ways nothing can prepare anybody for an assignment quite like this one."

He adds, "Being inside the White House press corps bubble is a privilege, an honor and an important responsibility, but they don't call it a bubble for nothing. The space inside the cramped White House briefing room, where reporters have to ask one another to move simply to sit down, is a good metaphor for the confining nature of reporting on the most powerful of American institutions."

The similarities to other beats, however, are also important. The goal of any beat reporter, as David has learned, is to hold accountable those who occupy positions of power and privilege. That accountability in journalism is vital to the health of the democracy, whether the beat is the White House or the courthouse.

Few beat reporters become media stars, as many White House reporters do, but none has escaped the changes brought by technology and economics. Additionally, as you saw in Chapter 1, the definition of news itself is getting broader. That change extends the range of beats. Along with such standard beats as local government, police, business and sports, cultural beats reflect the interests and activities of a changing America. Some beat reporters cover shopping malls. Some cover commuting. Some cover spiritual life. Some cover cyberspace.

Covering beats is among the most important work in journalism. Economic pressures have cut the staffs in most newsrooms, print and broadcast, leaving fewer reporters and stretching their assignments over multiple beats. Often, today's reporters are trying to do more, on several platforms, in less time. That's true on the White House beat, too.

"In the 24/7 hypermedia age, reporters have another challenge: to keep up with the speed and competition fostered by the Internet," David says. "I regularly tweet and blog, but even when I'm writing as fast as I can, I often am behind other reporters—or even reporters at my own publication who can watch the briefings and all of Obama's speeches online."

The more time journalists spend tweeting and blogging, the less time they have for developing sources and understanding complex issues.

David Nakamura again: "That brings up another inherent danger in the age of Twitter. Reporters, political operatives, congressional members and staffers, and White House staff are all using it to shape opinion, break news and debate one another—but increasingly the online space has become a place where the same relatively small number of Washington insiders are talking to themselves and shaping conventional wisdom that is harder and harder to break out of."

No matter the locale, beat reporters today are expected to tell their audiences not only what is happening but also how to get involved. Stories include telephone numbers, email addresses and often Twitter handles along with the names of decision-makers. Much of the most useful reporting is done in advance of public meetings, with the goal of enabling citizens to become participants instead of passive onlookers. Readers are regularly invited to use email or online bulletin boards to speak up on public issues. Journalists and officials alike encourage Twitter followers and Facebook friends. Even President Obama has a Twitter account. With all these changes, though, beat reporters remain the eyes and ears of their communities. Surrogates for their readers, they keep track of government, education, police, business and other powerful institutions that shape readers' lives.

The principles of good reporting apply to the coverage of any beat. The same principles also apply to specialized publications, including those aimed at particular industries, professions or ethnic groups. A reporter for *Women's Wear Daily* may cover fashion designers. A reporter for *Diario Las Américas* in Miami may cover Cuban exile politics. But each is doing the same job: discovering and writing news that's relevant and useful to the publication's readers.

Editors and audiences expect reporters on these specialized beats, like those in more traditional assignments, to provide information and understanding that will help readers improve the quality of their lives. That's important work, and it's rewarding work. But it's not easy.

PRINCIPLES FOR REPORTERS ON A BEAT

Whether you cover the public library or the Pentagon, the county courthouse or the White House, the principles of covering a beat are the same.

As David Nakamura points out, "Ultimately, that's where the White House beat is similar to any other—reporters must be dogged asking the right questions and relentless in demanding answers. They must be observant and able to identify important shifts in message and tactics, and they must be willing to challenge authority, even at the highest levels."

If you want to succeed as a reporter, you must be prepared, alert, persistent and wary. And, on any beat, you must be there. These qualities will help you win the trust of your sources, keep up with important developments on your beat and avoid the trap of writing for your sources instead of your readers. Let's take a closer look at what each of those rules means in practice.

Be Prepared

Where should preparation begin? For you, it has already begun. To work effectively, a journalist needs a basic understanding of the workings of society and its various governments. You need to know at least the rudiments of psychology, economics and history. That is why the best education for a journalist is a broad-based one, providing exposure to the widest possible sampling of human knowledge. But that exposure will not be enough when you face an important source on your first beat. You will need more specific information, which you can acquire by familiarizing yourself with written accounts or records or by talking to sources.

Reading for Background

In preparing to cover a beat, any beat, your first step is to learn as much as possible about the issues and personalities you'll be covering. Google is your friend. General and specialized search engines allow you to read not only the material that has been produced by your own organization but the relevant stories from other outlets worldwide. You can often access the contents of major newspapers, magazines, research publications and other reference libraries without regard to physical distance. Use the Internet to acquire background and to understand the context of local events and issues. Of course, you'll want to double-check anything you learn from unfamiliar online sources. For example, if your new beat is medicine, you might begin with the website of the Association of Health Care Journalists (healthjournalism.org). Television and Web-only newsrooms are less likely to have their own libraries. Online sources make that less of a handicap. Your local public and university libraries are also valuable resources, with their online catalogs and generally good collections of recent local periodicals.

In your local research, make notes of continuing issues, questions left dangling in previous stories or ideas for stories to come. Go back several years in your preparation. History might not repeat itself, but knowledge of it helps you assess the significance of current events and provides clues to what you can expect.

Library research is only the start of your preparation. You must become familiar with the laws governing the institution you cover. If a governmental organization is your beat, find the state statutes or the city charter that created the agencies you will be covering. Learn the powers, duties and limitations of each official. You might be surprised to discover that someone is failing to do all that the law requires. Someone else might be doing more than the law allows.

Look at your state's open-meetings and open-records laws, too. Every state has such laws, although they vary widely in scope and effectiveness. Knowing what information is open to the public by law can be a valuable tool for a reporter dealing with officials who may prefer to govern privately. (White House internal documents, as David Nakamura has learned, are exempt from the federal Freedom of Information Act.)

Talking to Sources

Now you're ready to start talking to people. You should conduct your first interviews in the newsroom with your predecessor on the beat, your assignment editor and any veterans who can shed light on the kinds of things that rarely appear in statute books or newspaper stories. Who has been a good source in the past? Who will lie to you? Who drinks to excess? Who seems to be living extravagantly? Whose friends are big land developers? Who wants to run for national office? Who has been hired, fired or promoted? Who has moved to a competing company? Remember that you are hearing gossip, filtered through the biases of those relating it. Be a little skeptical.

Some understanding of the workings of your own newsroom won't hurt, either. Has your predecessor on the beat been promoted? Has he or she been transferred because of unsatisfactory performance? Will an introduction from your predecessor help you or hurt you with your sources? And what are your boss's expectations? Is your assignment to report almost every activity of government, or will you have time to do some investigative work and analysis? Living up to your boss's expectations is easier if you know in advance what they are.

Only after gaining as much background as possible are you ready to face the people you will be covering. A quick handshake and a superficial question or two might be all you have time for in the first encounter, but within a week you should arrange for sit-down conversations with your most important sources. These are get-acquainted sessions. You are trying to get to know the sources, but don't forget that they need to know you, too, if they are going to respect and trust you.

You might have noticed that the preparation for covering a beat is similar to the preparation for an interview or for a single-story assignment. The important difference is that preparing for a beat is more detailed and requires more time and work. Instead of just preparing for a short-term task, you are laying the foundation for an important part of your career. A beat assignment nearly always lasts at least six months and often two years or more. Understanding that will help shape your first round of meetings with sources.

A story might emerge from those first interviews, but their purpose is much broader. You are trying to establish a relationship, trying to convert strangers into helpful partners in news gathering. To do that, you should demonstrate an interest in the sources as people as well as officials. Ask about their families, their interests, their philosophy, their goals. Make it clear with your questions that you are interested rather than ignorant. (Don't ask if the source is married. You should already know. Say, "I understand your daughter is in law school. Is she going into politics, too?" Similarly, don't ask if your source has any hobbies. Find out beforehand. Say, "So you collect pornographic comic books. Sure takes your mind off the budget, doesn't it?")

And be prepared to give something of yourself. If you both like to fish, or you both went to Vassar, or you both have children about the same age, seize on those ties. All of us feel comfortable with people who have something in common with us. This is

TIPS

Talking to Sources

» Talk to your predecessor on the beat, your assignment editor and veterans in the newsroom for background.

» Understand your boss's expectations.

» Establish a relationship with sources; demonstrate interest in them.

ON THE JOB

His Beat: The White House

You've met **David Nakamura**, who covers the White House for *The Washington Post*. He didn't begin with that assignment, of course. Fresh from journalism school, he took an internship at *The Post*. He has been there ever since, first in sports, then as a suburban reporter, then covering Washington city government, then a stint in Afghanistan. Here's how he describes the challenges and benefits of his current job:

"Over the course of one and a half years on the beat, I have asked President Obama three questions during press conferences and spoken to him a handful of other times in off-the-record settings on Air Force One or in private briefings arranged by his press aides.

"The White House has a huge press operation whose job is twofold: to offer official White House responses on issues of the day (usually called 'spin' by cynical reporters) and to shape the narrative by doling out 'news' items in a rapid, highly orchestrated fashion so that reporters are busy filing stories that the administration wants rather than having free time to pursue the ones it fears."

The pluses outweigh the negatives, though, he says.

"There is excellent journalism each day at the White House. Much of our jobs involves analyzing why decisions are made and what the consequences are—politically and practically—for the president, the political parties and the nation.

"White House reporters often say the main perk of the job is being able to tell friends they cover the president, but that the daily grind is far less glamorous. In truth, though, the job is immensely interesting, and there are moments that are so surreal as to be almost fictional. I traveled with President Obama to the Korean DMZ as he looked through binoculars into North Korea, and I was with him when he met democracy leader Ang San Suu Kyi in Burma—the first American president ever to visit that country. I've flown round the world on Air Force One and to Hawaii when Bo the First Dog and President Obama both came back to the press cabin to visit.

"Those are moments that anyone would be honored to witness and ones that help make all the other hours inside the bubble worthwhile."

the time, too, to let your sources know that you know something about their work and that you're interested in it.

Be Alert

Lisa Arthur learned her way around schools in three years on the education beat for *The Miami Herald*. When she was assigned to cover the shooting of a teacher in Fort Lauderdale, she was ready for any possibility. The shooting had attracted national attention, so a throng of journalists gathered outside the building. School officials announced that only a small group of reporters, called a *pool*, would be allowed inside. Faced with head-to-head competition from a Fort Lauderdale *Sun Sentinel* reporter, Lisa thought fast. Let her tell the story:

So I said, I covered schools in Broward for three years, and there are dozens of schools I have still never seen the inside of. Have you ever actually been to this school?

She says no. (The mind reels. If there ever was a time to flat-out lie, this was it.)

I said, Look, no offense, but if you knew them that well, they would have just picked you as the pool reporter and not sent you over here to fight it out with us folks they've never seen before. . . . My suggestion is we flip a coin.

She said okay. . . .

I flip. She calls heads. It lands in my palm ever-loving tails side up. . . .

We ended up being in there for about 30 to 40 minutes only. The leash was more like a choke chain. But it was understandable. I got lucky because the guy in there coordinating the mental health team was a psychologist from the Miami-Dade school district. So he was extremely helpful and went as far as he could.

Afterwards I had to give a debriefing to every outlet that wanted it. I literally gave everyone everything in my notebook . . . and all the quotes I used. But nobody could write the inside-the-school story the way we could without giving it a "from pool report" byline. . . .

I could have explained not getting in there to my bosses. No one expected me to. Just getting to the coin toss was a major victory for us. I don't know how she explained it.

Sometimes, being alert means thinking fast and seizing an opportunity. Sometimes, it means recognizing an important story when others don't. Important stories are seldom labeled as such. In many cases, the people involved might not realize the significance of what they are doing. Probably more often they realize it but hope nobody else will. The motivation for secrecy might be dishonesty, the desire to protect an image or a conviction that the public will misunderstand.

If your beat is a government agency, you will find that many public officials and public employees think they know more about what is good for the public than the public does. The theory of democratic government is that an informed citizenry can make decisions or elect representatives to make those decisions in its own best interests. If you are the reporter assigned to city hall, the school board or the courthouse, you carry a heavy responsibility for helping your audience put that theory into practice. To discharge that responsibility, you must probe beneath the surface of events in search of the "whys" and "hows" that lead to understanding.

When you are presented with a news release or hear an announcement or cover a vote, ask yourself these questions before passing the event off in a few paragraphs:

» **Who will benefit from this, and who will be hurt?** If the tentative answer to the first part suggests private interests, or the answer to the second part is the public, some digging is in order.
» **How important is this?** An event that is likely to affect many people for good or ill usually deserves more explanation than one affecting only a handful.
» **Who is for this, and who is against it?** Answers to these questions are often obvious or at least easy to figure out. When you know them, the answers to the first two questions usually become clearer.
» **How much will this cost, and who will pay?** An architect's design for renovating downtown may look less attractive when the price tag is attached. The chamber of commerce's drive to lure new industry may require taxpayers to pay for new roads, sewers, fire protection, and even schools and other services for an increased population.

Skilled reporters are persistent interviewers and insist on responsive answers. Make sure your questions are answered satisfactorily.

The answers to these questions allow you to judge that most important element of news value—impact.

Be Persistent

Persistence means two things to a reporter on a beat. First, it means that when you ask a question, you do not give up until you get an answer. Second, it means that you must keep track of slow-developing projects or problems.

Insisting on a Responsive Answer

One of the most common faults of beginning reporters is that they give up too easily. They settle for answers that are unresponsive to their questions, or they return to the newsroom not sure they understand what they were told. In either case, the result is an incomplete, confusing story.

"Why is it that our fourth-graders score below average on these reading tests?" you ask the school superintendent.

He might reply, "Let me first conceptualize the parameters of the socioeconomic context for you."

The real answer probably is "I only wish I knew."

Your job is to cut through the jargon and the evasions in search of substance. Often that is not an easy task. Many experts, or people who want to be regarded as experts, are so caught up in the technical language of their special field that they find it almost impossible to communicate clearly. Many others seek refuge in gobbledygook

TIPS

Insisting on a Responsive Answer

» Cut through the jargon and evasions in search of substance.

» Rephrase technical language in plain English.

or resort to evasion when they don't know an answer or find the answer embarrassing. Educators and lawyers are particularly adept at such tactics.

Listen politely for a few minutes while the school superintendent conceptualizes his parameters. Then, when he finishes or pauses for breath, lead him back toward where you want to go. One way is to say, "It sounds to me as if you're saying . . ." and rephrase what he has told you in plain English. At those times when you simply are in the dark—and that may be often—just confess your puzzlement and ask for a translation. And keep coming back to the point: "But how does all that affect reading scores?" "How can the problem be solved?" "What are you doing about it?"

All the while, you must ask yourself, "Does that make sense to me?" "Can I make it make sense to my readers?" Don't quit until the answer is yes. You should not be obnoxious, but you do have to be persistent.

Following Up on Slow Developments

Persistence is also required when you are following the course of slow-developing events. Gardeners do not sit and watch a seed germinate. They do, however, check every few days, looking for the green shoots that indicate that growth is taking place as it should. If the shoots are late, they dig in to investigate.

Beat reporting works much the same way. Officials announce a downtown redevelopment plan, say, or a revision in a school's curriculum. The story covers the plans and the hoped-for benefits. The seed is planted. If it is planted on your beat, make a note to yourself to check on it in a week or two. And a week or two after that. And a month after that. Start a file of reminders so you won't forget. Such a file often is called a **tickler** because it serves to tickle your memory.

Like seeds, important projects of government or business take time to develop. Often what happens during the long, out-of-public-view development is more important than the announcements at the occasional news conferences or the promises of the promotional brochures. Compromises are made. Original plans turn out to be impractical or politically unpalatable. Consultants are hired. Contracts are signed. Public money is spent. The public interest may be served, or it may not.

Sometimes the story is that nothing is happening. At other times the story might be that the wrong things are happening. Consulting contracts might go to cronies of the mayor. Redevelopment might enhance the property values of big downtown landowners. Curriculum revisions might be shaped by influential pressure groups.

Even if nothing improper is taking place, the persistent reporter will give readers an occasional update. At stake, after all, are the public's money and welfare.

Be There

In beat reporting, there is no substitute for personal contact. Trying to do it all by telephone or email won't work. The only way to cover a beat is to be there—every day, if possible. Joking with the secretaries, talking politics with council members and lawyers, worrying over the budget or trading gossip with the professional staff—you must make yourself a part of the community you are covering.

Remember that the sources who are most important to you probably are in great demand by others, too. They have jobs to do. Maneuver to get as much of their time as you need, but don't demand too much. Do your homework first. Don't expect a school superintendent to explain basic concepts of education. You can learn that information by talking with an aide or by reading. What you need to learn from the superintendent is how he or she intends to apply those concepts, or why they seem to be inapplicable here. Find out what a class I felony is before asking the police chief why they are increasing. You will get the time you need more readily if busy sources know their time will not be wasted.

There are other simple techniques you can use to build and maintain good relationships with the people on your beat. Here are some of them:

» **Do a favor when you can.** As a reporter, you spend much of your time asking other people to do favors for you—giving you their time, sharing information they need not share, looking up records and figures. If a source needs a favor in return, don't refuse unless it would be unethical. The favors asked are usually small things, like getting a daughter's engagement picture or a club announcement in the paper, procuring a print of a picture taken with the governor to decorate the official's wall, bringing in a few copies of a favorable feature you wrote.

» **Don't shun good news.** One ill-founded but common complaint is that news media report nothing but bad news. Admittedly, there is usually no story when people are doing what they are supposed to do. Sometimes there should be, if they do their duty uncommonly well or have done it for a very long time or do it under the burden of some handicap. Sources like these "good news" stories, and so do readers.

» **Protect your sources.** Many people in government—politicians and bureaucrats alike—are willing to tell a reporter things they are not willing to have their names attached to in print or otherwise. The same is true of people in private business, who might fear reprisals from their employers, co-workers or competitors. Sometimes such would-be anonymous sources are trying to use you to enhance their own positions. You have to protect yourself and your audience against that possibility. Confer with an editor if you have doubts. Most news organizations are properly wary of relying on unnamed sources. Sometimes, though, the requests for anonymity are valid, necessary to protect the source's career. Once you have agreed to protect a source, you must do it. Don't tell anyone but your editor. An inability to keep your mouth shut can cost you more than a source. It can cost you your reputation. (The protection of sources has legal as well as ethical implications. So-called shield laws in some states offer limited exemptions for journalists from legal requirements to disclose sources; see Chapter 21. But there are no blanket exemptions.)

» **Above all, be accurate.** Inaccurate reporting leads first to loss of respect from sources, then to loss of the sources themselves and finally to loss of the job. If you are a good, tough reporter, not all of the contacts on your beat will love you. But if you are an accurate reporter, they will respect you.

Remember, beat reporting is a lot like gardening. Both require you to be in the field every day, cultivating. And in both, the amount of the harvest is directly proportional to the amount of labor invested.

Be Wary

The point of all this effort—the preparation, alertness, persistence and personal contact—is to keep your audience informed. That is an obvious statement, but it needs to be made because every beat reporter is under pressures that can obscure the readers' importance. You must be wary of this problem.

Even with the interactivity offered by online, mobile and Twitter services, you will have little to do with most of your audience. They will not write you notes when you have done a story they like or call you when they dislike what you have said or written. They will not offer to buy you a cup of coffee or lunch, or stop you in the hall to urge you to see things their way. But your sources will.

If you report that city council members are thinking about raising the property-tax rate, you will probably hear complaints from council members about premature disclosure. If you report that the police department is racked by dissension, expect a less-than-friendly reaction from the chief. If you report that the CEO of a major business is looking for a new job, the chances are that he or she will deny it even though the story is true.

All sources have points of view, programs to sell, careers to advance, opponents to undercut. It is likely that they will try to persuade you of the merit of their viewpoint, try to sell their programs through your reporting, try to shape the news to help their careers.

Be wary of sources' efforts to use you. You can lose the critical distance a reporter must maintain from those being covered. When that happens, you start thinking like a participant rather than an observer. You begin reporting for your sources rather than your audience. This is a real danger. No one can spend as much time with sources as a beat reporter does or devote as much effort to understanding them without becoming sympathetic. You may forget that you are a surrogate for the outsiders when you associate so closely with the insiders.

BEAT REPORTING ACROSS MEDIA PLATFORMS

Online media offer the opportunity for instant reporting. With smartphones, digital cameras and laptop computers, reporters can and do file short reports and even photographs and video for posting on the Web as the story unfolds. For newspaper reporters, this is a high-tech return to the distant days of multiple editions, when instead of one deadline a day journalists had many. For radio and television reporters, the online opportunities match those of live reporting over the air. Research shows that increasing numbers of online readers rely on websites to stay in touch with news as it happens.

ANNOTATED MODEL **A Crime Story Across Media Platforms**

The news flash contains only bare-bones facts, with promise of follow-up.

Twitter feed (2 p.m.):

@COPSBEAT Another "bear hug" just reported; this @ Springfield College campus. More soon.

Web report (3 p.m.):

Springfield College campus police report that a female student was grabbed from behind by an unknown assailant at 1:25 p.m. on the college campus.

The reporter follows her tweet with an online report that includes as many details as are immediately available. The follow-up is posted as soon as possible after the first tweet.

This is the third such assault to be reported in the past two days. The first two both occurred on the university campus. Police suspect the same man is involved.

The suspect is described as a strongly built white male, in his 20s, with a reddish beard and bad breath. Police have produced a composite sketch, which is being circulated on both campuses.

In all three instances, the victim was walking alone in a relatively secluded area of the campus during daylight hours. None of the victims was seriously injured. None knew the assailant.

Newspaper story (following morning):

A university student has been arrested and charged with being the "bear hug" assailant who assaulted women on both the university and Springfield College campuses.

University police gave the suspect's name as Thomas Albright. He is identified as a 20-year-old sophomore from Chicago.

A police spokesman said that, after sketches of an unknown suspect were circulated on both campuses, police received an anonymous call naming Albright as the perpetrator. He was taken into custody about 8 p.m. and was identified by at least one of the victims.

The spokesman said Albright denied the accusations but admitted to having tried to find a former girlfriend he believes to be a Springfield College student.

The first incident took place Monday afternoon near the university's recreation center. The victim, a university senior, told police she screamed and the man who had grabbed her around the waist from behind turned and fled.

The second assault was later that day, in the Hitt Street parking garage. In that incident, the victim told police the assailant asked her if she was someone whose name she didn't recognize. When she said she wasn't, he mumbled something and released her, she said.

(continued)

A reporter on the crime beat starts reporting instantly via Twitter and then revises the story online and in print.

(continued)

The third assault was Tuesday afternoon on the Springfield College campus. That victim had much the same experience as in the second incident.

None of the victims was seriously injured.

Albright is in city jail awaiting a preliminary hearing.

"Cops Beat" blog (later that day):

The cops are trying to downplay this case of the Bear-Hug Bandit to avoid frightening any more women. They told me as much, but not for attribution, so we didn't use it in the paper. It seems to me and my editor, though, that students and administrators on both campuses should use this as a takeoff point for an examination of security, especially in more secluded areas, such as parking garages. Could have been much worse. What do you think?

With that opportunity, of course, comes obligation. As you see in the example of David Nakamura, beat reporters at all levels are expected to blog, send Twitter messages and post instant updates to Facebook and other social networking sites throughout the day. All that takes time and energy, often cutting into the reporter's opportunity for in-depth research or even the conversations that are important in developing sources.

Also, reporters are expected to gather and present to audiences more information, more detail and more points of view online than print, television or radio permit. Citizens who care enough to follow an issue online want and expect to see the source documents reporters use—and that policymakers use. They want and expect links to other websites that offer related information or further background.

But what really sets online and social media apart is interactivity. Social media such as Twitter and Facebook both facilitate interactivity—with sources as well as readers. It's common for a reporter to start covering a beat story with an on-site tweet that gives the basic facts in 140 characters or fewer. After taking some—but not much—time for research, the reporter might follow up with a Web story that gives more detail. By the next morning, she or he will have written a print story for the newspaper that contains even more detail and background. Finally, later that day, the reporter might return to the story, this time to write a post for the beat blog that readers respond to. See the annotated model "A Crime Story Across Media Platforms" beginning on page 297 for an example of how a beat story can progress across media platforms.

This fast-paced use of new media brings its own hazards. It's impossible to be nuanced in 140 characters, so it's easy for a reporter in a hurry to overstate or misstate something that then comes back to bite painfully. In the midst of a breaking news story, authorities don't always have the facts straight, yet the reporter often can't wait for information to be confirmed before getting it out. Finally, tweets are unedited, so the reporter has no editorial "safety net" to catch errors and questionable information. All these hazards make it critical for reporters to be as thorough as possible at every stage of a story.

COVERING THE MOST IMPORTANT LOCAL BEATS

Your political science courses will introduce you to the structure of government, but from a reporter's viewpoint, function is usually even more important than structure. You must learn who holds the real power, who has the most influence on the power-holders and who are the most likely sources of accurate information. The specifics vary from city to city, but there are some general principles that will help you when covering any type of state or local institution.

» **Information is power.** The holder of information may be a professional administrator (the city manager, school superintendent, police chief or court clerk) or an elected official (the mayor, chair of the county commission or chair of the school board). The job title is unimportant. Find the person who knows in detail how an organization really works, where the money goes and how decisions are made. Get to know that person because he or she will be the most important person on your beat.

» **The budget is the blueprint.** This principle is a corollary of the first. Just as detailed knowledge of how an organization works is the key to controlling that organization, a budget is the blueprint for the organization's activities. The budget tells where the money comes from and where it goes. It tells how many people are on the payroll and how much they are paid. It tells what programs are planned for the year and how much they will cost. Over several years' time, the budget tells where the budget-makers' priorities are, what they see as their organization's role in the community.

So, find copies of the last two or three years' budgets for your beat. Try to decipher them. Learn all you can from your predecessor and from newspaper clips. Then find the architect who drew up this blueprint—the budget director or the clerk or the assistant superintendent—and get a translation. Ask all the questions you can think of. Write down the answers.

When budget-making time arrives, follow every step. Attend every public hearing and every private discussion session you can. In those dollar figures are some of the most important stories you will write—stories of how much your readers will be paying for schools and roads and garbage pickup, stories of what they will get for their money.

» **Distributing power and money is politics.** While looking for your beat's power centers and unraveling its budget mysteries, you will be absorbing as well the most interesting part of beat reporting: politics.

At any level in any type of organization, power and money go hand in hand with politics. Politics provides the mechanisms through which limited resources are allocated among many competing groups. Neither elections nor political parties are necessary for politics. You will have to learn to spot more subtle forms of political maneuvering.

If you are covering city hall, for example, pay close attention as the city budget is being drafted. You may find the mayor's pet project being written in by the city manager. Nobody elects the city manager, but it is good politics for him or her to keep the mayor happy. Are the builders influential in town? If so, you will probably find plenty of road and sewer projects in the budget. Are the city employees unionized? Look for healthy wage and benefit increases if they are. Is there a vocal retirees' organization? That may account for the proposed senior citizens' center. None of those projects is necessarily bad just because it is political. But you and your readers ought to know who is getting what and why.

Now suppose an election is coming up, and the builders' campaign contributions will be heavy. A councilman who is running for mayor switches his vote from money for parks to money for new roads. Has a deal been made? Has a vote been sold? That's politics, too. Some digging is in order.

Power, money and politics are the crucial factors to watch in any beat reporting. With this in mind, let's take a closer look at the most important local beats.

City and County Government

Most medium-sized cities have council-manager governments. The mayor and council members hire a professional administrator to manage the day-to-day affairs of the city. The manager, in turn, hires the police and fire chiefs, the public works director and other department heads. Under the city charter, the council is supposed to make policy and leave its implementation to the manager. Council members are usually forbidden to meddle in the affairs of any department.

Some cities, such as New York and Chicago, have governments in which the mayor serves as chief administrator.

Whatever the structure of your city, you will have a range of good sources to draw on:

» **Subordinate administrators.** They know details of budgets, planning and zoning, and personnel matters. They are seldom in the spotlight, so many of them welcome a reporter's attention as long as the reporter does not get them into trouble. Many are bright and ambitious, willing to second-guess their superiors and gossip about politics, again providing you can assure them that the risk is low.

» **Council members.** Politicians, as a rule, love to talk. What they say is not always believable, and you have to be wary of their attempts to use you, but they will talk. Like most of us, politicians are more likely to tell someone else's secret or expose the other guy's deal. So ask one council member about the political forces behind another member's pet project while asking the other about the first's mayoral ambitions. This improves the odds that you will learn all there is to know.

» **Pressure groups.** You can get an expert view of the city's land-use policies from land developers and a different view from conservationists. The manager or the personnel director will tell one side of the labor-management story. The head of the employees' union will tell the other. How about the school board's record in hiring minorities? Get to know the head of the NAACP or of the local Urban League chapter. Public officials respond to pressure. As a reporter, you need to understand those pressures and who applies them.

» **Public citizens.** Consumer advocate Ralph Nader made the term "public citizens" popular, but every town has people—lawyers, homemakers, business executives, retirees—who serve on charter commissions, head bond campaigns, work in elections and advise behind the scenes. Such people can be sources of sound background information and useful assessments of officeholders.

» **Opponents.** The best way to find out the weaknesses of any person or program is to talk with an opponent. Seek out the board member who wants to fire the school superintendent. Look up the police captain demoted by the new chief. Chat with the leader of the opposition to the new hospital. There are at least two sides to every public question and every public figure. Your job is to explore them all.

Once you have found the sources, keep looking, listening and asking for tips, for explanations, for reactions, for stories. The fun is just starting.

Covering a county government is very much like covering a city government. In both cases you deal with politicians, with administrators, with budgets, with problems. The similarities may be obscured by differences in structure and style, however.

Cities are more likely to have professional administrators, for example. The administration of county governments is more likely to be in the hands of elected commissioners, supervisors or judges. Counties, too, are more likely to have a multitude of elected officials, from the sheriff to the recorder of deeds. City governments are more likely to be bureaucracies. One way to generalize about the differences is to say that city governments are often more efficient and county governments are more responsive.

These differences frequently mean, for a reporter, that county government is easier to cover. More elected officials means more politicians. That, in turn, can mean more talkative sources, more open conflict, more points at which constituents and reporters alike can gain access to the governmental structure.

The principles and the problems of reporting are the same. The budget remains the blueprint whether it is drafted by a professional administrator or an elected officeholder. Knowledge is power whether it is the city manager or the elected county clerk who knows where the money goes. Politics is politics.

The Schools

No institution is more important to any community than its schools. None is worse covered. And none is more demanding of or rewarding to a reporter. The issues that arise on the school beat are among the most important in our society. If it is your beat, be prepared to write about racial tensions, drug abuse, obscenity versus free

Writing for Readers

What does it mean to write for your audience instead of your sources? It means that you must follow several important guidelines.

Translate

The language of bureaucrats, educators, scientists and lawyers is not the same language most people speak. You need to learn the jargon of your sources, but you also need to learn how to translate it into standard English for your audience. The city's planning consultant might say, "Preliminarily, the concept appeared to permit attainment of all our criteria; but when we cost it out, we have to question its economic viability." Your lead could translate that statement as follows:

> The proposed plan for downtown redevelopment looks good on paper, but it may cost too much, the city's planning consultant said today.

Think of the Public Pocketbook

If the tax rate is going up 14 cents, how much will it cost the average homeowner? If employees of a firm are seeking a 10 percent raise, how much will that cost the employer? How much of that increase will be passed on to customers? If garbage collection fees are about to be increased, how will they compare to fees in comparable cities?

A city manager proposed "adjusting" the price of electricity to lower the cost to industrial customers and raise rates to private homes. A city hall reporter did a quick survey of comparable cities around the state. Then she wrote:

City residents, who already pay more for their electricity than residents of eight similar-sized cities around the state, would be charged an average of $4 per month more under a proposal announced Tuesday by City Manager Barry Kovac.

Industrial users, whose rate now is about average among the nine cities, would enjoy the second-lowest rate under Kovac's proposal.

Kovac defended his plan as "equitable and necessary to ensure continued economic growth for the city."

Get Out of the Office

City council votes are important, but far more people will have personal contact with government in the form of a police officer, a clerk or a bus driver than with a council member. Go to where government meets its constituents. Ride a bus. Visit a classroom. Patrol with a police officer. Not only will you get a reader's-eye view of your beat, but you may also find some unexpected stories.

Ask the Audience Members' Questions

Ask "Why?" "How much will it cost me?" "What will I get out of it?" You are the public's ombudsman.

Remember, a good beat reporter has to be prepared, be alert, be persistent, be wary and be there. If you always keep in mind the people you are writing for, you'll keep the customers—and the editors—satisfied.

speech, religious conflict, crime, labor-management disputes, politics, sex—and yes, education.

The process of learning and teaching can be obscured by the furor arising from the more dramatic issues. Even when everyone else seems to have forgotten, though, you must not forget that those are only side issues. The most important part of the school beat is what goes on in the classroom.

Whether those classrooms hold kindergartners or high school students, the principles for covering education remain the same. For the most part, the issues are the same, too. When the schools are private rather than public, you have fewer rights of access.

The classroom is not an easy place to cover. You may have trouble getting into one. Administrators frequently turn down such requests on the grounds that a reporter's presence would be disruptive. It would be, at first. But a good teacher and an unobtrusive reporter can overcome that drawback easily. Many papers, at the start of the school year, assign a reporter to an elementary school classroom. He or she visits frequently, gets to know the teacher and pupils, becomes part of the furniture. And that reporter captures for readers much of the sight and sound and feeling of education.

There are other ways, too, of letting readers in on how well—or how badly—the schools are doing their job. Here are some of them:

» **Examine standardized test scores.** The federal No Child Left Behind law has forced testing to the core of every conversation about school quality. The Obama administration's Race to the Top program in education has added complications. Every school system administers standardized tests designed to measure how well its students compare either with a set standard or with other students. The results of such tests are or ought to be public information. Insist on learning about them. Test scores are an inadequate measure of school quality, but they are good indicators. When you base a story on them, be sure you understand what is really being compared and what factors outside the schools may affect the scores. Find out what decisions are made on the basis of standardized test scores. For example, do schools with relatively low average scores get additional faculty? Do they get special-education teachers?

» **Be alert to other indicators of school quality.** You can find out how many graduates of your school system go to college, how many win scholarships and what colleges they attend. You can find out how your school system measures up to the standards of the state department of education. Does it hold the highest classification? If not, why not? National organizations of teachers, librarians and administrators also publish standards they think schools should meet. How close do your schools come?

» **Understand that in education, as in anything else, you get what you pay for.** How does the pay of teachers in your district compare with pay in similar-sized districts? How does the tax rate compare? What is the turnover among teachers?

» **Get to know as many teachers, administrators and students as possible.** You can learn to pick out the teachers who really care about children and learning. One way to do that is to encourage them to talk about their jobs. A good teacher's warmth will come through.

One reason schools are covered poorly is that the school beat often does not produce the obvious, easy stories of politics, personalities and conflict that the city hall and police beats yield. School board meetings usually produce a spark only when a side issue intrudes. Most school board members are more comfortable talking about issues other than education itself, which is often left to the professionals.

TIPS

Keeping Up with Issues on the Education Beat

» Subscribe to trade newsletters and magazines.

» Remember the most important part of the beat: what goes on in the classroom.

» Understand what standardized test scores mean.

» Get to know teachers, administrators and students.

The politics and the budgets of schools are very much like those of other institutions. The uniquely important things about schools are the classrooms and what happens inside them. Your reporting will suffer if you forget that fact. So will your audience.

Higher Education

Look around you. Relevant and useful stories are everywhere. From the next meeting of the governing board to the classroom of a popular professor, the same principles that apply to coverage of primary and secondary schools can be applied on the campus.

Politics, economics and pedagogy—all included as subjects in the course catalog—are also prime prospects for examination. Politics may be partisan, especially in public universities with elected or appointed governing boards, or it may be bureaucratic, as individuals or departments compete for power and prestige. The economics of higher education translates to budgets, salaries and tuition costs. Pedagogy, the art and science of teaching, is often overlooked by reporters, but it is really the point of the enterprise.

The Chronicle of Higher Education and campus newsletters are required background reading—the former for insights into national issues and trends, the latter for the nitty-gritty of local developments.

Suppose, for example, that *The Chronicle* reports a nationwide increase in the average cost of tuition. The obvious local story is what's happening on your campus and how that compares with the situation at peer institutions. A less obvious story may be how students are scraping up that tuition money. And an even better, though more difficult, story would be how rising costs affect who can afford to attend, and therefore the composition—by race, ethnicity, social class, even geography—of the student body.

To cover your campus, you'll have to overcome the natural hesitancy of many students to challenge professors, administrators and other authority figures. Try to think of them not as superior beings, but as sources and possible subjects of stories. Then treat them respectfully but not obsequiously, as you would any public official. If your campus is state-supported, they are public officials, after all. That means, among other things, that state laws governing open meetings and records apply.

Here are a few of the issues that should yield good stories on most campuses:

» **Politics.** Who are members of the governing board, and how are they chosen? What's their agenda? Within the campus, which are the favored departments? How strong is the fraternity and sorority system? How much clout does the athletic department wield with the campus administration or alumni? In an institution founded on free inquiry, just how free is speech for students, faculty and staff?

» **Finances.** How much does the president get paid? The faculty? The janitors? Where does the money to support the institution really come from? The state? Tuition? Alumni giving? Research grants and contracts? Where does that money go? How much is spent on intercollegiate athletics? How much on the English and history departments?

» **Pedagogy.** Who are the best (and worst) teachers on campus? Is good teaching rewarded as much as research is? Among the faculty, who gets tenure and who doesn't? Who does the teaching, anyway? Senior faculty? Graduate students? Part-timers?

You can practice good reporting without leaving your campus.

Police

The police beat probably produces more good, readable stories per hour of reporter time than any other beat. It also produces some of the worst, laziest reporting and generates many of our most serious legal and ethical problems. It is the beat many cub reporters start on and the beat many veterans stay on until they have become almost part of the police force. It offers great frustration and great opportunity. All these contradictions arise from the nature of police work and of reporting.

If you are going to be a police reporter—and nearly every reporter is, at least briefly—the first thing you have to understand is what police officers are and what they do. We hire police officers to protect us from one another. We require them to deal every day with the dregs of society. Abuse and danger are parts of the job, as is boredom. We pay police officers mediocre wages and accord them little status. We ask them to be brave but compassionate, stern but tolerant. Very often what we get is not what we ask for but what we should expect. Police work seldom attracts saints. Police officers are frequently cynical, often prejudiced, occasionally dishonest.

When you walk into a police station as a reporter for the first time, expect to be met with some suspicion, even hostility. Police officers often perceive young reporters as being radical, unkempt, anti-authority. How closely does that description fit you and your classmates?

Police departments are quasi-military organizations, with strict chains of command and strong discipline. Their members are sworn to uphold the status quo. The reasons that police and young reporters are mutually suspicious should be clear by now.

Then how do you cover the police?

» **Educate yourself in police lore.** Take a course in law enforcement, if you can, or take a course in constitutional law. You also might read Joseph Wambaugh's novels for a realistic portrait of the police.
» **Try to fit in.** Keep your hair neat, dress conservatively and learn the language. Remember that police officers, like the rest of us, are usually quicker to trust people who look and act the way they do.
» **Lend a sympathetic ear.** You enjoy talking about yourself to somebody who seems to be interested; so do most police officers. They know they have a tough job, and they like to be appreciated. Open your mind, and try to understand even the points of view with which you may disagree strongly.

TIPS

Covering the Police Beat

» Educate yourself in police lore.

» Try to fit in.

» Lend a sympathetic ear.

» Encourage gossip.

» Talk with other police watchers.

» **Encourage gossip.** Police officers may gossip even more than reporters do. Encourage such talk over a cup of coffee at the station, while tagging along in a patrol car or over a beer after the shift. The stories will be one-sided and exaggerated, but you may learn a lot. Those war stories are fascinating, besides. Just don't print anything you haven't verified.

» **Talk with other police watchers.** Lawyers can be good sources, especially the prosecutors and public defenders who associate every day with the police. Other law enforcement sources are good, too. Sheriff's deputies, for example, may be eager to talk about dishonesty or inefficiency in the city police department, and city police may be eager to reciprocate.

One important reason for all this work is that little of the information you need and want as a police reporter is material you are entitled to see under public-records laws. By law, you are entitled to see only the *arrest sheet* (also called the *arrest log* or **blotter**). This record tells you only the identity of the person arrested, the charge and when the arrest took place. You are not entitled by law to see the arrest report or to interview the officers involved.

Writing a story depends on securing more than the bare-bones information. Finding out details depends on the good will you have generated with the desk sergeant, the shift commander and the officers on the case.

The dangers—of being unfair, of damaging your reputation and that of your organization—are ever-present. Good reporting requires that you know what the dangers are and how to avoid them.

Sports

A good sports reporter is a good reporter. That's not always obvious, especially to beginners, because the love of sports lures them to the field in the first place. Most sports reporters were sports fans before they were journalists. That's not typical of other specialties. Reporters who cover government seldom attend city council meetings for fun. Medical reporters don't usually spend their days off observing operations. (Instead, they may watch a sports event.)

As a sports reporter and writer, you are likely to find your workplace organized in much the same way as the news department. Typically, in the sports department of a newspaper, there will be reporters, copy editors and an editor. The difference is likely to be the scale. On small papers, the sports editor may double as writer and may even take the photographs, too. On medium-sized papers, the sports reporters usually don't specialize as the news reporters may. One day you may be covering high school swimming; the next, football or a visiting rodeo.

At small and medium-sized broadcasting stations, a "sports department" is likely to consist of one person who serves as writer, photographer and sports anchor at various times of the day or night. The big crews, the "guys in the truck" you hear mentioned on ESPN, are at the network level. At most local stations, you'll be expected to report, to write, to shoot video and to deliver your work on camera. Sometimes, when time pressure is great or the game is big, you'll go on the air live, summarizing a game that has just ended or that may even be in progress. Then your skills at ad-libbing will be tested, a challenge print reporters don't face.

In the multiplatform world, of course, you should be prepared to do it all, including tweeting during the event and engaging with your audience during and after.

One more thing: Don't confuse sports reporters with play-by-play announcers. The latter may be reporters in a literal sense, but they usually aren't journalists. Their skill is in instant description, not the behind-the-scenes digging or the after-the-fact analysis expected of print and broadcast reporters. Often they are hired by the teams they follow or the sponsors they serve instead of by the station carrying their work.

Sports Reporting *Is* Beat Reporting

Before you even thought about sports reporting, chances are good that you were reading, watching and playing sports. In that sense, at least, preparing to be a sports reporter is easier than preparing to cover city hall. But there is more to preparation than immersing yourself in sports. Competition pushes people to their limits, bringing out the best and worst in them. So you need to know some psychology. Sports has played a major role in the struggles of blacks and women for equality. So you need to know some sociology and history. Sports, professional and amateur, is big business. So you need a background in economics. Some of our greatest writers have portrayed life through sports. So you need to explore literature.

To get to the "why" and "how" of a game's outcome, reporters need to dig beneath the mere results. They can bring a story to life by getting out of the press box to find an interesting story angle or to secure compelling quotes from players and coaches.

Meet T.J. Quinn, who reports for ESPN: "The myth of the job is that sports writers sit in the press box, eat hot dogs, live on expense accounts and get to travel all over the country. Mostly true. But covering a beat means keeping track of which players are doing what, who's injured, what a team needs to get better and where they might get it, who wants a contract, who's going to be a free agent, which pitcher is experimenting with a new grip on his slider, which coach is feuding with the owner, which power forward is angry with the point guard because she doesn't pass to the low post enough."

And here's the top of a story that resulted from paying close attention:

Mike Hampton was already a professional athlete the first time he beat his father at basketball.

Until that day, as an 18-year-old minor leaguer, he was oh-for-life against Mike Sr., never walking off the driveway of their Homosassa, Fla., home with so much as a gift win.

When Little Mike was 8 years old, Big Mike blocked his shots. When Little Mike tried to drive the lane, Big Mike would put his body in front of the boy and put him on the ground. The boy bled often but learned to cry less and less. His eyes puffy, his breath short, he would sometimes storm off, but he always came back to play the next day.

"It was gross how tough he was," the new ace of the Mets pitching staff said. "You fall down, get a scratch. 'Get up. It'll stop hurting. Get up; let's go.'"

Big Mike knew it was cruel, and wonders still whether he pushed the boy too hard. But the boy needed to learn that winning meant taking something, not waiting for a handout.

This is a story that entertains while it informs. It shows readers something of the character of an athlete and the meaning of tough love.

Here are a few tips to help you be alert to stories that go beyond the cliché:

» **Look for the losers.** Losing may not—as football coaches and other philosophers like to assert—build character, but it certainly bares character. Winners are likely to be full of confidence, champagne and clichés. Losers are likely to be full of self-doubt, second-guessing and surliness. Winners' dressing rooms are magnets for sports writers, but you usually can tell your readers more about the game and those who play it by seeking out the losers.

» **Look for the benchwarmers.** If you follow the reporting crowd, you'll end up in front of your local version of Alex Rodriguez or Venus Williams every time. Head in the other direction. Talk to the would-be football player who has spent four years practicing but never gets into a game. Talk to the woman who dreams of being a professional golfer but is not yet good enough. Talk to the baseball player who is growing old in the minor leagues. If you do, you may find people who both love their sport more and understand it better than do the stars. You may find less press agentry and more humanity.

» **Look beyond the crowds.** Some of the best and most important sports stories draw neither crowds of reporters nor crowds of fans. The so-called minor sports and participant sports are largely untapped sources of good stories. More Americans watch birds than play football. More hunt or fish than play basketball. More watch stock-car races than watch track meets. But those and similar sports are usually covered—if at all—by the newest or least talented reporter on the staff. Get out of the press box. Drop by a bowling alley, a skeet-shooting range, the local college's Ultimate Frisbee tournament. Anywhere you find people competing—against each other, against nature, against their own limits—you can find good stories.

Developing Contacts

Being there, of course, is half the fun of sports reporting. You're there at the big games, matches and meets. You're there in the locker rooms, on team buses and planes, with an inside view of athletics and athletes that few fans ever get. If you are to answer your readers' questions, if you are to provide insight and anecdote, you must be there, most of the time.

Sometimes you should try being where the fans are. Plunk down $20 (of your boss's money) for an end-zone seat and write about a football game from the average fan's point of view. Cover a baseball game from the bleachers. Cold hot dogs and warm beer are as much a part of the event as is a double play. Watch one of those weekend sports shows on television and compare the way a track meet or a fishing trip is presented to the way it is experienced in person. Join a city league softball team or a bowling league for a different kind of inside view.

A sports reporter must develop and cherish sources just as a city hall reporter must. You look for the same kinds of sources on both beats. Players, coaches and administrators—like city council members and city managers—are obvious sources. Go beyond them. Trainers and equipment managers have insiders' views and sometimes lack the fierce protectiveness that often keeps players, for example, from talking candidly.

Alumni can be excellent sources for high school and college sports stories. If a coach is about to be fired or a new fund drive is being planned, important alumni are sure to be involved. You can find out who they are by checking with the alumni association or by examining the list of major contributors that every college proudly compiles. The business managers and secretaries who handle the money can be invaluable for much-needed but seldom-done stories about the finances of sports at all levels. Former players sometimes will talk more candidly than those who are still involved in a program. As on any beat, look for people who may be disgruntled—a fired assistant coach, a benched star, a big contributor to a losing team. And when you find good sources, cherish them. Keep in contact, flatter them and protect them. They are your lifeline.

Digging for the Real Story

It is even harder for a sports reporter than it is for a political or police reporter to maintain a critical distance from the beat. The most obvious reason is that most of the people who become sports reporters do so because they are sports fans. To be a fan is precisely the opposite of being a dispassionate, critical observer. In addition, athletics—especially big-time athletics—is glamorous and exciting. The sports reporter associates daily with the stars and the coaches whom others, including cynical city hall reporters and hard-bitten managing editors, pay to admire at a distance. Finally, sports figures ranging from high school coaches to owners of professional baseball teams deliberately and persistently seek to buy the favor of the reporters who cover their sports.

We are taught from childhood that it is disgraceful to bite the hand that feeds you. Professional teams and many college teams routinely feed reporters. Major league baseball teams even pay reporters to serve as official scorers for the game. In one embarrassing incident, the reporter-scorer made a controversial decision that preserved a no-hit game for a hometown pitcher. His story of the game made little mention of his official role. The reporter for a competing paper wrote that if it had been his turn to be scorer, he would have ruled the other way.

Sports journalism used to be even more parasitic toward the teams it covered than it is now. At one time, reporters routinely traveled with a team at the team's expense. Good news organizations pay their own way today.

Even today, however, many reporters find it rewarding monetarily as well as psychologically to stay in favor with the teams and athletes they cover. Many teams

TIPS

Contacts for the Sports Beat

» Players, coaches, administrators

» Trainers

» Equipment managers

» Alumni (for high school and college sports)

» Business managers and secretaries who handle money

» Former players

» People who are disgruntled

TIPS

Digging for the Real Story

» Maintain your distance from the people you cover.

» Keep readers in mind.

» Answer readers' questions about the story behind the story.

» Follow the money.

» Find the real "why."

» Find the real "who."

pay reporters to write promotional pieces for game programs. And writing personality profiles or "inside" accounts for the dozens of sports magazines can be a profitable sideline.

Most sports reporters, and the editors who permit such activities, argue that they are not corrupted by what they are given. Most surely are not. But temptation is there for those who would succumb. Beyond that, any writer who takes more than information from those he or she covers is also likely to receive pressure, however subtle, from the givers.

Anywhere athletics is taken seriously, from the high schools of Texas to the stadiums of the National Football League, athletes and coaches are used to being given special treatment. Many think of themselves as being somehow different from and better than ordinary people. Many fans agree. Good reporters, though, regard sports as a beat, not a love affair.

Those sports reporters maintain their distance from the people they cover, just as reporters on other beats do, by keeping their readers in mind. Readers want to know who won, and how. But they also want to know about other sides of sports, sides that may require some digging to expose. Readers' questions about sports financing and the story behind the story too often go unanswered. Accountants have become as essential to sports as athletes and trainers. Talk to them. Readers have a legitimate interest in everything from ticket prices to the impact of money on the actual contests.

When a key player is traded, as much as when a city manager is fired, readers want to know the real "why." When athletes leave school without graduating, find out why. When the public is asked to pay for the expansion of a stadium, find out why. One of the attractions of sports is that when the contest is over, the spectators can see who won and how. Often that is not true of struggles in government or business. The whys of sports, however, frequently are as hard to discover as they are in any other area.

Sports figures often appear to their fans, and sometimes to reporters, to be larger than life. In fact, athletics is an intensely human activity. Its participants have greater physical skills, and larger bank accounts, than most other people, but they are people. Sports reporters know that their audience is interested in the real "who" behind the headlines.

SUGGESTED READINGS

Houston, Brant, and Investigative Reporters and Editors, Inc. *The Investigative Reporter's Handbook*. 5th ed. New York: Bedford/St. Martin's, 2009. This comprehensive guide to using public records and documents, written by members of Investigative Reporters and Editors, is a must for serious reporters. See also the suggested readings at the end of Chapter 19. They'll be useful in beat reporting, too.

Royko, Mike. *Boss: Richard J. Daley of Chicago*. New York: New American Library, 1971. This is a classic, brilliantly written study of urban machine politics.

Sports Illustrated. This magazine features some of the best examples of how sports should be reported and written about.

SUGGESTED WEBSITES

www.espn.go.com
As every sports fan knows, here you'll find multimedia reporting, commentary, statistics and lots of good story ideas.

www.pewstates.org/projects/stateline
This site, a service of the Pew Charitable Trusts, provides story tips and background information on state government and state-level issues.

www.poynter.org
We recommend this site repeatedly because it is useful in many ways. One feature is its links to nearly every professional journalism organization.

EXERCISES

1. **Team project.** With your classmates, form the class into a newsroom. Decide on the essential beats to cover. Assign a pool of reporters to each beat. Working with the other members of your group, take the necessary first step toward successful coverage and produce a background memo that identifies key issues and sources for your beat. Present your memo for class discussion. Listen to and comment on other groups' work.

2. Now get out of the classroom and spend some time actually covering one of these beats. Get acquainted with some of the sources your group has identified. Write a beat memo that describes several story ideas, with likely sources.

3. Complete the job by reporting and writing one of the stories identified in exercise 2. This would be a good opportunity for peer critiquing of one another's work.

4. **Journalism blog.** Spend some time exploring a news website. In a blog post, compare the news coverage and the features of the website with the content of the newspaper and the television outlet that cover the same area. Which of the three is more useful, more satisfying, more fun?

5. In the library or in a computer database, look up three recent national or international stories about a religious or scientific issue. Write a memo explaining how you would localize each story for your city. Include possible sources.

6. Using LexisNexis or another computer database, examine how two or three major newspapers cover a national beat, such as Congress or a federal agency. What similarities and differences do you see between that work and local coverage? The topics will be different, but what about sources? Do you see a different focus on reader interests?

7. Analyze a local news story about crime. Identify the sources. If you were reporting this story, what other sources would you consult? What specific questions would you try to get answered?

15

GET IN★
CHICAGO
SAFER COMMUNITIES, BRIGHTER FUTURES

IN★SPIRED IN★VOLVED IN★VESTED

Speeches, News Conferences and Meetings

WHEN REPUBLICANS from the U.S. House of Representatives met behind closed doors in Williamsburg, Va., to discuss their strategy on budget cuts and other issues, experienced reporters from television, newspapers and online news organizations waited outside. Rep. Paul Ryan, who chairs the House Budget Committee, emerged to hold a news conference. Here is the angle that *The Washington Post* took:

WILLIAMSBURG, Va.—House Republicans are weighing a plan to raise the nation's legal borrowing limit for just a few months, a move that could shift debate over the debt ceiling into March, when Congress will face other major fiscal decisions, Rep. Paul Ryan (R-Wis.) said Thursday.

But, speaking to reporters at the annual House Republicans retreat at Williamsburg's storied Kingsmill Resort, Ryan said Republicans are still in intense discussions about how to approach the difficult question of raising the debt ceiling. He said House leaders were using closed-door sessions Thursday to educate their own members, many of them itching for a fight with President Obama over the debt limit, about the potential consequences of failing to raise the limit.

Here is how CBSNews.com reported the news conference on its website:

Rep. Paul Ryan, R-Wis., suggested today that House Republicans could push for a short-term increase of the debt limit, likely around one month, to allow more time for Republicans to work with President Obama and Senate Democrats on spending cuts.

"We're discussing the possible virtue of a short-term debt limit extension so that we have a better chance of getting the Senate and the White House involved in discussions in March," Ryan, the chairman of the House Budget Committee, told reporters at the House Republican Conference annual retreat in Williamsburg, Va.

Despite covering the same news conference, the reporters took different approaches to tailor their stories to their audiences. Some emphasized the Republican leadership's efforts to get House members to fall in line; others emphasized the strategy of pushing back the deadline.

To write these stories, reporters have to be knowledgeable about the topic and to be there. Whatever beat you are covering, you must be prepared to cover three basic assignments: speeches, news conferences and meetings.

DISTINGUISHING AMONG SPEECHES, NEWS CONFERENCES AND MEETINGS

A *speech* is a public talk. Someone speaks to an audience in person or on radio or television. Regardless of the medium, a speech is one-way communication. The speaker speaks, and the audience listens, although sometimes a question-and-answer session follows.

Speakers are usually invited and sometimes paid to address an audience. That is not the case with those who hold a *news conference*. People "call" or "hold" news conferences. They do not send invitations to the general public, but they do alert members of the news media. The media respond because of the importance of the person calling the news conference and because the person might have something newsworthy to say. The person holding the news conference often begins with an opening statement and usually accepts questions from reporters. A news conference is meant to be two-way communication. Many politicians, who would rather not take questions, are using social media, particularly their websites and Twitter, to make announcements.

Unlike speeches and news conferences, *meetings* are not held with an audience in mind, although an audience might be present and allowed to participate. A meeting is primarily for communication among the members of a group or organization, whether a local parent-teacher association or the U.S. Congress. Reporters who are permitted to witness a meeting tell the public what is of interest and importance. This task of the news media is especially important if the participants are members of a governmental body that spends or allocates taxpayers' money.

GETTING READY TO COVER THE STORY

Good reporters know that preparation makes covering a story much easier, and they always do their homework. The preparation for speeches, news conferences and meetings is similar. Because these events are usually announced in advance, you often have time for thorough preparation.

Preparing for the Speech Story

Not every speech will demand a great deal of research. Many speakers and speeches will be dry and routine. The person giving the speech will be someone you know or someone you have covered before. If you are working for campus media, it could be a university official. If you are working for the professional press, it could be the mayor or the director of the local United Way. At other times you might get an assignment on short notice and be forced to find background information after hearing the speech. In either case, never take the speaker or the topic for granted. Failure to get enough background on the speaker and on the speech almost guarantees failure at writing a comprehensive speech story.

If you have not covered the speaker before, the first step in your research is to identify the person correctly. Middle initials are important, but sometimes even they are not enough. *USA Today* had to print a "clarification" after reporting that Larry King had made a $1,000 donation to a presidential campaign. The donor was Larry L. King, author and playwright, not Larry King, the former CNN show host.

Then, before doing research on the speaker, contact the group sponsoring the speech and ask for the topic. You might find you need to do some reading to prepare yourself to understand the subject. If you are lucky, you may get an advance copy of the speech. Next, check your organization's own library to see what other reporters have written previously about the speaker. If you have access to a national database of newspaper and magazine stories such as Factiva, use it.

If the speech is important enough, you might want to contact the speaker ahead of time for a brief interview. If he or she is from out of town, you might plan a meeting at the airport. You might also arrange ahead of time to interview the speaker after the speech. You might have questions or points to clarify.

Not every speech demands this much effort. But even the most routine speech assignment requires preparation. Sooner or later you may be called on to cover speeches by major political figures, perhaps even the U.S. president. For this task, too, you will need background—lots of it. Doing a good job demands that you read the news and know what is going on. You must keep up with current events. If you don't regularly read or listen to the news, subscribe to an RSS feed from one of the major news organizations, such as CNN or *The New York Times*. If you are on Facebook frequently, like the page of any of the big news organizations so you get postings from them.

Preparing for the News Conference Story

Preparing for a news conference is similar to preparing for a speech. You need up-to-date background on the person giving the news conference, and you must learn why the news conference is being held. Often the person holding the news conference has an announcement or an opening statement. Unless that statement is leaked to the press, you will not know its content ahead of time, but you can make some educated guesses. Check out any rumors. Call the person's associates, friends or secretary.

Consult your editor and other staff editors about specific information they want. Then draw up a list of questions to ask at the news conference. Once the news conference begins, you will not have time to think of questions; recording responses to other reporters' questions will keep you too busy. The better prepared you are, the better chance you will have of coming away with a coherent, readable story.

It may be impossible to arrange an interview before or after the news conference. If the person holding the news conference wanted to do interviews with individual

TIPS

Preparing for the Speech Story

» Be sure you have the right person.

» Contact the group sponsoring the speech and ask for the topic.

» Check your newspaper library and online sources for background on the speaker.

» If the speech is important enough, contact the speaker for a brief interview.

TIPS

Preparing for the News Conference Story

» Get up-to-date background on the person holding the news conference.

» Learn why the conference is being held.

» Check out any rumors beforehand.

» Try to arrange an interview before or after the news conference.

reporters, he or she probably would not have called the news conference. But you can always ask—you might end up with some exclusive information.

Preparing for the Meeting Story

TIPS

Preparing for the Meeting Story

» Contact some of the key figures.

» Try to find out what the meeting is about. You can then study and investigate issues before arriving.

Often the meetings of important organizations are preceded by an agenda or an advance, a report outlining the subjects and issues to be covered during the upcoming meeting. With nongovernmental, and even some governmental, meetings, you often do not know what to expect, so you must do your best to prepare. Who is holding the meeting? What kind of organization is involved? Who are the key figures? Again, the news library should be your first stop, and online research will yield more information. Then contact some of the key figures.

If there is no agenda, find out what the meeting is about. Talk to the organization's president. If you know the main subject to be discussed, you will be able to study and investigate the issues before arriving. Knowing what to expect and being familiar with the issues will make covering the meeting much easier. A reporter with a regular beat—an assigned area of responsibility—usually covers meetings of the most important organizations and groups on that beat, such as the city council, the school board or the county commission. (Beat reporting is discussed in detail in Chapter 14.) Beat reporters are most familiar with the organizations and issues involved.

COVERING SPEECHES, NEWS CONFERENCES AND MEETINGS

An old story is that of the reporter who prepared well for a speech assignment, contacted the speaker, got a copy of the speech, wrote the story and spent the evening in a bar. Not until after he handed in his story did he find out that the speech had been canceled.

And then there's the yarn about the young reporter assigned to cover a meeting who came back and told the city editor there was no story.

"Why not?" the city editor asked.

"Because the meeting was canceled."

"Why was that?"

"Well," replied the reporter, "when the meeting started, some of the board members got into this big argument. Finally, three of them walked out. The president then canceled the meeting because there was no quorum."

Of course, the canceled meeting and the circumstances surrounding its cancellation probably were of more interest to readers than the meeting itself would have been.

Preparing to cover an event is only the beginning. Knowing what to do when you get there is equally important. You must cover the entire event—the content of the speech, news conference or meeting; the time, place, circumstances and number of people involved; and the possible consequences of what was said or of the actions taken.

A story about a speech, news conference or meeting often requires direct quotes.

The Medium Matters

What you need to do at a speech, press conference or meeting depends on your final distribution medium. If you're writing a story for print, simply taking good notes, using an audio recorder and getting audience reaction might suffice. If you are shooting video, you have to consider the lighting and find a good place from which to shoot. (For tips on shooting video for the Web, see Chapter 12.)

These days, if the event is of enough interest, you probably will also be tweeting or posting texts to your organization's mobile users. You might be charged with writing a Web story, providing an audio clip and then writing yet another story for the newspaper. If you are working for a television station, you might be shooting coverage of the event, interviewing people afterward, tweeting some important lines during the event, editing the video and writing a Web version.

More and more nontelevision news organizations are adding video to their websites, which means you might have to learn something about videography. This makes reporting more challenging today than ever. Print, Web and video coverage require different approaches, and doing all of them at the same time isn't easy. With today's many ways of distributing news information, you need to learn to become a multimedia journalist. Doing so will make you more valuable to your employer.

TIPS

Achieving Total Coverage of Content and Event

» Get the content correct. Recorders can be helpful, but always take good notes. Quote people exactly and in context.

» Note the background, personal characteristics and mannerisms of the main participants.

» Cover the event. Look around the edges—at the audience (size, reactions) and sometimes at what is happening outside the building.

» Get there early, position yourself and hang around afterward.

Getting the Content Correct

You may find a digital audio recorder or video camera useful for covering the content of speeches, news conferences and meetings. Be aware, though, that audio recorders and video cameras often intimidate people who aren't accustomed to being interviewed, so always ask permission to record any interviews you get. Practice using the recorder or video camera until you are familiar with its idiosyncrasies. Make sure you know how sensitive the microphone is. Get to know the camera's operation as best you can.

When someone says something newsworthy, note the counter on the recorder so you can find the quote quickly. Even if you record an event, take notes. Malfunctions can occur, even with the best recorders, at the most inopportune times. (See Chapter 4 for more on recording audio and video interviews.)

Sooner or later every reporter adopts or creates some note-taking shortcuts. You will have to do the same, perhaps expanding on the note-taking shortcuts you've used in college lectures. Learn to abbreviate (*wh* for "which," *th* for "that," *bk* for "book," *st* for "street," *bldg* for "building," etc.) and use signs (*w/* for "with," *w/o* for "without," *acc/* for "according to"). Taking notes is most crucial when you wish to record direct quotes.

As you learned in Chapter 5, putting someone's words in quotation marks means only one thing: You are quoting the exact words the person spoke. Speeches, news conferences and meetings all demand that you be able to record direct quotes. Your stories will be lifeless and lack credibility without them. A speech story, for example, should contain many direct quotes.

Whether covering a speech, a news conference or a meeting, be careful to quote people in context. For example, if a speaker gives supporting evidence for an argument, you would be unfair not to report it. Quotes can be misleading if you carelessly or deliberately juxtapose them. Combining quotes with no indication that something was said in between them can lead to inaccuracies and to charges of unfairness. Suppose, for example, someone says:

> "Cutting down fuel costs can be an easy thing. If you have easy access to wood, you should invest in a good wood-burning stove. With little effort, you can cut your fuel bills in half."

A reporter who omits the middle sentence of that quote, even inserting an ellipsis, makes the speaker look ridiculous:

> "Cutting down fuel costs can be an easy thing. . . . With little effort, you can cut your fuel bills in half."

Describing the Participants

An audio recording does not capture a speaker's facial expressions and gestures. These are sometimes more important than the words themselves.

Simply reporting the words of a speaker (or of the person holding a news conference or participating at a meeting) does not indicate the volume and tone of voice, inflections, pauses, emphases and reactions to and from those in attendance. You might note that a speaker deliberately winked while reading a sentence. Or you might notice unmistakable sarcasm in the speaker's voice.

Regardless of who the speaker is or where the speech is taking place, you should always note the speaker's background. A person's words must often be measured against that individual's background. For example, if a former Communist is speaking on communism, this fact might have a bearing on what he says. If a former CIA agent is speaking about corruption in the CIA, you cannot adequately report her message if you do not mention her background.

Sometimes, purely physical facts about the speaker are essential to the story. A blind person pleading for funds to educate the blind, a one-armed veteran speaking about the hell of war, a gray-haired person speaking about care for the elderly—these speakers must be described physically for the story to be complete, accurate and understandable. Beware, however, of including gratuitous descriptions; it's problematic to include the information that a state senator advocating for gun control is black, for example.

You also should note what the person who introduces a speaker says. This may help you understand the significance of the speaker and the importance of what he or she has to say.

Being Observant

Keep an eye on the audience and on what's happening around the edges. Measure the mood of the audience by noting the tone of the questions. Are they sharply worded? Is there much laughter or applause? Perhaps members of the audience boo. Does the speaker or the person holding the news conference or the person presiding over the meeting remain calm and in control? Is there casual bantering or joking with the audience? Is the audience stacked with supporters or detractors?

Sometimes the real action takes place outside in the form of a picket line or protest. Sometimes police manage to keep protesters away from the site. Sometimes who is *not* there is news.

Don't overlook the obvious. For example, you should note the size of the audience. Reporting a "full house" means little unless you indicate the house capacity. One way to estimate attendance is to count how many people are sitting in a row or in a typical section. Then you multiply that number by the number of rows or sections in the hall. Use good judgment and common sense to adjust for some sections being more crowded than others. In large venues, you can find out the seating capacity ahead of time. In some locations, the fire department requires all public venues to post the maximum capacity of the space.

Arriving, Positioning Yourself and Staying On

Most reporters arrive early. At some events, special seating is set aside for reporters, but you should probably not count on that unless you know for sure.

TIPS

Using a Digital Audio Recorder

» Be familiar with the device. Practice using it. Make sure you understand its peculiarities. Check its sound capabilities.

» Set it where you can see that it's working. Use the digital counter to note newsworthy quotes.

» Take notes. The recorder might not be working, or it might not have captured the voices clearly.

TIPS

Covering an Event

» Be sure to record what the digital recorder misses— gestures and facial expressions.

» Remember that a person's words often must be measured against his or her background.

» Take note of the tone of questions.

» Note the size of the audience.

At a speech, sitting in the first row is not necessarily best. Instead, choose a location that lets you see the reaction of the audience. If there is a question-and-answer period, you might want to be able to see the questioner. And you certainly want to be in a good position to ask questions yourself.

At a news conference, your location might help you get the attention of the person holding the conference. You should have your questions prepared, but preparing them is not enough. You have seen presidential news conferences on television, and you know how difficult it is to get the president's attention. Indeed, sometimes there is even a list showing the order in which reporters will be recognized. All news conferences present the reporter with similar difficulties, though on a smaller scale. You have also seen how difficult it is for reporters to follow up on their own questions. At some news conferences you will not be called on twice.

But you must do more than try to get your own questions answered. You must listen to others' questions and be able to recognize the making of a good story. Too often a good question is dropped without follow-up because reporters are not listening carefully or are too intent on pursuing their own questions. Listen for what is newsworthy and pursue it. Sticking with an important subject will make the job of writing the story easier. Remember, when the news conference is finished, you will have a

Speeches, such as this one from President Barack Obama, require the reporter to be alert not only to what is said but also to the audience's reaction.

story to write. Piecing together notes on dozens of unrelated topics can be difficult, if not impossible.

At a meeting you should be able to see and hear the main participants. Ordinarily, a board or council will sit facing the audience. Before the meeting starts, you should know which members are sitting where. You might want to assign each participant a number so you do not have to write the person's name each time he or she speaks. You also can draw a sketch of where members are sitting. In this way you will be able to quote someone by number and if necessary find out his or her name later. Know who the officers are. The president or the secretary might distribute handouts before the meeting. After a meeting, the secretary might be able to help you fill in missing words or information.

As a general rule, when the speech, news conference or meeting is over, do not rush off unless you are on deadline. Some of the best stories happen afterward. You might have some questions to ask. You might need clarification or want to arrange to interview a key spokesperson. Listen for reactions from those in attendance.

TIPS

Five Ways to Master the Meeting Story

» Arrive early.

» Prepare your questions.

» Listen to others' questions.

» Pursue what is newsworthy.

» Don't rush off. Some of the best stories happen afterward.

STRUCTURING AND WRITING YOUR STORY

Writing the lead for the speech, news conference or meeting story is no different from writing the lead for any other story. All of the qualities of the inverted pyramid news lead discussed in Chapter 9 are important here as well.

You must be careful not to emphasize something about the event that is of great interest or curiosity but does not lead into the rest of your story. It's tempting, for example, to lead with a striking quote. But rarely does a speaker or someone holding a news conference highlight the content or the main point in a single, quotable sentence. As always, there are exceptions. As a lead for one of Dr. Martin Luther King Jr.'s most famous addresses, a good reporter might have begun with "I have a dream."

Because of the nature of the inverted pyramid news story, rarely should you follow the chronology of the event you are covering. But the flow of your story might demand *some* attention to chronology (see Chapter 11). If you pay no attention to chronology, you might distort, or cause readers to misinterpret, the meaning of the event.

Writing the Speech Story

Although you might not soon be called upon to cover the speeches of well-known politicians, you can learn a lot from the way the pros handle important political addresses. The annotated model "Speech Story" on page 322 shows the first 300 words of CNN's coverage of a speech in which President Barack Obama proposed new gun control laws. CNN accompanied this Web story with five video excerpts and background material.

The approach for a video reporter is somewhat different. For television or video on the Web, you'll introduce the subject and the speaker and then cut in video snippets of the speech itself. You might well end the piece with an interview of someone who attended and in the process get some audience reaction.

ANNOTATED MODEL   Speech Story

Pushback on Obama's Plan to Stem Gun Violence

By Dana Bash, Jessica Yellin and Tom Cohen, CNN

Summary lead →

Washington (CNN)—President Barack Obama on Wednesday proposed background checks on all gun sales and bans on military style assault weapons and high-capacity magazines as part of a package of steps to reduce gun violence in the wake of the Newtown school massacre last month.

← Transition sentence describes the environment of the speech.

Additional details summarize the speech. →

With relatives of some of the 20 children killed in the Connecticut rampage looking on, Obama signed 23 executive actions—which don't require congressional approval—to strengthen existing gun laws and take related steps on mental health and school safety.

Third paragraph offers specifics of the plan. →

He also called on Congress to reinstate an assault weapons ban that expired in 2004, to restrict ammunition magazines to no more than 10 rounds, and to expand background checks to anyone buying a gun, whether at a store or in a private sale at an auction or convention.

← Though long, the sentence is clear because it contains items in a series.

Hyperlink →

Senate Democrats hold key to passage of gun legislation

With proposals outlined, the story starts to give Obama's rationale. →

Referring to the young students killed in the Newtown shootings on December 14 and other victims of gun violence, Obama said the nation must do a better job of protecting its children, especially when they are in schools, shopping malls, movie theaters and other public places.

While some of the steps he proposed are given little chance of winning congressional approval in the face of the nation's powerful gun lobby, Obama said all efforts must be made to reduce chronic gun violence in the country.

"This is our first task as a society—keeping our children safe," the president said, adding that saving even one life would make the changes he seeks worth the effort.

← Reporters decided this was the most important quote in the speech.

Hyperlink →

Read Obama's proposals

Political speeches often require opposition response for fairness. →

Republicans immediately rejected the Obama proposals as an attack on the constitutional right to bear arms.

"Nothing the president is proposing would have stopped the massacre at Sandy Hook," said a statement by Sen. Marco Rubio, R-Florida, considered an up-and-coming GOP leader. "President Obama is targeting the Second Amendment rights of law-abiding citizens instead of seriously addressing the real underlying causes of such violence."

CNN's coverage of President Obama's gun control speech illustrates a typical approach to speech stories. Because this story appeared on CNN's website, it has hyperlinks.

Writing the News Conference Story

Writing the news conference story might be a bit more challenging than writing the speech story. Because you will go to the conference with different questions in mind from those your fellow reporters want to ask, you might come away with a different story. Your lead, at least, might be different from the leads of other reporters.

A news conference often covers a gamut of topics. Often it begins with a statement from the person who called the conference.

For example, when the mayor of Springfield holds a news conference to announce her candidacy for a second term, you can be sure that she will begin with a statement to that effect. Although her candidacy might be news to some people, you might want to ask her questions about the location of a new landfill that the city is rumored to be planning. Most citizens will admit the need for landfills, but their location is always controversial. And then there's that tip you heard about the city manager possibly resigning to take a job in a large city.

Other reporters will come with other questions. Will there be further cuts in the city budget? Will the cuts mean that some city employees will lose their jobs? What happened to the plans to expand the city jail?

After you leave a news conference that covered many topics, you have the job of organizing the material in some logical, coherent order. You can choose to write a multiple-element lead (see Chapter 9). But usually you will treat the most newsworthy subject first and deal with the other subjects in the order of their importance. Rarely would you report on them in the chronological order in which they were discussed.

Suppose you decide the location of the landfill is the most important item of the news conference—especially if the mayor revealed the location for the first time. You might begin your story this way:

> The city will construct its new landfill near the intersection of State Route 53 and Route E, four miles north of Springfield, Mayor Juanita Williams said today.
>
> "After nearly a year of discussion and the best advice we could obtain, we are certain the Route E location is best for all concerned," Williams said at a news conference.
>
> The mayor admitted there would be continued opposition to the site by citizens living in the general area, especially those in the Valley High Trailer Court. "No location will please everyone," Williams said.
>
> Williams called the news conference to make the expected announcement of her candidacy for a second term.

Now you have to find a way to treat the other topics of the conference. You might want to list them first in a series of bullet points:

> In other matters, Williams said:
> * City Manager Diane Lusby will not be resigning to take another post.
> * Budget constraints will not permit any new construction on the city jail this year.
> * Budget cuts will not cost any city employees their jobs. However, positions vacated by retiring personnel will not be filled.

TIPS

Technical Concerns for Television Journalists

Speeches, news conferences and meetings present several technical challenges. Here are three to keep in mind:

» Think visuals. What will your backdrop be? Will there be signs, photos, samples, logos or flip charts to help tell the story?

» Think sound. Will there be one microphone or a multi-box in which you can insert your mic, or will you be free to set up your own microphone?

» Think light. Will the event take place outdoors or in a well-lit room, or must you bring your own lighting? How far is the camera throw (the distance from the event to your camera)? Will there be a camera platform or a set space, or will you be free to set up your camera anywhere?

After this list, you will either go back to your lead, giving more background and quoting citizens or other city officials on the subject, or go on to discuss, one at a time, the matters you listed. Pay particular attention to making proper transitions from paragraph to paragraph so your story is coherent. "On other subjects, the mayor said . . . ," "The mayor defended her position on . . . ," "Again she stressed. . . ."

If one of the subjects is of special interest, you may want to write a sidebar, a shorter piece to go with your main story. For this story, you could do a sidebar on the mayor's candidacy, her record, her possible opponents and the like.

With a longer or more complicated story, you may want to make a summary list of all the main topics covered and place the list in a box or sidebar.

You probably wrote a story before the news conference to say the mayor was expected to announce her candidacy. When she makes the announcement, you probably tweet it. You probably also tweet the location where the city plans to locate the landfill.

Remember, your job is to give readers the news, as simply and clearly as possible. Remember, too, to cover the event itself as well as the content. Perhaps some picketers protested the mayor's remarks about a local abortion clinic. Sometimes what happens at a news conference is more newsworthy than anything the person holding the conference says. What happens there might well be the lead of your main story, or you may want to place it in a sidebar.

Writing the Meeting Story

Readers want you to take their place at the meeting you are covering. Let's look at a simple meeting story—in this case, a meeting of a local school board:

The decision of three national corporations to protest a formula used to compute their property taxes is causing more than $264,000 to be withheld from the Walnut School District's operating budget for the 2009–10 school year.

Superintendent Max Schmidt said at Monday's school board meeting that International Business Machines Corp., ACR Corp. and Xerox are arguing that the method used in computing their property taxes was no longer valid. Nine California counties are involved in similar disputes.

The taxes, totaling $264,688, are being held in escrow by the county until the matter is resolved. Some or all of the money eventually may be returned to the district, but the administration cannot determine when or how much.

"If we take a quarter million dollars out of our program at this time, it could have a devastating effect," Schmidt said. "Once you've built that money into your budget and you lost it, you've lost a major source of income."

Mike Harper, the county prosecuting attorney, and Larry Woods, the school district attorney, advised board members to take a "wait-and-see attitude," Schmidt said. He said that one alternative would be to challenge the corporations in court. A final decision will be made later.

The board also delayed action on repayment of $80,000 to IBM in a separate tax dispute. The corporation claims the district owes it for overpaid 2007 property taxes. The county commission has ruled the claim is legitimate and must be repaid.

ON THE JOB

Speeches, News Conferences and Meetings

Patrick Pierce's 2002 degree in journalism — with an emphasis in broadcast journalism and a minor in political science — has served him well. He began his career working as a sports reporter in Columbia, Mo., and West Monroe, La.

He quickly ventured into politics with a race for U.S. Congress in 2004 and for state representative in 2006, both in Missouri.

He worked briefly in marketing before using his reporting skills to work in public relations after a move to San Diego in 2008. He became a PR consultant for a variety of nonprofits, trade organizations, the hospitality industry, health companies and former professional athletes.

Pierce returned to journalism as a reporter for the *Mission Times Courier* in San Diego. He is currently Director of Communications and Membership Outreach for the San Diego and Imperial Counties Labor Council. Pierce continues to serve as a contributing writer for the *Mission Times Courier*.

Having been on both sides of the microphone as a reporter and newsmaker, he understands how important each side is in the news-gathering process. After covering speeches and delivering them, attending meetings and leading them, as well as asking questions at news conferences and being interviewed at them, Pierce has some advice that he is eager to share.

His chief tip: "Don't be afraid to ask the tough question." Pierce warns against allowing a few veteran reporters to control questions after a meeting or during a news conference.

"Remember, you have the power to change the pace of a news conference and to ask the tough question when it needs to be asked. Don't wait, or you might not be able to ask your question."

With the evolution of "news" now including the likes of Twitter, Facebook, YouTube, blogs, vlogs and websites, as well as traditional news stations and publications, reporters often forget to ask the tough question, Pierce says.

"Asking the tough question when the situation calls for it will earn you both respect and a reputation of being a firm but fair reporter. If you stick to your core beliefs of what a journalist is and does, including asking the tough question at the right time, you will be successful in your reporting career."

A possible source of additional income, however, could be House Bill 1002, Schmidt said. If passed, this appropriations bill would provide an additional $46 million for state education, approximately $250,000 of which could go to the Walnut School District.

Charles Campbell, the district architect, said plans for the area's new vocational technical school to be built on the Rock Bridge High School campus will be given to contractors in February. Bids will be presented at the March 15 board meeting.

The board voted to have classes on Presidents Day, Feb. 15, to make up for time missed because of the teachers' strike.

The issue of the meeting was money problems—a subject that concerns every taxpayer. The writer jumped right into the subject in the lead, giving the "what" in the first paragraph, and then in the second paragraph giving us the "who," "when" and "where." The reporter then dealt with specifics, naming names and citing figures, and quoted the key person at the meeting. In the last two paragraphs the writer dealt with other matters discussed in the meeting.

The issues discussed at a meeting are not your only considerations in covering a meeting story. Remember, too, to cover the event. Who was there? Who represented the public? How did people react after the meeting was over?

One reporter began her meeting story in this way:

> Even though they are footing the bill, only one of Boone County's residents cared enough to attend a Tuesday night hearing on the county's 2010 budget.
>
> With an audience of one citizen plus two reporters, County Auditor June Pitchford presented her official report on the $21 million budget to the Boone County Commission in a silent City Council chamber.

Even when covering routine, boring events, you are allowed to use your creativity. In addition to getting all the facts, your job is also to be interesting, to get people to read the story. Remember, two of the criteria for news are that it be relevant and useful. Another is that it be interesting.

If you're a video reporter, your approach to a meeting story will be quite different. There's almost nothing as boring as video of a city council meeting, so telling the story creatively is important. If you know the council will be debating increased garbage pickup rates, get some video of garbage trucks to show while you're narrating the gist of the story. Then, of course, interviews with council members or members of the public can be used to complete the story.

No matter which medium you work for, you will be expected to write well—even for a common event like a speech, news conference or meeting.

SUGGESTED READINGS

Biography and Genealogy Master Index. Detroit, Mich.: Gale Research, 1981 to present. This compilation of biographical directories lists people whose biographies have been written and indicates which date and volume of those reference books to consult for the actual biography.

Biography Index. Bronx, N.Y.: H.W. Wilson, 1946 to present. This reference helps you locate biographical articles that have appeared in 2,000 periodicals and journals, as well as in biographical books and chapters from collective biographies.

Current Biography. Bronx, N.Y.: H.W. Wilson, 1940 to present. This monthly publication about people in the news includes a photo of each subject. It is an excellent source for people not included in more formal biographical sources.

SUGGESTED WEBSITES

http://journalism-education.cubreporters.org/2010/08/how-to-cover-speeches.html
A former reporter offers tips on how to cover speeches.

www.bedfordstmartins.com/newscentral
When you visit News Central, you will find up-to-the-moment RSS feeds, research links and exercises to help you improve your grammar and AP style usage. In addition, the site's

VideoCentral: Journalism section hosts the videos highlighted in this chapter as well as additional clips of leading professionals discussing important media trends.

www.journalism.about.com/od/reporting/a/pressconf.htm
Tony Rogers offers some easy-to-remember tips for covering a news conference.

EXERCISES

1. **Team project.** Your instructor will divide the class into teams. Find out when your university's faculty council or similar faculty representative group is having its next meeting. As a team, plan the steps you will take to prepare for the meeting, and share the information you gather as you prepare. Then cover the meeting, taking notes. Discuss your notes with team members and then write individual stories for the student newspaper. Compare your stories. How similar are the leads and the story structures? How do they differ? Are direct quotations used effectively? How could the stories be improved?

2. Read President Obama's second inaugural speech (www .politico.com/story/2013/01/president-barack-obamas -2013-inaugural-address-full-text-86497.html). Discuss in class what you would use for your lead and why.

3. The site that contains the text of the inaugural speech also contains the video. After watching the video, decide what observations about the president's demeanor or delivery, audience reaction, or the setting you would add to your story.

4. Search at least two news organizations to find reports about the inauguration, and compare your suggestions with the professionals' work.

5. Journalist Andrea Mitchell is coming to town to speak on the current U.S. president's relationship with the press. Prepare to cover the speech. Record the steps you have taken to prepare for the speech and the information you have gathered on Mitchell.

6. Find out when a public figure in your area—a government official or a college administrator, for example—plans to give a speech on a specific topic. Prepare for and cover the speech, using a digital recorder. Then write two versions of your news story: one for immediate posting on a website and one for the print edition of a newspaper. For the Web version, what specific links would be useful? Suggest at least one possible sidebar.

7. **Journalism blog.** Attend a speech, news conference or meeting—preferably one occurring at the school you are attending. Then on your blog, post a 300-word item about the event, including its content. Be sure to include links to pertinent social media and other sites.

8. Prepare for and cover a meeting of a local government agency or committee—the school board, the city council, or a similar group. Try to interview one of the participants before or after the meeting. Then write your story in two versions—one for a website specializing in local events and one for a local radio news broadcast. How do the two stories differ? How does each story meet the criteria of usefulness, relevance and interest?

16

Other Types of Local Stories

In this chapter you will learn:

1. How to gather information for stories about crimes, accidents and fires, and court proceedings.

2. How to write such stories.

3. How to recognize special problems of crime and court reporting.

4. How to report and write obituaries and life stories.

ALMOST ALL REPORTERS will be expected at some time in their careers to write at least one obituary. Rex Huppke, a general assignment reporter and columnist for the *Chicago Tribune*, offers a bit of sound advice: "Remember that you are writing the final chapter of a person's life. This is not a responsibility to be taken lightly."

He followed his own rule, sort of, when he wrote an obituary for facts. Here's how he began the piece, which ran on the "Politics" page of the *Tribune*'s website:

Facts, 360 B.C.–A.D. 2012
In memoriam: After years of health problems, Facts has finally died.

A quick review of the long and illustrious career of Facts reveals some of the world's most cherished absolutes: Gravity makes things fall down; 2 + 2 = 4; the sky is blue.

But for many, Facts' most memorable moments came in simple day-to-day realities, from a child's certainty of its mother's love to the comforting knowledge that a favorite television show would start promptly at 8 p.m.

Then came the nut graph:

To the shock of most sentient beings, Facts died Wednesday, April 18, after a long battle for relevancy with the 24-hour news cycle, blogs and the Internet. Though few expected Facts to pull out of its years-long downward spiral, the official cause of death was from injuries suffered last week when Florida Republican Rep. Allen West steadfastly declared that as many as 81 of his fellow members of the U.S. House of Representatives are communists.

And the conclusion:

Facts is survived by two brothers, Rumor and Innuendo, and a sister, Emphatic Assertion.

Services are alleged to be private. In lieu of flowers, the family requests that mourners make a donation to their favorite super PAC.

Clearly, this is satire born of disgust at political fabrication. Equally clearly, though, this obituary for Facts illustrates several important facts about journalism today.

First, not all the news is deadly serious.

Second, audiences expect and welcome variety. This piece was shared nearly 90,000 times on Twitter, Facebook, email, Google+, Digg, Reddit and Tumblr.

Third, good reporters in any medium need imagination, writing skill and flexibility.

Now let's see how to apply your skills in a more serious way.

You may never have the opportunity for satire, but you are likely at some time to find yourself covering crime, chasing fire trucks or trying to make sense of court proceedings. This chapter will help. You also are likely to be assigned to tell the real life story of someone who has died. This chapter will help with that, too.

YOUR PREPARATION

When news breaks, you won't have much time to prepare before rushing out the door or picking up the phone. However, there is some instant research you can do, even if it requires using your smartphone on your way to the scene (preferably with someone else driving). Begin as you would with any other story—by checking your newsroom's electronic morgue. There you'll learn whether a similar crime has occurred before, whether accidents are common at the location of the latest one, whether similar suspicious fires have occurred or whether the person charged with the crime has been in trouble before. And don't overlook Google.

Preparing for the Crime Story

Meetings, news conferences, speeches and court proceedings are usually scheduled events, so on most occasions you should have ample time beforehand to do background research on the individual or topic to be covered. Obituaries also call for a first stop in the television station or newspaper library, but crime reporting may be different. If the police radio reports a murder in your area, you may be dispatched to the scene as the story is breaking. At that point, no one will know who is involved or what happened. There will be no time to check the library, and you will have to do your initial reporting at the scene.

Most information about crimes comes from three sources:

» Police officials and their reports.
» The victim or victims.
» The witness or witnesses.

The circumstances of the crime may determine which of the three is most important, which should be checked first or whether they should be checked at all. If the victim is available, as a reporter you should make every effort to get an interview. If the victim and witnesses are unavailable, the police and their reports become primary sources.

In the era of convergence, you'll need more than a pencil and notebook to gather information at the scene of a crime. A digital recorder will allow you to record your interviews for publication on your news organization's website, and a digital camera or phone camera might help record what happened at the scene. That's particularly true if you are covering the event alone without the help of a photojournalist or videographer. A smartphone will make it possible for you to tweet instant updates from the scene.

The point at which your editor assigns you to a crime story is important. If you are dispatched to the scene of the crime as it happens or soon afterward, you should attempt to interview the victim and witnesses first. The police report probably hasn't even been written yet. But if you are assigned to write about a crime that occurred the night before, the police report should be your starting point.

The timing affects what kinds of material you will be able to gather and which medium might use your information first. A major breaking story might warrant a mobile phone news bulletin or a television report. Something that happened the night before might require more sophisticated work, such as gathering information for a detailed information graphic of a crime scene.

Reporters can often use a smartphone or tablet computer to research background on a breaking story before arriving at the scene.

A police officer investigating a crime covers much of the same ground as you. The officer is interested in who was involved, what happened, when, where, why and how. Those details are needed to complete the official report of the incident, and you need them for your story. When you write about crime, always check the police report. It is often the source of basic information, such as:

» A description of what happened.
» The location of the incident.
» The name, age and address of the victim.
» The name, age and address of the suspect, if any.
» The offense police believe the suspect has committed.
» The extent of injuries, if any.
» The names, ages and addresses of witnesses, if any.

If you arrive at the scene of a crime as it is taking place or immediately afterward, you have the advantage of being able to gather much of the required information first-hand. When timely coverage is impossible, however, the police report allows you to catch up quickly. The names of those with knowledge of the incident usually appear on the report, and the reporter uses that information to learn the story.

Reporters sometimes write crime stories from the police report alone. Good journalists, however, demand more because police reports are frequently inaccurate. Most experienced reporters have read reports in which the names of those involved were misspelled, ages were wrong and other basic information was inaccurate. Sometimes such errors are a result of sloppy reporting by the investigating officer or mistakes in transcribing notes into a formal report. Occasionally, the officer may lie in an attempt to cover up shortcomings in the investigation or misconduct at the scene of the crime. Whatever the reason, you should do your own reporting and not depend solely on a police officer's account. Remember that editors frown on single-source stories of any kind. It's your job to do solid reporting, and you are expected to consult multiple sources.

Often, you will want to post the police report itself on your organization's website. The public has a right to see primary sources of this type. But be careful to protect the privacy of victims where appropriate. After a newspaper posted the police account of interviews with the victim of a sexual assault, editors were horrified to discover that the police had failed to remove the victim's name in several places. (Nearly all news organizations protect the identities of sex crime victims.) Another thing to remember is that police reports often contain graphic details some civilians find offensive.

For crime stories, you will usually do a background check in the newsroom's morgue after you return to the office. Check whether the morgue contains relevant information about those involved in the crime, for example. Has the suspect been arrested before? Has the store been robbed before? The morgue might help answer those kinds of questions.

Preparing for Accident and Fire Stories

If you are assigned to cover an accident or fire, you can expect some of the same problems you'd encounter in covering a crime. Much depends on whether the police or fire report is available before you are assigned to the story. If the accident or fire took place overnight, the official report is the place to start. It will give you most of the basic information you need. It will also lead you to other sources.

If you are sent to the scene of an accident or fire, your job is to collect much of the basic information yourself. As for crimes, the basic information you'll need includes:

» A description of what happened.
» The location of the incident.
» The name, age and address of the victim or victims.
» The extent of injuries, if any.
» The names, ages and addresses of witnesses, if any.

TIPS

What to Do at the Scene of an Accident

» Question the person in charge of the investigation.

» Try to find and interview witnesses.

» Try to find friends or relatives of the victims.

» If possible, interview the victims.

» Talk with others at the scene.

» Be sensitive to victims and their families.

Preparing for the Court Story

Most court stories you are likely to cover will be follow-ups to earlier stories. If a murder suspect is appearing for a preliminary hearing, details of the crime probably were reported earlier, and a check of the newsroom's morgue may give you ample background information as you prepare for your visit to the courtroom. Otherwise, a chat with the district attorney or the police chief or one of their assistants might provide ample background for writing the story.

Court stories are often difficult for beginners who do not understand the complex process used in criminal prosecutions. In addition, reporters might be asked to cover civil court proceedings, which are lawsuits that charge an individual or company with harming another. Here's our best advice on how to approach court stories: Ask plenty of questions of the judge and attorneys before or after the court proceeding or during recesses. It's much better to admit your lack of knowledge about the court process than to make a serious error in a story because you didn't understand what was happening.

WRITING THE STORY

Rex Huppke offers useful suggestions that apply to reporting crimes, fires or any other breaking news:

> First make sure you nail down the essential information you'll need. This is, in essence, the classic "who, what, when, where and why." At the very least you need to be able to write a simple story that details whatever has happened. Once you've got the basics covered, assuming you have time, open your eyes and ears and start taking notes. Capture a mental picture of the scene and put it in your notepad.
>
> When you sit down to write the story, take a quick moment to consider what you've just witnessed. Is there an anecdote that jumps out? Is there a scene you can recreate that gets at the heart of the story?
>
> If nothing comes to you, just start writing the straightforward story—lay out the basics. You have a deadline looming and you must at least make sure you've got a story in place. Once that's done, if there's still time, take another moment. Look at the simple house you've built. What can you do to jazz it up? Is there a more interesting way to get into the story, one that tells the news more vividly? Are there some details you can sprinkle in among the facts and quotes, tidbits that will boost the reader's mental image of the scene? If so, get them in there.
>
> Once you've done this several times, you'll start to relax more. Knowing that you've got the basics that you need for a story provides a calm, and that calm allows you to soak in more of the surroundings. The soaking part usually will yield the best material.

The Crime Story

Solid reporting techniques pay off for crime stories just as they do in other types of reporting; then it is a matter of writing the story as the facts demand. Sometimes the events are most effectively told in chronological order, particularly when the story is complex (see Chapter 11). More often, a traditional inverted pyramid style works best. The amount of time the reporter has to file the story also influences the approach. Let's take a look at how two accounts of a crime were developed over time and why a different writing style seemed appropriate for each.

Gathering facts from the many sources available and sorting through conflicting information can be time-consuming tasks. Sometimes, especially when you are posting online, you may have to write the story before all the facts are gathered. The result is a bare-bones account. The breaking news story shown in the annotated model comparison on page 335 illustrates this kind of treatment.

After meeting the Web deadline, the reporter had enough time to gather material for the follow-up story, also shown in the annotated model. That second story uses a chronology structure with a narrative emphasis to give a fuller picture of the sequence of events.

If a number of people witnessed or were affected by a crime, you can supplement the main story with a sidebar that deals with the personal impact of the crime — the "so what." The writer of the "Follow-Up Story" shown in the annotated model also decided to write a separate story on nearby residents who had little to add to the main story but became a part of the situation nonetheless:

In the grass at the edge of a woods near Pierpont Friday afternoon, the only remaining signs of James Phipps were a six-inch circle of blood, a doctor's syringe, a blood-stained button and the imprints in the mud where Phipps fell after he was shot by a Highway Patrol officer. Elsewhere in the area, it was a quiet, sunny, spring day in a countryside dotted by farms and houses. But inside some of those houses, dwellers still were shaken by the morning's events that had forced a police order for them to evacuate their homes.

Mrs. James G. Thorne lives on Cheavens Road across the clearing from where Phipps was shot. Mrs. Thorne had not heard the evacuation notice, so when she saw area officers crouching with guns at the end of her driveway, she decided to investigate.

"I was the surprise they weren't expecting," she told a Highway Patrol officer Friday afternoon. "I walked out just before the excitement."

When the officers saw Mrs. Thorne, "they were obviously very upset and shouted for me to get out of here," she said. "I was here alone and asked them how I was supposed to leave. All they said was, 'Just get out of here!'"

Down the road, Clarence Stallman had been warned of the situation by officers and noticed the circling airplane and helicopter. "I said, 'Are they headed this way soon?' and they said, 'They're here,'" said Stallman.

After Stallman notified his neighbors, he picked up Mrs. Thorne at her home and left the area just before the shooting.

On the next street over, Ronald Nichols had no intention of running.

"I didn't know what was happening," Nichols said. "The wife was scared to death and didn't know what to do. I grabbed my gun and looked for them."

Another neighbor, Mrs. Charles Emmons, first was alerted by the sound of the surveillance plane. "The plane was flying so low I thought it was going to come into the house," she said. "I was frightened. This is something you think will never happen to you."

Then Mrs. Emmons flashed a relieved smile. "It's been quite a morning," she said.

ANNOTATED MODEL   Comparison of a Breaking News Story and a Follow-Up Story

Breaking News Story

A short, inverted pyramid story may be posted online immediately after the news breaks.

A Highway Patrol marksman shot and killed a Kansas man in a rural area south of Springfield this morning after the victim threatened to blow off the head of his apparent hostage.

The summary lead captures the action and some of the drama.

A hitchhiker reportedly told police earlier this morning that his "ride" had plans to rob a service station on Interstate 70. That tip apparently followed an earlier report of a van leaving a station at the Millersburg exit of I-70 without paying for gasoline.

An ensuing hour-long chase ended at 9:30 a.m. in an isolated meadow in the Pierpont area when Capt. N.E. Tinnin fired a single shot into the stomach of the suspect, identified as Jim Phipps of Kansas City, Kan.

Phipps, armed with a sawed-off shotgun, and his "hostage," identified as Anthony Curtis Lilly, 17, also of Kansas City, Kan., eluded police by fleeing into a rugged, wooded area at the end of Bennett Lane, a dead-end gravel road off Route 163.

Then comes a chronological reconstruction, but without much detail or background.

Tinnin said he fired the shot with a .253-caliber sniper rifle when it appeared Phipps was going to shoot Lilly. Two troopers' efforts to persuade Phipps to throw down his weapon and surrender were unsuccessful, Tinnin said.

Follow-Up Story

With more time to learn the full story, the reporter can give readers a more complete account, either online or in print.

James Phipps and Anthony Lilly, a pair of 17-year-olds from Kansas City, Kan., were heading west on Interstate 70 at 7:30 a.m. Friday, returning from a trip to Arkansas.

The reporter can use narrative to bring interest to an ongoing story.

Within the next hour and a half, Phipps had used a sawed-off shotgun stolen in Arkansas to take Lilly hostage, and, after holding that shotgun to Lilly's head, was shot and killed by a Highway Patrol captain on the edge of a rugged wooded area south of Springfield.

As the episode ended, local officials had only begun to piece together a bizarre tragedy that involved a high-speed chase, airplane and helicopter surveillance, a march through a wooded ravine and the evacuation of several frightened citizens from their country homes.

After the lead (the first two paragraphs) comes a paragraph of scene-setting and foreshadowing.

One attribution (underlined) allows the reporter to narrate the story without repeating the source.

As police reconstructed the incident, Phipps and Lilly decided to stop for gas at the Millersburg exit east of Springfield at about 7:30 a.m.

With them in the van was Robert Paul Hudson Jr., a San Francisco-bound hitchhiker.

Hudson was not present at the shooting. He had fled Lilly's van at the Millersburg exit after he suspected trouble.

(continued)

With breaking news, a reporter might post the basic facts online immediately in an inverted pyramid story. Once the basic news is posted, the reporter has some time to gather additional facts and craft a chronological narrative that gives readers the full story.

Comparison of a Breaking News Story and a Follow-Up Story (continued)

The trouble began when Lilly and Phipps openly plotted to steal some gasoline at Millersburg, Hudson told police. He said the pair had agreed to display the shotgun if trouble arose with station attendants.

Here is a necessary bit of explanation.

Hudson said he persuaded Phipps to drop him off before they stopped for gas. He then caught a ride to Springfield and told his driver of the robbery plans he had overheard. After dropping Hudson off near the Providence Road exit, the driver called Springfield police, who picked up Hudson.

Then the narrative begins.

Meanwhile, Phipps and Lilly put $8.90 worth of gas in the van and drove off without paying. The station attendant notified authorities.

As he approached Springfield, Phipps turned onto U.S. 63 South, where he was spotted by Highway Patrol troopers Tom Halford and Greg Overfelt. They began a high-speed chase, which ended on a dead-end gravel road near Pierpont.

Transitions orient the reader and keep the story moving.

During the chase, which included a U-turn near Ashland, Phipps bumped the Highway Patrol car twice, forcing Halford to run into the highway's median.

Upon reaching the dead end, the suspects abandoned the van and ran into a nearby barn. At that point, Phipps, who Highway Patrol officers said was wanted in Kansas for escaping from a detention center, turned the shotgun on Lilly.

When Halford and Overfelt tried to talk with Phipps from outside the barn, they were met with obscenities. Phipps threatened to "blow (Lilly's) head off," and vowed not to be captured alive.

The reporter uses a direct quote to add color to the narrative.

Phipps then left the barn and walked into a wooded area, pressing the gun against Lilly's head. Halford and Overfelt followed at a safe distance but were close enough to speak with Phipps.

While other officers from the Highway Patrol, the Lincoln County Sheriff's Department and Springfield police arrived at the scene, residents in the area were warned to evacuate their homes. A Highway Patrol plane and helicopter flew low over the woods, following the suspects and the troopers through the woods.

The four walked through a deep and densely wooded ravine. Upon seeing a partially constructed house in a nearby clearing, Phipps demanded of officers waiting in the clearing that his van be driven around to the house, at which time he would release his hostage. Halford said, "They disappeared up over the ridge. I heard some shouting (Phipps' demands), and then I heard the shot."

Another direct quote lends authenticity while giving the story a dramatic conclusion.

After entering the clearing from the woods, Phipps apparently had been briefly confused by the officers on either side of him and had lowered his gun for a moment.

The story is wrapped up in the final paragraph.

That was long enough for Highway Patrol Capt. N.E. Tinnin to shoot Phipps in the abdomen with a high-powered rifle. It was about 8:45 a.m. Phipps was taken to Boone County Hospital, where he soon died.

The techniques of writing in chronological order and separating the accounts of witnesses from the main story worked well in this case. More often, however, crime stories are written in the classic inverted pyramid style because of time and space considerations.

Accident and Fire Stories

When you are assigned to cover an accident or a fire, many of the facts and all of the color are gathered at the scene. If the accident has just taken place, a visit to the scene is essential. Being there will give you the best picture of what happened, and you will be able to write a solid story. Too many reporters cover accidents and fires as purely passive observers. Indeed, you must observe. But you must also actively solicit information from those who are present. Many of them, including those directly involved, you may never be able to find again. Keep a digital recorder and digital camera at hand. You may be asked to prepare stories for multiple media.

When you are dispatched to the scene of an accident, move as quickly as possible to collect this information:

» The names, ages, addresses and conditions of the victims.
» Accounts of witnesses or police reconstructions of what happened.
» When the accident occurred.
» Where it occurred.
» Why or how it happened or who was at fault, as determined by officials in charge of the investigation.

If that list sounds familiar, it should. You could simplify it to read "who, what, when, where and why." As in any news story, that information is essential. You must gather it as quickly as possible after being assigned to the story.

Just as important is knowing what to do when you arrive on the scene of an accident. These suggestions will help:

» **Question the person in charge of the investigation.** This individual will attempt to gather much of the information you want. A police officer, for example, needs to know who was involved, what happened, when it happened and who was at fault. If you are able to establish a good relationship with the investigator, you may be able to secure much of the information you need from this one source, though single-source stories are usually inadequate.

   Remember that the spellings of names, addresses and similar facts must be verified later. Any veteran reporter can tell you that police officers and other public officials are notoriously bad spellers and often make errors in recording the names of victims. To avoid such errors, call relatives of the victims or consult the city directory, telephone book or other sources to check your information.
» **Try to find and interview witnesses.** Police and other investigators may lead you directly to the best witnesses. The most accurate account of what happened usually comes from witnesses, and the investigators will try to find them. You should, too. A good way to do that is to watch the investigators. Listen in as they interview

a witness, or approach the witness after they are finished. If there is time, of course, try to find your own witnesses. You cannot and should not always rely on investigators to do your work for you.

» **Try to find friends or relatives of the victims.** These sources are helpful in piecing together information about the victims. Through them you often get tips about even better stories.

» **If possible, interview the victims.** Survivors of an accident may be badly shaken, but if they are able to talk, they can provide firsthand details that you won't find in an official report. Make every attempt to interview those involved.

» **Talk with others at the scene.** If someone died at the scene of the accident, an ambulance paramedic or the medical examiner may be able to give you some indication of what caused the death. At the least you can learn where the bodies or the injured will be taken. That may help, because later the mortician or hospital officials may be able to provide information you need for your story.

» **Be sensitive to victims and their families.** You have a job to do, and you must do it. That does not mean, however, that you can be insensitive to those involved in an accident or fire.

» **Sketch elements of the scene on a piece of paper.** This sketch may be useful in helping an information graphics artist re-create the scene.

» **Record your interviews.** You might need a recording for your website or to help you make sure the information is correct.

Of course, your deadline will have a major impact on the amount of information you are able to gather. If you must meet a deadline soon after arriving at the scene, you will probably be forced to stick to the basics of who, what, when, where, why and how. Thus it is important to gather that information first. Then, if you have time, you can concentrate on more detailed and vivid information to make the story highly readable.

Accidents and fires present similar problems for the reporter, but at a fire of any size you can expect more confusion than at the scene of an accident. One major difference, then, is that the officer in charge will be busier. At the scene of an accident, the damage has been done and the authorities are usually free to concentrate on their investigation. At a fire, the officer in charge is busy directing firefighters and probably will be unable to talk with you. The investigation will not even begin until the fire is extinguished. In many cases, the cause of the fire will not be known for hours, days or weeks. In some cases, it may never be known. Seldom is that so in an accident, except perhaps for air accidents.

Another problem is that you may not have access to the immediate area of the fire. Barriers often are erected to keep the public—and representatives of the news media—from coming too close to a burning structure. Such barriers, erected to ensure safety, may hamper your reporting. You may not be able to get close enough to firefighters to learn about the problems they are having or to obtain the quotes you need to improve your story.

These problems usually make covering a fire more difficult than covering an accident. Despite the difficulties, you cover a fire in much the same way, interviewing

Hazards at the scene of a disaster, such as this fire resulting from a Los Angeles–area earthquake, can make a reporter's job difficult and dangerous.

officials and witnesses at the scene. You also should try to interview the property owner. Moreover, because the official investigation will not have begun, you must conduct your own. When covering a fire, you must learn:

» The location of the fire.
» The names, ages and addresses of those killed, injured or missing.
» The name of the building owner or, in the case of a grass fire or forest fire, the landowner.
» The value of the building and its contents or the value of the land.
» Whether the building and contents were insured for fire damage. (Open land seldom is.)

» When the fire started, who reported it and how many firefighters and pieces of equipment were called to the scene.

» What caused the fire, if known.

As in any story, the basics are who, what, when, where, why and how. But the nature of the fire will raise other questions that must be answered. Of primary importance is whether life is endangered. If it is not, the amount of property damage becomes the major emphasis of the story. Was arson involved? Was the building insured for its full value? Was there an earlier fire at the same location? Did the building comply with fire codes? Were any rare or extremely valuable objects inside? Did explosives inside the structure complicate fighting the fire and pose an even greater threat than the fire itself?

> " The news is no longer the news. . . . It's all about luridness. Body bags will be seen at 7, chasing ambulance at 8, victim's family at 9. "
>
> — Oliver Stone, film director

Your job is to answer these questions for your readers or viewers. You may be able to obtain some of this information later on from official fire reports if they are ready before your deadline. But most information will come from interviews that you conduct at the scene with the best available sources. Finding your sources may not be easy, but you can begin by looking for the highest-ranking fire official. Large departments may have a designated press officer whose job is to deal with you and other reporters.

Another important source is the fire marshal, whose job is to determine the cause of the fire and, if arson is involved, to bring charges against the arsonist. You should make every effort to talk with the fire marshal at the scene, if he or she is available.

The Court Story

Criminal justice proceedings can be very complicated, with a case moving through a number of stages, from occurrence of the crime, to police investigation, to actions by prosecutors and defense attorneys, to actual criminal trials, to legal punishments like incarceration and execution.

Throughout this cycle of events, a reporter has numerous opportunities to write stories. The extent to which the reporter does so depends on the importance of the case and the amount of local interest in it. In a major case, the filing of every motion may prompt a story; in other cases, only the verdict may be important. As in any type of reporting, news value is the determining factor.

Avoiding Libelous Statements

Accuracy also is important, as in any form of reporting. Perhaps no other area of writing requires as much caution as the reporting of crime and court news. The potential for libel is great.

Libel is damage to a person's reputation caused by a written statement that brings the person into hatred, contempt or ridicule or that injures a person's business or occupational pursuits (see Chapter 21). Reporters must be extremely careful about what they write. One of the greatest dangers is the possibility of writing that someone

ON THE JOB

"Every Story Is Important"

At the beginning of this chapter, you met **Rex Huppke** and saw a bit of his work as a general assignment reporter and columnist for the *Chicago Tribune* and chicagotribune .com. This isn't the job he landed fresh from school. In fact, he majored in chemical engineering, only to discover six months into his first job that he had made a big mistake. Eventually, he returned to graduate school, this time in journalism. His first reporting job was in Colorado. Then later on in Indiana, he joined the Associated Press while his wife earned her law degree.

He has never forgotten a lesson learned on his first assignment in Colorado Springs:

I was dispatched to a county fair with the mission of finding something "cute" to put in the next day's paper. There was, without question, a part of me that felt I was above

such a simple assignment. I was a journalism school graduate, after all.

But I went and found two sisters prepping their goats for a 4-H competition, and wound up spending about an hour with the girls and their mother learning the intricacies of goat upkeep and show prep. The family was so excited to have a reporter in their midst that the mother

insisted I pose for a picture with the girls and their goats.

I did, then went back to the newsroom and, charmed by the family, put together a nice feature story that ran inside the next day's feature section. About a week later, I received a letter and opened it to find a copy of the picture the mother took with a note that gushed about how much the article meant to those girls. It was something, the mother wrote, that they would keep forever.

I have kept that photo, and I look at it now and then to remind myself what matters in this business. Every story is important. You are never greater than the people who let you into their lives, whether it's at a time of triumph or tragedy or simple day-to-day existence.

Start each story with that one truth — every story is important — and you will do fine.

is charged with a crime more serious than is the case. After checking clippings in the newsroom library, for example, one reporter wrote:

> The rape trial of John L. Duncan, 25, of 3925 Oak St. has been set for Dec. 10 in Jefferson County Circuit Court.
>
> Duncan is charged in connection with the June 6 rape of a Melton High School girl near Fletcher Park.

Duncan had been charged with rape following his arrest. However, the prosecutor later determined that the evidence was insufficient to win a rape conviction, the charge was reduced to assault and the newspaper had to print a correction that identified the correct charge.

Many courts handle both civil and criminal cases. Media coverage often focuses on criminal cases, although civil actions — lawsuits involving disputes of one type or another — are often excellent sources of stories.

Any story involving arrests should raise caution flags. You must have a working knowledge of libel law and what you can and cannot write about an incident. Any reporter who writes the following, for example, is asking for trouble:

> John R. Milton, 35, of 206 East St. was arrested Monday on a charge of assaulting a police officer.

It would be safer, and more accurate, to write that he was arrested "on suspicion of" the assault. Only a prosecutor, not a police officer, may file charges. In many cases, a police officer may arrest a person with the intent of asking the prosecutor to file a certain charge, but the prosecutor may find that the evidence warrants only a lesser charge. For that reason, many journalists prefer to release the name of an arrested person only after the charge has been filed.

Reporters who cover court news encounter many such pitfalls. They are not trained as attorneys, and it takes time to develop a working knowledge of legal proceedings. The only recourse is to ask as many questions as necessary when a point of law is not clear. It is far better to display ignorance of the law and ask questions than to commit a serious error that harms the reputation of the accused and exposes the newspaper to costly libel litigation.

However, it is also important to know that anything said in open court is fair game for reporters. If, in an opening statement, a prosecutor says the defendant is "nothing but scum, a smut peddler bent on polluting the mind of every child in the city," then by all means report the comment in context in your story. But if a spectator makes that same statement in the hallway during a recess, you probably would not report it. Courts do not extend the qualified privilege to report court proceedings beyond the context of the official proceeding.

Types of Courts and Cases

The U.S. has two main court systems: federal and state. Federal district courts handle violations of federal crime statutes, interpretation of the U.S. Constitution, and matters dealing with civil rights, election disputes, commerce and antitrust laws, postal regulations, federal tax laws and similar issues. They also handle actions between citizens of different states when the disputed amount exceeds $50,000.

Each state has its own system, with many similarities from state to state. The average citizen is most likely to encounter city or municipal courts, which have jurisdiction over traffic and other minor violations. News from these courts is handled as a matter of record in many newspapers.

Violations of state statutes usually are handled in the state trial courts. These *courts of general jurisdiction* (often called *circuit* or *superior courts*) handle civil cases, such as contract disputes, as well as criminal cases.

Most state crimes are either misdemeanors or felonies. A *misdemeanor* is usually punishable by a fine, a county jail term not to exceed one year, or both. *Felonies* are punishable by a fine, a state prison sentence of more than one year, or death.

Now let's trace a criminal case from the time of arrest through the trial to show how a reporter might cover each step.

A Breaking-News Tweet

When arrested, a suspect is taken to a police station for fingerprinting, photographs and perhaps a sobriety test or a lineup. The police may take statements as evidence only if the person is informed of and waives the Miranda rights, which include the right to have an attorney and the right to remain silent. A charge must be filed, or the person must be released, usually within 24 hours.

The first report of a story can come in the form of a tweet as soon as the arrest is confirmed:

> Arrest made in Springfield murder. More to come.

A Typical First Story

Next comes a more detailed version of the story for the Web. You'll notice that unanswered questions remain. This bare-bones story, however, provides a glimpse of several key points in covering arrest stories:

> An unemployed carpenter was arrested today and charged with the Aug. 6 murder of Springfield resident Anne Compton.
>
> Lester L. Rivers, 32, of 209 E. Dillow Lane was charged with first-degree murder, Prosecuting Attorney Mel Singleton said.
>
> Chief of Detectives E.L. Hall said Rivers was arrested on a warrant after a three-month investigation by a team of three detectives. He declined to comment on what led investigators to Rivers.
>
> Compton's body was found in the Peabody River by two fishermen on the morning of Aug. 7. She had been beaten to death with a blunt instrument, according to Dr. Ronald R. Miller, the county medical examiner.

Notice that the reporter carefully chose the words "arrested . . . and charged with" rather than "arrested for," a phrase that may carry a connotation of guilt.

Another important element of all crime and court coverage is the tie-back sentence. This sentence relates a story to events covered in a previous story—in this case, the report of the crime itself. It is important to state clearly—and near the beginning of the story—which crime is involved. It is also important to provide enough information about it so that the reader recognizes it. Clarification of the crime is important even in major stories with ready identification in the community. This story does that by recounting when and where Compton's body was found and by whom. It also tells that she died after being hit with a blunt instrument.

Follow-Up Story: First Court Appearance

After the prosecuting attorney, who argues for the state, files charges, the defendant is usually brought before a judge, informed of the charges and reminded of the Miranda rights. Bail may be set.

For a misdemeanor, if the defendant pleads guilty, the judge usually handles the case immediately with a sentence or fine. If the plea is not guilty, a trial date is set.

For a felony, the defendant does not enter a plea. The judge sets a date for a preliminary hearing, unless the defendant waives the right to such a hearing. A defendant who waives this hearing is bound over to the general jurisdiction trial court; that is, the records of the case are sent to the trial court.

TIPS

Writing the Court Story

- » Possess a strong working knowledge of libel law.
- » Ask questions when a point of law is unclear.
- » Know that anything said in open court is fair game.
- » Early in the story, state clearly which crime is involved and provide enough information so the reader recognizes it.
- » Don't overstate facts.
- » Take good notes. Trial coverage is greatly enhanced with direct quotations of key exchanges.

In the Rivers case, the following morning the suspect was taken to Magistrate Court for his initial court appearance. Here is part of the story that resulted:

Lester L. Rivers appeared in Magistrate Court today charged with first-degree murder in connection with the Aug. 6 beating death of Springfield resident Anne Compton.

Judge Howard D. Robbins scheduled a preliminary hearing for Nov. 10 and set bail at $10,000. Robbins assigned Public Defender Ogden Ball to represent Rivers, 32, of 209 E. Dillow Lane.

Rivers said nothing during the 10-minute session as the judge informed him of his right to remain silent and his right to an attorney. Ball asked Robbins to set the bail at a "reasonable amount for a man who is unemployed." Rivers is a carpenter who was fired from his last job in June. Despite the seriousness of the charge, it is essential that Rivers be free to help prepare his defense, Ball said.

Police have said nothing about a possible connection between Rivers and Compton, whose body was found in the Peabody River by two fishermen on the morning of Aug. 7. She had been beaten to death.

The reporter clearly outlined the exact charge and reported on key points of the brief hearing. Again, the tie-back helps readers recognize and remember details of the crime.

Follow-Up Story: Preliminary Hearing

Next comes the *preliminary hearing*, in which the evidence linking the defendant to the crime is first revealed.

The hearing is usually held before a magistrate or a lower-level judge. The prosecutor tries to convince the judge that there is *probable cause* to believe the defendant committed a crime. The defendant can cross-examine the state's witnesses and present evidence, but normally does not. Because preliminary hearings are thus often one-sided, reporters must be careful to write a well-balanced story.

If the judge finds probable cause, the prosecuting attorney must file, within a short time period (usually 10 days), what is called an "information" based on the judge's finding.

Here's the story that resulted from Rivers' preliminary hearing:

Lester L. Rivers will be tried in Jefferson County Circuit Court for the Aug. 6 murder of Springfield resident Anne Compton.

Magistrate Judge Howard D. Robbins ruled today that there is probable cause to believe that a crime was committed and probable cause that Rivers did it. Rivers was bound over for trial in Circuit Court.

Rivers, 32, of 209 E. Dillow Lane is being held in Jefferson County Jail. He has been unable to post bail of $10,000.

At today's preliminary hearing, Medical Examiner Ronald R. Miller testified that a tire tool recovered from Rivers' car at the time of his arrest "could have been used in the beating death of Miss Compton." Her body was found floating in the Peabody River Aug. 7.

James L. Mullaney, a lab technician for the FBI crime laboratory in Washington, D.C., testified that "traces of blood on the tire tool matched Miss Compton's blood type."

In reporting the testimony, the reporter was careful to use direct quotes and not to overstate the facts. The medical examiner testified that the tire tool *could have been used* in the murder. If he had said it *had been used*, the reporter would have needed a stronger lead.

Defense attorneys usually use preliminary hearings to learn about the evidence against their clients and do not present any witnesses. This apparently was the motive here because neither the police nor the prosecutor had made a public statement on evidence in the case. They probably were being careful not to release prejudicial information that could be grounds for a new trial.

In most states, a person can also be brought to trial by a grand jury indictment. In federal courts, the Constitution requires indictment by a grand jury in felony cases.

In some states, grand jury hearings are secret, and potential defendants are not allowed to be present when testimony is given. The prosecuting attorney presents evidence that determines whether there is probable cause to prosecute.

A grand jury returns a "true bill" if it finds probable cause and a "no true bill" if not. The jury foreman or forewoman and the prosecuting attorney must sign the indictment, which then is presented in open court to a trial judge.

If the defendant is not already in custody, the judge orders an arrest warrant. Arraignment in the trial court follows.

Follow-Up Story: Arraignment

Arraignment, conducted in open court, is the first formal presentation of the information or the indictment to the defendant. The defendant enters a plea to the charge: guilty, not guilty, or not guilty by reason of mental disease or defect.

In the Rivers case, the prosecutor filed an information, as state law required. The defendant was arraigned in Circuit Court, and the result was a routine story that began as follows:

> Circuit Judge John L. Lee refused today to reduce the bail of Lester L. Rivers, who is charged with first-degree murder in the Aug. 6 death of Springfield resident Anne Compton. Rivers pleaded not guilty. Repeating a request he made earlier in Magistrate Court, Public Defender Ogden Ball urged that Rivers' bail be reduced from $10,000 so he could be free to assist in preparing his defense.

The not-guilty plea was expected, so the reporter concentrated on a more interesting aspect of the hearing—the renewed request for reduced bail.

At this point in criminal proceedings, *plea bargaining* sometimes occurs. A defendant changes a plea from not guilty to guilty in return for a lighter sentence, typically pleading guilty to a lesser charge. A charge of premeditated murder, for example, might be reduced to manslaughter. To save the time and expense of a trial, prosecutors often agree to this if they believe justice is served.

If the defendant enters a guilty plea, the judge may impose a sentence immediately, or a *presentencing investigation* of the defendant's background may be ordered to help the judge set punishment. Many jurisdictions require presentencing investigations, at least in felony cases. A sentencing date may be set.

If the defendant enters a plea of not guilty, the judge sets a trial date. Most jurisdictions require speedy trials.

As the prosecutor and defense attorney prepare for trial, they may file motions for disclosure of evidence, suppression of evidence and similar rulings. A defense attorney who feels that pretrial stories in the local media may prejudice potential jurors will often ask for a **change of venue**, which moves the trial to a county other than the one in which the crime occurred.

Follow-Up Story: First Day of the Trial

On the first day of a trial, a jury, usually 12 jurors and at least one alternate, is selected during a process called *voir dire* (vwar DEER). The prosecutor and defense attorney question the prospective jurors to identify jurors they hope will be sympathetic to their positions. In the federal system the judge often asks questions, but the prosecutor and defense attorneys may suggest questions for the judge to ask.

Each attorney can eliminate a certain number of people as jurors without having to state a reason and also dismiss an unlimited number *for cause* (if, for example, the prospective juror is related to the accused).

In the Rivers case, after a series of motions was reported routinely, the trial began. Here's the story written on the first day:

Jury selection began today in the first-degree murder trial of Lester L. Rivers, who is charged with the Aug. 6 beating death of Springfield resident Anne Compton.

Public Defender Ogden Ball, Rivers' attorney, and Prosecuting Attorney Mel Singleton both expect jury selection to be complete by 5 p.m.

The selection process started after court convened at 10 a.m. The only incident occurred just before the lunch break as Single-ton was questioning prospective juror Jerome B. Tinker, 33, of 408 Woodland Terrace.

"I went to school with that guy," said Tinker, pointing to Rivers, who was seated in the courtroom. "He wouldn't hurt nobody."

Singleton immediately asked that Tinker be removed from the jury panel, and Circuit Judge John L. Lee agreed.

Rivers smiled as Tinker made his statement, but otherwise sat quietly, occasionally conferring with Ball.

The testimony is about to begin, so the reporter set the stage here, describing the courtroom scene. Jury selection is often routine and becomes newsworthy only in important or interesting cases.

Once the jurors are sworn in, the prosecutor makes an opening statement that outlines how the state expects to prove each element of the crime. The defense attorney may follow with a statement, may wait until after the prosecution has introduced its evidence to make a statement, or may waive an opening statement altogether.

Follow-Up Story: Trial Testimony

A basic tenet of criminal law is that the prosecution must prove the defendant guilty beyond a reasonable doubt. The defendant is not required to prove anything or even to testify.

To establish what happened and to link the defendant to the crime, the state calls witnesses to testify. First, the prosecutor asks questions, and the witness responds. The defense attorney then cross-examines the witness. Frequently, one attorney will object to questions posed by the other, and the judge must rule on the objection.

When the defense attorney finishes cross-examination, the prosecutor conducts *re-direct examination* to clarify certain points or to bolster a witness's credibility. Cross-examination and re-direct examination continue until both sides have asked the witness all their questions.

Trial coverage can be tedious, but when the case is interesting, the stories are easy to write. As the Rivers trial progressed, the reporter picked the most interesting testimony to use in leads:

A service station owner testified today that Lester L. Rivers offered a ride to Springfield resident Anne Compton less than an hour before she was beaten to death Aug. 6.

Ralph R. Eagle, the station owner, was a witness at the first-degree murder trial of Rivers in Jefferson County Circuit Court.

"I told her I'd call a cab," Eagle testified, "but Rivers offered her a ride to her boyfriend's house." Compton had gone to the service station after her car broke down nearby. Under cross-examination, Public Defender Ogden Ball, Rivers' attorney, questioned whether Rivers was the man who offered the ride.

"If it wasn't him, it was his twin brother," Eagle said.

"Then you're not really sure it was Mr. Rivers, are you?" Ball asked.

"I sure am," Eagle replied.

"You think you're sure, Mr. Eagle, but you really didn't get a good look at him, did you?"

"I sold him some gas and got a good look at him when I took the money."

"But it was night, wasn't it, Mr. Eagle?" Ball asked.

"That place doesn't have the best lighting in the world, but I saw him all right."

The reporter focused on the key testimony of the trial by capturing it in the words of the participants.

After the prosecution witnesses have testified and the state rests its case, the defense almost always makes a motion for acquittal, arguing that the state has failed to prove its case beyond a reasonable doubt. Almost always, the motion is denied.

The defense then calls witnesses to support its case, and the prosecutor cross-examines them. Finally, when all witnesses have testified, the defense rests.

At this point, the prosecutor calls *rebuttal witnesses* in an attempt to discredit the testimony of the defense witnesses. The defense then has the right to present even more witnesses, called *surrebuttal witnesses*.

Follow-Up Story: Verdict

After these witnesses have testified, the judge instructs the jury about possible verdicts and key points of law. The prosecutor makes a closing argument, usually an impassioned plea for a guilty verdict addressed directly to the jury. The defense attorney's closing argument follows, and the prosecutor is allowed a final rebuttal. In the federal system, closing arguments precede the judge's instructions to the jury. The jury then retires to deliberate.

For the journalist covering the trial, there is eventually the verdict story, which is usually one of the easiest to write. Here's the verdict story in the Rivers case:

Lester L. Rivers was found guilty of first-degree murder today in the Aug. 6 beating death of Springfield resident Anne Compton.

Rivers stood motionless in Jefferson County Circuit Court as the jury foreman returned the verdict. Judge John L. Lee set sentencing for Dec. 10.

Rivers, 32, of 209 E. Dillow Lane could be sentenced to death in the electric chair or life imprisonment in the State Penitentiary.

Public Defender Ogden Ball, Rivers' attorney, said he will appeal.

After the verdict was announced, Mr. and Mrs. Lilborn O. Compton, the victim's parents, were escorted from the courtroom by friends. Both refused to talk with reporters.

Because a criminal trial requires a unanimous verdict, deliberations often are protracted. If jurors fail to agree (a hung jury), the judge may order a mistrial; then the entire case will be retried with a new jury. If a verdict is reached, the jury returns to the courtroom, where the verdict is read.

Sentencing and Appeals

In some states, juries may recommend sentences in guilty verdicts. But the final decision is always made by the judge unless a crime carries a mandatory sentence. Sentencing may be done immediately, but more likely a presentencing report will be ordered and a sentencing date set. For a really important criminal trial, reporters might be assigned to cover a sentencing hearing.

The defense often files a motion asking that a guilty verdict be set aside or requesting a new trial. These motions, though usually denied, are often prerequisites to the filing of an appeal. Appeals often follow guilty verdicts. Except in cases involving serious crimes, judges often permit a defendant to be released on bail pending the outcome of appeals.

Many other types of stories can be written about a trial. Lengthy jury deliberations, for example, might prompt stories about the anxiety of the defendant and attorneys and their speculations about the cause of the delay.

Covering court news requires care and good reporting. As in any kind of reporting, you must be well-prepared. If you understand the language of the courts and how they are organized, your job is simplified.

OTHER ISSUES IN CRIME AND COURT REPORTING

Covering crime and the courts is not a simple matter. While the complexity of court proceedings can be baffling to a beginning reporter, there are other pitfalls as well.

The Free Press/Fair Trial Controversy

The 1954 murder trial of Dr. Samuel Sheppard in Cleveland was the landmark case involving the perceived conflict between a defendant's right to a fair trial and the public's right to know. Sheppard was accused of murdering his wife. News coverage in the Cleveland newspapers, which included front-page editorials, was intense. In 1966, the U.S. Supreme Court said the trial judge had not fulfilled his duty to protect the jury from the news coverage that saturated the community and to control disruptive influences in the courtroom.

That case, more than any other, ignited what is known as the **free press/fair trial controversy**. This controversy raged during the O.J. Simpson case in the mid-1990s. On numerous occasions, Judge Lance Ito threatened to end television coverage of court proceedings to protect Simpson's rights during his criminal trial. Lawyers charged that the media were threatening the Sixth Amendment right of the accused to an impartial jury. The media countered with charges that lawyers were threatening the First Amendment.

Editors realize that coverage of a crime can make it difficult to impanel an impartial jury, but they argue that courts have available many remedies other than restricting the flow of information. In the Sheppard case, for example, the Supreme Court justices said a change of venue, which moves the trial to a location where publicity is not as intense, could have been ordered. Other remedies suggested by the court in such cases are to "continue" (delay) the trial, to grant a new trial or to head off possible outside influences during the trial by sequestering the jury. Editors also argue that acquittals have been won in some of the most publicized cases in recent years.

> " To make inroads into the mind-set that 'if the press reported it, it must be true' is the lawyer's most challenging task. "
>
> —Robert Shapiro, attorney

Gag Orders and Closed Trials

Despite the remedies the Supreme Court offered in the Sheppard case, trial judges continued to be concerned about impaneling impartial juries. Judges issued hundreds of gag orders in the wake of the Sheppard case. Finally, in 1976, in the landmark case of Nebraska Press Association v. Stuart, the Supreme Court ruled that a gag order was an unconstitutional prior restraint that violated the First Amendment to the Constitution. The justices did not go so far as to rule that all gag orders are invalid. But in each case, the trial judge has to prove that an order restraining publication would protect the rights of the accused and that no other alternatives would be less damaging to First Amendment rights.

That ruling, of course, did not end the concerns of trial judges. Rather than issue gag orders restricting the press from reporting court proceedings, some attempted to close their courtrooms. In the first such case to reach the U.S. Supreme Court, Gannett v. DePasquale, the press and public suffered a severe but temporary blow. On July 2, 1979, in a highly controversial decision, the justices said, "We hold that members of the public have no constitutional right under the Sixth and Fourteenth amendments to attend criminal trials." The case itself had involved only a pretrial hearing.

As a result of the decision and the confusion that followed, the Supreme Court of Virginia sanctioned the closing of an entire criminal trial. The accused was acquitted during the second day of the secret trial. The U.S. Supreme Court agreed to hear the appeal of the trial judge's action in a case known as Richmond Newspapers v. Virginia. On July 2, 1980, the court said that under the First Amendment "the trial of a criminal case must be open to the public." Only a court finding of an "overriding interest," which was not defined, would be grounds for closing a criminal trial.

Covering Sex Crimes

The reporting of sex crimes often causes controversy. Most news executives think of their products as family newspapers or broadcasts and are properly hesitant about reporting the lurid details of sex crimes.

Sex Crime Victims

One problem in reporting on sex crimes is the question of how to handle rape victims. Too often, rapes are not reported to police because victims are unwilling to appear in court to testify against the suspects. Defense attorneys sometimes use such occasions to attack the victim's moral character and imply that she or he consented to sexual relations. Many victims decline to press charges because of fear that their names will be made public in the media. Both of these things happened to the woman who accused basketball star Kobe Bryant of rape. There is, after all, still a lingering tendency to attach a social stigma to the rape victim, despite increasing public awareness of the nature of the crime. In some states, "rape shield" statutes prohibit a defendant's attorney from delving into the rape victim's prior sexual activity unless some connection can be shown with the circumstances of the rape charged.

Sex Crime Offenders

In Massachusetts, a judge excluded the public and press from the entire trial of a man accused of raping three teenagers. A Massachusetts law provided for the mandatory closing of trials involving specific sex offenses against minors. In 1982, the U.S. Supreme Court held in Globe Newspaper Co. v. Superior Court that the mandatory closure law violated the First Amendment right of access to criminal trials established in the Richmond Newspapers case. The justices ruled that when a state attempts to deny the right of access in an effort to inhibit the disclosure of sensitive information, it must show that the denial "is necessitated by a compelling governmental interest." The court indicated in the opinion that in some cases *in-camera proceedings* (proceedings that take place in a judge's chambers outside the view of the press and public) may be appropriate for youthful witnesses.

In Press-Enterprise v. Riverside County Superior Court, the U.S. Supreme Court ruled in 1984 that a court order closing the jury-selection process in a rape-murder case was invalid. The court ruled that jury selection has been a public process with exceptions only for good cause. In a second Press-Enterprise v. Riverside County Superior Court case, the U.S. Supreme Court said in 1986 that preliminary hearings should be open to the public unless there is a "substantial probability" that the resulting publicity would prevent a fair trial and there are no "reasonable alternatives to closure." In 1993, the Supreme Court continued its emphasis on the importance of open court proceedings. It struck down a Puerto Rican law that said preliminary hearings "shall be held privately" unless the defendant requests a public preliminary hearing.

Press-Bar Guidelines

These cases appeared to uphold the right of the press and the public to have access to criminal proceedings. Judges, however, have a duty to protect the rights of the accused. The Supreme Court of the State of Washington, in Federated Publications v. Swedberg, held in 1981 that press access to pretrial hearings may be conditioned on the agreement of reporters to abide by the voluntary press-bar guidelines that exist in some states. The decision involved a preliminary hearing in a Bellingham, Wash., murder case tied to the "Hillside Strangler" murders in the Los Angeles area. The state Supreme Court ruled that the lower-court order was "a good-faith attempt to accommodate the interests of both defendant and press." The lower court had required reporters covering the hearing to sign a document in which the reporters agreed to abide by press-bar guidelines. The state Supreme Court said the document should be taken as a moral commitment on the part of the reporters, not as a legally enforceable document.

The U.S. Supreme Court in 1982 refused to hear an appeal of that case. Fortunately, many states have statutes to the effect that "the setting of every court shall be public, and every person may freely attend the same." When such statutes are in place, the closed-courtroom controversy appears to be moot. In states that have no such statute, the result seems to be that:

» A criminal trial must be open unless there is an "overriding interest" that requires some part of it to be closed.
» Judges must find some overriding interest before closing pretrial hearings.

One effect of the Washington decision is that many media groups are withdrawing from state press-bar agreements in the few states that have such guidelines. Their reasoning is that the voluntary guidelines in effect could become mandatory.

Cameras in the Courtroom

In 1994, the U.S. Judicial Conference ended its three-year experiment with cameras in federal courts by banning them. Two years later, the Judicial Conference agreed to permit cameras in some lower federal courts. And 47 states do allow cameras in at least some state courtrooms. Only Indiana, Mississippi, South Dakota and the District of Columbia ban courtroom cameras.

The fact remains that there are many ways for judges to protect the rights of the accused without trampling on the right of the press and public to attend trials and pretrial hearings. Indeed, most editors are sensitive to the rights of the accused. Most exercise self-restraint when publishing or broadcasting information about a crime. And most have attempted to establish written policy on such matters, although others insist that individual cases must be judged on their merits.

Coverage of Minority Groups

Reporters and editors must share with judges the burden of protecting the rights of the accused. They also must ensure that certain groups within our society are not treated unfairly, either by the courts or in the media. In a study of crime reporting at the Gannett Center for Media Studies, Robert Snyder discovered that minorities tend to be covered by the media mainly in the context of crime news. Crime reporting is a staple of urban news, and urban areas are where minorities are concentrated. In large cities like New York and Los Angeles, some areas of the city often make news only because of crime. As it is reported now, Snyder says, crime is almost always a conversation about race. He concludes that if the media are to change that perception, they must cover minorities more broadly and sympathetically. The real story of crime, Snyder says, should be the "breaking down of communities and the real weakening of the social structure."

Many editors are concerned about the way minorities are portrayed in crime stories. In fact, many newspapers and broadcast stations studiously avoid gratuitous mentions of race. Their reporters are allowed to mention the race of a suspect only as part of the complete identification of a fugitive. For many years, it was common to read or hear references to a "six-foot-tall black man" wanted for a crime. Today such a description would be considered unacceptable. Too many men fit that description, and the racial reference merely reinforces the stereotype of blacks as criminals. However, if a complete description of a fugitive might help lead to an arrest, it is appropriate to mention race as a part of that description. Only when race becomes the central theme of a story should it be emphasized.

Similarly, most editors consider a person's sexual orientation off limits unless the story focuses on heterosexuality or homosexuality. Increasingly, though, gays and lesbians are willing to talk openly about their sexual orientation as a means of advancing the cause of gay rights. Such issues cannot and should not be ignored by the media. But tastefully handling crime news involving homosexual crimes often proves to be difficult. This was never more true than in the sensational murder trial of Milwaukee's

Jeffrey Dahmer, convicted of sexually molesting young boys and men, killing them and eating parts of their bodies. In such cases, the press walks a fine line between responsibly informing the public and pandering to its seemingly insatiable appetite for sensational crime news.

Coverage of Terrorism

Since the 2001 attacks on the World Trade Center and the Pentagon, much has been written about the rights of those arrested as alleged terrorists. Suspects have been held for years without charge at the U.S. naval base at Guantánamo Bay, Cuba, and interrogated by U.S. officials in foreign countries. Rights activists and the suspects' attorneys have challenged such actions as unconstitutional, and the courts have agreed. This ongoing battle is likely to be a matter of contention for the foreseeable future.

Issues of Taste and Ethics

News editors ponder a number of major issues involving taste and ethics in crime and court reporting:

» When should the media reveal details of how a murder or another crime was committed?
» When should the media reveal details about sex crimes or print the names of sex crime victims?
» When should the media reveal a suspect's confession or even the fact that the suspect confessed?
» When should the media reveal a defendant's prior criminal record?
» When should the media reveal the names of juveniles charged with crimes?

None of these questions can be answered to everyone's satisfaction, and it is doubtful whether rules can be established to apply in all such situations.

Reporting Details of a Crime

There have been charges that when the media reveal details of a murder, some people use the techniques described to commit additional murders. This charge is directed most frequently at television, but newspapers have not been immune and online media may also face this issue.

Reporting Confessions and Prior Convictions

Many editors will not publish or broadcast details of a suspect's confession in an effort to protect the suspect's rights. Revealing such information blocks the way for a fair trial perhaps more than anything else the media can do. Some newspapers and broadcast stations, however, continue to reveal assertions by police or prosecutors that a confession was signed. Many critics question whether such information isn't just as prejudicial as the confession statement itself.

Occasionally, journalists question whether to suppress an unsolicited confession. After a youth was charged with a series of robberies and was certified to stand trial as an adult, a newspaper reporter phoned the youthful defendant, who was free on bail, for an interview. The result was interesting. The defendant admitted to two other robberies in what amounted to a confession to the newspaper and its readers. The editor, who would not have printed a simple statement by police that the defendant had confessed to the crimes, printed this one. Why? The editor reasoned that information about a confession to police amounts to secondhand, hearsay information. The confession to a reporter, however, was firsthand information obtained by the newspaper directly from the accused.

Lawyers also view as prejudicial the publication of a defendant's prior criminal record. Even if authorities refuse to divulge that information, much of it may be in the morgue. Should it be reported? Most journalists believe it should be, particularly if a prior conviction was for a similar offense. Most attorneys disagree.

Identifying Juveniles

Whether to use the names of juveniles charged with crimes is a troublesome issue as well. Most states prohibit law enforcement officers and court officials from releasing the names of juveniles. The reasoning of those who oppose releasing juveniles' names is that the publicity marks them for life as criminals. Those who hold this view argue that there is ample opportunity for these individuals to change their ways and become good citizens—if the media do not stamp them as criminals. Others argue that juveniles who commit serious offenses, such as rape and armed robbery, should be treated as adults.

Questions such as these elicit divergent views from editors, some of whom regularly seek the advice of their lawyers. Little guidance for the reporter can be offered here. Because the decision to publish or not to publish is the editor's, not the reporter's, consultation is necessary. Each case must be decided on its merits.

OBITUARIES AND LIFE STORIES

In the online world, obituaries are big business. Newspaper websites sell advertising to funeral homes and auxiliary services because they have found that readers search for obituaries frequently. Even former residents of a city monitor obituaries. Some websites are devoted to obituaries and provide resources for readers and advertisers. One, legacy.com, which is partially owned by a newspaper, provides links and a searchable database to hundreds of newspapers, and it sells advertising to the funeral industry. It also allows readers to post memorials to friends and family members who have died.

Web editors and entrepreneurs are just discovering the drawing power of obituaries, but most newspaper editors have known about it for years. Chuck Ward, publisher of the *Olean (N.Y.) Times Herald*, once told his readers about the time his editor asked whether they should do a special obituary on the father of one of their employees: "My response was that unless the father (or any relative) of the employee met the criteria for a glorified obituary, the obituary should be treated as 99 percent of our obituaries are."

He then recounted that when he went to the visitation that evening, the line extended 50 yards outside the mortuary. He returned in an hour, and the line was still long. That got Ward thinking about his question earlier in the day: "What did he do?"

"All he did, apparently, was live a wonderful, loving life with a splendid family. During the course of that life, he must have touched the lives of countless people in our community. And they all were there to say goodbye."

Ward learned that people don't have to be public figures to deserve well-reported obituaries. Too many obituaries read as if they were written by a computer program—efficient but lifeless. This tendency persists despite readership surveys that show that about 50 percent of readers look at obituaries, about twice as many as those who look at most other features.

And obituaries are read critically. If the deceased was an Odd Fellow, you'd better not say he was an Elk. If the deceased belonged to the Shiloh Baptist Church, count on a phone call if you say she was a member of Bethany Baptist. Reporting and writing obituaries is important work, and you must get it right.

Despite this importance, many newspapers do not publish a news obituary unless the person who died was well-known. Television news generally follows the same policy. However, you're more likely to find staff-written obituaries in local publications, in print and online. Jim Nicholson of the *Philadelphia Daily News*, who wrote obituaries full-time and won the American Society of News Editors Distinguished Writing Award, explained why. Readers want to know, he said, "How did someone live a good life? How did they get through this world?"

An obituary is a news story. You should apply the same standards to crafting a lead and building the body of an obituary as you do to other stories.

Remember that obituary for Facts, the satirical piece that began this chapter? Even though he was writing in jest, the reporter sought out comment from someone who knew the deceased:

"It's very depressing," said Mary Poovey, a professor of English at New York University and author of "A History of the Modern Fact." "I think the thing Americans ought to miss most about facts is the lack of agreement that there are facts. This means we will never reach consensus about anything. Tax policies, presidential candidates. We'll never agree on anything."

TIPS

Five Safeguards for Obit Writers

» Confirm spellings of names on the mortuary form.

» Check the addresses. If a telephone book or city directory lists a different address, contact the mortuary about the discrepancy.

» Check the birth date against the age, noting whether the person's birthday was before or after the date of death.

» Verify with the mortuary or family any obituary phoned or faxed to the newspaper.

» Check your newspaper's library for stories about the deceased, but be sure you don't pull stories about someone else with the same name.

Crafting a Lead

You begin by answering the same questions you would answer in any news story: who (Michael Kelly, 60, of 1234 West St.), what (died), where (at Regional Hospital), when (Tuesday night), why (heart attack) and how (while jogging). With this information, you are ready to start the story.

The fact that Kelly died of a heart attack suffered while jogging may well be the lead, but the reporter does not know this until the rest of the information essential to every obituary has been gathered. You also must know:

» Time and place of funeral services.
» Time and place of burial.
» Visitation time (if any).
» Survivors.
» Date and place of birth.
» Achievements.
» Occupation.
» Memberships.

Any of these items can yield the nugget that will appear in the lead. However, if none of these categories yields notable information, the obituary will probably start like this:

> Michael Kelly, 60, of 1234 West St., died Tuesday night at Regional Hospital.

Another standard approach could be used later in the news cycle:

> Funeral services for Michael Kelly, 60, of 1234 West St., will be at 2 p.m. Thursday at St. Catherine's Roman Catholic Church.

However, good reporters often find distinguishing characteristics of a person's life. It may be volunteer service, an unusual or important job, service in public office or even just having a name of historical significance. Whatever distinguishes a person can be the lead of the obituary.

Building the Story

You will find most of the obituary information on a standard form from the mortuary. When the reporter relies only on the form, this is usually what results:

Michael Kelly, 60, of 1234 West St. died Tuesday night at Regional Hospital.

Kelly collapsed while jogging and died apparently of a heart attack.

Services will be at 2 p.m. Thursday at St. Catherine's Roman Catholic Church. The Rev. Sherman Mitchell will officiate.

Burial will be at Glendale Memorial Gardens in Springfield.

Friends may visit at the Fenton Funeral Chapel from 7 to 9 p.m. Wednesday.

Born Dec. 20, 1954, in Boston to Nathan and Sarah Kelly, Kelly was a member of St. Catherine's Roman Catholic Church and a

U.S. Navy veteran of the Vietnam War. He had been an independent insurance agent for the last 25 years.

He married Pauline Virginia Hatfield in Boston on May 5, 1974.

Survivors include his wife; a son, Kevin, of Charlotte, N.C.; and a daughter, Mary, who is a student at the University of North Carolina at Chapel Hill.

Also surviving are a brother, John, of Milwaukee, Wis., and a sister, Margaret Carter, of Asheville, N.C.

Writing Life Stories

The Kelly obituary is a dry biography, not a story of his life. There is no hint of Kelly's impact on friends, family or community. Good reporting produces stories of life, such as this one:

Frank Martin loved to garden and loved to share.

"When the ground began to thaw, he'd try to figure out how to grow things," friend and co-worker Walter Begley recalled.

Another friend, Caroline Newby, said he would come to her home to help take care of her small vineyard. He made wine from the grapes to share with his family during the holidays. When she had problems with her crop, Mr. Martin would drive over and open the trunk of his old Dodge to reveal a nursery of soil and gardening tools.

On the back of that car was a bumper sticker that read "Practice Random Acts of Kindness and Senseless Acts of Beauty." Newby said Mr. Martin lived by that phrase. . . .

The more traditional biographical information, along with information about visitation and funeral services, appears later in the story.

When writing a life story, you ask people what was important to the deceased and what the evidence for that is. If the subject volunteered, find out where and why and talk to the people served. Your goal is to capture the theme of the person's life. If family members and friends recognize the deceased in your story as the person they knew, you have done your job. Amy Rabideau Silvers, the obituary writer for the *Milwaukee Journal Sentinel*, provides such an example in the annotated model "A Life Story" on page 358.

Sources of Information

Writing an obituary or life story is like writing a feature story. You seek anecdotes that reveal the person. Your sources include the mortuary form, your publication's own library, and family and friends of the deceased (and possibly their paid funeral notices).

The Mortuary Form

For many reporters, the standard form from the mortuary is the primary source of information. The mortuary can be of further help if you need more information. Does your city editor want a picture of the deceased? Call the mortuary. They can usually obtain one quickly from the family. Is there some conflicting or unclear information on the form? Call the mortuary for clarification.

OBITUARY
A Life of Love Was Made Public in End
Couple Came Out, Testified at Capitol

By Amy Rabideau Silvers, Staff
Milwaukee Journal Sentinel

The opening teases, much like a feature story lead.

For nearly 49 years, Richard Taylor and Ray Vahey did not speak openly about their long and loving relationship.

They did not tell family. They did not tell friends at work.

Two short sentences in a separate paragraph bring attention to themselves.

That changed a year ago, after Vahey was asked if they might speak at PrideFest. Together, they wrote a speech. Vahey gave it, Taylor at his side.

This is the "so what." It establishes the impact Vahey and Taylor had on the state debate. This story is a history of an era told through the experience of two men, one of whom died.

They went on to other appearances, including a state hearing last November in Madison, speaking against the proposed amendment that would ban gay marriage and civil unions in Wisconsin. They spoke at area churches. They were asked to speak at PrideFest in June, but Taylor, hospitalized with cancer, was too ill to go.

"We wrote the speech together at his hospital bed," Vahey said. Then Taylor said something Vahey will never forget.

This strong anecdote motivates the reader to keep on reading.

"Ray, remember, I'm standing right beside you," he said.

"And I feel that now," Vahey said.

News peg. This is a variation of the focus structure.

Richard Taylor died Friday. He was 81.

By chance, his name appeared twice in the *Journal Sentinel* on Sunday. The longtime partners were mentioned in a "Crossroads" opinion piece opposing the proposed amendment. His death notice appeared in the same edition.

"We were from the silent generation," Vahey said. "It was an exaggerated version of don't ask, don't tell."

Vahey is the primary source because they lived together for nearly 50 years.

"I was 18 and he was 31" when they met in 1956, Vahey said. Both grew up in Ohio—Taylor in Cleveland and Vahey in Youngstown.

Taylor's service in the Navy becomes important later in the story.

"When Richard was 17, he convinced his father to allow him to join the Navy during World War II," Vahey said.

Taylor served aboard a naval tanker on convoy duty, first in the North Atlantic and then in the Mediterranean. His tanker next moved into the Pacific.

"His tanker fueled a cruiser while it bombarded Mount Suribachi on Iwo Jima, and then they went on to Okinawa, where they came under kamikaze attack," he said.

This life story uses the basic focus structure. All it lacks is a tie-back.

Taylor, who had a high school education, was also self-taught, widely read in economics and philosophy, history and politics. As the two men grew older, they came to see history in a new light.

Here is the impact of his Navy service.

"Richard voluntarily put himself into harm's way to protect his country and the rights of all Americans of that day, and all of the generations that have followed. Now there is an attempt to separate Richard from society and take away his right to equality under the law."

Over the years, they lived in Ohio, Illinois, California, New Jersey and Virginia. In 2000 they decided to move to Milwaukee, a city they knew from visits to Taylor's brother.

Finally, they decided to step out of the closet for good.

"I never told my sister about us until the night we testified in Madison," Vahey said, adding that she took the news without surprise or judgment.

This anecdote reveals the depth of their cover-up.

"It was like the elephant in the living room. It was there, but no one addressed it."

The official transcripts of hearings and stories in your newspaper library are good sources for quotes.

"Euphemisms like 'partnership' or 'union' set us apart from society," Vahey said at the legislative hearing last fall. "Substitute terms that categorize and separate us become our yellow Star of David badges. . . . Here at home, African-Americans learned long ago that 'separate but equal' is not equal."

Taylor and Vahey planned a wedding ceremony for Sept. 16, the 50th anniversary of their life together. But when Taylor became increasingly ill, they had moved up the date, marrying in a religious ceremony at the hospital on Memorial Day. Invitations now will be sent for a special memorial event Sept. 16, which also will be a fund-raiser for Fair Wisconsin's anti-amendment efforts.

Visitation will be from 5 to 7 p.m. today at the Suminski Family Funeral Home, 1901 N. Farwell Ave.

The story concludes with basic obituary information.

In addition to Vahey, Taylor is survived by brother Robert Morgan, nieces and nephews.

Writing obituaries from the mortuary's information alone is a clerk's work. As a reporter, you should go beyond the form. You should also confirm every fact on the sheet. Mortuary forms are notoriously inaccurate.

Sometimes, what the mortuary form doesn't tell you is as important as what it does. For the writer of the following obit, the first clue that the death notice was unusual was the age. The deceased was 12. That alone was enough for the reporter to start asking questions. The result was an obituary that moved from the records column to the front page:

TIPS

Policy Options for Handling Obits

» In an obituary, ignore any embarrassing information, and if necessary, omit the cause of death. If circumstances surrounding the death warrant a news story, run it separate from the obituary.

» Include embarrassing details and the cause of death in all obituaries.

» Include embarrassing details and the cause of death in an obituary only for a public figure.

» Put a limit on how far back in the person's life to use derogatory information such as a conviction.

» Print everything thought newsworthy that is learned about public figures but not about private figures.

» Print everything thought newsworthy about public and private figures.

» Decide each case as it comes up.

Sandra Ann Hill, 12, lost her lifetime struggle against a mysterious muscle ailment Wednesday night. The day she died was the first day she had ever been admitted as a hospital inpatient.

Although they knew it was coming, the end came suddenly for Sandra's family and school friends, said her father, Lester, of 1912 Jackson St.

Just last Friday, she attended special classes at the Parkdale School. "She loved it there," Hill said. "Like at recess, when the sixth graders would come in and read to her. She always wanted to be the center of attention."

"Bright as a silver dollar" was the way one of Sandra's early teachers described her. In fact, no one will ever know. Sandra couldn't talk.

"We didn't know what she knew or didn't know," her father said. Sandra's only communication with the world around her came in the form of smiles and frowns — her symbols for yes and no.

"There were times when I'd come around the corner and kind of stick my head around and say 'boo,'" her father recalled. "She smiled. She liked that."

The care and attention Sandra demanded makes the loss particularly hard for her family to accept, Hill said. "I can't really put it into words. You cope with it the best

you can, keep her comfortable and happy. We always took her with us."

Sandra came down with bronchitis Friday. Complications forced her to be admitted Wednesday to Lincoln County Hospital, where she died later that night.

Sandra's fight for life was uphill all the way. It started simply enough when she was 4 months old. Her mother, Bonnie, noticed she "wasn't holding up her head" like her other children.

Although her ailment was never firmly diagnosed, doctors found Sandra's muscles held only half the tissues and fibers in a normal child's body. The diagnosis: a type of cerebral palsy. The prognosis: Sandra had little chance to live past the age of 2. Medical knowledge offered little help.

Sandra was born in Springfield on Jan. 15, 1984. She is survived by her parents; one brother, Michael Eugene Hill; one sister, Terrie Lynn Hill, both of the home; and her grandparents, Gordon Hill of Seale, Ala., and Mrs. Carrie Harris of Phoenix, Ariz.

Services will be at 3:30 p.m. today at the Memorial Funeral Chapel with the Rev. Jack Gleason conducting. Burial will follow at the Memorial Park Cemetery.

The family will receive friends at the Memorial Funeral Home until time for the service.

The reporter who wrote this obituary obviously did a great deal of research beyond what was on the mortuary form. Because the girl was not a public figure, the reporter could not consult a reference work such as *Who's Who in America* or a national publication. But the reporter did have access to the newspaper library and could interview the girl's family and friends.

The Newsroom Library

In the newsroom library, you may find an interview with the deceased, an interesting feature story or clips indicating activities not included on the mortuary form. In an interview or feature story, the person may have made a statement about a philosophy of life that would be appropriate to include in the obituary. The subject also may have indicated his or her goals in life, against which later accomplishments can be measured. You can find the names of friends and co-workers in the clips as well. These people are often the source of rich anecdotes and comments about the deceased.

Your newsroom files are not the only source for information on people who have state or national reputations. You or your librarian should also search electronic databases for stories that have appeared elsewhere.

Interviews with Family and Friends

Journalists treat public figures in more detail than private citizens not only because they are newsworthy but also because reporters know more about them. Even though private citizens are usually less newsworthy, many good stories about them are never written because the reporter did not—or was afraid to—do the reporting. The fear is usually unfounded.

Cause of Death

If the person who died was not a public figure and the family does not wish to divulge the cause of death, some news organizations will comply. That is questionable news judgment. The reader wants to know what caused the death. A reporter should call the mortuary, the family, the attending physician and the appropriate medical officer. Only if none of these sources will talk should you leave out the cause of death.

A death certificate must be filed for each death, but obtaining it often takes days, and some states do not make the cause of death part of the public record. Even if the state lists the cause of death and the reporter has timely access to the death certificate, the information is often vague.

> **"** I don't write about death, I write about life. **"**
>
> —Michael Best, *The Detroit News*

If the deceased was a public figure or a young person, most newspapers insist on the cause of death. If the death is the result of suicide or foul play, reporters can obtain the information from the police or the medical examiner. Some newspapers include suicide as the cause of death in the obituary, others print it in a separate news story, and still others ignore it altogether. This is one way to report a suicide:

> Services for Gary O'Neal, 34, a local carpenters' union officer, will be at 9 a.m. Thursday in the First Baptist Church. Coroner Mike Pardee ruled that Mr. O'Neal died Tuesday of a self-inflicted gunshot wound.

Private or Embarrassing Information

Another newspaper policy affecting obituaries concerns private or embarrassing information. When the *St. Louis Post-Dispatch* reported in an obituary that the deceased had been disbarred and that he had been a key witness in a bribery scandal involving

TIPS

Sources for Obits

» Mortuary forms.

» Paid funeral notices.

» The newsroom's library.

» Interviews with family and friends of the deceased.

TIPS

Choosing Your Words

» Avoid euphemisms; such terms are out of place in a news story. People don't "pass away." They die. If a "lingering illness" was cancer, say so.

» Watch your language as you report the cause and circumstances of the death.

» Be careful with religious terms.

a well-known politician 13 years earlier, several callers complained. The paper's reader's advocate defended the decision to include that history in the obituary:

One who called to complain about the obit told me it reminded her of the quotation from Shakespeare's *Julius Caesar*, about how the good a man does is often buried with him and forgotten.

Yes, I said, and the first part of that quotation could be paraphrased to say that the news a man makes often lives after him.

When author W. Somerset Maugham died, *The New York Times* reported that he was a homosexual, even though the subject generally had not been discussed in public before. Yet many years later, when Susan Sontag died, few publications included the fact that she had acknowledged her bisexuality in a newspaper interview, even though Sontag herself clearly wasn't embarrassed by this information. When Bill Mauldin, a Pulitzer Prize–winning editorial cartoonist, died in 2003, the *Chicago Sun-Times*, where he had worked for years, wrote, "In his last years, Mr. Mauldin battled alcoholism and Alzheimer's."

The crucial factor in determining the extent to which you should report details of an individual's private life is whether the deceased was a public figure or a private person. A public figure is someone who has been in the public eye. A participant in civic or social activities, a person who spoke out at public meetings or through the mass media, a performer, an author, a speaker—these all may be public figures. A public official, an individual who has been elected or appointed to public office, is generally treated like a public figure.

Whether the subject is a public figure or a private citizen, the decisions newspapers must make when dealing with the obituary are sensitive and complicated. It is your obligation to be aware of your organization's policy. In the absence of a clear policy statement, consult an editor.

SUGGESTED READINGS

Center on Crime, Communities and Culture and *Columbia Journalism Review*. *Covering Criminal Justice*. New York: Graduate School of Journalism, Columbia University, 2000. This manual lists resources that will help reporters cover crime and the courts.

Giles, Robert H., and Robert W. Snyder, eds. *Covering the Courts: Free Press, Fair Trials and Journalistic Performance*. Piscataway, N.J.: Transaction, 1998. This book provides useful guidance from professional journalists.

Pulitzer, Lisa Beth. *Crime on Deadline: Police Reporters Tell Their Most Unforgettable Stories*. New York: Boulevard, 1996.

Real stories from nine of the nation's top crime reporters are featured in this book.

Siegel, Marvin, ed. *The Last Word*: The New York Times *Book of Obituaries and Farewells: A Celebration of Unusual Lives*. New York: Quill, 1998. Examples abound of well-written and compelling obituaries from *The New York Times*.

Singer, Eleanor, and Phyllis M. Endreny. *Reporting on Risk: How the Mass Media Portray Accidents, Diseases, Disasters and Other Hazards*. New York: Russell Sage Foundation, 1993. The authors take a critical look at media reporting of accidents and disasters.

SUGGESTED WEBSITES

www.fbi.gov
The FBI website provides useful information about crime.

www.fema.gov
The Federal Emergency Management Agency, part of the U.S. Department of Homeland Security, provides assistance during major emergencies. This site provides useful background information and contacts.

www.ntsb.gov
The National Transportation Safety Board website is an excellent source of accident information.

www.ojr.org
The *Online Journalism Review* has useful tips, articles and information about tools and techniques for reporting and storytelling online.

www.supremecourtus.gov
The U.S. Supreme Court is the nation's highest court. The Supreme Court's website outlines its operation.

EXERCISES

1. **Team project.** Working in teams, analyze the coverage of a major national crime, accident or fire story. Each team member should scrutinize the coverage of the story by a different news organization—print, online or broadcast. Then meet with the other members of your team to compare notes and discuss which stories are most satisfactory and why.

2. Monitor a day of local news. Take note of how many of the stories are the types covered in this chapter. Do they provide an accurate picture of your town? Do these stories meet the standards you've just learned? If not, how could they be improved?

3. **Journalism blog.** The obituary that began this chapter was a lighthearted treatment of a serious subject. Google "obituary for facts," and read the full obituary. What do you think of it? Does it work as a way to get people thinking? Why don't news organizations use this approach more often? Write a blog post in which you give your views.

4. Find an accident story in a local newspaper. List all the sources the reporter used in obtaining information for the story. List additional sources you would have checked.

5. Talk with a firefighter in your local fire department about the department's media policy at fire scenes. Using what you learn, write instructions for your fellow reporters on what to expect at fires in your city or town.

6. Cover a session of your local circuit court. Write a story based on the most interesting case of the day.

7. Research the coverage of constitutional rights as they pertain to terrorism suspects. Evaluate whether the media have done an adequate job of covering this issue. If you find fault with the coverage, describe what you would do differently.

8. Research and write the life story of a resident of your city.

17

Business and Consumer News

THE ELECTION OF 2012 sparked heated discussion on the state of the U.S. economy and how to create additional jobs for Americans. Journalists scrambled to determine whether the country was better off than four years before, when the Wall Street meltdown of 2008 plunged the country into what is being called the Great Recession. In recent years, headlines and news packages have told the stories of home foreclosures, job layoffs and a volatile stock market.

Business news is now big news. Turn on satellite or cable television in any country around the world, and you'll find 24-hour channels like CNBC or Bloomberg following the world stock markets and broadcasting that information in English, Chinese, Arabic, Spanish, Portuguese and German. And the speed of the Internet and TV adds complications to an already hard-to-understand topic. Print newspapers and specialized magazines—the legacy media—provide the foundation of information on which the electronic media elaborate.

Many young business journalists soon find themselves at the center of the world's most important stories. On a Sunday night in September 2008, a mere 14 months after graduating from journalism school, FoxBusiness.com reporter Ken Sweet found himself collaborating with editor Kathryn Vasel to piece together a story that would change the financial world. The investment bank Lehman Brothers had collapsed. "It was a Sunday night, and there were so many moving parts—we had Lehman collapsing and then the news broke that Bank of America was buying Merrill Lynch—any other day it would have been a huge story, but it was sidelined by Lehman, and then the problems at AIG came into the mix," says Vasel.

"First you have to get the straight news story out, but it doesn't end there—you have to add in company statements, reaction and what this means for the average consumer and other companies. You have to constantly massage the story to make sure it still flows with the latest add-ins while making sure the latest news is still in the lead," she says. On a major story, Vasel knew she had to get details precisely right, making sure she didn't overstate or mislead. "It was hard to swallow such a big story, but I also had to make sure to do the mundane tasks of double-checking names and titles to get it right."

Despite woes in many parts of journalism, business news has seen growth, and knowledgeable young journalists have attractive job prospects. Christopher Dieterich,

In this chapter you will learn:

1. Why business journalism is growing in importance.

2. How to report business stories.

3. Where to find business stories.

4. How to understand business numbers.

5. How to find and report consumer news.

a 2010 graduate, now covers daily New York stock markets for Dow Jones Newswires and, often, *The Wall Street Journal*. Jessica Smith and Victoria Craig found work soon after their 2012 graduation at Fox Business, a five-year-old network that has rapidly gained viewers. Austin Alonzo, another 2012 graduate, is back in his hometown of Kansas City, covering the construction industry for the *Kansas City Business Journal*.

So, how do you get started covering business news? First, you need to understand basic business terminology and basic math. You also need to learn how to read financial statements, which is surprisingly easy. Beyond that, you need the skills of any journalist: perseverance, curiosity and an ability to ask questions and get answers.

THE GROWING IMPORTANCE OF BUSINESS JOURNALISM

It's clear that government intervention into markets and business is here to stay, so it's especially important for political reporters to learn the basics of business. In 2012 and 2013, when Congress wrestled with reducing the federal deficit without sending the economy back into recession, journalists covering the story needed to understand the economic consequences of political decisions. With the passage of the Affordable Care Act, health issues are becoming increasingly related to economics, and reporters covering health care reform need to understand the business side of medical care so they can explain these new changes to their audiences. Influenza epidemics, like the one involving the H1N1 virus, have profound financial effects on the workforce and tourism.

All stories have some sort of business angle. A quick glance at an edition of *The Wall Street Journal* shows the breadth of news with an economic component—from admissions policies at Ivy League schools to how Apple iPhone sales can affect the gross domestic product of the U.S., to the latest technology employed by Procter & Gamble scientists in the $1.3 billion home hair-coloring industry.

Yet many news directors and editors still struggle with the focus of their business news. Who is their audience? Is it consumers, investors, local business executives or people looking for work? When gasoline prices rise in Texas, should reporters in Houston emphasize how high prices hurt consumers or how they increase the costs of goods shipped by highway? Or should they write about how higher oil profits will spur more oil exploration off the Texas Gulf Coast? Or should they focus on the potential loss of jobs at nearby refineries hurt by a decline in gasoline consumption? This array of ways to focus business stories provides an opportunity in the field of business journalism.

Business news is changing rapidly. Financial news, including up-to-the-second stock prices, is now available on mobile devices. Business executives use Twitter to send messages directly to customers, and the number of business-related Facebook sites continues to grow. When BP settled with the U.S. in 2012 over its role in the 2010 Deepwater Horizon oil rig explosion and resulting spill, it took to Facebook, YouTube and Twitter to post information about its restoration effort.

The increasing number of business news outlets is just one reason why business-trained journalists are in high demand. Even in a troubled newspaper industry, these specially trained journalists often command a 20 percent premium in salary, according to Detroit-based recruiter Joe Grimm, who blogs for the Poynter Institute.

Business journalism training is also important for those who seek jobs in corporate communications. More than 60 percent of Americans own stock, mostly through 401(k) retirement plans, and corporate communications divisions employ journalists to write about investor and consumer issues.

Specialized Business News

Local newspapers are shedding business staff members as part of a major employment decline, but those reporters are finding some job opportunities at the weekly journals that have grown and expanded in all major U.S. cities—from Fresno to Louisville to Hartford. American City Business Journals, based in Charlotte, N.C., publishes profitably in multiple cities.

Pick an industry and there is a magazine, Internet news site, newsletter or newspaper that specializes in covering it. Far from sleepy operations, these publications often are in the midst of breaking news. *CFO* magazine—whose audience is made up of chief financial officers in a wide range of industries—doesn't shy away from covering the scandals that have rocked the finance industry. The weekly trade news service *The Packer*, based in Lenexa, Kan., is covering the changes that have overwhelmed the cantaloupe industry after several recalls related to bacteria; it is now calling for more inspections and regulations to guarantee safety. Sean Sposito covers technology in the banking industry for *American Banker* magazine, and Sheena Martin covers petroleum refineries for Petroleum Listing Services, an industry news service in Houston.

Global Reach

Business journalism is a growing global industry. Business newspapers are now prevalent in China's major cities. *Shanghai Securities News*, founded in 1991, focuses on covering the Shanghai and Hong Kong Stock Exchanges as well as Asian economic news. American business media outlets have bureaus in major Asian cities and often employ multilingual reporters. It was a team of Chinese and American reporters for Dow Jones Newswires, the fee-based industry wire service, that broke the China copper-trading scandal in 2005. Those stories won several distinguished journalism prizes.

Business journalists who work for mainstream organizations must acknowledge the often-conflicting outcomes of economic events. A story about an outbreak of mad cow disease in Washington state could have multiple effects—depressing the earnings of McDonald's but boosting the price of Brazilian beef and leading to trade restrictions from a nervous Taiwan.

And business journalists must be able to see the big picture. While many Americans have lost jobs that went to workers in India or Mexico, an increasing number of Americans now work for global employers. It surprises many that the U.S. has often led the world in foreign direct investment; funds from other countries are building businesses in every state. Workers in South Carolina make small refrigerators for

Chinese-owned Haier Inc. Autoworkers in southern Indiana learn Japanese manufacturing techniques while manufacturing SUVs and minivans for Toyota. And though the 2008 recession was blamed on the mortgage crisis in the U.S., problems in eurozone countries like Greece and Spain were what sent the New York stock markets on an up-and-down roller coaster ride.

Wide Range of Topics

The range of possible business stories is as broad as the range of business itself. Some business stories are about a company's promotions and retirements, and some concentrate on company profits, which are of interest to investors and potential investors in that company. Other business stories cover personal finance issues that are of interest to lay readers rather than investment community insiders. Such stories explore issues such as these: Which is a better choice, a 15- or 30-year mortgage? Is art a good investment? Which mutual funds are high performers? Personal finance news is so popular that there are scores of websites devoted to this topic, like CNN's Money.com and the venerable Kiplinger, which started as a newsletter and now is a robust website. A business story might also be about new products, like the array of new tablet computers and e-readers released before every holiday season. These stories interest not just shareholders of the company but potential consumers as well. How does the latest smartphone stack up against its competitors? And what does that mean for investors? Interest in Apple products pushed the company's stock to record highs and made the Cupertino, Calif.–based tech firm one of the world's most valuable companies.

Many stories are both global and local. A story about a decision by the Federal Reserve Board's Open Market Committee to expand or tighten the money supply may seem far removed from your audience. But that decision can affect the rate your readers pay for a car or mortgage loan. A sizable trade deficit for the U.S. may weaken the value of the dollar and increase the price of a Korean-made TV, a Volkswagen car or a bottle of Cutty Sark Scotch whisky. It takes skill, but a good business journalist can make these seemingly esoteric stories clear and relevant to the audience.

Many important corporate and economic decisions that affect us all are made in Washington, New York, Chicago and a few other major metropolitan centers. But those cities do not have a monopoly on the creation and coverage of business news. Even in towns of a few thousand residents, businesses will be opening or closing, and manufacturing plants will be increasing or decreasing production, hiring or firing employees. Local residents will be spending money for houses, cars, vacations or tablet computers, or socking it away in local banks or savings and loan associations. There is a business story in every such development.

Increasingly, economics plays a strong role in disaster coverage. Hurricane Katrina caused at least $125 billion in economic damage when it swamped coastal areas in Louisiana, Mississippi, Alabama and Florida in 2005. Only half of that was covered by insurance. Hurricane Sandy, which devastated coastal areas in New Jersey, New York and Connecticut in 2012, cost that region more than $50 billion. The most expensive natural disaster in world history was the 2011 Tohoku earthquake and tsunami, which resulted in more than $235 billion in losses to the Japanese economy, according to the World Bank. The disaster, including the related meltdown of three nuclear reactors at the Fukushima Daiichi power plant, rocked manufacturing in Japan, caused parts shortages in Toyota plants worldwide and affected investment in the Japanese economy. The Bank of Japan was prompted to offer $180 billion in aid to keep the economy afloat.

In fact, the economic risk of natural disaster is of paramount interest to investment professionals, who abide by the investing wisdom "Buy on rumor and sell on news." Two days before Katrina hit, financial news outlets like Bloomberg News and Dow Jones Newswires were already reporting the potential impact on oil drilling and gasoline refineries in the Gulf of Mexico.

HOW TO REPORT BUSINESS STORIES

Business stories use the same structures as other types of stories: inverted pyramid, chronology, news narrative and focus. The preparation is the same as for any other beat, but business writers also have some unique challenges.

Avoiding Jargon and Finding the "So What"

What separates a business story from a soccer story—or, for that matter, a soccer story from a story about atomic particles—is the knowledge and language required to ask the right questions, to recognize the newsworthy answers and to write the story in a way that readers without specialized knowledge will understand. A reporter who understands the subject can explain what the jargon means.

Business reporters must use understandable language. But oversimplification can turn readers off. *The Wall Street Journal* avoids both traps by shunning jargon as much as possible, explaining any technical terms essential to the story, and linking to more detailed explanations. In one story, for example, *The Journal* explained the terms "Federal Open Market Committee," "federal funds rate," "M1," "M2" and "free-reserve position." Sophisticated readers might know what those terms mean, but many of the paper's readers would not. Those interested could also find more detailed explanations through online links.

Rather than imposing on busy readers, business reporters should develop the expertise to translate or explain technical terms. You may even have to do some math. For example, if banks change their lending rates, the personal finance reporter might be the person to write the story explaining that an increase of 1 percentage point could result in higher interest rates for car or home loans.

If West Coast longshoremen go on strike, one reporter covering local corporations might explore the impact on the supplies for a local manufacturer, while a retail reporter might talk to store owners about whether they'll have a popular toy on their shelves in time for Christmas. With terrorism continuing to affect the airline and travel markets, labor and transportation reporters at the *Orlando Sentinel*, near Walt Disney World and Universal Studios theme parks, often work together on a story about how security alert levels affect local employment.

TIPS

Reporting Business Stories

» Use language readers will understand, but don't oversimplify.

» Always be fair. You will win the trust and confidence of businesspeople—or at least their grudging respect.

» Appearances count. It may help you to dress as businesspeople do.

» The more you can demonstrate that you understand a business, the more likely you are to generate trust and draw out the information you seek.

» There are many sides to business stories—and you need to understand the viewpoint of shareholders, customers, competitors, suppliers and workers.

» Always remember that a company, government agency or pressure group may be using you to plant stories that serve some special interest.

Putting Sources at Ease

Sourcing presents a major challenge for business reporters: How do you get information from someone who does not legally have to tell you anything? It often takes more creative reporting skills to coax a story from a business source than from a government official. Almost all government information is public. Many business records are not.

The mistrust that many businesspeople have of the press can make it difficult to cover stories adequately, even when it would be in the business's interest to see that the story is told. Even if executives are willing to talk, they may become angry if the reporter quotes an opposing point of view or points out a flaw on the corporate visage. And of course, businesses know they can often sell their "spin" on a story by reaching the public directly through their websites and social media outlets.

The best antidote a reporter can use against this attitude is to report fairly and accurately what a business is doing and saying. By always being fair, you can win the trust and confidence of businesspeople—or at least their grudging respect.

Because business executives tend to be cautious when talking with reporters, it may help you to dress more like a business manager than a concert reviewer. Appearances count. Businesspeople, like reporters, feel more comfortable with their own kind. The more you demonstrate that you understand their business, the more likely you are to generate the trust that will draw out the information you seek. Public relations people are often helpful in providing background information and directing you to executives who can provide other comments and information, but you should try to get to know as many company executives as you can. Sometimes you can do this best through a background interview, one not generated by a crisis but intended simply to provide information about what the company is doing. Perhaps you can arrange to have lunch to see what the managers are thinking about and to give them a chance to see that you are probably not the demon that they may have thought you were.

Watching Out for Biases and Conflicts of Interest

Always remember that a company, government agency or pressure group may be trying to use you to plant stories that serve some special interest. Companies want stories that make them look promising to investors with the hope of driving up the price of their stock or that make them appear to be attractive merger partners. If you are suspicious, do some digging; talk to competitors and analysts, and ask detailed questions. Just because a company or some other group is pushing a story does not mean you have to write it.

Business journalists face conflict-of-interest challenges because they often write stories, some of which are unfavorable, about companies who buy advertising dollars from their media companies. Business editors across the country have become increasingly concerned as advertisers threaten to pull advertising over unfavorable coverage. For instance, a 2003 story in the *Orlando Sentinel* on the shoddy practices of homebuilders cost the newspaper $700,000 in canceled advertisements.

Because business news can affect market prices, business journalists must adhere to a strong code of ethics to avoid the appearance that their stories are being

ON THE JOB
Translating Business into English

Nik Deogun didn't set out to be a business reporter. It took an internship with *The Wall Street Journal* to change his mind. True, he had studied economics as an undergraduate, but his reporting courses in his master's program in journalism school had emphasized government and education. He sought the internship not because of *The Journal*'s niche in business coverage but because he hoped for the chance to do the kinds of news features that appear on its front page.

He got hooked on business. "This is where the power lies, and not many people are writing about it," he says. "Money is the source of all power, the source of all evil"—and thus the source of good stories.

Deogun, now senior vice president at CNBC business news network, thinks his generalist background, both in liberal arts and in journalism, prepared him well. Business writers need to understand the social and political context in which their subjects operate.

"I use here the same reporting skills you'd use on any beat," he says. "If tomorrow I had to go cover fly-fishing, I wouldn't know diddly. But I'd learn. You read a lot and ask people questions." Deogun understands he must be able to speak the technical language without falling into the trap of also writing it. "Most of your readers don't know that much about business," he observes.

Clear thinking and clear writing remain essential.

influenced. In addition, business journalists can be fined or even jailed if they violate U.S. securities laws and face jail time if they trade stocks based on inside information uncovered during the reporting process. In a famous case, R. Foster Winans, a former reporter for *The Wall Street Journal*, was convicted of illegal insider trading and mail fraud for tipping off a stockbroker to information he would later publish in his "Heard on the Street" columns. He served nine months in federal prison.

WHERE TO FIND BUSINESS STORIES

The starting point in writing a business story is similar to the first step in reporting any story: understanding the subject you're writing about. For the business reporter, that almost always means some basic research into the subject. For openers, check your organization's archives to learn what's been written locally about your topic or company.

A broad spectrum of Internet-accessible databases provides lists and summaries of stories published on a wide range of subjects. The truly adept can plumb raw data, including stock market transactions, to track the impact of announcements, mergers and personnel changes on stock prices. But everyone can use simple Internet searches to access annual reports, stock analyses, press releases and other announcements.

Of growing importance are databases that provide lists and summaries of stories published on a range of topics. Standard & Poor's, Dow Jones Factiva and Disclosure

TIPS

Where to Find Business Stories

» Conduct some basic research into the subject. Check the electronic and paper archives to learn what's been written locally about the topic or company.

» Turn to your computer. From a broad spectrum of databases you can obtain lists and summaries of stories published on a wide range of subjects. LinkedIn, the social media site, provides autobiographical employee profiles.

» Read print sources to find stories about your business or industry. Many trade journals are available online.

Inc. are some of the companies providing this information. Thomson Reuters, Dow Jones Factiva and Bloomberg Business News also provide background information on companies and securities, historical prices and real-time news on business and economic issues. In addition, companies like Business Wire and PR Newswire handle thousands of news releases daily from companies and nonprofit organizations, pumping out public relations news and videos through the Internet and social media. Sometimes that information causes investors to sell or buy stocks or bonds, even before journalists have the time to check that news for accuracy or "spin."

Journalists now rely on an array of aggregation websites focused on information for investors. Two examples are Yahoo Finance and MarketWatch, which compile news on companies and provide links to government-required Securities and Exchange Commission filings and charts of historical stock prices.

Records and Reports

Here are some good sources of information that you will find invaluable when writing business stories. Remember, many of these can be accessed through various online databases, so you can decide on a question, log on and get the information you need right away.

Corporate Data

Basic information on corporations can be found online, either on the company's own website or through government filings. Independent sources include Dun & Bradstreet Credibility Corp., which provides online information on large and small businesses. D&B also owns Hoovers.com, another business database. Standard & Poor's investigates the creditworthiness of companies and issues analysts' reports. To find suppliers and product news, check out ThomasNet.com's database.

Investment Data

To get specific information about the financial performance of a company or an industry, check reports prepared by Standard & Poor's, as well as ratings competitors Moody's and Fitch Ratings. Thomson Reuters First Call, Morningstar and Value Line discuss company prospects, forecast earnings and predict major trends. Also helpful are annual corporate scoreboards prepared by *Fortune*, Bloomberg and *Forbes*.

Financial Ratios

To assess a company's financial picture and management, compare your subject's financial ratios with the averages for other firms in the same industry. Industry ratios and averages can be found in reports prepared by Dun & Bradstreet, Moody's, and S&P's, in a number of trade journals, and on Yahoo Finance.

Company Filings

For years, the Securities and Exchange Commission operated under the guiding principle that companies should make available a maximum amount of information so that stockholders can make the most informed decisions regarding management's performance. The SEC preferred to keep out of corporate affairs and let the stockholders provide the necessary discipline. Much of the information companies provide to stockholders is made public through SEC filings.

You should start with the annual report, which will give you an overview of the company's operations and finances. The 10-K, a more detailed version of the annual report required by the SEC, also will give you the number of employees, a list of major real estate and equipment holdings, and information on any significant legal proceedings. Many other important documents, such as labor contracts, are listed by reference and can be acquired through the company, a Freedom of Information Act request or a private service such as Disclosure Inc. Annual reports often show up on the nightstands of business reporters. Carol Loomis, a prize-winning reporter for *Forbes* magazine, read 50 years' worth of company annual reports while researching a story on Bethlehem Steel.

Most filings are available free of charge through the SEC's online EDGAR system, but journalists often use the pay service 10KWizard, operated by Morningstar Document Research. Other outlets, such as MarketWatch and Yahoo Finance, will let you set up "alerts" notifying you of news and filings on companies of interest.

Another SEC filing, the *proxy statement*, which goes to shareholders before the annual meeting or other important meetings, provides an outline of issues to be voted on, as well as executive salaries and information on the company's board of directors. The proxy also sometimes contains leads about the company's business dealings. Interesting nuggets are found under mundane headings such as "Other Matters" or "Legal Proceedings." For example, now-bankrupt Enron Corp. disclosed some hints about its offshore partnerships in the footnotes of its SEC filings. Those footnotes generated some stories, but company officials did not disclose the true extent of the company's financial problems. In any filing, always read anything pertaining to lawsuits. That, in turn, can lead you to public documents regarding a particular suit.

All publicly traded companies now release their annual report, 10-K and proxy statement on their websites, and materials can be downloaded.

Trade Press

Beyond the newspapers and magazines you already know and read is another segment of journalism known as the *trade press*. In these journals and house organs you will find grocers talking with grocers, undertakers talking with undertakers and bankers talking with bankers. You will learn the important issues in a field, how an industry markets its products and services, and what legislation it fears and favors.

A number of trade publications are independent and objective. Among them are *Advertising Age, Aviation Week & Space Technology, Institutional Investor, American Banker, Editor & Publisher, The Wrap* and *Variety*, the last two of which cover the entertainment industry. Many more are very pro-industry; even so, they are still valuable for learning about current issues, marketing and lobbying strategies. To find trade publications, consult the *Standard Periodical Directory* or *Ulrich's International Periodicals Directory*. Most trade publications offer online versions, like www.ogj.com, the online version of the comprehensive trade publication *Oil & Gas Journal*. Topic-specific websites, such as the Medicare News Group, can also offer industry news.

Newsletters

Newsletters, which now have morphed into subscription and fee-free topic websites, have become an important source of inside information in recent years. Some are purely ideological, but others can be valuable. Among the best are *The Energy Daily*, *Nucleonics Week* and *Education Daily*. Peter Zollman, a former reporter for United Press International, runs a subscription-only print and online newsletter, *Classified Intelligence*, which covers the $7 billion online classified industry, which includes such companies as Monster.com and Craigslist.

Court Records

Most companies disclose only information required by the SEC. But when a corporation sues or is sued, an extensive amount of material becomes available. Likewise, criminal action against principals in a firm can provide the lead to a good story. It is important to check court testimony and records at all levels, including those of bankruptcy and divorce courts, all of which can be found on Pacer.gov or USCourts.gov. States also offer court records online through such sites as Iowa's www.iowacourts.state.ia.us. Journalists found information about the pay package and executive perks of former General Electric CEO Jack Welch in his divorce filing.

Local Regulators

Frequently, businesses want to enlarge their facilities or expand into new markets. To do so, they may seek funds from an industrial bond authority, which helps companies obtain large sums of money at below-market rates. When an institution such as a hospital wants to expand its services, often it must make a case for the expansion before a regional or local agency. In either case, documents filed to support the request may be revealing and may put into the public record information that previously was unobtainable. Local reporters who know how to find business plan filings in the county or city planning commission office gain insight into their area's economic development. These records are public but are often underutilized by reporters.

Other Sources

The preceding lists are certainly not exhaustive. Other relevant materials may be found at local tax and record-keeping offices, as well as in filings with the Federal Trade Commission, the Federal Communications Commission, the Food and Drug Administration, the Interstate Commerce Commission, the Bureau of Labor Statistics and various state agencies, such as the secretary of state's office, which compiles information on businesses registered in the state.

Don't overlook the Federal Reserve—the central bank of the U.S.—which employs scores of economic analysts at each of its 12 regional banks. Eight times a year, the Fed publishes a comprehensive book of regional statistics and analysis,

Publicly Held Companies' SEC Filings

The following is a list of places to look for publicly held companies' SEC filings:

» **13-D.** Lists owners of more than 5 percent of the voting stock. Must report increases and decreases of holdings and be filed within 10 business days.

» **13-F.** Quarterly report of ownership by institutional investors. Includes holders of less than 5 percent of the company.

» **8-K.** Report of a significant incident.

» **10-Q.** Quarterly financial statement.

» **10-K.** Annual financial statement. Includes number of employees, major real estate and equipment holdings, significant legal proceedings. Many other important documents, such as labor contracts, are listed by reference and can be acquired through the company, a Freedom of Information Act request or a private service.

» **Proxy statement.** Contains executive salaries, director information and shareholder voting issues.

» **Annual report to shareholders.** May lack much of the data found in 10-K.

» **Securities registration statement/prospectus.** Submitted when new stock is to be issued. Usually contains same information as 10-K and proxy but is more up-to-date.

nicknamed the "Beige Book," which is available online at www.federalreserve.gov. The Consumer Confidence Index, a survey of 5,000 sample households by the Conference Board, gauges consumer sentiment on the U.S. economy. This is an important monthly index, followed by market watchers as well as the Federal Reserve in setting interest rates.

The Department of Commerce's Bureau of Economic Analysis (www.bea.gov) now allows reporters to generate economic data by county, region or state. The BEA uses data from agencies that don't issue public reports, such as the Internal Revenue Service. The Census Bureau provides timely data on many economic functions, including business inventories and monthly retail sales. The bureau recently released a smartphone application that will allow reporters to access this information in the field. And graphic artists can use the Census Bureau's data visualization tools to create information graphics.

Human Sources

Who are the people you should talk to on the business beat? Here are some who are important sources of information.

Company Executives

Although many public relations people can be helpful, the most valuable information will probably come from the head of the corporation or corporate division. Chief executive officers are powerful people, either out front or behind the scenes, in your community. They are often interesting and usually well informed. Not all of them will be glad to see you, although many executives value open communication with the press. In 2000, in an effort to tighten up information that could lead to illegal stock trading based on inside information, the SEC adopted Regulation FD (Fair Disclosure). It governs how corporate executives release information about corporate finances and other material information. Though Regulation FD has an exemption for journalists, it has caused executives to be more cautious in releasing information. As a result of Regulation FD and the 2002 Sarbanes-Oxley Act, companies now release quarterly financial information via electronic news services like PR Newswire and Business Wire and discuss those results in Web-based public conference calls with analysts in which journalists can listen in, but not ask questions.

Public Relations Sources

Don't automatically assume the public relations person is trying to block your path. Many people working in corporate communications are truly professional, and providing information to journalists is part of their job. Remember, though, that they are paid to make the company look good, so they are likely to point you in the direction of the company's viewpoint. Public relations professionals aren't objective, but that doesn't mean that the information they provide is untrue. Instead, you should assume that it is being packaged to show the company in its best light.

Union meetings, such as this one of the United Food and Commercial Workers in Los Angeles, can be an excellent source of labor stories.

Academic Experts

Your college or university has faculty members with training and experience in business and economics. Often they are good sources for local reaction to national developments or analysis of economic trends.

Trade Associations

Although trade associations clearly represent the interests of their members, they can provide expert commentary on current issues or give explanations from the perspective of the industry. When *The New York Times* reported on the revival of the moving industry, the Household Goods Carriers Bureau, a major trade group, proved to be an important source. To find trade associations, check the federal USA.gov site, which maintains an alphabetized list.

Chamber of Commerce Officials

Chamber of commerce officials are clearly pro-business. They will seldom make an on-the-record negative comment about business, but they usually know who is who and what is what in the business community. The chamber may be involved in such projects as downtown revitalization and industry recruiting. State and regional areas all have economic development agencies that receive tax funds and are required to file reports of recruitment activities.

Former Employees

Many business reporters say that their most valuable sources are former employees. Business reporter and analyst Chris Welles writes, "Nobody knows more about a corporation than someone who has actually worked there." He warns, "Many, probably most, have axes to grind, especially if they were fired; indeed, the more willing they are to talk, the more biased they are likely to be." The good reporter will exercise care in using information obtained from former employees. A quick way to search is through the social media site LinkedIn. The site offers a tutorial for journalists.

Labor Leaders

For the other side of many business stories and for pieces on working conditions, contracts and politics, get to know local union officials. The workings, legal and otherwise, of unions make good stories, too.

Other Sources

Don't overlook the value of a company's customers, suppliers and competitors. You may also want to consult with local bankers, legislators, legislative staff members, law enforcement agents and regulators, board members, oversight committee members and the like. Don't forget those ubiquitous consultants, who are usually well informed and often willing to talk, if only for background. If the company you are covering is publicly traded, investor sites like Yahoo Finance offer a list of "peer" companies.

Announcements and Meetings

The source of much business news, and the starting point for many good stories, is an announcement by a company of a new product or the firm's reaction to some action by a government agency. News conferences can take many forms—in person or via a webcast. Companies also send out news releases via electronic outlets like PR Newswire or Business Wire, or a company PR person might send news to a reporter directly by email.

If you work in a city where one or more corporations are based, you may have the opportunity to cover an annual meeting, which invariably produces some news. Many companies will restrict those meetings to shareholders, but some do allow the media to observe.

Reporter Enterprise

As in other areas of journalism, often the best business news stories are generated by a reporter's initiative, sparked by a hunch or a tip passed along by an editor, a shareholder or a disgruntled employee or customer. Sometimes a self-promoting source can lead to a good story. When the president of a new commodity options firm called *The Boston Globe* to suggest a story on her company, reporter Susan Trausch was dispatched. The reporter quickly became suspicious of some things she saw and was told. The investigation that followed produced a series on abuses in an unregulated industry and won several national prizes. The original caller got her name in the paper all right, but hardly as she had expected.

In other cases, a news release may raise questions that turn into stories. For example, a routine announcement of an executive appointment may lead a curious reporter to a story about the financial problems that produced the change in leadership. Or a stockholder's question may result in a story about a new trend in corporate financing or a shift in emphasis on operations within the company. Or a former employee's call that a company is quietly laying off workers may produce a story about the firm's declining fortunes.

LOOKING AT THE NUMBERS

An understanding of the numbers that a business generates is essential to any intelligent analysis of a company or an industry. The most complete summary of the financial picture of a business is found in SEC filings.

More than 100 million copies of annual reports are pumped out each year, and almost all annual reports can be downloaded from the Internet, as can recent recordings of "conference calls"—or the conversations that company executives have with investment analysts.

Annual reports can often be complicated, and new journalists should look first at Microsoft's reports, which feature easy-to-read financial statements. A typical annual report includes:

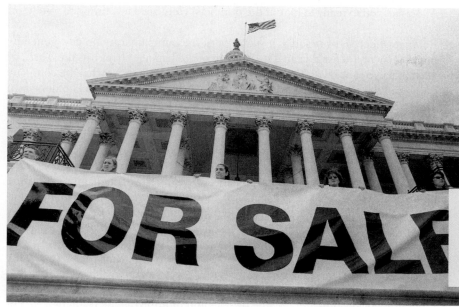

Consumer activist organizations can be a good source of background information on an issue. Remember to take the group's mission into consideration, though.

» An opening letter from the CEO
» Key financial data
» Results of continuing operations
» Market segment information
» New product plans
» Subsidiary activities
» Research and development activities on future programs
» Summarized disclosures from the 10-K report

Most veteran reporters, like Diana Henriques, investigative business reporter for *The New York Times*, start with the auditor's statement, which is generally located near the back of the annual report, and also examine basic financial data, footnotes and supplementary financial information. The basic auditor's report, from one to four paragraphs long, states that the material conforms to generally accepted auditing standards and that it fairly presents the financial condition of the company. But read the report closely. Sometimes auditors hint at trouble by deviating from the standard language.

Next, move on to the footnotes, where the seeds of many fascinating stories may be germinating among the innocuous prose and numbers that follow and supplement the company's basic financial data. Then, turn to the front of the annual report to find the report from the CEO. It is usually addressed "To our shareholders" and should give an overview of the company's performance.

After that, you're ready to look at the numbers. Here are a few things to watch for:

» **Balance sheet.** This report is a snapshot of the company on one day, generally the last day of the fiscal year. The left side of the balance sheet lists the *assets*, or what the company owns. On the right side are the *liabilities*, or what the company owes, and the *shareholders' equity*, or the dollar value of what stockholders own. The two sides must balance, so the balance sheet can be summarized with the following equation: assets equal liabilities plus shareholders' equity. The balance sheet shows how the year in question compares with the previous year. Reporters should note any significant changes worth exploring for a possible story.

» **Income statement.** This report, also referred to as an *earnings statement* or *statement of profit and loss*, answers this key question: How much money did the company make for the year? Look first at *net sales* or *operating revenues* and determine if they went up or down. If they increased, did they increase faster than they did last year and faster than the rate of inflation? If sales lagged behind inflation, the company could have serious problems.

» **Return on sales (ROS).** Company management and financial analysts calculate a number of ratios to gain better insights into the financial health of an organization. One important test of earnings is the relation of net income to sales, which is obtained by dividing net income by sales and multiplying the result by 100. For example, suppose a company has sales of $150,000 and, after expenses, has a net income of $30,000.

ROS = ($30,000 / $150,000) × 100
ROS = .2 × 100 = 20 percent

The ROS will tell you how much profit after expenses was produced by each dollar of sales. Reporters should remember that average percentages can vary widely by industry, but generally the higher the percentage, the better.

» **Return on equity (ROE).** This ratio, which shows how effectively a company's invested capital is working, is obtained by dividing net income minus preferred dividends by the common stockholders' equity for the previous year. Every year since 1997, Standard & Poor's Equity Research staff has compiled a list of the best returns on equity by U.S. companies of various sizes. ROE ratios are best compared within an industry, but generally speaking, between 15 and 20 percent is considered a good ROE.

» **Dividends.** These payments to shareholders are declared quarterly and generally are prominently noted in the annual report. Dividends are an inducement to shareholders to invest in the company. Because companies want to see dividends rise each quarter, they sometimes go so far as to change their accounting or pension assumptions so enough funds will be available to increase dividends. Other companies, such as Berkshire Hathaway Inc., declare no dividends because they prefer to reinvest profits internally. Shareholders of Microsoft Corp. complained for years that the software giant was holding on to too much cash and urged the board to return more money to its investors through higher dividends.

Now that you have an idea of how to examine an annual report and its numbers, it is time for some important words of caution. First, the numbers in an annual report, though certified by an auditor and presented in accordance with SEC regulations, are not definite because they are a function of the accounting assumptions used in their preparation. That leads to the second and third points: Look at a company's numbers both in the context of its industry and compared with several years' performance. To understand how well a firm is performing, examine the numbers along with those of other firms in the same industry. Look at how the company has performed for the last five to 10 years. Then you will discern trends instead of basing your conclusions on one year's performance, which may be atypical.

COVERING CONSUMER NEWS

The phrase "consumer news" is in its broadest sense arbitrary and redundant. All economic news is, directly or indirectly, about consumers. A story about the stock market may affect or be of interest to "consumers" of stocks and bonds even though those items aren't consumed in the same sense as cornflakes. A story about the price of crude oil affects consumers of gasoline and many other products refined from crude oil. A story about a drought that may drive up the price of wheat has an impact on consumers of hamburger buns.

Many news outlets, especially local and network television, run "consumer target" features that respond to consumer complaints of alleged fraud or unfair treatment by merchants or landlords.

Where to Find Consumer News

Sources of consumer news fall into three general categories: government agencies, consumer groups and private businesses. Let's consider each of these groups.

Government Agencies

Many municipalities, especially large cities, have a consumer advocate who calls public attention to problems that affect consumers. Most county prosecuting attorneys' offices also have someone—or even a whole department—who challenges business practices of questionable legality. These offices handle cases of consumer fraud in which people pay for something they do not receive or pay for something of a certain quality and receive something less.

Most states have a consumer affairs office that investigates consumer problems and orders or recommends solutions. In addition, state attorneys general investigate and prosecute cases of consumer fraud. Most states also have regulatory commissions that represent the public in a variety of areas. The most common commissions regulate rates and practices of insurance companies, rates and levels of service of utilities and transportation companies, and practices of banks and savings and loan

TIPS

Cautions When Examining an Annual Report

» Remember that the numbers on an annual report are not definite.

» Look at the company's numbers both in the context of its industry and compared with several years' performance.

» Remember that cash flow from operations, which are funds that companies get from products or services they sell, and not from the sale of assets, is the true measure of a company's performance. Earnings can also come from the sale of assets or from financing, which make the balance sheet look good but aren't sustainable.

» Use the knowledge you gain in this chapter to reach preliminary conclusions that you can pursue with experts and company officials.

associations. Another source is the state auditor's office, which may also uncover fraud and wrongdoing within government or government contracts.

At the federal level, government regulatory agencies involved in consumer affairs have the power to make rules and to enforce them:

» The Federal Trade Commission oversees matters related to advertising and product safety.
» The Food and Drug Administration watches over prices and safety rules for food, drugs and a variety of other health-related items.
» The Securities and Exchange Commission oversees the registration of securities for corporations and regulates the exchange, or trading, of those securities.
» The Interstate Commerce Commission regulates prices and levels of service provided by surface-transportation companies in interstate commerce.
» The Federal Energy Regulatory Commission regulates the rates and levels of service provided by interstate energy companies.
» The Occupational Safety and Health Administration has inspectors who routinely visit and report on safety in workplaces and factories and who investigate workplace accidents.

Consumer Groups

Nongovernment consumer groups are composed of private citizens who have organized to represent the consumer's interest. They, too, are often good sources of background information or comment.

Consumer Federation of America, an advocacy and education nonprofit, and Consumers Union, an independent group that publishes the popular *Consumer Reports*, are general in nature. Many states have public-interest research groups. Other organizations, such as the Sierra Club, which concentrates on environmental matters, are such strong advocates that their information might, at times, be anti-business. Other groups may be more local in scope. They may try to enact legislation that promotes recycling, or they may fight what they perceive as discrimination in the way banks and savings and loan associations make housing loans.

Private Businesses

Almost all large corporations and many smaller ones have public relations departments, which try to present the company in the most favorable light and attempt to mask the scars as much as possible.

Because of the successes of the consumer movement, a number of companies have taken the offensive and have instituted programs they deem to be in the public interest. Oil companies tell drivers how to economize on gasoline, electric utilities tell homeowners how to keep their electric bills at a minimum and even use solar and wind power, and credit card companies suggest ways to manage money better.

A new breed of websites, like Bankrate.com, are independent sources of information for consumers on lending rates and credit cards, though their advertising support comes from the credit industry.

A Business Mini-Glossary

Bonds

Governments and corporations issue bonds to raise money (capital). The bonds pay interest at a stated rate and are redeemable on a predetermined maturity date.

Constant Dollars

Because of inflation, $10 doesn't buy in 2013 what it did in 1991. Constant dollars take inflation into account by figuring their value compared with a base period. See Chapter 8 for more on writing about inflation.

Consumer Price Index

A measure of the relative price of goods and services, the CPI is based on the net change compared with a base period. An index of 115 means the price has increased 15 percent since the base period. Thus, to report the significance of a rise or drop in the CPI, you need to know the base year.

Dow Jones Industrial Average

The Dow is the principal daily benchmark of U.S. stock prices. It is based on the combined value of 30 major stocks, which are changed on a regular basis. Those stocks, despite the name, are no longer purely industrial, and they represent some companies listed on the NASDAQ and not the New York Stock Exchange. The

Dow exceeded 12,000 for the first time in 2006 but fell sharply in the 2008 Wall Street meltdown. Though the Dow is widely used, some prefer the accuracy of the Standard & Poor's index of 500 top U.S. companies, the S&P 500.

Individual Retirement Accounts

IRAs and Roth IRAs are restricted savings accounts whose earnings (as well as some contributions) are tax-free until withdrawal.

Mutual Funds

These funds are collections of bonds, stocks and other securities managed by investment companies. Individuals buy shares in them much as they buy shares of stock, but mutual funds provide more diversity.

Stocks

A share of stock represents a piece of a company. The price varies from day to day. Blue chip stocks are generally less volatile stocks that are meant for long-term investing. The price per share of blue chip stocks does not generally increase at any sort of going rate, but these stocks can give decent or large returns in the long term.

How to Report Consumer Stories

Consumer stories may be exposés, bringing to light a practice that is dangerous to consumers or that increases the price of a product or service. Research for such stories can be simple and inexpensive to conduct, and the findings may arouse intense reader interest. The project can be something as simple as buying hamburger meat at every supermarket in town to see if all purchases weigh what they are marked. Theo Keith, a reporter at WISC-TV in Madison, Wis., found that 50 local gas stations with faulty meters were shorting customers on gasoline purchases.

Susan Lundine, a reporter for the *Orlando Business Journal*, scoured Florida state insurance records to detail claims from the hurricanes that crisscrossed the state in 2004: Charley, Frances, Ivan and Jeanne. Lundine found, for example, that homeowners who lived in 12 counties on Florida's east coast, 370 miles from where Ivan made landfall, claimed more than $65 million in damages from that storm. The *Business Journal* ran a county-by-county map of claims for each of the four storms, which starkly showed how ludicrous some of the claims were. The state reacted, investigating additional cases of potential insurance fraud.

Consumer stories may also be informational, intended to help readers make wiser or less expensive purchases. Other consumer stories can be cautionary, warning readers of impending price increases, quality problems with products or questionable practices of business or consumer groups. Such stories can have great impact. Dozens of magazines and books focus on consumer news, from stories on what to look for when building a new house to advice on how to select a good nursing home.

Consumer stories can put news organizations at odds with advertisers. It was a consumer story that led to a lawsuit against *The Denver Post* when it published a story about a dry cleaner that consistently lost customers' clothes.

SUGGESTED READINGS

Houston, Brant, and Investigative Reporters and Editors. *The Investigative Reporter's Handbook: A Guide to Documents, Databases and Techniques*. 5th ed. New York: Bedford/St. Martin's, 2009. This valuable guide should be on every reporter's shelf. See especially the chapter on business.

Lewis, Michael. *The Big Short: Inside the Doomsday Machine*. New York: W. W. Norton, 2010. Lewis provides a gripping explanation of the housing and credit bubbles of the 2000s.

Morgenson, Gretchen. *The Capitalist's Bible: The Essential Guide to Free Markets—and Why They Matter to You*. New York: HarperCollins, 2009. This guide offers a good discussion of business terms and concepts.

Smith, Rebecca, and John R. Emshwiller. *24 Days: How Two Wall Street Journal Reporters Uncovered the Lies That Destroyed Faith in Corporate America*. New York: HarperCollins, 2003.

This is an inside-the-newsroom account of the Enron scandal, the biggest bankruptcy in recent business history.

Sorkin, Andrew Ross. *Too Big to Fail: The Inside Story of How Wall Street and Washington Fought to Save the Financial System—and Themselves*. New York: Viking Adult, 2009. This is an excellent chronicle of the Wall Street collapse in 2008.

Taparia, Jay. *Understanding Financial Statements: A Journalist's Guide*. Chicago: Marion Street Press, 2004. Taparia, a popular trainer in business journalism, walks journalists through complicated financial statements.

Wilkins, Lee, Martha Steffens, Esther Thorson, Greeley Kyle, Kent Collins and Fred Vultee. *Reporting Disaster on Deadline*. New York: Routledge, 2012. This handbook describes how to cover disasters in today's Internet age. See the chapters on economic damage and consumer fraud.

SUGGESTED WEBSITES

www.bea.gov, www.bls.gov and www.census.gov
These sites, from the U.S. Department of Commerce and the U.S. Department of Labor, offer overviews of the U.S. economy and exhaustive studies about each segment of the economy.

www.business.com
This directory of business websites offers information about individual companies and industries.

www.businessjournalism.org
This website, funded by the Donald W. Reynolds National Center for Business Journalism, offers tips and tutorials for business journalism professionals and students.

www.finance.yahoo.com
This portal is an accessible and free index of corporate financial filings, stock prices and corporate news.

www.investorwords.com
This is one of many commercial sites with reliable definitions of words used in finance.

www.ire.org/nicar/database-library
The National Institute for Computer-Assisted Reporting provides access to databases and training in how to use them to analyze business, economic and regulatory information.

www.sabew.org
The Society of American Business Editors and Writers can be a good source for contacts, story ideas and student training opportunities. Students can join the organization for a modest fee.

EXERCISES

1. **Team project.** The foreclosure crisis that began in 2008 led to many stories about the impact of foreclosures on communities, from rampant homelessness to the increase in illnesses caused by mosquitoes that breed unchecked in abandoned backyard swimming pools. Your instructor will divide the class into teams. Each team should choose an area of the country and research effects of the foreclosure crisis. How many families were affected? Why did families lose their homes? What kinds of mortgages were involved? How did state and local governments handle the crisis? Divide the research tasks among team members. Then meet to discuss and plan a series of stories you might write. If time permits, assemble your results into stories.

2. **Journalism blog.** Find newspaper, television and Internet stories on the same business topic, such as the latest employment statistics, which are released each Friday. Compare the stories in terms of their detail and sources used. Which is the most informative? Which is the most interesting? Write a blog post explaining your findings.

3. Identify a local business reporter. Study her or his work, and then interview the reporter. Ask about sources, story ideas and career opportunities.

4. Download a prospectus on a mutual fund, and study its investment rationale. Or read a prospectus on a stock offering, and study its price-earnings ratio, yield on dividends and other value indicators. Find commentary on the fund or stock on the Web, and explain its performance.

5. Use LexisNexis or the SEC's EDGAR database and edgr.com to find the 10-K report on a publicly traded company with a local operation.

18

Social Science Reporting

As the 2012 presidential campaign neared its conclusion, pundits of all political inclinations were nearly unanimous in declaring the contest too close to call. They discerned "momentum" for either President Barack Obama or Republican challenger Mitt Romney. They quoted the results of a multitude of polls.

One analyst disagreed. Nate Silver, creator of the FiveThirtyEight blog for *The New York Times*, declared Obama the favorite throughout the campaign. Silver's final post gave Obama a 90.9 percent chance of winning. His predictions drew widespread criticism from both columnists and politicians, especially Republicans. We know the results: Not only did Silver call the presidential race, but he correctly predicted the outcome in all 50 states. How did he do it?

It was pretty simple, he told Jon Stewart on *The Daily Show* shortly after the election. His secret: "arithmetic."

In fact, Silver had devised a complex algorithm that took into account a variety of polls, the political history of each state and the likely makeup of the electorate. He ran those numbers repeatedly and simply reported the results.

In the aftermath of the election, Kelly McBride of the Poynter Institute wrote, "Many are declaring the 2012 presidential election a victory for Nate Silver and his FiveThirtyEight blog." She described his success as "the reassertion of journalism as a discipline of verification."

It is also a vivid demonstration of the value of social science methods in a field that doesn't usually think of itself as scientific.

Many journalists would resist the very suggestion that they are scientists. But the best reporting has a great deal in common with the work of political scientists, historians and sociologists. Like these social scientists, reporters frame research questions or hypotheses. They seek answers to their questions through the careful accumulation of reliable data and the use of scientific formulas and statistics to analyze the information they've gathered. They double-check their findings for reliability. Then they report clearly and carefully what they have learned.

The social science tool journalists use most often is the public opinion survey, or poll. It is also the tool they misuse most often. Routinely, but especially during political campaigns, journalists report the headline numbers of a poll without taking into account two key factors. One is the methodology of the poll. The other is the margin of error.

In this chapter you will learn:

1. How computer-assisted journalism is creating new knowledge.

2. How to use participant observation, including dealing with the issues of invasion of privacy, involvement and generalization.

3. How to approach a systematic study of records.

4. How to understand field experiments, including hypotheses, variables, experiment control and randomization.

5. How to evaluate public opinion polls.

After the 2012 election, Nate Silver turned his analytic power on the polls themselves. He discovered that some were consistently more accurate than others and that some had built-in biases toward one party or the other.

The most accurate polls, he found, tended to be those taken online. Closely behind came the polls done by live telephone callers. Least accurate were the automated telephone polls. Polls relying on only landline telephones had a Republican bias, because so many young voters rely exclusively on cellphones. Overall, in 2012, the polling firm with the worst performance was the one most likely to be quoted by journalists: Gallup.

Clearly, caution is in order.

COMPUTER-ASSISTED REPORTING

American journalism—print, broadcast and online—relies on computers. Reporters write on computers. Photographers edit and transmit their pictures by computer. The almost unlimited storage capacity of computers and the flexibility of digital technology enable online journalists to combine text and video with links to original documents and to related information stored anywhere in the world. Increasingly, journalists are also using computers to analyze data and to create knowledge that nobody had before.

Computers assist reporting in two main ways:

» Journalists can access digital information from databases on the Internet. (See Chapter 6 for more about these resources and how to tap them.)
» Journalists can become knowledge creators by compiling and analyzing information that was previously not collected or not examined. (See Chapter 8 for more about using numbers.)

David Herzog, director of the National Institute for Computer-Assisted Reporting, teaches University of Missouri students and hundreds of practicing journalists from all over the world how to use their computers as more than word processors. His students learn how to acquire data from government agencies, nonprofit organizations and other researchers. Then they place the information into a searchable database, such as an Excel spreadsheet, so they can analyze the data. Often they match information from two or more databases to find something even policymakers didn't know.

Take, for instance, the topic of police shootings. Jo Craven McGinty was a graduate student at Missouri who mastered analytic techniques and worked part time for NICAR, helping professional journalists tell statistics-based stories. She came across an FBI database on the use of weapons by police officers. When she took an internship at *The Washington Post*, she took with her that knowledge and a story idea. Months later, as part of *The Post*'s investigative team, she helped tell the story that Washington, D.C., police used their guns to shoot civilians more often than police in any other city. The story won a Pulitzer Prize for *The Post*. Later she moved to *The New York Times*, where she is on the computer-assisted reporting team.

**bedfordstmartins.com
/newsreporting**

Watch **"Computer-Assisted
Reporting"**

» Computer-based research has become more and more common over the past twenty years—but it's not foolproof. What should journalists be cautious about when using computers for research?

» How do you typically use computers for research? Have you found information that would have been hard to locate by other methods?

Not all computer-assisted reporting leads to Pulitzers, but much of it reveals important information that otherwise would remain hidden in bureaucratic files. Sometimes those stories are hidden in plain sight, and the data must just be arranged to be understood. Herzog is an expert in computer mapping, which is the use of special software programs to display information in maps to reveal significant patterns. Crimes, for example, can be mapped to show the truly dangerous areas of a city. Outbreaks of disease can be mapped to help identify sources of infection. Patterns of immigration or unemployment or voting can be demonstrated more clearly by electronic maps than words alone could describe.

To learn more, or to get help with your own reporting, go to www.ire.org/nicar. There you can benefit from computer-assisted learning.

PARTICIPANT OBSERVATION

Audiences around the world watched in real time as America's wars in Iraq and Afghanistan unfolded. Viewers saw desert terrain spread out across their screens as cameras mounted on military vehicles captured the progress of American and British troops toward Baghdad. From Afghanistan came timeless images of Special Forces soldiers on horseback riding into battle. Correspondents wearing camouflage uniforms often slipped into the first-person plural as they described the experiences of the soldiers they were accompanying. In military jargon, those reporters were "embedded" with their units. A social scientist would say that they were engaged in participant observation.

Participant observation is a tool long used by anthropologists and sociologists to learn about unknown societies by becoming part of the scene they are studying. War correspondents have used it for just as long to provide firsthand accounts of campaigns. Other journalists have employed participant observation for **undercover reporting**, to expose crimes or social ills from the inside. All participant observers get close-up views of their subjects, insights they cannot obtain by studying statistics or formal interviewing. They can capture facts and feelings that otherwise would remain undiscovered.

Along with its unique advantages, participant observation also poses some unique problems. These problems may have no clear solutions, but you and your editors must at least consider them before you set out to become an ambulance attendant or a migrant worker. (Be aware that it's illegal to pretend to be a licensed professional, such as a cop or a physician.)

The Problem of Invasion of Privacy

Unless you identify yourself as a reporter, you are, in effect, spying on people—an ethically questionable activity. But if you do identify yourself, some of the advantages of participant observation are lost. In either case, sensitivity is essential, especially when the people you write about may be embarrassed by your reporting or have their jobs or safety jeopardized.

TIPS

Cautions About Participant Observation

» Sensitivity is essential; people don't always feel as you do. What you write about others may embarrass them or jeopardize their jobs or safety.

» Don't become so involved that you change the course of the events you're observing.

» Participant observation usually works best as a supplement to interviewing and examining documents.

The Problem of Involvement

There are two things to watch out for. First, do not become so involved that you change the course of the events you are observing. You may be on stage, but you are not the star performer. Second, do not assume that the people you are observing feel the same way you do. No matter how hard you work at fitting in, you remain an outsider, a visitor. The view from inside a migrant workers' camp or a psychiatric hospital is different when you know you will be there for two weeks instead of two years or a lifetime.

The first of these was the issue that drew the most criticism of the embedded reporters in Iraq. The reporters' perspective on the war was necessarily that of the units to which they were attached. One reporter for *USA Today* even wrote a column in which he described how, during a battle, he was asked to help a medic who was treating a wounded soldier. The reporter told how he put his "objectivity" aside to save the life of a man who might have saved the reporter's life if the fight had turned out differently.

The Problem of Generalization

Scientists know well the danger of generalizing from limited observations. Reporters don't always recognize that danger, or sometimes they forget it. Keep in mind that although participant observation yields a detailed picture of a specific situation, it tells you nothing reliable about any other situation. Participant observation is a good tool, but it is a limited one. It usually works best as a supplement to the standard techniques of interviewing and examining documents. This, too, was true of the war reporting. As the embedded journalists pointed out, theirs was not the only angle from which the war was reported. Other reporters at military headquarters, back home or even in besieged Baghdad all contributed to the overall account. That's a lesson to keep in mind.

SYSTEMATIC STUDY OF RECORDS

Kathleen Kerr and Russ Buettner of *Newsday* used the systematic study of records to discover whether New York City's criminal justice system discriminated against the poor. Their method was to acquire computer databases of city and state records on 27,810 prisoners and then to use their own computer to sort those cases by race and other criteria. They found that the poor, especially minorities, were often denied bail and forced to wait in jail for trials that often found them not guilty. No amount of traditional interviewing and observing could have produced such credible stories.

Scholars have long used the systematic study of records in their research. Its use by reporters is still limited but growing. The advantage of the detailed analysis of court records, budgets, voting records and other documents is that it permits reporters and readers to draw conclusions based on solid information. The widespread availability of powerful personal computers and easy-to-use analytic programs brings the systematic study of records within the reach of any news organization.

TIPS

Once You Begin a Study . . .

» Make sure it is systematic. Either examine all the pertinent records or choose the ones you examine in such a way that they are truly representative of the rest.

» Be sure to ask the right questions and record the information necessary to answer them.

» Remember that a computer can perform complicated analyses very quickly but cannot analyze facts that have not been input.

The main obstacles to such study are shortages of time and money. Major projects for a large metropolitan daily often require months of work by one or more reporters. On small papers, especially, you may have trouble freeing yourself for even several days. And reporters' time and computer time both cost money. Editors and publishers must be convinced that the return will be worth the investment before they will approve the project. Before launching your study, you probably should have at least some clues that wrongdoing, injustice or inefficiency exists.

Once you have begun a study, make sure that it is systematic. Either examine all the pertinent records or choose the ones you examine in such a way that they will be truly representative of the rest. Be sure to ask the right questions, and record the information necessary to answer them. A computer can perform complicated analyses quickly, but it cannot analyze facts that have not been input. People who use computers have a term for that problem: GIGO, the acronym for "garbage in, garbage out."

Don't set out on a systematic study without assurances of time and money, a clear idea of what you're looking for and expert technical advice. If the expertise is unavailable at your newspaper, look for it at the nearest college.

FIELD EXPERIMENTS

Reporters may not think of themselves as scientists, but they conduct a great many experiments. A common one is to examine the honesty of auto mechanics by taking a car in perfect condition to several shops and reporting on the "defects" that each finds. Consumer reporters also commonly check weights and measures: Does a "pound" of hamburger meat really weigh a pound? And they test for discrimination by having a black reporter and a white reporter apply for the same insurance policy or mortgage.

Here's a test you can do. Say you want to find out whether landlords in your town discriminate against nonwhite would-be renters. Send out teams of different races to visit the same rental agencies or to respond to the same advertisements. Then compare the results. Did the all-white teams receive more welcoming treatment than the others? A scientist conducting that kind of test would call it a **field experiment**. In all such experiments, researchers take some action in order to observe the effects.

If reporters' field experiments are to be successful, they must follow the same guidelines—and avoid the same pitfalls—that scientists' experiments must. A little scientific terminology is necessary here. It is fairly straightforward, though, and it will be useful if you ever have the opportunity to set up an experiment.

State the Hypothesis and Identify the Variables

Your field experiment must have a **hypothesis**, a statement of what you expect to find. Your hypothesis must be stated clearly and simply. A well-constructed hypothesis will help you focus your attention on the two elements of the experiment: the independent variable and the dependent variable. The **variables**, just as their name implies, are the things that change during the experiment. The *independent variable* is what

ON THE JOB
Computer-Assisted Reporting Has Many Uses

In this chapter you met **Jo Craven McGinty**, whose computer-assisted reporting expertise helped her win a Pulitzer Prize. Now a member of the CAR team at *The New York Times*, she contributed to election coverage by analyzing campaign contributions in House of Representatives races across the country. That was just one way computers are used in reporting.

McGinty says, "Our team is available to work with any section of the newspaper, but I frequently work with Metro — or 'New York,' as the section is now called.

Some stories of mine from this year do not seem overtly CAR related, but all evolved in some way from CAR. The editor with

whom I have been working most closely this year is an old-school journalist who believes that we should see a line of reporting through to the end, no matter where it leads.

"So, for example, a series that my colleague Ralph Blumenthal and I did earlier this year on parking in NYC (a CAR-heavy project) eventually led us to report on, among other things, the conduct of the commissioner of the city's Department of Finance and one particular parking judge."

you think may be a cause. You change it and observe what happens to the *dependent variable*, the effect.

Let's look again at the search for bias in renting. As a social scientist, you would state the hypothesis you're testing: "Landlords in our town discriminate against renters of color." The independent variable is race. The dependent variables are the forms of security, the kinds of identification and the rents charged to each team. You're looking to see how differences in the variable of race affect the dependent variables.

Control the Experiment and Choose Subjects Randomly

There are two other steps you must take to ensure a successful experiment. First, you must **control** the experiment. Every aspect of the experiment must be carefully structured to make sure that any change you observe is caused only by the independent variable you want to test. For example, your teams of would-be "renters" must be as much alike as possible in the financial details they provide, the way they dress, their gender and their age. Otherwise, any differences in the responses by the landlords might be due to something other than race, the variable you are interested in. Also, the applicants should visit the same landlords and speak to the same people. Without careful control of the experiment, you may end up being unable to say whether the results support your hypothesis or not. Then you've got no story.

The other step is called **randomization**, or random selection. In a small town you could run your experiment with every landlord. But in a big city, that would be impossible. So if you want to be reasonably sure that the results of the experiment apply to all the landlords in town, you must choose at random the ones to approach. Randomization allows you to assume that what you select—10 landlords, for instance—is representative of the whole (the total number of landlords in the city).

Choosing anything at random simply means that you employ a method for choosing that gives every person or thing an equal chance of being picked. The procedure for making a random selection is beyond the scope of an introductory reporting text. The Suggested Readings at the end of the chapter include books in which you can find material relating to the concepts introduced here. Much of that material deals with statistics. Many experiments require statistical analysis to ensure that what you have found is significant. Most polls and surveys require some statistical analysis, too. Explanations of the fairly simple math involved also can be found in the books listed in the Suggested Readings.

PUBLIC OPINION POLLS

Surveying is a powerful journalistic tool. It is also a tool that is often misused. We've already seen how overreliance on polls misled many commentators and some candidates in 2012. We've seen Nate Silver's analysis of pollsters' accuracy in that campaign. Despite the problems, many journalists, politicians, businesses and scholars today are using poll results because they show more reliably than anecdotes or ordinary interviews what the public thinks about important issues. Many news organizations now go beyond reporting the findings of national polling firms such as Gallup and Harris Interactive and conduct or commission their own surveys. Several journalism schools—including those at the universities of Alabama, Florida, North Carolina and Missouri—have developed scientific polling operations staffed by faculty and students to serve newspapers and broadcasters. Some pollsters are described as "Democratic" or "Republican." That's really a shorthand way of saying they usually work for candidates of one or the other party. It doesn't mean their results are slanted. An accurate sense of the public mood is at least as important to politicians as to journalists. Of course, if you report the results of one of these one-party pollsters, make sure you explain the connection.

Every day, new poll results illustrate what people think about various topics in the news. And just about every day, journalists confuse readers when they try to interpret the results.

The Margin of Error

The most important thing to keep in mind about polls and surveys is that they are based on samples of a population. Because a survey reflects the responses of a small number of people within a population, every survey has a *margin of error*—the difference between the entire population and the random sample. The results must be presented with the understanding that scientific sampling is not a perfect predictor for the entire population.

Suppose your news organization buys polling services that show that Candidate Hernandez has support from 58 percent of the people surveyed, Candidate Jones has

TIPS

**Poll Information to Share
with Your Audience**

» The identity of the poll's
   sponsor.

» The exact wording of the
   questions asked.

» A definition of the population
   sampled.

» The sample size and re-
   sponse rate.

» The margin of error.

» Which results are based on
   only part of the sample (for
   example, probable voters).

» When the interviews were
   conducted.

» How the interviews were
   conducted—in person, by
   mail, and so on.

—AP Managing Editors Association

support from 32 percent, and 10 percent are undecided. The polling service indicates that the margin of error of the poll is plus or minus 3 percentage points. The margins separating the candidates are well beyond the margin of error, so you can write that Hernandez is leading in the poll.

Candidate	Percentage of Support	Percentage of Support Adjusted for Margin of Error (+/− 3%)
Hernandez	58%	55–61%
Jones	32%	29–35%
Undecided	10%	7–13%

Now suppose Hernandez has 52 percent support and Jones has 48 percent. The difference between them is within the margin of error, less than plus or minus 3 percentage points. Thus you should report that the race is too close to call.

Candidate	Percentage of Support	Percentage of Support Adjusted for Margin of Error (+/− 3%)
Hernandez	52%	49–55%
Jones	48%	45–51%

When polls are conducted properly and reported carefully, they can tell us something we could not know otherwise and perhaps even lead to wiser public policies. But when they are badly done or sloppily reported, polls can be bad news for journalists and readers alike.

The chances are good that sometime in your reporting career you will want to conduct an opinion poll or at least help with one your employer is conducting. The Suggested Readings listed at the end of the chapter will tell you much of what you need to know for that. Even if you never work a poll, you almost certainly will be called on to write about polling results. What follows will help you understand what you are given and will help you make sure your readers understand it, too.

Poll Information to Share

The Associated Press Media Editors prepared a checklist of the information you should share with your audience about any poll on which you are reporting. Several of their points require some explanation:

» **Identity of the sponsor.** The identity of the survey's sponsor is important to you and your readers because it hints at possible bias. Most people would put more trust in a Gallup or Harris poll's report that, for instance, Hernandez is far ahead of Jones in the presidential campaign than they would in a poll sponsored by the Hernandez for President organization.

» **Exact wording of the questions.** The wording of the questions is important because the answers received often depend at least in part on how the questions were asked. (See Chapter 4 on interviewing for more detail.) The answer might well be different, for example, if a pollster asks, "Whom do you favor for president, Jones or Hernandez?" rather than "Wouldn't Jones make a better president than Hernandez?"

» **Population sampled.** In science, the *population* is the total number of people—or documents or milkweed plants or giraffes—in the group being studied. For an opinion survey, the population might be, for example, all registered voters in the state, black males under 25 or female cigarette smokers. To understand what the results of a poll mean, you must know what population was studied. The word *sampled* refers to the procedure in which a small number—or sample—of people is picked at random so as to be representative of the population.

» **Sample size and response rate.** The sample size is important because—all other things being equal—the larger the sample, the more reliable the survey results should be. The response rate is especially important in surveys conducted by mail, in which a low rate of response may invalidate the poll.

» **Margin of error.** The margin of error, or sampling error, of any survey is the allowance that must be made for the possibility that the opinion of the sample may not be exactly the same as the opinion of the whole population. For very large populations, such as the size involved in an election, the margin of error depends mainly on the size of the sample. For instance, all other things being equal, a sample of 384 would have a margin of error of 5 percentage points, and a sample of 1,065 would have a margin of error of 3 percentage points.

As we saw earlier, if a poll with a margin of error of 3 percentage points has Hernandez with 58 percent of the votes and Jones with 32 percent, you can be confident that Hernandez actually has between 55 and 61 percent and Jones actually has between 29 and 35 percent. The laws of probability say that the chances are 19 to 1 that the actual percentages fall within that range. Those odds make the information good enough to publish.

» **Which results are based on part of the sample.** The problem of sampling error helps explain why it is important to know which results may be based on only part of the sample. The smaller that part is, the greater the margin of error. In political

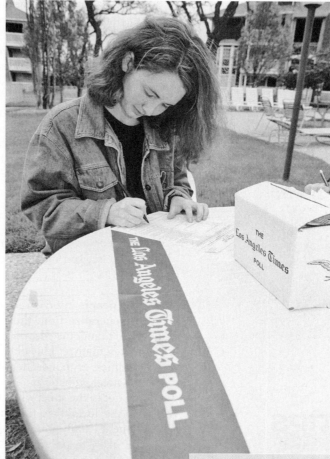

Polling voters on Election Day is an excellent way to forecast election results. However, polls must be conducted properly and interpreted carefully to produce reliable information.

polls, it is always important to know whether the results include responses from all eligible voters or only from individuals *likely* to vote. The opinions of the likely voters are more important than others' opinions.

» **When the interviews were collected.** When the interviews were collected may be of critical importance in interpreting a poll. During campaigns, for example, the candidates themselves and other events may cause voters' preferences to change significantly within a few days. Think of presidential primaries. As candidates join or drop out of the race, support for each of the other candidates changes. A week-old poll may be meaningless if something dramatic happened after it was taken. Candidates have been known to use such outdated results to make themselves appear to be doing better than they really are, or their opponents worse. Be on guard.

Caution in Interpreting Polls

Whether you are helping conduct a survey or only reporting on one produced by someone else, you must exercise caution. Be on guard for the following potential problems:

» **The people interviewed must be selected in a truly random fashion if you want to generalize from their responses to the whole population.** If the selection wasn't randomized, you have no assurance that the interview subjects are really representative. The old-fashioned people-in-the-street interview is practically worthless as an indicator of public opinion for this reason. The man or woman in the street probably differs in important ways from all those men and women who are not in the street when the questioner is.

Also invalid are the questionnaires members of Congress mail to their constituents. Only strongly opinionated—and therefore unrepresentative—people are likely to return them. For the same reason, the "question-of-the-day" feature that some newspapers and broadcast stations ask you to respond to online tells you nothing about the opinions of the great mass of people who do not respond. Even worse are the TV polls that require respondents to call or send a text message to a number to register their opinions. Because there is a charge for such calls, these pseudopolls produce not only misleading results but profits that encourage their use.

» **The closer the results, the harder it is to say anything definitive.** Look again at the example of the Hernandez-Jones campaign. Notice what happens when the poll shows Hernandez with 52 percent and Jones with 48 percent of the vote. Hernandez may or may not be ahead. With the margin of error of 3 percentage points, Hernandez could actually have only 49 percent, and Jones could have 51 percent. All that you could report safely about those results is that the race is too close to call. Many reporters—and pollsters—are simply not careful enough when the outcome is unclear.

TIPS

Cautions About Using Poll Data

» The people interviewed must be selected in a truly random fashion if you want to generalize from their responses to the whole population.

» The closer the results, the harder it is to say anything definitive.

» Beware of polls that claim to measure opinion on sensitive, complicated issues.

"*Next question: I believe that life is a constant striving for balance, requiring frequent tradeoffs between morality and necessity, within a cyclic pattern of joy and sadness, forging a trail of bittersweet memories until one slips, inevitably, into the jaws of death. Agree or disagree?*"

Some pollsters' questions seem designed to elicit a desired response.

» **Beware of polls that claim to measure opinion on sensitive, complicated issues.** Many questions of morality, or on social issues such as race relations, do not lend themselves to simple answers. Opinions on such matters can be measured, but only by highly skilled researchers using carefully designed questions. Anything less can be dangerously oversimplified and highly misleading.

Polling—like field experiments, systematic analysis and participant observation—can help you as a reporter solve problems you could not handle as well with other techniques. But these are only tools. How effectively they are used—or how clumsily they are misused—depends on you.

SUGGESTED READINGS

Campbell, Donald, and Julian Stanley. *Experimental and Quasi-Experimental Designs for Research*. Skokie, Ill.: Rand McNally, 1966. This classic guide to field experimentation is also useful in providing a better understanding of scientific research.

Demers, David Pearce, and Suzanne Nichols. *Precision Journalism: A Practical Guide*. Newbury Park, Calif.: Sage, 1987. A primer for students and journalists, this book is simply written and includes examples.

Houston, Brant. *Computer-Assisted Reporting: A Practical Guide*. 3rd ed. New York: Bedford/St. Martin's, 2004. Houston has written a practical introduction to data analysis and field reporting.

McCombs, Maxwell, Donald L. Shaw, and David Grey. *Handbook of Reporting Methods*. Boston: Houghton Mifflin, 1976. The authors offer examples of real-life uses of social science methods in journalism but do not provide enough on statistics to serve as a guide in employing those methods.

Meyer, Philip. *Precision Journalism*. 4th ed. Lanham, Md.: Rowman and Littlefield, 2002. This detailed introduction to surveying, conducting field experiments and using statistics to analyze the results was written by a reporter who pioneered the use of these methods in journalism. A theoretical justification of the techniques is included.

Seltzer, Richard A. *Mistakes That Social Scientists Make: Error and Redemption in the Research Process*. New York: St. Martin's Press, 1996. Seltzer has written a useful book about the kinds of errors often made by social scientists during their research.

Silver, Nate. *The Signal and the Noise*. New York: Penguin Press, 2012. The creator of the FiveThirtyEight blog explains how to evaluate predictions in fields ranging from politics to the weather.

SUGGESTED WEBSITES

www.aejmc.org
The Association for Education in Journalism and Mass Communication is a professional organization for journalism teachers and researchers. For a journalist or journalism student, perhaps the most useful feature of this site is accessibility to the organization's research publications. Many of the reports in those publications use and explain the techniques discussed in this chapter.

www.gallup.com
The Gallup organization is one of the most reputable of the national polling companies. This site contains the results of a wide variety of public polls and explains their methodology.

www.ire.org/nicar
At the website of the National Institute for Computer-Assisted Reporting, you'll find many stories reported using CAR techniques, plus tips for doing this kind of reporting yourself.

www.journalistsresource.org
At this site, from the Joan Shorenstein Center at Harvard, you'll find an array of authoritative explanations of research. One entry, for example, translates the language of statistics into understandable English.

www.people-press.org
This is the site of the Pew Research Center for the People and the Press. Here you'll find not only the results of polls but also explanations of their methodology and limitations.

EXERCISES

1. **Team project.** Your instructor will divide your class into teams of four or five. Working as a team, design a field experiment: Brainstorm ideas for an experiment that could yield results for news stories. Develop and state a hypothesis, identify the dependent and independent variables, and describe the controls that you would use. Write up your plan, and present your experiment idea to the class for discussion.

2. As a class, choose from among the experiments the teams designed in exercise 1. Assign tasks, and carry out the chosen field experiment. Pool all the results, and write individual stories using the field experiment data.

3. **Journalism blog.** In a blog post, consider the social science tools described in this chapter. Which seem to be the most practical for working journalists? Which have you seen in action? Which tool would you be most likely to pick up? Give suggestions for how you might use the tool.

4. Go to the Pew website (www.people-press.org), choose any of the polls that are reported and measure it against the elements of sound polling discussed in the chapter. If you do this exercise in class, you can discuss your findings with classmates.

5. Go to www.ire.org or www.ire.org/nicar, and find at least one story that uses one or more of the social science techniques discussed in this chapter. Analyze the reporting and writing. How do the stories you found differ from stories that rely on interviewing? What possible sources of practical or ethical problems can you identify?

6. As a class, transform yourselves into survey researchers. Design a simple survey using the technique described by Philip Meyer in *Precision Journalism* (see the Suggested Readings). Then carry out the survey, and report your results.

19

Investigative Reporting

HERE'S HOW Mark Horvit, executive director of the national organization Investigative Reporters and Editors, sees the current state of investigative reporting:

> I'm not saying everything is better now. It isn't.
> I'm not saying the cutting and the furloughs are over. They're not.
> I'm not saying we don't have a lot more work to do. We do.
> But there's no point in dwelling on what we've lost. Our time is much better spent looking at those who are working to rebuild, and how we're refocusing on journalism that really matters. There are plenty of examples out there.

The same issue of *The IRE Journal* that carried Horvit's summary included a few of those relevant examples—projects that won 2012 IRE awards:

» KQED, San Francisco's public television station, won in the "Multiplatform" category for a 19-month investigation in which reporters dug through 30,000 documents, created online maps and databases and visited schools throughout California to show that officials' failures have left thousands of students in schools vulnerable to earthquake collapses. The story was published and broadcast across the state. It led to new safety standards and increased inspections.

» Two reporters for the Sarasota, Fla., *Herald-Tribune* won in the "Print/Online" category for their analysis of databases and shoe-leather reporting that found hundreds of Florida police officers with questionable backgrounds, including convictions for crimes. The state's governor ordered an official investigation.

» NPR reporters won in the "Radio" category for uncovering a pattern of abuse and neglect of mental health patients in psychiatric hospitals. The series led to stronger legislation.

Investigative reporting is alive and well in America.

INVESTIGATIVE REPORTING: AN AMERICAN TRADITION

Investigative reporting has a rich history in American journalism. The fiercely partisan editors of the Revolutionary era dug for facts as well as the mud they hurled at

In this chapter you will learn:

1. How the tradition of investigative reporting grew.

2. What the process of investigative reporting is.

3. How to find and use human and written sources.

4. How new technology helps reporters pursue traditional goals.

VideoCentral

**bedfordstmartins.com
/newsreporting**

Watch **"Investigative
Reporting Resources."**

» How does investigative
reporting differ from the
usual reporting journalists
do?

» What different challenges
do government, nonprofit
and commercial sources
pose for investigative
reporting?

their opponents. In the early 20th century, investigative reporting flowered with the "muckrakers," a title bestowed angrily by Theodore Roosevelt and worn proudly by journalists. Lincoln Steffens explored the undersides of American cities, one by one, laying bare the corrupt combinations of businessmen and politicians that ran them. Ida Tarbell exposed the economic stranglehold of the oil monopoly. And Theodore Dreiser, Upton Sinclair and Frank Norris revealed the horrors of working life in factories and meatpacking plants.

Just as the work of the muckrakers appeared in magazines, nonfiction books and even novels, the work of today's investigative reporters is produced beyond traditional newsrooms. The most prominent example of 21st-century muckraking is a new nonprofit called ProPublica. Funded initially by foundation grants and led by a former editor of *The Wall Street Journal*, ProPublica's staff of experienced journalists tackles major investigations of national significance, often in partnership with traditional news organizations.

As economic pressures force staff cuts in those traditional newsrooms, other investigative innovations are emerging at local and regional levels, too. For example, reporter Andy Hall, who decided to leave his newspaper when the staff was reduced, has launched the Wisconsin Center for Investigative Journalism (WisconsinWatch .org), a nonprofit cooperative that seeks to pick up where diminished newsrooms are

Ida Tarbell, one of the original muckrakers, helped set the pattern for investigative reporting with her exposé of Standard Oil.

The Social Media Complication

"Twitter is no longer a toy," Tom Lee of the Sunlight Foundation wrote in *The IRE Journal*. Indeed, it has become the medium of choice for millions, a valuable source of tips for reporters, and a quick and easy way to keep in touch with colleagues, audience members and human sources. It can, however, also be a trap.

For one thing, the handle that identifies a Twitter user may or may not have any relationship to that person's true identity. It's easy to pretend to be someone you're not on Twitter. So use tweets as story material with great caution.

A different problem arises from the tweets sent by reporters themselves. It's deceptively easy in a shorthand conversation to say something that can come back to haunt you. Even the most experienced professionals have learned this to their sorrow. In 2012, for example, the Jerusalem bureau chief for *The New York Times* stirred controversy with comments on social media that appeared to reveal bias or that went beyond provable facts. She posted a note on Facebook, for example, that described Palestinians as "ho-hum" about deaths in the Gaza uprising. Israelis, Palestinians and media critics all pounced. The *Times* ombudsman devoted a column to the problem and the proposed solution: An editor was assigned to go over the bureau chief's social media musings before she posted them.

So take advantage of social media, but don't get taken by them.

leaving off. Another pair of veteran journalists have formed the New England Center for Investigative Reporting (necir-bu.org), another nonprofit funded by startup grants and staffed by experienced reporters. Similar efforts are under way across the country.

These professional heirs of the original muckrakers bring to their work the same commitment to exposure and reform. They use refinements of many of the same techniques: in-depth interviews, personal observation, document analyses. But modern muckrakers have a powerful tool their predecessors didn't dream of. The computer allows today's reporters to compile and analyze masses of data, to perform complicated statistical tests and to create charts and graphs to enhance understanding. This tool, in turn, requires of reporters numeracy as well as literacy. It requires the addition of another set of skills to every serious journalist's repertoire.

Computer-assisted reporting gives young reporters the opportunity to be admitted to the major league of journalism. If you develop your computer-research skills and acquire the techniques taught in this chapter, you will be equipped for the 21st century.

THE PROCESS

Most investigations start with a hunch or a tip that something or someone deserves a close look. If a preliminary search bears out that expectation, a serious investigation begins. When enough information has been uncovered to prove or modify the reporter's initial hunch, it's time to analyze, organize and write the story.

Beginning the Investigation

No good reporter sets out on an investigation unless there is some basis for suspicion. That basis may be a grand jury report that leaves something untold or a tip that some public official is on the take. It may be a sudden upsurge in drug overdoses, or it may be long-festering problems in the schools. If you don't have some idea of what to look for, an investigation is too likely to turn into a wild-goose chase.

Acting on the tip or suspicion, together with whatever background material you have, you form a hypothesis. Reporters hardly ever use that term, but it is a useful one because it shows the similarity between the processes of investigative reporting and scientific investigation (see Chapter 18). In both, the hypothesis is the statement of what you think is true. Your informal hypothesis might be "The mayor is a crook" or "The school system is being run incompetently." It is a good idea to clearly state your hypothesis when you begin your investigation. By doing so, you focus on the heart of the problem and lessen the possibility of any misunderstanding with your editor or other reporters who may be working with you.

Once the hypothesis is stated, the reporter—like the scientist—sets out to support it or show that it is not supportable. You should be open to the possibility that your first assumption was wrong. Reporters—like scientists—are not advocates. They are seekers of truth. No good reporter ignores or downplays evidence just because it contradicts his or her assumptions. In journalism, as in science, the truth about a situation is often sharply different from what is expected. Open-mindedness is an essential quality of a good investigative reporter. Remember, too, that you may have a good story even if your hypothesis is not supported.

Carrying Out the Investigation

The actual investigative work usually proceeds in two stages. The first is what Robert W. Greene, a legendary reporter and Pulitzer Prize–winning editor for *Newsday*, named the **sniff**. After you form a hypothesis, you nose around in search of a trail worth following. If you find one, the second stage, serious investigation, begins.

Preliminary checking should take no more than a day or two. Its purpose is not to prove the hypothesis but to determine the chances of proving it. You make that effort by talking with the most promising source or sources, skimming available records and consulting knowledgeable people in your newsroom. The two questions you are trying to answer at this stage are these: (1) Is there a story here? and (2) Am I going to be able to get it? If the answer to either question is no, there is little point in pursuing the investigation.

When the answer to both questions is yes, the real work begins. It begins with organization. Your hypothesis tells you where you want to go. Now you must figure out how to get there. Careful organization keeps you on the right track and prevents you from overlooking anything important as you go. Many reporters take a kind of perverse pride in their illegible notebooks and cluttered desks. As an investigative reporter, you may have a messy desk, but you should arrange your files of information clearly and coherently. Begin organizing by asking yourself these questions:

» Who are my most promising sources? Who is likely to give me trouble? Whom should I go to first? Second? Last?
» What records do I need? Where are they? Which are public? How can I get to the ones that are not readily accessible?
» What is the most I can hope to prove? What is the least that will still yield a story?
» How long should the investigation take?

Then draw up a plan of action, such as the one shown in Figure 19.1. Experienced reporters often do this mentally. But when you are a beginner, it's a good idea to write out a plan and go over it with your editor. The editor may spot some holes in your planning or have something to add. And an editor is more likely to give you enough time if he or she has a clear idea of what has to be done.

Allowing flexibility for the unexpected twists that most investigations take, carry out your plan. During your first round of interviews, keep asking who else you should talk to. While you are checking records, look for references to other files or other people.

Be methodical. Many investigative reporters spend an hour or so at the end of every day adding up the score, going through their notes and searching their memories to analyze what they have learned and what they need next. Some develop elaborate, cross-indexed files of names, organizations and incidents. Others are less formal. Nearly all, however, use a code to disguise the names of confidential sources so that those sources will remain secret even if the files are subpoenaed. The method you use isn't important as long as you understand it. What is vitally important is that you have a method and use it consistently. If you fail to keep careful track of where you're going, you may go in the wrong direction, or in circles.

Getting It Right

The importance of accuracy in investigative reporting cannot be overstated. It is the essential element in good journalism of any kind. But in investigative reporting especially, inaccuracy leads to embarrassment, to ruined reputations and sometimes to lawsuits. The reputations ruined are often those of the careless reporter and the newspaper. Most investigative stories have the effect of accusing somebody of wrongdoing or incompetence. Even if the subject is a public official whose chances of suing successfully for libel are slim (see Chapter 21), fairness and decency require that you be sure of your facts before you put them in print.

Many experienced investigators require verification from two independent sources before they include an allegation in a story. That is a good rule to follow. People make mistakes. They lie. Their memories fail. Documents can be misleading or confusing. Check and double-check. There is no good excuse for an error.

Writing the Story

Most investigative stories require consultation with the newspaper's lawyer before publication. As a reporter, you will have little or nothing to say about the choice of

2/26/14   Plan for Mayor Jane Jones story

Hypothesis: Mayor Jones accepted improper campaign contributions from Top Construction as a council member, and as mayor she later awarded the company a contract to build a new high school.

Initial source: During the course of a conversation, XX casually suggested info about the campaign contribution.

Draft: Due 3/7.

Questions
--How much of this hypothesis can I prove?
--Is XX trustworthy? What does XX have to gain? Will XX go on the record?
--Will documents support the hypothesis? What records are important?
--What other people should I interview—on both sides?
--Will I have at least two credible sources for each fact?
--How can I make sure the story is relevant, useful and interesting?
--Is this one story or a series?
--What extras (documents, audio, video) can I get for the online version?

Plan
Request and review relevant documents:
--Any docs from XX.
--Campaign contribution records; get Stacy to help w/ this.
--Contract bids for HS; ask Manuel how to compare.

Interview major people:
--XX, to follow up on initial info.
--Schools chancellor about bids.
--Mayor's campaign manager (Roberts?) about contributions.
--Pres. of Top Construction (Smythe?) about contributions.
--Mayor.

Write outline:
--What's the lead?
--Story structure: inverted pyramid?
--Enough facts? details? anecdotes? quotes?
--Don't forget those online elements.

Write draft:
--Is the story complete? easy to follow? convincing? compelling?

Next steps:
--Editor? legal department?
--Need more facts? details?
--Revise and finalize draft?
--With editors, decide what to post online and when.

FIGURE 19.1

A plan of action lists the hypothesis and the steps the journalist will take to gather information and draft a story.

your paper's lawyer. That lawyer, though, will be an important part of your investigative career. The lawyer will advise on what you can print safely and what you cannot. Most editors heed their lawyers' advice. If you are lucky, your paper's lawyer will understand and sympathize with good, aggressive journalism. If he or she does not, you may find yourself forced to argue for your story. You will be better equipped for such an argument—few reporters go through a career without several—if you understand at least the basics of the laws of libel and privacy. Chapter 21 outlines those laws, and several good books on law for journalists are listed in the Suggested Readings at the end of that chapter.

> Go to the scene of the disaster and don't let the breaking story stop you from thinking ahead. There, you will find almost all of the sources to tell you what went wrong in responding to the disaster. Though you will have to get your proof through public-record requests, you will get your leads at the scene.
>
> —James Grimaldi, *The Wall Street Journal*

The last step before your investigation goes public is the writing and rewriting of the story. After days or weeks of intense reporting effort, the actual writing strikes some investigative reporters as a chore—necessary but unimportant. That attitude is disastrous. The best reporting in the world is wasted unless it is read. Your hard-won exposé or painstaking analysis will disappear without a trace unless your writing attracts readers and maintains their interest. Most reporters and newspapers that are serious about investigative reporting recognize this. They stress good writing almost as much as solid reporting.

Selecting an Effective Story Structure and Lead

How do you write the results of a complicated investigation? The general rule is, as simply as you can. One approach is to use a **hard lead** (an inverted pyramid lead that reports newly discovered facts), displaying your key findings in the first few paragraphs. Another option is to adopt one of the alternative approaches to storytelling explained in Chapter 11.

Mei-ling Hopgood helped report and write a *Dayton Daily News* investigation of the dangers of the Peace Corps. Here's how that series began:

AGUA FRIA, El Salvador—On a clear Christmas night near a moonlit stretch of Pacific beach, a man with a pistol came from the darkness and forced Diana Gilmour to watch two of her fellow Peace Corps volunteers being gang-raped while a male volunteer was pinned helpless on the ground.

One of the men—his breath reeking of alcohol—raped Gilmour, too. Then the attackers herded the volunteers at gunpoint to a field of high grass where they feared they would be executed.

"I was constantly waiting to hear a shot in the dark," Gilmour said.

Suddenly another volunteer approached with a flashlight, and the attackers fled.

The best stories are usually about people, and this one is no exception. The drama of one case introduces readers to the bigger story. A few paragraphs later, Hopgood and colleague Russell Carollo show that big picture:

Records from a never-before-released computer database show that reported assault cases involving Peace Corps volunteers increased 125 percent from 1991 to 2002, while the number of volunteers increased by 29 percent, according to the Peace Corps. Last year, the number of assaults and robberies averaged one every 23 hours.

The *Dayton Daily News* spent 20 months examining thousands of records on assaults on Peace Corps volunteers occurring around the world during the past four decades.

Moving from the particular to the general is both a logical progression and an effective way to show readers both the humanity and the full scope of the investigation.

Including Proof of the Story's Credibility

Notice that the last paragraph quoted above also lets readers know something about how the information was developed. That's important, too, if you want to be believed. In this case, the paper's editor also wrote a column explaining both the motivation and the methods of the investigation. That's another good idea. You owe it to your audience to be as open as possible about not only what you know but how you know it. In this era of diminished credibility, it's especially important to do everything you can to be honest and open about your work.

Striving for Clear, Simple Explanations

Writing an investigative story so that it will be read takes the same attention to organization and to detail as does any good writing. Here are a few tips that apply to all types of writing but especially to investigative stories:

» **Get people into the story.** Any investigation worth doing involves people in some way. Make them come alive with descriptive detail, the kind we were given in the Peace Corps story.

» **Keep it simple.** Look for ways to clarify and explain complicated situations. When you have a mass of information, consider spreading it over more than one story—in a series or in a main story with a sidebar. Think about how charts, graphs or lists can be used to present key facts clearly. Don't try to print everything you know, just enough to support your conclusions. More than that is too much.

» **Tell the reader what your research means.** A great temptation in investigative reporting is to lay out the facts and let the reader draw the conclusions. That is unfair to you and your reader. Lay out the facts, of course, but tell the reader what they add up to. A reporter who had spent weeks investigating the deplorable conditions in his state's juvenile corrections facilities wrote this lead: "Florida treats her delinquent children as if she hated them." Then he went on to show the reality that led to that summary. If the facts are there, drawing the obvious conclusions is not editorializing. It is good and helpful writing.

» **Organize before you write.** Careful organization is as important in writing the investigative story as it is in reporting it. The job will be easier if you have been organized all along. When you are ready to write, examine your notes again.

ON THE JOB

A TV Reporter Sets the Investigative Pace

John Ferrugia has done it all. He has been a CBS correspondent in Washington. He has traveled the world on reporting assignments. For a decade now, he has been an investigative reporter leading a team of five for station KMGH-TV in Denver. Perhaps his most important investigation uncovered widespread and deliberately concealed sexual abuse at the U.S. Air Force Academy. That led to firings, demotions and reforms throughout the military.

Through it all, Ferrugia has applied the lessons he learned in journalism school: "I learned that hard work, research and digging can pay off with a significant story." Investigative reporting, he says, "is really a way of thinking. You've got to see the broader issues."

You've also got to have the tools. This is his advice for anyone who wants to follow in his footsteps:

Learn absolutely as much as you can about all aspects of new and traditional media.

Writing is essential in whatever path you choose, and good writing comes from reading the best writers and columnists. Learn how to shoot video and edit video and audio on your laptop.

Understand how to use databases, social media and the Web to research stories. Learn how to organize information in spreadsheets for easy access and meshing databases.

But always remember, even with all the new media and computer-assisted reporting, there is no substitute for personal contact with sources. As a journalist, you are always selling your own credibility and integrity to potential sources, and the biggest sales are always made in person.

Make an outline. Pick out your best quotes and anecdotes. Some reporters, if they are writing more than one story, separate their material into individual folders, one for each story. However you do it, know what you are going to say before you start to write.

» **Suggest solutions.** Polls have shown that readers prefer investigative stories that show how to correct the problems described in the stories. Many of today's best newspapers are satisfying readers' demands by going beyond exposure in search of solutions. Are new laws needed? Better enforcement of present laws? More resources? Better training? Remember that the early-20th-century progressive movement (of which the original muckrakers were a part) produced reforms, not just good stories.

» **Use the Web to support your story.** Readers are skeptical. They want to be shown, not just told. So use the expanded capacity of your organization's website to post supporting documents, photographs, audio or transcripts of key interviews. And include any responses or defenses offered by the people or institution you're examining. Fairness is essential.

Think of writing as the climax of a process that begins with a hypothesis, tests that hypothesis through careful investigation, checks and double-checks every fact, and satisfies the concerns of newspaper editors and lawyers. Every step in that process is vital to the success of any investigative story.

THE SOURCES

Investigative reporters—like other reporters—get their information from people or documents. The perfect source is a person who has the pertinent documents and is eager to tell you what those documents mean. Don't count on finding the perfect source. Instead, expect to piece together the information you need from a variety of people and records. Some people will not be at all eager to talk to you, and some of the records will be difficult to obtain—and, if you do gain access to them, difficult to understand. Let's consider human sources first.

Human Sources

Suppose you get a tip that the mayor received campaign contributions under the table from the engineering firm that just got a big city contract. Who might talk?

» **Enemies.** When you are trying to find out anything bad about a person, his or her enemies are usually the best sources. More often than not, the enemies of a prominent person will have made it their business to find out as much as possible about that person's misdeeds and shortcomings. Frequently, they are happy to share what they know with a friendly reporter.

» **Friends.** Friends are sometimes nearly as revealing as enemies. In trying to explain and defend their friend's actions, they may tell you more than you knew before. Occasionally, you may find that someone your subject regards as a friend is not much of a friend after all.

» **Losers.** Like enemies, losers often carry a grudge. Seek out the loser in the last election, the losing contender for the contract, the loser in a power struggle. Bad losers make good sources.

» **Victims.** If you are investigating a failing school system, talk with students and their parents. If your story is about nursing home abuses, talk with patients and their relatives. The honest and hardworking employees caught in a corrupt or incompetent system are victims, too. They can give you specific examples and anecdotes. Their case histories can help you write the story. Be wary, though. One thing enemies, losers and victims have in common is that they have an ax to grind about your subject. Confirm every allegation they make.

» **Experts.** Early in many investigations, there may be a great deal that you don't understand. You may need someone to explain how the campaign finance laws could be circumvented, someone to interpret a contract, someone to decipher a set of bid specifications. Lawyers, accountants, engineers or professors can help you understand technical jargon or complicated transactions. If they refuse to comment on your specific case, fit the facts you have into a hypothetical situation.

» **Police.** Investigative reporters and law enforcement agents often work the same territory. If you are wise, you will make friends with carefully selected agents. They can—and frequently will—be of great help. Their files may not be gold mines, but they have investigative tools and contacts you lack. When they get to

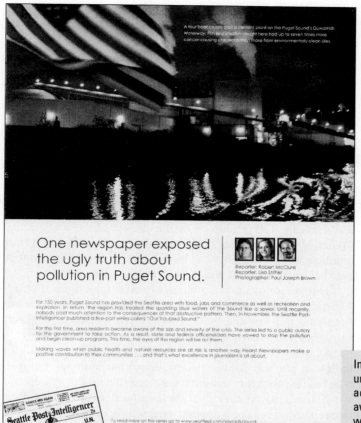

One newspaper exposed the ugly truth about pollution in Puget Sound.

Reporter: Robert McClure
Reporter: Lisa Stiffler
Photographer: Paul Joseph Brown

For 150 years, Puget Sound has provided the Seattle area with food, jobs and commerce as well as recreation and inspiration. In return, the region has treated the sparkling blue waters of the Sound like a sewer. Until recently, nobody paid much attention to the consequences of that destructive pattern. Then, in November, the Seattle Post-Intelligencer published a five-part series called "Our Troubled Sound."

For the first time, area residents became aware of the size and severity of the crisis. The series led to a public outcry for the government to take action. As a result, state and federal officeholders have vowed to stop the pollution and begin clean-up programs. This time, the eyes of the region will be on them.

Making waves when public health and natural resources are at risk is another way Hearst Newspapers make a positive contribution to their communities . . . and that's what excellence in journalism is all about.

To read more on this series go to www.seattlepi.com/specials/sound

Hearst Newspapers

> Investigative reporters have uncovered scandals and illegal activity and have raised public awareness of issues such as water pollution.

know and trust you, they will share. Most police like seeing their own and their organizations' names in the paper. They know, too, that you can do some things they cannot. You need less proof to print that the mayor is a crook than it may take to convince a jury. Most police investigators want to corner wrongdoers any way they can. You can use that attitude to your advantage.

» **People in trouble.** Police use this source and so can you, although you cannot promise immunity or a lesser charge, as prosecutors can. A classic case is the Watergate affair, in which members of President Richard Nixon's administration recruited five men to break into the headquarters of the Democratic National Committee to wiretap phones illegally. Once the Nixon administration started to unravel, officials trying to save their careers and images began falling all over one another to give their self-serving versions of events. People will react similarly in lesser cases.

As an investigative reporter, you cultivate sources in the same ways a reporter on a beat does. You just do it more quickly. One excellent tactic is to play on their self-interest. Losers and enemies want to get the so-and-so, and thus you have a common aim. (But don't go overboard. Your words could come back to haunt you.) Friends want their buddy's side of the story to be explained. So do you. If you keep in mind that no matter how corrupt your subject may be, he or she is still a human being, it may be easier to deal sympathetically with that person's friends. That attitude may also help ensure that you treat the subject fairly.

Experts just want to explain the problem as you present it. And you just want to understand. People in trouble want sympathy and some assurance that they still merit respect. No reporter should have trouble conveying either attitude.

Another way to win and keep sources is to protect them. Occasionally a reporter faces jail unless he or she reveals a source. Even jail is not too great a price to pay to keep a promise of confidentiality. More often, the threats to confidentiality are less dramatic. Other sources, or the subject of the investigation, may casually ask, "Where'd you hear that?" Other reporters, over coffee or a beer, may ask the same question. Hold your tongue. The only person to whom a confidential source should ever be revealed is your editor.

Human sources pose problems as well as solve them. To hurt an enemy or protect a friend, to make themselves look better or someone else look worse—and sometimes simply for fun—people lie to reporters. No reporter is safe, and no source is above suspicion. They may use you, too, just as you are using them. The only reason most people involved on any side of a suspicious situation will talk about it is to enhance their own position. That is neither illegal nor immoral, but it can trip up a reporter who fails to take every self-serving statement with the appropriate grain of salt.

Sources may change their stories as well. People forget. Recollections and situations change. Pressure is applied. Fear or love or ambition or greed intrudes. A source may deny tomorrow—or in court—what he or she told you today.

Finally, sources will seldom want to be identified. Even the enemies of a powerful person are often reluctant to see their names attached to their criticisms in print. Even friends may be reluctant to be identified. Experts, while willing to provide background information, often cite their codes of ethics when you ask them to go on the record. Stories without identifiable sources have less credibility with readers, with editors and even with colleagues.

Written Sources

Fortunately, not all sources are human. Records and documents neither lie nor change their stories, they have no axes to grind at your expense and they can be identified in print. Many useful documents are public records, available to you or any other citizen on request. Others are nonpublic but still may be available through your human sources.

Remember that most, if not all, of the relevant documents—especially the public records kept by government agencies—are likely to be accessible online. Google and other search engines shouldn't be your only tools, but they are powerful ones. Use them early and often. And don't overlook the revelations, some of them unintentional, that turn up on Web-based networking sites like LinkedIn and Facebook.

Public Records

As the examples earlier show, a great deal can be learned about individuals and organizations through records that are available for the asking, if you know where to ask. Let's take a look at some of the most valuable public records and where they can be found. Nearly all, in nearly all jurisdictions, are available online today.

» **Property records.** Many investigations center on land—who owns it, who buys it, how it is zoned, how it is taxed. You can find out all that information and more from public records. Your county recorder's office (or its equivalent) has on file the ownership of every piece of land in the county as well as the history of past owners. In most offices, the files are cross-indexed so you can find the owner of the land if you know its location, or the location and size of the property if you know the owner. Those files also will tell you who holds a mortgage on the land. The city or county tax assessor's office has on file the assessed valuation of the land, which is the basis for property taxes. Either the assessor or the local zoning agency can tell you for what use the property is zoned. All requests for rezoning are public information, too.

» **Corporation records.** Every corporation must file a document showing the officers and principal agent of the company. This document must be filed with the state in which the corporation is formed and with every state in which it does business. The officers listed may be only "dummies"—stand-ins for the real owners—but you can find out at least who the stand-ins are. But that is only the beginning.

Publicly held corporations must file annual reports with the Securities and Exchange Commission in Washington. The reports list officers, major stockholders, financial statements and business dealings with other companies owned by the corporation. Nonprofit corporations—such as foundations and charities—must file with the Internal Revenue Service an even more revealing statement, Form 990, showing how much money came in and where it went. Similar statements must be filed with the attorneys general of many states.

Corporations often are regulated by state or federal agencies as well. They file regular reports with the regulating agency. Insurance companies, for instance, are regulated by state insurance commissioners. Nursing homes are regulated by various state agencies. Broadcasters are overseen by the Federal Communications Commission, truckers by the Interstate Commerce Commission. Labor unions must file with the U.S. Department of Labor detailed statements called *5500 forms* showing assets, officers' salaries, loans and other financial information.

Once you have corporation records, you must interpret them. Your public library has books that tell you how. Your news organization's own business experts may be willing to help.

» **Court records.** Few people active in politics or business go through life without becoming involved in court actions of some sort. Check the offices of the state and federal court clerks for records of lawsuits. The written arguments, sworn statements and answers to questions (*interrogatories*) may contain valuable details or provide leads to follow. Has your target been divorced? Legal struggles over assets can be revealing. Probate court files of your subject's deceased associates may tell you something you need to know.

» **Campaign and conflict-of-interest reports.** Federal—and most state—campaign laws now require political candidates to disclose, during and after each campaign, lists of who gave what to whom. Those filings can yield stories on who is supporting the candidates. They also can be used later for comparing who gets what from which officeholder. Many states require officeholders to file statements of their business and stock holdings. These can be checked for possible conflicts of interest or used as background for profile stories.

» **Loan records.** Commercial lenders usually file statements showing property that has been used as security for loans. Known as *Uniform Commercial Code filings*, these can be found in the offices of state secretaries of state and sometimes in local recorders' offices.

» **Minutes and transcripts.** Most elected and appointed governing bodies, ranging from local planning and zoning commissions to the U.S. Congress, are required by law to keep minutes or transcripts of their meetings.

The states and the federal government have laws designed to ensure access to public records. Many of these laws—including the federal **Freedom of Information Act**, which was passed to improve access to government records—have gaping loopholes and time-consuming review procedures. Still, they have been and can be useful tools when all else fails. Learn the details of the law in your state. You can get information on access laws and their interpretations by contacting the Freedom of Information Center at the University of Missouri, 127 Neff Annex, Columbia, MO 65211.

Nonpublic Records

Nonpublic records are more difficult, but often not impossible, to obtain. To get them, you must know that they exist, where they are and how to gain access. Finding out about those things requires good human sources. You should know about a few of the most valuable nonpublic records:

» **Investigative files.** The investigative files of law enforcement agencies can be rich in information. You are likely to see them only if you have a good source in a particular agency or one affiliated with it. If you do obtain such files, treat them cautiously. They will be full of unsubstantiated allegations, rumor and misinformation. Be wary of accepting as fact anything you have not confirmed yourself.

» **Past arrests and convictions.** Records of past arrests and convictions increasingly are being removed from public scrutiny. Usually these are easier than investigative files to obtain from a friendly police or prosecuting official. And usually they are more trustworthy than raw investigative files.

» **Bank records.** Bank records would be helpful in many investigations, but they are among the most difficult types of records to get. Bankers are trained to keep secrets. The government agencies that regulate banks are secretive as well. A friend in a bank is an investigative reporter's friend indeed.

» **Income tax records.** Except for those made public by officeholders, income tax records are guarded carefully by their custodians. Leaks are rare.

» **Credit checks.** Sometimes you can get otherwise unavailable information on a target's financial situation by arranging through your newspaper's business office for a credit check. Credit reports may reveal outstanding debts, a big bank account, major assets and business affiliations. Use that information with care. It is unofficial, and companies that provide it intend it to be confidential.

Problems with Written Sources

Even when you can obtain them, records and other written sources present problems. They are usually dull. Records give you names and numbers, not anecdotes or sparkling quotes. They are bare bones, not flesh and blood.

Documents can be misleading and confusing. Many highly skilled lawyers and accountants spend careers interpreting the kinds of records you may find yourself pondering without their training. Misinterpreting a document is no less serious an error than misquoting a person. And it's easier to do.

Documents usually describe without explaining. You need to know the "why" of a land transaction or a loan. Records tell you only the "what."

Most investigative reporters use both human and documentary sources. People can explain what documents cannot. Documents prove what good quotes cannot. You need people to lead you to documents and people to interpret what the documents mean. And you need documents to substantiate what people tell you. The best investigative stories combine both types of sources.

NEW TOOLS, TRADITIONAL GOALS

As you've seen, the computer is the most important new tool of investigative reporting. Once you know how to use it, the computer allows you to obtain, analyze and present information in ways that would have been impossible 20 years ago, let alone in the era of the original muckrakers. But useful as it is, the computer is only a tool. Many modern investigative reporters are guided by goals that their predecessors of a century ago would easily recognize.

Today's investigators, like the original muckrakers, are not satisfied with uncovering individual instances of wrongdoing. They look at organizations as a whole, at entire systems. They seek not only to expose but to explain. In many cases, they also seek to change the problems and abuses they reveal. Many, perhaps most, investigative reporters think of themselves as more than chroniclers of fact or analysts. They also see themselves as reformers. This, too, was true of the muckrakers.

The drive to expose abuses is something the public welcomes and expects from journalists. Studies have shown that the consumers of journalism support investigative reporting when it leads to reforms. There's no conflict between investigative reporting and the journalistic standard of objectivity, either. You'll remember from Chapter 1 that objectivity doesn't have to mean neutrality. In journalism, as in science, objectivity is the method of searching for the truth. Just as scientists are not expected to be neutral between disease and cure, journalists don't have to be neutral between good and evil. What objectivity requires of both scientists and journalists is honest, open-minded investigation and truthful reporting of the results of that investigation.

SUGGESTED READINGS

Houston, Brant. *Computer-Assisted Reporting: A Practical Guide.* 3rd ed. New York: Bedford/St. Martin's, 2003. Houston, the executive director of Investigative Reporters and Editors, has written an invaluable how-to guide for using the newest and most powerful reporting tool.

Houston, Brant, and Investigative Reporters and Editors. *The Investigative Reporters' Handbook: A Guide to Documents, Databases and Techniques.* 5th ed. New York: Bedford/St.

Martin's, 2009. This handbook tells you how to get and how to use the most important records and documents.

The IRE Journal. Publication of Investigative Reporters and Editors Inc., 138 Neff Annex, Missouri School of Journalism, University of Missouri, Columbia, MO 65211. Every issue has articles on investigations, guides to sources and documents, and a roundup of legal developments. Edited transcripts of IRE conferences are also available.

SUGGESTED WEBSITES

www.icij.org
This site takes you to the work of the International Consortium of Investigative Journalists, which did the tobacco smuggling project and other groundbreaking pieces of cross-border digging.

www.ire.org
Begin here. Investigative Reporters and Editors, headquartered at the University of Missouri, is the world's leading source of expertise, story ideas and professional and personal support for investigative reporters.

www.ire.org/nicar
The National Institute for Computer-Assisted Reporting, a partnership of IRE and the Missouri School of Journalism, teaches the skills and provides the consulting you'll need to get and analyze the data for richer, more revealing stories.

www.opensecrets.org
The Center for Responsive Politics specializes in collecting, analyzing and making available information on money and politics. The center's handbook, *Follow the Money*, is an invaluable resource for any reporter interested in the impact of money on self-government.

EXERCISES

1. **Team project.** Much of the best investigative reporting is done in teams. You'll find plenty of examples at the IRE website. Your instructor will divide your class into three- or four-person teams. With your team, pick a topic to investigate and then design your project. Use the format shown in Figure 19.1 as a guide. Then assign responsibilities and devise a system for coordinating your findings. If there's time, dig in. Otherwise, submit the complete plan for class discussion.

2. **Journalism blog.** Use your blog to share discoveries, frustrations and lessons learned during the team project. Comment on your teammates' blog posts, and invite other classmates to compare their experiences.

3. Visit John Ferrugia on the Web (www.denverchannel.com). What can you learn about his story choices, his methods and the man himself? Is his career path one you would like to follow?

4. Go to www.ire.org, and find the stories that have won recent IRE awards. Choose one story from each of at least three categories. Compare the sources and techniques used. What similarities and differences do you find in different media? Which stories seem to you most complete and most satisfying? Why?

5. School board member Doris Hart reported at last week's meeting of the board that major flaws, including basement flooding and electrical short circuits, have plagued the new elementary school. She noted that this is the third straight project designed by consulting architect Louis Doolittle in which serious problems have occurred. School Superintendent Margaret Smith defended Doolittle vigorously. Later, Hart told you privately that she suspects Doolittle may be paying Smith off to keep the consulting contract, which has earned the architect more than $100,000 per year for the past five years. Describe how you will investigate the following:

   a. The sniff.
   b. Human sources. Who might talk? Where should you start? Whom will you save for last?
   c. What records might help? Where are they? What will you be looking for?
   d. What is the most you can hope to prove? What is the least that will yield a story?

6. Choose a public official in your city or town, and compile the most complete profile you can, using only public records.

7. Use one or more of the computer databases described in Chapter 6 to learn as much as you can about your representative in Congress. Write the most complete investigative profile you can from the databases. In a memo, explain what additional information you'd need to complete your story and where it might be found.

20

Working in Public Relations

HE STRUCK OUT on three pitches.

Adam Greenberg had waited seven years, two months and 24 days for his first real at-bat in the major leagues. That was after his first attempt in Major League Baseball, while playing for the Chicago Cubs, when the very first pitch he faced, a 92-mph fastball, hit him in the head and caused a severe concussion. Greenberg returned to play in the minors the following year before the Cubs released him. He had never had an official MLB at-bat.

Enter filmmaker and fanatical Cubs fan Matt Liston. Liston was determined to get Greenberg listed as a major leaguer, and that meant Greenberg had to have at least one official at-bat. Liston never studied or worked in public relations, but he knew how to go about it. He established a website (oneatbat.com); he tweeted; he used Facebook and YouTube; he gathered 25,000 petition signatures on change.org; he contacted major league teams personally; he appeared on the *Today Show* with Greenberg.

The Chicago Cubs turned him down, as did other clubs. Ironically, it was another lowly, last-place team, the Miami Marlins, that offered Greenberg a one-day contract.

And so it was that the hapless Cubs missed a golden opportunity for national and even international publicity at little or no expense and passed it on to another team equally in need of it—the team that was playing the Cubs when Greenberg's career was destroyed. It matters little that he struck out on three pitches for a last-place team against the Mets in a meaningless and penultimate game of the season. He had achieved his lifelong goal of getting an official major league at-bat.

You and all public relations professionals can learn from Matt Liston. The whole incident might seem a silly matter of getting a young man an at-bat in the major leagues, but the story is much, much bigger than that. It involves human dreams and persistence and that magic word "comeback."

Unquestionably, if you intend to work in any area of public relations, you need to have expertise in social media, like Liston. Social media are not just for people who represent celebrities or who handle management or crisis communications. Internal public relations and corporate communicators want their employees to monitor social media for potential public relations crises and opportunities and to report them immediately. They also use the social media to spread the good word about their organizations.

In this chapter you will learn:

1. How public relations differs from journalism.

2. Why message, audience and media, including social media, are important in public relations writing.

3. How to write persuasively.

4. How to write a news release that gets attention.

5. How to put together a digital news release.

If you are planning to work in the public relations field, you need to be prepared to use all types of media—not just print, television and radio, but also digital media, including social media networks—to get your job done.

PUBLIC RELATIONS: A DIFFERENT APPROACH TO NEWS

Regardless of your situation, professionals agree that the skill most required of public relations people is good writing. Journalism schools traditionally require a course in news writing for students interested in public relations, and many public relations professionals like to hire people with some news writing experience. Only by studying news and how news organizations operate will you be successful in public relations or in offices of public information. Knowing how reporters deal with news releases will help you write better releases. Of course, studying the news also helps you enormously in the advertising world and in what is now frequently called *strategic marketing* or *strategic communication*.

Not only do skilled public relations or public information practitioners know how to write news, but they also apply all the principles of good news writing in their news releases. Thus, a good news release meets the criteria of a good news story. Like a good story, it should have some staying power, as organizations often keep recent news releases available on their websites. You can see a typical news release in Figure 20.1. Notice that the release begins with the name of the organization putting out the release and includes the contact person's name, title, phone number and email address. If the news is for immediate release, say so. Otherwise, indicate a release date.

Public relations professionals also know that doing internal and external communications for an organization demands a specific perspective and, in many cases, a specific kind of writing. Of course, good writing is good writing, and what you have learned so far applies to public relations writing. But you also will be called on to do writing that is different from the kinds of writing journalists do.

Defining Public Relations

Rex Harlow, called by some the "father of public relations research" and perhaps the first full-time public relations educator, claimed to have found 472 definitions of public relations. One definition, in use from 1982 to 2012 according to the Public Relations Society of America, was simple: "Public relations helps an organization and its publics adapt mutually to each other."

In 2012, PRSA selected this definition by a public vote: "Public relations is a strategic communication process that builds mutually beneficial relationships between organizations and their publics."

Not that the new definition—or any definition—will stop the critics of public relations. Rick Rice, an independent consultant with more than 35 years of experience in public relations, says, "It takes more than a new definition to change the way people perceive the public relations industry." The public "has a fundamental lack

Contact: Mary Ann Beahon
Director of University Relations
(573) 592-1127
mbeahon@williamwoods.edu
www.thewoods.edu

December 3, 2014
FOR IMMEDIATE RELEASE

William Woods Senior Art Students Showcase Work

FULTON, Mo.—Demonstrating what they've learned during the past four years, three William Woods University seniors are displaying their talents at the annual Senior Art Show. The show runs through Dec. 12 in the Mildred Cox Gallery of the Gladys Woods Kemper Center for the Arts.

The exhibit features the work of Hillary Reed of Castle Rock, Colo.; Adam Dresden of Granite City, Ill., and Kelly Trustee of Huntsville, Mo. Included in the show are examples of ceramics, oil painting, charcoal, pencil, watercolor and graphic design.

The Mildred Cox Gallery is open 9-4 p.m. Monday through Friday, and 1-4 p.m. Saturday and Sunday. Admission is free and open to the public. For more information about the exhibit, call (573) 592-4245.

###

FIGURE 20.1

A traditional news release is double-spaced and follows AP style. Note that this release includes the line "For immediate release."

of respect for PR practitioners," he says. This lack of respect can only be corrected in two ways:

1. By focusing on measurement and accountability.
2. By improving training and development.

This chapter will help you with your training and development. It will be up to you to increase the respect people have for what you do.

We've looked at the new definition of public relations. In *Public Relations: Strategies and Tactics*, Dennis Wilcox and Glen Cameron write that these key terms are essential to understand public relations:

» **Deliberate:** The "activity is intentional . . . designed to influence, gain understanding, provide feedback, and obtain feedback."
» **Planned:** "organized . . . systematic, requiring research and analysis."
» **Performance:** "based on actual policies."
» **Public interest:** "mutually beneficial to the organization and to the public."
» **Two-way communication:** "equally important to solicit feedback."
» **Management function:** "an integral part of decision-making by top management."

Public relations, then, is not just publicity, which seeks to get the media to respond to an organization's interests. Nor is it advertising or marketing, which are more directly concerned with sales. Through advertising, an organization pays to get the attention of the public, and marketing combines a whole host of activities to sell a product, service or idea.

A Range of Interests

If you wish to write in the field of public relations, you have many areas from which to choose.

» **Media relations:** seeking publicity and answering questions posed by the media.
» **Government affairs:** spending time with legislatures and regulatory agencies and doing some lobbying.
» **Public affairs:** engaging in matters of public policy.
» **Industry relations:** relating to other firms within the industry and to trade associations.
» **Investor, financial or shareholder relations:** working to maintain investor confidence and good relationships with the financial world.

More and more today, the term **strategic communication** is replacing "public relations." Some joke that one simple reason for this change is that the term "public relations" has always suffered a "PR problem." But of course the reasons are much more serious than that.

The demands made of public relations professionals are greater today than they were a generation ago. As Ronald Smith explains in *Strategic Planning for Public Relations*:

No longer is it enough merely to know *how* to do things. Now the effective communicator needs to know *what* to do, *why* and how to *evaluate* its effectiveness. Public relations professionals used to be called upon mainly for tasks such as writing news releases, making speeches, producing videos, publishing newsletters, organizing displays and so on. Now the profession demands competency in conducting research, making decisions and solving problems. The call now is for strategic communicators.

In short, the strategic communicator must take a more scientific approach, do some research, make careful choices and, when finished, evaluate the effectiveness of the completed program. Such a communicator would certainly be expected to write clearly and precisely, but differently from reporters.

Objectivity and Public Relations Writing

In traditional reporting, journalists strive to remain unbiased. They should not set out to prove something. Certainly, they should not be advocates for a point of view. They should get the facts, and let the facts speak for themselves.

By contrast, columnists do have a point of view, and good ones find ways to support it convincingly. Editorial writers use facts to persuade people to change their minds, to confirm their opinions, or to get people to do something or to stop doing something. (See Figure 1.1 in Chapter 1 for a comparison of how reporters and commentators approach accuracy, fairness and bias in writing.)

That's also what public relations writers do. Though sometimes they wish only to inform their audiences, they most often want to do what editorial writers do: persuade the audience to accept a particular position.

However, there's one major difference. News commentators serve the public. Public relations writers work for an organization or for a client other than a news operation. Their job is to make that organization or client appear in the best possible light. Effective public relations writers dare not ignore facts, even when the facts are harmful or detrimental to the cause they are promoting. But because they are promoting a cause or looking out for the best interests of the people for whom they are working, they will interpret all news, even bad news, in the most favorable light.

Public relations writers work much the way attorneys work for clients—as advocates. They should not lie or distort, but they might play down certain facts and emphasize others. In its "Official Statement on Public Relations," the Public Relations Society of America says:

> Public relations helps our complex, pluralistic society to reach decisions and function more effectively by contributing to mutual understanding among groups and institutions. It serves to bring private and public policies into harmony. . . . The public relations practitioner acts as a counselor to management and as a mediator, helping to translate private aims into reasonable, publicly acceptable policy and action.

The PRSA has a code of ethics for the practice of public relations. The code, given in full on its website (www.prsa.org), requires members to "adhere to the highest standard of accuracy and truth," avoiding extravagant claims or unfair comparisons and giving credit for ideas and words borrowed from others. It also requires members not to "knowingly disseminate false or misleading information."

THE MAIN FOCUS OF PUBLIC RELATIONS WRITING

Public relations personnel are concerned with three things: the message, the audience and the media used to deliver the message.

The Message

To be an effective public relations professional, you must know the message your organization wants to send. That message might focus on a product, a program or the organization itself. For every message you work on, you must first know what you hope to accomplish, even if your purpose is just to inform.

That's why it's so important for you to be a reporter first, to know how to gather information and to do so quickly. Like any reporter, you might be called on in an instant to deal with a crisis in the company for which you work.

When a security guard at San Francisco's Contemporary Jewish Museum asked two women who were holding hands to leave the premises, the couple asked to speak to the head of security. The head of security immediately fired the guard and apologized to the women. Then the director and CEO of the museum, Connie Wolf, relayed the incident to the museum's board and staff. Her words later appeared on the museum's Facebook page. In part, the statement said the following:

> The guard's behavior — something that has never happened at this museum in the past — resulted in an event that cannot be allowed to happen again. The CJM has a zero tolerance policy concerning any type of prejudiced or racist word or action — whether directed at CJM visitors or staff. . . . On behalf of the Museum, its staff, and Board of Trustees, we are truly sorry that this incident occurred in our facility.

Five days after the event, the museum announced, in the news release shown in the annotated model, a "Hand Holding Day at the CJM" and invited "visitors to come stroll hand in hand through the galleries no matter who you love and to celebrate the LGBT families in our community."

That's the way to handle a crisis.

You might not have a boss as enlightened about public relations as Connie Wolf, but as a PR professional, it is your job to try to be candid and truthful with the press and the public.

The Audience

Almost as important as knowing all you can about the message is knowing the audience to whom you are directing it. The better you target your audience, the more effective you will be. As in advertising, the demographics and psychographics of your target audience determine the way you write your message, the language you choose and the simplicity or complexity of the piece you create.

Who are these people, what are their attitudes, and what do they do for work and recreation? You will answer these questions somewhat differently if you write for internal audiences (employees or managers) or external audiences (the media, shareholders, constituents, volunteers, consumers or donors).

Many times a PR crisis has little to do with what a company does or does not do. Vacation rental site Airbnb proclaims itself as "a community marketplace for (travelers) to list, discover, and book unique spaces around the world." It goes on to say, "With listings in over 18,000 cities and 186 countries, you're sure to find something inspiring. And now, with Social Connections, you're sure to find someone you know."

ANNOTATED MODEL News Release Responding to a Crisis

HOME VISIT CALENDAR ON VIEW PROGRAMS EDUCATION MEMBERSHIP/SUPPORT ABOUT CONNECT STORE

Press Release

HAND HOLDING DAY at the CJM

Sunday, July 24, 2011

9 AM–5 PM

San Francisco, CA, July 21, 2011—It's time for a show of hands this Sunday, July 24 at the Contemporary Jewish Museum as we celebrate Hand Holding Day! In the aftermath of a widely publicized incident in our galleries in which a contract security guard, acting in his individual capacity, told two women holding hands that it was not allowed,* the Museum demonstrates its ongoing commitment to diversity by encouraging visitors to come stroll hand in hand through the galleries no matter who you love and to celebrate the LGBT families in our community.*

◄— News release publicizes an event designed to respond to a negative incident.

"We are excited about welcoming everyone to the Museum for a day of celebration," says CJM Director and CEO Connie Wolf. "When we learned that a contract security officer was not in alignment with the Museum's values and policies, he was immediately removed from the Museum and reprimanded. The Museum is dedicated to engaging all visitors in the diversity of culture, history, art, and ideas. Sunday at the Museum will be an extraordinary opportunity to share in the diversity of people, ideas, and community."

◄— The museum's swift corrective action is highlighted.

The release restates —► the museum's position on the issue.

The morning features several previously scheduled activities just for families with young children in conjunction with the current *Seeing Gertrude Stein: Five Stories* exhibition including special art-making activities, tours of the exhibition, and performances by the SF Lesbian/ Gay Freedom Band, the Voices Lesbian Choral Ensemble, and Lesbian/ Gay Chorus of San Francisco. The LGBT Family Morning of Stein takes place 9 AM to 12 PM and is appropriate for young children (preschool through nine years old) and their families. All families are welcome, and youth 18 and under are always free. Learn More.

◄— Details of the event make the museum's position clear.

◄— This link enables the reporter to get more information.

(continued)

This news release confronts negative publicity head-on and promotes the organization's corrective actions.
Source: Contemporary Jewish Museum, July 24, 2011.

News Release Responding to a Crisis *(continued)*

Later that day, loved ones can hold hands as they enjoy a special free performance by actress Laura Sheppard entitled *Paris Portraits: Stories of Picasso, Matisse, Gertrude Stein and their Circle*, her one-woman show based on the new memoir of Gertrude Stein by Harriet Levy from Heyday Books. The 30-minute performance starts at 2 PM and is followed by a conversation with Sheppard and historians Frances Dinkelspiel and Fred Rosenbaum. Get Tickets.

This link provides a service to the reader.

A fun day is at hand so shake a leg and come join us! It's all free with regular admission.

*For more information, view "The Contemporary Jewish Museum Responds to Incident in Gallery" press release.

This link to an earlier release about the incident provides background.

About the Contemporary Jewish Museum

With the opening of its new building on June 8, 2008, the Contemporary Jewish Museum (CJM) ushered in a new chapter in its twenty-plus year history of engaging audiences and artists in exploring contemporary perspectives on Jewish culture, history, art, and ideas. The facility, designed by internationally renowned architect Daniel Libeskind, is a lively center where people of all ages and backgrounds can gather to experience art, share diverse perspectives, and engage in hands-on activities. Inspired by the Hebrew phrase "L'Chaim" (To Life), the building is a physical embodiment of the CJM's mission to bring together tradition and innovation in an exploration of the Jewish experience in the 21st century.

For media information or visuals visit our online press gallery or please contact:

Contemporary Jewish Museum

Nina Sazevich
Public Relations
415.752.2483
Nina911@pacbell.net

Full contact info makes the journalist's job easier.

Daryl Carr
Director of Marketing & Communications
415.655.7834
dcarr@thecjm.org

Online: thecjm.org/press | thecjm.org/imagegallery

Unfortunately, when Airbnb arranged for a guest to stay in the San Francisco home of someone named EJ, the guest trashed the place.

In a blog, Airbnb CEO and co-founder Brian Chesky tried to "explain the situation," but in a subsequent blog, he admitted, "We have really screwed things up," noting that his blog earlier in the week did not reflect his "true feelings."

Further he said, "There have been a lot of questions swirling around, and I would like to apologize and set the record straight in my own words. In the last few days we have had a crash course in crisis management."

The company announced a new safety section on its website with a number of offerings, including an Airbnb guarantee of up to $50,000 to cover any loss or damage or theft caused by an Airbnb guest. Among other things, it initiated a 24-hour customer hotline and doubled its customer-support team. Airbnb said it would also be more vigilant in screening possible guests.

Sometimes you have to have a crisis to learn how to avoid future ones.

As Airbnb discovered, a major way of maintaining a good relationship with your audience is to facilitate two-way communication. If you involve your audience in what you are trying to achieve, your chances of achieving it increase. Establishing a website that encourages feedback is an excellent way to get people's ideas and reactions.

Sometimes you might have to deal with frivolous lawsuits. When a California woman accused Taco Bell of having too little "seasoned beef" in many of its tacos and burritos, the company launched a nationwide advertising campaign costing at least $3 million to combat the negative publicity, saying, "We thank you for suing us."

The lawsuit said the beef taco filling contained less than 50 percent beef; Taco Bell said it actually contained 88 percent beef and 12 percent "signature recipe."

"We gave them the facts, which we could have given them three months ago before this was filed, and when they saw the facts, they withdrew the lawsuit," CEO Greg Creed said in an interview with Reuters' Jonathan Stempel. "It's that simple."

At Penn State, rather than trying to hide the Jerry Sandusky sex scandal, suppose university officials had done the opposite. Michael Hiestand wrote in *USA Today*:

> Rece Davis (ESPN anchor) wondered how dumb it had to have been if anybody at Penn State worried that exposing Sandusky would be bad PR: "What in the world would have been better publicity than ferreting out a pedophile and stopping him?"

How could the university be so poorly informed about its audience? If Penn State had trusted its loyal audience and immediately dealt with the sex offender, the university might have actually gained some good public relations.

When J.C. Penney chose Ellen DeGeneres for its spokesperson, the conservative anti-gay group One Million Moms thought the company made a big mistake. It threatened a boycott. J.C. Penney trusted its choice and continued letting the popular talk-show host do the talking in ads nationally. The ads were a great success, and the boycott ended as quickly as it began.

ON THE JOB
Public Relations Writing

After **Brad Whitworth** received his journalism degree, he joined the staff of a small magazine covering Illinois politics. When the magazine abruptly folded six months later, he moved into corporate communications, where he worked first for a small association and then for a large insurance company.

Whitworth has spent the past 30 years doing public relations, speechwriting and internal communications for Silicon Valley companies, including high-tech giants Hewlett-Packard and Cisco Systems. For 10 of those years, business travel took him to Asia Pacific, Latin America and Europe.

"For global audiences, it's important to keep your words and sentences as simple as possible," says Whitworth. "In fact, the more complex or technical your subject matter, the simpler your words need to be.

"Selfishly, I'm glad the language for doing business around the world is English.

But for many audiences, it's their second language. Everything I learned in journalism school about making communications clear, concise, consistent and complete is even more critical when connecting with co-workers or customers halfway around the world."

Today he stays in touch around the clock with his global contacts using technology:

everything from high-definition video teleconferencing to hand-held instant messaging. His meetings start early in the morning with European colleagues and often finish late at night with Asian co-workers. In addition to high-tech tools, Whitworth continues to rely on a human network: the International Association of Business Communicators.

"I landed my job at HP through IABC's job bank and have hired dozens through the network." He's given back to IABC, too, serving as president of two local chapters and as the youngest chairman ever of the 16,000-member not-for-profit organization.

"It's really important to stay connected with others who are doing the same kind of work," he says. "You can share best practices, learn about job opportunities and take part in seminars, conferences and workshops. Your learning doesn't stop when you leave campus."

Other groups used public relations over the J.C. Penney issue to their advantage. The Gay and Lesbian Alliance Against Defamation used the controversy to call attention to the fact that in 29 states a person could be fired just for being gay. Membership in GLAAD increased by 50,000. A Facebook group called "1 Million People Who Support Ellen for JC Penney" quickly attracted more members than One Million Moms.

The Media

Once you have mastered the message or product and targeted the audience, you have to choose the media through which to deliver that message.

Research shows that the more media you use, the better chance you have to succeed. That's why effective public relations people, like those in advertising, think in terms of campaigns and strategies. A campaign assumes that you can't just tell an audience once what you want them to learn, retain and act on. It's far more effective to send the message in a mix of media in a carefully timed or orchestrated way. To do this, you must learn what each medium does best.

Television, Radio and Newsstand Publications

For a message that nearly everyone wants or needs to know, television might be your best medium. Television offers color and motion; television can show rather than tell.

Radio listeners usually are loyal to one radio station. They will listen to your message over and over. The more often they hear it, the more likely they are to retain it.

Print media such as newspapers and magazines are better for complicated messages and sometimes for delicate messages. People can come back again and again to a print message. Some argue that print still has more credibility than other media.

The Internet: An All-in-One Medium

Perhaps the best way to do public relations today is through digital media. More and more people are getting the information and products they need online—from their laptop, desktop computer, smartphone or tablet computer. Here you have the advantages of every medium—print, video and audio—all in one. Remember, people who spend a lot of time online generally are better educated and more affluent than those who do not. They love the control they have over the messages they find online. They can click on only the information they want, and they can do so in any order they choose. They can be involved and engaged and can respond to one another.

What is so challenging about digital media is the high degree of individualization; the online world is one of "mass customization." You must present the message at different levels to different people so that everyone feels as if you are writing only to him or her. It's all about individual choices and involving your readers so they will interact with you. As Web usability expert Jakob Nielsen puts it, online readers are "selfish, lazy and ruthless." Just remember, successful communication online means ideally making use of video and audio, as well as print, to get your story across. (For more about writing for the digital media, review Chapter 12.)

Social Networking Media

It is no exaggeration to say that social media networks have radically changed the way professionals do public relations. David Avitabile, president of JFK Communications, writes, "In many ways, social media was made for public relations and vice versa."

The advantages are enormous. As Avitabile notes, "The ability to develop a story over time, to weave in new messages, to engage with customers in meaningful ways and respond to their feedback are all features of social media."

According to a study by Booz & Co. and Buddy Media, 48 percent of companies have social media in the public relations function, but 88 percent use it for PR purposes. Social media coach Sally Falkow says, "Nearly 60 percent of companies polled said they plan to hire in-house social media talent. If you are looking for a job in PR or marketing, social media training and experience would be your best bet."

Nearly every area of our lives is under the influence of social media. For example, Steve Bryant and Laurie Demeritt, in a joint study "Clicks and Cravings: The Impact of Social Technology on Food Culture," found that social media are now "replacing mom as the go-to culinary source." Almost half of consumers are learning about food

TIPS

For PR Pros, Nine Rules Taken Directly from Kindergarten

1. Say please.
2. Say I'm sorry.
3. Be friendly.
4. Share.
5. Play fair.
6. Don't litter.
7. Never hurt others.
8. Say excuse me.
9. Listen to others.

—Richie Escovedo,
Next Communications

TIPS

The 10 Most Popular Social Networking Sites

These sites ranked highest in unique monthly visitors, as of February 2013:

» Facebook
» Twitter
» LinkedIn
» Pinterest
» Myspace
» Google+
» deviantART
» LiveJournal
» Tagged
» Orkut

—eBizMBA

TIPS

Avoid Overused Words

Some PR workers consider certain words and phrases overused in news releases. Here are some examples you might want to avoid:

» Announcement

» Award-winning

» Cutting edge

» Exciting

» Exclusive

» Groundbreaking

» Innovative

» Proactive

» Revolutionary

» Unprecedented

through social networks such as Twitter and Facebook, and 40 percent through websites, apps or blogs, they report.

Everything has become personal in today's public relations world. For example, Bryant and Demeritt report that "today's consumers want to hear from people who eat and cook food more than they want to hear from the entities who sell."

Twitter, Tumblr and other microblogging sites make it possible to send short text messages and Internet links to large groups of subscribers instantaneously. In addition, social media giants like Facebook, Google+, LiveJournal and Myspace have the capacity to reach large groups with targeted messages.

All of this developed rapidly, and most experts believe that we've seen only the beginning. Print will not disappear, but the arrival of the microblog might change the way we write nearly everything.

Internal Publications, Brochures and Billboards

If you work in internal communications, you might decide to publish a newsletter or magazine for employees. A large number of corporations are now communicating with employees throughout the day using an **intranet**, an internal online service accessible only to employees. They are also using social media. As a result, most organizations have abandoned their regularly published, internal print publications.

For messages that need more explanation or study, such as health-care matters, perhaps a printed brochure will do the job best. Externally, for matters that might concern the community, you might want to use billboards in addition to paid print ads or radio and television ads. Or you might choose to write news releases and leave it to others to interpret your message.

Sometimes, however, there's no quick fix. What took a long time to build can come tumbling down quickly, and then a long rebuilding process is necessary.

PERSUASIVE WRITING

Most of the time, you will write to try to persuade people. To succeed, you must study the techniques of persuasion and use them carefully.

Your Attitude

To persuade people, you need to believe three things:

» **People are essentially good.** If you are convinced of this, you will appeal to people's basic goodness and fairness.

» **People are intelligent or at least educable.** Don't talk down to people; don't assume that you can trick or fool them. Of course, don't assume that just because they are intelligent and educated, they know the subject matter as well as you do. A good rule: Never underestimate the intelligence of your audience, and never overestimate what they know. A college professor with a Ph.D. in

Six Alternatives to Sending a News Release

PR professional Claire Celsi suggests you write a news release to gather your thoughts but then not send it. Instead, do one of the following:

1. Send an email pitch. More than 90 percent of reporters say they want email pitches.
2. Make a website posting.
3. Send a tweet.
4. Send a Facebook message.
5. Pick up the phone.
6. Offer to meet the reporter for coffee if you're in the same city.

—Public Relations Princess

philosophy might be brilliant in that area but might know nothing about the financial markets.

» **People are changeable.** You must believe not only that people are changeable but also that you can change them.

Credibility and Trust

More than anything else, you need to establish and maintain your credibility and the credibility of the organization you represent. Aristotle wrote that the character of the speaker is the most essential and powerful component of persuasion. Without a doubt, character is the most important attribute public relations people need to have and to develop. A sterling reputation takes a long time to build—and it can be lost in an instant.

In addition, you must assume good will on the part of your audience. You cannot persuade people by abusing them or by calling them names. You are foolish to look at a client or the public as your enemy. This is particularly true regarding your attitude toward the press. Too many public relations professionals consider the press to be the enemy, not to be trusted with the truth, to be stonewalled at every opportunity.

> " The next time you become incensed about something the media has done—or you want to go on a crusade—call your travel agent and go on a golfing vacation instead. "
>
> —Bill Huey, president of Strategic Communication, *O'Dwyer's PR Report*

Executives and politicians continue to avoid answering questions and discussing issues by attacking the press. Some say Newt Gingrich won the CNN Republican presidential primary debate in South Carolina in January 2012 by doing just that. When asked about what his ex-wife said was his request for an open marriage, Gingrich replied to moderator John King:

> I think the destructive, vicious, negative nature of much of the news media makes it harder to govern this country, harder to attract decent people to run for public office. And I am appalled that you would begin a presidential debate on a topic like that.

For those words, Gingrich received a standing ovation.

Some called it good public relations. It was not. Even though he won the debate, Gingrich did not win the Republican nomination. A better approach might have been for him to use the question to explain his side of the story in a way that would help him with his longer-term goal of gaining the nomination.

NEWS RELEASES THAT GET ATTENTION

Perhaps nothing that you will be called on to write is more important than news releases. This is true, in spite of what people such as Simon Dumenco, the "Media Guy" columnist for *Advertising Age*, have written: "The long-suffering, much-maligned press release, I'd argue, finally died this summer, thanks particularly to Jet-Blue and BP, with a little moral support from Kanye West and just about every other celebrity with thumbs."

(For what it's worth, a Google search for "death of the press release" shows upward of 2.9 million results. But don't be deceived. Not all of those results are about its death.)

In an article entitled "Not So Fast" on WiredPen.com, Kathy Gill wrote, "What press releases—or blog posts—can do is provide an accessible back story that cannot or will not be included in a 30-second TV news story or a six-column-inch news story. One thing tweets do well is provide a link to more detailed information: the press release, whether its form is a classic release or the modern blog post."

> **"** If you don't understand good journalistic style and format (who, what, when, where and why) for writing a press release, you harm your company and yourself. **"**
>
> —G.A. Marken, president of Marken Communications, *Public Relations Quarterly*

A 2010 survey of 750 journalists in 15 countries found that 75 percent believed emailed news releases are still effective, assuming the content is "high quality and well targeted."

Even the smallest newspaper or radio or television station gets dozens of news releases daily. Myriads of print and electronic publications such as those in the American Business Media and the Specialized Information Publishers Association also receive dozens of public relations releases daily. Most releases are now sent electronically or through public relations wire services. Regardless of how you send your news, your problem is still the same: How do you break through the clutter and attract the attention of the gatekeepers at these publications?

Here are some guidelines to help you get your message to your intended audience.

Know What News Is and How to Write It

The news media will not pay attention to fluff—copy that is laced with opinion or self-serving quotations. Worse, they will ridicule your work and discard it immediately. Avoid statements such as this: "Monroe College is recognized as the foremost and most prestigious college of liberal arts in the entire Midwest." Who says?

To write for most publications, certainly for news media and the majority of print and electronic publications, you need to know Associated Press style. (See Appendix 2 for a summary of the style followed by most news publications.) Correct spelling, usage and grammar are essential, of course, but adhering to AP style is just as important. Why should news editors take you seriously if you don't bother to write in the style of their publications? That includes knowing how to write in the inverted pyramid format (see Chapter 9). Later in this chapter you will learn different approaches to writing news releases.

Some newspapers and magazines have their own stylebooks. Quite a few magazines follow *The Chicago Manual of Style*. Be sure you know what you're doing.

Know the Structure and Operations of Newsrooms

If you do not get actual experience in a television, radio, newspaper or convergence newsroom in college, find ways to spend some time in at least one of these. Use your public relations skills to get inside and to experience what goes on there.

The simplest and most important thing you can learn about newsrooms is that they have deadlines. Learn the deadlines of the media in your area, and respect them. This means that you should not call in a story to a television news station a half-hour before airtime. Not only will the station not use your story, but station employees will resent you and not forget the interruption at a critical time. News organizations will tell you what time you must submit a story to make the news that day.

> " Employers want people who can write and communicate ideas—who can pull complex or fragmented ideas together into coherent messages. This requires not only technical skill but also intelligence. It also requires a love of writing. "
> —Thomas H. Bivins, *Public Relations Writing*

Be sure that you make yourself available—by phone, email, fax, online, or in person—24 hours a day. Nothing is more important for a public relations practitioner. A reporter on deadline will write the story with or without you. It's *always* best that you talk to the reporter.

Know the People in the News Media and the Jobs They Hold

It's especially important to know who does what at the newspapers you contact. Sending a release addressed simply to a newspaper can be a waste of time and make you look as if you do not know what you are doing. Sending a release to the business editor or to the features editor makes more sense. Addressing by name the editor of the section in which you wish the story to appear works best.

Read what Chris Anderson, editor-in-chief of *Wired* magazine, has to say on this subject in his blog:

Sorry, PR people: yo're blocked.

I've had it. I get more than 300 e-mails a day and my problem isn't spam . . . it's PR people. Lazy flacks send press releases to the Editor in Chief of *Wired* because they can't be bothered to find out who on my staff, if anyone, might actually be interested in what they're pitching. . . . So fair warning: I only want two kinds of e-mail: those from people I know, and those from people who have taken the time to find out what I'm interested in and composed a note meant to appeal to that (I love those e-mails; indeed, that's why my e-mail address is public).

News Releases That Get Used

Fraser P. Seitel, author, communications consultant and teacher, identifies the following as the eight news release topics that are most likely to be used:

1. New products or projects.
2. Personnel promotions—at least of important people.
3. Trends.
4. Conflict.
5. Topicality—"relating your news to pressing issues of the day."
6. Local heritage—tying news to community roots or history.
7. Human interest.
8. Insanity—the truly bizarre or unusual.

If the people to whom you send news releases know and trust you, they are more likely to pay attention to your releases. Sometimes you can call them with a story idea and let them write their own stories. There's nothing writers like more than to get wind of good stories. Remember, your job is to help reporters write good stories. If you can help them do that and at the same time serve your client's interests, you will be a successful public relations practitioner.

Know the Style of Writing That Fits the Medium

Do not make the mistake of sending to a radio or television station the same news release that you send to a newspaper. Do not expect busy journalists to translate your newspaper release into broadcast copy. If you can write radio or television copy (see Chapter 13), you have a much better chance of getting the copy read over the air. Remember, too, that writing for digital media (see Chapter 12) can differ from writing for print.

In our social media world, sometimes you can even tweet a news release. Your headline must inform and grab, but keep it well below 140 characters so that people can retweet it with a brief comment.

Wendy's used only 84 characters to win the 2011 Twitter Golden Tweet Award for the most retweeted post of the year. Wendy's paid for the promotional ad. All it said was this: "RT for a good cause. Each retweet sends 50¢ to help kids in foster care. #tweetItFwd." The ad ran on Father's Day as part of the company's annual promotion for the Dave Thomas Foundation for Adoption, and it raised $50,000.

In addition, you must make your news release search-engine friendly. You must help people find you online by making clear the words that identify your client. Search-engine optimization, or SEO, doesn't count for everything, but you must be aware of it. Become acquainted with Google Insights, Google's AdWords, Keyword Discovery and Wordtracker for help with choosing the right words. Vanessa Bugasch, of the PR software and services company Cision, warns against overlinking, which might cause confusion. But she does advise writers to use one or two key words in the headline or subhead. She tells us that using them in the first two paragraphs has more impact than placing them lower in the release and cites research that shows that news releases "with pictures, video and other multimedia get at least 80 percent more search traffic than text-only releases."

You must be aware that just as some newspapers will use your news releases almost verbatim—some have sections of verbatim releases about events, promotions and so on—some radio and television stations will use your audio and video releases without editing them. In 2005, a *New York Times* investigation found that during the Bush administration at least 20 federal agencies, including the Defense Department, were distributing VNRs that made everyone and everything in government look good—including the war in Iraq. The government paid private public relations firms millions to produce messages that looked like traditional reporting—and stations used them.

The nonprofit group Center for Media and Democracy reported in 2006 that over a 10-month period at least 77 television stations used VNRs. Not one told viewers who had produced them. In some VNRs, publicists acted as news reporters.

In a 2009 hearing of the Consumer Protection, Product Safety, and Insurance Subcommittee of the Commerce Committee, Sen. Claire McCaskill called the use of VNRs "unconscionable." She said, "Our news folks have enough problems with credibility right now without fake news being aired." But VNRs continue to be broadcast without explanation. In 2012, for example, CNN ran a VNR for vaccines before the start of the school year.

The Public Relations Society of America still awards a Bronze Anvil each year for the best VNR. In 2013, MediaSource won the award for its multimedia release for the American Society of Plastic Surgeons. According to MediaSource: "More than a billion people saw or read the story around the world."

Know How to Distribute Information Online

Of course, not even the largest newspapers or radio or television networks can reach as many people as digital media can. With millions of websites, there are practically no limits to the audiences that can be reached on the Internet. First, you must establish your own credible, up-to-date, interactive website. Second, you must be thoroughly familiar with websites such as Online Public Relations, PR Newswire and Synaptic Digital so that you can distribute your releases online and keep up with what's happening in public relations. Third, you must become expert at using digital media to get across your organization's messages (see Chapter 12).

DIGITAL NEWS RELEASES

To be effective in their jobs, writers of news releases need to learn all the techniques that journalists use in writing news stories.

The straight, no-nonsense inverted pyramid news release remains the staple of the public relations professional. Many believe that news professionals will not take any other approach seriously. (See Chapter 9 for more on the inverted pyramid.) For an example of a traditional news release, see Figure 20.1 earlier in this chapter.

A less traditional news release, written in a lighter style, can be more engaging. Take another look at the news release, shown in the annotated model on page 425, that the Contemporary Jewish Museum released in connection with the hand-holding incident mentioned earlier. Notice the excellent first sentence, in which the emphasis on "hands" turns a negative occurrence at the museum into an occasion for celebration. The release goes on to acknowledge the "widely publicized incident" to which the museum is responding and to give details about the upcoming Hand Holding Day events. The ending—which ties back to the hand theme and adds "so shake a leg"—is an unexpected and delightful ending for a news release.

Despite the continued use of traditional news releases, today's savvy public relations professionals are sending social media news releases. Here are some of the steps, summarized and condensed, that digital PR expert Sally Falkow recommends for successful social media news releases:

» Write a short, concise headline.
» Answer the five W's in the first paragraph.
» List the core news facts in bullet points.
» Add approved quotes.
» Write the rest in narrative form; use relevant keywords so that journalists and others can find the release through search engines or social sites.
» Add links to research, facts, statistics or trends.
» Include an original, high-quality image that tells the story.
» Provide the source URL for the image so that bloggers and journalists can use it easily and quickly.
» Add more images, icons and, if possible, a short video, plus more supporting materials, such as charts and infographics.
» Provide an embed code with these items so that they can be easily republished. (An embed code acts like a link to video content.)
» Add the "About Us" boilerplate and contact person.
» Make the release available in an RSS news feed.
» Add sharing buttons so that the release can be shared through social networking sites.

Study the annotated model "Social Media News Release" for an example. Notice how the information leaps out at you, and note how many choices the release gives the readers and how many connections it provides.

The social media news release has changed the way public relations professionals think about doing news releases. And the social media have changed the way they think about doing public relations.

ANNOTATED MODEL   Social Media News Release

Social Media Release – Faces of Diversity 2011

Eye-catching design makes use of strong graphic elements.

April 13, 2011

National Restaurant Association's 2011 Faces of Diversity Awards Winners Illustrate the American Dream of Entrepreneurship

Heading and deck use terms easily found in an Internet search.

CONTACT INFORMATION

Annika Stensson | (202) 973-3677 | astensson@restaurant.org | Twitter@WeRRestaurants

Contact info is prominent.

2011 FACES OF DIVERSITY AWARDS

The Faces of Diversity Awards, created by the National Restaurant Association in partnership with PepsiCo Foodservice, celebrate diversity in the restaurant and foodservice industry and among the industry's nearly 13 million employees.

Theme gives the "so what."

Beautifully presented logo.

NEWS HIGHLIGHTS

Key news points are given in a bulleted list.

- The National Restaurant Association today honored four restaurant entrepreneurs and a renowned culinary college with its 2011 Faces of Diversity awards.

- The award celebrates members of the restaurant and foodservice industry who have embraced diversity and inclusion at their own business operations and achieved the American dream in the process. . . .

Important news here of American Dream Award winners, briefly stated and again bulleted.

- This year's American Dream Award winners are:
  - **Berekti and Akberet Mengistu, Mesob restaurant, Montclair, N.J.**: These Ethiopian-born sisters . . .

  - **Amporn Vasquez, Pizza by Elizabeths, Greenville, Del.**: This executive chef . . .

  - **Richard Castro, McDonald's franchisee, El Paso, Texas**: As a child . . .

A special award.

- The Inspiration Award winner is:
  - **The Culinary Institute of America, Hyde Park, N.Y., and Silver Ventures Inc., San Antonio**: In an attempt to increase the number of Hispanic managers and restaurant owner-operators in business . . .

Link to a longer, more detailed news release.

- Read the full news release.

(continued)

A nontraditional news release makes the most of what the digital media offer.

Social Media News Release *(continued)*

QUOTE

Relevant quote is labeled and clearly displayed.

- "The restaurant industry is one of the most diverse industries in the United States, and we are celebrating that by honoring these individuals and companies with our 2011 Faces of Diversity awards. It is a true pleasure to recognize their personal and professional achievements, which underscore how hard work and determination lead to success in our industry."

— *Dawn Sweeney, president and CEO for the National Restaurant Association*

VIDEO: 2011 FACES OF DIVERSITY WINNERS

You may also watch each winner's video individually:

The release gives video links that can be embedded into a story.

- The Culinary Institute of America
- Richard Castro
- Amporn Vasquez
- Berekti and Akberet Mengistu

FACES OF DIVERSITY IMAGE GALLERY

Download photos of the 2011 Faces of Diversity award winners, and the Faces of Diversity logo.

The release gives photos and graphics that journalists can use.

Berekti and Akberet Mengistu

Logo

The Culinary Institute of America

LINKS

Links to other sources give reporters access to more info.

- News release on the 2011 Faces of Diversity winners
- News release on 2011 Inspiration Award winner The Culinary Institute of America
- The Culinary Institute of America San Antonio campus . . .

BOILERPLATE

The history of the organization is also included, with its URL.

- Founded in 1919, the National Restaurant Association is . . . For more information, visit our website at www.restaurant.org.

SOME FINAL ADVICE

In addition to writing news releases, public relations professionals are involved with many other important functions that increase the value of public relations, including planning and carrying out successful press conferences and dealing with the foreign press.

You might be hired as a speechwriter or to do something as specialized as write an organization's annual report. Corporations and institutions such as hospitals and universities hire thousands of communicators to get their messages out to the public. Or you might work for a public relations agency that is hired to do this work for organizations. Many people make a good living working out of their homes for just a half dozen or fewer clients. No matter where you work, public relations demands that you never stop developing your skills and continuing your education.

TIPS

What Professionals Look for When Hiring a PR Person

» Kindness

» Creativity

» Passion

» Hustle

» Smarts

—Kathleen Henson, *PR News*

SUGGESTED READINGS

Bivins, Thomas H. *Public Relations Writing: The Essentials of Style and Format*. 6th ed. New York: McGraw-Hill, 2007. Bivins covers the wide variety of writing expected of public relations professionals.

Brown, Rob. *Public Relations and the Social Web: How to Use Social Media and Web 2.0 in Communications*. Philadelphia: Kogan Page, 2009. This book discusses the whole range of social media, including social media releases, Twitter and wikis.

Holtz, Shel. *Public Relations on the Net*. 2nd ed. New York: Amacom, 2002. Anything Holtz says or writes about online subjects is worth paying attention to. See also www.holtz.com /blog.

Horton, James L. *Online Public Relations: A Handbook for Practitioners*. Westport, Conn.: Quorum Books, 2001. A superb primer and more, this book begins by explaining terminology and ends with 85 industry and general information topics about placing news and gathering information. Horton also developed and maintains www.online-pr.com, an up-to-date resource that lists more than 500 media sites, nearly 800 public relations resources, and more than 1,200 general links to such things as dictionaries, quotation checkers, search engines and maps.

Howard, Carole, and Wilma Mathews. *On Deadline: Managing Media Relations*. 5th ed. Prospect Heights, Ill.: Waveland Press, 2013. This excellent practical book shows how organizations should deal with the news media.

Lattimore, Dan, Otis Baskin, Suzette Heiman and Elizabeth Toth. *Public Relations: The Profession and the Practice*. New York: McGraw-Hill, 2011. This good survey is divided into four parts covering the profession, the process, the publics and the practice.

Newsom, Doug, and Jim Haynes. *Public Relations Writing: Form and Style*. 9th ed. Belmont, Calif.: Wadsworth, 2010. A truly thorough classic, this book even has a section on grammar, spelling and punctuation.

Phillips, David, and Philip Young. *Online Public Relations: A Practical Guide to Developing an Online Strategy in the World of Social Media*. 2nd ed. Philadelphia: Kogan Page, 2009. The authors discuss many new ways for creative people to reach large audiences.

Seitel, Fraser P. *The Practice of Public Relations*. 10th ed. New York: Prentice Hall, 2006. You can tell Seitel has been a teacher. He writes simply, clearly and engagingly.

Seitel, Fraser P. "'Used' News Releases." *O'Dwyer's PR Report* (September 2006): 31, 42. Seitel's columns on professional development appear regularly in this publication.

Smith, Ronald. *Strategic Planning for Public Relations*. New York: Routledge, 2009. This book explains well the shift from public relations to strategic communications.

Wilcox, Dennis L., and Glen T. Cameron. *Public Relations Strategies and Tactics*. 10th ed. Boston: Allyn and Bacon, 2012. These two outstanding professors keep you up-to-date in the field.

Wilcox, Dennis L., and Bryan H. Reber. *Public Relations Writing and Media Techniques*. 7th ed. Boston: Pearson, 2013. You can be sure that any book in this field that has Wilcox's name on it will be excellent.

SUGGESTED WEBSITES

www.bedfordstmartins.com/newscentral
When you visit News Central, you will find up-to-the-moment RSS feeds, research links and exercises to help you improve your grammar and AP style usage. In addition, the site's Video-Central: Journalism section hosts the videos highlighted in this chapter as well as additional clips of leading professionals discussing important media trends.

www.instituteforpr.com
This website offers information about public relations research, measurement, programs, seminars, publications, scholarship and so on from the Institute for Public Relations, which explores "the science beneath the art of public relations."

www.odwyerpr.com
On this website, you can also find *O'Dwyer's PR Report*, an excellent monthly publication that devotes each issue to a public relations specialty field. This independent website and publication is often highly critical of the profession.

www.online-pr.com
Amazingly helpful for anyone interested in public relations, this site includes links to thousands of websites and other sources of information.

www.prsa.org
The website of the Public Relations Society of America has general information about the society, lists its chapters and sections, and offers information on publications, membership and accreditation, recognition and awards, conferences and seminars.

www.prwatch.org
This website, from the Center for Media and Democracy, investigates "public relations spin and propaganda." It sends out more than 1,000 news releases each day.

EXERCISES

1. **Team project.** Your instructor will organize the class into teams. Imagine that a classmate is killed in a car accident. A few thousand dollars are raised to set up a scholarship to honor his memory, but much more money is needed to endow the scholarship. Several students in the class have been training to run in the Chicago Marathon. A group of students decides to solicit money for each mile the runners complete. Plan a campaign on your campus to get people to pledge or donate money. Answer these questions:

   a. Who are your target audiences? Each team should take a different target audience if possible.
   b. Which medium would be most effective in reaching your audience? With your team, discuss the pros and cons of each medium, and decide as a group.
   c. How will you make use of social media throughout your campaign?
   d. How much will the campaign cost, and how long will it take? Work as a team to develop a budget and schedule for completing the campaign.

   When the teams are finished, the entire class will work together to compile a report that details how to proceed with the campaign.

2. **Journalism blog.** On your blog, write a post explaining why you would like to work in public relations—or why you would not.

3. Visit the public relations or public affairs department of a local college, hospital, corporation or association, and interview the person in charge about all aspects and responsibilities of her or his job. Then write a 1,000-word report summarizing what you learned.

4. Examine the news release from William Woods University (Figure 20.1). Suggest ways you could turn this traditional news release into a social media news release. Create an eye-catching design for your revision, and email it to your classmates.

5. Interview a student from a small town. Then write a news release about his or her life and activities at the university, and email it to the town's newspaper.

21

THE FIRST AMENDMENT states:

> Congress shall make no law respecting an establishment of religion, or prohibiting the free exercise thereof; or abridging the freedom of speech, or of the press; or the right of the people peaceably to assemble, and to petition the Government for a redress of grievances.

That's it: 45 words setting forth the basis for a free press in the U.S. It's deceptively simple, for no other constitutional amendment has generated as much controversy or as many cornerstone judicial opinions giving meaning to its provisions.

THE FIRST AMENDMENT: JOURNALISTS' RIGHTS AND RESPONSIBILITIES

The first five words of the First Amendment tell us a great deal about the Founding Fathers' intent: "Congress shall make no law. . . ." Rather than enumerate a bunch of rights granted by the amendment, it begins instead with a clear prohibition on the reach of the state into our ability to express ourselves.

But surely the framers of the Constitution did not mean literally "no law" under any circumstances, did they? The U.S. Supreme Court has never thought so, upholding a wide variety of restrictions on speech through the years. By imposing broad limits on the power of the government to restrict speech and expression, the First Amendment creates a system that protects the vast majority of speech in the U.S.

Such powerful protection is justified by the importance of free speech to democracy. The philosopher Alexander Meiklejohn provided the strongest explanation for free speech in a democratic society. Meiklejohn wrote that the Constitution is based on a two-tiered political agreement. First, all authority, whether to exercise control or determine common action, belongs to the people. Second, free people govern themselves, and to do so effectively, they must have access to a free flow of accurate information. When people govern themselves, "it is they—and no one else—who must pass judgment upon unwisdom and unfairness and danger," he wrote.

In this chapter you will learn:

1. What rights you have as a journalist and the source of those rights.

2. How to spot potentially libelous situations and what to do about them.

3. When you might be invading someone's privacy.

4. What kinds of problems you may face when protecting confidential sources.

5. What rights you have when obtaining access to courtrooms and court documents.

6. What you should know about copyright and fair use.

So the free flow of ideas is necessary in a democracy because people who govern themselves need to know about their government and about those who run it, as well as about the social and economic institutions that greatly affect their day-to-day lives. Most people get that information through newspapers, the Internet, radio and television. Increasingly, citizen journalists are communicating through blogs. While professional journalists debate whether blogs should be considered "real" journalism, the legal system is grappling with the issue of how to apply constitutional precedents to them.

The speed with which information can spread across social networks makes it more important than ever to understand the basics of media law. You don't have to be an expert. You just need to know when it's time to slow down and think a bit before hitting the "send" button.

Digital publishing raises all kinds of issues that journalists never had to consider before. Breaking news online raises all sorts of potential legal pitfalls. For example, a State College, Pa., student news site, Onward State, tweeted news of legendary Penn State football coach Joe Paterno's death at 8:45 p.m. on Saturday, Jan. 21, 2012. The tweet was short and authoritative:

> Our sources can now confirm: Joseph Vincent Paterno
> has passed away tonight at the age of 85.

But as we learned a day later, the report was false. Paterno did not die until the next day, a fact confirmed by his family.

By that point, Onward State's erroneous tweet had spread to a report on a local FM radio station, and then to CBS Sports, which published an obituary on its site, declaring that Paterno "has died," seemingly based on the Onward State report but without direct attribution. *The Huffington Post* followed minutes later with its own report, again passing along the Onward State version of the truth, unattributed. (*The Huffington Post* later acknowledged in a correction that it "did not properly attribute the source.")

Twelve minutes after the initial, erroneous report, Mark Viera of *The New York Times* tweeted:

> Dan McGinn, the Paterno family spokesman, at 8:57
> p.m. on reports about Joe Paterno's death: "Absolutely
> not true."

In twelve minutes, a story of national importance ricocheted across the Internet, putting into stark relief the promise and peril of journalism in the age of instantaneous publication.

The growth of digital communication brings new challenges to government transparency as well. In 1966, Congress passed the Freedom of Information Act to assist the public in finding out what is happening in federal agencies. The act was amended in 1996 by the Electronic Freedom of Information Act to improve access to computerized government records and was amended again in 2008 to ease the process of making requests. All 50 states have similar **open-records laws**. Though of great assistance to the press, these laws are also used by individuals and businesses to gain information previously kept secret by the government. Other laws ensure access to government transactions. The federal government and all the states have **open-meetings laws**—often called *sunshine laws*—requiring the public's business to be conducted in public. However, all of these access laws contain exemptions that keep some records and meetings private.

The First Amendment, the Freedom of Information Act and the sunshine laws demonstrate America's basic concern for citizen access to information needed for the "unfettered interchange of ideas." Nevertheless, some laws do reduce the scope of freedom of the press.

LIBEL

Traditionally, most of the laws limiting the absolute principle of freedom of the press have dealt with libel. These laws result from the desire of legislatures and courts to help individuals protect their reputations. Their importance was explained by U.S. Supreme Court Justice Potter Stewart in a 1966 libel case:

> The right of a man (or woman) to the protection of his (or her) own reputation from unjustified invasion and wrongful hurt reflects no more than our basic concept of the essential dignity and worth of every human being—a concept at the root of any decent system of ordered liberty.

Protection for reputations dates back centuries. In 17th-century England, individuals were imprisoned and even disfigured for making libelous statements. One objective was to prevent criticism of the government. Another was to maintain the peace by avoiding duels. Duels are rare today, and government is freely criticized, but the desire to protect an individual's reputation is just as strong.

Identifying Libel

A case concerning Israeli Gen. Ariel Sharon (sha-RONE) is helpful in understanding libel. The extensively covered trial was held in the winter of 1984–1985 in the federal courthouse in Manhattan. The case was based on a 1983 *Time* magazine cover story, "Verdict on the Massacre," about Israel's 1982 judicial inquiry into the massacre of several hundred civilians in two Palestinian refugee camps in Lebanon.

The *Time* article suggested that Sharon, then Israel's defense minister and later its prime minister, had ordered the massacre. The general sued *Time*. His attorneys knew they would have to show that their client had suffered hatred, contempt or ridicule because these statements were serious attacks on his reputation and not just unpleasant comments.

The jury's decision was in three parts. The first part of the verdict was in answer to this question: Was the paragraph concerning Sharon defamatory? The jury said it was. This meant the *Time* article had damaged Sharon's reputation and had exposed him to hatred, contempt or ridicule.

The second question for the jury was this: Was the paragraph concerning Sharon false? Again the jury answered affirmatively. If the answer had been no, the case would have ended there. Truth is a complete defense for libel.

The third question for the jury concerned whether the paragraph was published with "actual malice"—with knowledge that it was false or with reckless disregard of whether it was false ("serious doubt" that it was true). The jury answered no. Thus the trial ended in favor of *Time* magazine, despite the jury's ruling that the article was defamatory.

Courts use four categories to help jurors like those in the Sharon case decide if someone's reputation has been damaged because he or she has been brought into hatred, contempt or ridicule:

1. **Accusing someone of a crime.** This may have been the basis for the Sharon suit.
2. **Damaging a person in his or her public office, profession or occupation.** If the statements by *Time* against Sharon did not accuse him of crimes, they did damage him in his profession as a military man.
3. **Accusing a person of serious immorality.** The example lawyers often use is accusing a woman of being unchaste. Many states have statutes that make an accusation of unchastity a cause of action in a libel suit.
4. **Accusing someone of having a loathsome (that is, contagious) disease.** This category was fading as a source of defamation until the AIDS epidemic gave it new life.

This does not mean you can never say a person committed a crime, was unethical in business, was adulterous or had a loathsome disease. It does mean you must be certain that what you write is true.

Libel Suit Defenses

There are three traditional defenses against libel: truth, privilege, and fair comment and criticism. Two other constitutional standards—the actual malice and negligence tests—also help libel defendants. The court case clarifying these standards involved traditional media, but the principles are now being applied to the Internet, including blogs. In 2006, a blogger in Georgia lost the first of these electronic libel cases. He was ordered to pay $50,000 to a lawyer he had criticized. The diagram in Figure 21.1 shows the various defenses to a libel suit, which are also discussed below.

Truth

Truth is the best defense against libel. In libel cases involving matters of public concern, the burden of proof is on the plaintiff. This placement of the burden, however, does not change the reporter's responsibility to seek the truth in every possible way.

Defamation

Is a statement defamatory?
1. Damaging to reputation?
2. "Published" to third person?
3. Is plaintiff identified?
4. Injury?
5. Fault?

Spoken words of limited reach

Written (or broadcast) words

Slander

Libel

Damages presumed at common law

Slander *per se*
(Damages presumed at common law)
1. Crime
2. Loathsome disease
3. Bad in business
4. Sexual misconduct (women)

Not *per se*
Must show special damages

Libel *per se*

Libel *per quod*
Extrinsic facts necessary

Defenses to libel and slander

Truth
Absolute defense

Opinion
Fair comment
Rhetorical hyperbole

Retraction
Mitigation of damages

Qualified privilege
Fair and accurate report
Neutral reporting privilege

Absolute privilege
Participants in official proceedings

"Constitutional" privileges

Public officials, public figures
Must prove statement made with knowledge of falsity or in reckless disregard of whether true or false

Private plaintiffs
Must show defendant was "at fault" (usually negligent)

Damages
Actual damages cannot be presumed, must be proved
Punitive damages require proof of knowledge of falsity or reckless disregard whether statement was true or false

© Dr. Sandra Davidson

FIGURE 21.1

An understanding of libel and related concepts is essential for journalists.

You cannot be certain, for example, whether a person charged with arson actually started the fire. Who told you that Joe Jones started the fire? The first source to check is the police or fire report. If a police officer or fire marshal says that Jones started a fire, you can report not that Jones did it but that he has been accused of doing it. Unless you have information you would be willing to present in court, you should go no further. Be sure you report no more than what you *know* is true. And if you have a document in your hands that proves what you write, you're in even better shape.

> **"** Journalists don't believe . . . the Freedom of Information Act was created to be turned on us as an excuse to hide information. **"**
> —Sarah Overstreet, columnist

When a newspaper in Oklahoma reported that a wrestling coach had been accused of requiring a sixth-grader, who wanted to rejoin the team, to submit to a whipping by his fellow students while crawling naked through the legs of team members, the coach sued. He claimed damage to his reputation.

In cases like this, the reporter has to be certain not just that one or more participants told of the incident but also that the statements were true. In court, some participants might testify to an occurrence, and others might testify the incident never took place. A jury would have to decide on the credibility of the participants.

Although you must always strive for absolute truth in all of your stories, the courts will settle for what is known as **substantial truth** in most cases. This means that you must be able to prove the essential elements of all you write.

The Georgia case and others show that the courts are holding bloggers to the same standard established for traditional media. In the Georgia case, a disappointed client accused his former attorney, in a blog, of bribing judges. The lawyer sued and won when the blogger couldn't show that his charge was true.

Privilege

In addition to truth, the courts traditionally have allowed another defense against libel: **privilege**. This defense applies when you are covering any of the three branches of government. The courts allow legislators, judges and government executives the **absolute privilege** to say anything—true or false—when acting in their official capacities. The rationale is that the public interest is served when an official is allowed to speak freely and fearlessly about making laws, carrying them out or punishing those who do not obey them. Similarly, a participant in a judicial proceeding, such as an attorney, court clerk or judge, is absolutely privileged to make false and even defamatory statements about another person during that proceeding.

In the executive branch it isn't always clear whose statements are privileged and when. The head of state and the major officers of executive departments of the federal and state governments are covered. However, minor officials might not enjoy the protection of absolute privilege.

As a reporter, you have a **qualified privilege**, sometimes called *neutral reporting* or *conditional privilege*, at the federal level and in some states, to report what public officials say. Your privilege is conditioned on your report's providing full, fair and accurate coverage of the court session, the legislative session or the president's press conference, even if any one of the participants made defamatory statements. You can quote anything the president of the U.S. says without fear of losing a libel suit, even if the president is not acting in an official capacity. Reporters have a qualified privilege to report unofficial statements.

But there are many other levels of executives in federal, state and local governments. Mayors of small towns, for instance, often hold part-time positions. Although you are conditionally privileged to report on what those officials say when they are acting in their official capacities, a problem can arise when the part-time mayor says something defamatory when not acting in an official capacity. Courts in some jurisdictions might grant a qualified privilege; other courts might not.

Fair Comment and Criticism

In some types of writing, you may be commenting or criticizing rather than reporting. The courts have protected writers who comment on and criticize the public offerings of anyone in the public eye. Included in this category are actors and actresses, sports figures, public officials and other newsworthy people. Most often, such writing occurs in reviews of plays, books or movies, or in commentary on service received in hotels and restaurants.

The courts call this **fair comment and criticism**. You are protected as long as you do not misstate any of the facts on which you base your comments or criticisms and as long as you do not wrongly imply that you possess undisclosed, damaging information that forms the basis of your opinion. Merely labeling a fact as an opinion will not result in opinion protection, the U.S. Supreme Court ruled in 1990.

The Actual Malice Test and Public Officials

It was a small but momentous step from fair comment and criticism to the case of *The New York Times* v. Sullivan. In 1964, the U.S. Supreme Court decided that First Amendment protection was broader than just the traditional defenses of truth and privilege and that the press needed even greater freedom in its coverage of public officials.

The case started with an advertisement for funds in *The New York Times* of March 29, 1960, by the Committee to Defend Martin Luther King Jr. and the Struggle for Freedom in the South. The advertisement contained small, inconsequential factual errors concerning the police, according to Montgomery, Ala., Commissioner L.B. Sullivan. He thought the errors damaged his reputation, and he won a half-million-dollar judgment against *The New York Times* in an Alabama trial court.

The Supreme Court said it was considering the case "against the background of a profound national commitment to the principle that debate on public issues should be uninhibited, robust and wide open." Thus Justice William Brennan wrote that the Constitution requires a federal rule prohibiting a public official from recovering damages from the press for a defamatory falsehood relating to his or her official conduct, unless the public official can prove the press had knowledge that what was printed was false or that the story was printed with reckless disregard of whether it was true or not. The justices called this the **actual malice test**.

The actual malice test was applied later in a case involving a story on CBS's *60 Minutes* about a retired U.S. Army officer. Col. Anthony Herbert contended the broadcast falsely portrayed him as a liar. He tried to prove that producer Barry Lando recklessly disregarded whether or not it was a false broadcast. Herbert asked some questions that Lando claimed were protected by the First Amendment because they inquired into his state of mind and into the editorial processes during the production of the program. Eventually, the U.S. Supreme Court decided the "state of mind" case in Col. Herbert's favor.

The decision in the Sharon case discussed earlier in the chapter is an example of the burden of proving actual malice against the press. The jury decided that when the article in question was printed, *Time* did not know that its statement about Gen. Sharon was false.

In 1991, the Supreme Court decided Masson v. *The New Yorker*, the so-called fabricated quotes case. Jeffrey Masson, a psychologist, had sued the magazine and journalist Janet Malcolm, accusing them of making up quotes he never said. Over-ruling a lower court's decision that journalists could fictionalize quotations by making rational interpretations of speakers' remarks, the Supreme Court protected the sanctity of quotation marks. But the court also made clear that not every deliberate change in a quotation is libelous. Only a "material change in the meaning conveyed by a statement" poses a problem. Although Masson won the right to try his case, he lost against all defendants in 1994.

The Actual Malice Test and Public Figures

The actual malice protection was expanded in two cases in 1967 to include not only public officials but also *public figures*—people in the public eye but not in public office.

The first case stemmed from a *Saturday Evening Post* article that accused Coach Wally Butts of conspiring to fix a 1962 college football game between Georgia and Alabama. At the time of the article, Butts was the athletic director of the University of Georgia. The article, titled "The Story of a College Football Fix," was prefaced by a note from the editors of *The Post* stating:

> Not since the Chicago White Sox threw the 1919 World Series has there been a sports story as shocking as this one. . . . Before the University of Georgia played the University of Alabama . . . Wally Butts . . . gave (to Alabama's coach) . . . Georgia's plays, defensive patterns, all the significant secrets Georgia's football team possessed.

The Post reported that, because of an electronic error about a week before the game, George Burnett, an Atlanta insurance salesman, had accidentally overheard a telephone conversation between Butts and the head coach of Alabama, Paul Bryant.

ON THE JOB
The Keys to Avoiding Libel

Ken Paulson earned a law degree after graduating from journalism school. He then practiced journalism for 18 years. After serving as senior vice president of the Freedom Forum in Arlington, Va., and executive director of the First Amendment Center at Vanderbilt University, he returned to the newsroom as editor of *USA Today*. He moved again, to head the Newseum in Washington, D.C., before returning to the First Amendment Center, when he is currently president and CEO.

"Having a law degree has been helpful as a journalist," Paulson says, "but the key to avoiding libel suits really boils down to a few fundamentals."

Those fundamentals are rooted in professionalism and common sense. Paulson suggests that journalists ask themselves these questions:

- Have I reported fully?
- Have I reported factually?
- Have I reported fairly?
- Have I reported in good faith?

"If you can answer those four questions in the affirmative, the law will take care of itself," he says.

Coach Butts sued Curtis Publishing, publishers of *The Post*, and won a verdict for $60,000 in general damages and $3 million in punitive, or punishment, damages. Curtis Publishing appealed the case to the Supreme Court and lost. The trial judge reduced the amount of the damages to $460,000.

The second case was decided the same day. Gen. Edwin Walker sued the Associated Press for distributing a news dispatch giving an eyewitness account by an AP staffer on the campus of the University of Mississippi in the fall of 1962. The AP reported that Gen. Walker personally had led a student charge against federal marshals during a riot on the Mississippi campus. The marshals were attempting to enforce a court decree ordering the enrollment of a black student.

Walker was a retired general at the time of the publication. He won a $2 million libel suit in a trial court, but the Supreme Court ruled against him.

In both cases, the stories were wrong. In both, the actual malice test was applied. What was the difference between the Butts and Walker cases?

The justices said the football story was in no sense "hot news." They noted that the person who said he had heard the conversation was on probation in connection with bad-check charges and that *Post* personnel had not viewed his notes before publication. The court also said, as evidence of actual malice on the part of *The Post*, that no one looked at the game films to see if the information was accurate; that a regular staffer, instead of a football expert, was assigned to the story; and that no check was made with someone knowledgeable in the sport. In short, *The Post* had not done an adequate job of reporting.

The evidence in the Walker case was considerably different. The court said the news in the Walker case required immediate dissemination because of the riot on campus. The justices noted that the AP received the information from a correspondent who was present on the campus and gave every indication of being trustworthy and competent.

In the Butts and Walker cases, the court used two definitions of public figure. The first is a person like Butts who has assumed a role of special prominence in the affairs of society—someone who has pervasive power and influence in a community. The second is a person like Walker who has thrust himself or herself into the forefront of a particular public controversy in order to influence the resolution of the issues involved.

In the 1970s, the Supreme Court decided three cases that help journalists determine who is and is not a public figure. The first case involved Mrs. Russell A. Firestone, who sued for libel after *Time* magazine reported that her husband's divorce petition had been granted on grounds of extreme cruelty and adultery. Mrs. Firestone, who had married into the Firestone Tire and Rubber Co. family, claimed that those were not the grounds for the divorce. She also insisted that she was not a public figure with the burden of proving actual malice.

The Supreme Court agreed. Even though she had held press conferences and had hired a clipping service, the court ruled that she had not thrust herself into the forefront of a public controversy in an attempt to influence the resolution of the issues involved. The court admitted that marital difficulties of extremely wealthy individuals may be of some interest to some portion of the reading public but added that Mrs. Firestone had not freely chosen to publicize private matters about her married life. The justices said she was compelled to go to court to "obtain legal release from the bonds of matrimony." They said she assumed no "special prominence in the resolution of public questions." The case was sent back to Florida for a finding of fault, and a new trial was ordered. Eventually, the case was settled out of court.

The second case involved Sen. William Proxmire of Wisconsin, who had started what he called the Golden Fleece Award. Each month he announced a winner who, in his opinion, had wasted government money. One such winner was Ronald Hutchinson, a behavioral scientist who had received federal funding for research designed to determine why animals clench their teeth. Hutchinson had published articles about his research in professional publications. In deciding that Hutchinson was not a public figure, the court ruled that he "did not thrust himself or his views into public controversy to influence others." The court admitted there may have been legitimate concerns about the way public funds were being spent but said this was not enough to make Hutchinson a public figure.

The third case concerned an individual found guilty of contempt of court in 1958 for his failure to appear before a grand jury investigating Soviet espionage in the U.S. Ilya Wolston's name had been included in a list of people indicted for serving as Soviet agents in a 1974 book published by the Reader's Digest Association. In fact, Wolston had not been indicted on that charge, and he sued.

The Supreme Court, in deciding that Wolston was not a public figure, found that he had played only a minor role in whatever public controversy there may have been concerning the investigation of Soviet espionage. The court added that a private individual is not automatically transformed into a public figure merely by becoming involved in or being associated with a matter that attracts public attention.

As a journalist, do you have the same protection from a libel action when you write about a person somewhat connected with a news event as you do when you are certain a person is a public figure or public official? A 1974 Supreme Court decision says the answer is usually no. In the landmark Gertz v. Welch case, the justices said states may give more protection to private individuals if a newspaper or radio or television station damages their reputations than if the reputations of either public officials or public figures are damaged. Generally, you have protection from a libel action when you write about people who have thrust themselves into the forefront of a controversy or event. More recent cases have cemented this rule, as the courts tend to look broadly at those involved in newsworthy events as public figures.

The Negligence Test and Private Citizens

Private citizens who sue for punitive damages must meet the same actual malice test as public officials and public figures do. Because of the Gertz case, states have been allowed to set their own standards for libel cases involving private citizens who sue only for actual damages. A majority of states and the District of Columbia have adopted a **negligence test**, which requires you to use the same care in gathering facts and writing your story as any reasonable reporter would use under the same or similar circumstances. If you make every effort to be fair and answer all the questions a reasonable person may ask, you probably would pass the negligence test.

One state, New York, has adopted a gross irresponsibility test. A few states have established a more stringent standard that requires private citizens to prove actual malice. Some states simply require a jury to find "fault."

Libel Remains a Danger

Despite all the available defenses, libel remains a serious risk to journalists' financial health, as the following example demonstrates. In 1997, a Texas jury awarded a record $222.7 million to a defunct bond-brokerage firm against Dow Jones & Co., which owns *The Wall Street Journal*. The judge threw out $200 million in punitive damages but let stand the $22.7 million in actual damages for a *Journal* story about "bond daddies."

For citizen journalists, such as bloggers, even awards that are much smaller could be devastating. If you blog, you should meet the same standards of fairness and accuracy that are expected of traditional media.

Libel and the Internet

As we have seen, individuals who libel others over the Internet can be held responsible. But the Internet raises the interesting question of whether an online service provider like AOL or MSN can be held responsible for the libelous messages of their users.

In 1991, CompuServe successfully defended itself against a libel suit in a New York federal trial court. CompuServe had entered a contract with another company to provide an electronic bulletin board in the form of a newsletter about journalism. The second company then used a third company to create the newsletter. Because CompuServe did not try to exercise any editorial control over the newsletter, the court let CompuServe off the hook for libel. The court also reasoned that no library can be held responsible if a book that the librarian has not reviewed contains libel. CompuServe, the court said, was providing an "electronic, for-profit library."

In 1995, however, another online service provider, Prodigy, lost a similar libel case. To promote itself as a family-oriented Internet company, Prodigy controlled the content of its computer bulletin boards by using screening software to look for forbidden words, and its editorial staff blocked allegedly offensive posts. Unfortunately for Prodigy, no screening software could identify libelous material. A New York trial court said that by holding itself out as exercising editorial control, Prodigy was "expressly differentiating itself from its competition and expressly likening itself to a newspaper." Thus the court treated Prodigy like a newspaper and held it liable for libel posted on one of its bulletin boards.

Congress did not agree with the Prodigy decision, however, and effectively overruled the case in 1996 by passing "protection for 'Good Samaritan' blocking and screening of offensive material." Congress obviously did not support the idea that the failure to screen meant protection from libel but that limited screening could lead to liability. Federal courts have uniformly upheld the rule.

INVASION OF PRIVACY

Libel is damage to an individual's reputation. **Invasion of privacy** is a violation of a person's right to be left alone.

As a reporter, you may be risking an invasion of privacy suit under any of these circumstances:

» You physically intrude into a private area to get a story or picture—an act closely related to trespass.
» You publish a story or photograph about someone that is misleading, and thus you portray that person in a "false light."
» You disclose something about an individual's private affairs that is true but that is also offensive to a person of ordinary sensibilities.

Invasion of privacy may also be claimed if someone's name or picture is used in an advertisement or for similar purposes of trade. Such *appropriation* will not affect you when you are performing your reporting duties.

Consent is a basic defense in invasion of privacy suits. Make sure, however, that your use of the material does not exceed the consent given.

Another basic defense in an invasion of privacy suit is that you're a reporter covering a newsworthy situation. The courts usually protect members of the press against invasion of privacy suits when they are reporting matters of legitimate public interest. There are the three exceptions listed earlier, however: trespassing, portraying in a "false light," and causing unwanted publicity.

Trespassing

The first exception arises when you enter private property without permission to get a story. You cannot trespass on private property to get a story or to take a picture, even if it is newsworthy. The courts will not protect you when you are a trespasser.

Two *Life* magazine staffers lost an invasion of privacy suit because, posing as patients, they went into a man's home to get a story about a faith healer. They lost the case even though they were working with the district attorney and the state board of health.

You may enter private property only when you are invited by the owner or renter. And you should never use deception to gain entry to property you otherwise have no legal right of access to.

Portraying in a "False Light"

The courts also will not protect you if you invade someone's privacy by publishing misleading information about that person. For example, a legal problem arises if a photograph or information from a true story about a careful pedestrian struck by a careless driver is used again in connection with a story about, say, careless pedestrians. The pedestrian who was hit could file a lawsuit charging libel, "false light" invasion of privacy or even both in some states.

Some states do not recognize "false light" invasion of privacy and insist that libel is the appropriate form of suit. But "false light" suits can cover situations in which a picture or story is misleading but not defamatory. Even flattering material can place a person in an unwanted, false light.

Causing Unwanted Publicity Offensive to a Person of Ordinary Sensibilities

The third type of invasion of privacy that the courts recognize—unwanted publicity—arises from stories about incidents that, because they are true, are not defamatory but can be offensive to a person of ordinary sensibilities. The courts say that in order for privacy to be invaded, there must be a morbid and sensational prying into private lives. Merely being the subject of an unflattering or uncomfortable article is not enough. An example is a picture published by *Sports Illustrated* in which a football fan's pants zipper was open. The fan sued for invasion of privacy but lost.

Also in the area of unwanted publicity, the Supreme Court held in 1975 and again in 1989 that truthfully reporting the name

> " There are only two occasions when Americans respect privacy. . . . Those are prayer and fishing. "
> —Herbert Hoover, 31st U.S. president

of a rape victim is permitted. In 1976 and in 1979 the justices upheld the right of the press to publish the names of juveniles involved with the law because the information was truthful and of public significance.

PROTECTION OF SOURCES AND NOTES

Another area you must know about is your ability—or inability—to protect your sources and notes. The problem may arise in various situations. A grand jury that is investigating a murder may ask you to reveal the source of a story you wrote about the murder. Or you may be asked to testify at a criminal or civil trial.

The conflict that arises is between a reporter's need to protect sources of information and the duty of every citizen to testify to help the courts determine justice. Your work as a reporter will take you to events that are important and newsworthy. Anyone wanting the facts about an event can subpoena you to bring in all the details. Journalists usually resist. They work for their newspaper or radio or television station, not a law enforcement agency. Their ability to gather information would be compromised if sources knew that their identities or their information could go to the police.

By 2012, some protection against testifying—shield laws—had been adopted by these 41 states and the District of Columbia:

Alabama	Kentucky	North Dakota
Alaska	Louisiana	Ohio
Arizona	Maine	Oklahoma
Arkansas	Maryland	Oregon
California	Michigan	Pennsylvania
Colorado	Minnesota	Rhode Island
Connecticut	Montana	South Carolina
Delaware	Nebraska	Tennessee
Florida	Nevada	Texas
Georgia	New Hampshire	Utah
Hawaii	New Jersey	Washington
Illinois	New Mexico	West Virginia
Indiana	New York	Wisconsin
Kansas	North Carolina	

Shield law protection is important because without it, journalists do go to jail. In 2001–2002, Vanessa Leggett, a freelance journalist in Houston, spent a record 168 days in jail for refusing to hand over notes and interview tapes she had made while writing a book about the murder of a Houston socialite. Texas had no shield law at the time. In 2004–2005, Jim Taricani, a broadcast reporter in Providence, R.I., spent four months under house arrest for refusing to tell who gave him an FBI videotape that showed a Providence official taking a bribe from an undercover FBI agent. A federal judge had ordered Taricani to reveal his source. Although Rhode Island has a shield law, the federal government does not.

Perhaps *New York Times* reporter Judith Miller has garnered the most publicity for being jailed to protect a source. Her saga started when conservative columnist Robert Novak revealed the name of a CIA undercover agent, Valerie Plame. Plame's husband, retired diplomat Joseph Wilson, had said the Bush administration misrepresented the facts when it claimed that President Saddam Hussein of Iraq had tried to buy depleted uranium from Niger. The disclosure about Plame came after Wilson's assertions.

Miller did not use Plame's name in her stories, but she went to jail on July 6, 2005, for refusing to reveal the source who had provided her with information about the agent. Because it is a violation of federal law for an official to reveal the identity of an undercover CIA agent, a special prosecutor was assigned to investigate that leak. Several other journalists did testify after receiving permission from their sources. Miller and her bosses at *The Times* took the position that her promise to hold confidential her sources' names was not one she could break. The U.S. Supreme Court refused to hear her appeal. Although her imprisonment inspired bills in Congress calling for a federal shield law, Congress has not yet passed such a law.

Miller was released after serving 85 days in jail when her source gave her permission to reveal his identity. The only criminal charge to result from the investigation

After refusing to disclose to a judge his source for a 1971 article about the trial of mass murderer Charles Manson, reporter William Farr was taken to jail in a police van.

was a charge against Lewis "Scooter" Libby, assistant to Vice President Dick Cheney, of lying to investigators. Libby was convicted in federal court.

In 1980, Congress did pass the Privacy Protection Act. Under that act, federal, state and local law enforcement officers generally may not use a search warrant to search newsrooms. Instead, they must get a subpoena for documents, which instructs reporters and editors to hand over the material. Officers may use a warrant to search newsrooms only if they suspect a reporter of being involved in a crime or if immediate action is needed to prevent bodily harm, loss of life or destruction of the material.

> " (The media) seek to maintain a balance on the constantly shifting tightrope of personal privacy, access to information and government accountability. "
>
> —John R. Finnegan Sr., former newspaper editor

The difference between a search warrant and a subpoena is great. Officers with a search warrant can knock on the door, enter the newsroom and search on their own. A subpoena does not permit officers to search the newsroom. A subpoena for specific documents requires reporters to turn over the material to authorities at a predetermined time and place. In addition, it gives reporters time to challenge in court the necessity of surrendering the material.

Even in states with shield laws, judges in most criminal cases involving grand juries will not allow you to keep your sources secret. In other criminal cases, courts may allow confidentiality if a three-part test is met. Supreme Court Justice Potter Stewart suggested this test in his dissent in Branzburg v. Hayes, decided in 1972:

> Government officials must, therefore, demonstrate that the information sought is clearly relevant to a precisely defined subject of government inquiry. . . . They must demonstrate that it is reasonable to think the witness in question has that information. . . . And they must show that there is not any means of obtaining the information less destructive of First Amendment liberties.

In civil litigation, you may be permitted to keep sources confidential in most cases unless the court finds that the information sought is unavailable from other sources and highly relevant to the underlying litigation or of such critical importance to the lawsuit that it goes to the heart of the plaintiff's claim.

If you are sued for libel, you will find it difficult both to protect your sources and to win the lawsuit. The court might well rule against you on whether a statement is true or false if it came from a source you refuse to name.

The best way to avoid such confrontation with the courts is not to promise a source you will keep his or her name confidential. Only for the most compelling reason should you promise confidentiality.

In 1991, the U.S. Supreme Court ruled in Cohen v. Cowles Media Co. that the First Amendment does not prevent a source from suing a news organization if a reporter has promised the source confidentiality but the newspaper publishes the source's name anyway.

The latest controversy over journalistic privilege involves the status of bloggers and other digital authors under state shield laws. Shield laws for the most part were written before blogs existed, and thus often limit protection to members of bona fide news organizations. The law struggles to keep pace with emerging digital news operations and independent bloggers, with predictable results.

A New Jersey Superior Court judge recently ordered a blogger to defend her status as a journalist and explain why the state's shield law applied to her in her effort to avoid revealing the names of government officials she accused of wrongdoing.

Union County prosecutors subpoenaed blogger Tina Renna for the names of 16 government officials she accused of misusing county generators after Hurricane Sandy. Renna, who runs the website The County Watchers, claimed her sources would be revealed if she handed over the officials' names. A similar suit in Oregon raised the same issue: Are bloggers "journalists" and entitled to the protection of shield laws? In many states, the answer is far from clear.

ACCESS TO COURTS

The Supreme Court held in 1979 that "members of the public have no constitutional right" under the Sixth Amendment to attend criminal trials. In a reversal exactly one year later, the justices held that the public and the press have a First Amendment right to attend criminal trials. The justices said the right was not absolute but trial judges could close criminal trials only when there was an "overriding interest" to justify such closure. The basic concern of judges when they close trials is to protect the accused person's Sixth Amendment right to an "impartial jury"—often translated by attorneys as "a fair trial."

In addition, the First Amendment prevents the government from conducting business—even trials—in secret. In the Richmond Newspapers case in 1980, Chief Justice Warren Burger traced the unbroken and uncontradicted history of open judicial proceedings in England and the U.S. He concluded that there is a "presumption of openness" in criminal trials and pointed out the important role of the news media as representatives of the public.

By 1984, the Supreme Court had decided that openness in criminal trials "enhances both the basic fairness of the criminal trial and the appearance of fairness so essential to public confidence in the system." Public proceedings vindicate the concerns of victims and the community in knowing that offenders are being brought to account for their criminal conduct "by jurors fairly and openly selected." Proceedings of jury selection could be closed, the chief justice said, only when a trial judge finds that closure preserves an "overriding interest" and is narrowly tailored to serve that interest.

Judges are using that option. For instance, when John Gotti was convicted of organized crime activities in New York, the jurors' names were kept secret. Gotti's attorneys unsuccessfully challenged their anonymity. Jurors' names in the Rodney King case, which resulted in riots in Los Angeles in 1992, also were withheld.

In 1986, the Supreme Court said that only an overriding interest found by a trial judge can overcome the presumption of openness of criminal proceedings.

Today, 47 states allow cameras in at least some state courtrooms. Cameras are permitted in some lower federal courts but are excluded from the U.S. Supreme Court.

COPYRIGHT AND FAIR USE

The purpose of copyright law is to ensure compensation to authors for contributing to the common good by publishing their works. The Constitution provides for this in Article 1, Section 8, by giving Congress the power to secure "for limited times to authors and inventors the exclusive right to their respective writing and discoveries." The same section indicates that this provision is intended "to promote the progress of science and useful arts" for the benefit of the public. Copyright laws both protect your work and prohibit you from using significant amounts of others' writings without permission, which may in some cases require payment of a fee.

Key elements of copyright law include the following:

» Copyrightable works are protected from the moment they are fixed in tangible form, whether published or unpublished.
» Copyright protection begins with a work's "creation and . . . endures for a term consisting of the life of the author and 70 years after the author's death."
» Works for hire and anonymous and pseudonymous works are protected for 95 years from publication or 100 years from creation, whichever is shorter.
» There is a "fair use" limitation on the exclusive rights of copyright owners. In other words, it may be permissible to quote small excerpts from a copyrighted work without permission. According to the Supreme Court, these factors govern fair use:
  1. The purpose and character of the use.
  2. The nature of the copyrighted work.
  3. The size and significance of the portion used in relationship to the copyrighted work as a whole.
  4. The effect on the potential market for or value of the copyrighted work.

Although a work is copyrighted from the moment it is fixed in tangible form, the copyright statute says certain steps are necessary for the work to receive statutory protection. The author or publisher must:

» Publish or reproduce the work with the word "copyright" or the symbol ©, the name of the copyright owner and the year of publication.
» Deposit two copies of the work with the Library of Congress within three months of publication. (Failure to do so will not affect the copyright but could lead to the imposition of fines.)
» Register the work at the Library of Congress by filling out a form supplied by the Copyright Office and sending the form, the specified number of copies (usually one copy of an unpublished work and two copies of a published work), and a $35

fee to the Copyright Office. The copies and registration fee may be sent together and usually are.

Copyright law has a special provision for broadcasters of live programs. Broadcasters need only make a simultaneous tape of their live broadcasts in order to receive copyright protection. The tape fulfills the requirement that a work be in a "fixed" form for copyright protection. Because a digital form is a "fixed" form, editors of online newspapers already meet that copyright requirement.

Some aspects of U.S. copyright law changed in 1989, when the U.S. finally joined the 100-year-old Berne Convention, an international copyright treaty, primarily to prevent the pirating of American film productions in other countries. The changes include the following:

» Placing a copyright notice on a work is no longer necessary to protect a copyright after publication. This is in line with the Berne Convention principle that copyright protection should not be subject to formalities. The copyright notice, however, is still widely used because it acts as a bar to an infringer's claim of innocent infringement.

» Copyright registration is no longer a prerequisite for access to the federal courts for an infringement action. But registration is required for a copyright owner to recover statutory damages. (Without registration, the copyright owner can recover only the damages he or she can prove, plus court costs and "reasonable" attorney's fees.) The amount of statutory damages is determined by the judge. If the infringer was not aware he or she was infringing a copyright, the court may award as little as $200. If the infringement was willful, the court can award up to $150,000. Thus, like the copyright notice, copyright registration remains highly advisable.

Online journalism has created new copyright concerns. Using online content from others without permission can raise significant copyright issues, as the courts are still wrestling with the extent of the fair use doctrine when it comes to online usage. The safe route, and the ethical choice, is to seek permission before using the work of others and to link to other news sites if you wish to direct readers to other content online.

The digital media also have changed the rules of the game for freelancers and other content providers. In 2001, the U.S. Supreme Court, ruling against media companies, said freelance writers have the power to decide whether the articles they sold to print publications may be reproduced in an electronic form. In a 7-2 decision, the justices ruled that *The New York Times* must either pay its freelance authors when redistributing their articles online or negotiate other conditions for republication.

SUGGESTED READINGS

Carter, T. Barton, Marc A. Franklin, and Jay B. Wright. *The First Amendment and the Fourth Estate*. 8th ed. Westbury, N.Y.: Foundation Press, 2000. This text focuses on the relationship between the First Amendment and the press itself.

Middleton, Kent R., Robert Trager, and Bill F. Chamberlin. *The Law of Public Communication*. 6th ed. Boston: Allyn and Bacon, 2003. This is a valuable and authoritative treatment of free speech and free press issues.

Overbeck, Wayne. *Major Principles of Media Law*. Toronto: Thomson Wadsworth, 2004. This standard text covers all important aspects of law as it applies to the mass media.

SUGGESTED WEBSITES

www.firstamendmentcenter.org
At this Freedom Forum site, you'll find the "State of the First Amendment" report by Donna Demas, which discusses the public's ambivalence about First Amendment issues.

www.medialaw.org
This is the site of the Media Law Resource Center, "a non-profit information clearinghouse" organized in 1980 by leading media groups "to monitor developments and promote First Amendment rights in the libel, privacy and related legal fields." The site features a 50-state survey of media libel law.

www.rcfp.org
The Reporters Committee for Freedom of the Press maintains online publications and guides on First Amendment and freedom of information issues. Here you'll find current hot stories, plus archives and much more.

EXERCISES

1. **Team project.** Your instructor will divide your class into teams of four or five. With your teammates, select one situation from the following list.

   a. A reporter is on an assignment with a photographer who enters a house without permission and photographs the sale of illegal drugs. Should the reporter publish the photos?

   b. Your team is launching an independent news blog. What should your policy on the use of confidential sources look like? What legal factors should you consider in adopting the policy? Examine the latest cases involving bloggers and shield laws for guidance when formulating your policy.

   c. A team of reporters is working on a series of articles about possible corruption in the city agency responsible for zoning. One reporter gets an anonymous call from a senior official offering to give information about wrongdoing, but only on condition of anonymity. Should the reporter agree to anonymity for the source?

   d. A journalist comes into possession of a private email sent by a well-known person to an apparent lover and considers quoting the email and the recipient's name in a blog. Should the reporter use the email and the recipient's name?

   Discuss with your teammates the issues raised in the situation you've chosen. Brainstorm possible actions a journalist could take. Come up with a list of pros and cons for each action, and decide which action would, journalistically and legally, be the most responsible.

2. Using a search engine, identify a current First Amendment controversy of local interest. What are the issues? Write a two-page essay outlining the arguments and predicting the outcome of the controversy based on First Amendment analysis.

3. *The New York Times* v. Sullivan, 376 U.S. 254 (1964), was a landmark decision in favor of the press. Discuss, in a short essay, the consequences for the press if the decision had been different.

4. Using the LexisNexis database, determine how the U.S. Supreme Court has used Richmond Newspapers v. Virginia, 448 U.S. 555 (1980), in later cases dealing with openness in criminal proceedings.

5. **Journalism blog.** Find a news story generated by a public records request. One way to do this is by searching the "FOI at work" tag at www.theartofaccess.com, a blog dedicated to freedom of information news. Write a blog post summarizing the story and explaining why access to governmental information was important to the story.

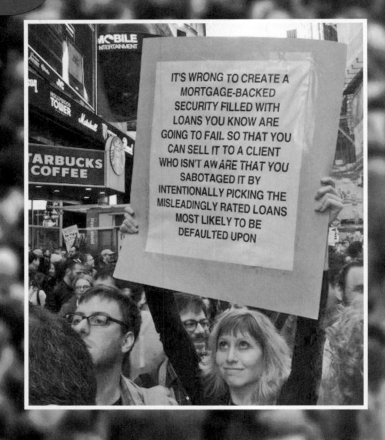

22

Ethics

JOURNALISTS, like most people, confront ethical decisions every day. Some would say more than most people.

» A review by Media Matters for America (MediaMatters.org) revealed that at least 32 Fox News figures publicly backed Republican campaigns in more than 300 instances in the 2011–2012 elections nationally and in more than 40 states.

» *The Sacramento Bee* fired award-winning photographer Bryan Patrick for digitally manipulating a photo of a great egret catching a frog. He combined it with one of a snowy egret reaching to grab a frog. After conducting a review, the *Bee* found that Patrick had previously altered two other photos.

» *The Oregonian* fired editor Kathleen Glanville for writing a story for the paper that editorial page editor Bob Caldwell had died in his parked car after suffering a fatal heart attack. He had actually died in a $200-an-hour prostitute's apartment while engaging in sex with a 23-year-old. Glanville moved Caldwell's car from the scene. While Caldwell was in charge of the editorial page, the paper ran 16 unsigned editorials deploring prostitution. Under his leadership, the paper won a Pulitzer Prize for editorial writing in 2006.

» After six of his staff members signed a petition to recall Gov. Scott Walker from office, *Wisconsin State Journal* editor John Smalley told them journalists shouldn't do that.

» *New Yorker* writer Jonah Lehrer resigned after admitting he had made up quotes attributed to Bob Dylan in his nonfiction book *Imagine*. He had also recycled work in articles and blogs and in his book.

The journalists involved in these incidents did not break any laws, but they knowingly committed serious ethical violations.

U.S. citizens have never had much regard for journalists' ethics. In 2000, Gallup reported that only 20 percent rated journalists' ethics as high or very high. In 2011, it was 25 percent.

Whom do poll respondents include and exclude when they use the term "journalists"? Do they equate "media" with journalism? Journalists work in the mass media, but in no way should journalism be identified as the mass media. The mass media

In this chapter
you will learn:

1. How the public perceives journalism ethics.

2. Three philosophical approaches that can help you find answers to ethical questions.

3. How to apply a method of principled reasoning to ethical problems.

4. What ethical questions are of special importance to journalists.

5. How to recognize and avoid plagiarism.

6. How to apply ethics to Twitter messages.

**bedfordstmartins.com
/newsreporting**

Watch **"Journalism Ethics:
What News Is Fit to Print?"**

» Who decides what news
is fit to publish, post or
broadcast? Who decides
issues such as whether to
publish the names of sexual
assault victims? Who should
decide, and why?

» How might convergence
make it harder for
journalists to maintain long-
held ethical standards?

*❝ If bloggers had no ethics, blogging would have
failed, but it didn't. So let's get a clue. ❞*

—Jay Rosen, media critic, author and scholar

include movies, fictional television series and music—none of which purport to be journalism.

You can, of course, find journalism in blogs, in Twitter messages and in every form of social media. And the principles and guidelines for being ethical apply to all media that can correctly be categorized as journalism. But journalism ethics do not necessarily apply to shows featuring political satirists, activist TV commentators or celebrity watchers, for example. Such shows may have the veneer of journalism, but they use current events only for entertainment purposes or commentary.

THE PUBLIC PERCEPTION OF JOURNALISM ETHICS

Often people who accuse the news media of being unethical have no clear notion of what journalism and journalism ethics are all about. Yet most of these people will say they have no trust in the press because they consider journalism ethics to be an oxymoron (a contradiction in terms). Despite this public perception, journalism has never been practiced in a more ethical way in this country and in a host of other countries around the globe. How can that be? Let's look at two factors influencing the theory and practice of journalism today.

Bloggers as Watchdogs

Some of the credit for the increased ethical behavior of journalists belongs to bloggers and many others on the Internet who are serving as watchdogs of the press and calling attention to every irregularity they see. Twitter users are quick to find errors, exaggerations and other problems with news coverage. As a result, journalists have responded by becoming much more transparent and by discussing their mistakes and failings.

David Leonhardt, Washington bureau chief for *The New York Times*, wrote in his Reddit chat: "I think the Web has created a more responsible press, with higher standards. Think how much easier it is for readers to point out flaws (or perceived flaws!) in a story today than in the past."

Journalism Codes of Ethics

Like many other professions, journalism in its many forms has codes of ethics. Some professions have the power to keep people from practicing unless they have member-ship or a license to practice. These professions can also censure practitioners in a meaningful way, perhaps even keeping members from practicing if they violate the code of the profession.

Despite journalists' increased accountability, journalism as a profession has not established a mandatory and enforced code. Although there are voluntary societies in journalism, no association has the authority to enforce restrictions on journalists' behavior. That's because of a fear that such an association and such a code might in some way infringe upon freedom of the press.

Examples of journalistic professional societies that have codes include the Society of Professional Journalists, the Public Relations Society of America, the International Association of Business Communicators, the American Society of Business Press Editors, the American Society of Magazine Editors and the American Business Media. CyberJournalist.net has a model bloggers' code of ethics that is similar to the code of the Society of Professional Journalists. However, journalists do not *have* to belong to such organizations to practice their profession.

Some critics condemn codes of ethics either for being hopelessly general and therefore ineffective or for being too restrictive. Some argue that strict codes help improve journalists' credibility; others say they merely make journalists easy targets for libel suits. Still, a majority of news organizations have established and enforced codes that restrict employees in their work. Journalists who have plagiarized, for example, have been suspended or fired from their news organizations.

Your employer might or might not have a code of ethics. Either way, you should devise your own ethical values and principles. Your upbringing, your education, and perhaps your religious training have already helped prepare you to do this.

Journalists too often and too easily justify all of their actions by citing the First Amendment. Because of the wide range of the First Amendment and the relatively few legal restraints on journalism, journalists need to discuss proper conduct—perhaps more than members of any other profession. As the famous Commission on Freedom of the Press concluded in 1947, unless journalists set their own limits on what is acceptable and responsible, government will eventually and inevitably do it for them.

THREE ETHICAL PHILOSOPHIES

Your personal ethics might derive from the way you answer one fundamental question: Does the end justify the means? In other words, should you ever do something that is not good in itself in order to achieve a goal that you think is good? Here's how adherents to three different ethical philosophies would answer that question.

The Ethics of Duty

Some ethicists hold quite simply that we have a duty to do what is right. They believe that some actions are always right and some always wrong; that is, there exists in nature (or, for those with religious faith, in divine revelation) a fixed set of principles or laws from which we should not deviate. For these people, the end *never* justifies the means.

That belief is why some refer to this ethical philosophy as **absolutism** or *legalism*. An absolutist sees one clear duty: to discover the rules and to follow them. For example:

» Suppose you believe that it's always wrong to lie. If you learn that a friend cheated on an exam and you are asked about your friend's actions by a college administrator, you would answer truthfully. You might be torn by loyalty to your friend, but you would not lie.

» Suppose you believe that it's wrong to keep someone else's property without permission. If you find a wallet with $500 in it, you would make every effort to return the wallet to its rightful owner.

One such absolutist was Immanuel Kant (1724–1804). Kant proposed the "categorical imperative," a moral law that obliges you to do only those things that you would be willing to have everyone do as a matter of universal law. Once you decide what the correct action is, you must regard your decision as unconditional and without exception, and you must do what you decide.

Many people draw support for their rigid sense of duty from their religious beliefs. They cite the Bible, the Quran or another religious source. If they themselves cannot resolve an ethical problem, they might turn to a minister, priest, rabbi, imam or guru for the answer. The absolutist is concerned only with doing what is right and needs only to discover what the right action is.

The journalist with this sense of duty is concerned only with whether an event is newsworthy. If an event is interesting, timely, significant or important, it is to be reported, regardless of the consequences. The duty of the journalist is to report the news. Period. Newscaster Walter Cronkite once said that if journalists worried about all the possible consequences of reporting something, they would never report anything.

Journalists who believe they have a duty to tell the news discount any criticism of the press for any stories it delivers to the public. Stop blaming the messenger, they say. We don't make events happen; we just report them.

The Ethics of Final Ends or Consequences

Many people believe that what makes an act ethical is not the act itself but the consequences of the act. In other words, they believe that the end can and often does justify the means. Actions that have "right consequences" are ethical actions. In this philosophy, ethics are more *relativistic* than absolutist. For example:

» Suppose your sister tells you that her husband is abusing her and she is moving to a shelter for battered women. If the husband asks you where your sister is, you would be justified, as one who practices relativism, in lying to protect her from him.

» Suppose a friend swears you to secrecy before telling you that he is feeling suicidal. If you believe that the consequences of an action determine its ethics, you would be justified in breaking your promise and getting help for your friend from a counselor or the friend's family.

An important consideration in relativism, the belief that nothing is objectively right or wrong, is the intention of the person performing the act. What one person

ON THE JOB

Develop Your Ability to Identify Ethical Situations

Jean McHale earned her bachelor's degree in journalism and worked in editorial roles at membership, employee and trade publications, followed by increasingly responsible positions in public information and public relations. She currently works at a professional association performing a variety of writing, media relations and executive communication assignments.

McHale says she has faced ethical choices throughout her career, but few situations presented themselves as neatly packaged defining moments.

"I've learned to recognize when my internal caution light is flashing," she says. "It is often a time when I cannot muster the energy to start a simple task, or when I feel the urge to rush through an assignment to get it off my plate, or when I'm in a creative rut."

McHale says that a personal or professional value often was being challenged in situations that triggered her impatience or hesitation.

"I can't overemphasize the importance of trusting your unique values, education and experiences to guide the professional and ethical decisions you will encounter throughout your career."

would declare unethical, another person would do for a good purpose or a good reason. For example, police often work undercover, concealing their identity in order to apprehend criminals. In the course of this work, if they must lie or even get involved in criminal activity, they would accept that. Their purpose is to protect the public; their intention is to work for the good of society. The end justifies the means.

Some journalists would not hesitate to do the same. Some might require that certain conditions be in place before they would steal or use deceit, but then they would proceed. They believe their purpose is to be the watchdog of government, to protect the common good, to keep the public fully informed. Whatever they must do to accomplish these goals, they argue, is clearly ethical.

Situation Ethics: The Ethics of Specific Acts

When asked whether the end justifies the means, a person subscribing to **situation ethics** would reply, "It all depends." Here are four philosophies that make use of some form of situation ethics.

No Moral Absolutes

Some believe there are no moral absolutes and that there is only one operative principle: Every person or every situation is unique, and to resolve an ethical problem by applying principles held by others or principles that apply in other cases is unethical. They believe that because each situation is unique, each ethical problem must be judged entirely on its own merits.

Love of Neighbor

Another type of situation ethics is based on the golden rule, essentially "You shall love your neighbor as yourself." This ethic holds that all principles are relative to one absolute: love of neighbor. Although you might think of love of neighbor as an essential Christian value with roots in Judaism, the fact is that most religions, as well as secular humanism, hold human values as the highest good.

To state it more simply, this form of situation ethics always places people first. In every ethical dilemma, you must always do what is best for people. Sometimes you must choose between love for one person and love for a larger community of people.

The Greatest Good for the Greatest Number

Love of neighbor can lead you to choose the action that is most likely to yield the greatest good for the greatest number. Some people add the words "over a long period of time" because some actions might seem wrong if one looks merely at the present situation.

Most journalists probably subscribe to this ethic. They know, for example, that publishing a story about the infidelities of a public official might destroy the person's reputation or hurt his or her family, but taking a greatest-good-for-the-greatest-number view, they decide that for the greater good, the public should have this information. The decision to publish will seem even more justifiable if the public official is involved in embezzlement or bribery or a possible threat to national security.

Ayn Rand's Rational Self-Interest

Ayn Rand's ethical philosophy of rational self-interest is the opposite of the greatest good for the greatest number and certainly of any form of altruism. Someone subscribing to her notion of ethical egoism would never sacrifice himself or herself for the good of others. An ethical egoist always looks out for his or her own self-interest first, believing that if everyone acted in this manner, we all would be better off.

Journalists who are ethical egoists do not mind using people for stories, even if the people they use have no idea how embarrassing the story might be to them. Photographers might take pictures of dying or dead children and of their grieving parents. Newscasters might not hesitate to show people committing suicide. In their opinion, whatever helps them get good stories and thus advance in the profession is ethical.

Some critics accuse journalists of embracing rational self-interest merely to sell publications or to increase traffic or ratings. However, on many occasions journalists report stories that anger both their readers and their advertisers.

RESOLVING ETHICAL ISSUES

Far too often, newsroom decisions are made on the basis of what will get the most views on the Web or what will get the viewers' attention. If you subscribe to the ethics of duty, you have no decisions to make. If you know the news, report it. But most ethicists believe that reasonable people must make reasoned or principled decisions.

These must be based on principles that will help you decide on proper or moral ways to act.

Principled reasoning assumes that you are not acting ethically if you do something simply because you have been told to do it or because that's what everyone else does. You are not ethical if you report a story just to beat the competition.

> *" I tell the honest truth in my paper, and I leave the consequences to God. "*
> —James Gordon Bennett, newspaper publisher, 1836

To help journalists and others make ethical decisions, ethicists Clifford Christians, Kim Rotzoll and Mark Fackler adapted a model of moral reasoning devised by Dr. Ralph Potter of Harvard Divinity School. Called the Potter Box (Figure 22.1), the model has four elements:

» **Appraising the situation.** Making a good ethical decision begins with good reporting. You cannot make an ethical decision unless you know all the facts. Sometimes when you don't appraise a situation fully and get all of the facts, you end up being highly embarrassed. The same can happen when you edit out facts so as to change a story.

The *Today* show broadcast a clip of a 911 call during the coverage of the fatal shooting of Trayvon Martin in Miami that made it look as if George Zimmerman, the shooter, immediately identified Martin as black when in fact he did so only in response to a dispatcher's question. A *New York Post* editorial called the edited 911 dispatch "pretty damning evidence of willful misconduct by NBC News" and suggested that racial violence could result from such "irresponsible news coverage." The editing error cost the Miami-based producer his job. He said he had cut the segment to meet a time requirement.

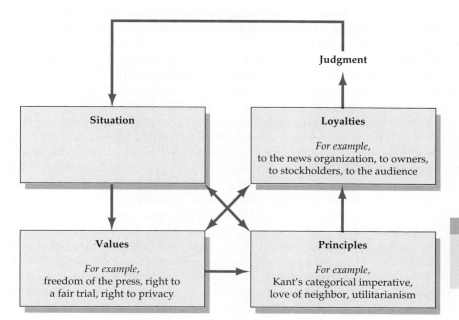

FIGURE 22.1

The Potter Box can help journalists analyze and resolve ethical problems.

TIPS

The SPJ's professional code of ethics cautions journalists to watch out for the following:

» Conflicts of interest, real or perceived.

» Associations and activities that may compromise integrity or damage credibility.

» Gifts and favors, secondary employment, political involvement, public office, and service in organizations that might compromise journalistic integrity.

» Favored treatment to advertisers and special interests.

» Bidding for news.

When *US Uncut* posted a fake GE news release that said that GE would return its $3.2 billion tax cut, it fooled *USA Today* and AP. Said *US Uncut* spokesperson Carl Gibson, "This action showed us how the world could work. For a brief moment people believed that the biggest corporate tax dodger had a change of heart and actually did the right thing." But obviously, *USA Today* and AP did not do the right thing either. They did not check the facts. During the brief period of the hoax, GE's stock plunged 0.6 percent, far more than $3.2 billion. It quickly recovered.

» **Identifying values.** What are your personal values, your news organization's values, your community's values, the nation's values? For example, you might place high value on your personal credibility and on that of your news organization.

When 27-year veteran and three-time Pulitzer Prize–winning *Washington Post* reporter Sari Horwitz was caught copying and pasting material from *The Arizona Republic* twice in six days, it wasn't just *The Post* that was harmed. As Dennis Wagner, the reporter who did most of the work on the original story, said, "It's bad because it undermines the credibility not just of *The Washington Post* but of journalists in general. People think we take shortcuts and cheat, and it's hurtful to all of us."

» **Appealing to ethical principles.** Look at the various ethical principles discussed previously. Contrary to what many believe, it's not always sufficient to follow your gut. If that were true, the world would have only ethical people in it. Nor are the principles meant to be a shopping list from which you choose items that serve your personal interest. To be ethical, you might have to choose a principle or principles that are far from expedient.

When veteran *Chicago Sun-Times* reviewer Paige Wiser left a "Glee Live" concert because one of her children became ill, she failed to note this in her review. In fact, she included one song she didn't see and another one that was not even performed. "What I should have done was written that I had to leave early, but I didn't want to let the paper down, so I tried to make the review seem complete by including the encore 'Friday' that I'm familiar with. Big mistake. I didn't see it there. So it was a lie." Expedient, but dumb. Wiser was fired.

» **Choosing loyalties.** Without question, your most important loyalty must be to your own principles and values. You must be able to look yourself in the mirror; you must be able to sleep at night. Your second most important loyalty is to your readers, listeners or viewers. You have a bond with them, and you dare not break their trust. Third, be loyal to the news organization for which you work. Sometimes this involves a bit of compromise, but you must consider seriously what your boss wants from you. You do need a job. Fourth, you must be loyal to your sources and to the people about whom you are reporting.

Sometimes being loyal to yourself and your principles gets you thrown in jail or fired. Caitlin Curran believed that it was wrong for brokerage houses to sell worthless mortgage-backed securities. A photo of her carrying a sign of her belief went viral on the Web, and she was fired from her part-time job as a Web producer with a Public Radio International show on WNYC in New York. Curran knew the rules against activism, and she chose to do something she deemed more important.

You need not consider the four elements in the Potter Box in any particular order. Also, don't stop reasoning after you have touched upon the four elements. Principled reasoning should continue, and be sure to use it in the discussion of other ethical problems. The main objection to the Potter Box is that using it takes too much time and is impractical in the deadline-driven business of journalism. However, as you become better acquainted with ethical principles and more practiced at principled reasoning, you will be able to make ethical decisions much more quickly and reasonably.

ETHICAL PROBLEMS FOR JOURNALISTS

Because of the First Amendment, American society has relatively few "rules" for journalists despite the special problems they face. The Web has introduced new ethical issues for journalists, and many times, those who write news for the Web have had no training in journalism ethics.

Without a doubt, the news often is not vetted the way it used to be before appearing in a newspaper or in a regular newscast. Cutbacks in newsroom staffs have also added to the difficulty of maintaining accuracy and credibility. Reporters are now expected to be involved in social media, and that, too, takes precious time.

All of this does not excuse the ethical violations discussed here. If anything, journalists need to be more versed in applying ethical principles than ever before.

> " Ethics is a system of principles, a morality or code of conduct. It is the values and rules of life recognized by an individual, group or culture seeking guidelines to human conduct and what is good or bad, right or wrong. "
>
> —Conrad C. Fink, professor, author

Deceit

When is it permissible to lie, misrepresent yourself or use a hidden audio recorder or camera? When may you steal documents? For those subscribing to the ethics of duty, the answer is simple: Never! The simple reason is that they would never want lying or concealing one's identity to become a universal law. For others, the answer is not easy.

Journalists and other writers have often concealed their identity in pursuit of a story. One reporter got a job in a grocery store to expose it for selling bad meat; an atheist became close to churchgoers to write a book about the evangelical church. Yet Fred Barnes, an editor at *The Weekly Standard*, says that if you're a journalist, it's dishonest to profess to be someone you're not.

A group of journalists in an ethical decision-making seminar at the Poynter Institute devised a list of criteria to justify the use of deceit. The box "Conditions Justifying the Use of Deceit by Journalists" synthesizes their conclusions. All the conditions listed there must be present to justify deceit.

> " Journalists demean themselves and damage their credibility when they misrepresent themselves and their work to news sources and, in turn, to the public at large. "
>
> —Everette E. Dennis, Dean and CEO of Northwestern University in Qatar

Conditions Justifying the Use of Deceit by Journalists

» An issue of profound public importance:
  - Of vital public interest, revealing system failure at high levels.
  - A preventive measure against profound harm to individuals.
» All other alternatives exhausted.
» Eventual full disclosure of the deception and the reason for it.
» Full commitment to the story by everyone involved.
» The harm prevented outweighs any harm caused.

» A meaningful, collaborative and deliberative decision-making process that takes into account:
  - Short- and long-term consequences of the deception.
  - The impact on credibility.
  - Motivations for actions.
  - Congruence between the deceptive act and the organization's editorial mission.
  - Legal implications.
  - Consistency of reasoning and action.

TIPS

Ethical Problems That Journalists Face

» Deceit.

» Conflicts of interest:
  - Friendship.
  - Payola.
  - Freebies.
  - Checkbook journalism.
  - Participation in the news.

» Advertising pressure.

» Invasion of privacy.

» Withholding information.

» Incorrect and incomplete information.

» Plagiarism.

Conflicts of Interest

Conflicts of interest can crop up anywhere, especially in the area of politics. Michele Norris of National Public Radio said she would resign her position on *All Things Considered* because her husband had taken a job with the Obama re-election campaign. In contrast, George Will, a syndicated columnist, saw no problem when his wife joined Gov. Rick Perry's presidential campaign. Will had criticized presidential candidate Mitt Romney in his column.

Conflicts of interest can occur outside the political arena, too. The Public Relations Society of America's Member Code of Ethics states that a member shall "disclose financial interest (such as stock ownership) in a client's organization." Should business reporters be allowed to cover companies in which they own stocks? Should all reporters be required to list the companies in which they hold stocks? Should religion writers cover news and events of the religion to which they belong?

Friendship

Friendship might be the greatest obstacle to the flow of information. No one knows whether friendship causes more stories to be reported or more stories to be killed. Either way, it sets up a powerful conflict of interest. If you are ever assigned to a story that involves a personal acquaintance, ask your supervisor to give the assignment to someone else.

Payola

Journalists may not accept payment for a story other than from their employer. Also, news organizations frown upon reporters doing promotional work for people they cover.

Economist Ben Stein was fired as a *New York Times* columnist because he was paid to be in advertisements for a company charging people to get their "free credit scores." Stein denied a conflict of interest because he never wrote about credit scores.

But he was an economist, and therefore, to the editors of the *Times*, there was a clear perception of a conflict of interest.

Other conflicts of interest are perhaps not as obvious. Should news agencies prohibit journalists from accepting speakers' fees? Should Congress attempt to legislate full disclosure of journalists' income and associations?

Freebies

When journalists accept freebies from people they cover, the gifts always come with a price. They raise these questions:

» Can reporters remain objective?
» Do gifts cause reporters to write stories they otherwise would not write?
» Does the public perceive the reporter who accepted or is suspected of accepting freebies as objective?

As with other conflicts of interest, it's the perception that is paramount. Some argue that the least reporters must do is disclose prominently in their stories any freebies they accepted. As in any case of deceit, reporters must disclose how they were able to get the story and why accepting freebies was necessary.

For example, travel writers are offered free trips, free cruises, free hotel accommodations and other freebies by companies that expect them to write about what they experience. Many small news outlets cannot afford to send their travel writers on expensive tours. Travel writers who accept freebies must mention doing so in their stories and allow readers to decide whether to trust the reporting.

Most news organizations have rules against accepting freebies. The Scripps-Howard newspaper group says, "When the gifts exceed the limits of propriety, they should be returned." The Society of Professional Journalists says, "Nothing of value shall be accepted." Is a cup of coffee something of value? The Associated Press expects its staff members to return gifts of "nominal value." Is a baseball cap of nominal value?

> " Conflict of interest is practically the only place in ethics where perceptions matter almost as much as what is the case. "
>
> —Lee Wilkins, co-author of *Media Ethics: Issues and Cases* and editor of the *Journal of Mass Media Ethics*

Checkbook Journalism

Paying a source for information brings up a number of ethical questions.

» Must you always report that you had to pay a source for information?
» Should reporters be in the business of keeping other reporters from getting a story?
» Are paid sources likely to have an ax to grind?
» Do paid sources come forward only for financial gain?
» Will the audience believe your story if you paid your source for it?

ABC News first denied and then admitted paying $200,000 to accused murderer Casey Anthony for "exclusive rights to an extensive library of photos and home video

ON THE JOB

Nurturing a Healthy Ethical Process in an Ever-Changing Environment

Every morning **Kelly McBride** walks into her office at the Poynter Institute, clicks on ESPN, boots up TweetDeck, Facebook and a dozen aggregation sites, and scans the developments of the day.

Then her phone starts to ring. Five years ago, the calls came from professional journalists working in newsrooms. Now many come from bloggers, freelancers and political activists. Although the callers differ widely, they have one thing in common: They're all making ethical choices that have significant consequences.

"Every journalist must 'do ethics' in every story," McBride says. "Young journalists make a common mistake when they fail to identify everyday decisions as ethical choices. Journalists of all experience levels make an even bigger mistake: They assume they should know the answer to every ethical question. Both mistakes undermine a healthy ethical process."

McBride spent 14 years as a reporter at *The Spokesman-Review* in Spokane, Wash. As the journalism landscape has dramatically changed in recent years, McBride has often been the champion of ethical reasoning in an environment that seems to have few widely accepted notions of right and wrong.

"I've stopped trying to figure out who is a journalist and who isn't. Instead, I focus on information that acts like journalism," she says. "If a certain piece of information acts like journalism, then there should be an ethical process behind it because it impacts the democratic process.

"Young journalists and small bloggers have more power than they imagine in growing this process," McBride says.

She learned that in a healthy newsroom, reporters constantly turn to one another for exchanges. The pathways between the editors' and reporters' desks are busy, two-way streets. At the intersections, journalists cluster in conversation. The most encouraging sign of all occurs when a huddle briefly loosens up and more people are invited into the discussion.

"When a culture is sick, decisions are made in secret, behind closed doors," McBride says. "Surprises show up in the paper or on the air without explanation, and no one knows how the decisions were made. People are afraid to ask questions. There is very little talking."

The same ethical process occurs in new forms of media, but often the conversations happen in virtual spaces like Twitter.

From the Poynter Institute, McBride gets a larger view. "The underlying values of journalism are becoming more and more diffuse, the further we get along in this revolution. In the future, we will get journalism from a variety of sources, including but not limited to professional journalists. The prevailing values of truth and accuracy are going to look different, depending on the source creating the story. I worry about the effect that will have on democracy."

McBride is a senior faculty member at the Poynter Institute and the lead writer on the Poynter-ESPN Review Project. You can send her questions at kmcbride@poynter .org and read her regular columns at www .poynter.org and at www.espn.com.

---

for use by our broadcasts, platforms, affiliates and international partners." Less than two weeks later, ABC abandoned checkbook journalism altogether. The new president of ABC News, Ben Sherwood, "concluded that the cash-register approach to journalism was starting to tarnish the network's credibility, even though the practice was relatively infrequent."

Surely, good reporting demands that you pay sources only when necessary and only if you can get other sources to corroborate your findings. You'd also better be sure that your bosses know that you're doing it.

Nick Denton of Gawker Media, who regularly pays sources for stories and doesn't apologize for doing so, says he sees no difference between his paying a source for a story and a news medium paying a reporter. He also says he's happy that "old journalists" do not pay sources because "it keeps the price down." He's a big supporter of the journalistic commandment of not paying sources—"as it applies to other organizations."

Participation in the News

At times, journalists receive severe criticism for doing what seems to be right and humane. When network correspondents were seen on television performing medical treatment in Haiti, Dr. Carl Elliott of the University of Minnesota Center for Bioethics called it "a classic PR tactic using humanitarian aid as a public relations device, in order to drive up ratings for their network."

> " But I don't believe that paying sources is unethical, as long as it's disclosed to the reader; in some cases I think it makes for better journalism. It gives a fair share of the profits to sources who spend time and take risks. "
> —John Tierney, from "Newsworthy," reprinted from the New York Times Company

Bob Steele, who teaches journalism ethics at DePauw University, concurs. He told blogger Matea Gold of the *Los Angeles Times*: "If it's imperative that (a reporter) intervene and help medically, then take him out of his journalistic role and do that. But don't have him covering the same stories in which he's a participant. It muddles the journalist reporting. It clouds the lens in terms of the independent observation and reporting."

Must journalists be passive citizens? Must they give up all activity that advocates or shows a point of view? Must a religion reporter be an atheist? Richard Harwood, *Washington Post* ombudsman at the time, told a conference of journalists: "You have every right in the world to run for office, or participate in a political activity or lobbying activity. You don't have the 'right' to work for *The Washington Post*."

Poynter's Julie Moss quotes *Wisconsin State Journal* editor John Smalley, who told his staffers:

> People accept work-related policies and restrictions all the time. If you want to sell high-end clothing, you can't wear cut-off jeans to work. If you want to deliver Coca-Cola, you can't drink Pepsi in your truck.
>
> And if you want to be a journalist, you keep your politics to yourself. That's just the way it is, and it's a deal every journalist accepts when he or she joins the profession.

Advertising Pressure

It's likely you won't work long at a news organization before you realize some subjects are taboo to write about and others are highly encouraged. If you are lucky, you will work for a paper, station or magazine with a solid wall of separation between editorial and advertising, sometimes referred to as "the separation of church and state."

However, in some places, advertising salespeople are allowed to peek over that wall and see what stories the publication or station is planning to run. That information might help sell some advertising. Some say, what could be wrong with that?

The next step is for the advertising department to climb over the wall and suggest that editorial do a story on some subject so that advertising can be sold.

And then the next step isn't too far away. Advertising salespeople begin to suggest or even to dictate what must and must not be printed in the newspaper, said on radio or shown on television, or even displayed on the website. In print media, advertisers might want the layout, design and type of their ads or sections to look like the publication's normal layout and design. They might also insist that the word "advertising" appear in small print or at the bottom of the page or be dropped altogether. Some advertisers prefer the term "sponsored by," which they believe softens the pure sales pitch of their message.

> " If you're not involved in the community at all and you're totally neutralized, you end up not knowing enough about the community, not being able to get enough leads and so on in order to do your job. "
> —Ethicist Louis W. Hodges, quoted by Tony Case in *Editor & Publisher*

In early 2010, newspaper consultant Alan Mutter reported in his blog that 17 percent of newspapers had returned to an earlier practice of placing ads on their front pages. Magazines are doing the same. Frank Anderson, writing under the head "Magazine Cover Advertisements: A Necessary Evil—Or Just Evil," wonders why anyone would believe a magazine with an ad on the cover.

Magazines and "New Financial Pillars"

The Atlantic Monthly has brought journalists and policymakers together for off-the-record conversations for years, with each meeting sponsored by a different corporation. Eric Alterman, a senior fellow at the Center for American Progress, quotes *Atlantic Monthly* Media Chairman David Bradley as saying such meetings are necessary because "the economic foundation beneath journalism is falling away." The article quotes Bradley further: "The imperative, as I see it, is to rebuild journalism on different financial pillars. One of them, and not inconsequential to us, is events—of all types."

The dangers in these practices are twofold. The policymakers involved in these friendly chats are more likely to demand friendly stories from the writers or, perhaps worse, no stories at all. No stories would deprive readers of information they need or should have.

Invasion of Privacy

Most journalists would cry out against an invasion of their own privacy. Yet many of them argue for a vague "right to know" when they report on others, especially if those others are public officials or public figures. The head-on collision of the right to know and the right to privacy will confront you every day of your reporting life. The Constitution mentions neither "right."

There are many ways to invade people's privacy with hidden cameras and microphones. Now nearly everyone with a cellphone has become a photographer, and no place is private outside one's home.

Some say that a major reason Gov. Mitt Romney lost his bid for the presidency in 2012 was that he thought he was speaking to a closed, private room of fundraisers where he said, "There are 47 percent of the people who will vote for the president no matter what," and his role "was not to worry about them." Perhaps the room was closed, but the world heard his words and saw him say them.

One thing we know for sure. Nothing you write on the Internet is secure. *New York Times* reporter Nicole Perlroth quotes Internet security researcher Dan Kaminsky:

> What people don't realize is that hacking and spying went mainstream a decade ago. They think hacking is some difficult thing. Meanwhile, everyone is reading everyone else's emails—girlfriends are reading boyfriends', bosses are reading employees'—because it's just so easy to do.

True, there are some ways to slow people down from reading your emails, but Kaminsky says, "The reality is if you don't want something to show up on the front page of *The New York Times*, then don't say it." The ethical question that remains for you is this: Is it ever ethical to quote someone's personal email? If doing so would prevent a serious evil from occurring (stopping the bombings at the 2013 Boston Marathon), a teleological ethicist would justify it. Otherwise, privacy would demand refraining from using it.

Crime Victims

The most obvious and talked-about issue related to the right to privacy is naming crime survivors, especially rape and sex-crime survivors. The state of Florida legislated against publishing rape survivors' names, only to have the law struck down by a Florida district court. The U.S. Supreme Court has held that news agencies cannot be punished for publishing lawfully obtained information or information from a public record. Meanwhile, legislators in many states are looking for ways to close the records on rape and to punish police, hospitals, court clerks and other officials who release survivors' names.

So the issue comes down to a matter of ethics, and as usual, there is not complete agreement. Not publishing the name continues the stigma that somehow the rape was the survivor's fault. Publishing the survivor's name heaps more suffering upon that person. Few news outlets would publish a rape survivor's name without the person's approval.

And there's always the possibility that the accusation is false. A 17-year-old girl cried rape in Palos Heights, Ill., but five days later she admitted she had made the whole thing up. According to a report by Kim Janssen on SouthtownStar.com, everyone knew who she was. Janssen reported that Northwestern University journalism ethics professor Jack Doppelt said he would print her name. Kelly McBride of the Poynter Institute said she wouldn't but would not blame editors who would.

Solving ethical questions is not easy. Suppose you had been the editor in Kennebunk, Maine, a town of 10,500, and were handed a list of more than 150 names of residents, including some prominent community figures, who were secretly taped having sexual encounters with 29-year-old Zumba instructor Alexis Wright.

» Would you publish all of the names? What is your policy for publishing misdemeanors?

» Would you publish only the names of the prominent community figures?

» Would it make a difference if your paper publishes a police log as a matter of routine?

» What if you know other papers in the area will publish the names?

» If you do not publish the names, are you concerned that innocent men might be thought to be among the 150?

Juvenile Offenders

Another ethical issue concerns publishing the names of juvenile offenders. News agencies traditionally have not published them because they have held that juveniles are entitled to make juvenile mistakes, even if those mistakes are crimes. After all, juvenile court records are sealed. Again, the courts have upheld the right to publish juvenile offenders' names that are on the public record.

Some media critics, such as *The Fresno Bee*'s former editor and ombudsman Lynne Enders Glaser, have applauded the publication of the names of juvenile offenders. Glaser wrote: "It doesn't take a rocket scientist to figure out that more and more violent crimes are being committed by young people. And in increasing numbers, *Bee* readers have challenged the law and the media to stop protecting the identity of criminals because of their age."

However, in addition to the stigma forever attached to the juvenile offender's name and the embarrassment to his or her parents and family, some worry that in some groups a youth's notoriety will encourage other young people to violate the law. Others argue that shame will stop other juveniles from committing crimes.

Victims of Child Abuse and Their Families

Victims of child abuse are often ashamed to talk about it, even to their parents, and their parents are even more ashamed. But once one victim has the courage to speak, others often follow. The lessons of the child abuse accusations at Penn State University are obvious.

The Philadelphia Inquirer reported that, after the Penn State scandal broke, the hotline of the Rape, Abuse and Incest National Network had its busiest month since it started in 2006. The average number of sessions a month jumped from 2,500 to 3,100. A lawyer in Miami who represents victims of sexual abuse reported that his website, which ordinarily receives 5,000 hits a month, received 15,000 in one month after the scandal broke. In the six weeks after the scandal became public, the Survivors Network of Those Abused by Priests said that "it had been deluged with emails and phone calls from survivors, many breaking their silence for the first time."

Perhaps reporters have inborn respect and admiration for certain people and professions. Are they too prone to see only the heroics of sports stars? Is that why not a single reporter checked on anything that Notre Dame's Manti Te'o was saying about his fictional girlfriend? How could Father Lawrence Murphy have sexually abused as many as 200 boys in a school for the deaf in St. Francis, Wis., without anyone in the press knowing about it? How could so much sexual abuse by Roman Catholic priests have gone on for so long without more investigations from the news media?

Is there any class or profession or institution that journalists should not be skeptical of? Should the news media pay more attention to rumors?

Questions remain, for example, about the silence of *The (Harrisburg, Pa.) Patriot-News* and ESPN when they first heard allegations about jailed Penn State assistant coach Jerry Sandusky. Were they ethical in remaining silent? Should they have reported their investigation in order to quell rumors? Would others have stepped up?

And how far, how graphic, should the news media go in describing what victims are made to suffer? Should reporters visit their parents?

Sexual Orientation

Perhaps no issue is as muddled and contentious as when to reveal someone's sexual orientation. Not even the members of the National Lesbian and Gay Journalists Association have agreed on a policy. However, when a public figure or a religious leader has made a point of attacking gays or opposing same-sex marriage and that person is secretly leading a gay life, most would agree it is ethical to out that person.

Public Figures

These are just a few of the myriad privacy issues you will face. Journalists are still protected when writing about public officials and public figures—most of the time. But what about the children of politicians or celebrities?

Websites exist that have files on nearly everyone. Some allow you to see what anyone has ever posted in a chat room. What may journalists use? Legitimate, respectable journalism does not permit, let alone use, material obtained by hacking. Some corporations, however, claim the right to know what employees write on company computers during work time. The federal government sometimes claims the right to capture emails for national security reasons.

Photos and Video

Photographers and videographers must be especially concerned with privacy. How often and under what circumstances should they stick cameras into people's grieving and anxious faces?

Photographers must respect people's dignity at crime and disaster scenes, and they need to be invited to a funeral unless it is for a public figure. With permission of the family, they may now photograph coffins containing deceased soldiers from U.S. military actions.

Judgments about using photos are often a matter of taste more than ethics. Here are three examples.

Many U.S. newspapers thought it best not to run what were thought to be photos of the bloodied corpse of Osama bin Laden, in part because President Obama asked them not to, fearing that the photo would inflame tensions in the Muslim world. However, the websites of five British newspapers briefly displayed a photo purported to be that of bin Laden. *The Guardian* revealed that the photo displayed on the websites had been taken two years earlier and altered with the photo-editing software Photoshop.

The *Los Angeles Times* published two photos of U.S. soldiers posing with dead Afghan soldiers. The soldiers' action was a violation of Army standards, and U.S. military officials asked the *Times* not to publish the photos, which they said were more than two years old. Poynter quoted *Times* editor Davan Maharaj's explanation of the paper's decision to publish:

> After careful consideration, we decided that publishing a small but representative selection of the photos would fulfill our obligation to readers to report vigorously and impartially on all aspects of the American mission in Afghanistan, including the allegation that the images reflect a breakdown in unit discipline that was endangering U.S. troops.

Freelance photographer R. Umar Abbasi was waiting for a train on the platform of the 49th Street subway station in Manhattan when he saw a man on a subway track about to be killed by an oncoming train. Jeff Sonderman quotes the photographer in *Poynter* as saying, "I just started running, running, hoping that the driver could see my flash." What his flashes did capture were pictures of a desperate man trying to save his life. The engineer saw the flashes but said he could not stop.

The *New York Post* could have stopped. It did not have to run the resulting photo—at least not on a full front page—but it did. It's one thing to ask whether the photographer should have dropped his camera and tried to save the man's life. There were others present who could have done so. Some people defended the photographer. But it is another question to ask whether the *Post* had any reason to run the photo—and on the front page.

Some people defended the newspaper's decision. But most people, including journalism professors and scholars, condemned the *Post* for being sensationalistic and insensitive. *USA Today* quoted Poynter's Kelly McBride as saying that printing the picture had no "journalistic purpose." She explained that it did "not bear witness to something people need to know about."

Withholding Information

Sometimes the government asks news organizations to withhold information from their audiences. When Raymond Davis, a former U.S. Special Forces soldier, shot and killed two Pakistani citizens, President Obama asked the Pakistani government for the release of "our diplomat in Pakistan." In reality, Davis was a member of the CIA. A number of media outlets, including *The New York Times*, knew this but, at the request of the Obama administration, kept it quiet.

In January 2011, for the first time in history, a U.S. government advisory board asked scientific journals not to publish scientific information. The reason? The board feared that the information could be used by terrorist groups.

Is it ever permissible to withhold information from the news organization for which you work? If you are a working journalist writing what you hope will be a best-selling book, may you save some "news" until after the book is published?

If you work as a journalist, are you ever off-duty? A doctor isn't. Doctors take an oath to treat the sick. If you witness something at a friend's house or at a party, do you tell your news director about it? One reporter was fired when his boss discovered that he had attended a rock band's post-concert party, where lines of cocaine were openly available. The reporter did not include this information in his coverage of the band. His defense was that if he reported the illegal drug use, he would never get interviews with or access to other rock groups, and he would be finished as a music critic. His excuse didn't save his job.

When should you withhold information because the police ask you to or because it may jeopardize a case? When a suspect in the BTK serial murder case in Wichita, Kan., was finally arrested, *Seattle Times* reporter Cathy Henkel recalled the copy of a two-page memo she had that BTK sent to the police in the 1970s when Henkel was working for the weekly *Wichita Sun*. The letter, filled with graphic content and bad grammar, discussed four types of knots the murderer used to strangle his victims. Because the police felt the release of the information would hurt their case, the paper thought it best to do nothing with the information, despite the public's right to know. *The Wichita Eagle* and ABC affiliate television station KAKE had even more information about BTK the year before his arrest, but both said nothing.

McBride says, "Cutting deals to withhold information is dangerous. It should be done with great caution, much forethought and only in rare circumstances." She also warns that "we too readily agree with police and keep information from the public."

Incorrect and Incomplete Information

One situation in which some media organizations withhold information occurs when they have published incorrect information. Print publications that get the news wrong customarily inform readers of these mistakes in a corrections column, usually on the second page of the publication. Some online news sites, however, act as if they never make mistakes. They simply post new stories with updated information or act as if the first stories never appeared. The Canadian Association of Journalists has these recommendations for online corrections:

» Be transparent with your online audience, telling them when you've made an error—be it a spelling mistake or new information in a developing story.

» Engage your readers: Ask them to point out mistakes, verify the information they provide in corrections and make this an easy process.

» Be timely with your corrections.

» Place your corrections with or as part of the article. There's no real "Page 2" online that mirrors the newspaper tradition when it comes to corrections.

» Have the same standard for accuracy and corrections across all platforms. If people clicked through via Twitter, Facebook, LinkedIn or Google+, the correction and corrected items should also be found in these spots.

Online journalists often make up for incomplete information by using hyperlinks to external sites. Are raw data journalism? How much and how often may you link to raw data, and with what warnings or interpretations? There's little doubt that readers appreciate links to source data so they can make judgments for themselves. At the same time, good websites help readers navigate that information. Journalists are still trying to find the right balance between the two.

Beware of Plagiarism!

Roy Peter Clark of the Poynter Institute cautions against the following acts of plagiarism:

» Taking material verbatim (word for word) from the newspaper library.

» Using material verbatim from the wire services.

» Using material from other publications.
» Using news releases verbatim.
» Using the work of fellow reporters.
» Using old stories over again.

PLAGIARISM

No one wants you to use his or her work as your own. Everyone condemns **plagiarism**—journalism's capital offense.

Plagiarism regularly raises its ugly head everywhere. Rookies and veterans in every area of journalism ruin their personal reputations and sully the reputations of the news organizations for which they work.

» Jon Flatland, columnist, former president of the North Dakota Newspaper Association and one-time newspaper owner, was exposed by humor writer Dave Fox, who estimates that 80 to 90 percent of Flatland's columns contained plagiarized material; virtually none of it was his original work. Flatland had worked on newspapers in Missouri, Minnesota and North Dakota and had won numerous awards.

» The editor of *Anchor Weekly*, Steve Jeffrey, resigned after being accused of using others' work in 42 of his last 52 issues. Jeffrey had changed a few details. He said he used others as inspiration, "but I would say that I have not plagiarized anything."

» Columnist and television host Fareed Zakaria lifted paragraphs from another writer for his column in *Time* magazine and was suspended for one month. Zakaria said he made "a terrible mistake." Later, after careful review, *Time* and CNN concluded what he did was an unintentional and isolated incident for which he had apologized. He was reinstated.

» Penn State's newspaper suspended a writer because she not only plagiarized, but she made up quotes by Sue Paterno, widow of football coach Joe Paterno. Editor-in-chief Casey McDermott said it was not the student's first offense.

Although one could go on and on listing incidents of plagiarism (three student newspapers were affected in one month in 2012), David Swartzlander, president of the College Media Association, says he is "unconvinced" that it is occurring more frequently than in the past. Mallary Jean Tenore quotes Swartzlander in *Poynter* as saying he believes "we have a sense that it is happening more because of digital media, which can expose these practices more widely and with much more ease than in previous generations."

Perhaps the greatest temptation is to plagiarize material published online. But you also might be tempted to lift words from your own news organization's stories or from a wire report. Some reporters have felt justified taking quotes and verbatim sentences from news releases and inserting them into their stories. Make sure you're not plagiarizing when you think you're paraphrasing (see Figure 22.2). You always

Plagiarism, Quotation and Paraphrase

Using an Attributed Quotation—Acceptable
The journalist fully identifies the source of the quotation and puts the source's exact words in quotation marks.

As William A. Henry III writes in *Time* magazine, reporters have a "First Amendment bond" with their readers. "Plagiarism," he writes, "imperils that bond, not because it involves theft of a wry phrase or piquant quote, but because it devalues meticulous, independent verification of fact—the bedrock of a press worth reading."

Paraphrasing a Quotation—Acceptable
The journalist identifies the source and restates the source's original idea in the journalist's own words.

William A. Henry III writes about the destructive effect on journalism that plagiarism can have, suggesting that it compromises the integrity of the reportorial research process.

Plagiarizing—Unacceptable
Even though the source is identified, the journalist errs by using the source's original words (in bold) without putting them in quotation marks. Simply using distinctive words and phrases without quotation marks can constitute plagiarism.

In writing about how plagiarism **imperils** a reporter's **bond** with readers, William A. Henry III says the practice goes beyond stealing **a wry phrase or piquant quote**. It **devalues the meticulous, independent verification of fact** that journalism depends on.

Plagiarizing—Unacceptable
The journalist has not identified the source and has not put the source's original words (in bold) in quotation marks. Changing the occasional word (for example, "striking" rather than "piquant") or the structure of a sentence is not sufficient to avoid plagiarism.

Plagiarism damages the reporter's **bond** with his or her readers. It goes beyond the **theft of a wry phrase or** striking **quote** and diminishes the foundation of journalism—**the meticulous, independent verification of facts**.

FIGURE 22.2

Writers sometimes misunderstand the nature of paraphrase. Simply altering a few words of a quotation, with or without attribution, often results in plagiarism rather than paraphrase.

TIPS

Three Final Guidelines

» Be free of obligations to anyone or to any interest except the truth. The primary obligation of the journalist is to be free.

» Be fair. Even children know when you treat them unfairly or when they are being unfair. So do you.

» Remember good taste. Some actions and stories might be ethical, but they might be in bad taste.

serve your readers best when you get your own quotations. Don't even reuse your own material or stories or columns without letting your readers know what you are doing. Remember, Internet users are quite effective at spotting many of these practices. Bloggers and Twitter users will catch and expose you!

Though it might seem impossible, some people believe writers can plagiarize and have absolutely no idea they are doing so. They say that sometimes something you have read becomes so familiar that you later consider it your own. Sometimes plagiarism results from sloppy note taking.

You must fight every impulse to use others' work, question everything, check any doubts, and avoid any hint of plagiarism. And just as certainly you must resist temptations to make up people, to fabricate events and to invent quotations.

TWITTER ETHICS

Twitter has become a most useful and even necessary tool for obtaining tips and leads to stories. All the guidelines of journalism ethics apply to reporters' use of Twitter. Journalist and media strategy consultant David Brewer summarizes the main ethical issues as they apply to Twitter:

» **Accuracy:** well-sourced information based on solid evidence.
» **Impartiality:** fair and open-minded, exploring of all significant views.
» **Fairness:** transparent, open and honest, based on straight dealing.
» **Offense:** delivering challenging journalism that is sensitive to audience expectations.
» **Integrity:** dealing with groups keen to use the media for their own advantage.
» **Privacy** must be respected and not invaded unless it is in the public interest.

All of this within 140 characters. If Twitter does nothing else for you, it forces you to think ethically while being concise.

SUGGESTED READINGS

Christians, Clifford G., Mark Fackler, Peggy J. Kreshel, Robert H. Woods Jr., and Kathy Brittain McKee. *Media Ethics: Cases and Moral Reasoning*. 8th ed. Boston: Allyn and Bacon, 2008. The authors apply the Potter Box method of principled reasoning to dozens of journalism, advertising and public relations cases.

Christians, Clifford G., and Lee Wilkins. *Handbook of Mass Media Ethics*. New York: Lawrence Erlbaum, 2009. In this handbook, scholars look at the intellectual history of mass media ethics over the past 25 years and summarize past and possible future research.

Fletcher, Joseph. *Situation Ethics: The New Morality*. Louisville, Ky.: Westminster John Knox Press, 1997. First published in 1966, this classic work on Christian situation ethics is for some a breath of fresh air, for others pure heresy.

Kovach, Bill, and Tom Rosenstiel. *The Elements of Journalism: What Newspeople Should Know and the Public Should Expect*. New York: Random House, 2007. This book should be required reading for every journalism student and journalist.

Meyers, Christopher, ed. *Journalism Ethics: A Philosophical Approach*. New York: Oxford Univ. Press, 2010. Even a quick look at this book's table of contents tells you it brings together the best journalism scholars writing about journalism's most vital topics.

Wilkins, Lee, and Philip Patterson. *Media Ethics, Issues and Cases*. 6th ed. Burr Ridge, Ill.: McGraw-Hill Humanities, Social Sciences and World Languages, 2010. This book offers an excellent discussion of journalism ethics with up-to-date cases.

SUGGESTED WEBSITES

www.bedfordstmartins.com/newscentral
When you visit News Central, you will find up-to-the-moment RSS feeds, research links and exercises to help you improve your grammar and AP style usage. In addition, the site's Video-Central: Journalism section hosts the videos highlighted in this chapter as well as additional clips of leading professionals discussing important media trends.

www.ijnet.org
This is the website of the International Journalists' Network. Here you can find the codes of ethics of nearly every country or press association that has one. It also reports on the state of the media around the world and contains media directories.

www.journalism.indiana.edu/resources/ethics
This site, from the School of Journalism of Indiana University, contains a large set of cases to help you explore ethical issues in journalism. The initial cases were published in *FineLine*, a newsletter by Barry Bingham Jr.

www.spj.org
(Click on "Journalist's Resources" on the top of the screen. Then scroll down to "Ethics.") The ethics site of the Society of Professional Journalists provides the SPJ code of ethics, ethics news, an ethics hotline, an SPJ ethics listserv, ethics case studies and other ethics resources.

EXERCISES

1. **Team project**. Your instructor will divide the class into three groups. Each group will search for at least five articles on whether to publish the names of one of the following:

   Juvenile criminal suspects and defendants.
   Victims of rape, molestation or other sex crimes.
   Gay men and lesbians who have not publicly stated their sexual orientation.

   Set a time for the groups to meet, and then outline an article you could write on the subject.

2. **Journalism blog.** Using what you have learned in this chapter, write a blog post answering this question: Does the end ever justify the means? Give at least two examples.

3. You've learned that the daughter of a local bank president has been kidnapped. The kidnappers have not contacted the family, and police officials ask you to keep the matter secret for fear the abductors might panic and injure the child. Describe how an absolutist, a person who believes the end justifies the means and a situation ethicist would make their decisions about how to handle the situation.

4. You're assigned to write a piece on a new bus service from your town to Chicago. Your editor tells you to ask the bus company for a free round-trip ticket. What will you do, and why?

5. **Journalism blog.** For at least a year, reporters on your paper have heard rumors that a retirement home is negligent in its care of the elderly. Your editor asks you to get a job there as a janitor and to report what you find. How will you respond, and why? Write a post on your journalism blog explaining your position. Include links to the blog posts of classmates who agree and disagree with you.

6. You are a photographer. Your editor has told you to keep an eye out for any instances of police brutality. You happen to see a policeman knock down a homeless man and begin kicking him. Will you take photos, or will you attempt in some way to discourage the policeman from hurting the homeless man? Explain.

7. You are the theater critic for your news organization. A producer has offered you free tickets to an upcoming premiere performance. Should you accept the tickets? Why or why not?

20 Common Errors of Grammar and Punctuation

GRAMMAR PROVIDES our language's rules of the road. When you have a green light, you proceed on faith that other drivers will not go through their red light. That's because drivers have a shared understanding of the rules of the road. Similarly, writers have a shared understanding of the grammar rules that ensure we understand what we are reading. Occasionally, as on the road, there is a wreck. We dangle participles, misplace modifiers and omit commas. If we write "Running down the street, his pants fell off," we are saying a pair of pants ran down a street. If we write "He hit Harry and John stopped him," the missing comma makes the meaning, on first reading, "He hit Harry and John."

To say what you mean—to avoid syntactic wrecks—you must know the rules of grammar. We have compiled a list of 20 common errors that we find in our students' stories and in the stories of many professionals. Avoid them, and you'll write safely.

To take quizzes based on this list of 20 common errors of grammar and punctuation, go to Exercise Central for AP Style at http://bcs.bedfordstmartins.com/apexercises2. There you will find advice and activities that go beyond grammar; Exercise Central also offers exercises on Associated Press style—the style that makes news writing distinctly journalistic.

1. Incorrect comma in a series in Associated Press style

Use commas to separate the items in a series, but do not put a comma before *and* or *or* at the end of the series unless the meaning would be unclear without a comma.

Incorrect comma before *and*	The film was fast-paced, sophisticated, and funny.
Clear without comma	The film was fast-paced, sophisticated and funny.

A comma before *and* or *or* can prevent confusion.

Unclear without comma	He demanded cheese, salsa with jalapeños and onions on his taco.

Adding a comma before *and* prevents readers from wondering if he demanded salsa containing both jalapeños and onions or if the salsa and the onions were two separate toppings.

Clear with comma	He demanded cheese, salsa with jalapeños, and onions on his taco.

The sentence can be revised to mean salsa with both jalapeños and onions.

> **Clear revision without comma**   He demanded cheese and salsa with jalapeños and onions on his taco.

2. Run-on sentence

An independent clause contains a subject and a predicate and makes sense by itself. A run-on sentence—also known as a *comma splice*—occurs when two or more independent clauses are joined incorrectly with a comma.

> **Run-on**   John Rogers left the family law practice, he decided to become a teacher.

You can correct a run-on sentence in several ways. Join the clauses with a comma and one of the coordinating conjunctions—*and, but, for, nor, or, yet* or *so*—or join the clauses with a semicolon if they are closely related. Use a subordinating conjunction such as *after, because, if* or *when* to turn one of the clauses into a dependent clause. Or rewrite the run-on as two separate sentences.

Correcting a run-on with a comma and a coordinating conjunction
John Rogers left the family law practice, for he decided to become a teacher.

Correcting a run-on with a semicolon
John Rogers left the family law practice; he decided to become a teacher.

Correcting a run-on by making one independent clause a dependent clause
John Rogers left the family law practice when he decided to become a teacher.

Correcting a run-on by writing two separate sentences
John Rogers left the family law practice. He decided to become a teacher.

3. Fragment

A fragment is a word group that lacks a subject, a verb or both, yet is punctuated as though it were a complete sentence. Another type of fragment is a word group that begins with a subordinating conjunction such as *because* or *when*, yet is punctuated as though it were a complete sentence.

> **Fragments**   After she had placed her watch and an extra pencil on the table. Without feeling especially sorry about it.

Correct a fragment by joining it to the sentence before or after it or by adding the missing elements so that the fragment contains a subject and a verb and can stand alone.

Correcting a fragment by joining it to another sentence

After she had placed her watch and an extra pencil on the table, the student opened the exam booklet.

Correcting a fragment by turning it into a sentence

She apologized to her boss for the outburst without feeling especially sorry about it.

4. Missing comma(s) with a nonrestrictive element

A nonrestrictive element is a word, phrase or clause that gives information about the preceding part of the sentence but does not restrict or limit the meaning of that part. A nonrestrictive element is not essential to the meaning of the sentence; you can delete it and still understand clearly what the sentence is saying. Place commas before and (if necessary) after a nonrestrictive element.

Unclear	The mayor asked to meet Alva Johnson a highly decorated police officer.
Clear	The mayor asked to meet Alva Johnson, a highly decorated police officer.
Unclear	His wife Mary was there.
Clear	His wife, Mary, was there.

5. Confusion of *that* and *which*

The pronoun *that* always introduces restrictive information, which is essential to the meaning of the sentence; do not set off a *that* clause with commas. The pronoun *which* introduces nonrestrictive, or nonessential, information; set off a nonrestrictive *which* clause with commas.

Incorrect	The oldest store in town, Miller and Co., <u>that</u> has been on Main Street for almost a century, will close this summer.
Correct	The oldest store in town, Miller and Co., <u>which</u> has been on Main Street for almost a century, will close this summer.
Incorrect	The creature, <u>which</u> has been frightening residents of North First Street for the past week, has turned out to be a screech owl.
Correct	The creature <u>that</u> has been frightening residents of North First Street for the past week has turned out to be a screech owl.

6. Missing comma after an introductory element

A sentence may begin with a dependent clause (a word group that contains a subject and a verb and begins with a subordinating conjunction such as *because* or *when*), a prepositional phrase (a word group that begins with a preposition such as *in* or *on* and ends with a noun or pronoun), an adverb such as *next* that modifies the whole sentence, or a participial phrase (a word group that contains a past or present participle, such as *determined* or *speaking,* that acts as an adjective). Use a comma to separate these introductory elements from the main clause of the sentence.

Dependent clause	<u>After the applause had died down,</u> the conductor raised his baton again.
Prepositional phrase	<u>Without a second thought,</u> the chicken crossed the road.
Adverb	<u>Furthermore,</u> the unemployment rate continues to rise.
Participial phrases	<u>Waiting in the bar,</u> José grew restless.
	<u>Saddened by the news from home,</u> she stopped reading the letter.

Although it is always correct to use a comma after an introductory element, the comma may be omitted after some adverbs and short prepositional phrases if the meaning is clear.

Suddenly it's spring.

In Chicago it rained yesterday.

Always place a comma after two or more introductory prepositional phrases.

In May of last year in Toronto, Tom attended three conventions.

Here are more examples:

Incorrect	Shaking her head at the latest budget information the library administrator wondered where to find the money for new books.
Correct	Shaking her head at the latest budget information, the library administrator wondered where to find the money for new books.

Incorrect	After a week of foggy, rainy mornings had passed he left Seattle.
Correct	After a week of foggy, rainy mornings had passed, he left Seattle.

7. Missing comma(s) between coordinate adjectives

Adjectives are coordinate if they make sense when you insert *and* between them or place them in reverse order.

Coordinate adjectives	The frightened, angry citizens protested the new policy.
	The frightened and angry citizens protested the new policy.

The adjectives make sense with *and* between them, so they are coordinate.

The angry, frightened citizens protested the new policy.

The adjectives make sense in reverse order, so they are coordinate. Separate coordinate adjectives with commas.

| Incorrect | The gaunt lonely creature was also afraid. |
| Correct | The gaunt, lonely creature was also afraid. |

8. Missing comma(s) in a compound sentence

Two or more independent clauses—word groups containing a subject and a verb and expressing a complete thought—joined with a coordinating conjunction (*and, but, for, nor, or, yet* or *so*) form a compound sentence. Place a comma before the conjunction in a compound sentence to avoid confusion.

| Unclear | She works as a pharmacist now and later she plans to go to medical school. |
| Clear | She works as a pharmacist now, and later she plans to go to medical school. |

9. Misused semicolon

In a compound sentence that has a coordinating conjunction joining the clauses, place a comma before the conjunction, not a semicolon.

| Incorrect | The Chicago Cubs did not play in the World Series; but they did win their division. |
| Correct | The Chicago Cubs did not play in the World Series, but they did win their division. |

10. Misplaced or dangling modifier

Modifiers are words or phrases that change or clarify the meaning of another word or word group in a sentence. Place modifiers immediately before or directly after the word or words they modify. A *misplaced modifier* appears too far from the word or words it is supposed to modify in the sentence. A *dangling modifier* appears in a sentence that does not contain the word or words it is supposed to modify. A modifier at the beginning of a sentence should refer to the grammatical subject of the sentence.

	subject
Misplaced modifier	Having predicted a sunny morning, the downpour surprised the meteorologist.
	subject
Correct	Having predicted a sunny morning, the meteorologist did not expect the downpour.
	subject
Dangling modifier	Working in the yard, the sun burned her badly.
	subject
Correct	Working in the yard, she became badly sunburned.

11. Missing or misused hyphen(s) in a compound modifier

A compound modifier consists of two or more words used to modify a single noun. When a compound modifier precedes a noun, you should hyphenate the parts of the compound unless the compound consists of an adverb ending in *-ly* followed by an adjective.

Incorrect   His <u>over the top</u> performance made the whole film unbelievable.

The <u>freshly-printed</u> counterfeit bills felt like genuine dollars.

The local chapter of Parents Without Partners will sponsor a <u>come as you are</u> party on Saturday.

Correct   His <u>over-the-top</u> performance made the whole film unbelievable.

The <u>freshly printed</u> counterfeit bills felt like genuine dollars.

The local chapter of Parents Without Partners will sponsor a <u>come-as-you-are</u> party on Saturday.

12. Missing or misused apostrophe

Do not confuse the pronoun *its*, meaning "belonging to it," with the contraction *it's*, meaning "it is" or "it has." Although the possessive form of a noun uses an apostrophe (*Tom's*), possessive pronouns (*its, hers, his, ours, yours, theirs*) never take apostrophes.

Incorrect   The car is lying on <u>it's</u> side in the ditch.

<u>Its</u> a blue 2009 Ford Taurus.

That new car of <u>her's</u> rides very smoothly.

Correct   The car is lying on <u>its</u> side in the ditch.

<u>It's</u> a blue 2009 Ford Taurus.

That new car of <u>hers</u> rides very smoothly.

For clarity, avoid using the contraction ending in *-'s* to mean "has" instead of "is."

Unclear   <u>She's</u> held many offices in student government.

Clear   <u>She has</u> held many offices in student government.

13. Incorrect pronoun case

A pronoun that is the subject of a sentence or clause must be in the subjective case (*I, he, she, we, they*). A pronoun that is the direct object of a verb, the indirect object of a verb, or the object of a preposition must be in the objective case (*me, him, her, us, them*). To decide whether a pronoun in a compound construction—two or more nouns or pronouns joined with *and* or *or*—should be subjective or objective, omit everything in the compound except the pronoun and see whether the subjective or objective case sounds correct.

Incorrect   He took my wife and <u>I</u> to dinner.

Try that sentence without the first part of the compound, *my wife and*. It sounds incorrect.

> Correct   He took my wife and <u>me</u> to dinner.

Here's another example.

> Incorrect   <u>Her</u> and her family donated the prize money.

Try that sentence without the second part of the compound, *and her family*. It sounds incorrect.

> Correct   <u>She</u> and her family donated the prize money.

The pronouns *who* and *whom* often cause confusion. *Who* (or *whoever*) is subjective; *whom* (or *whomever*) is objective. If the pronoun appears in a question, answer the question using a pronoun (such as *I* or *me*) to determine whether to use the subjective or objective form.

> Incorrect   <u>Who</u> does Howard want to see?

Answering the question—*Howard wants to see me*—reveals that the pronoun should be objective.

> Correct   <u>Whom</u> does Howard want to see?

When *who* or *whom* is not part of a question, it introduces a dependent clause. Determine the case of the pronoun in the clause by removing the clause from the sentence and replacing *who* or *whom* with *I* and *me* to see which form is correct.

> Incorrect   She welcomed <u>whomever</u> knocked on her door.

The dependent clause is *whomever knocked on her door*. Replacing *whomever* with *I* and *me*—*I knocked on her door; me knocked on her door*—reveals that the subjective form, *whoever*, is correct.

> Correct   She welcomed <u>whoever</u> knocked on her door.

14. Lack of agreement between pronoun and antecedent

Pronouns must agree in number (singular or plural) and person (first, second or third) with their *antecedents*—the nouns or pronouns to which they refer. Do not shift, for example, from a singular antecedent to a plural pronoun, or from a third-person antecedent to a first- or second-person pronoun.

> Incorrect   The <u>class</u> meets on Thursdays to check <u>their</u> work.
>
> Correct   The <u>class</u> meets on Thursdays to check <u>its</u> work.
>
> Class <u>members</u> meet on Thursdays to check <u>their</u> work.

15. Biased language

Avoid stereotypes and biased language. Take special care to avoid gender-specific pronouns.

Biased	A reporter must always check <u>his</u> work.
Acceptable	Reporters must always check their work.
	If you are a reporter, you must always check your work.

Biased	Local politicians and their <u>wives</u> attended a dinner in honor of the visiting diplomat.
Acceptable	Local politicians and their spouses attended a dinner in honor of the visiting diplomat.

Biased	Dr. Jones, a <u>deaf-mute</u>, spoke about the challenges she faced in medical school.
Acceptable	Dr. Jones, who cannot hear or speak, spoke about the challenges she faced in medical school.

16. Lack of agreement between subject and verb

Subject and verb must agree in number. Use the form of the verb that agrees with a singular or plural subject. Be especially careful to identify the subject correctly when words, such as a prepositional phrase, separate subject from verb.

Incorrect	The bag with the green stripes <u>belong</u> to her.
Correct	The <u>bag</u> with the green stripes <u>belongs</u> to her.

A compound subject with parts joined by *and* is always plural.

Incorrect	A mystery writer and her daughter <u>lives</u> in the house by the river.
Correct	<u>A mystery writer and her daughter live</u> in the house by the river.

When parts of a compound subject are joined by *or*, make the verb agree with the part of the compound closest to the verb.

Incorrect	Either Mike or his sisters <u>has</u> the spare key.
Correct	Either Mike or <u>his sisters have</u> the spare key.

17. Incorrect complement with linking verb

A linking verb such as *be, appear, feel* or *become* links a subject with a word or words that identify or describe the subject. When the identifying word—called a *subject complement*—is a pronoun, use the subjective case for the pronoun.

Incorrect	That was <u>him</u> on the telephone five minutes ago.
Correct	That was <u>he</u> on the telephone five minutes ago.

A word or words that describe the subject and follow a linking verb must be adjectives.

Incorrect   She feels <u>terribly</u> about the things she said.
Correct   She feels <u>terrible</u> about the things she said.

18. Incorrect use of subjunctive mood

Conditions contrary to fact require a verb to be in the subjunctive mood. Apply this rule in stories about all pending legislation at all levels of government. Use the subjunctive mood in "that" clauses after verbs of wishing, suggesting and requiring; in other words, use the subjunctive in clauses, dependent or independent, that do not state a fact.

Incorrect   The bylaws require that he <u>declares</u> his candidacy by April 10.
Correct   The bylaws require that he <u>declare</u> his candidacy by April 10.

Incorrect   The bill <u>will</u> require everyone to register for the draft at age 18.
Correct   The bill <u>would</u> require everyone to register for the draft at age 18.

19. Wrong word

Wrong-word errors include using a word that sounds similar to, or the same as, the word you need but means something different (such as writing *affect* when you mean *effect*) and using a word that has a shade of meaning that is not what you intend (such as writing *slender* when you want to suggest *scrawny*). Check the dictionary if you are not sure whether you are using a word correctly.

Incorrect   Merchants who appear <u>disinterested</u> in their customers may lose business.
Correct   Merchants who appear <u>uninterested</u> in their customers may lose business.

Incorrect   The guests gasped and applauded when they saw the <u>excessive</u> display of food.
Correct   The guests gasped and applauded when they saw the <u>lavish</u> display of food.

20. Incorrect verb form

Every verb has five forms: a base form (*talk*; *see*), a present-tense form (*talks*; *sees*), a past-tense form (*talked*; *saw*), a present-participle form used for forming the progressive tenses (*is talking*; *is seeing*), and a past-participle form used for forming the passive voice or one of the perfect tenses (*has talked*; *has seen*).

Dropping the ending from present-tense forms and regular past-tense forms is a common error.

Incorrect   The police are <u>suppose</u> to protect the public.
Correct   The police are <u>supposed</u> to protect the public.

Incorrect   The city <u>use</u> to tax all clothing sales.

Correct   The city <u>used</u> to tax all clothing sales.

Regular verbs end in *-ed* in the past tense and past participle, but irregular verbs do not follow a set pattern for forming the past tense and past participle (for example, *saw, seen*), so those forms of irregular verbs are frequently used incorrectly. Look up irregular verbs if you are uncertain of the correct form.

Incorrect   The manager was not in the restaurant when it was robbed because he had <u>went</u> home early.

Correct   The manager was not in the restaurant when it was robbed because he had <u>gone</u> home early.

Incorrect   The thieves <u>taked</u> everything in the safe.

Correct   The thieves <u>took</u> everything in the safe.

Wire-Service Style Summary

MOST PUBLICATIONS adhere to rules of style to avoid annoying inconsistencies. Without a stylebook to provide guidance in such matters, writers would not know whether the word *president* should be capitalized when preceding or following a name, whether the correct spelling is *employee* or *employe* (dictionaries list both), or whether *Twelfth Street* or *12th Street* is correct.

Newspapers use the wire-service stylebooks to provide such guidance. For consistency, most newspapers follow rules in *The Associated Press Stylebook*. Many also list their own exceptions to AP style in a separate style sheet. There often are good reasons for local exceptions. For example, AP style calls for spelling out *First Street* through *Ninth Street* but using numerals for *10th Street* and above. But if a city has only 10 numbered streets, for consistency it might make sense to use *Tenth Street*.

This appendix is an abbreviated summary of the primary rules of wire-service style. (See Chapter 13 for more on radio and television style.) This summary should be helpful even for those without a stylebook, but we provide it assuming that most users of this book have one. Why? Because this section includes only the rules used most frequently, arranged by topic to make them easier to learn. Only about 10 percent of the rules in a stylebook account for 90 percent of the wire-service style you will use regularly. You will use the rest of the rules about 10 percent of the time. It makes sense, therefore, to learn first the rules you will use most often.

ABBREVIATIONS AND ACRONYMS

Punctuation of Abbreviations

» Generally speaking, abbreviations of two letters or fewer have periods:
600 B.C., A.D. 1066
8 a.m., 7 p.m.
U.N., U.S., R.I., N.Y.
8151 Yosemite St.
EXCEPTIONS: *AM radio, FM radio, 35 mm camera, the AP Stylebook, LA smog, D-Mass.,*
R-Kan., IQ, TV, EU
» Most abbreviations of three letters or more do not have periods:
CIA, FBI, NATO
mpg, mph
EXCEPTION: *c.o.d.* for *cash on delivery* or *collect on delivery*

Symbols

» Always write out *%* as *percent* in a story, but you may use the symbol in a headline.

» Always write out *&* as *and* unless it is part of a company's formal name.

» Always write out *¢* as *cent* or *cents*.

» Always use the symbol *$* rather than the word *dollar* with any actual figure, and put the symbol before the figure. Write out *dollar* only if you are speaking of, say, the value of the dollar on the world market.

Dates

» Never abbreviate days of the week except in a table.

» Don't abbreviate a month unless part of a specific date:
August 2013; Aug. 17; Aug. 17, 2013

» The five months spelled with five letters or fewer are never abbreviated:
March; April 20; May 13, 2013; June 1956; July of that year

» Never abbreviate *Christmas* as *Xmas*, even in a headline.

» *Fourth of July* is written out.

» *Sept. 11* and *9/11* are both acceptable.

People and Titles

» Some publications still use courtesy titles (*Mr., Mrs., Ms., Miss*) on second reference in stories, although most seem to have moved away from them as sexist. Many publications use them only in quotations from sources. Others use them only in obituaries and editorials, or on second reference in stories mentioning a husband and wife. In the last case, some newspapers prefer to repeat the person's whole name or, especially in features, use the person's first name. The Associated Press suggests using a courtesy title when someone requests it, but most journalists don't bother to ask.

» Use the abbreviations *Dr.* (for a medical doctor, not someone with a Ph.D. degree), *Gov., Lt. Gov., Rep., Sen.* and *the Rev.*, as well as abbreviations of military titles, on first reference; then drop the title on subsequent references. Some titles you might expect to see abbreviated before a name are not abbreviated in AP style: *Attorney General, District Attorney, President, Professor, Superintendent.*

» Use the abbreviations *Jr.* and *Sr.* after a name on first reference if appropriate, but do not set them off by commas as you learned to do in English class.

Organizations

» Write out the first reference to most organizations in full rather than using an acronym: *National Organization for Women.* For *GOP, CIA* and *FBI*, however, the acronym may be used on the first reference.

» You may use well-known abbreviations such as *FCC* and *NOW* in a headline even though they would not be acceptable on first reference in a story.

» Do not put the abbreviation of an organization in parentheses after the full name on first reference. If an abbreviation is that confusing, don't use it at all. Instead, call the organization something like "the gay rights group" or "the bureau" on second reference.

» Use the abbreviations *Co., Cos., Corp., Inc.* and *Ltd.* at the end of a company's name even if the company spells out the word; do not abbreviate these words if followed by other words such as "of America." The abbreviations *Co., Cos.* and *Corp.* are used, however, if followed by *Inc.* or *Ltd.* (These latter two abbreviations are not set off by commas even if the company uses commas.)

» Abbreviate political affiliations after a name in the following way:
Sen. Claire McCaskill, D-Mo., said . . .
   Note the use of a single letter without a period for the party and the use of commas around the party and state abbreviations.

» Never abbreviate the word *association*, even as part of a name.

Places

» Don't abbreviate a state name unless it follows the name of a city in that state:
Nevada; Brown City, Mich.

» Never abbreviate the six states spelled with five or fewer letters or the two noncontiguous states:
Alaska, Hawaii, Idaho, Iowa, Maine, Ohio, Texas, Utah

» Use the traditional state abbreviations, not the Postal Service's two-letter ones:
Miss., not *MS*
EXCEPTION: Use the two-letter postal abbreviations when a full address is given that includes a ZIP code.

Here are the abbreviations used in normal copy:

Ala.	Fla.	Md.	Neb.	N.D.	Tenn.
Ariz.	Ga.	Mass.	Nev.	Okla.	Vt.
Ark.	Ill.	Mich.	N.H.	Ore.	Va.
Calif.	Ind.	Minn.	N.J.	Pa.	Wash.
Colo.	Kan.	Miss.	N.M.	R.I.	W.Va.
Conn.	Ky.	Mo.	N.Y.	S.C.	Wis.
Del.	La.	Mont.	N.C.	S.D.	Wyo.

» Use state abbreviations with domestic towns and cities unless they appear in the wire-service list of cities that stand alone in datelines. Many publications add to the wire-service list their own list of towns well-known in the state or region. Use a nation's full name with foreign towns and cities unless they appear in the wire-service list of cities that stand alone in datelines. Once a state or nation has been identified in a story, it is unnecessary to repeat the name unless clarity demands it. The lists of cities in the U.S. and the rest of the world that the wire services say may stand alone without a state abbreviation or nation are too lengthy to include here. Consult the appropriate stylebook. A handy rule of thumb is if it's an American city that has a major sports franchise, it probably stands alone. Likewise, if it's a foreign city most people have heard of, it probably stands alone.

» Don't abbreviate the names of thoroughfares if there is no street address with them:
Main Street, Century Boulevard West

» If the thoroughfare's name has the word *avenue, boulevard, street* or any of the directions on a map, such as *north* or *southeast*, abbreviate those words with a street address:
1044 W. Maple St., 1424 Lee Blvd. S., 999 Jackson Ave.

» In a highway's name, always abbreviate *U.S.*, but never abbreviate a state's name. In the case of an interstate highway, the name is written in full on first reference, abbreviated on subsequent ones:
U.S. Highway 63, Massachusetts 2
Interstate 70 (first reference), *I-70* (second reference)
» Never abbreviate *Fort* or *Mount*.
» Always use the abbreviation *St.* for *Saint* in place names.
EXCEPTIONS: *Saint John* in New Brunswick, *Sault Ste. Marie* in Michigan and Ontario
» Abbreviate *U.S., U.K.* and *U.N.* as both nouns and adjectives.

Miscellaneous

» Use the abbreviation *IQ* (no periods) in all references to *intelligence quotient*.
» Abbreviate and capitalize the word *number* when followed by a numeral: *No. 1*.
» Use the abbreviation *TV* (no periods) as an adjective or noun as an abbreviated form of *television*.
» Use the abbreviation *UFO* in all references to an *unidentified flying object*.
» Generally, spell out *versus*, but use the abbreviation *vs.*, not *v.*, for *versus* in short expressions: *guns vs. butter*. Use *v.* for court cases: *Marbury v. Madison*.

CAPITALIZATION

» Proper nouns are capitalized; common nouns are not. Unfortunately, this rule is not always easy to apply when the noun is the name of an animal, food or plant or when it is a trademark that has become so well-known that people mistakenly use it generically.
» Regions are capitalized; directions are not: *We drove east two miles to catch the interstate out West.*
» Adjectives and nouns pertaining to a region are capitalized: *Southern accent, Southerner, Western movie.*
» A region combined with a country's name is not capitalized unless the region is part of the name of a divided country: *eastern U.S., North Korea.*
» A region combined with a state name is capitalized only if it is famous: *Southern California, southern Colorado.*
» When two or more compound proper nouns are combined and have a word in common, the shared plural is lowercased: *Missouri and Mississippi rivers, Chrisman and Truman high schools.*
» Government and college terms are not always consistent.
  • *College departments* follow the animal, food and plant rule: Capitalize only words that are already proper nouns in themselves: *Spanish department, sociology department.* By contrast, always capitalize *a specific government department*, even without the city, state or federal designator and even if it's turned around with *of* deleted: *Police Department, Fire Department, Department of State, State Department.*
  • *College and government committees* are capitalized if the formal name is given rather than a shorter, descriptive designation: *Special Senate Select Committee to Investigate Improper Labor-Management Practices; rackets committee.*

- *Academic degrees* are spelled out and lowercased: *bachelor of arts degree, master's degree*. Avoid the abbreviations *Ph.D., M.A., B.A.*, etc., except in lists.
- Always capitalize (unless plural or generic) *City Council* and *County Commission* (but alone, *council* and *commission* are lowercased). *Cabinet* is capitalized when referring to advisers. *Legislature* is capitalized if the state's body is formally named that. *Capitol*, the building, is capitalized, but *capital*, the city, is not. Capitalize *City Hall* even without the city name but not *county courthouse* without the name of the county.
- Never capitalize *board of directors* or *board of trustees* (but formal governing bodies, such as *Board of Curators* and *Board of Education*, are capitalized). *Federal, government* and *administration* are not capitalized. *President* and *vice president* are capitalized only before a name and only when not set off with a comma:
  President Barack Obama
  Vice President Joe Biden
  the president, Barack Obama, said . . .
- *Military titles* (*Sgt., Maj., Gen.*) are capitalized before a name, as are *Air Force, Army, Marines* and *Navy* if referring to U.S. forces.
- *Political parties* are capitalized, including the word *party*: *Democratic Party, Socialist Party*. However, capitalize words such as *communist, democratic, fascist* and *socialist* only when they refer to a formal party rather than a philosophy.

» Terms related to the Internet are not always consistent.
- *Internet* and *the Net* (acceptable in later references) are capitalized. Some other Internet and technology terms are capitalized; some are not: *BlackBerry(s), blog, cellphone, chat room, click-thru(s), crowdsourcing, home page, Listserv* (trademarked software), *retweet, smartphone, social media* (n., adj.), *tweet* (n., v.), *Wi-Fi*.
- *World Wide Web, the Web* and *Web page* are capitalized. But *website, webcam, webcast* and *webmaster* are lowercased.
- *Email* (note lack of hyphen) and other similar terms (*e-book, e-commerce, e-business*) are lowercased.
- *IM* is acceptable for a second reference to *instant message*; also *IMing, IMed*.
- The proper names *iPad, iPhone* and *iPod* should be capitalized at the start of a sentence or headline (*IPad, IPhone, IPod*).

» Some religious terms (including holidays) are capitalized; most are not: *bar mitzvah, nirvana, Hanukkah, Ramadan*.
- *Pope* is lowercased except before a name: *the pope, Pope Francis*.
- *Mass* is always capitalized.
- Pronouns for *God* and *Jesus* are lowercased.
- Names of religious figures are capitalized: *Prophet Muhammad, Buddha*.
- Names of holy books are capitalized: *Talmud, Quran* (preferred to *Koran*). *Bible* is capitalized when meaning the Holy Scriptures and lowercased when referring to another book: *a hunter's bible*.
- Sacraments are capitalized if they commemorate events in the life of Jesus or signify his presence: *Holy Communion* but *baptism, communion*.

» Proper names and adjectives for races, ethnicities, and nationalities and religions are capitalized, but color descriptions are not: *African American, Arab, Asian* (preferred to *Oriental* for people), *Caucasian, Cherokee, Chinese* (singular and plural), *French Canadian, Muslim, Negro* (used only in names of organizations and quotations), *white, black*.

(Note that *Arab*, which denotes ethnicity, and *Muslim*, which refers to religion, are not interchangeable. For example, many Arabs are Christian, and Muslims may be Indian, Indonesian, Turkish, American, etc.)

» Formal titles of people are capitalized before a name, but occupational names are not: *President Barack Obama, Mayor Laura Miller, Coach Roy Williams, Dean Jaime Lopez, astronaut Ellen Ochoa, journalist Fred Francis, plumber Phil Sanders, pharmacist Roger Wheaton*

Some titles are not easy to recognize: *managing editor, chief executive officer*. When in doubt, put the title after the name, set it off with commas, and use lowercase.

» Formal titles that are capitalized before a name are lowercased after a name: *Barack Obama, president of the U.S.; Mike Rawlings, mayor of Dallas; Roy Williams, coach of the North Carolina Tar Heels; Fred Wilson, dean of students*

» Formal titles that are abbreviated before a name are written out and lowercased if they follow a name:
Gov. Andrew Cuomo; Andrew Cuomo, governor of New York
Sen. Lindsey Graham of South Carolina; Lindsey Graham, senator from South Carolina

» The first word in a direct quotation is capitalized only if the quote meets both of these criteria:
- It is a complete sentence. Don't capitalize a partial quote.
- It stands alone as a separate sentence or paragraph, or it is set off from its source by a comma or colon.

» A question within a sentence is capitalized:
My only question is, When do we start?

NUMBERS

» Cardinal numbers (numerals) are used in:
- Addresses. Always use numerals for street addresses: *1322 N. 17th St.*
- Ages. Always use numerals, even for days or months: *3 days old; John Burnside, 56.*
- Aircraft and spacecraft: *F-4, DC-10, Apollo 11*. Exception: *Air Force One.*
- Clothes sizes: *size 6.*
- Dates. Always use the numeral alone — no *st, nd, rd* or *th* after it: *March 20.*
- Decades: *the 1980s, the '80s, the early 2000s* (or *first decade of the 21st century*).
- Dimensions: *5-foot-6-inch guard* (but no hyphen when the word modified is one associated with size: *3 feet tall, 10 feet long*).
- Highways: *U.S. 63.*
- Millions, billions and trillions: *1.2 billion, 6 million.*
- Money. Always use numerals, but starting with a million, write like this: *$1.4 million.*
- Numbers: *No. 1, No. 2.*
- Percentages. Always use numerals except at the beginning of a sentence: *4 percent.*
- Recipes. All numbers for amounts take numerals: *2 teaspoons.*
- Speeds: *55 mph, 4 knots.*
- Sports. Use numerals for just about everything: *8-6 score, 2 yards, 3-under-par, 2 strokes.*
- Temperatures. Use numerals for all except *zero*. Below zero, spell out *minus: minus 6,* not *-6* (except in tabular data).

- Times: *4 a.m., 6:32 p.m., noon, midnight, five minutes, three hours.*
- Weights: *7 pounds, 11 ounces.*
- Years: Use numerals without commas. A year is the only numeral that can start a sentence: *1988 was a good year.*

» Numerals with the suffixes *st, nd, rd* and *th* are used for:

- Political divisions (precincts, wards, districts): *3rd Congressional District.*
- Military sequences: *1st Lt., 2nd Division, 7th Fleet.*
- Courts: *2nd District Court, 10th Circuit Court of Appeals.*
- Streets after *Ninth.* For *First* through *Ninth,* use words: *Fifth Avenue, 13th Street.*
- Amendments to the Constitution after *Ninth.* For *First* through *Ninth,* use words: *First Amendment, 16th Amendment.*

» Words are used for:

- Numbers less than 10, with the exceptions noted above: *five people, four rules.*
- Any number at the start of a sentence except for a year: *Sixteen years ago . . .*
- Casual numbers: *about a hundred or so.*
- Fractions less than one: *one-half.*

» Mixed numbers are used for fractions greater than one: *1 1/2.*

» Roman numerals are used for a man who is the third or later in his family to bear a name and for a king, queen, pope or world war: *John D. Rockefeller III, Queen Elizabeth II, Pope John Paul II, World War I.*

SUGGESTED WEBSITE

www.apstylebook.com
The Associated Press provides its stylebook in several formats, including as a traditional printed book, an online subscription and a mobile device (smartphone or tablet) application.

Society of Professional Journalists' Code of Ethics

PREAMBLE

Members of the Society of Professional Journalists believe that public enlightenment is the forerunner of justice and the foundation of democracy. The duty of the journalist is to further those ends by seeking truth and providing a fair and comprehensive account of events and issues. Conscientious journalists from all media and specialties strive to serve the public with thoroughness and honesty. Professional integrity is the cornerstone of a journalist's credibility. Members of the society share a dedication to ethical behavior and adopt this code to declare the society's principles and standards of practice.

SEEK TRUTH AND REPORT IT

Journalists should be honest, fair and courageous in gathering, reporting and interpreting information.

Journalists should:

» Test the accuracy of information from all sources and exercise care to avoid inadvertent error. Deliberate distortion is never permissible.
» Diligently seek out subjects of news stories to give them the opportunity to respond to allegations of wrongdoing.
» Identify sources whenever feasible. The public is entitled to as much information as possible on sources' reliability.
» Always question sources' motives before promising anonymity. Clarify conditions attached to any promise made in exchange for information. Keep promises.
» Make certain that headlines, news teases and promotional material, photos, video, audio, graphics, sound bites and quotations do not misrepresent. They should not oversimplify or highlight incidents out of context.
» Never distort the content of news photos or video. Image enhancement for technical clarity is always permissible. Label montages and photo illustrations.
» Avoid misleading re-enactments or staged news events. If re-enactment is necessary to tell a story, label it.

Sigma Delta Chi's first Code of Ethics was borrowed from the American Society of Newspaper Editors in 1926. In 1973, Sigma Delta Chi wrote its own code, which was revised in 1984 and 1987. The present version of the Society of Professional Journalists' Code of Ethics was adopted in September 1996.

» Avoid undercover or other surreptitious methods of gathering information except when traditional open methods will not yield information vital to the public. Use of such methods should be explained as part of the story.

» Never plagiarize.

» Tell the story of the diversity and magnitude of the human experience boldly, even when it is unpopular to do so.

» Examine their own cultural values and avoid imposing those values on others.

» Avoid stereotyping by race, gender, age, religion, ethnicity, geography, sexual orientation, disability, physical appearance or social status.

» Support the open exchange of views, even views they find repugnant.

» Give voice to the voiceless; official and unofficial sources of information can be equally valid.

» Distinguish between advocacy and news reporting. Analysis and commentary should be labeled and not misrepresent fact or context.

» Distinguish news from advertising and shun hybrids that blur the lines between the two.

» Recognize a special obligation to ensure that the public's business is conducted in the open and that government records are open to inspection.

MINIMIZE HARM

Ethical journalists treat sources, subjects and colleagues as human beings deserving of respect. Journalists should:

» Show compassion for those who may be affected adversely by news coverage. Use special sensitivity when dealing with children and inexperienced sources or subjects.

» Be sensitive when seeking or using interviews or photographs of those affected by tragedy or grief.

» Recognize that gathering and reporting information may cause harm or discomfort. Pursuit of the news is not a license for arrogance.

» Recognize that private people have a greater right to control information about themselves than do public officials and others who seek power, influence or attention. Only an overriding public need can justify intrusion into anyone's privacy.

» Show good taste. Avoid pandering to lurid curiosity.

» Be cautious about identifying juvenile suspects or victims of sex crimes.

» Be judicious about naming criminal suspects before the formal filing of charges.

» Balance a criminal suspect's fair trial rights with the public's right to be informed.

ACT INDEPENDENTLY

Journalists should be free of obligation to any interest other than the public's right to know. Journalists should:

» Avoid conflicts of interest, real or perceived.

» Remain free of associations and activities that may compromise integrity or damage credibility.

» Refuse gifts, favors, fees, free travel and special treatment, and shun secondary employ-
  ment, political involvement, public office and service in community organizations if they
  compromise journalistic integrity.
» Disclose unavoidable conflicts.
» Be vigilant and courageous about holding those with power accountable.
» Deny favored treatment to advertisers and special interests and resist their pressure to
  influence news coverage.
» Be wary of sources offering information for favors or money; avoid bidding for news.

BE ACCOUNTABLE

Journalists are accountable to their readers, listeners, viewers and each other.
    Journalists should:

» Clarify and explain news coverage and invite dialogue with the public over journalistic
  conduct.
» Encourage the public to voice grievances against the news media.
» Admit mistakes and correct them promptly.
» Expose unethical practices of journalists and the news media.
» Abide by the same high standards to which they hold others.

Glossary

absolute privilege   The right of legislators, judges and government executives to speak without threat of libel when acting in their official capacities.

absolutism   The ethical philosophy that holds that there is a fixed set of principles or laws from which there is no deviation. To the absolutist journalist, the end never justifies the means.

actual malice   Reckless disregard for the truth. Actual malice is a condition in libel cases.

actual malice test   Protection for reporters to write anything about an officeholder or candidate unless they know that the material is false or they recklessly disregard the truth.

add   A printed page of copy following the first page. "First add" would be the second page of printed copy.

advance   A report covering the subjects and issues to be dealt with in an upcoming meeting or event.

advertising department   The newspaper department responsible for advertisements. Most advertising departments have classified and display ad sections.

aggregated journalism   The viral dissemination of the news by members of the public, who often use social media for this purpose.

anchor   A person in a television studio who ties together a newscast by reading the news and providing transitions from one story to the next.

anecdote   An informative and entertaining story within a story.

angle   The focus of, or approach to, a story. The latest development in a continuing controversy, the key play in a football game or the tragedy of a particular death in a mass disaster may serve as an angle.

annual percentage rate   The annual cost of a loan expressed as a percentage. The basic method for computing APR is set forth in the Truth in Lending Act of 1968.

AP   The Associated Press, a worldwide news-gathering cooperative owned by its subscribers.

APME   Associated Press Media Editors, an organization of managing editors and other editors whose papers are members of the Associated Press.

app   Short for *computer application*. Software, usually for a smartphone or tablet computer, that helps users perform a particular task. For example, a news app might enable users to access a news website efficiently.

arithmetic mean   See *average*.

assessed value   The amount that a government appraiser determines a property is worth.

assistant news director   The second in command in a television station newsroom.

attribution   Identification of the source of the information or quotation.

average   (1) A term used to describe typical or representative members of a group. (2) In mathematics, the result obtained when a set of numbers is added together and then divided by the number of items in the set.

background   Information that may be attributed to a source by title but not by name; for example, "a White House aide said."

backgrounder   A story that explains and updates the news.

beat   A reporter's assigned area of responsibility. A beat may be an institution, such as a courthouse; a geographic area, such as a small town; or a subject, such as science. The term also refers to an exclusive story.

blog   Short for *Web log*. A Web-based publication in which articles or diarylike entries, issued periodically, appear in reverse chronological order.

blotter   An old-fashioned term for the arrest sheet that summarizes the bare facts of an arrest. Today this information is almost always stored on a computer.

book   Assembled sheets of paper, usually newsprint, and carbon paper on which reporters once prepared stories. Books are not used with modern computerized processes.

Boolean search command   The language of searching computer databases in which the search is narrowed through the use of operators such as AND, OR or NOT.

bureau   A news-gathering office maintained by a newspaper somewhere other than its central location. Papers may have bureaus in the next county; in the state capital; in Washington, D.C.; or in foreign countries.

byline   A line identifying the author of a story.

calendar year   The 12-month period from January through December.

change of venue   The transfer of a court proceeding to another jurisdiction for prosecution. This often occurs when a party in a case claims that local media coverage has prejudiced prospective jurors.

chat room   An online site for meeting and communicating by text and sometimes by webcam (a video camera connected to a computer).

circulation department   The department responsible for distribution of the newspaper.

citizen journalist   One who practices a new form of media in which citizens actively participate in gathering and writing information, often in the form of news. Also called *participatory journalist.*

city editor   The individual (also known as the *metropolitan,* or *metro, editor*) in charge of the city desk, which coordinates local news-gathering operations. At some papers the desk also handles regional and state news from its own reporters.

click-through rate   The measurement of how often online readers open individual links/stories.

clip   A story clipped from a newspaper.

closed-ended question   A direct question designed to draw a specific response—for example, "Will you be a candidate?"

community portal   A website designed as a general entry point for Internet users in a city and its nearby suburbs.

compound interest   Interest paid on the total of the principal (the amount borrowed) and the interest that has already accrued.

conditional privilege   See *qualified privilege.*

constant dollars   Monetary amounts adjusted for inflation.

Consumer Price Index   A tool used by the government to measure the rate of inflation. CPI figures, reported monthly by the Bureau of Labor Statistics of the U.S. Department of Labor, compare the net change in prices between the current period and a specified base period. Reporters should use these data to accurately reflect the actual costs of goods and services.

content aggregator   A company that collects and distributes news from traditional media sources but does little or no independent news gathering.

contextual advertising   Website advertising directed to likely users of the site according to demographic profiles.

contributing editor   A magazine columnist who works under contract and not as an employee of the magazine.

control   To structure an experiment so that the only forces affecting the outcome are the variables you are observing.

convergence   A term defined in different ways by different people in the media industry but generally used to describe the coordination of print, broadcast and online reporting in a news operation.

copy   What reporters write. A story is a piece of copy.

copy desk   The desk at which final editing of stories is done, headlines are written and pages are designed.

copy editor   A person who checks, polishes and corrects stories written by reporters. Usually copy editors write headlines for these stories; sometimes they decide how to arrange stories and pictures on a page.

cover   To keep abreast of significant developments on a beat or to report on a specific event. The reporter covering the police beat may be assigned to cover a murder.

crowdsourcing   The practice of inviting unpaid readers and viewers to submit their own stories, photographs and video and sometimes to lend their expertise to help solve community problems.

cutline   The caption that accompanies a newspaper or magazine photograph. The term dates from the days when photos were reproduced with etched zinc plates called *cuts.*

deadline   The time by which a reporter, editor or desk must have completed scheduled work.

deep background   Information that may be used but that cannot be attributed to either a person or a position.

delayed-identification lead   The opening paragraph of a story in which the "who" is identified by occupation, city, office or any means other than by name.

desk   A term used by reporters to refer to the city editor's or copy editor's position, as in "The desk wants this story by noon."

desk assistant   An entry-level position in television newsrooms. Desk assistants handle routine news assignments, such as monitoring wire services and listening to police scanners.

developing story   A story in which newsworthy events occur over several days or weeks.

dialogue   A conversation between two or more people, neither of whom normally is the reporter.

direct quote   A quote inside quotation marks that captures the exact words of the speaker.

documentary   In-depth coverage of an issue or event, especially in broadcasting.

e-book reader   An electronic device whose primary function is the digital storage of books, though most e-book readers also offer other features.

editor   The top-ranking individual in the news department of a newspaper, also known as the *editor-in-chief.* The term may refer as well to those at any level who edit copy.

editorial department   The news department of a newspaper, responsible for all content of the newspaper except advertising. At some papers this term refers to the department responsible for the editorial page only.

editorialize To inject the reporter's or the newspaper's opinion into a news story or headline. Most newspapers restrict opinion to analysis stories, columns and editorials.

editorial page editor The individual in charge of the editorial page and, at larger newspapers, the op-ed page. See also *op-ed page*.

executive producer The television executive with overall responsibility for the look of the television newscast.

explanatory journalism Journalism that explains not only what happened but how. The use of this technique often distinguishes professional journalism from citizen journalism.

e-zine Magazines and newsletters distributed by email.

Facebook The world's most-used social networking website, which allows people to share updates, photos and news in a series of personalized feeds.

fair comment and criticism Opinion delivered on the performance of someone in the public eye. Such opinion is legally protected as long as reporters do not misstate any of the facts on which they base their comments or criticism, and it is not malicious.

feature A story that includes little or no breaking news.

field experiment A research technique in which the reporter deliberately takes some action to observe the effects. For example, a perfectly tuned automobile could be taken to several repair shops to find out if the mechanics would invent problems that required fixing.

field producer A behind-the-scenes television reporter who often does much of the fieldwork for a network's on-camera correspondents.

fiscal year Any 12-month period used to calculate annual revenues and expenditures.

flat-file database A simple database program that allows users to keep track of almost any type of data. A simple address book is an example.

focus structure A story organization that begins with the story of an individual person, broadens to include a trend or issue, and then brings the issue back to the person featured at the beginning of the story.

follow A story supplying further information about an item that has already been published. *Folo* is an alternate spelling.

foreshadowing A technique that teases readers with material coming later in the story as a way of encouraging them to keep reading.

Freedom of Information Act A law passed in 1966 to make it easier to obtain information from federal agencies. The law was amended in 1974 to improve access to government records.

free-form database A database that is not limited in structure and allows almost any type of content to be included.

free press/fair trial controversy The conflict between a defendant's right to an impartial jury and a reporter's responsibility to inform the public.

full-text database A database that permits searches of any text in an article.

futures file A collection—filed according to date—of newspaper stories, letters, notes and other information to remind editors of stories to assign. See also *tickler*.

gatekeepers Editors who determine what readers or viewers read, hear and see.

graf A shortened form of *paragraph*, as in "Give me two grafs on that fire."

graphics editor Usually, the editor responsible for all non-photographic illustrations in a newspaper, including information graphics, maps and illustrations.

handout See *news release*.

hard lead A lead that reports a new development or newly discovered fact. See also *soft lead*.

hard news Coverage of the actions of government or business, or the reporting of an event, such as a crime, an accident or a speech. The time element often is important. See also *soft news*.

HTML The abbreviation for *hypertext markup language*, the coding language used to create text on the Web.

hyperlink A connection between two places on the Web.

hyperlocal Information that is intensely local in its emphasis.

hypermedia Web links to audio, video and pictures.

hypertext A Web document coded in HTML.

hypothesis In investigative reporting, the statement a reporter expects to be able to prove, as in, "The mayor took a bribe from that massage parlor." In an experiment, the statement of what a researcher hopes to find.

immediate-identification lead The opening paragraph of a story in which the "who" is reported by name.

income tax An annual tax on an individual's income or a business's profit. It is levied by the federal government and in some cases by state and local governments. It is calculated as a percentage.

indirect quote A paraphrase of the speaker's words. Because it is a paraphrase, the words are not in quotation marks.

inflation The rising cost of living as time goes by. See also *Consumer Price Index*.

infomedium Short for *information medium*, a term coined to represent the merger of the Internet, television, wireless and other technologies as the medium of the future.

information graphic A visual representation of data.

interest (1) A measure of the cumulative effect of all the news values. The more elements of each of the six news values that appear in the story, the more interesting that story will be to readers. (2) Money earned or paid on a base amount and calculated as a percentage.

Internet The vast network that links computers around the world.

interviewing Having conversations with sources.

intranet An internal online service accessible only to employees of a particular company or organization.

invasion of privacy Violation of a person's right to be left alone.

inverted pyramid The organization of a news story in which information is arranged in descending order of importance.

investigative piece A story intended to reveal material not generally known.

investigative reporting The pursuit of information that has been concealed, such as evidence of wrongdoing.

IRE Investigative Reporters and Editors, a group created to exchange information and investigative reporting techniques. IRE has its headquarters at the University of Missouri School of Journalism.

lay out (v.) To prepare page drawings to indicate where stories and pictures are to be placed in the newspaper.

layout (n.) The completed page drawing, or page dummy.

lead (1) The first paragraph or first several paragraphs of a newspaper story (sometimes spelled *lede*). (2) The story given the best display on Page 1. (3) A tip.

lead-in An introduction to a filmed or recorded excerpt from a news source or from another reporter.

legacy media Traditional media outlets such as newspapers, magazines, broadcast television and the like.

libel Damage to a person's reputation caused by a false written statement that brings the person into hatred, contempt or ridicule or injures his or her business or occupational pursuit.

line-item budget A budget showing each expenditure on a separate line.

macroediting Editing for the big picture, such as whether the story is missing anything and whether it is organized properly. See also *microediting*.

maestro The leader of a news-gathering team. Reporters, copy editors, editors and graphic designers work with a maestro to create special reports.

managing editor The individual with primary responsibility for the day-to-day operation of the news department.

margin of error The difference between results from the entire population (all registered voters in your county, for example) and a random sample of the population. It is usually expressed as plus or minus x points. The x depends on the size of the sample. The larger the sample, the smaller the margin of error.

media fragmentation A proliferation of media outlets leading to smaller audiences for traditional media and a resulting decline in the ability to target audiences.

median The middle number in a series arranged in order of magnitude; it is often used when an average would be misleading. (If the series has an even number of items, the median is the average of the two "middle" numbers.) See also *average*.

metadata Keywords attached to an online story, but not necessarily within it, that help search engines index material for display in search results. See also *search-engine optimization*.

microediting Editing for details such as grammar, punctuation and spelling. See also *macroediting*.

micropayment A small payment for reading an article on the Web.

millage rate The tax rate on property, determined by the government.

mobile media Portable digital devices, such as smartphones and tablet computers.

moblog A type of Internet blog in which the user publishes blog entries directly to the Web from a smartphone or other mobile device.

more A designation used at the end of a page of copy to indicate that one or more pages follow.

morgue The newsroom library, where published stories, photographs and resource material are stored for reference.

multimedia assignment desk In a converged newsroom, the news desk where the efforts of print, broadcast and online reporters are coordinated. See also *convergence*.

multimedia editor An editor responsible for coordinating or producing news content for various media.

multimedia journalist A journalist capable of producing content in more than one medium, such as radio and newspapers.

multiple-element lead The opening paragraph of a story that reports two or more newsworthy elements.

narration The telling of a story, usually in chronological order.

negligence test The legal standard that requires reporters gathering facts and writing a story to use the same degree of care that any reasonable individual would use in similar circumstances.

network correspondent A television reporter who delivers the news on camera. Network correspondents do not necessarily do the actual news gathering for their stories.

new media Emerging forms of computer-delivered news.

news conference An interview session in which someone submits to questions from reporters. Also called a *press conference*.

news director The top news executive of a local television station.

news editor The supervisor of the copy desk. At some newspapers, this title is used for the person in charge of local news-gathering operations.

news narrative A story that sums up the news in the first paragraph or two and then describes events chronologically rather than ranking them in descending order of importance.

news release An item that is sent out by a group or individual seeking publicity. Also called a *handout* or *press release*.

news story A story, often written in inverted pyramid style, that emphasizes the facts.

news value The measure of how important or interesting a story is.

niche A specific subset of a part of a general audience. A magazine or website directed at weavers or bow hunters would be a niche publication.

nominal dollars Monetary amounts not adjusted for inflation.

not for attribution An expression indicating that information may not be ascribed to its source.

nut paragraph A paragraph that summarizes the key element or elements of a story. Nut paragraphs usually are found in stories not written in inverted pyramid form. Also called a *nut graf*.

off-camera reporter A reporter who gathers news for television but does not report on the air.

off the record An expression that usually means "Don't quote me." Some sources and reporters use it to mean "Don't print this." Phrases with similar, and equally ambiguous, meanings are "not for attribution" and "for background only."

online editor The editor of a website for a newspaper or television station.

online media See *new media*.

online videoconferencing An Internet-enabled, real-time communication where participants can both see and hear each other.

op-ed page The page opposite the editorial page in a printed newspaper, or the corresponding opinion pages in an online publication, frequently reserved for columns, letters to the editor and personality profiles.

open-ended question A question that permits the respondent some latitude in the answer—for example, "How did you get involved in politics?"

open-meetings law A state or federal law, often called a *sunshine law*, guaranteeing public access to meetings of public officials.

open-records law A state or federal law guaranteeing public access to many—but not all—kinds of government records.

parallelism A technique of presenting ideas in similar grammatical forms.

paraphrase A technique that digests, condenses or clarifies a quotation to convey the meaning more precisely or succinctly than the speaker's words do; an indirect quotation. Quotation marks are not used with paraphrases.

participant observation A research technique in which the reporter joins in the activity he or she wants to write about.

payola Money or gifts given in the expectation of favors from journalists.

PDF file A computerized document that preserves formatting.

per capita A Latin term meaning "by heads." A per capita amount is determined by dividing a total figure—such as a budget—by the number of people to which it applies.

percentage A mathematical way to express the portion of a whole; literally, a given part of every hundred. A percentage is determined by taking the number of the portion, dividing by the number of the whole and moving the decimal point two places to the right. For example, 15 divided by 30 equals .50, or 50 percent.

percentage change A number that explains by how much something goes up or down.

percentage point A unit of measure used to express the difference between two percentages. For example, the difference between 25 percent and 40 percent is 15 percentage points.

photo editor The individual who advises editors on the use of photographs in the newspaper. The photo editor also may supervise the photography department.

piece See *story*.

plagiarism The act of using any part of another person's writing and passing it off as your own.

play A shortened form of *display*. A good story may be played at the top of Page 1; a weak one may be played inside.

podcasting A method of distributing multimedia files, usually audio or video, to mobile devices or personal computers so that consumers can listen or watch on demand. The term is derived from Apple Computer's iPod, but podcasts may be received by almost any music player or computer.

population   In scientific language, the whole group being studied. Depending on the study, the population may be, for example, voters in St. Louis, physicians in California or all residents of the U.S.

press   (1) The machine that prints newspapers. (2) Also a synonym for *journalism*, as in the phrase "freedom of the press." Sometimes used to denote print journalism, as distinguished from broadcast journalism.

press box   The section of a stadium or arena set aside for reporters.

press conference   See *news conference*.

press release   See *news release*.

primary source   A person who witnesses or participates in an event, or an authentic document from an event.

principal   The amount of money borrowed.

principled reasoning   Reasoning that reflects ethical principles.

Privacy Protection Act   A law passed in 1980 that requires federal, state and local enforcement officers to get a subpoena—rather than a search warrant—to obtain documents from reporters and newsrooms, unless the reporter is involved in a crime or immediate action is needed to prevent bodily harm, loss of life or destruction of the material.

privilege   A defense against libel that claims journalists have the right to repeat what government officials say or do in their official capacities.

production department   The department of a newspaper that transforms the work of the news and advertising departments into the finished product. The composing room and pressroom are key sections of this department.

profile   A story intended to reveal the personality or character of an institution or person.

program budget   A budget that clearly shows what each agency's activities cost.

property tax   An annual tax, figured as a percentage, on the value of houses, buildings and land. Property taxes are usually levied by local or state governments.

proportion   An explanation that relates one specific number to another or to the quantity or magnitude of a whole.

public figure   A person who has assumed a role of prominence in the affairs of society and who has persuasive power and influence in a community or who has thrust himself or herself to the forefront of a public controversy. Courts have given journalists more latitude in reporting on public figures than on private citizens.

public information utility   A commercial online service such as CompuServe.

public journalism   The new (or rediscovered) approach to journalism that emphasizes connections with the community rather than separation from it. Among the newspapers best known for practicing public journalism are *The Wichita (Kan.) Eagle* and *The Charlotte (N.C.) Observer*.

publisher   The top-ranking executive of a newspaper. This title often is assumed by the owner, although chains sometimes designate the top local executive as publisher.

Pulitzer Prize   The most prestigious of journalism awards. It was established by Joseph Pulitzer and is administered by Columbia University.

qualified privilege   The right of journalists to report what government officials say or do in their official capacities if the report is full, fair and accurate. Also called *conditional privilege*.

quote   As a noun, a source's exact words, as in "I have a great quote here." As a verb, to report a source's exact words inside quotation marks.

randomization   The mathematical process used to ensure that every member of a population being studied has an equal chance of being chosen for questioning or observation.

rate   The amount or degree of something measured in relation to a unit of something else or to a specified scale. In statistics, rate often expresses the incidence of a condition per 100,000 people, such as a murder or suicide rate. Rate also can reflect the speed at which something is changing, such as inflation or the percentage increase in a budget each year.

records column   A regular newspaper feature that contains such information as routine police and fire news, births, obituaries, marriages and divorces.

relational database   A database program that permits users to determine relationships between two or more dissimilar databases. For example, a relational database program would enable a reporter to compare one database of people convicted of drunken driving with another database of school-bus drivers. The result would show how many bus drivers had drunken-driving convictions.

relevance   The impact of a story as measured by the number of readers it affects and how seriously it affects them.

reporter   A person whose job is to gather and write the news for a publication or a broadcast outlet.

roundup   A story that includes a number of related events. After a storm, for example, a reporter might do a roundup of accidents, power outages and other consequences of the storm.

RSS   Short for *really simple syndication*, a form of content distribution over the Internet that relies on a common markup language, XML (extensible markup language).

sales tax   A tax, figured as a percentage, on the price of goods. It is usually levied by a local or state government and is paid by the consumer to the retailer at the time of purchase.

sample   A portion of a group, or population, chosen for study as representative of the entire group.

search-engine optimization   The practice of writing stories and headlines to increase the likelihood that search engines such as Google will index them. Behind-the-scenes metadata also influence SEO.

secondary source   A source who talked to a witness, such as a public safety official investigating a crime. The witness would be a primary source.

second-cycle story   A second version of a story already published, also called a *second-day story*. It usually has new information or a new angle.

senior editor   A person who edits a section of a major magazine.

senior writer   A title reserved for a magazine's best and most experienced reporters.

series   Two or more stories on the same or related subjects, published on a predetermined schedule.

service journalism   An aspect or type of journalism that recognizes usefulness as one of the criteria of news. Taking into consideration content and presentation, service journalism presents useful information in a usable way—for instance, by placing key information in a list or graphic box.

setup   In broadcasting, an introductory statement to pique the interest of listeners or viewers. In written accounts, the material between the opening of a narrative story and the body. It generally consists of the transition to the theme paragraph, the nut paragraph, and, when appropriate, the "so what" and "to be sure" statements and foreshadowing.

shield law   Legislation giving journalists the right to protect the identity of sources.

shovelware   Stories posted on the Web exactly as they appeared in print.

show producer   A television news specialist who produces individual newscasts and who reports to the executive producer.

sidebar   A secondary story intended to be run with a major story on the same topic. A story about a disaster, for example, may have a sidebar that tells what happened to a single victim.

simple interest   Interest paid on the principal (the amount borrowed).

situation ethics   The philosophy that recognizes that a set of rules can be broken if circumstances indicate that the community would be served better by breaking them. For example, a journalist who generally believes that deceiving a news source is unethical may nevertheless be willing to conceal his or her identity to infiltrate a group operating illegally.

slug   A word that identifies a story as it is processed through the newspaper plant or at a broadcast news station. A slug is usually placed in the upper left-hand corner of each take of a newspaper story. See also *take*.

smartphone   A mobile phone with an operating system that expands its uses from just talking and texting to connecting to the Web and using a variety of applications.

sniff   The preliminary phase of an investigation.

social networking   The practice of connecting with others for business or social purposes. Social networking sites make it easy for individuals to connect with others who have similar interests or goals.

soft lead   A lead that uses a quote, anecdote or other literary device to attract the reader. See also *hard lead*.

soft news   Stories about trends, personalities or lifestyles. The time element usually is not important. See also *hard news*.

sound bite   An audio recording that accompanies a story in radio or television news or, more recently, that is available even on newspaper websites as a supplement to the printed product.

sources   People or records from which a reporter gets information. The term often is used to describe people, as opposed to documents.

spot news   A timely report of an event that is unfolding at the moment.

spreadsheet program   A computer program used for analyzing numbers. It is often used to track changes in budgets and expenditures.

story   The term most journalists use for a newspaper article. Another synonym is *piece*, as in "I saw your piece on the mayor." A long story may be called a *takeout* or a *blockbuster*.

strategic communication   A "new" name for public relations that emphasizes the stronger role of professionals in this field in conducting research, solving problems and making decisions. Strategic communication sometimes includes advertising.

stylebook   A book of rules on grammar, punctuation, capitalization and abbreviation in newspaper text. The AP and UPI publish similar stylebooks that are used by most papers.

substantial truth   The correctness of the essential elements of a story.

summary lead   The first paragraph of a news story in which the writer presents a synopsis of two or more events rather than focusing on any one of them.

sunshine law   See *open-meetings law*.

tablet computer   A self-contained, flat-panel computer, like an iPad, that is portable. Most tablets are about the size of a book.

take   A page of printed copy for newspaper use.

teleprompter   A mechanical or electronic device that projects broadcast copy next to the television camera lens so that a newscaster can read it while appearing to look straight into the lens.

30   A designation used to mark the end of a newspaper story. The symbol # is an alternate designation.

tickler   A file of upcoming events kept on paper or stored electronically at the assignment desks of most news organizations. See also *futures file*.

tie-back   (1) The sentence or sentences relating a story to events covered in a previous story. Tie-backs are used in follow-up or continuing stories or in parts of a series. (2) The technique of referring to the opening of a story in the story's ending.

"to be sure" paragraph   In stories focusing on one person or perspective, a statement reflecting the opinions of those who disagree with the person featured, as in "To be sure, not everyone agrees."

truth   Actuality or reality. Truth is the best defense against libel.

Twitter   A microblogging site that allows users to post short status updates in 140 characters or fewer, and follow the updates of friends, celebrities, news organizations and others.

undercover reporting   A technique in which a reporter pretends to be someone else in order to gain access to otherwise unobtainable information.

universal desk   A copy desk that edits material for all editorial departments of a newspaper.

update   A type of follow that reports on a development related to an earlier story. See also *follow*.

UPI   United Press International, a worldwide news-gathering organization that is privately owned.

URL   Short for *uniform resource locator*, the address of an Internet site.

usefulness   A quality of news that increases the impact of the story. The story has information that readers can use to act on, such as notification of a meeting before it occurs.

variable   In an experiment, one of the elements being observed. The *independent variable* is what is thought to be a cause; the *dependent variable* is the effect of that cause.

videographer   A television camera operator.

videoprompter   See *teleprompter*.

viral marketing   The practice of using social networking media such as Facebook or Myspace to seed links to a more traditional media form, thus increasing traffic to the other medium.

webcast   An audio or video report available on a website.

website   A location on the World Wide Web, the Internet service that connects hypertext data.

Wi-Fi   Wireless Internet access.

wiki   A type of website that allows users to add or alter content. Wikipedia, for example, is a user-written and user-updated encyclopedia.

Wikinews   A wiki on which users can post or update information in news format.

wrap-up   (1) The completion of commentary that comes at the end of a taped segment in broadcasting. (2) A strong ending to a report.

"you" lead   The first paragraph of a story, written using the informal, second-person pronoun "you."

Acknowledgments *(continued from page iv)*

Chapter 2

J. D. Lasica, "Six Types of Citizen Journalism" from "What Is Participatory Journalism?," *Online Journalism Review*, August 7, 2003. J. D. Lasica/Socialmedia.biz. Reprinted by permission of the author.

Sarah Rupp, "On the Job" Interview. Reprinted by permission of Sarah Rupp.

Chapter 4

Wright Thompson, "Comments on a story about a former college football player and a memorable interview with Heisman Trophy winner Eric Crouch." Reprinted by permission of the author.

Chapter 5

Associated Press, "Terror Sting Thwarts Car Bomb Attempt," as appeared in *Columbia Daily Tribune*, October 18, 2012. Reprinted by permission of Associated Press.

Bruce Horovitz, "Advertisement Put Obese People in Spotlight," *USA Today*, October 4, 2012. Copyright © 2012 Gannett. Reprinted by permission.

T. J. Quinn, "On the Job" Interview. Reprinted by permission of T. J. Quinn.

Chapter 6

Erik Ulken, "On the Job" Interview. Reprinted by permission of Erik Ulken.

Stan Ketterer, journalist and journalism professor. "Guidelines for Evaluating Information of the Web." Reprinted by permission of the author.

Susanne Rust, Meg Kissinger and Cary Spivak, "Chemical Fallout: Bisphenol A Is in You," *Milwaukee Journal Sentinel*, December 2, 2007. Copyright © 2007 by Journal/Sentinel, Inc. Reprinted by permission of Journal/Sentinel, Inc.

Chapter 7

Lara Jakes, "On the Job" Interview. Reprinted by permission of Lara Jakes.

Humane Society of Missouri, "Humane Society of Missouri Confirms: Guilty Pleas Entered in Federal Court to Charges from Largest Dog Fighting Raid and Rescue in U.S. History," news release, September 14, 2009. Copyright © 2009. Reprinted by permission of the *Humane Society of Missouri*.

Chapter 8

Jennifer LaFleur, "On the Job" Interview. Reprinted by permission of Jennifer LaFleur.

Chapter 9

AP Leads, excerpts from several Associated Press leads. Reprinted with permission of The Associated Press.

Asif Lakhami, "Parks and Recreation, City Council discuss plans for parks tax," *Columbia Missourian*, November 29, 2010. Reprinted by permission of the Columbia Missourian.

Tina Macias, "On the Job" Interview. Reprinted by permission of Tina Macias.

Tina Macias, education reporter. "A Case Study of Leads." Reprinted by permission of the author.p

Elizabeth Phillips, "Man Arrested in Attack, Charged with Child Endangerment," *Columbia Missourian*, November 17, 2006. Copyright © 2006 Columbia Missourian. Reprinted by permission.

Chapter 10

Mark Landler and Eric Dash, "Drama Behind a $250 Billion Banking Deal," *The New York Times*, October 15, 2008 Issue, p. A1. Copyright © 2008 New York Times. All rights reserved. Reprinted by permission.

Justin Heckert, "On the Job" Interview. Reprinted by permission of Justin Heckert.

Amy Ellis Nutt, "48 hours: Before, during, and after Hurricane Sandy in Seaside Heights and Cape May," *The Star-Ledger*, November 4, 2012. Copyright © 2012. Reprinted by permission.

Chapter 11

Kristen Gelineau and Ravi Nessman, "Ill-fated train ride tears Indian boy from mother, sparks 25-year worldwide hunt for home," Associated Press, June 11, 2012. Reprinted by permission of Associated Press.

John Tully. "Horse Power" from *Columbia Missourian*, November 27, 2006, p. 1. Copyright © 2006 *Columbia Missourian*. Reprinted by permission of the Columbia Missourian.

Jane Meinhardt, "Mother Accused of Being Criminal Ringleader," *St. Petersburg Times*, October 21, 1994. Copyright © 1994 by St. Petersburg Times. Reprinted by permission.

Matt Pearce, "Web plays incendiary role in Ohio high school rape case," *Los Angeles Times*, January 7, 2013. Reprinted by permission of the Los Angeles Times.

Chapter 12

Jenifer Langosch, "On the Job" Interview. Reprinted by permission of Jenifer Langosch.

David Carr, "In $2.5 Million Judgment, Court Finds Blogger Is Not a Journalist," Media Decoder blog, *The New York Times*, December 8, 2011. Copyright © 2011 New York Times Co. Reprinted by permission.

Jeré Longman, "Waiting for Power in the Cajun Prairie," *The New York Times*, BLOG section, September 3, 2008. Copyright © 2008 The New York Times Co. Reprinted by permission.

Chapter 13

Associated Press, "Sheriffs in five South Carolina counties are offering people a chance to turn in explosives, no questions asked," October 24, 2012. Reprinted by permission of Associated Press.

Associated Press, "Couple found shot dead in Jefferson City," September 28, 2009. Reprinted by permission of Associated Press.

Associated Press, "Attorney General Bars Florida Telemarketer," December 6, 2011. Reprinted by permission of Associated Press.

Devlin Barrett and Pete Yost, "Scientist appears in court in secrets case," October 20, 2009. Copyright © 2009 Associated Press. Reprinted by permission.

Associated Press, "Roadside Fish Memorial," October 30, 2012. Reprinted by permission of Associated Press.

Chapter 14

Derrick Goold, "On the Job" Interview. Reprinted by permission of Derrick Goold.

Chapter 15

Rosalind S. Helderman and Ed O'Keefe, "House Republicans weighing short-term debt limit increase," *The Washington Post*, January 17, 2013. Copyright © 2013. Reprinted by permission.

Dana Bash, Jessica Yellin and Tom Cohen, "Pushback on Obama's plan to stem gun violence," CNN, January 17, 2013. Copyright © 2013. Reprinted by permission.

Chapter 16

Rex Huppke, "Facts, 360 B.C.–A.D. 2012, In memoriam: After years of health problems, Facts has finally died," *Chicago Tribune*, April 19, 2012. Copyright © 2012. Reprinted by permission.

Amy Rabideau Silvers, "A life of love was made public in end: Couple came out, testified at Capitol," *The Milwaukee Journal Sentinel*, August 2, 2006. Reprinted by permission.

Chapter 17

Nik Deogan, "On the Job" Interview. Reprinted by permission of Nik Deogan.

Chapter 20

Contemporary Jewish Museum, Press Release, "Hand Holding at the CJM," July 23, 2011. Reprinted by permission of the Contemporary Jewish Museum.

Chris Anderson, "Sorry PR people: you're blocked," *Wired* blog network, October 29, 2007. Reprinted by permission of the author.

Richie Escovedo, "For PR pros, 9 rules taken directly from Kindergarten," October 29, 2009, www.ragan.com. Copyright © 2009. Reprinted by permission of *Ragan Communications*.

Brad Whitworth, "On the Job" Interview. Reprinted by permission of Brad Whitworth.

Chapter 21

Ken Paulson, "On the Job" Interview. Reprinted by permission of Ken Paulson.

Jean McHale, "On the Job" Interview. Reprinted by permission of Jean McHale.

Chapter 22

Society of Professional Journalists, "Act Independently" from "Code of Ethics." Copyright © 1996-2007 Society of Professional Journalists. Reprinted with permission. All rights reserved. www.spj.org.

Bob Steele, "Ask These 10 Questions to Make Good Ethical Decisions." Copyright © 1995–2007 The Poynter Institute. Reprinted by permission of the author.

Roy Peter Clark, "Beware of Plagiarism!" Reprinted with permission of The Poynter Institute.

Index

Note: Page numbers in *italics* indicate material presented in boxes. Page numbers followed by an italicized *f* indicate figures. Page numbers in **boldface** indicate terms that appear in the Glossary.

Abbasi, R. Umar, 482
abbreviations, 499–502
  in broadcast news, 281
  dates, 500
  miscellaneous, 502
  names and titles, 500
  organizations, 500–501
  places, 501–2
  punctuation for, 499
  symbols, 500
ABC News, 475–76
Abramson, Jill, 90
absolute privilege, 447*f*, **448**
absolutism, **467**–68
accents, quotations with, 92–94
accident stories
  attributions for, 98
  deadlines in, 338
  preparing for, 330, 332
  sources for, 337–38
  tips for, 332
  writing, 337–40
accountability, ethics and, 508
accuracy
  in beat reporting, 295
  in crime stories, 340–42
  fact checking, 11, 89, 164, 189
  importance of, 5, 13–14, 17, 189–90
  in information gathering, 112–15
  in interviewing, 75–78
  in investigative reporting, 405
  in news releases, 142
  of numbers, *163*, 164
  in obituaries, 355, 356
  of online sources, *124–25*
  prepublication review for, 64, 89–90, 189–90
  public perceptions of, 31
  of published sources, 120
  of quotations, 78, 85–90, 91, 189–90

  recording devices for, 89, 91
  of social media reporting, 111, *124*, 277
  verifying names, 173, 315, 337
acronyms, 500
active voice, *269*, 270
activist journalism, 7–8
actual malice test, 446, **449**–53
adjectives
  compound, 494
  coordinate, 492–93
  demonstrative, 201, *202*, 203
advances, **183**
  for meetings, 316
  memo-structure for, 183
adverbs
  intensive and qualifying, 204, *205*
  in introductory elements, 491–92
advertising
  conflict of interest and, 370
  consumer stories and, 384
  ethical problems with, 477–78
  focus structure and, 230
  jobs in, *55*, 132
  obituaries and, 354
  strategic marketing, 420
  Web-based journalism and, 242, 354
age, in leads, 171
age bias, 208
agenda-setting, 11–12
aggregators. *See* content aggregators
Al Jazeera, 48
Alonzo, Austin, 366
Alterman, Eric, 478
Amanpour, Christiane, 275*f*
American Banker magazine, 367
American Business Media, 432, 467
American City Business Journals, 367
American Society of Business Press
    Editors, 467

American Society of Magazine Editors, 467
American Society of News Editors, 195, 211, 355
analogies, 207
Anderson, Chris, 433
Anderson, Frank, 478
anecdotes, **213**
  closed-ended questions for, 71
  for ending stories, 235
  for maintaining interest, 234–35, 333
  in narration, 213–14
  in obituaries, 357, 358
  opening with, 230
announcement news releases, 133–35, 137–38
announcements, for business news, 378
annual meetings, 378
annual percentage rate (APR), **155**
annual reports, 162–63, 373, 375, 378–81
anonymous sources, 104–6
  attributions for, 99, *100*
  background interviews, 106
  New York Times' policy for, *104*
  problems with, 104
  protecting, 295, 412, 456–59
  terminology disagreement about, 105
  See also confidential sources
antecedents, 495
Antelope Valley Press, 50
AP. *See* Associated Press
apostrophes, 494
appeals, court, 348
appropriation, 454
apps, **23**. *See also* mobile media
arithmetic mean, 153
Arizona Republic, The, 149, 150*f*
Arkansas Democrat-Gazette, 50
arraignments, 345–46
arrest records, 414

arrest sheets, 306
arrest stories, 342–43
Arthur, Lisa, 291–92
assessed value, **159**
Associated Press, 90, 167, 178, 266, 268, 271, 451–52, 475
Associated Press Media Editors, 394
Associated Press style, 96, 97, 137–38, 208, 432–33, 489, 499, 505. *See also* wire service style
Atlantic Monthly, The, 92, 478
attributions, 81, **98–104**
   for anonymous sources, 99, *100*, 104–6
   for background interviews, 106
   in broadcast news, 282
   checking accuracy of, 189–90
   effective use of, 86, 99–103
   for online sources, *125*
   for opinions, 172
   past tense usage in, 103
   placement of, 101–2
   for separating partial and complete quotes, 102
   when to use, 98–99
   wording of, 99–101
   for written sources, 103–4
audience engagement
   citizen journalism, 35–37
   news blogs and, 4, 6
   in service journalism, 236*f*
   social media and, 6, 7, 298
   in Web-based media, 244–45, 247, 254, 255–56, 257
audiences
   in beat reporting, *302*
   for business news, 366
   distrust of media, 8–9, 31–32, 465, 466–67
   expectations of digital media, 243–51, 298
   fragmentation of, 24–25
   growth of news, 22–23, 24, 38
   international, 248
   keys to attracting, 52–53
   multimedia journalism and, 9, 245–46
   news values and, 5
   persuading, 430–31
   for public relations, 424–28
   in speech, news conference, and meeting stories, 319, 326
   translating jargon for, 302

types of, 29–30
   See also citizen journalism; news consumption
auditor's statements, 379
Autrey, James, 238
averages, **153**–54, *155*
Avitabile, David, 429

background, **105**
   interviews, 106, 370
   researching, 289–90, 315
balance sheets, in annual reports, 380
Banaszynski, Jacqui, *210*, 231
bank records, 415
Bankrate.com, 382
Barlett, Donald, 203
Barnes, Fred, 473
BBC, 36, 241–42, *248*, 249
Be the Media: How to Create and Accelerate Your Message . . . Your Way (Mathison), 49
beat reporting, 287–310
   accuracy in, 295
   across media platforms, 288, 296–99
   alertness in, 291–93
   dealing with sources, 277, 290–91, 294–96
   government beat, 299–301
   higher education beat, 304–5
   important factors for, 299–300
   meetings, 316
   persistence in, 293–94
   personal contact in, 294–96
   police beat, 305–6
   preparing for, 289–91
   principles of good, 288–96
   school beat, 291–92, 301–4
   slow-developing stories, 294
   sports beat, 306–10
   tips for, 289, 290, 293, 300, 303, 305, 309
   wariness in, 296
   writing for readers, *302*
Benchley, Robert, 93
Bennett, James Gordon, *471*
Bensley, Russ, 275
Bentley, Clyde, 258
Bergman, Lowell, 64
Berne Convention, 461
Berzon, Alexandra, 11

Best, Michael, *361*
bias
   in business journalism, 370–71
   in coverage of minority groups, 352–53
   in interviewing, 75, 76
   in language usage, 207–9, 496
   in news coverage, 8, 14–15, 17
   in news releases, 132
   in polls and surveys, *163*, 388, 393, 394
   in sources, 127
   in use of quotations, 93
Bing, 117, 118
Bivins, Thomas H., *433*
Black, Hugo, *446*
Blais, Madeleine, *201*
Blekko, 117, 118, 119
blogs
   for beat reporting, 261, 298
   citizen journalism and, 8, 36, 37, 46, 444
   code of ethics for, 467, 468
   gathering information from, 119
   growing popularity of, 4
   legacy media's use of, 4, 6, 242, 260, 261
   libel suits and, 446, 448, 453
   professional standards for, 261
   for public relations, 259, 427, 430, 432
   quotations from, 87
   reader interactivity on, 6, 36, 37
   shield laws and, 458–59
   as watchdogs, 466
   writing for, 259–61
   See also social media
Bloomberg News, 50, 168, 365, 369, 372
blotter, **306**
BlufftonToday.com, 36
Blumenthal, Ralph, 392
blurbs, 237*f*
Boggs, Alison, 195
bonds, 383
Bonime, Andrew, 242, 249
Boolean search commands, 118
Boston Globe, The, 25, 197, 247, *248*, 378
Boston.com, *248*
boxes
   for service journalism, 236*f*–37*f*, 238
   summary, 181

Bradley, David, 478
Branzburg v. Hayes, 458
Brennan, William, 449
Brewer, David, 486
broadband accessibility, 22
broadcast news
    citizen sites, 37
    copyright laws for, 461
    interviewing for, 64–66
    See also radio and television news writ-
        ing; radio news; television news
brochures, 430
Broder, David, 251
Bryant, Howard, 95, 96
Bryant, Steve, 429–30
budgets, 159–62
    basics of, 160
    as blueprints, 159, 299–300
    expenditures in, 160
    finding stories in, 160–62
    summary page of, 161f–62f
Buettner, Russ, 390
Bugasch, Vanessa, 434–35
bullets
    for news conference stories, 323
    in Web-based writing, 243f, 253–54,
        255
Bureau of Economic Analysis, 375
Bureau of Labor Statistics, 374
Burger, Warren, 459
business journalism, 365–84
    announcements and meetings, 378
    audience for, 366
    bias and conflicts of interest in, 370–71
    corporate information, 372–73, 375,
        378–81
    global reach of, 367–68
    glossary of terms for, 383
    growing importance of, 365–69
    human sources for, 375–77
    inverted pyramid for, 168, 169
    jargon in, 369, *371*
    numbers in, 378–81
    online sources for, 371–72
    for-profit websites, 50
    putting sources at ease, 370
    range of topics in, 368–69
    records and reports for, 372–75,
        378–81
    reporter initiative in, 378
    specialized business news, 367

    tips for, 369, 372, 381
    unique challenges for, 369–71
Business Wire, 372, 376

cable television news
    credibility problems for, 30
    partisan politics and, 31
    popularity of, 24–25, 28, 30
    See also radio and television news
        writing; television news
Caldwell, Bob, 465
cameras
    for accident and fire stories, 337
    in courtroom, 349, 352, 460
    for crime stories, 331
    See also recording devices; video
        reporting
Cameron, Glen, 421
campaign reports, 414
Canadian Association of Journalists, 483
capitalization, 502–4
Cappon, Jack, *198, 207*
CareerBuilder.com, 49
Carollo, Russell, 407–8
Carr, David, *208, 260*
categorical imperative, 468
cause-promoting news releases, 135,
    139
CBSNews.com, 313
cell phones. *See* mobile media
Celsi, Claire, *431*
Census Bureau, 375
Center for American Progress, 478
Center for Media and Democracy, 435
CFO magazine, 367
chamber of commerce officials, 377
change of venue, **346**, 349
chat rooms, 87, 257
checkbook journalism, 475–77
Chicago Tribune, 25
child abuse victims, 480–81
Christians, Clifford, 471
Chronicle of Higher Education, The, 304
chronology, 199, 203, 220–26
    for crime stories, 333–37
    endings for, 222f, 225–26, 235
    foreshadowing in, 224
    in news narratives, 226, 227, 228
    nut paragraph for, 222f, 224
    vs. other story structures, 222f–23f

    sample outline for, 221–24
    for speech, news conference, and
        meeting stories, 321
    time lines for, 221
    "to be sure" paragraphs in, 224–25
chunking, 243f, 254–55
Churchill, Winston, 272
citizen journalism, 35–37
    beat reporting and, 288
    blogs, 8, 36, 37, 46, 444
    convergence news and, 34
    crowdsourcing, 4
    forms of, 37
    limitations of, 8, 36–37, 46–47
    rise of, 7–8, 35–36, 242, 245
    social media sites and, 36, 111, 241
    volunteerism and, 4, 7
    websites, 6, 7–8, 37, 41, 46–47
    See also blogs; social media; Twitter
citizen journalists, 7
city and county government. *See* govern-
    ment beat reporting
city directories, 126
clarity
    in broadcast news, 269, 272–73
    in Web-based writing, 251, 252
Clark, Roy Peter, 484
Classified Intelligence, 374
click-through rate, **182**, 262
closed-ended questions, **71**
CNBC, 365
CNN, 31, 35f, 36, 169, 181, 266, 321,
    322
codes of ethics, 466–67, 472, 474. *See
    also* ethics
Cohen v. Cowles Media Co., 104, 458
coherence, 199–203
    conjunctions for, 200–201
    outlining for, 199–200
    parallelism for, 203
    sentence structure and, 200
    transitions for, 201–3, 324
College Media Association, 484
college terminology, 502–3
colloquialisms, 85, 92–94, 269, 271
ColumbiaHeartBeat.com, 43
comma splices, 490
commas
    in broadcast copy, 283
    in compound sentences, 209–10, 493
    coordinate adjectives and, 492–93

commas *(continued)*
   introductory elements and, 491–92
   with nonrestrictive elements, 491
   run-on sentences and, 490
   in series, 489–90
commentaries
   news stories vs., 14*f*, 17, 31
   public relations vs., 423
Commercial Appeal (Memphis), The,
   211–12
commercial database services, 119–20
Commission on Freedom of the Press,
   467
Committee of Concerned Journalists, 10
community news. *See* local news
   coverage
complex sentences, 200
compound interest, **155**–56
compound modifiers, 494
compound sentences, 200, 493
compound subjects, 496
CompuServe, 454
computer-assisted reporting, *158,* 388–89
   computer mapping, 389
   custom databases for, 122–24
   database matching techniques, 122,
      388
   government databases for, 120–22
   for investigative reporting, 120–24,
      278, 388, 390, 392, 403, 415
   special-interest databases for, 122
   systematic study of records, 390–91
   See also online sources
conciseness
   in broadcast news, 269, 271–72
   editing for, *205*
   in news writing, 203–6
   in Web-based writing, 251, 252, 253,
      256
concrete examples, 196–97
conditional mood, 207
conditional privilege, 448–49
confessions, reporting, 353–54
confidential sources, 104–6
   disguising names of, 405
   lawsuits by, 458
   protections for, 456–59
   See also anonymous sources
conflict
   as news value, 5, 15
   in stories, *234*

conflict-of-interest reports, 414
conflicts of interest, 474–77
   in business journalism, 370–71
   checkbook journalism, 475–77
   code of ethics and, 507–8
   freebies, 475
   friendships, 474
   participation in news, 477
   payola, 474–75
conjunctions, 200–201, 490
constant dollars, 383
"constitutional" privileges, 447*f*
Consumer Confidence Index, 375
Consumer Federation of America, 382
consumer fraud protections, 381–82
consumer news coverage, 381–84
   field experiments and, 391
   sources for, 381–82
   types of stories, 383–84
Consumer Price Index, 157, 383
Consumers Union, 382
content aggregators, 3, 48
   blogs, 261
   for business news, 372
   gathering information from, 117, 119
content management systems, *123*
contractions, *269,* 270, 494
controls, in experiments, **392**–93
convergence, **4**–5
   for beat reporting, 296–99
   in broadcast news, 266
   definition of, 34
   enhanced Web coverage, 33–34
   with inverted pyramid story, 187–89
   media fragmentation and, 32–35
   in news media careers, 9
   synchronized coverage in, 34–35
conversational style, for broadcast news,
   269, 270–71
conviction records, 354
coordinating conjunctions, 201, 490, 493
copy editors, *123*
copy-flow pattern, 116*f*
copyright laws, 48, 119, 460–61
Corbett, Gerard, 88
Corbett, Philip B., 89
corporate communications, 367, 376
corporate data and reports, 372–73, *375,*
      378–81, 413. *See also* records and
      reports
council-manager governments, 300

County Watchers, The, 459
court access, 349–51, 459–60
court procedures
   camera coverage of, 349, 352, 460
   change of venue, 346, 349
   criminal justice proceedings, 342–48
   free-press/fair-trial controversy, 349–51,
      459–60
   gag orders and closed trials, 349–50
   press-bar guidelines, 351
   types of courts and cases, 342
court records
   for business news, 374
   for investigative reporting, 414
court stories
   on arraignments, 345–46
   arrest stories, 342–43
   closed-courtroom controversy, 349–51,
      459–60
   on initial court appearances, 343–44
   libel and, 340–42
   on preliminary hearings, 344–45, 351
   preparing for, 330, 333
   sentencing and appeals, 348
   sex crimes, 350–51
   taste and ethics issues, 353
   tie-backs in, 343
   tips for, 343
   on trial proceedings, 346–48
   on verdicts, 348
   writing, 340–48
   See also crime stories
Craig, Victoria, 366
credibility
   anonymous sources and, 104, 412
   including proof of, 408
   new media forms and, 46
   of news media, 9, 30
   public relations and, 431–32
credit checks, 415
crime stories
   across media platforms, *297*–98
   coverage of minority groups, 352–53
   coverage of terrorism, 353
   invasion of privacy and, 455–56,
      479–80
   on juveniles, 353, 354, 480
   libel and, 340–42
   preparing for, 330–32
   reporting confessions and prior convic-
      tions, 353–54

samples of, 297–98, 335–36
sex crimes, 350–51, 352–53, 479–80
sidebars for, 334
sources for, 330–32
structuring and writing, 333–37
taste and ethics issues, 353
undercover reporting, 389
See also court procedures; court stories
crime victims. *See* victims
Crizer, Zach, *124*
Cronkite, Walter, 468
crowdsourcing, **4**, 119, 276
"cuing in," in broadcast news, 273
cultural beats, 287
cultural differences
bias-free language for, 208
interviewing and, 75
Curran, Caitlin, 472
CyberJournalist.net, 467

Dallas Morning News, The, 158
dangling modifiers, 493
databases
for business news, 371–72
commercial services, 119–20
custom, 122–24
government, 120–22
news archives, 117–18
special-interest, 122
Dateline NBC, 267
dates
in broadcast copy, 282
wire service style for, 500
Dayton Daily News, 407
de Vise, Daniel, 90
deadlines, 338, 433
Deam, Jenny, 233
deceptive practices, 473, *474*
deep background, **105**
defamation, 447*f. See also* libel
DeGregory, Lane, 62–63, 64
delayed-identification leads, **177**, *184*
Demeritt, Laurie, 429–30
democracy
free speech and, 443–44
journalism and, 5, 8–9, 10–12, 28, 292
uninformed citizens and, 28
Democracy in America (Tocqueville), 8
Dennis, Everette E., 473
Denton, Nick, 477

Denver Post, The, 384
Deogun, Nik, *371*
dependent clauses, 272, 273, 490, 491–92
details
concrete examples, 196–97
describing scenes, 210–12
in good writing, 196–98
Deuze, Mark, 254
dialect, quotations with, 92–94
dialogue, **84**, 212–13
Dieterich, Christopher, 365–66
digital media
accuracy issues, 111, *124,* 190, 277
audience expectations of, 243–51, 298
broadband access and, 22
building audiences with, 52–53
compared with print media, 243*f*
copyright laws for, 461
credibility problems for, 30
demographics for, 29–30
ethics and, 466, 473, 486
growing popularity of, 3–4, 21–23, 25, 28, 29, 30
libel and, 446, 448, 453–54
media law and, 444
news values and, 6
plagiarism and, 484–85
privacy and security issues, 479
public relations and, 131, 424, 427, 429–30, *431,* 434–38
shield laws and, 458–59
terminology, capitalization of, 503
viral marketing and, 52–53
See also mobile media; social media; Web-based journalism
digital recorders. *See* recording devices
Dillon, Karen, *12*
Dimoudi, Christina, 254
direct quotes, **81**. *See also* quotations
disabled people, 208
disaster stories, 337, 368–69
Disclosure Inc., 371–72, 373
Discovering the News (Schudson), 16
dividends, in annual reports, 380
Doppelt, Jack, 479
Dow Jones Factiva, 371, 372
Dow Jones Industrial Average, 383
Dow Jones Newswires, 367, 369
Dreiser, Theodore, 402
Drudge, Matt, 12
Drudge Report, 37

Dubow, Craig, 34
DuckDuckGo, 117, 118
Duffy, Margaret, 46, 47
Duin, Steve, 198
Dumenco, Simon, 432
Dun & Bradstreet, 372

e-book readers, 22*f,* 38
earnings statements, 380
editorial process
for conciseness, *205*
grammar and punctuation, 209–10, 489–98
layered, 115, 116*f, 124*
for quotations, 95–97
Twitter and, 262, 298–99
verification of information, 114–15
for Web-based journalism, 29, *123*
editorial writers, 423
election coverage
fact checking and, 11, 164
impact of medium on, 3–4
polling and predictions, 387–88, 393, 396
public view of, 9
Electronic Freedom of Information Act, 444–45
Elements of Journalism, The (Kovach, Rosenstiel), 10, 16, 114
ellipses, in quotations, 92, 96, 318
email
interviews, 59, 60, 66–67
polls, 257
privacy and security issues, 479
public relations pitches, *431*
quotations from, 87
"embedded" journalism, 389, 390
engagement, as news value, 6. *See also* audience engagement
entrepreneurs. *See* media entrepreneurs
ESPN, 306, 307, 481
ethical egoism, 470
ethical problems, 473–83
advertising pressures, 477–78
conflicts of interest, 474–77
deceit, 473, *474*
incorrect and incomplete information, 483
invasion of privacy, 478–82
payola, 474–75

ethical problems (continued)
    plagiarism, 484–86
    withholding information, 482–83
ethics, 465–86
    for bloggers, 467, 468
    in business journalism, 370–71
    codes of ethics, 466–67, 472, 474,
        506–8
    in crime and court reporting, 353
    in decision-making, 470
    digital media and, 466, 473, 486
    of duty, 467–68
    of final ends or consequences, 468–69
    healthy ethical process, 476
    principled reasoning for, 470–73
    public perception of, 466–67
    in public relations, 423
    Reuters' 10 absolutes, 467
    situation, 469–70
    Society of Professional Journalists'
        code, 506–8
    tips for, 467, 470, 472, 474, 486
    watchdog bloggers and, 466
Evans, Harold, 28
examples
    concrete, 196–97
    in focus structure, 234
expenditures, 160
exposition, 210, 234

Facebook, 3, 430
    beat reporting and, 288, 298
    news consumption on, 3, 6, 22, 276
    promoting news on, 52–53, 261–62
    for source information, 60, 315, 413
    See also social media
Fackler, Mark, 471
Factiva, 118, 120, 121f, 315
facts
    accuracy checks, 11, 89, 164, 189
    avoiding, in quotations, 83
    concrete examples, 197
    in journalism, 12–13
fair comment and criticism, 449
fair use limitations, 460
fairness
    in business journalism, 370
    code of ethics and, 506–7
    importance of, 5, 13–14, 17
    in interviewing, 75–78

    in journalism, 114–15, 127
    in using quotes, 81, 85–90
Falk, Adam, 47
Falkow, Sally, 429, 436
Farr, William, 457f
features, 226
    news narratives vs., 226
    news stories vs., 233
Federal Communications Commission,
        97, 374, 413
federal district courts, 342
Federal Energy Regulatory Commission,
        382
Federal Reserve, 374–75
Federal Trade Commission, 374, 382
Federated Publications v. Swedberg, 351
felonies, 342
Ferrugia, John, 409
field experiments, 391–93
figures of speech, 206–7, 269, 272
financial and investor relations, 422
financial challenges
    charging for Web content, 50
    foundation support for, 43, 45–46, 47,
        52
    for general news sites, 50
    government-financed approach to, 52
    growing Web advertising revenues,
        242
    for legacy media, 24–27, 42, 478
    new forms of journalism and, 42–44
    See also media entrepreneurs
financial news. See business journalism
financial ratios, 372
financial reports, 162–64. See also records
        and reports
Fink, Conrad C., 473
Finkel, David, 76, 211
Finnegan, John R., Sr., 457
Finneman, Teri, 9
fire stories
    collecting information for, 338–40
    preparing for, 330, 332
    sources for, 337–38
    writing, 337–40
First Amendment
    actual malice test and, 449–50
    closed-courtroom controversy and,
        349–51, 459
    ethics and, 467, 473
    freedom protections of, 8, 443, 445

    plagiarism and, 485f
    source confidentiality and, 104
Fitch Ratings, 372
FiveThirtyEight blog, 387
flair, leads with, 182–83, 226
Flandreau, Michelle, 278
flat-file databases, 122
Flatland, Jon, 484
focus structure, 228–35
    body for, 234–35
    endings for, 223f, 235
    foreshadowing in, 231–32
    leads for, 223f, 230
    nut paragraph in, 223f, 230–31
    vs. other story structures, 222f–23f
    setup in, 230–33
    "so what" strategy for, 232
    "to be sure" paragraph in, 233
    transitions in, 230–31, 232
follow-up questions, 77
Food and Drug Administration, 374, 382
Forbes, 372, 373
foreshadowing, 214–15
    in focus structure, 231–32
    nut paragraph and, 224
Fortune, 372
foundation-supported media, 43, 45–46,
        47, 52
Fourteenth Amendment, 350
Fowler, Gene, 174
Fox News, 31, 276
fragments, sentence, 271, 490–91
Franklin, Jon, 234
free-press/fair-trial controversy, 349
freebies, as conflict of interest, 475
Freedom of Information Act, 290, 373,
        375, 414, 444–45
freedom of press
    challenges to, 8
    democracy and, 443–44
    ethics codes and, 467
    Hutchins Commission on, 17
    importance of, 8
    See also First Amendment
friendships, as conflict of interest, 474
Frievogel, Margaret, 41

gag orders, 349–50
Galbraith, John Kenneth, 206
Gallup, 388

Gannett Co., 34, 48–49, 352
Gannett v. DePasquale, 350
gate-keeping, 12
Gawker Media, 477
Gelineau, Kristen, 219–20
general jurisdiction courts, 342
Gertz v. Welch, 453
Gibb, Don, 205
Gibson, Carl, 472
Gill, Kathy, 432
Glanville, Kathleen, 465
Glaser, Lynne Enders, 480
Globe Newspaper Co. v. Superior Court, 350
glossary boxes, 237f
Google, 117, 118, 258, 289, 330, 412–13
Google+, 430
Google News, 3, 48, 119, 123, 257
Google's Blogger, 119
Gotham Gazette, 41, 46
government affairs, 422
government agencies
    consumer news stories and, 381–82
    getting public records from, 414, 444–45
    minutes and transcripts from, 414
    open-meetings laws and, 445
government beat reporting, 292, 299–301
    budgets as blueprint for, 159–62, 299, 300
    local regulators, 374
    political maneuvering and, 299–300
    power of information in, 299
    sources for, 300–301
government databases, 117, 120–22, 124
government-financed media, 52
government terminology, 502–3
Graham, Lamar, 111
grammar
    in broadcast news, 272
    common errors in, 209, 489–98
    correcting in quotations, 95–96
grand jury indictment, 345
graphic devices
    interactive graphics, 34
    in service journalism, 236f–37f
    summary boxes, 181
    See also visuals
greatest-good-for-greatest-number ethics, 470
Greene, Robert W., 404

Grimaldi, James, 407
Grimm, Joe, 367
gross irresponsibility test, 453
Guardian, The, 481

Half the Sky: Turning Oppression into Opportunity for Women Worldwide (Kristof, WuDunn), 11
Hall, Andy, 402
handouts, 131. See also press releases
hard leads, 407
Harlow, Rex, 420
Harrington, Walt, 198
Harris, Craig, 149, 150f
Hart, Jack, 99
Hart, John, 276
Harwood, Richard, 477
health care reporting, 366
Hearn, Lorie, 51–52
Hearst, William Randolph, 24, 25f
Heckert, Justin, 196
Henriques, Diana, 379
Henry, William A., III, 485f
Herald-Tribune (Sarasota, Fla.), 401
Hersh, Seymour, 74
Herzog, David, 388, 389
Heslam, Jessica, 88
Hewitt, Don, 268
Hiestand, Michael, 427
higher education beat, 304–5
Hodges, Louis W., 478
Holtz, Shel, 251
HootSuite, 241
Hoover, Herbert, 455
Hopgood, Mei-ling, 407
Horovitz, Bruce, 86
Horvit, Mark, 401
Horwitz, Sari, 472
Houston Chronicle, 11
Howard, Carole, 132
Hoyt, Clark, 104
Huey, Bill, 431
Huffington, Arianna, 44f
Huffington Post, 3, 43, 90
Huppke, Rex, 329, 333, 341
Hutchins Commission, 17
hyperlinks, 256
    characteristics of, 249
    external connections, 256–57, 258
    internal connections, 256, 258

for layering content, 243f, 249, 250
    to raw data, 483
    in Web-based writing, 255–57
hypermedia, 249
hyphens
    in broadcast copy, 279, 281, 283
    in compound modifiers, 494
hypotheses
    in field experiments, 391
    in investigative reporting, 404, 406f

image-building news releases, 135–36, 139–40
immediacy
    in broadcast news, 267, 268–69, 270
    of Web-based media, 244, 251
    See also timeliness
immediate-identification leads, 176–77
impact, as news value, 5
income statements, 380
income taxes, 157–58, 415
independent clauses, 490, 493
indirect quotations, 91–92, 98–104, 282.
    See also quotations
Individual Retirement Accounts (IRAs), 383
industry relations, 422
indymedia.us, 8
inflation, 156–57
information
    in broadcast news, 267
    incorrect and incomplete, 483
    insider, 371, 376
    as power, 299
    public access to, 414, 444–45
    withholding of, 482–83
information gathering, 111–27
    accuracy in, 112–15
    for beat reporting, 289–91
    commercial databases, 119–20
    custom databases, 122–24
    government databases, 120–22
    for interview questions, 68–69
    multiple sources for, 112–14
    news archives, 117–18, 125–26
    for news releases, 142–44
    from news websites, 119
    online sources for, 115–24
    reference sources, 126–27
    search engines, 118–19

information gathering *(continued)*
　from social media, 60, 111–12, 119
　special-interest databases, 122
　tips for, 117, 118
　traditional sources, 124–27
　verification and, 76, 114–15
　See also sources
initial appearance, in court proceedings, 343–44
instant messaging (IM) interviews, 67
interactivity. *See* audience engagement
interest, of news, 5, 170, 174
interest and compounding, 155–56
International Association of Business Communicators, **428**, 467
Internet. *See* digital media; mobile media; online sources; social media; Web-based journalism
Interstate Commerce Commission, 374, 382, 413
interviewing, **59**–78
　accuracy in, 75–78
　approaches to, 73–75
　audio and video, 64–66
　background sessions, 106
　for beat reporting, 290–91
　checklist for, 61*f*
　cultural differences and, 75
　email and IM interviews, 66–67
　establishing rapport, 66, 72–75
　face-to-face, 59–60, 66
　follow-up questions, 77
　for investigative reporting, 60, 63–64, 73–74
　for news conference stories, 315–16
　for news releases, 142–44
　for news stories, 60, 61–62, 73
　note-taking and recording for, 66, 75–76, 78
　observing, 77
　online videoconferencing, 67
　pauses in, 78
　preparing for, 60–64
　profiles, 60, 62–63, 73
　questions for, 68–71
　quotations from, 98, 99
　setting up, 68
　sources for, 60
　for speech stories, 315
　telephone interviews, 66

tips for, 75, 76
written requests for, 64
intranet, **430**
introductory elements, 491–92
invasion of privacy, **454**–56
　of child abuse victims, 480–81
　of crime victims, 479–80
　defenses against, 454–55
　digital media and, 479
　ethics and, 478–82
　of juvenile offenders, 480
　in participant observation, 389
　with photos and videos, 481–82
　portraying in "false light," 455
　of public figures, 481
　sexual orientation and, 481
　trespassing, 455
　unwanted publicity, 455–56
inverted pyramid, **167**–90
　across media platforms, 187–89
　for crime stories, 334–37
　decline in use of, 31
　delayed-identification leads, 177, *184*
　immediate-identification leads, 176–77
　importance of, 168–70
　leads for, 170–83, 222*f*
　limitations of, 169
　for memo-structure stories, 183, *185*
　multiple-element leads, 179–82
　for multiple-element stories, 185–87
　for news releases, 433, 436
　for one-subject stories, 183, *184*
　vs. other story structures, 222*f*–23*f*
　samples of, *175*, *184–85*, *188*
　"so what" strategy for, 170–76
　for speech, news conference, and meeting stories, 321
　story organization for, 183–87, 222*f*
　summary leads, 178–79
　techniques for writing leads, 171–74
　tips for, 170, 171, 173, 186
　for Web-based writing, 168–69, *180*, 187–89, 243*f*, 246–47
　"what's next" strategy for, 176
　"you" leads, 176
　See also story structures
Investigative News Network, 46
Investigative Newsource, 51–52
Investigative Reporters and Editors, 89, *158*, 401

investigative reporting, 401–16
　accuracy in, 405
　across media platforms, *409*
　anonymous sources in, *105*
　computer-assisted, 120–24, *158*, 278, 388, 390, 392, 403, 415
　current state of, 401, 402–3
　forming hypotheses, 403–4
　gathering information for, 64, 120–24
　human sources for, 410–12
　impact of decline of, 27–28
　interviewing for, 60, 63–64, 73–74
　investigative work, 404–5
　media law and, 405–6
　muckrakers, 402–3, 415
　multiple sources for, 112–14
　objectivity in, 416
　organization in, 404–5, 406*f*, 408–9
　proof of credibility in, 408
　story structure and leads for, 407–8
　suggesting solutions in, 409
　tips for, 404, 408–9
　using numbers, 149, 150*f*, 158
　Web support for, 409
　writing process for, 405–9
　written sources for, 412–15
investment data, 372
its/it's, 494

Jakes, Lara, *134*
Janssen, Kim, 479
jargon, 207
　in business journalism, 369, *371*
　translating, 293–94, 302
Jay, Timothy, 97
Jeffrey, Steve, 484
Jenner, Mike, 36
jobs, in journalism, 53–55. *See also* On the Job
Jones, Alex S., 27
Journal of the Hyperlinked Organization, 247
journalism
　accuracy and fairness in, 5, 13–14, 17
　bias in, 14–15, 17
　changes in business of, 42–44
　convergence in, 4–5, 32–35
　current challenges to, 8–9, 38
　democracy and, 5, 8–9, 10–12, 28, 292

First Amendment and, 443–45
impact of technology on, 3–4, 21–23
jobs in, 53–55
mass media vs., 465–66
objectivity in, 15–16, 114–15
performance reports on, 10
principles of good, 10
qualified privilege and, 448–49
truth in, 12–15
vital functions of journalists, 10–12
Journalism Buzz, 261
JournoResources, 261
jury deliberation, 348
jury selection, 346, 351
JustinTV.com, 37
juvenile offenders, revealing names of, 353, 354, 456, 480

Kaminsky, Dan, 479
Kansas City Star, The, 59, 88
Kant, Immanuel, 468
Karp, Scott, 36
Keith, Theo, 383
Keller, Jon, 88
Kerr, Kathleen, 390
Ketterer, Stan, *124*
keywords, for search-engine optimization, 251, 258–59
Kilpatrick, James, 194
Kipling, Rudyard, *213*
Kiplinger, 368
Koetting, Tom, 214
KOMO-TV, 276, 277
Kovach, Bill, 10, 16, 114–15
KQED, 401
Kravitz, Derek, *63*
Kristof, Nicholas D., 11

labor leaders, 377
LaFleur, Jennifer, *158, 164*
Langosch, Jenifer, 53, 252
language
    bias-free, 207–9, 496
    correct and effective usage, 206–10
    figures of speech, 206–7
    grammar and punctuation, 209–10, 489–98
    word choice, 198, 207

LaRocque, Paula, 81, *189,* 204
Larson, Erik, 231–32
Las Vegas Sun, 11
Lasica, J. D., 37
Lawrence (Kan.) Journal-World, 32f
layered structure, for Web-based media, 243f, 248–51
lead-ins, **274**
leads, **170**
    for broadcast news, 273–74
    case study of, *178*
    delayed-identification, 177, *184*
    emphasizing news values in, 174
    with flair, 182–83, 226
    in focus structure, 223f, 230
    as foreshadowing, 214–15
    hard leads, 407
    hooking the reader with, *196*
    immediate-identification, 176–77
    in inverted pyramid, 170–83, 222f
    in investigative reporting, 407
    length of, 172, 173
    multiple-element, 179–82, 323
    in news narratives, 223f, 226, 227
    for news releases, 137, 138, 144
    numbers in, 173
    for obituaries, 356, 358
    problems with, 182
    six basic questions for, 170–76
    "so what" strategy for, 170–76
    for speech, news conference, and meeting stories, 321, 323, 325
    summary, 178–79
    techniques for writing, 171–74
    tips for, 170, 171, 173
    for Web-based writing, 247, 258–59
    "what's next" strategy for, 176
    "you" leads, 176, 226
"Lede, The," 260
Lee, Tom, *403*
legacy media, 8
    audiences for, 29–30
    citizen journalism and, 8, 35–37, 242
    convergence news and, 32–35
    declining audience for, 3, 21, 24, 28, 30
    financial challenges for, 3, 24–27, 42
    future of, 38
    jobs in, *55*
    new technologies and, 3–5

public distrust of, 8–9, 31–32
    for public relations, 429
    as source of news, 3, 27–28
    thriving aspects of, 42
    use of blogs and social media, 4, 6, 242, 248, 260, 261
    Web-first focus of, 32–35, 42, *123,* 242, 244
    Web profitability and, 48–49
    See also news media; newspapers; radio news; television news
legal issues. *See* libel; media law
legalism, 467–68
Leggett, Vanessa, 456
Lehrer, Adrienne, 85
Lehrer, Jonah, 465
Leonhardt, David, 466
letters to the editor, 257
libel, **340,** 445–54
    actual malice test, 446, 449–53
    court stories and, 340–42
    dangers of, 453
    digital media and, 446, 448, 453–54
    fair comment and criticism protections, 449
    identifying, 445–46
    investigative reporting and, 405
    keys to avoiding, *451*
    negligence test, 453
    prepublication review and, 89
    private citizens and, 453
    privilege as defense against, 448–49
    protections for reputations, 445–46
    public officials and figures and, 449–53
    quotations and, 89, 450
    and related concepts defined, 447f
    truth as defense against, 446–48
    See also media law
Life magazine, 455
life stories, 357. *See also* obituaries
Lim, Victoria, 277
Limbaugh, Rush, 31
line-item budget, **160**
LinkedIn, 22, *74,* 377, 413
links. *See* hyperlinks
Liston, Matt, 419
lists
    in service journalism, 236f
    in Web-based writing, 243f, 253–54, 255

LiveJournal, 430
loan records, 414
local news coverage
    business news and, 368, 369
    cause-promoting news releases, 139
    citizen journalism and, 7
    focus structure for, 230
    importance of, 6, 11
    importance of names in, 177
    obituaries, 355
    public opinion of, 32
    public service announcements, 133
    television, decline in, 27
    Web-based, 6, 7, 41, 46–47
    See also beat reporting
local regulators, for business news, 374
Loeb, Penny, 120
Longman, Jere, 260
Loomis, Carol, 373
Lord, Barbara King, 93
Los Angeles Times, 25, 123, 482
*Losing the News: The Future of the News
    That Feeds Democracy* (Jones), 27
Lost Remote, 276
love-of-neighbor ethics, 470
Lundine, Susan, 383–84

Macias, Tina, *178*, *180*
Maddow, Rachel, 17, 31
Madison, James, 5
magazines
    advertising influences and, 478
    approach to news stories, 7
    business, 367
    commercial databases for, 119–20
    jobs in, 55
    profitability of, 25, 42, 43f
    service journalism and, 237f, 238
Maharaj, David, 482
margin of error, **152**, 387, 393–94,
    395–96
Marken, G. A., *432*
MarketWatch, 50, 372, 373
Márquez, Gabriel García, 78
Marshall, Josh, 12
Martin, Sheena, 367
Masson v. Malcolm, 98
Masson v. *The New Yorker*, 450
Mathews, Wilma, 132
Mathison, David, 7, 49

McBride, Kelly, 387, 476, 479, 482, 483
McClatchy Co., 90
McDermott, Casey, 484
McGinty, Jo Craven, 388, 392
McGraw, Mike, 59
McHale, Jean, *469*
mean, 153, 154
"Media Decoder" blog, 260
media entrepreneurs
    building audiences, 52–53
    jobs available for, 55
    niche journalism, 49–50
    not-for-profit models, 44–47, 51–52
    for-profit models, 47–50
    in San Diego, 51–52
    social media sites and, 52–53
    Web-based journalism and, 42–44, 47
media fragmentation, **24**–25, 32–35
media law, 443–61
    access to information, 444–45
    copyright and fair use, 460–61
    court access, 459–60
    digital media and, 444
    First Amendment and, 443–45
    invasion of privacy, 454–56
    investigative reporting and, 405–6
    libel, 445–54
    protection of sources and notes, 456–59
Media Matters for America, 465
media relations, 422
medians, **153**–54
MediaSource, 435
Meet the Press, 276
meeting stories
    advances for, 316
    in business journalism, 378
    characteristics of meetings, 314
    describing participants and audience,
        318–19
    impact of medium on, 317
    note-taking for, 318
    preparing for, 316
    quotations in, 318
    reporter behavior during, 319–21
    structuring and writing, 321, 324–26
    tips for, 316, 318, 319, 321, 323
Meiklejohn, Alexander, 443
Meinhardt, Jane, 226, 227
memo-structure stories, 183, *185*
metadata, **52**
metaphors, 207

Meyer, Philip, 114
Miami Herald, The, 104, *250*, 257
millage rate, **159**
Miller, Judith, 457
Milwaukee Journal Sentinel, 112–14
MinnPost.com, 41, 43, 46
minority groups, biased coverage of,
    352–53
Miranda rights, 343
misdemeanors, 342
misplaced modifiers, 493
Missourian, 246f
MLB.com, 49, 53, 252
mobile media, **21**
    broadcast news on, 266, 276
    building audiences with, 53
    for business news, 366
    citizen journalism and, 35–36
    convergence news and, 32
    for crime stories, 330, 331
    designing content for, 245–46
    gathering information from, 117
    news-based apps, 23, 35, 117, 242,
        246f, 276
    news consumption on, 21–23, 24, 25,
        28, 29, 30, 38, 242
    popular activities on, 23
    "push" delivery method for, 266
    "two-screen viewing" and, 276
    See also social media; Twitter
moblogs, **36**
mode, *154*
modifiers, 201, 493–94
Moehringer, J. R., 93
Money.com (CNN), 368
Moody's, 372
Moore, Maloy, 122–23
moral absolutes, 469
moral law, 468
moral reasoning, 470–73
morgue. *See* news archives
Morkes, John, 251, *256*
mortuary forms, 356, 357–60
Moss, Julie, 477
MSNBC, 31, 266
muckrakers, 402–3, 415
multimedia career paths, *9*, *74*, *123*, *234*
multimedia content
    audience appeal and, 245–46
    importance of, 317
    Web-based, 245–46, *248*, *249*, *255*

multiple-element leads, **179**–82, 186, 323

multiple-element stories, 185–87

multiple-source journalism, 112–14, 332

municipal courts, 342

Murdoch, Rupert, 50

Mutter, Alan, 478

mutual funds, 383

Myspace, 430

Nakamura, David, 287, 288, 290, *291*, 298

names and titles
    abbreviations for, 500
    in broadcast news, 272, 274, 279–80
    capitalization of, 503–4
    in leads, 176–77
    verification of, 173, 315, 337

narration, 210–15
    anecdotes in, 213–14
    in crime stories, 335–36
    describing scenes, 210–12
    dialogue in, 212–13
    foreshadowing in, 214–15
    in news stories, 7, 31, 193–94
    tips for, 215
    See also news narratives

National Institute for Computer-Assisted Reporting, 388

National Journal, 90

National Lesbian and Gay Journalists Association, 481

National Public Radio, 4, 31, 42, 52, 276, 401

NBC News, 276

Nebraska Press Association v. Stuart, 349

negative news, impact of, 6–7

negligence test, **453**

neighborhood newsletters, 46

Nessman, Ravi, 219–20

neutral reporting, 448–49

New England Center for Investigative Reporting, 403

New York Post, 471, 482

New York Times, The, 4, 11, 17, 31, 34–35, 104, *104*, 124, 244, 245, 257, 260, 261, 392, 435, 457, 461, 474–75

New York Times, The v. Sullivan, 449

New Yorker, The, 450

news
    defined, 5–8
    elements of good story, 5–7
    as journalist's responsibility, 10–11
    as storytelling, 7, 11, 31

news alerts, 242, 266

news archives
    for beat reporters, 289
    for court stories, 333
    for fast-breaking stories, 330
    for obituaries, 360–61
    online sources, 117–18
    print sources, 125–26
    for speech stories, 315

news conference stories
    attributions in, 98
    in business journalism, 378
    characteristics of new conferences, 314
    describing participants and audience, 318–19
    different approaches to, 313
    impact of medium on, 317
    note-taking for, 318
    preparing for, 315–16
    quotations in, 318
    reporter behavior during, 319–21
    structuring and writing, 321, 323–24
    tips for, 315, 318, 319, 323

news consumption
    age and medium disparities, 3–4
    decline for young people, 28
    growth of Web-based, 21–23, 24
    partisan politics and, 31–32
    shifting patterns of, 28–30
    on social media, 3, 22–23
    types of audiences, 29–30
    See also audiences

news media
    advertising influences and, 477–78
    convergence of, 32–35
    fragmentation of, 24–25
    jobs in, 53–55
    public opinion of, 8–9, 31–32, 465, 466–67
    strengths and limitations of different, 7

news narratives, 219–20, 221, **226**–28
    features vs., 226
    leads in, 223f, 226, 227
    with narrative emphasis, 228, 229
    with news emphasis, 226–28
    vs. other story structures, 222f–23f

outlines for, 226
samples of, 227, 229

news releases, **131**–45
    accuracy and fairness in, 142
    alternatives to, *431*
    announcement, 133–35, 137–38
    appealing topics for, *434*
    attention-getting, 432–35
    in business journalism, 378
    cause-promoting, 135, 139
    digital media for, 131, 434–38
    image-building, 135–36, 139–40
    importance of, 131–32
    reading fine print in, *134*, 142
    refrigerator journalism for, 237f
    release dates and, 137
    rewriting, 136–45
    samples of, 421f, 425–26, 437–38
    search-engine optimization for, 434–35
    sending, 433–34
    as sources for stories, 131–32, *134*
    style of medium and, 434–35
    tips for, 141, 430
    types of, 132–36
    video new releases (VNRs), 435
    writing style for, 420, 432–33
    See also public relations

news room searches, 458

news stories
    accuracy and fairness in, 14f, 189–90
    across media platforms, 187–89, 277, 296–99
    commentaries vs., 14f, 17, 31
    comparison of print and Web, 243f
    features vs., 233
    "good news," 295
    interviewing for, 60, 61–62, 73
    sources for ideas, 118, 131–32

news values, 5–6, 174

Newsbank, 120

newsletters
    for business news, 374
    for internal communications, 430

Newspaper Research Journal, 189

newspaper websites, 22
    convergence news and, 33–35
    gathering information from, 117, 119
    initial approaches of, 242
    inverted pyramid and, 169
    longer content on, 249

newspaper websites (continued)
pay walls on, 50
shovelware market, 244
See also Web-based journalism
newspapers
approach to news stories, 7, 31
commercial databases for, 119–20
declining audience for, 24, 30, 38
financial challenges for, 25, 27, 31,
38, 50
front page ads in, 478
jobs in, 55
past profitability of, 24
profitability of local, 42
service journalism and, 237f, 238
as source of news, 27–28
Web-first focus of, 32–35, 123, 242
wire service style for, 499–505
See also legacy media; newspaper
websites
newsroom library. See news archives
Newsweek, 25
Newsy.com, 43, 47, 48, 119
niche journalism, 46–47, 49–50
Nicholson, Jim, 355
Nielson, Jakob, 251, 253, 254, 256, 429
Nishimura, Scott, 74
nonpublic records, 414–15
nonrestrictive elements, 491
Norris, Frank, 402
Norris, Michele, 474
Northwest Voice, 37
not for attribution, 105
not-for-profit models, 44–47, 51–52
note-taking
checking accuracy of, 189
for interviews, 75, 76, 78
protection for notes, 456–59
for speeches, news conferences, and
meetings, 318
See also recording devices
novelty
leads emphasizing, 182–83
as news value, 6, 15, 174
numbers, 149–64
accuracy of, 76, 163
averages and medians, 153–54, 155
avoiding, in quotations, 83
in broadcast news, 269, 272–73, 282
budgets, 159–62
in business journalism, 378–81

financial reports, 162–64
focus structure for, 228
guidelines for reporting, 162
inflation, 156–57
interest and compounding, 155–56
in leads, 173
mixing with words, 164
percentages, 151–53
problems and distortions with, 155,
163, 164
proportion, 151–55
rates, 154
symbols, 500
taxes, 157–59
tips for using, 151, 152, 154, 155, 156,
157, 159, 160
wire service style for, 499, 504–5
nut paragraphs, 224
in chronology, 222f, 224
in focus structure, 223f, 230–31
Nutt, Amy Ellis, 193–94, 195, 197

obituaries, 354–62
accuracy in, 355, 356
cause of death in, 361
embarrassing information in, 360,
361–62
interviewing family and friends, 361
leads for, 356, 358
as life stories, 357
mortuary form for, 356, 357–60
news libraries for, 360–61
profitability of, 354
sample of, 358–59
tips for, 356, 360, 361, 362
Web-based, 354–55
word choice in, 362
objectivity
in investigative reporting, 416
in journalism, 15–16, 114–15
in participant observation, 390
public relations and, 422–23
obscenity, in quotations, 97
Occupational Safety and Health
Administration, 382
off the record, 105
Ogilvy, David, 237f
On Deadline: Managing Media
Relations (Howard, Mathews),
132

On the Job
avoiding libel, 451
broadcast news, 277, 278
business journalism, 371
computer-assisted reporting, 392
editing Web-based news, 29, 123
ethics, 469, 476
hook in the opening, 196
importance of every story, 341
interviewing, 63
inverted pyramid, 180
investigative reporting, 409
multimedia journalism, 9, 74, 234
news releases, 134
off-the-record interviews, 105
public relations, 428
speeches, news conferences, and
meetings, 325
sports news, 252
Web startups, 47
White House beat, 291
working with numbers, 158
one-subject stories, 183, 184
Online Journalism Review, 37
Online Public Relations, 435
online sources, 115–24
authoritative websites, 117
for beat reporting, 289
for business news, 371–72
common address extensions, 125
currency of, 125
databases, 119–24
evaluating, 124–25
news archives, 117–18
news sites and content aggregators,
119
quotations from, 87
search engines, 118–19
social media, 119
See also information gathering; sources
online videoconferencing, 67
open-ended questions, 65, 70–71
open-meetings laws, 289–90, 445
open-records laws, 289–90, 445
OpenSecrets.org, 122
opinions, attributing, 172
order-of-importance structure, 199, 220,
226
O'Reilly, Bill, 17
organizations, abbreviations for, 500–501
Orlando Business Journal, 383–84

Orlando Sentinel, 26f, 370
Ornstein, Charles, 122–23
Outing, Steve, 247
outlines
    for chronology, 221–24
    for coherence, 199–200
    for news narrative, 226
    for storytelling, *234*
Overstreet, Sarah, *448*

Packer, The, 367
parallelism, 179, **203**
paraphrases, **91**, 96
    in broadcast news, 282
    plagiarism and, 485f
Parents Television Council, 97
partial quotations, 91–92
participant observation, **389–90**
participial phrases, 491–92
partisan politics
    distrust of media and, 31–32
    polls and, 388, 393, 394, 396
passive voice, 269, 270, 271
past tense, *270*
    for attributions, 103
    in broadcast news, 269
Patriot-News (Harrisburg, Pa.), The, 481
Patterson, Thomas, 6
Paulson, Ken, *451*
payola, 474–75
PDF files, **118**, 244
Penn, Steve, 88
people
    focus for broadcast news, 268
    in investigative reporting, 407, 408
    prominent, as news value, 6
    See also names and titles; public figures
per capita comparisons, 154
percentage change, **152–53**
percentage points, **152**
percentages, 151–53
Perlroth, Nicole, 479
personal finance news, 368, 369
persuasion, public relations and, 423, 430–32
Peter, Laurence J., 89
Pew Research Center, 8, 21, 28, 29
Pexton, Patrick B., 90
Philadelphia Inquirer, The, 33, 480

photographs, invasion of privacy and, 481–82. *See also* visuals
Pierce, Patrick, 325
places
    abbreviations for, 501–2
    capitalization of, 502
plagiarism, 99, 467, **484**–86
play, **138**, 139
plea bargaining, 345
podcasts, 118, 266
Pohlmann, Ken C., 242, 249
police, interviewing, 330, 331, 337, 338, 410–11
police beat reporting, 305–6
police reports, 331–32
Politico.com, 43, 50
politics
    distrust of media and, 31–32
    in government beat, 299–300
    in higher education beat, 304
    speech stories, 313
    See also election coverage
PolitiFact.com, 164
polls. *See* public opinion polls
population, **151**
    for opinion polls, 393, 395
    percentages of, 151–52
possessive form, 494
Potter Box, 471–73
Potter, Ralph, 471
power, monitoring of, 11, 15, 299
Poynter Institute, 65, 89, 367, 473, *476*, *484*
PR Newswire, 132, 372, 376, 435
preliminary hearings, 344–45, 351
prepositional phrases, 273, 491–92
prepublication review, 89–90, 189–90
present tense, for broadcast news, 268–69, *270*
presentencing investigations, 346
press-bar guidelines, 351
Press-Enterprise v. Riverside County Superior Court, 351
press releases, 131. *See also* news releases
PressDisplay.com, 118
primary sources, **60**
principal, **155**
privacy. *See* invasion of privacy
Privacy Protection Act, 458
private citizens, libel standards for, 447f, 453

privilege, as defense against libel, 447f, **448**–49
Prodigy, 454
profanity, in quotations, 97
profile stories, 60, 62–63, 73, 112
program budget, **160**
Project for Excellence in Journalism, 3, *4*, 10, 23
prominence, as news value, 6, 15, 176–77. *See also* public figures
pronouns, 75, 207, 494–95, 496
pronunciation, in broadcast news, 280–81
property records, 413
property taxes, 159
proportion, **151**–55
ProPublica, 4, 43, 45–46, 52, 123, *158*, 402
ProQuest Newsstand, 120
proximity, as news value, 6
proxy statements, 373, 375
public affairs, 422
Public Broadcasting System, 52
public figures
    actual malice test and, 450–53
    definitions of, 452
    invasion of privacy of, 481
    libel standards for, 447f, 449
    news releases about, 135–36, 139–40
    obituaries for, 360, 361–62
    quotations from, 85, 87
public image, news releases for, 135–36
Public Insight Network, 4
public officials
    actual malice test and, 449–50
    conflict-of-interest reports for, 414
    invasion of privacy of, 481
    libel standards for, 447f, 448–49
public opinion polls, 393–97
    analysis of accuracy of, 387, 388, 393
    explanatory notes for audiences, 394–96
    growing popularity of, 393
    margin of error, 393–94, 395
    on news media, 8–9, 31, 465
    political bias in, 388, 393, 394, 396
    problems with, 387–88, 396–97
    randomization in, 396
    sample size and response rate, 395
    sponsorship of, 394
    tips for, 394
    wording of questions, 395

public records
   accessing, 414, 444–45
   for investigative reporting, 413–14
   See also records and reports
public relations, 419–39
   alternatives to news releases, *431*
   audiences for, 424–28
   code of ethics for, 423
   consumer protections and, 382
   for crisis management, 424–27
   definitions of, 420–22
   digital media for, 419, 424, 427,
      429–30, *431*, 434–38
   internal communications, 430
   knowledge of news media for, 432–34
   main focus of, 423–30
   media choices for, 428–30, 434–35
   message in, 423–24
   news releases, 131–32, 420, 432–35
   objectivity and, 422–23
   persuasion and, 423, 430–32
   as sources for stories, 376
   specialties in, 422
   tips for, 429, 430, 439
   See also news releases
Public Relations Society of America, 88,
      420, 423, 435, 467, 474
Public Relations: Strategies and Tactics
      (Wilcox, Cameron), 421
public service announcements, 133
Pulitzer Prize, 11, 45, 195, 211, 388
punctuation
   for abbreviations, 499
   in broadcast copy, 283
   common errors in, 209–10, 489–98
   for quotations, *103*

qualified privilege, 447f, **448**–49
question-and-answer columns, 237f
question-and-answer stories, 66
questions
   asking for readers, 302
   asking tough, 325
   in beat reporting, 292
   closed-ended, 71
   follow-up, 77
   for interviewing, 68–71
   in investigative reporting, 405, 406f
   leads as, 182
   for news conferences, 315, 320, 323
   open-ended, 65, 70–71

phrasing of, 69–71
   for public opinion polls, 395
   researching, 68–69
   six basic, 170–76
   for television interviewing, 65
Quinn, Sally, 266
Quinn, T. J., *105*, 307
quotations, 81–106
   accuracy of, 78, 85–90, 91, 189–90
   alternatives to direct, 91–98
   attributions for, 81, 98–104
   avoiding facts and statistics in, 83
   in broadcast news, 282
   capitalization in, 504
   correcting grammar in, 95–96
   with dialect or accent, 92–94
   dialogue vs., 84, 212
   effective use of, 86
   ellipses in, 92, 96, 318
   from emails, 87
   fabricated, 98, 103, 450
   fairness of, 81, 85–90
   guidelines for choosing, 82–85
   by important people, 85
   indirect, 91–92
   mixing order of, 94–95, 318
   for moving story forward, 83–84
   in news narratives, 336
   obscenity, profanity, and vulgarity in, 97
   on- and off-the-record information,
      104–6
   from online sources, 87
   paraphrasing, 91, 96, 485f
   partial quotes, 91–92
   prepublication review of, 89–90,
      189–90
   punctuating, *103*
   removing redundancies, 96–97
   from speeches, news conferences, and
      meetings, 318, 321
   tips for, 83, 91, 99, 105
   unique material for, 84–85
   using someone else's, 88, 99
   verification of, 87
   See also attributions
quotes, **82**

racial terminology, 207, 208, 503–4
radio and television news writing, 265–83
   abbreviations in, 281
   characteristics of, 268–73

conciseness and clarity in, 269, 271–73
   conversational style for, 269, 270–71
   criteria for selecting news, 266–68
   format for, 278–79, 280f, 281f
   immediacy in, 267, 268–69, 270
   lead-ins and wrap-ups, 274
   leads, 269, 273–74
   names and titles in, 279–80
   numbers and symbols, 268, 272–73,
      282
   preparing copy, 278–83
   pronunciation, 280–81
   punctuation, 283
   quotations and attributions, 87, 96,
      282
   samples of, *270*, 279f, 280f, 281f
   story structure for, 273–76
   tips for, 268
radio news
   approach to stories, 7
   digital media for, 33, 266, 267, 276–77
   financial challenges for, 24–25
   important role of, 265–66
   jobs in, *55*
   talk radio, 31
   See also radio and television news
      writing
Rand, Ayn, 470
randomization, **392**–93, 396
rape victims. *See* victims
rapport, establishing, 66, 72–75
rates, **154**
rational self-interest, 470
recording devices
   for accident and fire stories, 337, 338
   for accuracy, 89, 91
   for crime stories, 331
   for interviewing, 61f, 66, 75–76
   invasion of privacy and, 481–82
   for speeches, news conferences, and
      meetings, 318, 319
   for Web content, *255*
   See also video reporting
records and reports, 372–75
   budgets, 159–62
   corporate data and filings, 372–73,
      375
   financial reports, 162–64, 378–81
   nonpublic, 414–15
   public, 413–14
   public access to, 414, 444–45
   systematic study of, 390–91

redundancies
    eliminating, 204, *205*
    in quotations, 96–97
reference boxes, 237*f*
reference sources, 126–27
"refrigerator journalism," 235, 236*f*–37*f*
*Regret the Error: How Media Mistakes
    Pollute the Press and Imperil Free
    Speech* (Silverman), 89
Regulation FD (Fair Disclosure), 376
relational database programs, **122**
relativism, 468–69
relevance, of news, 5, 170, 174, 176,
    232
religion, ethics and, 468, 470
religious terminology, 503–4
Renna, Tina, 459
repetition
    in broadcast news, 269, 272
    for coherence, 203
    in parallelism, 203
    in Web-based writing, 249
research. *See* information gathering
return on equity ratios, 380
return on sales ratios, 380
Reuters, 266, 467
revenues, 160
Reynolds, Donald W., 24
Rice, Rick, 420–21
Richmond Newspapers v. Virginia, 350,
    459
Roberts, Gene, 210
Rocky Mountain News, 25
Rosen, Jay, *466*, 468
Rosenstiel, Tom, 10, 16, 114–15
Rotzoll, Kim, 471
RSS feeds, 266, 315
run-on sentences, 490
Rupp, Sarah, 29

Sacramento Bee, The, 465
Sacramento Press, The, 7
Saffo, Paul, *42*
sales taxes, 157
samples, **152**, 395–96
sampling errors. *See* margin of error
San Diego News Network, 51
San Diego Union-Tribune, The, 51–52
Sarbanes-Oxley Act (2002), 376
satire, 329–30
Saturday Evening Post, 450–52

scenes, in storytelling, 77, 210–12, 230,
    234–35
Schieffer, Bob, 64–65
Schmidt, Eric, 48
school beat reporting, 291–92, 301–4
Schudson, Michael, 16
science, journalism and, 16, 114
Scripps-Howard news service, 475
search-engine optimization, **52**, *123*, 247,
    258–59, 434–35
search engines, 117, 118–19, 413. *See
    also* online sources
search warrants, 458
Seattle Post-Intelligencer, 25
secondary sources, **60**
Securities and Exchange Commission
    (SEC), 372–73, 374, 375, 382,
    413
securities registration statements, 375
Seitel, Fraser P., *434*
semicolons, 490, 493
senses, using in writing, 210–12
sentence structure
    for broadcast news, 269, 270, 271, 272,
        273–74
    coherence and, 200
    correct grammar and, 209–10, 489–98
    fragments, 490–91
    run-on sentences, 490
    types of, 200
    for Web-based writing, 251
sentencing, court, 348
series of items, commas with, 489–90
service journalism, **235**–38
setup, **230**–33
sex crimes, covering, 332, 350–51,
    352–53, 479–80
sexist language, 207–8, 209, 496
sexual abuse, 480–81
sexual orientation
    in crime stories, 352–53
    invasion of privacy and, 481
    in obituaries, 362
    terminology for, 75, 208
Shafer, Jack, 45
Shanghai Securities News, 367
Shapiro, Robert, 349
Shaw, George Bernard, 83
Sheppard, Samuel, 349
Sherwood, Ben, 476
shield laws, 295, 350, 456–59
shovelware, **242**, 244

"show, don't tell" writing, 197–98
sidebars, **182**, 221
    for crime stories, 334
    for news conference stories, 324
    for service journalism, 236*f*–37*f*, 238
    for Web-based content, 243*f*, 254
Sierra Club, 382
Silver, Nate, 387, 388, 393
Silverman, Craig, 89
Silvers, Amy Rabideau, 357, 358–59
similes, 206–7
simple interest, **155**
simple sentences, 200
simplicity
    in investigative reporting, 408
    for Web-based writing, 251, 252
    in writing process, 205–6
Sinclair, Upton, 402
situation ethics, **469**–70
six basic questions, 170–76, 337
Sixth Amendment, 349, 350, 459
60 Minutes, 267, 268, 450
Skype interviews, 67
slander, 447*f*
slang, 269, 271
Slashdot.org, 37
Slate magazine, 251
slugs, **279**
Small, Bill, 270
Smalley, John, 465, 477
smartphones, **21**. *See also* mobile media
Smith, Gary, 71
Smith, Jessica, 366
Smith, Ronald, 422
sniff, **404**
Snyder, Robert, 352
"so what" strategy
    in business journalism, 369
    in chronology, 224
    in focus structure, 232
    in inverted pyramid, 170–76
social media
    for beat reporting, 288, 297, 298–99
    breaking news stories on, 23, 36, 111,
        119, 187, 244, 342–43
    for broadcast news, 266, 276–77
    for business news, 366, 377
    concise writing for, 203
    crowdsourcing on, 276
    ethics for, 486
    gathering information from, 60, 117,
        119, 315, 413

social media (continued)
  guidelines for using, 277, 403
  legacy media's use of, 242, 248
  media law and, 444
  most popular sites, 429
  news consumption on, 3, 22–23
  for news releases, 131, 434, 436–38
  political uprisings and, 36, 111, 241
  promoting news on, 52–53, 74, 119,
    248, 261–62
  for public relations, 419, 424, 429–30,
    431, 434
  quotations from, 87
  reader interactivity on, 6, 7, 298
  shield laws and, 458–59
  for speeches, news conferences, and
    meetings, 317
  verifying sources from, 111–12, 124,
    277, 403
  for viral marketing, 52–53
  watchdog journalism and, 466
  See also blogs; Twitter
social science reporting, 387–97
  computer-assisted reporting, 388–89,
    392
  field experiments, 391–93
  participant observation, 389–90
  public opinion polls, 393–97
  systematic study of records, 390–91
  tips for, 389, 390, 394, 396
Society of Professional Journalists, 467,
  475
  code of ethics, 472, 506–8
solutions
  in investigative reporting, 409
  as news value, 6–7
Sonderman, Jeff, 262
sound bites, **65**
sources
  for accident and fire stories, 337–38
  anonymous, 99, 100, 104–6, 295
  attributions for, 98–104
  background interviews, 106
  for beat reporting, 277, 290–91,
    294–96
  building and maintaining, 294–96
  for business news, 371–78
  for consumer news, 381–82
  for crime stories, 330–32
  cultivating, 412
  for government beat reporting, 300–301

  for interviewing, 60
  for investigative reporting, 410–15
  for obituaries, 357–61
  online, 115–24
  paying for, 475–77
  primary and secondary, 60
  problems with human, 412
  problems with written, 415
  protecting, 295, 412, 456–59
  putting at ease, 370
  reference sources, 126–27
  for sports reporting, 308–9
  for story ideas, 118, 131–32
  traditional print, 124–27
  using multiple, 112–14
  See also anonymous sources; informa-
    tion gathering
special-interest databases, 122
Specialized Information Publishers
  Association, 432
speech stories
  attributions in, 98
  background information in, 319
  characteristics of speeches, 314
  describing participants and audience,
    318–19
  impact of medium on, 317
  note-taking for, 318
  preparing for, 314–15
  quotations in, 318
  reporter behavior during, 319–21
  sample of, 322
  structuring and writing, 321–22
  tips for, 315, 318, 319, 323
Spencer, Jim, 48, 49, 53
Spokesman-Review (Spokane, Wash.),
  The, 195
Sports Illustrated, 455
sports reporting
  as beat reporting, 306–10
  careers in, 252
  developing contacts, 308–9
  digging for stories, 309–10
  for-profit websites, 49, 252
  tips for, 309
  verbatim quotes in, 95–96
Sposito, Sean, 367
spot news, **27**
St. Louis Beacon (stlbeacon.com), 4, 41,
  43, 46
St. Louis Post-Dispatch, 41, 152

St. Paul Pioneer Press, 244, 245f
Standard & Poor's, 371, 372, 380
Standard Periodical Directory, 373
Star-Ledger (Newark, N.J.), The, 193–94
state manuals, 126
"State of the News Media" assessments,
  10
statistics. See numbers
Steele, Bob, 477
Steele, Daniel, 470
Steele, James, 203
Steffens, Lincoln, 402
Stein, Ben, 474–75
Steinberg, Dan, 261
Stewart, Jon, 12
Stewart, Potter, 445, 458
stocks, 383
Stolzfus, Duane, 189
Stone, Oliver, 340
story highlights list, 181, 186
story structures
  for broadcast news, 273–76
  chronology, 199, 220–26
  comparison of different types,
    222f–23f
  focus structure, 228–35
  inverted pyramid, 167–90
  in investigative reporting, 407–8
  memo-structure stories, 183, 185
  multiple-element stories, 185–87
  news narratives, 219–20, 226–28
  one-subject stories, 183, 184
  order of importance, 199, 220, 226
  outlining, 199–200
  service journalism, 235–38
  for Web stories, 243f, 248–51
storytelling
  important elements in, 234
  news as, 7, 11, 31
  in television news, 65–66
  See also narration
strategic communication, 420, **422**
Strategic Planning for Public Relations
  (Smith), 422
style. See wire service style
subheads
  in memo-structure stories, 185
  in service journalism, 237f
  for Web content, 255, 258
subject complements, 496
subject-verb agreement, 496

subjunctive mood, 497
subordinating conjunctions, 200, 490
substantial truth, **448**
suicides, obituaries and, 361
Sullivan, Bartholomew, 211
Sullivan, Julie, 207
summary boxes, 181, 186, 324
summary leads, **178**–79, 335
sunshine laws, 445
Supreme Court
    on closed-courtroom controversy,
        349–51, 459–60
    on copyright laws, 460, 461
    on freedom of press, 443
    libel rulings of, 98, 449–50, 451–53
    on source confidentiality, 104, 458
    on unwanted publicity, 455–56, 479
surveys, bias in, *163. See also* public
        opinion polls
Swartzlander, David, 484
Sweet, Ken, 365
symbols
    in broadcast news, 282
    wire service style for, 500
Synaptic Digital, 435

tablet computers, **21**. *See also* mobile
        media
Tampa Bay Online, 33
Tarbell, Ida, 402
Taricani, Jim, 456–57
taxes, 157–59
telephone interviews, 59, 60, 66
teleprompters, **279**
television news
    approach to stories, 7
    declining audience for, 24, 30
    digital media for, 33, 244, 249, 266,
        267, 276–77
    emotional content in, 65
    financial challenges for, 24–25, 27
    important role of, 265–66
    interviewing for, 64–66
    jobs in, 55
    newsmagazine formats, 267
    ratings for, 31
    speech, news conference, and meeting
        stories, 321, 323
    video new releases (VNRs), 435
    visual impact in, 267

writing to video in, 253, 275–76
    See also radio and television news
        writing
10-K reports, 373, 375, 379
10KWizard, 373
terrorism
    coverage of, 353
    freedom of press and, 8
that/which, 491
thin media, 37
Thomas, Helen, 257
Thomas Reuters, 372
Thompson, Wright, 72, 77, 234
Thorson, Esther, 46, 47
"3-2-2-1" format, 258
tickler files, **294**
tie-backs, **235**, 343
Tierney, John, *477*
Time magazine, 445–46, 450
time references
    in broadcast news, 269
    as transitions, 202, 203
timeliness
    in broadcast news, 267
    getting facts and, 12–13
    as news value, 6, 226
    in Web-based journalism, 243*f,* 244,
        251
Times-Picayune (New Orleans), The, 25
titles. *See* names and titles
"to be sure" paragraphs, **224**–25, 233
Tocqueville, Alexis de, 8
Today show, 471
Tompkins, Al, 65, 66
trade associations, 377
trade press, 373–74
traditional media. *See* legacy media
transitions
    for coherence, 201–3, 324
    in focus structure, 223*f,* 230–31, 232
    in news narratives, 226, 336
Trausch, Susan, 378
travel writers, ethics for, 475
trespassing, 455
trial balloons, 104
trial courts, 342
trial proceedings, 346–48
Truesdell, Jeff, 70
truth
    code of ethics and, 506–7
    as defense against libel, 446–48

in journalism, 12–15
    objectivity and, 15–16
Tuchman, Gaye, 16
Tully, John, 228, 229
Tumblr, 430
Twain, Mark, *163*
20/20, 267
Twitter, **3**, 430
    beat reporting and, 288, 297, 298–99
    breaking news stories on, 23, 111, 187,
        342–43
    editorial problems with, 262, 298–99
    ethics for, 486
    growing importance of, *403*
    inverted pyramid style and, 167, 187
    news consumption on, 3, 6, 23, 276
    news releases on, 434
    promoting news on, 119, 261–62
    service journalism and, 235–38
    verifying sources from, *124, 403*
    watchdog journalism and, 466
    See also social media

Ulken, Eric, *123*
*Ulrich's International Periodicals
        Directory,* 373
undercover reporting, **389,** 473
Uniform Commercial Code filings, 414
unwanted publicity, 455–56
US Uncut, 472
USA Today, 83–84, 86, 190, 390
USAToday.com, 49
usefulness
    of news, 5, 170, 174
    service journalism and, 235, 236*f*

variables, in experiments, **391**
Vasel, Kathryn, 365
verbs
    agreement with subject, 496
    incorrect form of, 497–98
    linking, 496–97
    mood of, 497
    tense, in broadcast news, 268–69, 270
    transitive, 270
    in tweets, 262
verdicts, 348
verification
    of information, 76, 114–15

verification *(continued)*
　layered editing process for, 116*f, 124*
　of quotations, 87
　See also accuracy
victims
　interviewing, 330–31, 338, 410
　revealing names of, 455–56, 479–80
　of sex crimes, 332, 350, 353, 456, 479
video new releases (VNRs), 435
video reporting
　in convergence news, 34
　interviewing, 64–66
　invasion of privacy and, 481–82
　for speeches, news conferences, and
　　meetings, 317, 321, 323, 326
　in television news, 267, 275–76, 323
　Web-based, 48, *255*
viral marketing, 52–53
visuals
　invasion of privacy and, 481–82
　manipulation of, 481
　in service journalism, 236*f*, 237*f*
　sources for, 118, 126
　in television news, 267
　for Web-based media, 243*f, 250,* 253,
　　258
vodcasts, 118
Voice of San Diego, 51
voir dire, 346
Voltaire, *177*
vulgarity
　avoiding, 269, 271
　in quotations, 97

Walker, Stanley, *168, 182*
Wall Street Journal, The, 31, 50, 228,
　231–32, 235, 366, 369
war reporting, 389, 390, 482
Ward, Chuck, 355
Washington Post, The, 87, *124,* 261, 287,
　313, 388
watchdog journalism, 15, 28, 52, 112–14,
　466
Web-based journalism, 241–62
　advertising revenues and, 242, 354
　audience expectations for, 243–51, 298
　beat reporting, 288, 296–99
　blog writing, 259–61
　broadcast news content, 33, 244, 249,
　　266, 267, 276–77
　chunking information, 254–55

citizen journalism and, 7–8, 36, 242
contact information in, 257, *258*
content aggregators, 3, 48, 117, 119,
　372
convergence news and, 32–35
copyright laws and, 461
customized content, 247, 429
editorial process for, 29, *123*
effective writing for, 251–58
financial models for, 42–50
for-profit models, 47–50
hyperlinks, 249, 255–57, 483
immediacy of, 244, 251
incorrect and incomplete information
　in, 483
innovative approaches to, 48–49
international audiences and, 248
inverted pyramid format for, 168–69,
　180, 187–89, 246–47
jobs in, 55
layered structure for, 243*f,* 248–51
leads for, 247, 258–59
legacy media's focus on, 32–35, 42, 50,
　123, 242, 244
lists and bullets for, 243*f,* 253–54, 255
for local news coverage, 6, 7, 41,
　46–47
memo-structure stories for, 183
mobile media formats, 245–46
multimedia content, 245–46, *248,* 249,
　255
nonprofit sites, 41, 44–47
obituaries, 354–55
ongoing news updates, 188–89
political uprisings and, 241–42, 248
print media vs., 243*f*
producing video for, *255*
for public relations, 429, 434–35
public view of, 9
reader interactivity in, 4, 6, 244–45,
　254, 255–56, 257
search-engine optimization, *123,* 247,
　258–59
service journalism and, 237*f,* 238
social media and, 22–23, 261–62
sports news, 49, 252
"3-2-2-1" format for, 258
as unique media form, 7, 242
verbal and visual thinking, 253
visuals in, 243*f, 250,* 253, 258
See also digital media; mobile media;
　newspaper websites; social media

webcasts, **60**
Weber, Tracy, 122–23
Weinberg, Steve, 64, 89
Weinberger, David, 247, 255
Weiss, Philip, 89
Welles, Chris, 377
WestSeattleBlog.com, 43
"what" strategy, 170–76, 273
"what's next" strategy, 176
White House beat, 287, 288, *291*
Whitworth, Brad, 428
"who" leads, 176–77
who/whom, 495
Wi-Fi, **22**
Wikipedia, 119, *124*
Wilcox, Dennis, 421
Wilkerson, Isabel, 73, 87
Wilkins, Lee, *475*
Will, George, 474
Williams, Brian, 17
Williams, Walter, 10
Winans, R. Foster, 371
wire service style, 499–505
　abbreviations, 499–502
　AP style, 96, 97, 137–38, 208, 489,
　　499
　capitalization, 502–4
　numbers, 504–5
wire services, 266
Wired magazine, 433
Wisconsin Center for Investigative Jour-
　nalism, 402–3
Wise, Mike, 95
Wiser, Paige, 472
witnesses
　in court proceedings, 347
　interviewing, 330, 331, 337–38
Wolf, Connie, 424
Wolverton, Troy, 53
Woolley, Buzz, 51
word choice
　avoiding biased, 207–9
　conciseness in, 203–6
　errors in, 497
　in obituaries, 362
　precision in, 198, 207
　simplicity in, 205–6
WordPress, 119, *123*
wrap-ups, **274**
Writing for Story (Franklin), *234*
writing skills, 193–215
　for accident and fire stories, 337–40

bias-free language, 207–9
coherence, 199–203
conciseness, 203–6
for crime and court stories, 333–37, 340–48
details, 196–98
figures of speech, 206–7
good reporting as basis of, 195
grammar and punctuation, 209–10, 489–98
importance of, 193–95
for investigative reporting, 405–9
language usage, 206–10
narrative tools, 210–15

for numbers, 164
for obituaries, 354–62
opening hooks, *196*
order of elements, 199–200
outlining, 199–200
print vs. online, 243*f*
for public relations, 420, 432–35
sentence structure, 200
simplicity, 205–6, 251, 252
for speech, news conference, and meeting stories, 321–26
tips for, 199, 204, 208, 209, 215
transitions, 201–3
using conjunctions, 200–201

for Web-based journalism, 251–58
word choice, 198, 207
WuDunn, Sheryl, 11

Yahoo, 117, 118, 258
Yahoo Finance, 372, 373
Yahoo News, 48, 119
"you" leads, **176**, 226

Zakaria, Fareed, 99, 484
Zarrella, Dan, 262
Zollman, Peter, 374

Annotated Models

Model	Chapter	Page
BREAKING NEWS		
Comparison of a Breaking News Story and a Follow-Up Story	16	335
A Crime Story Across Media Platforms	14	297
News Narrative with Narrative Emphasis	11	229
News Narrative with News Emphasis	11	227
News Release Responding to a Crisis	20	425
BROADCASTING AND MULTIMEDIA		
A Crime Story Across Media Platforms	14	297
Layering Content on a Web Page	12	250
Social Media News Release	20	437
Use of Verb Tenses in a TV Story	13	270
EDITING AND MECHANICS		
Editing for Conciseness	10	205
Integrating Multiple Sources into a Story	6	113
Using Quotes Effectively	5	86
Using Transitions	10	202
TYPES OF STORIES		
The Classic Inverted Pyramid Story	9	188
Comparison of a Breaking News Story and a Follow-Up Story	16	335
A Life Story	16	358
A Memo-Structure Story	9	185
Integrating News Release Information	7	145
A Sample Inverted Pyramid Story	9	175
A Single-Subject Inverted Pyramid Story	9	184
Speech Story	15	322
Using Anonymous Sources	5	100

Copy Editing and Proofreading Symbols

Writing and editing for today's media are done almost exclusively on computers. Only in the book industry are most manuscripts still prepared on paper. Nevertheless, at some small newspapers and magazines, editors prefer to edit on paper. For that reason, failure to learn the copy editing symbols used in manuscript preparation is a mistake. There is a good chance you will need to use those symbols at some point in your career, if only to satisfy the occasional editor who prefers doing things the old-fashioned way.

You are even more likely to use proofreading symbols, which are used on galley proofs and page proofs to correct typeset copy. While there are some similarities in the two sets of symbols, there also are differences. The chart on the opposite page shows the most common copy editing symbols (used in manuscript preparation), and the chart below illustrates the most common proofreading symbols (used to correct typeset copy).

Proofreading Symbols

∧	Insert at this point.	✓✓	Space evenly.
⊥	Push down space.	◯	Close up entirely.
ℓ	Take out letter, letters or words.	⊏	Move to left.
⸏	Turn inverted letter.	⊐	Move to right.
lc	Set lowercase.	⊔	Lower letter or word.
wf	Wrong font letter.	⊓	Raise letter or word.
ital	Reset in italic type.	out see copy	Words are left out.
rom	Reset in roman (regular) type.	//=	Straighten lines.
bf	Reset in boldface type.	¶	Start new paragraph.
⊙	Insert period.	no ¶	No paragraph. Run together.
⌃	Insert comma.	tr	Transpose letters or words.
⌃	Insert semicolon.	?	Query; is copy right?
⊨	Insert hyphen.	⊢	Insert dash.
⩑	Insert apostrophe.	□	Indent 1 em.
⩔ ⩔	Enclose in quotation marks.	□□	Indent 2 ems.
≡	Replace with a capital letter.	□□□	Indent 3 ems.
#	Insert space.	stet	Let it stand.